Lecture Notes in Computer Science   10069

Commenced Publication in 1973
Founding and Former Series Editors:
Gerhard Goos, Juris Hartmanis, and Jan van Leeuwen

T0212482

More information about this series at http://www.springer.com/series/7409

Carmelo R. García · Pino Caballero-Gil
Mike Burmester · Alexis Quesada-Arencibia (Eds.)

Ubiquitous Computing and Ambient Intelligence

10th International Conference, UCAmI 2016
San Bartolomé de Tirajana, Gran Canaria, Spain,
November 29 – December 2, 2016
Proceedings, Part I

 Springer

Editors

Carmelo R. García
University of Las Palmas de Gran Canaria
Las Palmas
Spain

Pino Caballero-Gil
Departamento de Estadistica
Universidad La Laguna
La Laguna
Spain

Mike Burmester
Florida State University
Tallahassee, FL
USA

Alexis Quesada-Arencibia
University of Las Palmas de Gran Canaria
Las Palmas
Spain

ISSN 0302-9743   ISSN 1611-3349 (electronic)
Lecture Notes in Computer Science
ISBN 978-3-319-48745-8   ISBN 978-3-319-48746-5 (eBook)
DOI 10.1007/978-3-319-48746-5

Library of Congress Control Number: 2016955505

LNCS Sublibrary: SL3 – Information Systems and Applications, incl. Internet/Web, and HCI

Printed on acid-free paper

This Springer imprint is published by Springer Nature
The registered company is Springer International Publishing AG
The registered company address is: Gewerbestrasse 11, 6330 Cham, Switzerland

Preface

The UCAmI Conference brings together the fields of ubiquitous computing (UC), which is defined as the integration of human factors, computer science, engineering and social sciences, with a paradigm built upon UC, called ambient intelligence (AmI), which refers to sensitive electronic environments responsive to the presence of people. Thus, altogether, the core of the conference is a complete notion that mutually inspires UC and AmI. In particular, UCAmI 2016 focused on research topics related to ambient assisted living, Internet of Things, smart cities, ambient intelligence for health, human–computer interaction, ad hoc and sensor networks, and security.

This year we celebrated in Gran Canaria, Canary Islands, Spain, the 10th International Conference on Ubiquitous Computing and Ambient Intelligence (UCAmI 2016), which included the International Work Conference on Ambient Assisted Living (IWAAL), and the International Conference on Ambient Intelligence for Health (AmIHEALTH). The program of this joint event included a rich variety of technical sessions to cover the most relevant research topics of each conference. Since its first meeting back in 2005 the event has grown significantly, as shown by its increasing number of participants. For UCAmI 2016, a total of 145 submissions were received, and the acceptance rate for long papers and doctoral consortium papers was 51 %. All submissions were peer reviewed by at least three members of the Program Committee. The reviewers' comments and recommendations were taken into consideration while selecting submissions for inclusion in the proceedings, and were communicated to the authors. Authors whose manuscripts were accepted were asked to address the reviewers' comments. We would like to thank all the authors who submitted their work for consideration and also the reviewers for providing their detailed and constructive reviews in a timely manner.

Furthermore, in an effort to increase the visibility of the contributions of UCAmI, selected papers were invited for submission as extended versions in the journals: *Sensors, Mobile Information Systems, Journal of Ambient Intelligence and Humanized Computing*, and *International Journal of Computational Intelligence Systems*. We would like to thank the distinguished editors of these journals for providing us with these opportunities.

Finally, we would like to thank all organizers (i.e., University of Las Palmas de Gran Canaria and MAmI Research group), and the reviewers (members of the Program Committee) for helping us by contributing to a high-quality event and proceedings book on the topics of ubiquitous computing and ambient intelligence. Special thanks are due to the staff of Springer in Heidelberg for their valuable support.

November 2016

Carmelo R. García
Pino Caballero-Gil
Mike Burmester
Alexis Quesada

Organization

General Chair

Jose Bravo   University of Castilla La Mancha, Spain

Local Organizing Chair

Alexis Quesada   University of Las Palmas de Gran Canaria, Spain

UCAmI PC Co-chairs

Carmelo R. García   University of Las Palmas de Gran Canaria, Spain
Pino Caballero-Gil   University of La Laguna, Spain
Mike Burmester   University of State of Florida, USA

Publicity Chairs

Jesús Fontecha Diezma   University of Castilla-La Mancha, Spain
Vladimir Villarreal   Technological University of Panama, Panama

Web Master

Iván González Díaz   University of Castilla-La Mancha, Spain

Steering Committee

Xavier Alaman, Spain
Jose Bravo, Spain
Jesus Favela, Mexico
Juan Manuel García Chamizo, Spain
Luis Guerrero, Costa Rica
Ramón Hervás, Spain
Rui Jose, Portugal
Diego López-De-Ipiña, Spain
Chris Nugent, UK
Sergio F. Ochoa, Chile
Gabriel Urzáiz, Mexico
Vladimir Villareal, Panama

Organizing Committee

Jezabel Molina-Gil, Spain
Cádido Caballero-Gil, Spain
Candelaria Hernández-Goya, Spain
Alexandra Rivero-García, Spain
Iván Santos-González, Spain
Tania Mondéjar, Spain
Justyna Kidacka, Spain
Merce Naranjo, Spain
Elitania Jiménez, Spain
Carlos Gutiérrez, Spain
Esperanza Johnson, Spain
María Martínez, Spain
Carlos Dafonte, Spain

Tracks Chairs

AAL (IWAAL)

Riitta Hellman, Norway
Jesus Fontecha, Spain
Juan M. García-Chamizo, Spain

Health (AmIHEALTH)

Ramón Hervás, Spain
Oresti Baños, Spain

Ad-Hoc Sensor Networks

Jezabel Molina-Gil, Spain
Mike Burmester, USA

Security

Pino Caballero-Gil, Spain
Slobodan Petrovic, Norway

Human-Computer Interaction

Jesús Favela, Mexico
Nadia Bethouze, UK

Smart Cities

Diego López-De-Ipiña, Spain
Erik Mannens, Belgium

IoT

Candido Caballero-Gil, Spain
Haibo Chen, UK

Program Committee

Hindusthan A.V. Senthil	Hindusthan College of Arts and Science, India
Ricardo Aguasca-Colomo	Universidad de Las Palmas de Gran Canaria, Spain
Ramón Aguero Calvo	Universidad de Cantabria, Spain
Mónica Aguilar Igartua	Universidad Politécnica de Cataluña, Spain
Xavier Alamán	UAM, Spain
Francisco Alayón	Universidad de Las Palmas de Gran Canaria, Spain
Rosa Arriaga	Georgia Institute of Technology, USA
Mohamed Bakhouya	University of Technology of Belfort Montbeliard, France
Nelson Baloian	University of Chile, Chile
Jean-Paul Barthès	UTC, France
Oresti Baños	University of Twente, The Netherlands
Paolo Bellavista	University of Bologna, Italy
Jessica Beltrán	CICESE, Mexico
Nadia Berthouze	University College London, UK
Stephane Bouchard	Uqo, Canada
Ljiljana Brankovic	The University of Newcastle, UK
Jose Bravo	Universidad de Castilla La Mancha, MAmI Research Lab, Spain
Willem-Paul Brinkman	Delft University of Technology, The Netherlands
Mike Burmester	Florida State University, USA
Cándido Caballero-Gil	Universidad de La Laguna, Spain
Pino Caballero-Gil	Universidad de La Laguna, Spain
Eduardo Calvillo	City of San Luis Potosí, Mexico
Karina Caro	CICESE, Mexico
Giorgio Carpino	CIR, University Campus Bio-Medico of Rome, Italy
Luis Castro	Instituto Tecnologico de Sonora, Mexico
Filippo Cavallo	The BioRobotics Institute, Italy
Sophie Chabridon	Institut Telekom and Management SudParis/CNRS UMR SAMOVAR, France
Haibo Chen	University of Leeds, UK
Walter Colitti	ModoSmart S.L., Spain
Diane Cook	Washington State University, USA
Ray Cornejo	Northwestern, USA
Domenico Cotroneo	University of Naples Federico II, Italy
Michael P. Craven	University of Nottingham, UK
Dagoberto Cruz	CICESE, Mexico
Gabriel de Blasio	Universidad de Las Palmas de Gran Canaria, Spain
Fabio De Felice	Università degli Studi di Cassino, Italy

Boris De Ruyter	Philips Research, The Netherlands
Stefan Decker	RWTH Aachen, Germany
Anna Doreen Robin	University of India, India
Rachael Dutton	Accord Group, UK
Kholoud Elbast	Gaza University, Palestine
Lizbeth Escobedo	UABC, Mexico
Jesus Favela	CICESE, Mexico
Anna Fensel	Semantic Technology Institute (STI) Innsbruck, University of Innsbruck, Austria
Antonio Fernández-Caballero	Universidad de Castilla-La Mancha, Spain
Carlo Ferrari	University of Padova, Italy
Giuseppe Fico	Universidad Politécnica de Madrid, Spain
Laura Fiorini	The BioRobotics Institute, Italy
Jesus Fontecha	Universidad de Castilla La Mancha, MAmI Research Lab, Spain
Antonio Fratini	Aston University, UK
Andrea Gaggioli	Catholic University of Milan, Italy
Juan Manuel Garcia-Chamizo	University of Alicante, Spain
Carmelo R. García	University of Las Palmas de Gran Canaria, Spain
Jorge García Vidal	Universidad Politécnica de Cataluña, Spain
Lilia Georgieva	Heriot-Watt University, UK
Roberto Gil Pita	University of Alcala, Spain
Victor Gonzalez	Instituto Tecnológico Autónomo de México, Mexico
Dan Grigoras	UCC, Ireland
Terje Grimstad	Karde AS, Norway
Luis Guerrero	Universidad de Chile, Chile
Juan Carlos Guerri Cebollada	Universidad Politécnica de Valencia, Spain
Antonio Guerrieri	University of Calabria, Italy
Bin Guo	Institut Telecom SudParis, France
Sofiane Hamrioui	University of Haute Alsace, France
Maria Haritou	Institute of Communication and Computer Systems - National Technical University of Athens, Greece
Jan Havlik	Czech Technical University in Prague, Czech Republic
Riitta Hellman	Karde AS, Norway
Daniel Hernandez	CICESE, Mexico
Netzahualcoyotl Hernández	CICESE, Mexico
Candelaria Hernández-Goya	Universidad de La Laguna, Spain
Valeria Herskovic	Pontificia Universidad Católica de Chile, Chile
Ramon Hervas	Universidad de Castilla La Mancha, MAmI Research Group, Spain
Jesse Hoey	University of Waterloo, Canada
Alina Huldtgren	Eindhoven University of Technology, The Netherlands
Marjan Hummel	University of Twente, The Netherlands

Eduardo Jacob	Universidad del País Vasco, Spain
Martin Jaekel	ZHAW Zurich University of Applied Sciences, Switzerland
Alan Jovic	University of Zagreb, Croatia
Martin Kampel	Vienna University of Technology, Computer Vision Lab, Austria
Wolfgang Kastner	TU Vienna, Austria
Mariano Lamarca Lorente	Ayuntamiento de Barcelona, Spain
Sungyoung Lee	KyungHee University, South Korea
Ernst Leiss	University of Houston, USA
Lenka Lhotska	Czech Technical University in Prague, Czech Republic
Jaime Lloret Mauri	Universidad Politécnica de Valencia, Spain
Vincenzo Loia	Università degli Studi di Salerno, Italy
Tun Lu	Fudan University, China
Jens Lundström	Högskolan i Halmstad, Sweden
Wolfram Luther	University of Duisburg-Essen, Germany
Diego López-De-Ipiña	Deusto Institute of Technology, University of Deusto, Spain
Elsa María Macías López	Universidad de Las Palmas de Gran Canaria, Spain
Ratko Magjarevic	University of Zagreb, Croatia
Domingo Marrero Marrero	University of Las Palmas de Gran Canaria, Spain
Alicia Martinez	CENIDET, Mexico
Ana Martinez	CICESE, Mexico
Francisco José Martínez Saldivar	Universidad Politécnica de Cataluña, Spain
Oscar Mayora	CREATE-NET, Italy
Paolo Melillo	Second University of Naples, Italy
Vicente E. Mena Santana	ULPGG, Spain
Singidunum Milos Stojmenovic	Singidunum University, Serbia
Jezabel Molina-Gil	Universidad de La Laguna, Spain
Alberto Moran	UABC, Mexico
Tatsuo Nakajima	Waseda University, Japan
Julián Navajas Fernández	Universidad de Zaragoza, Spain
Rene Navarro	Universidad de Sonora, Mexico
Panagiota Nikopoulou-Smyrni	Brunel Univesrity, UK
Chris Nugent	University of Ulster, UK
Sergio Ochoa	Universidad de Chile, Chile
Mof Otoom	Yarmouk University, Jordan
Mwaffaq Otoom	Yarmouk University, Jordan
Gabino Padrón	Instituto de Ciencias y Tecnologías Cibernéticas, Universidad de Las Palmas de Gran Canaria, Spain
Philippe Palanque	ICS-IRIT, University Toulouse 3, France
Nicolas Pallikarakis	University of Patras, Greece
Pablo Pancardo	Universidad Juárez Autónoma de Tabasco, Mexico

Additional Reviewers

Acerbi, Giorgia
Aguilera, Unai
Almeida, Aitor
Alvarez-Díaz, Néstor
Azkune, Gorka
Brewer, Robin
Buján-Carballal, David
Emaldi, Mikel
Fankhauser, David
Fernbach, Andreas
Fiorini, Laura
Fuentes, Carolina
González Díaz, Iván
Guidi, Gabriele
Iadanza, Ernesto
Ibarra-Esquer, Jorge Eduardo

Landaluce, Hugo
Limosani, Raffaele
Lodeiro-Santiago, Moisés
Lopez, Unai
López-De-Armentia, Juan
Marrero Marrero, Domingo
Pijoan, Ander
Pretel, Ivan
Raich, Philipp
Razzaq, Asif
Rivero-Cáceres, Alexandra
Rivero-García, Alexandra
Rodriguez, Iyubanit
Santana, Jose
Santos-González, Iván
Suárez-Armas, Jonay

Contents – Part I

Human-Computer Interaction

Contents – Part II

Ad-hoc and Sensors Networks

IoT

Smart Cities

Security

Health (AmIHEALTH)

Fuzzy Intelligent System for Supporting Preeclampsia Diagnosis from the Patient Biosignals

Macarena Espinilla[1(✉)], Sixto Campaña[2],
Jorge Londoño[3], and Ángel-Luis García-Fernández[4]

[1] Computer Science Department, University of Jaén, Jaén, Spain
mestevez@ujaen.es
[2] Universidad Nacional Abierta y a Distancia - UNAD, ECBTI, Pasto, Colombia
sixto.campana@unad.edu.co
[3] Universidad Pontificia Bolivariana - UPB, Medellín, Colombia
jorge.londono@upb.edu.co
[4] Computer Science Department, University of Jaén, Jaén, Spain
algarcia@ujaen.es

Abstract. This contribution presents a proposal for generating linguistic reports based on the study of biomedical signals of human patients. Although this topic is dealt in many previous works, there are challenges still open for the scientific community, such as the development of systems to produce reports and alerts using a human-friendly language. We present a brief review of some relevant previous works, as well as our proposal of a system based on fuzzy linguistic approach applied to the diagnosis of the preeclampsia disease that may affect pregnant women. Our system transforms numerical values of biomedical signals into linguistic values that are understandable information for the patients and the medical staff. The dataset used for testing the system contains real data from a study carried out by the Davinci UNAD Group (Colombia) on patients that suffer from preeclampsia.

Keywords: Fuzzy logic · Fuzzy linguistic intelligent systems · Biomedical systems · Preeclampsia

1 Introduction

We live in the era of data. Our everyday lives are surrounded by sensors that capture information associated to objects, humans or environments, such as vision sensors, motion sensors, light sensors, medical sensors, etc. The so-called Internet of Things (IoT) is all around us, producing a huge amount of data that needs to be automatically organized and processed in order to produce easy to understand reports for the users, as trying to deal with this data directly is far from the human capabilities.

Data analysis is at the core of a relevant amount of recently published works, many of them focusing on data mining techniques to extract useful knowledge

© Springer International Publishing AG 2016
C.R. García et al. (Eds.): UCAmI 2016, Part I, LNCS 10069, pp. 3–14, 2016.
DOI: 10.1007/978-3-319-48746-5_1

from the data and shape it so that the users understand what is happening and act accordingly. The research on methods to communicate this knowledge in a user-friendly way has led to the concept of linguistic descriptions [1], which allow to abstract useful data into different levels and dimensions, therefore providing interpretability.

Our work considers a case study in the health care area, given its relevance nowadays [2], although the presented techniques could be applied in other areas as well.

Modern health care systems make use of many technological advances to measure biomedical signals that produce large amounts of raw data. The development of methods for analysing this data relies mostly on *soft computing techniques* whose results in most cases still require some level of expertise to understand and use them properly. This is the motivation for the development of linguistic report techniques, which rely on fuzzy logic principles to communicate important information obtained from the analysis of the data. In our work, biomedical signals will be used to identify risk conditions and generate linguistic reports for the medical staff.

Submitting user-friendly reports to support the diagnosis and monitoring of a given disease is a problem that has not been completely solved yet, as sometimes a rigid interpretation of the data can lead to misdiagnosis. Therefore we propose in this paper a new system based on fuzzy linguistic approach focused on this process.

This work is structured as follows: Sect. 2 describes a series of related works; Sects. 3 and 4 introduce a fuzzy intelligent system that is used in our proposal; Sect. 5 presents the result of applying the fuzzy intelligent system to a preeclampsia case study, and finally, Sect. 6 summarizes our conclusions and future work.

2   Related Works

Nowadays data mining is one of the major topics in the research on data analysis. The work from Karahoca et al. [3] presents a scientific review of the needs that have motivated many researchers to study new ways of organizing and interpreting data in order to find out and/or understand the activity that is monitored and notify the users about it, so that they can use that information for any further action.

The search for new ways to understand the data generated in different contexts has resulted in the development of intelligent systems and linguistic descriptions [1]. These descriptions allow to abstract easy to understand information from raw data, organize it into different levels and dimensions and shape it into a useful format for the users who demand it.

Other interesting works related to this topic include the one from Bhunia et al. [4] who present the design of a system for health surveillance and remote monitoring of patients, able to detect any abnormal situation by applying fuzzy rules; this system is also able to produce alerts for the health care staff when necessary. Although the system from Bhunia et al. produces technical reports, it lacks the capacity of producing a linguistic description of its results.

Baig et al. [5] give a thorough review of the research works related to the application of intelligent environments to health monitoring. In their work, the application of fuzzy logic to the identification of abnormal conditions and the generation of linguistic descriptions for the medical staff is said to be a still open topic, as very little has been done on it up to now.

Different reviews have been published on the application of fuzzy systems [6], health care systems [7] and data mining on medical sensor data [8]. All these works make patent the need of having systems able to generate linguistic descriptions easy to read and interpret.

The application of fuzzy logic systems to health care has been dealt in a series of already published works: Yuan et al. [9] propose a fuzzy reasoning system for remotely monitoring chronic patients which generates reports on their behaviour; Latifi et al. [10] present an expert system that applies fuzzy logic to assist in diagnosing leukemia in children; Sen et al. [11] introduces a data mining system that makes use of fuzzy logic for predicting coronary heart disease; Ekong et al. [12] focus their system on the diagnosis of depression; Nnamoko et al. [13] present a fuzzy expert system for monitoring diabetes mellitus; and finally, Dennis et al. [14] propose an adaptive genetic fuzzy system for classifying medical data.

The generation of linguistic summaries in order to generate health alerts has been studied by Jain et al. [15]; Wilbik et al. [16] also worked on a system to linguistically summarize sensor data related to eldercare. An expert system to support a preeclampsia prevention program was also presented by Matamoros et al. [17], but to the best of our knowledge, it is the only published work linking fuzzy systems and preeclampsia; moreover, that work does not deal with the generation of linguistic reports in the way that we propose.

According to Acampora et al. [18], there are still many challenges to face, especially those related to the generation of user-friendly reports on data from sensors that monitor medical variables that affect humans. This task requires intelligent systems to manage and process the data, and generate the expected results.

3 Previous Concepts

Fuzzy linguistic modelling makes possible the representation of qualitative descriptions that describe words or statements in natural or artificial language by means of linguistic variables [19]. These variables take numerical values such as measurements and can be transformed into statements more understandable to the end user. The elements of an intelligent fuzzy system [20] are the fuzzy rules, the knowledge base and finally, the inference engine. All of them are briefly described in this section.

3.1 Fuzzy Rules

Fuzzy rules are statements of the form "IF - THEN". These rules allow the identification of actions to be performed when a certain condition is met. For example, if the temperature is high, then send the alert "high temperature". In our case, the rules take the form "If x is A then y is B", given a set of input and output pairs [21] in which the output is an alert or an action that is performed in response to the variation of a monitored variable.

The input-output pairs are part of the fuzzy universe of the intelligent fuzzy system. It is common in fuzzy logic the combination of one or more input fuzzy sets (Antecedent), which in turn generate an output fuzzy set (Consequent) [22]. For the case of two fuzzy input sets the rule is as follows

$$\text{IF } x \text{ is } \mathbf{A} \text{ AND } y \text{ is } \mathbf{B} \text{ THEN } z \text{ is } \mathbf{C} \tag{1}$$

Where x, y and z are linguistic variables and A, B and C are fuzzy sets defined in the universe of x, y and z.

3.2 Knowledge Base

The knowledge base supports the set of fuzzy rules [20]. It may include facts and expert opinions on the subject. In some cases the facts are absolute and certain (a body temperature above 37.5 °C corresponds to fever). In other cases it may depend on the opinion of the expert who advises or assists the system (given their high body temperature, the patient may go into convulsions). There are clinical protocols [23] which determine certain actions to be taken given the diagnosis and/or the medical condition of a patient. These protocols are also part of the knowledge base for the intelligent system. In this work, we have also received medical expert advice on the selected topic.

3.3 Inference Engine

The inference engine uses the knowledge base to draw conclusions from the inputs, and produces proper responses. In the case of biomedical signal monitoring, the inference engine links the changes in the monitored variables to the alerts or reports that are generated in the process. There are different inference engine models, the ones from Mamdani and Takagi-Sugeno being the most popular [24]. In this work, the inference engine by Mamdani is used.

The rules in the Mamdani fuzzy model are represented as follows:

$$R^i : \text{IF } x_1 \text{ is } \mathbf{A}_1^i \text{ AND } x_2 \text{ is } \mathbf{A}_2^i \text{ ... AND } x_n \text{ is } \mathbf{A}_n^i \text{ THEN } y \text{ is } \mathbf{B}^i \tag{2}$$

Where x_i and y are linguistic variables, and $\mathbf{A}_j^i$ and $\mathbf{B}$ represent linguistic values that the variables can take.

According to the above, we propose a set of fuzzy rules for monitoring patients and supporting the diagnosis of the preeclampsia disease from the biosignal values of the patient. This rules are the model of the fuzzy intelligent system that runs a standard inference engine.

4 Fuzzy Intelligent System for Supporting Preeclampsia Diagnosis

Preeclampsia (PE) is a medical condition that is mainly characterized by high blood pressure (BP) and proteinuria, which refers to the excess of proteins in the urine, and to a lesser extent, by high body temperature (T). This condition may be mild or severe [25] and occurs usually after 20 weeks of pregnancy. The protocol that applies in this type of pathology is as follows [26]:

Protocol diagnostic phase of preeclampsia (PE):

1. Measure the patient blood pressure (BP) twice, and compute the average of the two measurements. The BP consists of two values: the systolic blood pressure (SBP) and the diastolic blood pressure (DBP). Measure other vital signs of the patient, like the body temperature.
2. If either SBP or DBP are high, proceed to perform a urine test.
3. Perform a physical examination on the patient to search for oedemas or reddened body parts.
4. If the results of the above tests are abnormal, the patient may suffer from preeclampsia. The seriousness of the illness has to be evaluated:
   (a) Mild PE if: SBP between 140 and 160 mmHg and DBP between 90 and 110 mmHg; proteinuria is between $2\,g/24\,h$ y $5\,g/24\,h$; no oedema
   (b) Severe PE if: SBP is greater than 160 and DBP is greater than 110; proteinuria is greater than $5\,g/24\,h$; presence of oedema; T greater than 36.5 °C.
5. According to the type of preeclampsia, the doctor determines the procedure to be followed.

In the following subsection we propose the linguistic variables (SBP, DBP and T) and their linguistic terms that will be used by our proposed system.

4.1 Measured Variables and Linguistic Terms

As stated above, Our contribution will work with only three linguistic variables: systolic and diastolic blood pressure and body temperature, as these three values can be easily measured at home. Regarding blood pressure, there exist a series of portable, non-invasive sensors that may be used together with smartphones, like the ones from iHealth Labs, that provide the systolic pressure (SBP) and diastolic blood pressure (DBP) values [27], both measured in mmHg. Body temperature (T) can be measured in different ways [28]; temperature sensors have been considered in the literature [29,30] and are now commercially available [31].

Our system has a single linguistic output that is the proposal of diagnosis for the patient: DP $\in$ {Absence of PE, Possible mild PE, Possible severe PE}. Table 1 shows the relationship between the type of PE and the value ranges of SBP and DBP, and Table 2 shows the relationship between PE and the T value.

The linguistic variables associated to the three measured values are described as follows:

Table 1. Classification of blood pressure ranges [32]

Variable	Normal	Abnormal (mild)	Abnormal (severe)
SBP	120–140	141–160	>160
DBP	80–90	91–105	>110

Table 2. Classification of body temperature ranges

Variable	Normal	High	Low
Temperature	36 °C–36.5 °C	>36.5 °C	<36 °C

– *Systolic Blood Pressure (SBP)*: universe of discourse: [120, 220] mmHg; linguistic term sets: SBP ∈ {normal, abnormal (mild), abnormal (severe)}. (Figure 1)
SBP values below 120 mmHg are not a preeclampsia symptom, and therefore they will not be taken into account in this study.
– *Diastolic Blood Pressure (DBP)*: universe of discourse: [80, 120] mmHg; linguistic term set: DBP ∈ {normal, abnormal (mild), abnormal (severe)}. (Figure 2)
DBP values below 80 mmHg are not a preeclampsia symptom, and therefore they will not be taken into account in this study.
– *Temperature (T)*: universe of discourse: [35, 45] °C; linguistic term set: T ∈ {normal, high, low}. (Figure 3)

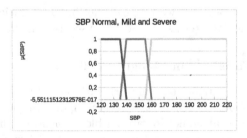

Fig. 1. SBP fuzzy membership functions: normal, abnormal (mild) and abnormal (severe)

4.2 Fuzzy Rules

For the case of preeclampsia, we have defined the fuzzy rules that are shown in Table 3.

Table 3. Fuzzy rule set connecting preeclampsia with blood pressure and body temperature

Rule	Antecedent	Consequent
1	IF ((SBP is normal) OR (DBP is normal) OR (T is normal))	THEN (DP is absence of PE)
2	IF ((SBP is normal) OR (DBP is normal) OR (T is high))	THEN (DP is absence of PE)
3	IF ((SBP is normal) OR (DBP is normal) OR (T is Low))	THEN (DP is absence of PE)
4	IF ((SBP is abnormal (mild)) OR (DBP is normal))	THEN (DP is possible mild PE)
5	IF ((SBP is normal) OR (DBP is abnormal (mild)))	THEN (DP is possible mild PE)
6	IF ((SBP is abnormal (mild)) OR (DBP is abnormal (mild)))	THEN (DP is possible mild PE)
7	IF ((SBP is abnormal (severe)) OR (DBP is abnormal (mild)) OR (T is high))	THEN (DP is possible severe PE)
8	IF ((SBP is abnormal (mild)) OR (DBP is abnormal (severe)) OR (T is high))	THEN (DP is possible severe PE)
9	IF ((SBP is normal) OR (DBP is abnormal (severe)) OR (T is high))	THEN (DP is possible severe PE)
10	IF ((SBP is abnormal (severe)) OR (DBP is normal))	THEN (DP is possible severe PE)
11	IF ((SBP is abnormal (severe)) OR (DBP is normal))	THEN (DP is possible severe PE)
12	IF ((SBP is normal) OR (DBP is abnormal (severe)))	THEN (DP is possible severe PE)
13	IF ((SBP is abnormal (severe)) OR (DBP is abnormal (severe)) OR (T is high))	THEN (DP is possible severe PE)

4.3 Inference Engine

The inference engine of our system is based on the Mamdani model [24], and applies the rules from Table 3 using the OR operator.

The trapezoidal-shaped membership functions of the engine are shown in Eq. 3. In these functions, x represent the value of the measured variable, a and d correspond to the "feet" of the trapezoid (the limits of the membership range for the variable), and b and c correspond to the "shoulders" of the trapezoid (the limits of the range for which the membership function takes its maximum value).

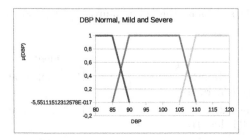

Fig. 2. DBP fuzzy membership functions: normal, abnormal (mild) and abnormal (severe)

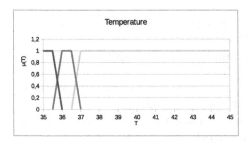

Fig. 3. T fuzzy membership functions: low, normal and high

$$A(x) = \begin{cases} 0 & \text{IF } ((x \leq a) \text{ OR } (x \geq d)) \\ (x-a)/(b-a) & \text{IF } x \in (a, b) \\ 1 & \text{IF } x \in [b, c] \\ (d-x)/(d-c) & \text{IF } x \in (b, d) \end{cases} \quad (3)$$

In Sect. 5 we will show the application of this engine to some example data.

5   Results

In order to prove the effectiveness of the proposed system, we have applied it to a series of real data from patients with preeclampsia that attended the University Hospital of the Nariño department in Colombia. Here we present three example cases:

– **Case 1:** Table 4 shows the SBP, DBP and T values of the patient.
  The results of the inference engine for this case are the following: Rule 1 (Table 3) produces the highest degree of membership, due to the fact that the values of SBP, DBP and T are labeled as *normal*, all of them with a degree of membership equal to 1. Rules 2 and 3 could also be partially considered, given the values of the monitored variables. The final proposal of diagnosis is "absence of PE" with a degree of membership equal to 1.

Table 4. Measured values of the patient from Case 1

Variable	Value
SBP	130 mmHg
DBP	84 mmHg
Temperature	36.5 °C

Table 5. Measured values of the patient from Case 2

Variable	Value
SBP	137 mmHg
DBP	89 mmHg
Temperature	36.2 °C

– **Case 2:** Table 5 shows the SBP, DBP and T values of the patient.
  The results of the inference engine for this case are the following: Rule 5 (Table 3) produces the highest degree of membership, due to the fact that the value of SBP is labeled as *normal* with a degree of membership of 0.6 and the value of DBP is labeled as *abnormal(mild)* with a degree of membership of 0.8. Rules 4 and 6 could also be partially considered, given the values of the monitored variables. The final proposal of diagnosis is "Possible mild PE", with a degree of membership equal to 0.8.
– **Case 3:** Table 6 shows the SBP, DBP and T values of the patient.

Table 6. Measured values of the patient from Case 3

Variable	Value
SBP	158 mmHg
DBP	88 mmHg
Temperature	36.8 °C

The results of the inference engine for this case are the following: the value of SBP is labeled as *abnormal(mild)* with a degree of membership equal to 0.4, and as *abnormal(severe)* with a degree of 0.6; the value of DBP is labeled as *normal* with a degree of membership equal to 0.4, and as *abnormal(mild)* with a degree of membership equal to 0.6; finally, the value of T is labeled as *normal* with a degree of membership equal to 0.4, and as *high* with a degree of membership equal to 0.6.

Given the labels for the measured biosignals, Rule 10 (Table 3) produces the highest degree of membership, while Rules 7, 8, 9, 11, 12 and 13 could also be partially considered. The final proposal of diagnosis is "Possible severe PE", with a degree of membership equal to 0.6.

6   Conclusions and Future Work

One of the most important tasks in medicine is the interpretation of the results of the different tests that are performed on the patients, as the choice of one or the other treatment depends on it. Fuzzy models can give support to this task, as fuzzy logic is a well-known technique that can be adapted to many application areas. However, the creation of a general model for creating linguistic descriptions of the fuzzy system results is still an unsolved problem.

In this work we have presented a model for the analysis of biomedical signals that applies fuzzy logic principles as a step towards the development of an intelligent system that allows the generation of user-friendly linguistic descriptions. Our aim for future works is the development of a system able to monitor biomedical signals over the time and identify possible pathologies using pattern matching techniques. For this purpose, we will have support by medical experts for defining the fuzzy sets and rules for the system.

References

1. Ramos-Soto, A., Bugarin, A.J., Barro, S., Taboada, J.: Linguistic descriptions for automatic generation of textual short-term weather forecasts on real prediction data. IEEE Trans. Fuzzy Syst. **23**(1), 44–57 (2015)
2. Uribe, T.M.: El autocuidado y su papel en la promoción de la salud. Investigación y Educación en Enfermería, vol. 17, no. 2 (2013)
3. Karahoca, A., Karahoca, D., Şanver, M.: Survey of Data Mining and Applications (Review from 1996 to Now) (2012)
4. Bhunia, S.S., Dhar, S.K., Mukherjee, N.: iHealth: a fuzzy approach for provisioning intelligent health-care system in smart city. In: 2014 IEEE 10th International Conference on Wireless and Mobile Computing, Networking and Communications (WiMob), pp. 187–193 (2014)
5. Baig, M.M., Gholamhosseini, H.: Smart health monitoring systems: an overview of design and modeling. J. Med. Syst. **37**(2), 1–14 (2013)
6. Kar, S., Das, S., Ghosh, P.K.: Applications of neuro fuzzy systems: a brief review and future outline. Appl. Soft Comput. **15**, 243–259 (2015)
7. Touati, F., Tabish, R.: U-healthcare system: state-of-the-art review and challenges. J. Med. Syst. **37**(3), 1–20 (2013)
8. Banaee, H., Ahmed, M.U., Loutfi, A.: Data mining for wearable sensors in health monitoring systems: a review of recent trends and challenges. J. Sens. **13**(12), 17472–17500 (2013)
9. Yuan, B., Herbert, J.: Fuzzy cara-a fuzzy-based context reasoning system for pervasive healthcare. Procedia Comput. Sci. **10**, 357–365 (2012)
10. Latifi, F., Hosseini, R., Mazinai, M.: A fuzzy expert system for diagnosis of acute lymphocytic leukemia in children. Int. J. Inf. Secur. Syst. Manage. **4**(2), 424–429 (2015)
11. Sen, A.K., Patel, S., Shukla, D.P.: A data mining technique for prediction of coronary heart disease using neuro-fuzzy integrated approach two level. Int. J. Eng. Comput. Sci. ISSN 2319-7242 (2013)
12. Ekong, V.E., Inyang, U.G., Onibere, E.A.: Intelligent decision support system for depression diagnosis based on neuro-fuzzy-CBR hybrid. Modern Appl. Sci. **6**(7), 79 (2012)

13. Nnamoko, N.A., Arshad, F.N., England, D., Vora, J.: Fuzzy expert system for Type 2 Diabetes Mellitus (T2DM) management using dual inference mechanism. In: AAAI Spring Symposium: Data Driven Wellness (2013)
14. Dennis, B., Muthukrishnan, S.: AGFS: Adaptive Genetic Fuzzy System for medical data classification. Appl. Soft Comput. **25**, 242–252 (2014)
15. Jain, A., Keller, J.M.: Textual summarization of events leading to health alerts. In: 2015 37th Annual International Conference of the IEEE on Engineering in Medicine and Biology Society (EMBC), pp. 7634–7637 (2015)
16. Wilbik, A., Keller, J.M., Alexander, G.L.: Linguistic summarization of sensor data for eldercare. In: 2011 IEEE International Conference on Systems, Man, and Cybernetics (SMC), pp. 2595–2599 (2011)
17. Matamoros, A., Torrealba, A., Rivas, F., González, S., Sánchez, R., Molina, L., Rivas-Echeverría, C.: Expert system for the preeclampsia prevention program. In: Proceedings of the 4th WSEAS International Conference on Computational Intelligence, Man-machine Systems and Cybernetics, (MSC 2005), Miami, USA, pp. 146–149 (2005)
18. Acampora, G., Cook, D.J., Rashidi, P., Vasilakos, A.V.: A survey on ambient intelligence in healthcare. Proc. IEEE **101**(12), 2470–2494 (2013)
19. Zadeh, L.A.: The concept of a linguistic variable and its applications to approximate reasoning, pp. 43–80 (1975)
20. Ortiz, F., Liu, W.Y.: Modelado y control PD-difuso en tiempo real para el sistema barra-esfera, México DF (2004)
21. Rodríguez, F.O., Liu, W.Y.: Modelado y control PD-difuso em tiempo real para el sistema barraesfera. Master's thesis, Universidad de Mexico (2004)
22. Díaz, B., Morillas, A., et al.: Minería de datos y lógica difusa. Una aplicación al estudio de la rentabilidad económica de las empresas agroalimentarias en Andalucía. Estadística Española **46**(157), 409–430 (2004)
23. PARA, EPIDEMIOLOGÍA: Los protocolos clínicos. Med Clin (Barc), vol. 95, pp. 309–316 (1990)
24. Llano, L., Zapata, G., Ovalle, D.: Sistema de Inferencia Difuso para Identificar Eventos de Falla en Tiempo Real del STE usando Registros SOE [Fuzzy Inference System for Identifying Fault Events in STE Real Time Using SOE Registries]. Revista Avances en Sistemas e Informática [Advances in Systems and Informatics Journal] Escuela de Sistemas [School of Systems] de la Universidad Nacional de Colombia Sede Medellín **4**(2) (2007). Special Edition. ISSN: 1657-7663
25. Soli, S.B.: Presentación y evolución de las pacientes ingresadas en la Unidad de Cuidados Intensivos con diagnóstico de Preeclampsia-Eclampsia (2013)
26. Gutiérrez, A., Herráiz, M.A., Bellón, M., Martell, N., Escudero, M.: Protocolo de actuación ante la preeclampsia. Nuestra experiencia (2002)
27. Pérez, J.H., Unanua, A.P.: Hipertensión arterial (2002)
28. Padilla-Raygoza, N., Ruiz-Paloalto, M.L., Díaz-Guerrero, R., Olvera-Villanueva, G., Maldonado, A., del Pilar Raygoza-Mendoza, M.: Correlación de mediciones de temperatura corporal con 3 termómetros: ótico, cutáneo y digital, en niños mexicanos. Enfermería Clínica **4**(3), 175–182 (2014)
29. Ng, K.-G., Wong, S.-T., Lim, S.-M., Goh, Z.: Evaluation of the cadi thermosensor wireless skin-contact thermometer against ear and axillary temperatures in children. J. Pediatr. Nurs. **25**(3), 176–186 (2010)
30. Ávila, D., Cervantes, H., Hipólito, J.I., Nieto, L., de Dios, J., Sánchez, R., Martınez, M.E., Calvo, A.H.: Arquitectura de e-Salud basada en Redes Inalámbricas de Sensores. DIFU100ci@, vol. 6, no. 2, pp. 54–61 (2012)

31. Beurer, G.: Body temperature from Beurer. Soeflinger Strasse, Alemania. Recuperado de: https://www.beurer.com/web/es/products/body_temperature/body_temperature.php (2016)
32. Sanchez, R.A., Ayala, M., Baglivo, H.: otros: Guias Latinoamericanas de Hipertension Arterial. Revista chilena de cardiologia 29 (2010)

Non-intrusive Bedside Event Recognition
Using Infrared Array and Ultrasonic Sensor

Asbjørn Danielsen[✉]

UiT – The Arctic University of Norway, Narvik, Norway
Asbjorn.Danielsen@uit.no

Abstract. Falls in hospitals, in residential care facilities and in home of elderly commonly occur near the bed. Recognizing bedside events may give caretakers the opportunity to intervene, thereby preventing a fall from happening. Most approaches today either use cameras which invade privacy, or sensor devices attached to bed. In this paper an experimental approach for recognizing bedside events using a ceiling mounted 60 × 80 longwave infrared array combined with an ultrasonic sensor device is presented. This novel approach makes it possible to monitor activity while preserving privacy in a non-intrusive manner.

Keywords: Bedside event detection · Fall detection · Longwave infrared array · Ultrasonic sensor · Decision tree

1 Introduction

Investigations into where falls happen done by the Public Health Agency of Canada shows that around 20 % of all registered falls occur in hospital or intervention settings [1, 2]. These falls happen to people that already has problems, either cognitively or physically, and amplifies to the already complicated situation. This increase the healthcare costs not only for the hospitals, but also for the patients and their family [3]. Most falls in nursing homes occur in the resident's room, especially during attempts to get in or out of bed [6, 7, 11, 19]. This is also true in a hospital setting [6, 12, 19].

Systems using sensors attached to the body [9], bed [8] and floor [7] exist in the market despite the lack of evidence that such equipment reduce the number of falls or severity of falls [13–15]. The presence of multiple bed exit alarm devices in the market is however evidence that clinicians are searching for methods to alert them to patients or residents trying to get out of bed so that they might be able to intervene with the hope of possibly preventing a fall.

Bedside event recognition systems are one approach being employed clinically, and trialed in research to provide staff with warning that patients with increased risk of falls (often older patients with cognitive impairment and multiple comorbidities) are about to get up from the bed or chair without the required supervision or assistance [9]. How effective in terms of reducing falls the bed-exit alarms are, is however not clear. In hospital wards the fall rate is relatively low compared to what is observed in nursing homes or subacute wards with the cognitively impaired [20]. An older underpowered study (n = 70) in a geriatric hospital ward found no reduction in falls or fall related

© Springer International Publishing AG 2016
C.R. García et al. (Eds.): UCAmI 2016, Part I, LNCS 10069, pp. 15–25, 2016.
DOI: 10.1007/978-3-319-48746-5_2

injury with pressure sensor bed exit alarms [3]. Similarly, a more recent, larger cluster randomized control trial did not find a reduction in falls rate even though there was increased use of pressure sensor alarms [13]. Shee et al. [20] did a single cohort study evaluating the effectiveness of an electronic sensor alarm in reducing falls in patients (n = 34) with cognitive impairment. The study used a repeated measure (A-B-A) single cohort design to examine the effectiveness of the electronic sensor bed/chair alarm on fall outcomes. The electronic alarm system was found to be a feasible, effective, and acceptable fall prevention strategy for patients with cognitive impairment and they observed a significant decrease in number of falls in the intervention period compared to pre- and post-intervention periods.

It is likely that the lack of evidence of bed-exit alarms as a valuable tool for reducing falls is based on evaluations of the installations of the devices as a single intervention tool only. It seems however that the bed-exit system and protocol need to be tuned differently based on cognitive capabilities of the individual being monitored. Shee et al. [20] used the bed-exit alarms in a ward with cognitively impaired (mean Mini-Mental State examination score: 12.2) patients to signal nurses about individuals that was getting out of bed. With individuals not being cognitively impaired, different approaches may be more effective. In a larger six-month study performed in 2009, Dykes et al. [16] found a positive correlation between awareness of fall risk and the actual number of falls, both in hospital settings and intervention settings. If awareness of fall risk of the individual being hospitalized was altered according to the actual fall risk by recognizing specific actions prior to rising up from bed or sitting down in bed, we expect bed-exit systems to become most valuable. A discussion and design of a fall risk awareness protocol that may be suitable for such an approach is provided by Danielsen et al. [29]. It is however imperative to recognize fall risk awareness as not only a process involving the bed-exiting individual, but moreover a process involving everyone with formal or informal responsibilities in respect to care of the person being monitored [16–18].

This paper presents a novel approach towards bed-event recognitions using a FLIR Lepton 80 × 60 infrared array combined with ultrasonic radar as sensors and a BeagleBone Black as processing device.

2   Related Work

There have been several studies presenting approaches on automatic sensing systems inside hospital rooms to recognize falls out of bed, patients leaving bed, and bed occupancy. In [8] Madokoro et al. developed a sensor using piezoelectric film between two layers of polyethylene terephthalate (PET) plates of laminated polyester. These sensors where placed strategically in bed to detect movement. The signals where amplified, noise cancelling performed, and the output was fed into Counter Propagation Networks (CPNs) – a supervised learning algorithm based on self-organizing maps (SOMs), recognizing 7 distinct behaviors with a mean recognition accuracy of 75 %.

Capezuti et al. [9] investigated two types of bed-exit alarms to detect bed-exiting body movements: a pressure-sensitive, and a pressure sensitive combined with infrared beam detectors (dual sensor system). They also evaluated the occurrence of nuisance alarms, or alarms that are activated when a participant does not attempt to get out of bed. In the investigation they concluded that dual sensor (pressure sensitive plus infrared beam detectors) bed-exit alarm was more accurate than the pressure sensitive alarm in identifying bed-exiting body movements and reducing the incidence of false alarms. Poisson regression modeling was used to recognize alarm conditions.

In [10] Ranasinghe et al. investigated the accuracy of a continuously wearable, battery less, low power and low cost monitoring device (Wearable Wireless Identification and Sensing Platform - WISP) with a single kinematic sensor capable of real-time monitoring. Three-dimensional acceleration readings and the strength of the transmitted signal from the WISP were interpreted to identify bed exit events and sensitivity, specificity and Receiving Operator Curves (ROC) were determined. Two sensor locations was evaluated, over sternum or attached to mattress. The best sensor location was determined to be over sternum. It performed with sensitivity and specificity values of 92.8 % and 97.5 % recognizing bed entry events, and respectively 90.4 % and 93.80 % for detecting bed exit events.

In addition to the approaches that use sensors attached to the actual bed or body, camera-based solutions have been investigated as well. Ni et al. [22] developed a system analyzing depth images on the Microsoft Kinect Depth platform. They recognized the "patient gets up from the bed" event and was able to get an overall accuracy rate of 98 %. Rantz et al. [23] used a similar platform to detect falls from a standing position, from a bed, and rolling out of a bed. They reported a sensitivity of 92 % and 95 % specificity.

The number of approaches towards fall detection, activity or bed-side event recognition using infrared arrays is however very limited. In [24] Sixsmith et al. used a 16×16 thermal array to recognize falls. The system recognized 30 % of all falls. More recently Mashiyama et al. [26] have reported on 8×8 low-cost infrared array mounted in ceiling, which use a k-nearest neighbor (k-NN) algorithm as classifier on a dataset consisting of 20 consecutive frames to detect falls with a fairly high accuracy of approximately 95 %. We have not been able to find any reports on using infrared arrays to recognize bed-side events or bedside falls, neither alone or in combination with other sensors.

3 Experiment

The hardware setup consisted of a BeagleBone Black (BBB) processing platform, a FLIR Lepton 80×60 infrared array, and a Maxbotix ultrasonic sensor, all integrated into a single unit and mounted in the ceiling. The BeagleBone Black [25] is a credit-card sized, low-cost, community-supported development and processing platform running Debian Linux with 512 MB memory, 4 GB 8-bit eMMC on-board flash storage, and a 1 GHz ARM Cortex A8 processor.

The FLIR Lepton 80×60 Infrared Array [28] is a long-wave infrared (LWIR) camera module with 51° Horizontal Field of View and 63.5° Diagonal Field of View. It captures infrared radiation input in its nominal response wavelength band (from 8 to 14 microns) and outputs a uniform thermal image using the Serial Peripheral Interface Bus (SPI) as video interface with an 8.6 framerate. Each frame is transferred as a sequence of integer numbers that represent the temperature in each pixel of the frame. The thermal sensitivity in the infrared array is 0.05° Celsius. The sensor is controlled using a two-wire I2C-like serial-control interface. Due to the nominal response wavelength band, the FLIR Lepton do not need any external light source to function. The data put into the image are purely heat measurements.

The Maxbotix Ultrasonic Sensor MB-1202 I2CXL-MaxSonar EZ0 [21] use I2C two-wire serial control for access and control, and is able to take up to 40 readings per second. Distance readings range from 25 cm up to around 220 cm in our setting.

The FLIR-sensor was mounted in the FLIR Breakout Board [5] and interfaced to the BBBs I2C-bus along with the Maxbotix ultrasonic sensor. The size of the unit containing both sensors and processing unit was 8 × 12 × 3 cm.

3.1   Recognizing the Location of the Bed

The experiments were executed in a hospital bedroom at UiT nursing school in Narvik, Norway. The layout of the room used during experiment is shown in Fig. 1a. The bed used was an ordinary hospital bed with rails. During the experiment the bed was altered into three positions, as shown in Fig. 1b, c and d.

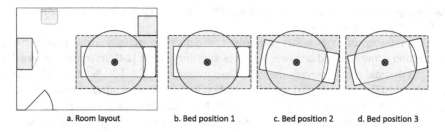

a. Room layout   b. Bed position 1   c. Bed position 2   d. Bed position 3

Fig. 1. Room layout and positions of bed during experiment (Color figure online)

The dark red point over the bed is the location of the ceiling mounted sensors and processing device. The square blue area is the area registered by the FLIR sensor, and the circular area is the area monitored by the ultrasonic sensor.

Temperature is usually not evenly distributed in a room. The floor tends to be slightly colder than the upper parts of the room. This feature suggests that objects in different heights in a room will have slightly different temperatures. In the experiment the bed was positioned around 50–70 cm above the floor and the outline of the bed, with or without bed linen, was clearly visible in the infrared representation due to The FLIR sensor thermal sensitivity of 0.05° Celsius. In Fig. 2a the infrared image captured by the FLIR sensor is presented with a temperature range from 11° to 20° Celsius. The graph presented in Fig. 2a show the temperature distribution in the actual frame. Based on this observation a bed-detection algorithm was developed which executed periodically when a person was not detected in 10 consecutive frames. The bed-detection algorithm uses the Sobel (Fig. 2c) and Canny (Fig. 2d) edge detection algorithms on each frame. On the 20 frames resulting from the 10 frames, a Hough line detection is executed, extracting the two longest and most parallel lines which are furthest apart. Since no heat signature from a person is present in the room obscuring the view, the result is two lines representing the two longest sides of the bed. In Fig. 2b these two lines are superimposed on an IR representation image ranging from 10° to 38° Celsius. The graph presented in Fig. 2b shows the temperature distribution in the actual frame based on this scale.

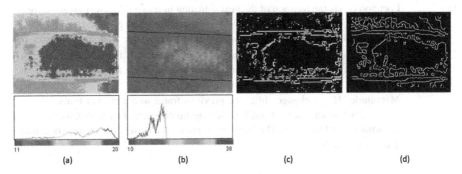

Fig. 2. Bed outline recognition

3.2   Extracting Features

The heat signature of a person is defined to be from 25° Celsius and above. Images without heat signatures are used to filter out the background of the images with individuals in. In addition, the features presented in Table 1 are used for evaluation purposes. The event detection algorithms use the features in Table 1 for analyzing N consecutive frames leading up to the current frame recognizing transitions as shown in Fig. 3.

Residual heat left in bed when an individual leave the bed is detected based on a heat disposal algorithm using the identical N consecutive frames used for event recognition in addition with detection of movement based on M_f. The heat disposal is recognized using temperature trends in areas with sudden temperature changes.

In Fig. 3, the locations where the body heat signature is detected is separated using dashed blue lines (N/A, Floor, Bed, and Bedrail). The oval shapes indicate postures (N/A, Standing, Sitting, Laying) recognized in the different locations. The solid arrows between postures show how postures change. Any change of Posture into Laying or Sitting posture on Floor is interpreted as a Fall-event. Other events recognized are Area Entry/Exit and Bed Entry/Exit.

The approach presented use the size of the heat imprint in-bed (P_{fmax_in}) and out-of-bed (P_{fmax_out}) to determine location (L_f) along with the maximum temperature observed in-bed (T_{fmax_in}) and out-of-bed (T_{fmax_out}). The maximum temperature spot, independent of location, will in most cases be an individual's head, and as such a strong suggestion of the location of the body. Secondly, the size of the heat imprint in or out of bed is a further indication. This approach towards determining location make recognition of location less sensitive towards the use of bed linen.

Table 1. Features extracted for evaluation

P_{fmax_in}	The number of heat pixel found within boundary of bed in frame f
P_{fmax_out}	The number of heat pixels outside the boundary of the bed in frame f
T_{fmax_in}	Max temperature registered within boundary of bed in frame f
T_{fmax_out}	Max temperature registered outside bed boundaries in frame f
D_f	Distance (D_f) is the number of centimeters from the ceiling mounted ultrasonic sensor to the closest reflecting object in frame f
L_f	Location (L_f) is the location of the heat signature in frame f. It is recognized as one of: Bed, Floor, Bedrail, and N/A. N/A indicates no heat signature (above 25° Celsius) in the image or heat signature is not determinable as a single person
PO_f	Posture in frame (PO_f) is posture recognized in frame f. It is evaluated to one of the following: Laying, Sitting, Standing, or N/A. N/A indicates that not sufficient information is available to determine posture
M_f	Magnitude (M_f) of changes from the previous frame to the current frame f. Expressed as an integer from 0 indicating no changes other than normal disturbance, and upwards. The larger the number, the more changes have occurred
Δt	Time between frames

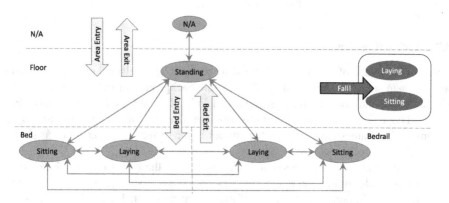

Fig. 3. Transitions and event identification (Color figure online)

3.3 Training

The training set consist of 829 frames out of a total of 8032 frames. One person was used in training set to simulate all transitions expressed in Fig. 3. The data generated from the 8032 frames are P_{fmax_in}, P_{fmax_out}, T_{fmax_in}, T_{fmax_out}, and D_f.

Decision Tree #1. In the first part P_{fmax_in}, P_{fmax_out}, T_{fmax_in}, T_{fmax_out} and D_f, have been manually labeled with the correct location L_f for teaching purposes. This was used to generate a C4.5 [4] generated decision tree using the J48 implementation of WEKA. The generation uses a 10-fold cross validation test mode; resulting in a pruned tree with a 94.5 % correctly recognized instances (783) and 5.5 % incorrectly recognized instances (46).

Decision Tree #2. The second tree use the training set result of Decision Tree #1 where location was correctly recognized (783 instances), the correct posture PO_f was manually added to the result for teaching purposes. This data, consisting of P_{fmax_in}, P_{fmax_out}, T_{fmax_in}, T_{fmax_out}, D_f, L_f, and PO_f, was used to generate a C4.5 [4] generated decision tree using the J48 implementation of WEKA. The generation uses a 10-fold cross validation test mode; resulting in a pruned tree with a 98 % correctly recognized instances (767) and 2.0 % incorrectly recognized instances (16).

3.4 Event Recognition

Event recognition is done analyzing N consecutive frames in terms of Location (L_f) and Posture (PO_f) in frame f, with corresponding distance readings (D_f). The Fall event is recognized as a change from any other posture or location resulting in a situation which the individual is recognized with L_f = Floor and posture PO_f = (Laying | Sitting), in N -1 consecutive frames. The recognition of the fall event uses $N = 10$ frames for this purpose. In addition, in each frame D_f (distance from ultrasonic sensor device to reflecting object) is evaluated to ensure that frames with incorrectly recognized L_f and PO_f are dismissed. M_f is analyzed due to a fall often being a violent incident which significantly alter the heat-impression between frames. Finally, in case an individual falls out of bed, the number of heat impression pixels along with the value of the heat impression in the bed should steadily decrease, while the number of heat impression pixels outside the bed should abruptly increase and then become fairly stable.

The Area Entry and Area Exit events detect situations in which a heat signature totally leave or enter the IR sensory area.

The Bed Entry and Bed Exit events use a similar approach as detection of Fall event, but evaluates on whether the heat signature enter or leave the bed using threshold values. Consequently, a fall incident from bed may trigger two events; Bed Exit and Fall.

3.5 Instructions

Four different predefined sessions were defined to be executed by all participants as shown in Table 2. The hospital bed was positioned in different positions as shown in Fig. 1. The instructions, as expressed in Table 2, were given orally, but no guidance on how to execute the instructions was given.

3.6 Execution

A total of 28 recordings were done by 7 participants, 3 women and 4 men, all young and healthy. The first recording of Scene 1, 2 and 3 by person #1 was used as learning set to create the decision trees. The rest of the dataset, 25 recordings in total, was used for testing. All participants did all four scenes independently of each other. Time between infrared frames, Δt, was 1 s. The bed had full bed linen and some of the participants used this. The participants were instructed to perform an activity, but not

Table 2. Timing scene instructions to participants

Time	Scene 1	Scene 2	Scene 3	Scene 4:
00:00	Enter room Sit down on bed	Enter room Falling down beside bed (knees on the floor)	Enter room Lay down on the bed	Enter room Lay down on the bed
01:00	Lay down on the bed	Try to stand up (do not succeed)	Changing poses randomly during 1–2 min	Laying during one-two minutes, and changing poses
02:00	Laying down changing poses	Sit down or lay down on the floor Change poses	Slip down from the bed to floor Change poses	Sit on the bed
03:00	Sit on the bed Move if you want			Fall down when trying to stand up
03:30	Stand up, walking around the bed			Sit down or lay down on the floor
04:00	Exit room			Exit room

specifically how to perform the activity. The hospital bed was also adjustable, and some of the participants played around with this during the experiment, changing the height/angle back support in the bed.

3.7 Results

During the experiment, a total of 7203 frames where analyzed. The recordings consisted of 130 events. Out of these events 113 events was correctly identified. Table 3 gives a detailed overview of the results from the approach used in this experiment.

Table 3. Event recognition results

	Fall	Bed Entry	Bed Exit	Area Entry	Area Exit
Actual Events	25	23	23	41	18
Recognized	29	14	21	34	15
False Positive	4	2	3	6	5
False Negative	0	11	5	13	8
True Positive	25	12	18	28	10
True Negative	101	105	104	83	107
Accuracy	96,9 %	90,0 %	93,9 %	85,4 %	90,0 %
Precision	86,2 %	85,7 %	85,7 %	82,4 %	66,7 %
Sensitivity	100,0 %	52,2 %	78,3 %	68,3 %	55,6 %
Specifity	96,2 %	98,1 %	97,2 %	93,3 %	95,5 %

4   Discussion

The recognition of the Fall event is very good with a Sensitivity of 100 % and Accuracy of 96,9 %. This is due to the usage of the D_f as a controlling parameter in terms of recognizing the location of an individual to be below the bed. In our setup, this is recognized as $D_f > 180$ during initial startup. The Fall event algorithm detected all falls and an additional 4 false positives. The false positives recognitions were all recognized as secondary falls as a result of an attempt to getting up from the floor, but failing to do so. No false positives were recognized independently of these situations.

The recognition of Bed Entry and Exit events along with the Area Entry and Exit events do not perform as well as the Fall event recognition. This is mainly due to a simplistic approach on detecting these events that should be further developed.

The experiment was executed in a controlled environment, both in terms of air and room temperature, and other factors like sunlight reflecting on floor or wall, air conditioning devices, etc. The approach presented here should be investigated in terms on how external factors influence the recognition rate and which adaptations to make to maintain the recognition rate.

Using an infrared array in activity or event recognition in this context have historically performed unsatisfactory, e.g. Sixsmith et al. [24]. Recently Mashiyama et al. [26] reported on an Accuracy of 95 % using an 8×8 infrared array to detect falls using a ceiling-mounted infrared array in an experimental setting. The approach presented in this paper offer both higher Accuracy and higher Sensitivity.

Microsoft Kinect based platforms have been used in similar contexts. A 92 % Sensitivity and 95 % Specificity was reported by [23] on a 100-week dataset recorded in a hospital setting. These are very good results. Li et al. [27] report 93.0 % and 94.5 % overall Accuracy on recognizing bed posture using the Kinect.

It is evident that the depth imaging capabilities of the Kinect platform is very potent. However, some problems exist. First of all, the Kinect platform use its own infrared light source to create a specter of dots that are used by the two infrared cameras to read distance from the dots and to the camera. If two or more Kinects are used in close proximity and this light specter overlaps between the two Kinects, neither will be able to read distance in the overlapping regions. Secondly, the Kinect platform includes an RGB camera that may be interpreted as invading privacy. The FLIR sensor used in this paper is both low resolution and detect temperature only, thus minimizing privacy issues. Finally, the approach presented may be easily adapted into a home environment, intervention settings or hospitals due to its compact size ($8 \times 12 \times 3$) compared to the Microsoft Kinect ($8 \times 28 \times 8$). In addition, the Kinect approach need a separate processing unit while the approach presented include the processing unit.

5   Conclusions and Future Work

The experiments got a very high Sensitivity and Accuracy detecting falls out of bed using a ceiling-mounted 80×60 infrared sensor combined with an ultrasonic sensor, and using a BeagleBone Black as the processing device. The results from the experiment showed no false negatives in respect to the fall event (all falls that happened was recognized). Further that all false positives (falls that was recognized as falls, but was not falls) was detected as a secondary fall of a previous recognized fall within the same sequence of frames.

The recognition sensitivity of Bed Entry and Bed Exit events is not satisfactory due to the present low-resolution algorithms for event recognition. This is being worked on. When a better recognition rate is achieved with lower False Positives and False Negatives, the system is planned to be tested out in hospital or intervention settings.

A novel approach for recognizing bed-side events by implementing a ceiling-mounted platform which use a FLIR Lepton infrared array sensor for capturing heat impressions and an ultrasonic sensor for registering proximity from the senor devices to the closest reflecting object, have been presented. The processing and recognition of Location and Posture is done using two C4.5 generated decision trees. This information is then used to recognize bedside events using a continuous sliding 10-frame window for event recognition.

References

1. Public Health Agency of Canada: Report on Seniors' fall in Canada (2005). http://publications.gc.ca/collections/Collection/HP25-1-2005E.pdf. Accessed 9 Mar 2016
2. Public Health Agency of Canada: Senior's fall in Canada – Second Report (2014). http://www.phac-aspc.gc.ca/seniors-aines/publications/public/injury-blessure/seniors_falls-chutes_aines/assets/pdf/seniors_falls-chutes_aines-eng.pdf. Accessed 9 Mar 2016
3. Inouye, S.K., Brown, C.J., Tinetti, M.E.: Medicare nonpayment, hospital falls, and unintended consequences. New Eng. J. Med. **360**, 2390–2393 (2009)
4. Quinlan, J.R.: C4.5: Programs for Machine Learning. Morgan Kaufmann Publishers, San Francisco (1993)
5. flir.com: FLIR Lepton Camera Breakout 1.4. http://www.flir.com/uploadedFiles/CVS_Americas/Cores_and_Components_NEW/Resources/flir-lepton-breakout-product-brief.pdf. Accessed 30 May 2016
6. Shojania K.G., Duncan B.W., McDonald K.M., Wachter R.M., Markowitz A.J.: Making Health Care Safer: A critical analysis of patient safety practices. Evidence Report/Technology Assessment, Number 43 (2001). http://archive.ahrq.gov/clinic/ptsafety/pdf/ptsafety.pdf. Accessed 30 May 2016
7. Capezuti, E., Maislin, G., Strumpf, N., Evans, L.: Siderail use and bed-related fall outcomes among nursing home residents. J. Am. Geriatr. Soc. **50**, 90–96 (2002)
8. Madokoro, H., Shimoi, N., Sato, K.: Bed-leaving detection using piezoelectric unrestrained sensors and its measurement system regarding QOL. Nurs. Health **1**(2), 36–45 (2013)
9. Capezuti, E., Brush, B.L., Lane, S., Rabinowitz, H.U., Secic, M.: Bed-exit alarm effectiveness. Arch. Gerontol. Geriat. **49**, 27–31 (2009)
10. Ranasinghe, D.C., Shinmoto Torres, R.L., Hill, K., Visvanathan, R.: Low cost and batteryless sensor-enabled radio frequency identification tag based approaches to identify patient bed entry and exit posture transitions. Gait Posture **39**, 118–123 (2014)
11. Rapp, K., Becker, C., Cameronv, K., Büchele G.: Epidemiology of falls in residential aged care: analysis of more than 70,000 falls from residents of Bavarian nursing homes. J. Am. Med. Dir. Assoc. **13**, 187.e1–187.e6 (2012)

12. Hanger, H.C., Ball, M.C., Wood, L.A.: An analysis of falls in the hospital: can we do without bedrails? J. Am. Geriatr. **47**, 529–531 (1999)
13. Shorr, R.I., Chandler, A.M., Mion, L.C., Waters, T.M., Liu, M., Daniels, M.J., Kessler, L.A., Miller, S.T.: Effects of an intervention to increase bed alarm use to prevent falls in hospitalized patients: a cluster randomized trial. Ann. Intern. Med. **157**, 692–699 (2012)
14. Tideiksaar, R., Feiner, C.F., Maby, J.: Falls prevention: the efficacy of a bed alarm system in an acute-care setting. Mount Sinai J. Med. New York **60**(6), 522–527 (1993)
15. Bruyneel, M., Libert, W., Ninane, V.: Detection of bed-exit events using a new wireless bed monitoring assistance. Int. J. Med. Inform **80**, 127–132 (2011)
16. Dykes, P.C., Carroll, D.L., Hurley, A., Lipsitz, S., Benoit, A., Chang, F., Meltzerm, S., Tsurikova, R., Zuyov, L., Middleton, B.: Fall Prevention in Acute Care Hospitals: a randomized trial. JAMA, J. Am. Med. Assoc. **304**, 1912–1918 (2010)
17. Lee, D.-C.A., Pritchard, E., McDermott, F., Haines, T.P.: Falls prevention education for older adults during and after hospitalization: a systematic review and meta-analysis. Health Educ. J. **73**, 530–544 (2014)
18. Ryu, Y.M., Roche, J.P., Brunton, M.: Patient and family education for fall prevention: involving patients and families in a fall prevention program on a neuroscience unit. J. Nurs. Care Qual. **24**, 243–249 (2009)
19. Fonda, D., Cook, J., Sandler, V., Bailey, M.: Sustained reduction in serious fall-related injuries in older people in hospital. Med. J. Aust. **184**, 379–382 (2006)
20. Shee, A.M., Phillips, B., Hill, K., Dodd, K.: Feasibility, acceptability, and effectiveness of an electronic sensor bed/chair alarm in reducing falls in patients with cognitive impairment in a subacute ward. J. Nurs. Care Qual. **29**, 253–262 (2014)
21. maxbotix.com, "I2CXL-MaxSonar® - EZ™ Series Datasheet". http://www.maxbotix.com/documents/I2CXL-MaxSonar-EZ_Datasheet.pdf. Accessed 30 May 2016
22. Ni, B., Nguyen, C.D., Moulin, P.: RGBD-camera based get-up event detection for hospital fall prevention. In: IEEE International Conference on Acoustics, Speech and Signal Processing (ICASSP), pp. 1405–1408. IEEE Press, New York (2012)
23. Rantz, M.J., Banerjee, T.S., Cattoor, E., Scott, S.D., Skubic, M., Popescu, M.: Automated fall detection with quality improvement "Rewind" to reduce falls in hospital rooms. J. Gerontol. Nurs. **40**, 13–17 (2014)
24. Sixsmith, A., Johnson, N.: A smart sensor to detect the falls of the elderly. IEEE Pervas. Comput. **3**, 42–47 (2004)
25. beagleboard.org: "BeagleBone Black" (2016). https://beagleboard.org/black. Accessed 30 May 2016
26. Mashiyama S., Hong J., Ohtsuki T.: A fall detection system using low resolution infrared array sensor. In: IEEE 25th Annual International Symposium on Personal, Indoor, and Mobile Radio Communication (PIMRC), pp. 2109–2113. IEEE Press, New York (2014)
27. Li, Y., Berkowitz, L., Noskin, G., Mehrotra, S.: Detection of patient's bed statuses in 3D using a Microsoft Kinect. In: 36th Annual International Conference of the IEEE Engineering in Medicine and Biology Society, pp. 5900–5903. IEEE Press, New York (2014)
28. flir.com: "FLIR LEPTON® - Longwave Infrared (LWIR) Camera Module. http://www.mds-flir.com/datasheet/FLIR-Lepton-datasheet.pdf. Accessed 30 May 2016
29. Danielsen, A., Olofsen, H., Bremdal, B.A.: Increasing fall risk awareness using wearables: A fall risk awareness protocol. J. Biomed. Inform. **63**, 184–194 (2016)

Vision Based Gait Analysis for Frontal View Gait Sequences Using RGB Camera

Mario Nieto-Hidalgo[(⊠)], Francisco Javier Ferrández-Pastor,
Rafael J. Valdivieso-Sarabia, Jerónimo Mora-Pascual,
and Juan Manuel García-Chamizo

Department of Computing Technology, University of Alicante,
Campus San Vicente del Raspeig, Alicante, Spain
{mnieto,fjferran,rvaldivieso,
jeronimo,juanma}@dtic.ua.es
http://www.dtic.ua.es

Abstract. In this paper we propose a vision based gait analysis approach to work with frontal view sequences. The main issue of sagittal
view gait sequences is the physical space required to record them. We
propose two different approaches to obtain heel strike and toe off with
frontal gait, both of them are based in the time series of the difference
of component y of both feet. In the former, the zero crosses are used
to determine the range in which heel strike and toe off occurs. In the
latter, the maxima and minima are used instead. Testing our approach
with our own dataset show that it is possible to obtain heel strike and
toe off events using only frontal view gait sequences recorded with an
RGB camera. Results show as well that it is possible to classify between
normal and abnormal gait using frontal view.

Keywords: Gait analysis · Computer vision · RGB camera · Heel
strike · Toe off

1 Introduction

The main objective of the project we are working on is the early detection
of frailty and dementia syndromes using gait analysis. Physical activity is one
of the main component involved in frailty syndrome evaluation [3,12]. Gait is
identified as a high cognitive task in which attention, planning, memory and
other cognitive processes are involved [4,8].

Through gait analysis, quantification of measurable information of gait and
its interpretation [7], frailty and dementia syndromes can be diagnosed. This
process is carried out by specialist and is based on estimations through visual
inspection of gait.

In this work we propose a computer vision approach that could aid the specialists providing them with objective measurements of gait and, thus, improving
the objectivity of the gait analysis performed.

© Springer International Publishing AG 2016
C.R. García et al. (Eds.): UCAmI 2016, Part I, LNCS 10069, pp. 26–37, 2016.
DOI: 10.1007/978-3-319-48746-5_3

We propose the use of video cameras to record the gait of the subject and provide computer vision algorithms able to analyse those sequences to extract spatio-temporal gait parameters. These parameters are analysed by a classifier that is able to determine the presence of abnormalities.

This paper is organised as follows. Section 2 describes related works. Section 3 states the differences between frontal and sagittal gait sequences and why we decided to include frontal view. Section 4 provides the frontal gait approach and experimentation. Finally, Sect. 5 provides the conclusion.

2 Related Works

A set of different gait features is analysed in [17] for person identification. They extract the silhouette and then obtain the contour. Then they extract 4 features: evolution of the width/height proportion, of maximum and minimum width of the bounding box, of the silhouette area and of the center of gravity (COG). These 4 features follow a cyclic pattern that match the gait cycle and are used to identify a person through deterministic learning.

The suitability of the Kinect sensor to measure gait parameters during a treadmill walking in frontal view is examined in [15]. They compare the heel strike (HS) and toe off (TO) obtained with their approach with those obtained with a motion tracking system. HS show less error than TO because it happens closer to the sensor.

The method proposed in [2] is composed of three modules: extraction and post-process of the silhouette, subject classification using Procrustes Shape Analysis (PSA) and Elliptic Fourier Descriptor (EFD), and combination of both results. For silhouette extraction they use background subtraction and morphologic operations to remove noise. PSA module analyses a group of shapes using matching of geometrical location points of a silhouette. They calculate the stride length using the width of the bounding box. EFD allows to characterize the contour of the subject in key points of a gait phase.

Leu et al. propose a method to extract skeleton joints from sagittal and frontal view [6]. The method proposed uses the horizontal and vertical projection of the silhouette pixels to obtain the neck joint, then an anatomical model is applied to obtain hip, knees and ankles. Another method for extracting skeleton joints is proposed by Yoo and Nixon [16]. They also use an anatomical model to segment the silhouette, then they obtain the mean points of each segment and then apply linear regression to obtain a line that represent the bones. During double support gait phase they apply motion tracking to estimate the location of the occluded points. Similarly Khan et al. [5] obtained the skeleton by computing the mean points of each body segment. They obtain legs movement and the posture inclination and compare it with a normal gait model to recognise parkinsonian gait.

There are also some proposals for normal and abnormal gait classification. Wang et al. [13] proposed a method based on optical flow to calculate a histogram of silhouette-masked flows, then an eigenspace transformation is performed.

Then they compare with a normal gait template to calculate a deviation. Bauck-hage et al. [1] proposed a homeomorphisms between 2D lattices and binary shapes to obtain a vector space where the silhouette is encoded. They perform successive bounding box splittings to obtain different lattices, then Support Vector Machine (SVM) is used for classifying.

Most of the vision based gait analysis proposals use sagittal view because it provides more information to work with. However, there are some benefits of a frontal gait analysis. Section 3 analyse the differences between sagittal and frontal view and why we decided to incorporate frontal view to our system.

3   Differences Between Sagittal and Frontal Gait Sequences

In our previous work [9,10], we use sagittal gait video sequences and we rely on feet movement and gradient analysis to determine HS and TO events.

The reason to initially aboard the sagittal plane is because according to Whittle [14] there are more gait abnormalities that can be observed from a sagittal view than from a frontal view. We decide to add frontal gait analysis for the following reasons:

– There are some abnormalities that can only be observed from a frontal point of view. Whittle [14] mention that circumduction, hip hiking, abnormal foot contact and rotation among others are better observed from a frontal view.
– Large amount of physical space required to record sagittal gait sequences, while only a small hall or corridor is required for frontal gait sequences.

Some workarounds are to use a treadmill although it could alter the gait patterns specially with frailty people. Another workaround is to use a motorised camera that follows the subject although it is expensive and could complicate the background subtraction as the background is moving as well.

Sagittal images show a clear view of the movement of the feet and enough information to locate heel and toe of each foot so our previous method works with sufficient accuracy. However, in frontal view it is not easy to determine where the heel and toe are located in each foot. Therefore a different approach is required for frontal sequences.

In sagittal view, the silhouette of the subject, essentially, maintains its size during all the trajectory, however in frontal view the size of the silhouette increases during the trajectory so a normalization might be required.

4   Frontal Gait Approach

The proposed algorithm is very similar to the sagittal one proposed in our previous work [9,10]. It has the same phases: preprocessing, feet location, feature extraction, skeleton detection and classification. Feet location and feature extraction phases that conform the Heel Strike and Toe Off Detection (HSTOD) algorithm are different and the classification phase requires different features to work with. The diagram of the frontal gait approach is shown in Fig. 1.

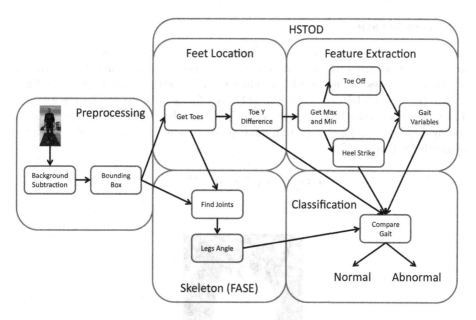

Fig. 1. Diagram of the frontal gait approach.

4.1   Preprocessing

In this phase we extract the subject silhouette by performing a background subtraction using Mixture of Gaussians [18]. Then we apply morphological operation to remove noise. This phase is the most computationally expensive since it has to deal with the entire image and it is also critical because the rest of the algorithm depends on the extraction of the silhouette. An optimization could be to limit the background subtraction to an area slightly bigger than the previously computed silhouette and thus reducing the amount of pixels analysed.

Once the silhouette is extracted we proceed to obtain its bounding box by computing the x, y positions using Eq. 1, then those points are converted to a rectangle $(x, y, width, height)$ using Eq. 2.

$$min_x = \arg\min_{x,y}(\forall_{x,y} \in silhouette : x)$$
$$max_x = \arg\max_{x,y}(\forall_{x,y} \in silhouette : x)$$
$$min_y = \arg\min_{x,y}(\forall_{x,y} \in silhouette : y) \tag{1}$$
$$max_y = \arg\max_{x,y}(\forall_{x,y} \in silhouette : y)$$

$$boundingBox = (min_x, min_y, max_x - min_x, max_y - min_y) \tag{2}$$

4.2 Feet Location

In frontal view both toes are always visible but heels are occluded constantly so heels cannot be properly located. Therefore we rely on toe information only.

To obtain toes we proceed by dividing the silhouette in four parts according to the human model established in [11]. We focus only on the feet segment. Then we split vertically that segment in half. We obtain the left and right foot toe by locating the pixel with minimum y component in the left and right half respectively (Eq. 3) (Fig. 2).

$$\arg\min_{x,y}(\forall_{x,y} \in silhouette : y) \tag{3}$$

Fig. 2. Silhouette obtained after background subtraction and toes obtained by marking the minimum Y of each halves of the silhouette.

4.3 Feature Extraction

The previous phase provides the position of each toe for each frame. That is the information we have to obtain HS and TO. We propose two different approaches to obtain HS and TO with frontal gait. Both of them are based in the time series obtained by subtracting the vertical component of both feet. In the former, the zero crosses are used to determine the range in which HS and TO occurs. In the latter, the maxima and minima are used instead. The former approach obtains good results with normal gait but not with abnormal. This issue is solved by the latter approach.

First Approach. We propose to use the difference of the y component of the toes obtaining a curve in which zero crosses indicate the feet adjacent gait phase. HS and TO of each foot are located between each zero cross as shown in Fig. 3. We can estimate HS and TO by assuming HS is produced before TO and HS is produced in the first half of each region and TO in the second half. Therefore we can estimate HS and TO following Eqs. 4 and 5 respectively, where zc_i is the frame in which a zero cross point occurs and zc_{i-1} is the frame of the previous zero cross point.

$$HS = zc_{i-1} + \frac{(zc_i - zc_{i-1}) \times 3}{4} \tag{4}$$

$$TO = zc_i - \frac{zc_i - zc_{i-1}}{4} \tag{5}$$

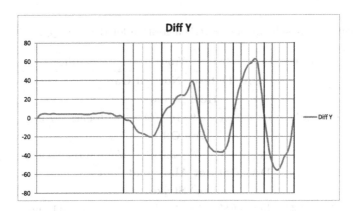

Fig. 3. Graph showing the difference of component Y of each foot. A red vertical line marks the instant at which a HS is produced and a green vertical line marks TO. (Color figure online)

We performed some experiments using our own dataset of frontal gait. To record the dataset we place a camera in front of a corridor of 8 m and ask the person to walk towards it. There are a total of 24 samples of normal gait and 20 samples of abnormal.

We use as ground truth a manual marking of the HS and TO events of each gait sequences of the dataset. The error margin of this manual marking is ±1 frame because that is the minimum measure. We also assume an error of ±1 frame in the algorithm output. So the global error margin is ±2 frames. Then the difference in frames between the ground truth and the proposed algorithm is analysed. We consider acceptable any difference less or equal to the global error margin. Then the root mean square error (RMSE) of the differences is computed using the Eq. 6.

$$RMSE = \sqrt{\frac{1}{n}\sum_{i=0}^{n}(m_i - a_i)^2} \tag{6}$$

Where n is the number of events (HS or TO in this case), m_i is the frame of the event i in the manual marking and a_i is the frame of the event i in the algorithm output.

Table 1 shows the amount of correct detections (less than 2 frames of difference between algorithm and manual marking), undetected cases, wrong detection (more than 2 frames of difference) and the root mean square error of both correct and wrong cases. The RMSE of both HS and TO in normal gait are a bit bigger than the error margin of 2 frames, but they are much bigger in the case of abnormal gait. Therefore, results are acceptable for normal gait but not so for abnormal. A different approach that deals with abnormal gait is required.

Table 1. Results of the HSTOD algorithm for the first approach.

Correct	Undetected	Wrong	RMSE
DAI Dataset Normal Gait			
Heel Strike			
94 (83.2 %)	16 (12.4 %)	19 (16.8 %)	2.02 frames (67 ms)
Toe Off			
75 (66.4 %)	16 (12.4 %)	38 (33.6 %)	2.73 frames (90 ms)
DAI Dataset Abnormal Gait			
Heel Strike			
96 (64.9 %)	49 (24.9 %)	52 (35.1 %)	3.38 frames (111 ms)
Toe Off			
62 (41.9 %)	48 (24.5 %)	86 (58.1 %)	4.1 frames (135 ms)
Total			
Heel Strike			
185 (72.5 %)	65 (20.3 %)	70 (27.5 %)	2.88 frames (95 ms)
Toe Off			
132 (51.8 %)	64 (20.1 %)	123 (48.2 %)	3.60 frames (119 ms)

Second Approach. The previous approach works well with normal gait patterns, however, in some abnormal gait patterns it could not detect some events, e.g., when a foot is always behind the other or is dragged due to some injure or pain. Figure 4 shows a case of foot dragging where in some cases the curve does not cross zero during swing phase. To solve this issue we propose another approach. Using the same curve from the previous approach (the difference of y

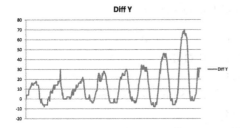

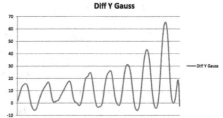

Fig. 4. Difference of component Y of each foot with abnormal foot dragging.

Fig. 5. Difference of component Y of each foot after several gaussian filters.

component of each foot), we proceed by applying several Gauss filters to remove noise (Fig. 5 shows the curve of Fig. 4 after applying several Gauss filters), then we obtain the local maxima and minima. These maxima and minima are located more or less at the center of each pair of zero crosses. But, in this case, the curve does not have to cross zero to produce a maximum or minimum, solving the issue of the previous approach.

HS are located before a maximum or minimum and TO after. We know that both events are located in that region. Empirically adjusting them we obtain that the HS is located at 1/4 of the distance between one maximum (or minimum) and the previous (Eq. 7) and TO is located at 1/8 of the distance between one maximum (or minimum) and the next one (Eq. 8).

Being M an ordered set of maxima and minima in ascending chronological order:

$$M = \{m_1, m_2, m_3 \ldots m_n\}$$

HS of m_i is obtained as:

$$HS_i = m_i - \frac{m_i - m_{i-1}}{4} \tag{7}$$

and TO is obtained as:

$$TO_i = m_i + \frac{m_{i+1} - m_i}{8} \tag{8}$$

The same experiment performed in the first approach is performed for the second one and results are shown in Table 2.

As shown in there, the RMSE of both HS and TO in normal gait are smaller than the error margin of 2 frames, but they are slightly bigger in the case of abnormal gait. Therefore, results are acceptable and the abnormal gait accuracy is improved. Most of the error is produced in the first steps when the silhouette is smaller (the subject is the farthest from the camera).

The results obtained with our sagittal view approach [10] are similar for normal gait. We obtained there 1.2 frames for HS and 1.24 for TO, those were slightly better than the frontal approach (1.89–1.65) but very similar. However in the case of abnormal gait we obtained 1.48 frames for HS and 2.09 for TO which where way better than the obtained with the frontal view approach (2.68–3.03).

Table 2. Results of the HSTOD algorithm for the second approach.

Correct	Undetected	Wrong	RMSE
DAI Dataset Normal Gait			
Heel Strike			
115 (89.1 %)	0 (0 %)	14 (10.9 %)	1.89 frames (62 ms)
Toe Off			
115 (89.1 %)	0 (0 %)	14 (10.9 %)	1.65 frames (54 ms)
DAI Dataset Abnormal Gait			
Heel Strike			
102 (68.9 %)	6 (3.9 %)	46 (31.1 %)	2.68 frames (88 ms)
Toe Off			
91 (61.5 %)	6 (3.9 %)	57 (38.5 %)	3.03 frames (100 ms)
Total			
Heel Strike			
217 (78.3 %)	6 (2.1 %)	60 (21.7 %)	2.34 frames (77 ms)
Toe Off			
206 (74.4 %)	6 (2.1 %)	71 (25.6 %)	2.48 frames (82 ms)

Although a different dataset and recording environment was used in Xu et al. [15] we can do a comparison between our approach and theirs. We can only compare our results for normal gait as their approach uses only that. For HS they obtained a standard deviation of 1.45 frames (1.3 for right foot and 1.6 for left foot) and our result was 1.89 frames, a fairly similar result. However for TO they obtained a standard deviation of 3.55 frames (3.4 for right foot and 3.7 for left foot) whether we obtained 1.65 frames, a better result. Xu et al. stated in their paper that a greater error in TO was due to the TO occurring at a far distance to the camera where the depth error was bigger, in our case we do not have that problem. As we stated before, Xu et al. used a different dataset and a different recording environment so the conclusion of the comparison is that both approaches show similar results although our approach uses only RGB image.

4.4 Skeleton Detection

This phase deals with locating some characteristic points of the human body. The process is the same as in our previous work [10]. We start by dividing the silhouette using an anatomical model to obtain head, torso, thighs and feet segments. Then for head and torso segments we split them horizontally and compute the COG of both halves. We move the COGs obtained to top and bottom of their respective segments and average the points of upper torso and lower head to connect both points. For the thighs segment we proceed like in head and torso and then we also split it vertically to obtain another two COGs, those COGs are moved to bottom to obtain knee points. The upper thighs COG is averaged with lower torso COG to obtain the hip point. Finally, feet points are already located in the previous phase (Foot Location).

Once the points are obtained, we calculate legs angle using the hip and feet points to obtain the angle between the two lines formed by hip - left foot and hip - right foot. The other points are not used, but we intend to use them for classification purposes in the future.

4.5   Classification

To perform a classification between normal and abnormal gait we use the stride (difference between y component of each foot) and legs angle time series. We use the classifier K-Nearest Neighbours (KNN) with Dynamic Time Warping (DTW) as distance function. We perform the classification with two different methods:

- Testing each gait cycle separately.
- Testing each gait cycle of each recording sample and outputting the result that appears in most cases.

The results of the classification experiments are shown in Table 3. As shown in there, testing each recording sample produce better results as it tends to eliminate outliers.

Table 3. 10-fold and leave-one-out cross-validation results of each classifier.

Classifier	10-Fold	Leave-one-out
Stride each cycle	74.64 %	79.3 %
Legs angle each cycle	71.42 %	77.19 %
Stride each subject	80 %	83.72 %
Legs angle each subject	87.5 %	88.37 %

As a first experiment we focused in obtaining a classification between normal and abnormal gait to assess the suitability of the proposed algorithm to differentiate between the two of them. For this test we considered knee pain and foot dragging as abnormal gait. The results obtained suggest that the classifier can differentiate between normal and abnormal gait, therefore, future work will focus in classifying different abnormal gaits.

5   Conclusion

In this paper we propose an approach to obtain HS and TO and some skeleton joints using frontal gait sequences. Using frontal view we face some problems when obtaining heels position so we focus in toes instead. Results are acceptable providing a good approximation to HS and TO. Comparing with our sagittal view approach, results were similar but the accuracy of the sagittal view was better. We also compare the results with those obtained by Xu et al. [15] with Kinect showing similar results too with the advantage that we only rely on RGB image.

We also provide some features to perform a classification between normal and abnormal gait from frontal view. Results show classification rates greater than 80 % in some cases.

The ability to perform gait analysis using frontal view allow to reduce the physical space required for the tests. In addition, this method does not rely on silhouette movement (our previous approach did) so it is also suitable for treadmill gait sequences therefore the space could be reduced even more in cases where the alteration of gait patterns that the treadmill could cause are not important.

Future work will focus in improving the accuracy of HS and TO for abnormal gait and classifying different abnormal gait types.

Acknowledgements. This research is part of the FRASE MINECO project (TIN2013-47152-C3-2-R) funded by the Ministry of Economy and Competitiveness of Spain.

References

1. Bauckhage, C., Tsotsos, J.K., Bunn, F.E.: Automatic detection of abnormal gait. Image Vis. Comput. **27**(1), 108–115 (2009)
2. Choudhury, S.D., Tjahjadi, T.: Gait recognition based on shape and motion analysis of silhouette contours. Comput. Vis. Image Underst. **117**(12), 1770–1785 (2013)
3. Fried, L.P., Tangen, C.M., Walston, J., Newman, A.B., Hirsch, C., Gottdiener, J., Seeman, T., Tracy, R., Kop, W.J., Burke, G., et al.: Frailty in older adults evidence for a phenotype. J. Gerontol. A Biol. Sci. Med. Sci. **56**(3), M146–M157 (2001)
4. Hausdorff, J.M., Yogev, G., Springer, S., Simon, E.S., Giladi, N.: Walking is more like catching than tapping: gait in the elderly as a complex cognitive task. Exp. Brain Res. **164**(4), 541–548 (2005)
5. Khan, T., Westin, J., Dougherty, M.: Motion cue analysis for parkinsonian gait recognition. Open Biomed. Eng. J. **7**, 1 (2013)
6. Leu, A., Ristić-Durrant, D., Gräser, A.: A robust markerless vision-based human gait analysis system. In: 2011 6th IEEE International Symposium on Applied Computational Intelligence and Informatics (SACI), pp. 415–420. IEEE (2011)
7. Mahoney, F.I.: Functional evaluation: the barthel index. Maryland State Med. J. **14**, 61–65 (1965)
8. Mulder, T., Zijlstra, W., Geurts, A.: Assessment of motor recovery and decline. Gait Posture **16**(2), 198–210 (2002)
9. Nieto-Hidalgo, M., Ferrández-Pastor, F.J., Valdivieso-Sarabia, R.J., Mora-Pascual, J., García-Chamizo, J.M.: Vision based extraction of dynamic gait features focused on feet movement using RGB camera. In: Bravo, J., Hervás, R., Villarreal, V. (eds.) AmIHEALTH 2015. LNCS, vol. 9456, pp. 155–166. Springer, Heidelberg (2015). doi:10.1007/978-3-319-26508-7_16

10. Nieto-Hidalgo, M., Ferrández-Pastor, F.J., Valdivieso-Sarabia, R.J., Mora-Pascual, J., García-Chamizo, J.M.: A vision based proposal for classification of normal and abnormal gait using rgb camera. J. Biomed. Inform. **63**, 82–89 (2016)
11. Tafazzoli, F., Safabakhsh, R.: Model-based human gait recognition using leg and arm movements. Eng. Appl. Artif. Intell. **23**(8), 1237–1246 (2010)
12. Waltson, J., Fried, L.: Frailty and the old man. Med. Clin. North Am. **83**(5), 1173–1194 (1999)
13. Wang, L.: Abnormal walking gait analysis using silhouette-masked flow histograms. In: 18th International Conference on Pattern Recognition, ICPR 2006, vol. 3, pp. 473–476. IEEE (2006)
14. Whittle, M.W.: Gait Analysis: An Introduction. Butterworth-Heinemann, London (2014)
15. Xu, X., McGorry, R.W., Chou, L.S., Lin, J.H., Chang, C.C.: Accuracy of the microsoft kinect for measuring gait parameters during treadmill walking. Gait Posture **42**(2), 145–151 (2015)
16. Yoo, J.H., Nixon, M.S.: Automated markerless analysis of human gait motion for recognition and classification. Etri J. **33**(2), 259–266 (2011)
17. Zeng, W., Wang, C., Yang, F.: Silhouette-based gait recognition via deterministic learning. Pattern Recogn. **47**(11), 3568–3584 (2014)
18. Zivkovic, Z., van der Heijden, F.: Efficient adaptive density estimation per image pixel for the task of background subtraction. Pattern Recogn. Lett. **27**(7), 773–780 (2006)

Application of Feature Subset Selection Methods on Classifiers Comprehensibility for Bio-Medical Datasets

Syed Imran Ali[1(✉)], Byeong Ho Kang[2], and Sungyoung Lee[1(✉)]

[1] Department of Computer Engineering,
Kyung Hee University Seocheon-dong, Giheung-gu,
yongin-si, gyeonggi-do, Republic of Korea
{imran.ali,sylee}@oslab.khu.ac.kr
[2] Department of Engineering and Technology,
Information and Communication Technology,
University of Tasmania, Hobart, Australia
byeong.Kang@utas.edu.au

Abstract. Feature subset selection is an important data reduction technique. Effects of feature selection on classifier's accuracy are extensively studied yet comprehensibility of the resultant model is given less attention. We show that a weak feature selection method may significantly increase the complexity of a classification model. We also proposed an extendable feature selection methodology based on our preliminary results. Insights from the study can be used for developing clinical decision support systems.

Keywords: Feature subset selection · Model comprehensibility · Data classification · Data mining · Clinical decision support system

1 Introduction

Data classification is one of the important tasks in data mining for knowledge acquisition. The main purpose of a classification algorithm is to model relationship between independent features and a response variable. An inferred model constructed by a classification algorithm may produce either a comprehensible model or an incomprehensible model. This paper deals with comprehensible models. Decision tree and rule-based decision list are the two most common used comprehensible models [1]. Aforementioned models are depicted in Figs. 1 and 2, respectively. Along with predictive accuracy, comprehensibility of a model is also an important characteristic for a classification algorithm in certain domains [1].

2 Related Work

This section deals with some of the important related studies. Fast Correlation Based Feature Selection (FCBFS) [2] is one of the highly effective filter methods. It accounts for both feature relevancy and redundancy. H. Liu et al. [3] proposed a consistency

© Springer International Publishing AG 2016
C.R. García et al. (Eds.): UCAmI 2016, Part I, LNCS 10069, pp. 38–43, 2016.
DOI: 10.1007/978-3-319-48746-5_4

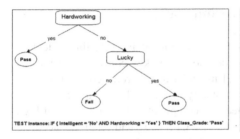

Fig. 1. Decision Tree model

Fig. 2. Decision List model

based feature selection mechanism. We have used genetic algorithm in this method (referred hereafter GA-Consist). Correlation-based Feature subset Selection (CFS) evaluates usefulness of a subset of attributes based inter and intra feature correlation [4]. This study is based on four commonly used comprehensible models namely C4.5, CART, RIPPER and Ant-Miner. Table 1 summarized some of the important studies.

Table 1. Summarized related work

Ref	Main contribution	Limitation(s)
[5]	Survey FSS methods, proposed categorizing framework and an integrated platform for automatic selection of FSS based on dataset characteristics	No emprical experiments classifier comprehensibility not discussed
[6]	Survey FSS methods for intrusion detection sysytem, empirical experimentation mainly based on predictive accuracy only	Classifier comprehensibility not discussed, no integrated framework proposed
[7]	Proposed a scoring measure to compare results of different FSS methods, Emprical experimentation is performed to contrast the ability of the different FSAs to hit a solution with respect to irrelevance, redundancy and sample size	No comprehensible framework on the basis of FSS and classifier complexity proposed
[8]	Survey state of the art FSS methods for micro-array datasets, dataset shift and imbalanced ration also discussed, empirical experiment mainly based on predictive accuracy only	Effects of FSS on model size are not studied, no integrating framework proposed
[9]	Proposed a framework for cost based feature, detailed empirical experimentation based on classifier error and total cost of the selected features	Model's complexity is not discussed, no categorizing framework explored

3   Proposed Methodology and Experimentation

Based on the empirical study, we proposed a methodology for selecting a feature selection method based on a number of considerations. The key consideration for this study is the nature of the classification model intended to be produced i.e. true base model or rule based model. Accuracy and complexity of the model are also addressed. For example if a rule based model is intended and complexity of the model is of high consideration then FCBF is recommended otherwise CFS can yield relatively accurate results with comparatively a more complex model. Figure 3 depicts feature selection methodology in a graphical manner. It is important to note that this is a preliminary study which lays foundation for further studies on the intersection of effective data reduction methods and classifier comprehensibility.

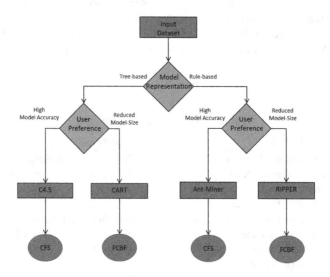

Fig. 3. Feature selection methodology

The purpose of the proposed methodology is to assist in selecting a feature selection method based on user's requirements. Moreover, only those feature selection methods are retained which enhances some aspect of the classifier e.g. compact model size, predictive accuracy, reduced training/testing time, etc. Since, GA-Consist couldn't provide any extra advantage over either CFS or FCBF therefore it is not depicted in Fig. 3. Datasets used in this study are easily accessible from University of California, Irvine (UCI) machine learning repository [10] and related openly accessible dataset repositories. Table 2 enlists datasets along with basic statistics i.e. number of features, instances and classes in each dataset. It is important to note that all the datasets employed in this study are from the bio-medical domain. All the experiments from Tables 3, 4, 5 and 6 are performed using 10-fold cross validation. These datasets are of varied complexity i.e. from medium to large dimensionality, high number of instances,

Table 2. Datasets characterisitcs

No.	Dataset	Features	Instances	Classes
1	Breast-Cancer	9	286	2
2	Diabetes	8	768	2
3	Heart-c	13	303	2
4	Heart-h	13	294	2
5	Heart-Statlog	13	270	2
6	Hepatitis	19	155	2
7	Hypothyroid	29	3772	2
8	Lymph	18	148	4
9	Primary Tumor	17	339	21
10	Splice	60	3175	3
11	Lung Cancer	56	32	3

imbalanced feature-instance ratio, etc. Hence, insights gathered from the study can be extended to data driven decision support systems.

In order to construct comprehensible classifiers all the datasets with numeric features are discretized. In this study effect of data discretization on model construction is not studied. Four state of the art classifiers are used i.e. C4.5, CART, RIPPER and Ant-Miner. Three filter methods, FCBF, CFS and GA-Consistency are used for feature subset selection. Detailed experimentation is performed. Due to the page limitation only the summarized results are discussed. As mentioned in Table 3 with no feature selection C4.5 achieved an average accuracy of 76.47 %. Average tree size and number of leaves are 42.63 and 31.81, respectively. In case of feature selection it can be observed that all the feature selection methods achieved a reduced dataset. FCBF selected the smallest number of features i.e. on average 7.63 features were retained, while the tree size was also reduced significantly. Average accuracy of C4.5 is slightly reduced with FCBF as compared to no feature selection. CFS also achieved smaller tree size as compared to without feature selection. Moreover, its accuracy is slightly better than the feature selection methods considered in the study. Case of GA-Consist is interesting. It could not perform well for classification accuracy although it retained only half of the feature set on average which is a lot of feature reduction. Tree size in case of GA-Consist is far more complex than with any of the other feature selection algorithms or with no feature selection. It can be easily observed that due to the failure in selecting useful features it not only affects the accuracy of the classifier but the model size also complicates more so than using all the features. It is an important observation which allows for more study on the effects of feature selection methods on the resultant model's complexity.

Table 3. Experimental results for C4.5   **Table 4.** Experimental results for CART

	Average Features	Average Accuracy	Average Tree Size	No. of Leaves		Average Features	Average Accuracy	Average Tree Size	No. of Leaves
Total	23.18	76.47	42.63	31.81	Total	23.18	72.89	16.09	8.54
FCBF	7.63	74.5	33.9	26.36	FCBF	7.63	74.86	16.63	8.81
CFS	9.45	75.97	38	27.81	CFS	9.45	73.40455	16.63	8.81
GA-Consist	12	71.65	66.76	49.07	GA-Consist	12	70.9	19	10

CART classifier achieved an average accuracy of 72.89 % with no feature selection. Resultant tree size and number of leaves are 16.09 and 8.54, respectively. CART could achieve lower accuracy as compared to C4.5 with a much reduced tree size on average. FCBF achieved highest accuracy on CART yet couldn't much improve on the model size. GA-Consist resulted in lower accuracy on average and a comparatively large model size.

For rule-based classifiers we have opted for a popular model complexity metric i.e. number of rules and conditions per rule [1]. RIPPER achieves an average accuracy of 72.41 % with no feature selection. On average 4.81 rules were created with a 1.96 conditions-to-rule ratio. Moreover, FCBF achieved slightly higher accuracy than CFS. Model size of FCBF was also slightly larger than with no feature selection, as is the case with other two feature selection methods. Hence, it can be observed that in case of RIPPER classifier feature selection methods couldn't improve on the model size of the algorithm. So here we can observe the trade-off between classifier's accuracy and its model size. If a user has a preference for the former case then FCBF would be preferred while no feature selection method may be preferred for the latter case.

Table 5. Experimental results for RIPPER   **Table 6.** Experimental results for Ant-Miner

	Features	Accuracy	Rules	Conditions	Conditions/ Rules		Features	Accuracy	Rules	Conditions	Conditions/ Rules
Total	23.18	72.41	4.81	9.45	1.96	Total	23.18	74.64	8.04	19.21	2.38
FCBF	7.63	75.1	4.9	10	2.03	FCBF	7.63	79.13	7.01	9.87	1.4
CFS	9.45	75	6	13.75	2.29	CFS	9.45	80.14	7.62	12.93	1.69
GA-Consist	12	71.52	8.16	20	2.44	GA-Consist	12	72.35	8.25	16.66	2.01

Table 6 mentions results for Ant-miner classifier. On average Ant-miner algorithm achieves higher accuracy than RIPPER. Moreover, average model size of Ant-miner is comparatively larger than that of RIPPER. CFS achieved the highest accuracy, with a slightly larger model size then FCBF. Although GA-Consist couldn't achieve higher accuracy but it did achieve a lower model size. So we can infer that the effects of a feature selection method on the model size vary from one classifier to another. Hence, effects of feature selection on comprehensibility of the classifier are more subtle. Since Ant-miner is a population-based stochastic algorithm [11] it has incurred the highest training time of all the classifiers considered in this study.

4   Conclusion and Future Work

In this study we evaluated effects of feature selection methods on comprehensibility of the classifiers. Classifier comprehensibility has received relatively less attention while selecting for an appropriate feature selection method. We have shown that different feature selection methods have a varied effect on the comprehensibility of classifiers.

Acknowledgments. This work was supported by the Industrial Core Technology Development Program (10049079, Develop of mining core technology exploiting personal big data) funded by the Ministry of Trade, Industry and Energy (MOTIE, Korea) and This work was supported by the National Research Foundation of Korea (NRF) grant funded by the Korea government (MSIP) NRF-2014R1A2A2A01003914.

References

1. Freitas, A.A.: Comprehensible classification models: a position paper. ACM SIGKDD Explor. Newslett. **15**(1), 1–10 (2014)
2. Yu, L., Liu, H.: Feature selection for high-dimensional data: A fast correlation-based filter solution. ICML **3**, 856–863 (2003)
3. Liu, H., Setiono, R.: A probabilistic approach to feature selection-a filter solution. ICML **96**, 319–327 (1996)
4. Hall, M.A.: Correlation-based feature selection for machine learning. Diss. The University of Waikato (1999)
5. Liu, H., Yu, L.: Toward integrating feature selection algorithms for classification and clustering. IEEE Trans. Knowl. Data Eng. **17**(4), 491–502 (2005)
6. Chen, Y., Li, Y., Cheng, X., Guo, L.: Survey and taxonomy of feature selection algorithms in intrusion detection system. In: Lipmaa, H., Yung, M., Lin, D. (eds.) Inscrypt 2006. LNCS, vol. 4318, pp. 153–167. Springer, Heidelberg (2006)
7. Belanche, L.A., González, F.F.: Review and evaluation of feature selection algorithms in synthetic problems. arXiv preprint arXiv:1101.2320 (2011)
8. Bolón-Canedo, V., Sánchez-Maroño, N., Alonso-Betanzos, A., Benítez, J.M., Herrera, F.: A review of microarray datasets and applied feature selection methods. Inf. Sci. **282**, 111–135 (2014)
9. Bolón-Canedo, V., Porto-Díaz, I., Sánchez-Maroño, N., Alonso-Betanzos, A.: A framework for cost-based feature selection. Pattern Recogn. **47**(7), 2481–2489 (2014)
10. Lichman, M.: UCI Machine Learning Repository. University of California, School of Information and Computer Science, Irvine (2013). http://archive.ics.uci.edu/ml
11. Parpinelli, R.S., Lopes, H.S., Freitas, A.A.: Data mining with an ant colony optimization algorithm. IEEE Trans. Evol. Comput. **6**(4), 321–332 (2002)

First Approach to Automatic Measurement of Frontal Plane Projection Angle During Single Leg Landing Based on Depth Video

Carlos Bailon[1](✉), Miguel Damas[1], Hector Pomares[1], and Oresti Banos[2]

[1] Department of Computer Architecture and Computer Technology,
CITIC-UGR Research Center, University of Granada, Granada, Spain
cbailon37@correo.ugr.es, {mdamas,hector}@ugr.es
[2] Telemedicine Group, University of Twente, Enschede, Netherlands
o.banoslegran@utwente.nl

Abstract. Knee alignment measurements are one of the most extended indicators of knee-complex injuries such as anterior cruciate ligament injury and patellofemoral pain syndrome. The Frontal Plane Projection Angle (FPPA) is widely used as a 2-D estimation of knee alignment. However, traditional procedures to measure this angle suffer from practical limitations, which leads to huge time investments when evaluating multiple subjects. This work presents a novel video analysis system aimed at supporting experts in the dynamic measurement of the FPPA in a cost-effective and easy way. The system employs Kinect V2 depth sensor to track reflective markers attached to the patient leg joints to provide an automatic estimation of the angle formed by the hip, knee and ankle joints. Information registered by the sensor is processed and managed by a computer application that simplifies expert's work and expedites the analysis of the test results.

Keywords: Knee alignment · Frontal Plane Projection Angle · Reflective markers · Anterior cruciate ligament · Patellofemoral pain syndrome · Depth video · Kinect · 2-D analysis

1 Introduction

The knee alignment angle – also known as knee valgus – measured during dynamic tasks is commonly used among the scientific community as a risk indicator of many biomechanical injuries and disorders related to leg joints. Altered knee alignment seems to contribute to the occurrence of anterior cruciate ligament (ACL) injuries and patellofemoral pain syndrome (PFPS) [1,2]. A recent study [3] also associates the midfoot mobility and the ankle joint dorsiflexion range with the knee valgus angle. Furthermore, other studies [4,5] show that the knee joint complex injuries are one of the most commonly occurring injuries in a number of sports (Fig. 1), meaning long rehabilitation periods and, in the worst-case scenario, the end of sport practice.

© Springer International Publishing AG 2016
C.R. García et al. (Eds.): UCAmI 2016, Part I, LNCS 10069, pp. 44–55, 2016.
DOI: 10.1007/978-3-319-48746-5_5

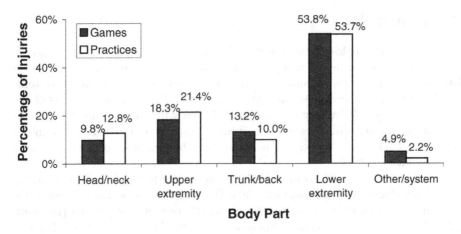

Fig. 1. Distribution (percentages) of injuries by body part for games and practices for 15 sports [5].

In order to quantify knee alignment, Wilson et al. [6] introduced the Frontal Plane Projection Angle (FPPA), presenting good within-day reliability (ICC[1] = 0.88). The FPPA is the projection of the knee angle onto the frontal body plane, resulting in the deviation of the hip-knee line from the knee-ankle line. Subsequent researches [7–9] have demonstrated the relationship between FPPA measurements and the previously mentioned injuries.

In the light of the present limitations of FPPA measurement methods and the significant results that can be extracted from them, as well as the potential of digital technologies, this work presents a novel automatic video analysis system intended to support experts in the dynamic measurement not only of FPPA, but also of any biomechanics 2-D angle with an inexpensive, easy-to-use, single-camera solution. In order to calculate the FPPA value, the system makes use of reflective markers placed on desired subject's body joints, and tracks them through a depth sensor. All the information registered is processed by a computer application, which aims to support and simplify expert's normal routine, helping to mitigate human errors – thus increasing precision – and accelerate the analysis of the results. This paper is structured as follows. Section 2 presents an overview of the state-of-the-art in methods to obtain FPPA values. In Sect. 3, fundamental principles of most frequently used tests for evaluating the FPPA are outlined. The proposed system is described in Sect. 4. The paper discussion is presented in Sect. 5. Section 6 summarizes final conclusions and highlights future work and prospects of the system.

---

[1] Intraclass correlation coefficient.

2   Related Work

To measure the angles of the lower limb joints, a great range of technologies can be used. Nevertheless many of them present essential drawbacks, which has motivated the development of this work. Inertial sensor-based systems [10,11] get very accurate data of 3-D rotations and the relative positions of the joints, but they involve having sensors and even wire connections attached to the subject's body, which results in movement restriction. Furthermore, another main drawback of inertial sensors is non-deliberated sensor displacement during dynamic tasks [12,13].

For those reasons, video analysis has become the main analysis method for lower limb kinematics analysis. Powerful 3-D marker-based motion tracking video systems are available, such as Vicon cameras [14] or Optotrak system [15], both *gold-standards* in biomechanical analysis. However, despite their reliability and accuracy, high financial and spatial resources are needed [7], making the 3-D video analysis not practical for most clinical settings, including the FPPA measurement.

Therefore, 2-D techniques, which employ less expensive, portable and easy-to-use equipment, may be more useful. Many studies have introduced 2-D video analysis of the FPPA measurement in a variety of tests and have contrasted its validity against existing 3-D techniques [7,9]. Allan G. Munro et al. [8,16] also showed the reliability of 2-D techniques when assessing knee injury risk and established measurement error values for this type of analysis. They also emphasized the need for further investigation on these screening tools. However, it is worth considering that FPPA is not informative of true joint 3-D motion [1,7] and cannot determine joint rotations – only 23 % to 30 % of their variation. Nevertheless, although 2-D analysis is not a substitute for 3-D measurements of lower limb kinematics, the previously mentioned researches demonstrated it to be useful for screening knee-joint FPPA to identify high-risk injury subjects.

Current systems based on 2-D analysis present an important limitation: they are based on offline video analysis with software tools, where experts have to manually plot the joint markers on freeze video frames. Offline video analysis demands huge time expenses, and increase human-made errors due to video freezing at correct frames and marker positioning. The proposed system tries to cope with this limitation, offering an automatic tracking system which provides real-time FPPA computing and processing, with no need for offline analysis. In order to achieve this, the Kinect V2 sensor has been used. This sensor provides accurate depth video frames which are used to track reflective markers attached to the subject's body. Moreover, due to its reduced cost and single-camera portability, it accomplishes the desired requirements: easiness-of-use and time-and-cost-effectiveness in contrast to other high-end cameras.

3   Knee Alignment Measurement Tests

There exist a great range of tests on which knee alignment can be measured, regardless of the physical condition of the assessed subject. The results obtained

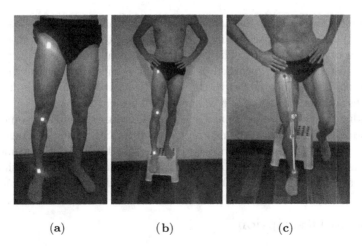

(a)   (b)   (c)

Fig. 2. SSL test procedure: (**a**) marker placing, (**b**) test start position, (**c**) test end position with FPPA displayed

for a given patient help experts determine their status relative to the injuries mentioned in Sect. 1 (ACL and PFPS).

Several functional tests to measure FPPA at dynamic conditions can be found in the literature. Most-widely used ones are single leg squat (SLS) [6,7,17], drop vertical jump (DVJ) [2], drop landing (DL) [18] and single leg landing (SLL) [19], as they simulate real movements and interactions produced during sport practice. During those tests, a health professional ought to determine the start of the execution, and its end based on some previously established criteria.

In this work, the SLL test has been implemented, due to its promptness and simplicity, saving time to experts and making it easier for subjects to understand the procedure. In order to perform the test, the method proposed in [18] is followed and explained in the following paragraphs.

As explained in [20], unilateral landings are a more common ACL injury mechanism than bilateral landings. In order to simulate the landings encountered during athletic participation, the SLL test requires the subject to perform a unilateral step landing task (Figs. 2b, c). This involves stepping off a 30-cm-high bench landing with the opposite leg onto a mark positioned 30 cm from the bench, and holding on the position for at least 2 s. During the test, subjects have to keep the hands on their hips and ensure that the contralateral leg makes no contact with any other surface. The sensor is placed at the subject's knee level, 2 m away from the landing target and aligned perpendicular to the frontal plane. It is recommended to perform various landings with each leg, and the final FPPA value should be measured based on them – e.g. the average value. While the bench height, the landing target separation and the sensor height are recommended indications for a correct test performance, the markers should be strictly placed on the anatomic points described in the next paragraph to obtain a reliable FPPA measurement.

Three reflective markers are attached at the anatomic points proposed in [6] (Fig. 2a): (i) Anterior Superior Iliac spine, (ii) middle of tibiofemoral joint and (iii) middle of ankle mortise. The markers alignment draws two lines, whose frontal projected angle is recorded as FPPA. It is measured at the maximum flexing point. If the knee moves to the subject's sagittal plane, it is known as knee valgus; if it moves outside, it is known as knee varus [21].

According to the aforementioned scientific literature, there are some established normal FPPA values for men and women for SLL tests. Average FPPA values for men are ($\pm$ confidence interval) values are $4.9 \pm 3.5°$. For women, values are significantly higher, reaching $7.1 \pm 2.5°$. Likewise, those values should be symmetrical for both legs in the range of $1–9°$ for males and $5–12°$ for females.

4   System Description

This work presents an innovative system to support practitioners during FPPA measurement procedures. It consists of a depth sensor, which captures video frames and tracks the position of three reflective markers placed on the subject's body, and a computer application that processes the data on-the-fly and stores them, offering experts the opportunity to obtain real-time FPPA values and analyse them. In the following, key features of the system are thoroughly described.

This system has been designed to operate on the depth data provided by the Kinect V2 sensor. Although Kinect is well-known for being a markerless system, some researches demonstrate that Kinect's pose estimation algorithm is not accurate enough for quantitative and precise clinical applications [22,23]. To solve this issue, reflective markers are used. These markers not only give experts certainty that the system is tracking exactly the desired points but also allow for tracking points that are not joints – for instance, the breastbone. Nevertheless, as it will be explained in the next subsection, Kinect's pose estimation algorithm is used to avoid tracking any reflective element in scene that is not a marker.

4.1   Reflective Marker Tracking

Based on the aforementioned test procedure, marker tracking is one of the main tasks of the current work. Using normal color cameras would force us to light up the scene with external light sources, in detriment of the portability and easiness-of-use objectives of the system. For this reason, the depth camera of Kinect V2 sensor is used. It allows us to use the system in any light conditions.

The Kinect's depth sensor is based on the time-of-flight principle [24], it emits an infrared (IR) pattern and captures the image simultaneously with a CMOS camera that is fitted with an IR-pass filter [25]. Its resolution is 512×424 pixels and its depth range goes from 0.5 m to 8 m, losing accuracy farther than 4.5 m. Sampling rate is 30 Hz. Each data frame is composed by a 512×424 array of 16-bit IR intensity values for each pixel [26], which are normalized to a scale from 0 to 1, thus removing light of external light sources and allowing us to get the same image regardless of light conditions. However, it is recommended not to expose it to unnecessary light sources to avoid possible interferences on IR light reflection. Finally, for each data frame, normalized values are encoded in a bitmap, which is shown as the video frame.

Taking into account the previously mentioned sensor resolution (512 × 424), the origin of the bitmap coordinate system is set at the top left corner of the image. Then, each intensity value is high-pass filtered, so those which exceed a sufficiently high intensity threshold are considered part of a marker and stored into a pixel buffer. The pixel's coordinates are extracted from the pixel's index into the frame array.

The next step is to identify which pixel corresponds to each marker (Fig. 3), and here is where the pose estimation algorithm is applied. The estimated hip, knee and ankle 3-D coordinates are obtained from Kinect's body frame and mapped from camera space point (3-D) to depth space point (2-D) [27]. Then, a neighbourhood of pixels is set around each joint, so that the pixels stored in the buffer whose coordinates are inside one neighbourhood belong to the marker of this joint. By applying this process, not only the markers are classified, but also any possible reflective element outside any neighbourhood − which is not part of a marker − is ignored, thus reducing the algorithm workload and improving its robustness.

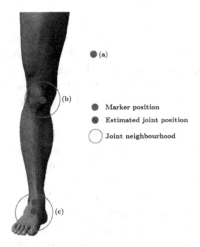

Fig. 3. Reflective pixels: (**a**) reflective element which is not part of a marker, not tracked, (**b**) knee marker pixel, (**c**) ankle marker pixel

It is worth noting that after classifying the reflective pixels, a bidimensional point cloud is stored for each marker. In order to increase accuracy and make it independent of the subject's distance to the sensor and the marker size, the midpoint of each point cloud is computed. This point represents the coordinates of the marker. Following this procedure, markers positions are calculated for each sensor frame, thus performing the marker tracking.

4.2 FPPA Computing

Once markers position is obtained, those three points tracked give us enough information to calculate FPPA. As it is a projected angle, it can be calculated based on 2-D coordinates of markers. With this aim, two vectors are created from the aforementioned points:

$$v_1 = (x_{hip} - x_{knee}, \, y_{hip} - y_{knee}) \tag{1}$$
$$v_2 = (x_{ankle} - x_{knee}, \, y_{ankle} - y_{knee}) \tag{2}$$

v_1 goes from knee to hip and v_2 from knee to ankle. As FPPA is a relative angle and depends only on those vectors, this measurement is robust against accidental camera rotations. Finally, FPPA is simply measured as:

$$FPPA = 180° - \angle(v_1, \, v_2) \tag{3}$$

4.3 Application Description

In this section, the computer application used to process and store the depth sensor data is described. The test results are stored in the system database, which can be edited by the expert, adding, editing or removing users. Each user is identified by an unambiguous personal ID, which is accompanied by personal information, such as name, height, weight and user's personal directory path – created automatically at this stage –, as well as some comments about possible health conditions.

Once the users have been added to the database, the SLL test can be performed (Fig. 4). In order to ensure the right sensor connection, all features are disabled until the sensor becomes available, and a status bar shows both sensor connection state and overall test progress. For a better FPPA visualization, a see-through canvas is positioned over the sensor's image, with the same resolution, where red circles are placed onto the markers, and yellow lines between them, in order to improve the FPPA visualization. Those shapes are attached to the markers coordinates, so they modify their position dynamically as the subject moves. If any marker is not tracked, those shapes related to it are not displayed.

This application gives experts full control over the test progress. They can select the desired subject from the database and the desired leg, as well as trigger the test start. The test finalizes either when the expert stops it or when approximately the same position is held for two seconds. During the test performance, FPPA is shown at runtime and each frame value is stored, with the exception of frames where a marker is not properly detected, which are ignored. The proposed system gives experts the chance to perform from 1 to 3 attempts with each leg, offering individual results and information for each attempt. Once any of them is finished, it is possible to visualize a plot of all data captured during the test, showing the evolution of the FPPA angle (see Sect. 5). This allows experts to go further than just analysing the FPPA value at the maximum flexing point. Although this value is stored into the database, full test data are saved to a comma-separated values file (.csv) with the aim of giving the chance to perform an offline data post-processing, and an image snapshot of the moment of maximum FPPA is stored into subject's personal directory.

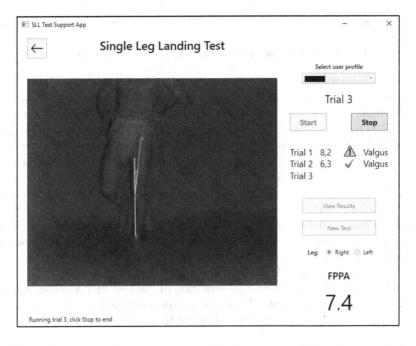

Fig. 4. System application snapshot: SLL test window (Color figure online)

Finally, the last feature of the application is an historical representation of any user-test combination. When single user and test are selected from two pull-down lists, the corresponding historical data values are displayed on a chart for each leg (Fig. 5), allowing experts to inspect the subject's FPPA progress.

4.4   Application Implementation

The application has been implemented using Microsoft .NET framework, which provides hardware platform independence – the programs written for .NET framework execute in a software environment, in contrast to hardware environment ones. For the UI design, Windows Presentation Foundation (WPF) framework has been used, so the application has been deployed as standalone desktop program.

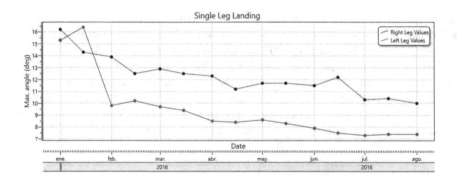

Fig. 5. System application snapshot: historical value chart

The test results data and the patient profile information are stored in a local database, as explained in Sect. 4.3. The system storage functionality relies on a local SQLite database [28] deployed in the user's computer storage disk. SQLite has been chosen due to system characteristics such as small amount of stored data and non-concurrent queries. This database engine adjusts to the characteristics of this system, since the amount of data managed is able to fit in a single disk file and there will not be concurrent writers. It offers a good trade-off between performance and simplicity, making it better for our system than a client/server database engine. Two tables have been created for this case, to decouple sensitive information and procure data anonymisation. The first one stores subjects' personal information while the second one stores test data, and both are related by subject ID number.

In order to provide graphical representation of the test FPPA values and the historical results, Dynamic Data Display open-source library [29] has been used, which allows us to create interactive 2-D plots in an easy way.

5   Discussion

The automatic marker tracking system presented in this work provides real-time FPPA computing, thus requiring much less time investment than offline video analysis, which is the main improvement of this work in relation to the offline analysis. In addition, the application described in Sect. 4.3 provides the opportunity to analyse not only the final FPPA value, but also all values registered during the SLL test performance (Fig. 6), which is significantly time consuming through offline analysis. The application also manages the information of both patients and tests results, simplifying the expert's normal routine.

However, despite all the aforementioned improvements, it is still a 2-D analysis system, so it suffers from the practical limitations of this type of analysis – limited joint rotation measurement –, and its effectiveness cannot be compared with 3-D analysis. However, as mentioned in Sect. 2, 2-D analysis has been demonstrated to be effective in screening knee-joint FPPA.

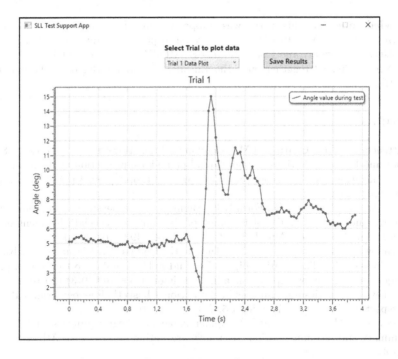

Fig. 6. SLL test data

6   Conclusions

Offline 2-D video analysis is an extended method to quantify knee FPPA, which has been demonstrated to be effective in estimating ACL and PFPS risk. However, traditional procedures like 2-D offline video analysis require large time investments. In this paper we have presented an automatic 2-D video analysis system to support experts during the FPPA measurement. The process involves using a depth sensor to track the position of three reflective markers attached to the subject's hip, knee and ankle joints. The FPPA is dynamically measured based on the marker's position, during a SLL test.

We also presented the main features of a computer application which computes the FPPA and stores the results of the test, allowing experts to analyse FPPA evolution during the whole test, and a historical representation of the evolution of the subject's knee angle.

We are working on many improvements that will be introduced soon and could lead to an extended version of this paper. An important one will be that the system autonomously gives the experts indications about subject's injury risk and possible actions to take, based on both current and previous FPPA values existent in the database. In addition, the spread of the measurements could be analysed in order to automatically detect potentially wrong results of the test and recommend the performance of more attempts. More tests will be also introduced in the system, as well as new useful measurements for these tests.

Acknowledgements. This work was supported by the University of Granada Research Starting Grant 2015. This work was also partially supported by the Spanish Ministry of Economy and Competitiveness (MINECO) Projects TIN2015-71873-R and TIN2015-67020-P together with the European Fund for Regional Development (FEDER).

References

1. Bittencourt, N.F., Ocarino, J.M., Mendonça, L.D., Hewett, T.E., Fonseca, S.T.: Foot and hip contributions to high frontal plane knee projection angle in athletes: a classification and regression tree approach. J. Orthop. Sports Phys. Ther. **42**(12), 996–1004 (2012)
2. Hewett, T.E., Meyer, G.D., Ford, K.R.: Biomechanical measures of neuromuscular control and valgus loading of the knee predict anterior cruciate ligament injury risk in female athletes. Am. J. Sports Med. **33**(4), 492–501 (2005)
3. Wyndow, N., Jong, A.D., Rial, K., Tucker, K., Collins, N., Vicencino, B., Rusell, T., Crossley, K.: The relationship of foot and ankle mobility to the frontal plane projection angle in asymptomatic adults. J. Foot Ankle Res. **9**(3) (2016)
4. Starkey, C.: Injuries and illnesses in the national basketball association: a 10-year perspective. J. Athletic Training **35**, 161–167 (2000)
5. Hootman, J.M., Dick, R., Agel, J.: Epidemiology of collegiate injuries for 15 sports: summary and recommendations for injury prevention initiatives. J. Athletic Training **42**, 311–319 (2007)
6. Wilson, J.D., Ireland, M.L., Davis, I.: Core strength and lower extremity alignment during single leg squats. Med. Sci. Sports Exerc. **38**, 945–952 (2006)
7. Wilson, J.D., Davis, I.S.: Utility of the frontal plane projection angle in females with patellofemoral pain. J. Orthop. Sports Phys. Ther. **38**(10), 606–615 (2008)
8. Munro, A., Herrington, L., Carolan, M.: Reliability of 2-dimensional video assessment of frontal-plane dynamic knee valgus during common athletic screening tasks. J. Sport Rehabil. **21**, 7–11 (2012)
9. McLean, S.G., Walker, K., Ford, K.R., Myer, G.D., Hewett, T.E., van den Bogert, A.J.: Evaluation of a two dimensional analysis method as a screening and evaluation tool for anterior cruciate ligament injury. Brit. J. Sport Med. **39**, 355–362 (2005)
10. Favre, J., Jolles, B.M., Aissaoui, R., Aminian, K.: Ambulatory measurement of a 3D knee joint angle. J. Biomech. **42**, 1029–1035 (2008)
11. Hu, W., Charry, E., Umer, M., Ronchi, A., Taylor, S.: An inertial sensor system for measurement of tibia angle with applications to knee valgus/varus detection. In: 2014 IEEE Ninth International Conference on Intelligent Sensors, Sensor Networks and Information Processing (ISSNIP) (2014)
12. Banos, O., Toth, M.A., Damas, M., Pomares, H., Rojas, I.: Dealing with the effects of sensor displacement in wearable activity recognition. Sensors **14**(6), 9995–10023 (2014)
13. Banos, O., Damas, M., Pomares, H., Rojas, I.: On the use of sensor fusion to reduce the impact of rotational and additive noise in human activity recognition. Sensors **12**(6), 8039–8054 (2012)
14. Vicon Motion Systems Ltd.: Vicon cameras. https://www.vicon.com. Accessed 06 June 2016
15. Northern Digital Inc.: Optotrak certus. http://www.ndigital.com/msci/products/optotrak-certus. Accessed 06 June 2016

16. Munro, A.G.: The use of two-dimensional motion analysis and functional performance tests for assessment of knee injury risk behaviours in athletes. Ph.D. thesis, School of Health Sciences, University of Salford, Salford, UK (2013)
17. Zeller, B.L., McCrory, J.L., Kibler, W.B., Uhl, T.L.: Differences in kinematics and electromyographic activity between man and women during the single-legged squat. Am. J. Sports Med. **31**(3), 449–456 (2003)
18. Herrington, L., Munro, A.: Drop jump landing knee valgus angle; normative data in a phisically active population. Phys. Ther. Sport **11**, 56–59 (2009)
19. Lawrence, R.K.I., Kernozek, T.W., Miller, E.J., Torry, M.R., Reuteman, P.: Influences of hip external rotation strength on knee mechanics during single-leg drop landings in females. Clin. Biomech. **23**, 806–813 (2008)
20. Faude, O., Junge, A., Kindermann, W., Dvorak, J.: Injuries in female soccer players: a prospective study in the german national league. Am. J. Sports Med. **33**(11), 1694–1700 (2005)
21. Kamath, A.F., Israelite, C., Horneff, J., Lotke, P.A.: Editorial: What is varus or valgus knee alignment? a call for a uniform radiographic classification. Clin. Orthop. Relat. Res. **468**(6), 1702–1704 (2010)
22. Bonnechère, B., Scholukha, V., Moiseev, F., Rooze, M., Van Sint, J.S.: From Kinect to anatomically-correct motion modelling: Preliminary results for human application. In: Games for Health: Proceedings of the 3rd European Conference on Gaming and Playful Interaction in Health Care, pp. 15–26. Springer Fachmedien Wiesbaden (2013)
23. Wiedmann, L.G., Planinc, R., Nemec, I., Kampel, M.: Performance evaluation of joint angles obtained by the kinect v2. In: IET International Conference on Technlogies for Active and Assisted Living (TechAAL) (2015)
24. Li, L.: Time-of-flight camera - an introduction. Technical report, Texas Instruments (2014)
25. Andersen, M.R., Jensen, T., Lisouski, P., Mortensen, A.K., Hansen, M.K., Gregersen, T., Ahrendt, P.: Kinect depth sensor evaluation for computer vision applications. Technical report, Department of Engineering, Aarhus University (2012)
26. Lower, B., Relyea, B.: Programming Kinect for Windows v2: Jump start. https://mva.microsoft.com/en-US/training-courses/programming-kinect-for-windows-v2-jump-start. Accessed 17 Feb 2016
27. Pterneas, V.: Understanding kinect coordinate mapping. http://www.codeproject.com/Articles/769608/Understanding-Kinect-Coordinate-Mapping. Accessed 08 June 2016
28. SQLite. http://www.sqlite.org. Accessed 17 April 2016
29. Microsoft: Dynamic Data Display library. https://dynamicdatadisplay.codeplex.com. Accesed 08 June 2016

Detecting Human Movement Patterns Through Data Provided by Accelerometers. A Case Study Regarding Alzheimer's Disease

Rafael Duque[1]([✉]), Alicia Nieto-Reyes[1], Carlos Martínez[2],
and José Luis Montaña[1]

[1] Departamento de Matemáticas, Estadística y Computación,
Universidad de Cantabria, Avenida de Los Castros S/N, 39005 Santander, Spain
{rafael.duque,alicia.nieto,joseluis.montana}@unican.es
[2] Departamento de Ciencias de la computación y la Decisión,
Universidad Nacional de Colombia, Facultad de Minas, Cra 80 65-223,
Bloque M8A, Of. 206, Medellín, Colombia
amartin@unal.edu.co

Abstract. A methodology for mining data coming from mobile phone accelerometers is proposed in order to discover movement patterns in Alzheimer patients and to explore the relation of these patterns with the stage of the disease. This methodology processes the data provided by the accelerometer to extract features of the patient movement patterns. This information is used to train a neural network that relates the patient movement patterns with the stage of the disease (early, middle or late). This proposal based on neural network classifiers is compared with other machine learning classifiers. Moreover, this methodology is applied in a case study with 35 patients. Initial experiments are promising with a success rate up to 83 percent. The projection and exploitation of the results of our analysis are subject to ulterior extensive validation of the proposed technique.

Keywords: Alzheimer · Healthcare · Pattern recognition · Supervised classification · Ubiquitous computing

1 Introduction

During the last decade there has been an important development of microelectronics, enabling mobile devices with remarkable unusual characteristics. Their small size, high computational power, and low economic cost allow people to interact with these devices as part of their daily living. This was the origine of Ubiquitous Computing, a research area with the aim of extracting knowledge from the data acquired by pervasive sensors. The ubiquitous computing paradigm [13] introduced important changes in the way of interacting with software systems. One of the main innovations of this paradigm was the reduction of the user's effort to interact with the system. Thus, the users do not have to perform

C.R. García et al. (Eds.): UCAmI 2016, Part I, LNCS 10069, pp. 56–66, 2016.
DOI: 10.1007/978-3-319-48746-5_6

interactions explicitly because the system analyses the users context [7] at every time and recognizes automatically their requirements.

This paradigm can be considered particularly useful in the healthcare area when the patients suffer from diseases that hinder their interaction with the system [1]. In these cases the purpose of the system is to check, in a continuous manner, parameters that evaluate, for example, the stage of a pathology [12] with no effort by the users to be monitored.

Current smartphones include accelerometers that use sensors to determine the orientation and acceleration of the movements of the device. Therefore, by means of these accelerometers, the user movements are monitored. A suitable analysis of data collected by the accelerometer enables us to identify anomalies in the user movement patterns that indicate, for example, periods of disorientation or crisis in patients with a neurological disease (Alzheimer's, dementia, etc.). Machine learning techniques have been used effectively to develop mechanisms that process the accelerometer data and identify the type of activity carried out by the user at every time [14]. These machine learning techniques require the user to train them so that the system recognizes the performed activities. However such proposals are not in line with the principles of ubiquitous computing that considers the computer as an *invisible* entity that minimizes the effort to interact with it. Other studies have used the data generated by accelerometers to confirm that patients with certain neurological diseases, such as Alzheimer, have movement patterns that differ from those of cognitively healthy subjects [9]. However, these studies do not provide software support to detect and characterize these alterations.

This paper proposes a method for automatically processing the data generated by the smartphone accelerometers to identify movement patterns in Alzheimer's patients and to relate this information with the stage of the disease in which they are.

Alzheimer's disease is a brain disorder characterized by a progressive dementia that occurs in middle or late life (to describe the pathology the interested reader is referred to [10]). According to McKhann et al. [10], Alzheimer's disease typically progresses in three general stages: early-stage, middle-stage, and late-stage. The symptoms of Alzheimer's disease worsen over time, although the rate at which the disease progresses varies. On average, a person with Alzheimer's lives between four and eight years after diagnosis; the maximum being approximately 20 years. In patients of Alzheimer, changes in the brain related to the disease begin years before the symptoms of the disease appear, which is referred to as preclinical Alzheimer's disease. It is generally difficult to place a person with Alzheimer's in a specific stage as stages may overlap. This is one of the main motivations of our work.

To address the problem of Alzheimer's patients classification according to disease stage a working group formed by members of the Department of Mathematics, Statistics and Computer Science of the University of Cantabria in collaboration with nurses belonging to the Alzheimer's Foundation of the city of Santander (Spain) has been created. The aim is to provide a rapid low cost categorization of the stage of the disease of the patient using data coming from the accelerometer of the mobile phone carried by the patient while being at a day centre. Our work does not intend to substitute professional diagnosis but to provide a mechanisms that helps the healthcare professional make the suitable diagnosis of the stage of the disease using highly economic procedures and, at the same time, to warn of the possibility of a progression of the disease to a more severe stage.

The reminder of the paper is organized as follows. Section 2 reviews the main contributions related to the use of accelerometers for analyzing human movement patterns in the healthcare field. Section 3 describes our methodological proposal to identify human movement patterns and its application in a case study regarding Alzheimer's disease. Finally, Sect. 4 analyses the conclusions drawn from this work.

2   State of the Art

The literature includes several proposals that use machine learning techniques to predict from data registered by accelerometers the behaviors or practices of their users. For instance, Casale et al. [4] propose a method that identifies the movement patterns of the user when he/she is walking. These movement patterns are used as an access control mechanism that identifies and authenticates the user. Anguita et al. [2] carry out a study to identify everyday situations of the user (walk, sit, lie down, climbing stairs, etc.). For this purpose, they videotape the activities of 30 people and label manually the name of these activities in a database that also contains the data registered by a accelerometer while performing the activities. Thus, this work also uses the accelerometer as an effective tool to predict the actions of the users by identifying movement patterns.

In the healthcare field, anomalies in the movement patterns of patients with neurological diseases, such as Alzheimer's, are one of the first manifestations of the disease. This is concluded by a study carried out by Kirste et al. [9] to analyze daily activities using data from accelerometers. The study analyzes the behavior of 46 people: a study group of 23 Alzheimer's patients and a control group of 23 healthy people. The study concludes that in 91 % of the cases there exist differences in movement patterns between the two groups. This study, however, does not characterize these patterns to identify abnormal movements.

Chung et al. [5] use a task in which nine Alzheimer's patients and three healthy controls walk along a straight line of 40 m at normal speed. The Alzheimer's disease patients present a significantly shorter mean stride length and slower mean gait speed than the healthy controls. This factor can allow us to design an algorithm that relate these movement patterns with the stage of the Alzheimer's disease.

Mobile technologies are a tool not only to analyze the impact of the Alzheimer's disease in the movement patterns but also to monitor the daily activities of the patients. For instance, Bravo et al. [3] use mobile phones to monitor the patients activities at a day centre environment and a home-based setting. Thus, the caregivers' tasks are dynamically determined with an analysis of the patients' needs at each moment [6].

To sum up, several research works have approached the analysis of the data provided by the accelerometer to identify human movement patterns which is a useful information in the healthcare field. Several works monitor the patients activities and do not analyse their movement patterns. Other proposals identify the movement patterns in specific situations as walking along a straight line. This paper has the goal of identifying the patient movement patterns during their daily activities to explore the relation of these patterns with the stage of the disease.

3   Methodology

This section describes our proposal to generate neural networks that identify movement patterns of Alzheimer patients and relate these patterns with the stage of the disease. This methodology takes as input a dataset with information on the movement patterns. For this purpose, we study a dataset with information on the movement patterns of 35 patients of Alzheimer. The Global Deterioration Scale [11] was used to classify the patients as follows:

- Early-stage: 7 patients (2 and 3 levels of the scale).
- Middle-stage: 18 patients (4 and 5 levels of the scale).
- Late-stage: 10 patients (6 and 7 level of the scale).

The movements of these patients were observed daily for approximately a week in a day care center using the accelerometer device of an Android smartphone. Therefore, the purpose of this experience is to analyze the movement patterns of the patients under the following two conditions: (i) the use of the accelerometer of the smartphone and not of a specific wearable device to observe the movements and (ii) the free movement of the patients not conditioned to the performability of specific exercises or tasks. Thus, through the use of personal smartphones, the study effectively identifies movement patters in the daily activities of the patients that are related to their stage of the disease.

The accelerometers of these smartphones are devices that measure the acceleration forces detected on the three axes of the space (see Fig. 1) using the International System of Units (meter/second^2). These acceleration forces are produced by the gravity force and by the user' forces to generate movements. In order to analyze the patients' movement patterns, a smartphone is introduced in a pocket of the patient and the accelerometer records measurements of the accelerations generated by him/her. Several measurements are taken per second and stored in a text file that is later analyzed.

3.1   Feature Extraction: Generation of the Dataset with Training Patterns

In this study we analyze $n = 187$ measurements, $a_1, \ldots a_n$, provided by an accelerometer carried by Alzheimer's patients while, as mentioned above, being

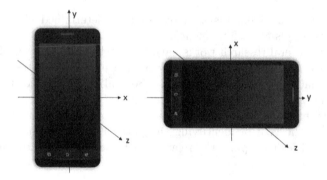

Fig. 1. Three axes used to measure the accelerations.

in a non-controlled activity with free walk around the space. The recorded measurements are $n = 187$, despite the number of patients being 35, due to the accelerations of each patient being recorded for a number of distinct periods of time, for instance between two and eight depending on the patient.

For each $i = 1, \ldots, n$, the accelerometer provides

$$a_i(t) := (x_i(t), y_i(t), z_i(t))$$

for $t \in \{i_1, \ldots, i_{t_i}\}$, where $x_i(t)$, $y_i(t)$ and $z_i(t)$ respectively denote the acceleration at time t in each of the coordinates axis of $\mathbb{R}^3$. To visualize the type of data we handle, in Fig. 2 it is plotted the x coordinate for three patients during one of the period of times in which their accelerations are measured. The three patients selected are at different stages of the disease, which is not depicted by the eye from the plots. The Android accelerometer also provides the euclidean norm of $a_i(t)$, for $t \in \{i_1, \ldots, i_{t_i}\}$, but as it is a redundant measure we do not use it in the analysis.

The accelerometer does not measure the acceleration in a continuous manner but on a grid of time-points, which is natural when recording real data through time. This type of data has, however, a richer topology than most data recorded through time. First, for any given $i, j = 1, \ldots, n$ with $i \neq j$, a_i and a_j are measured on a different time-grid; that is $i_k \neq j_k$ for any $k \leq \min\{t_i, t_j\}$. Second, a_i and a_j are measured for a different time length; that is $|i_{t_i} - i_1| \neq |j_{t_j} - j_1|$. This is easily observed from Fig. 2 as the time length on the left panel is visually shorter than the other two.

Therefore, a preprocess of the data is required in order to make them comparable. First, to account for the differences on time grid, we aggregate the data in seconds, and separately in minutes. This is done in the following manner. Given a_i, let s_i denote the ceiling of i_{t_i} to seconds, and respectively m_i to minutes. That is, if $i_{t_i} = 2500.34\,\text{s}$, then $s_i = 2501\,\text{s}$ and $m_i = 42$ minutes. The aggregation is done such that for each of the three coordinates of a_i and each $t \in \{1, \ldots, s_i\}$ we record the sum, median and mean of the accelerations at times $\{T \in \{i_1, \ldots, i_{t_i}\} : t - 1 < T \leq t\}$; and for each

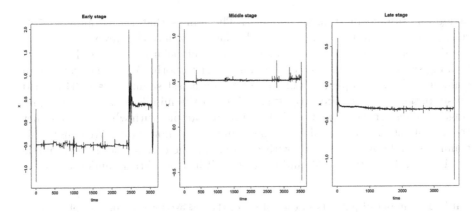

Fig. 2. Acceleration on the x coordinate for three patients at different stage of the disease: early (left), middle (central) and late (right).

$t \in \{1, \ldots, m_i\}$ we also record the sum, median and mean of the accelerations at times $\{T \in \{i_1, \ldots, i_{t_i}\} : t - 1 < T/60 \leq t\}$. Thus, we obtain three random functions when aggregated in seconds and another three when in minutes for each of the axis of $\mathbb{R}^3$.

It remains still, however, the fact that each a_i has a different time length, and so, a different dimension, which complicates the direct application of supervised classification procedures. As classification procedures extract the characteristics of the data that differ among the classes in which we aim to classify the data, for instance early, middle and late stage, our proposal is to extract first some characteristics of the datasets and apply the classification procedure to these characteristics. By extracting the same set of characteristics from each dataset, we apply the classification procedure to sets of the same dimension. The characteristics we propose to extract for each a_i are the sum, mean, median, minimum and maximum of the accelerations aggregated in seconds as above; and respectively in minutes. Thus, we obtain 30 real random variables for each of the axis of $\mathbb{R}^3$ (15 when aggregated in seconds and another 15 when in minutes).

It is well-known that important information of acceleration curves is usually noticeable by integrating them along time, once, obtaining the velocity, and twice, obtaining the distance. Therefore, using trapezoidal integration, the above preprocessing of the data has also been carried out on the velocities and distances; leading so to a set of ninety real random variables for each of the axis of $\mathbb{R}^3$. Therefore, denoting the data after the preprocessing by $A_1, \ldots A_n$, where $A_i := (X_i, Y_i, Z_i)$, we have that $X_i \in \mathbb{R}^{90}$, $Y_i \in \mathbb{R}^{90}$ and $Z_i \in \mathbb{R}^{90}$, for all $i = 1, \ldots, n$.

3.2 Processing the Dataset Using Machine Learning Classifiers

In this section we apply a neural network classifier to our dataset and compare our results to the obtained by other well-known supervised classifiers. First, we divide our sample in training and test. The aim is that the training sample constitutes approximately the 80 % of the data of each of the three classes while the data corresponding to each particular patient belongs in full either to the training sample or to the test sample; but never to both. We do the splitting in training and test sample at random and obtain a test sample of size 34 formed by six patients, one in the early stage, three in the middle and two in the late stage. The rest of the patients form the training sample, with which we construct the neural network. See Table 1 for the summarized information. We denote this training sample by $A_{t_1}, \ldots, A_{t_r}$ with $r = 153$ and the corresponding test sample by $A_{T_1}, \ldots, A_{T_e}$ with $e = 34$, and referred to it as the splitting under study.

Table 1. Number of patients in each stage of the disease for each of the splittings in training and test sample performed.

	Training sample				Test sample			
Splitting	Early	Middle	Late	Total	Early	Middle	Late	Total
Studied	6	15	8	29	1	3	2	6
1	5	15	8	28	2	3	2	7
2	5	14	8	27	2	4	2	8

Just to show that it is possible to obtain other splittings under the same randomization criteria, we have split the data, into training and test, two more times; obtaining what we referred as Splitting 1 and Splitting 2 respectively (see Table 1). Thus, the test sample 1 is of size 38 and is formed by seven patients (two in the early stage, three in the middle and two in the late) while the test sample 2 has size 39 and is formed by eight patients (two in the early stage, four in the middle and two in the late).

In order to select the appropriate neural network, we construct neural networks based on the training sample for eleven different layers [8]. In Fig. 3 the eleven different layers are represented by the numbers one to eleven. Due to the randomness intrinsic to neural networks, we construct 100 neural networks per training sample and layer and plot in Fig. 3 (left panel) the percentage of misclassified patients after applying each of the obtained neural networks to the test sample. As $A_{T_1}, \ldots, A_{T_e}$ are grouped into a few patients, for instance six in our case, we classify each of the patients of the test sample into the group in which the majority of it's corresponding $A_{T's}$ are classified.

For the sample under study, we obtain that the best neural network misclassifies one patient, of the test sample, in each of the layers (83 % of success rate), but for the third layer that misclassifies two. Furthermore, it is observable from the box-plot (Fig. 3, left panel) that, in terms of misclassifications, the best layers to use are the sixth, the tenth or the eleventh. The details of the neural network selected can be seen in Table 2. In the next section we compare these results with other supervised classifiers, see Table 3.

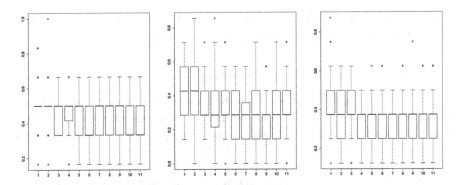

Fig. 3. Misclassification rates over 100 iterations for each of the 11 layers of the test data corresponding to the splitting, on training and test sample, under study (left), to Splitting 1 (middle) and to Splitting 2 (right).

Table 2. Configuration of the neural network selected

Neural network parameters	Values
Package	neuralnet
Input neurons	90
Hidden neurons	175
Output neurons	1
Bias	1 per hidden layer
Max iterations	1000
Activation function	logistic
Algorithm	esilient backpropagation with weight backtracking (rprop+)

Table 3. Misclassification and success rate obtained in the supervised classification of the test sample using the splitting under study. NN stands for neural networks and SVM for support vector machine.

Technique	Missclassifications				Success rate			
	Early	Middle	Late	Total	Early	Middle	Late	Total
NN	0	0	1	1	100 %	100 %	50 %	83 %
Random trees	1	0	2	3	0 %	100 %	0 %	50 %
Random forest	1	0	2	3	0 %	100 %	0 %	50 %
SVM	1	0	2	3	0 %	100 %	0 %	50 %

We have also pursued the above study for the other two splittings. In Splitting 1 the best neural network obtained has one misclassification with the first and third layer and none with the rest (Fig. 3, middle panel). Meanwhile, the best neural network obtained with the Splitting 2 has a misclassification in every layer (Fig. 3, right panel). Additionally, it is observed from the corresponding box-plots (Fig. 3, middle and left panel) that the best layer to use is the ninth for Sample 1 and either the fourth or seventh for Sample 2.

3.3 Other Machine Learning Classifiers

In this section we compare our results with those obtained by other well-known methods for supervised classification. As in the above case of neural networks, a patient of the test sample is classified into a group when the majority of its corresponding $A_{T's}$ are classified into that group.

Particularly, in this section we use the methodologies: random trees, random forest and support vector machine. When these methodologies are applied to the split sample under study, it is obtained that all of them misclassified three patients of the test sample (see Table 3). In fact, the same three patients are misclassified for the different procedures. These three patients are the patient in the early stage of the disease and the two patients in the late stage. This clearly points out the difficulty in analyzing this type of data. These methods do an appropriate classification of the patients in the middle stage of the disease; but this is the group with a larger amount of patients, and periods of acceleration recorded.

The computations have been carried out with R. Particularly, it is used the package *neuralnet* for the computation of the neural networks, *tree* and *rpart* for the computation of the random trees, *randomForest* for the computation of random forests and *rpart* for support vector machine.

4   Conclusions

We have described a methodology to analyze human movement pattern through data provided by accelerometers of smartphones. This methodology processes these data to learn a neural network that classifies the movement pattern of the user. This methodology has been applied to identify the movement patterns of Alzheimer patients to relate them with their stage of the disease.

A case study has been carried out to experiment with the proposed methodology. Thirty-Five Alzheimer patients participated in this case study. The methodology generated a neural network that takes as input the dataset provided by the accelerometer and outputs a description of the stage of the disease with one misclassification in the test sample (83 % of success rate).

We are working on validating the methodology with new case studies in which a higher number of patients will participate. If these new validations confirm the result of this paper, we will build an environment that will include a mobile application to collect the accelerometer data and classify it according to the neural network; then, communicate this information to a medical system used by health professionals. Thus, the doctor will manage additional information related to the patients' evolution and diagnosis.

Acknowledgments. This work was partially supported by project PAC::LFO of the Spanish Programa Estatal de Fomento de la Investigación Científica y Técnica de Excelencia under grant MTM2014-55262-P, by project BASMATI of the Spanish Programa Nacional de Investigación, Ministerio de Ciencia e Innovación, under grant TIN2011-27479-C04-04 and by the Spanish Ministerio de Economía y Competitividad under grant MTM2014-56235-C2-2-P. We gratefully acknowledge the "Asociación de Familiares de Enfermos de Alzheimer en Cantabria" and Pablo Cobo García for their participation in the various studies.

References

1. Acampora, G., Cook, D.J., Rashidi, P., Vasilakos, A.V.: A survey on ambient intelligence in healthcare. Proc. IEEE **101**(12), 2470–2494 (2013)
2. Anguita, D., Ghio, A., Oneto, L., Parra, X., Reyes-Ortiz, J.L.: Energy efficient smartphone-based activity recognition using fixed-point arithmetic **19**(9), 1295–1314 (2013). http://www.jucs.org/jucs_19_9/energy_efficient_smartphone_based
3. Bravo, J., López-de-Ipiña, D., Fuentes, C., Hervás, R., Peña, R., Vergara, M., Casero, G.: Enabling NFC technology for supporting chronic diseases: a proposal for alzheimer caregivers. In: Aarts, E., Crowley, J.L., de Ruyter, B., Gerhäuser, H., Pflaum, A., Schmidt, J., Wichert, R. (eds.) AmI 2008. LNCS, vol. 5355, pp. 109–125. Springer, Heidelberg (2008)
4. Casale, P., Pujol, O., Radeva, P.: Personalization and user verification in wearable systems using biometric walking patterns. Pers. Ubiquit. Comput. **16**(5), 563–580 (2011). http://dx.doi.org/10.1007/s00779-011-0415-z
5. Chung, P., Hsu, Y., Wang, C., Lin, C., Wang, J., Pai, M.: Gait analysis for patients with alzheimer's disease using a triaxial accelerometer. In: ISCAS, pp. 1323–1326. IEEE (2012)
6. Corchado, J.M., Bajo, J., Abraham, A.: Gerami: Improving healthcare delivery in geriatric residences. IEEE Intell. Syst. **23**(2), 19–25 (2008)
7. Dourish, P.: What we talk about when we talk about context. Pers. Ubiquit. Comput. **8**(1), 19–30 (2004). http://dx.doi.org/10.1007/s00779-003-0253-8
8. Kasabov, N.K.: Foundations of Neural Networks, Fuzzy Systems, and Knowledge Engineering, 1st edn. MIT Press, Cambridge (1996)
9. Kirste, T., Koldrack, P., Schubert, S., Teipel, S.: Ambient Assisted Living: 7. AAL-Kongress 2014 Berlin, Germany, January 21–22, 2014. Detecting the Effect of Alzheimer's Disease on Everyday Motion Behaviorpp. 149–156. Springer International Publishing, Cham (2015). http://dx.doi.org/10.1007/978-3-319-11866-6_12
10. McKhann, G., Drachman, D., Folstein, M., Katzman, R., Price, D., Stadlan, E.M.: Clinical diagnosis of alzheimer's disease: Report of the nincdsadrda work group* under the auspices of department of health and human services task force on alzheimer's disease. Neurology **34**(7), 939 (1984). http://www.neurology.org/content/34/7/939.abstract
11. Reisberg, B., F.S.d.L.M.C.: The global deterioration scale for assessment of primary degenerative dementia. Am. J. Psychiatry **139**(9), 1136–1139 (1982). pMID: 7114305
12. Villarreal, V., Hervas, R., Fontecha, J., Bravo, J.: Mobile monitoring framework to design parameterized and personalized m-health applications according to the patient's diseases. J. Med. Syst. **39**(10), 1–6 (2015). http://dx.doi.org/10.1007/s10916-015-0324-1

13. Weiser, M.: The computer for the 21st century. In: Human-Computer Interaction, pp. 933–940. Morgan Kaufmann Publishers Inc., San Francisco (1995). http://dl. acm.org/citation.cfm?id=212925.213017
14. Zheng, Y., Wong, W.K., Guan, X., Trost, S.: Physical activity recognition from accelerometer data using a multi-scale ensemble method (2013). http://aaai.org/ ocs/index.php/IAAI/IAAI13/paper/view/6373

Personalised Support System for Hypertensive Patients Based on Genetic Algorithms

Víctor Vives-Boix[✉], Daniel Ruiz-Fernández, Antonio Soriano-Payá,
Diego Marcos-Jorquera, Virgilio Gilart-Iglesias,
and Alberto de Ramón-Fernández

Department of Computer Technology, University of Alicante, Alicante, Spain
{vvives,druiz,soriano,dmarcos,vgilart,aderamon}@dtic.ua.es

Abstract. Hypertension is a common and dangerous condition, which is the most important preventable cause of stroke and heart disease. Long-term conditions result in a reduced quality of life that can be improved through self-management and empowerment of patients using information technologies. Current support systems include self-management and empowerment in patients, but both features are not personalised in terms of patient preferences and decision-making. In this work an adaptive genetic algorithm is proposed for personalised support systems in hypertensive patients by including patient blood pressure data in the generational replacement step of evolutionary computing.

Keywords: Genetic algorithms · Adaptive algorithms · Hypertension · Self-management · Empowerment · Personalised support system

1 Introduction

Hypertension, also known as high blood pressure, is defined by the World Health Organization (WHO) as a common and dangerous chronic condition in which the blood vessels have persistently raised pressure. Normal adult blood pressure is defined as 120 mm Hg when the heart beats (systolic) and 80 mm Hg when the heart relaxes (diastolic). When systolic is equal to or above 140 mm Hg and/or diastolic is equal to or above 90 mm Hg, a person is considered hypertensive [1].

Long term health conditions often result in a reduced quality of life that can be improved through self-management and empowerment [2]. Self-management denotes the active participation of chronic patients in their treatment, which aim is to minimise the impact of a particular condition in their health status [3]. Moreover, self-management support involves a patient-physician collaborative approach to promote patient empowerment, a process through which people reach greater control over decisions affecting their health.

Thus, in recent years, a new research area of information technologies to support patients in self-managing of long term health conditions has emerged. Support systems are powerful tools that facilitate self-management in patients

© Springer International Publishing AG 2016
C.R. García et al. (Eds.): UCAmI 2016, Part I, LNCS 10069, pp. 67–73, 2016.
DOI: 10.1007/978-3-319-48746-5_7

with chronic diseases [4]; however, the empowerment feature requires a personalisation that is not clearly defined at present in terms of technology.

Evolutionary computing and genetic algorithms are a common and reliable solution in current self-management support and recommender systems. However, health empowerment is often determined by patient monitoring, feedback, readability and/or gamification, and is not used as a value added proposal in the development of expert systems for personalised patient support. Even so, multiple remote devices are used for empowerment as in telemedicine [5], but a manual interaction is required and some users are resistant to use it.

In this paper we propose an adaptive genetic algorithm for a personalised support system for hypertensive patients, which includes self-management and empowerment based on their lifestyle preferences. The proposed algorithm enhances the generational replacement by introducing new patient data (collected with smart devices) with the aim of obtaining short-term goals introduced by a physician. The algorithm tries to fit patient data with the encoded value given as goal by evaluating similarity between them. Thus, each generation in the algorithm permits analysing data and establishing lifestyle recommendations based on the daily patient decision-making.

Patient data have been simulated assuming proper adherence to the treatment and recommendations made. The use of real data has not yet been possible in this work due to the scope of the problem, the absence of related datasets and the required monitoring in patients.

2   Related Work

Personalised decision support systems are a current field of study in healthcare [6]. Moreover, many personalised self-management systems have been proposed in recent years and it has been shown that they improve lifestyle in patients with chronic conditions [7]. In [8], a cloud-based system with a computerised physician order entry (CPOE) is proposed, which achieves a better blood pressure control in hypertensive patients. Experiences in self-management support are often positive; however, only receiving and managing information is not enough for patients and they want to be involved in medical decision-making [9].

Patient empowerment in self-management activities is considered in [10] by introducing an ICT framework with multiple services for diabetic patients. Nevertheless, manual entry data is usually a difficult task in patients without affinity with new technologies. In [11], hypertensive patients experience with an interactive mobile phone-based system is studied, where a prior training in users is required and only some responsive patients were adhered to the treatment.

Thus, automated data collection and processing for personalised support systems is required. In [12], a smart wristband is used for health empowerment through activity tracking. Moreover, the proposed self-management platform in [13] also uses a blood pressure monitor and a scale. Evolutionary computing is currently used in collaborative recommender systems. In [14], genetic algorithms are also applied to optimise feature weights in a collaborative filter, which are used to measure similarity between users. A complete review of research papers using evolutionary computing for user recommendations can be found in [15].

3   Background

In a genetic algorithm, potential solutions to a problem are usually represented by binary strings of a certain length, which is imposed by the number of existing variables in the solution and the number of bits to encode them. Following the vocabulary of biological systems, the term used to describe these binary strings is chromosome, and chromosomes are composed by binary values named genes. A chromosome c^t in a generation t can be represented as $c^t = (b_1^t...b_n^t)$, where $b_i^t \in \{0, 1\}$, $i = 1, ..., n$ (n = number of bits). The choice on how to represent the solutions of a problem becomes very important in evolutionary computing and can directly limit the way in which the system interprets its environment.

The usual mechanism to measure the fitness of a solution is to evaluate their phenotype, where the phenotype is the decoded chromosome c^t, through the fitness function f of the problem being solved. Thus, the evaluation function $eval$ corresponds to the fitness function f of the problem. Given a chromosome c^t and its phenotype x^t, fitness can be obtained as $f^t = eval(c^t) = f(x^t)$.

The term individual is often used to refer the information related with a phenotype and its fitness in the solution environment. Thus, an individual X^t in a generation t can be represented as $X^t = (c^t, x^t, f^t)$ and a population made by m individuals, where m is the population size given by an input parameter, is represented in a generation t as $P(t) = \{X_1^t, ..., X_m^t\}$.

Once all the solutions of the population in a generation t have been evaluated, the process evolves into a new generation t_{next}. The population in the next generation will suffer a transformation, carried out in a basic operating scheme by applying the following probabilistic transition rules: selection and sampling, genetic operators (crossover and mutation) and generational replacement.

Last, a general replacement is performed by the evaluation of selected, crossed and mutated chromosomes. New individuals in a population are selected from the current population and descendants, both crossed and mutated, thus avoiding the possibility that local minima occur in the function.

4   Method

Patient data have been represented using two parameters, systolic and diastolic blood pressure, whose aim is to be in a normal range. Thus, a chromosome is represented by the blood pressure values taken by a patient throughout a week, three times a day for better accuracy (morning, midday and night), where systolic and diastolic values are encoded as described in Table 1.

Each chromosome c^t in a generation t is represented as $c^t = (b_1^t b_2^t...b_7^t)$, where $b_i^t = (r_{i1}^t r_{i2}^t r_{i3}^t)$, being r_{ij}^t three daily blood pressure takings ($j = 1, 2, 3$) in a day (morning, midday and night respectively), each defined as:

$$r_{ij}^t = (sys_{ij1}^t sys_{ij2}^t dia_{ij1}^t dia_{ij2}^t), \tag{1}$$

where sys_{ij1}^t, sys_{ij2}^t, dia_{ij1}^t and dia_{ij2}^t are systolic and diastolic encoded blood pressure values in Table 1, thus setting 84 genes by chromosome.

Table 1. Blood pressure ranges and encoding

Condition	Systolic (mm Hg)	sys_1	sys_2	Diastolic (mm Hg)	dia_1	dia_2
Hypertension	≥ 140	0	0	≥ 90	0	0
Prehypertension	<140 and ≥ 120	0	1	<90 and ≥ 80	0	1
Normal pressure	<120 and ≥ 90	1	0	<80 and ≥ 60	1	0
Hypotension	<90	1	1	<60	1	1

The evaluation function compares the binary string of a chromosome c^t with the binary string of the target chromosome. Chromosomes are evaluated by their fitness, a value given by the fitness function that represents how close is the chromosome to the solution, where the higher the value, the better the fitness. In this paper the possibility of modifying a target in order to establish short-term goals is added, fact that improves self-management in chronic patients [2]. If this happens, all chromosomes change their fitness, directly affecting the generational replacement in the subsequent generation.

The selection scheme used is selection ranking, in which individuals are ordered in a list according to their fitness (best to worst individual) and the selection is performed based on their positions in the sorted list. Before selection, an initial population $P(t)$ is randomly generated. After selection, uniform crossover and mutation are used as genetic operators.

For crossover operator, each gene in a child is created with the corresponding genes of parents using a crossover mask. Genes of first child are taken from first parent if there is a 1 in the mask, and taken from second parent if there is a 0. Second child is created using the inverted method. For mutation operator is used a random mask, which define the genes to be mutated.

Chromosomes generated by encoding the blood pressure doses are included each generational replacement step, influencing the ranking selection and genetic operators in the subsequent generation. Thus, each generational leap can be used for evaluating the patient behaviour and defining personalised recommendations in terms of patient lifestyle preferences.

5   Results

The proposed adaptive genetic algorithm has been tested with synthetic data by simulating the behaviour of a patient and assuming an adherence to the treatment and given recommendations. Real data cannot be used due to the absence of related databases and the difficulty of generating such amount of information. The algorithm results are represented by the best chromosome's fitness on the Y axis and iterations or weeks on the X axis.

A goal can be manually modified during the process, if the physician considers it necessary, in order to achieve a normal blood pressure range by decreasing the target values progressively. The algorithm adapts itself and tries to fit the current patient status with the new target established. Thus, patients are continuously improving their blood pressure based on their own decision-making. This adaptive behaviour is showed in Fig. 1 where a short-term goal is modified every 40 weeks (iterations).

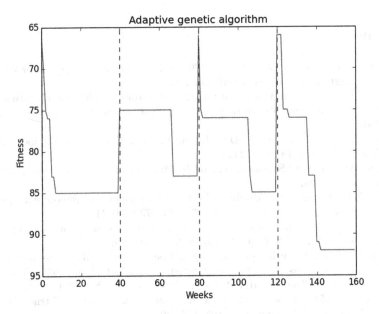

Fig. 1. Convergence with short-term goals each 40 weeks: hypertension to normal blood pressure by decreasing the goal in 10 mm Hg each 40 weeks

6   Conclusions and Future Work

The proposed adaptive genetic algorithm satisfies the expected goals. Recommendations can be made by comparing and decoding best chromosomes in a generation and patient data, being able to identify wrong patient behaviour in particular dates. Thus, a personalised support system for hypertensive patients based on adaptive genetic algorithms is proposed.

In future research, we suggest adding more smart devices, such as a smart wristband and a digital scale, in order to achieve more specific recommendations. Moreover, using real patients with different hypertension ranges, ages, activity and lifestyle preferences will produce more varied results. Both suggestions can complement and improve this work, which is a common topic in research of personalised support systems for healthcare.

Conflict of Interest

The authors declare no conflict of interest.

Acknowledgments. This work has been granted by the Ministerio de Economía y Competitividad of the Spanish Government (ref. TIN2014-53067-C3-1-R) and cofinanced by FEDER.

References

1. WHO - World Health Organization (2016). Hypertension. http://www.who.int/topics/hypertension/en/. Accessed May 2016
2. Nolte, E.E., McKee, M.: Caring for people with chronic conditions: a health system perspective. European Observatory on Health Systems and Policies Series XXI, 259 p. (2008)
3. Koch, T., Jenkin, P., Kralik, D.: Chronic illness self-management: locating the 'self'. J. Adv. Nurs. **48**, 8–9 (2004)
4. Barrett, M.J.: Patient Self-management Tools: An Overview. California Healthcare Foundation, Oakland (2005)
5. Anker, S.D., Koehler, F., Abraham, W.T.: Telemedicine and remote management of patients with heart failure. Lancet **378**, 731–739 (2011)
6. Douali, N., et al.: Personalized decision support system based on clinical practice guidelines. Stud. Health Technol. Inform. **211**, 308–310 (2015)
7. Zheng, H., et al.: Towards a decision support personalised self management system for chronic conditions. In: Networking, Sensing and Control, pp. 1521–1524 (2008)
8. Lee, P., et al.: Cloud-based BP system integrated with CPOE improves self-management of the hypertensive patients: a randomized controlled trial. Comput. Methods Programs Biomed. **132**, 105–113 (2016)
9. Dwarswaard, J., et al.: Self-management support from the perspective of patients with a chronic condition: a thematic synthesis of qualitative studies. Health Expect. Int. J. Public Participation Health Care Health Policy **2**, 194–208 (2016)
10. Lee, J.W., Lee, Y.J., Kim, H.K., Hwang, B.H., Ryu, K.H.: Discovering temporal relation rules mining from interval data. In: Shafazand, H., Tjoa, A.M. (eds.) EurAsia-ICT 2002. LNCS, vol. 2510, pp. 57–66. Springer, Heidelberg (2002). doi:10.1007/3-540-36087-5_7
11. Hallberg, I., Ranerup, A., Kjellgren, K.: Supporting the self-management of hypertension: patients' experiences of using a mobile phone-based system. J. Hum. Hypertens. **2**, 141–146 (2016)
12. Nelson, E.C., Verhagen, T., Noordzij, M.L.: Health empowerment through activity trackers: an empirical smart wristband study. Comput. Hum. Behav. **62**, 364–374 (2016)
13. Patterson, T., et al.: KeepWell: a generic platform for the self-management of chronic conditions. In: XIV Mediterranean Conference on Medical and Biological Engineering and Computing (2016)

14. Hwang, C.-S., Su, Y.-C., Tseng, K.-C.: Using genetic algorithms for personalized recommendation. In: Pan, J.-S., Chen, S.-M., Nguyen, N.T. (eds.) ICCCI 2010. LNCS (LNAI), vol. 6422, pp. 104–112. Springer, Heidelberg (2010). doi:10.1007/978-3-642-16732-4_12

15. Horváth, T., de Carvalho, A.: Evolutionary computing in recommender systems: a review of recent research. Nat. Comput. 1–22 (2016). doi:10.1007/s11047-016-9540-y. ISSN: 1567-7818

Business Process Management for the Crohn's Disease Clinical Process

Alberto de Ramón-Fernández[✉], Diego Marcos-Jorquera, Antonio Soriano-Payá,
Virgilio Gilart-Iglesias, Daniel Ruiz-Fernández[✉], and Javier Ramirez-Navarro

Department of Computer Technology, University of Alicante, Alicante, Spain
{aderamon,dmarcos,soriano,vgilart,druiz,
jramirez}@dtic.ua.es

Abstract. Crohn's disease belongs to the group of inflammatory bowel diseases. The current process of disease management has significant weaknesses that cause high cost for health systems and a significant loss of quality of life for the patient. This paper shows a new approach to redesign process for the management of Crohn's disease based on Business Process Management strategy. This approach seeks to improve the patient empowerment and self-management, reducing costs and obtaining constant and updated information throughout the process.

Keywords: Business Process Management · Empowerment · Self-management · Crohn's disease

1 Introduction

According to World Health Organization (WHO), chronic diseases (CD) are by far the leading cause of mortality in the world, representing 60 % of all deaths. They are diseases of long duration and generally slow progression. In 2008, 36 million people died from chronic disease, 29 % were under 60 years old and half were women [1]. Crohn's disease produces inflammation of the gastrointestinal tract and it can affect any area from the mouth to the rectum. This article focuses on reducing problems associated with the current clinical process, with the clear objective of improving the quality of life of patients and reducing the cost associated. One of the most recent management strategies to reach this purpose is Business Process Management (BPM) focused on continuous improvement of business processes using information technologies (IT's) as one of its fundamental principles for the realization process [2].

2 State of the Art

Chronic diseases require special attention from a wide variety of medical specialists.
To improve the remote patient monitoring, some frameworks have been developed. They are based on data that come from sensors coupled to the patients in a non-invasive way (u-health services) [3]. In recent years, other devices based on artificial intelligence

© Springer International Publishing AG 2016
C.R. García et al. (Eds.): UCAmI 2016, Part I, LNCS 10069, pp. 74–79, 2016.
DOI: 10.1007/978-3-319-48746-5_8

have also been developed improving the access of the Crohn patients to the information. This is thanks to the development of Web services and their integration into mobile devices [4]. Business Process Management (BPM) consists on a set of integrated, closed-loop management and analytic processes supported by technology. The research works [5, 6] support the successful use of information technologies (ITs) on the field of health. However, they are not managed by the process, which turns them into partial solutions again. An integrated solution based on BPM that uses all the factors involved in a clinical process, such as Crohn's disease, will be useful for a continuous process improvement. Some parts of the process could also be automated, which will reduce the cost of the health service and increase the satisfaction of the patient.

3 Crohn's Disease Clinical Process

In this section, the clinical process of Crohn's disease is defined from its diagnosis until its treatment. The main goal is to understand how the process is currently developed (AS_IS view) and how many factors are involved in. The analysis carried out in this work is supported by some international clinical guides (Canada, United Kingdom) [7, 8]. The procedure starts with the first clinical evaluation performed by the medical and nursing specialists (see P1 in Fig. 1). In case of medium-high risk, the doctor will perform a physical exam supported by an abdominal X-ray, blood pressure values, heart rate and temperature (see P2 in Fig. 1). The third stage of the diagnosis implies the valuation of the specialist doctor in digestive system. He will carry out a complete analysis as well as the faecal calprotectin test. This test allows the specialist to discard false positive results (see P3 in Fig. 1). Finally, the patient is subject to several tests carried out by different health specialist. In the case that any of them are positives, they allow the doctor to confirm the Crohn's disease (see P4 in Fig. 1).

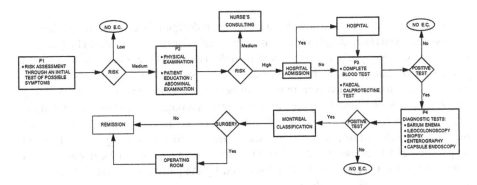

Fig. 1. Current diagnosis and treatment Crohn's disease process.

Once the patient is diagnosed with the Crohn's disease, it is classified in one of the disease phases. In that moment, it will decide if the patient needs a surgical intervention or he is derived to the induction stage, where he is monitored. In the case of the patient needs a surgical intervention, the possibility of deriving the digestive tract to a stoma is studied. Therefore, whether the surgical intervention is performed or not, the patient will be continuously valuated in the follow-up stage. In this phase, the tests related to the diagnosis are performed again with the purpose of looking for possible complications and re-classifying the disease degree of the patient.

4   Weaknesses in the Current Crohn's Disease Clinical Process

At present, the management of the Crohn's disease clinical process presents important deficiencies both in the diagnosis and in the treatment phase. In Spain, one of the main problems of the treatment is the lack of standardized clinical guidelines level and the time it takes to be diagnosed. Faecal calprotectine test is carried out only in the final step of the diagnostic phase [9]. The lack of psychological support during the process is among the most significant deficiencies [10]. From the point of view of the patient, factors such as the continuous visits to the primary care centres, absenteeism and the large number of tests to perform have affect the quality of life [11]. Another important aspect that negatively affects the quality of life is the lack of clear and updated information throughout the clinical process [12]. The annual cost of caring for patients with Crohn is one of the aspects that have more relevance throughout the process. The hospitalization rate is increased and this represent a significantly higher cost than keep the patient in remission. In [13] it was estimated that the costs related to surgery accounted for about 40 % of the total costs of the process. The BPM strategy will be used for the redesign of the clinical process, implementing the necessary improvements, and minimizing the most of the deficiencies identified, using ITs as a key element to achieve the objectives.

5   Redesign Process

The object of study of this article focuses on the redesign of clinical Crohn's disease process once it has been diagnosed and the implementation of improvements by business management strategy BPM. Its agile and flexible use allows the process to be adapted to unexpected changes. With the proposed development (see Fig. 2), a global model that integrates all processes involved in the treatment of the disease is obtained, including the phase of psychological support to the patient. Through specific user applications integrated with the system by means of web services, the patient can make self-assessment tests which will be integrated into the system in order to be analysed by the team of psychologist (empowerment action 1). Thus, a standardized clinical guideline is obtained and the psychological impact suffered by the patient is managed, two of the weaknesses previously identified.

Through web services, the patient can also send information related to various risk factors, blood tests values and other useful information referred to physical examination (empowerment action 2). In addition, data concerning about their blood pressure, physical activity and body mass index are incorporated automatically by communication between the expert system with a blood pressure monitor, a smart band and a digital scale respectively (empowerment action 3). To rule out misdiagnosis and shorten the

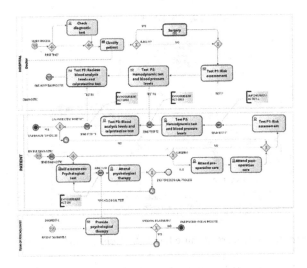

Fig. 2. Redesign model Crohn's disease process

process, a device measures the faecal calprotectin and this information is integrated into the system via Bluetooth (empowerment action 4). Thus, the medical team have an update medical history, reducing the number of visits to the medical centre that cause loss of quality of life for the patient and increase the costs borne by the health system.

Moreover, the expert system will provide recommendations based on information received by artificial intelligence algorithms behaving like a clinical decision support system. Thus, the patient participates actively in the process, promoting their empowerment and self-management of their disease and having updated information of its clinical status, overcoming one of the main deficiencies identified in the current process.

6   System Architecture

To carry out the above model, an architecture has been proposed (see Fig. 3) This architecture has three main areas: patient, medical team and data centre.

The area of patient is focused on data acquisition through wireless devices: smart band, blood pressure meter, digital balance and calprotectin meter. These devices will send automatically values of clinical interest to a smart device (mobile phone, tablet...) via Bluetooth. This information will be processed based on artificial intelligence algorithms offering, through User Agents (UA), customized recommendations based on patient's behaviour, predetermined goals and recommendations made by the medical team. Thus, a Decision Support System (DSS) is developed, improving patient empowerment. Data center will serve to store and manage data. BPMS allows us to model the clinical process developing task and processes. The DDS will made recommendations based on the data provided by the patient, collaborative filtering and the recommendations of the medical team. The transfer of data is bidirectional between different areas of the system using APIs Rest for communication between them.

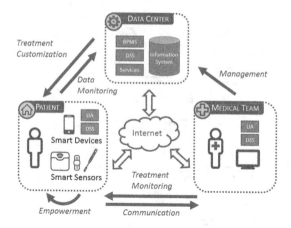

Fig. 3. System architecture for Crohn's disease management

A case study is described below to illustrate the proposed architecture: to verify whether the diet given to a patient is being effective, the patient control its weight daily with a balance. The balance collects the data (kg) and sends it via bluetooth to the mobile device, which synchronizes and resends the data to the center. The DDS data center evaluates the data based on the trend of the patient and the pre-set goals. If the results are within the pre-established limits informs the patient that its progression is adequate and should therefore continue with the diet. Otherwise, it proposes a series of recommendations to the patient (changing eating habits, increasing physical activity, readjusting the diet…) in order to correct their behaviour and achieve the pre-set goals. For more control, the data center will report the suggested changes to the medical team. This will allow them to monitor the patient's behaviour. Thus, the information is shared between the three areas defined in the architecture, obtaining an updated medical history and an increased supervision by the medical team.

7   Conclusions

Our proposal is focused on the use of BPM to the clinical process of Crohn in order to coordinate globally all elements involved in managing the clinical process of Crohn's disease. The main novelty of our approach is the use of Business Processes Management strategies and ITs together with artificial intelligence algorithms and different wireless sensors to allow the monitoring of the patient and provide information to the expert system. Thus, a dynamic model that adapts to the needs of the patient is achieved, improving the empowerment of the patient and overcoming the deficiencies in the current clinical process.

Conflict of Interest
The authors declare no conflict of interest in this article.

Acknowledgements. This work has been granted by the Ministerio de Economía y Competitividad of the Spanish Government (ref. TIN2014-53067-C3-1-R) and cofinanced by FEDER.

References

1. World Health Organization. Chronic disease and health promotion programme. http://www.who.int/topics/chronic_diseases/es/
2. Smith, H., Fingar, P.: Business Process Management: The Third Wave. Morgan Kaufmann, California (2002)
3. Patterson, T., Cruciani, F., Cleland, I., Nugent, C.D., Black, N.D., McCullagh, P.J., Zheng, H., Donnelly, M.P., McDonough, S., Boyd, A.: KeepWell: a generic platform for the self-management of chronic conditions. In: Journal of Health Politics, Policy and Law, pp. 891–896 (2016)
4. Pedersen, N.: EHealth: Self-management in Inflammatory Bowel Disease and in Irritable Bowel Syndrome Using Novel Constant-Care Web Applications. Herlev University Hospital, Herlev (2016)
5. Harmon, P.: Business Process Change: A Manager's Guide to Improving, Redesigning, and Automating Processes. Morgan Kaufmann, San Francisco (2003)
6. Becker, J., Fischer, R., Janiesch, C., Scherpbier, H.: Optimizing U.S. healthcare processes: a case study in business process management. In: Association for Information Systems - 13th Americas Conference on Information Systems, AMCIS 2007, Reaching New Heights, pp. 2236–2247 (2007)
7. O'Connor, M., Gaarenstroom, J., Kemp, K., Bager, P., van der Woude, C.J.: N-ECCO survey results of nursing practice in caring for patients with Crohn's disease or ulcerative colitis in Europe. J. Crohns. Colitis. **8**, 1300–1307 (2014)
8. Halpin, S.J., Ford, A.C.: Prevalence of symptoms meeting criteria for irritable bowel syndrome in inflammatory bowel disease: systematic review and meta-analysis. Am. J. Gastroenterol. **107**, 1474–1482 (2012)
9. Meuwis, M.A., Vernier-Massouille, G., Grimaud, J.C., Bouhnik, Y., Laharie, D., Piver, E., Seidel, L., Colombel, J.F., Louis, E.: Serum calprotectin as a biomarker for Crohn's disease. J. Crohn's Colitis. **7**, e678–e683 (2013)
10. Maunder, R.G.: Evidence that stress contributes to inflammatory bowel disease: evaluation, synthesis, and future directions. Inflamm. Bowel Dis. **11**, 600–608 (2005)
11. Nurmi, E., Haapamäki, J., Paavilainen, E., Rantanen, A., Hillilä, M., Arkkila, P.: The burden of inflammatory bowel disease on health care utilization and quality of life. Scand. J. Gastroenterol. **48**, 51–57 (2013)
12. Torrejón Herrera, A., Masachs Peracaula, M., Borruel Sainz, N., Castells Carner, I., Castillejo Badía, N., Malagelada Benaprés, J.R., Casellas Jordá, F.: Aplicación de un modelo de asistencia continuada en la enfermedad inflamatoria intestinal: la Unidad de Atención Crohn-Colitis. Gastroenterol. Hepatol. **32**, 77–82 (2009)
13. Odes, S.: How expensive is inflammatory bowel disease? A critical analysis. World J. Gastroenterol. **14**, 6641–6647 (2008)

Artificial Intelligence Applied in the Multi-label Problem of Chronic Pelvic Pain Diagnosing

Vinicius Oliverio$^{(\boxtimes)}$ and Omero Bendicto Poli-Neto

Universidade de São Paulo, Ribeirão Preto, SP 14049-900, Brazil
vinicius.oliverio@usp.br, polineto@fmrp.usp.br

Abstract. Chronic pelvic pain is a common clinical condition with negative consequences in many aspects of women's life. The clinical presentation is heterogeneous and the involvement of several body systems impairs the identification of the exact etiology of the problem. At the same time, a clinical treatment of good quality depends on the professional and the learning process is slow. The goal of the paper is to show techniques used to create an artificial intelligence system capable of indicating the probable causes of this condition in order to help the doctors in the diagnosing process. This system uses a supervised learning algorithm along with multi-label problem modeling techniques and attribute selection algorithms to achieve the desired goal.

Keywords: Artificial intelligence · Machine learning · Chronic pelvic pain · Diagnosis · Multi-label

1 Introduction

Chronic pelvic pain (CPP) is a common clinical condition worldwide and is defined as a pain in the lower abdomen and/or in the pelvis, persisting for at least six months and intense enough to cause functional incapacity, demanding clinical or surgical treatment [1].

This condition is difficult to control because frequently the primary cause is not identified. The etiology is not clear and, usually results from a complex interaction between the gastrointestinal, urinary, gynecological, musculoskeletal, neurological, psychological and endocrine systems, also influenced by sociocultural facts [2].

The disease implies a direct expense exceeding two billion dollars per year in the United States and has a considerable impact on the socioeconomic national scenario, directly due to elevated expenses and secondarily due to the incapacity caused by this condition [3].

At the same time, the importance of computing has been increasing over the years in a wide variety of fields, including medicine, in which the use of computational systems is extensive. Ranging from X-ray scanners to computerized robotic surgeries, computing has been used in many tasks. One of these tasks

© Springer International Publishing AG 2016
C.R. García et al. (Eds.): UCAmI 2016, Part I, LNCS 10069, pp. 80–85, 2016.
DOI: 10.1007/978-3-319-48746-5_9

is the possibility to enable the acquisition and reliable storage of selected clinical data that can be very useful for scientific research, including the field of chronic pelvic pain, by the creation of systems that record and manage structured forms [4]. Another important task would be to obtain artificial intelligence systems that would help with the diagnosis of the real cause of this condition using the databases created by those computational structured forms.

By discussing these questions, the goal of this paper is to promote reflection among clinical professionals and researchers about the benefits of computing systems, such as artificial intelligence systems, for supporting the development of good quality research and helping professionals in understanding better the diseases.

1.1 Naive Bayes

The Naive Bayes algorithm was chosen to be the classifier algorithm because bayesian learning algorithms that calculate explicit probabilities for hypotheses, are among the most practical approaches to certain types of learning problems [6]. In [9] a detailed study comparing the Naive Bayes classifier to other learning algorithms is provided, and it shows that the Naive Bayes classifier is competitive with decision trees, neural networks and other learning algorithms in many cases and in some cases it outperforms these other methods.

The Naive Bayes classifier bases itself in the simplified supposition that the attributes are conditionally independent given the target value (the class y). In other words, the suposition that the target value of one instance i, the probability of the conjunction of the elements of x_i ($\{x_i,1, x_i,2, \ldots, x_i,m\}$) is given by the multiplication of the probabilities of the individual attributes: $P(x_1, x_2, \ldots, x_i \mid y_j) = \prod_i P(x_i, y_j)$.

The Naive Bayes not always brings a very accurate probability of each class, but tends to have a good success rate in finding the most probable class. The reason which the estimated probability given by the naive bayes algorithm is not always precise is because of the simplification made by it when it disregards the relations between the attributes, assuming they are conditionally independent given the class.

2 Modeling

The chronic pelvic pain diagnose problem is a multi-label problem since each patient can have one or more diseases that are causing the condition. In the present paper each instance (patient) can have up to 7 diagnoses (labels), these possible diseases are constipation, pelvic inflammatory disease (PID), endometriosis, neuralgias (it covers ilioinguinal neuralgia and pudendal neuralgia), painful bladder syndrome, pelvic congestion syndrome and irritable bowel syndrome.

As it is a multi-label problem, it requires a multi-label strategy (modeling) since the classic Naive Bayes algorithm is a single-label classification algorithm. The next subsection shows how this problem can be solved.

2.1 Multi-label Classification

In multi-label classification, the examples are associated with one or more labels. In the beginning, multi-label classification was mainly motivated by the tasks of text categorization and medical diagnosis, for instance, in medical diagnosis, a patient may be suffering for example from endometriosis and constipation at the same time [10].

In [10,11], the authors made a survey of multi-label classification approaches and they show some problem transformation methods for adapting a multi-label problem to a single-label algorithm, the two used methods will be discussed.

The first chosen problem transformation method (called PT4) was used in several papers, such as, [10–13], and it consists in splitting the original data set into n data sets (where n is the number of classes) containing all examples of the original, labeled as l if the labels of the original example contained l and as ¬l otherwise. Then it is necessary to build one single label classifier to each data set. This approach is one of the two used in this paper in the experimentation process, it does not ignore any data and allows the classification to be done using a single label classifier such as Naive Bayes.

The second chosen approach (called PT5) was shown in [10] and consists of decomposing each example that has more than one label in n examples (where n is the number of labels that this example has). Then it learns one single-label classifier from the transformed data set. This approach was also one of the two used in this paper in the experimentation process, it also does not ignore any data and allows the classification to be done using Naive Bayes as well.

3 Experimentation

The training data set used to train the algorithm is a database of real diagnosed cases from the Clinics Hospital of Ribeirão Preto of the University of São Paulo (HCFMRP/USP). It consists of 346 instances (patients) with 106 attributes from the form filled by the doctors in each medical consultation of those patients, these forms contains the full history of the patient from the first consultation until the final diagnose.

The experimentation process consisted in four experiments, the first and the second one using the PT5 method, and the third and fourth experiment using the PT4 method. Since there are 106 attributes (symptoms, examinations, etc.), it is not known if all attributes are important for the diagnosis of all the diseases, so in the experiments two and four after the problem transformation method was applied, the database passed through the Correlation-based Feature Subset Selection algorithm [14] in order to discover which attributes were relevant to the classification process, this way, it is possible to check which classification will be better, the one with all attributes or the one with selected attributes.

In the second experiment the attribute selection algorithm was executed once in the transformed data set, and in the fourth experiment for each of the resulting data sets the attribute selection algorithm was executed in order to find out which variables are relevant to each one of the diseases (classes).

In the end of all experiments the resulting data sets were provided to the Naive Bayes classifier to train the algorithm, and its accuracy was validated using k-fold cross-validation [15] method, using a 10-fold size. The attribute selection algorithm and the Naive Bayes classifier were made using the Weka 3.9 software [16].

4   Results

In the experiments 2 and 4, the first step after the problem transformation methods were executed, was to run an attribute selection algorithm in order to reduce the amount of attributes used in the classification process. In experiment 2 the attribute selection algorithm selected 33 attributes, and in experiment 4 it selected 6 attributes for the constipation classifier, 7 for the PID classifier, 33 for the endometriosis classifier, 7 for the neuralgias classifier, 6 for the painful bladder classifier, 15 for the pelvic congestion classifier and 7 for the irritable bowel classifier.

As shown before, the first two experiments used PT5 and a single classifier. Initially the accuracy of the algorithm was very low, having a success rate of 23.57 % (experiment 1), then after the attribute selection step the success rate increased to 45.5 % (experiment 2). The result of the consecutive two tests (experiments 3 and 4), that used the PT4 method, can be seen in Fig. 1.

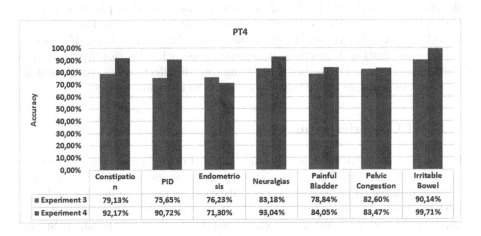

	Constipation	PID	Endometriosis	Neuralgias	Painful Bladder	Pelvic Congestion	Irritable Bowel
■ Experiment 3	79,13%	75,65%	76,23%	83,18%	78,84%	82,60%	90,14%
■ Experiment 4	92,17%	90,72%	71,30%	93,04%	84,05%	83,47%	99,71%

Fig. 1. Results from experiments 3 and 4.

As shown in Fig. 1 the accuracy of all classifiers used to process the data sets created by PT4 are better than the one classifier used for PT5. Also, in almost all cases the classifier that used only the selected attributes had better results than the classifiers that used all attributes, the only case that it didn't is the classifier for Endometriosis. One more interesting case is the case of the Irritable Bowel Syndrome, that achieved a success rate of 99.71 %, this is explainable because

Table 1. Sensitivity and specificity of the classifiers on experiment 3.

	Constipation	PID	Endometriosis	Neuralgias	Painful bladder	Pelvic congestion	Irritable bowel
Sensitivity	0.353	0.548	0.687	0.64	0.816	0.345	0.697
Specificity	0.839	0.777	0.818	0.847	0.784	0.87	0.923

Table 2. Sensitivity and specificity of the classifiers on experiment 4.

	Constipation	PID	Endometriosis	Neuralgias	Painful bladder	Pelvic congestion	Irritable bowel
Sensitivity	0.441	0.355	0.782	0.6	0.796	0.241	1
Specificity	0.974	0.962	0.662	0.956	0.848	0.889	0.997

this disease has a known set of characteristics that determine if the patient has it or not, and the selected attributes were exactly the ones used to determine it.

Another important result from the tests were the sensitivity and specificity of the classifier in experimentations 3 and 4, and these values can be seen on Tables 1 and 2.

Though the specificity in almost all cases were better than the sensitivity it is also good for this diagnosing problem. Despite the fact that the multidisciplinary approach is fundamental, the specific diagnose of the cause of the CPP is necessary for a good therapeutic planning. In this point there is another relative difficulty that is the multiplicity of symptoms. Many patients presents diverse symptoms that might suggest the commitment of several systems. The ability of the professional to list the most significant may optimize the process of complementary investigation. Consequently, besides propitiating a rational path to the diagnose, having a good specificity might improve the effectiveness-cost, avoiding the request of multiple exams, that in most of the cases are unnecessary.

5   Final Considerations

This paper shows a Naive Bayes classifier adapted to the multi-label problem of diagnosing the Chronic Pelvic Pain etiology, i.e., the diseases that are causing it. It was possible to achieve a good classification accuracy by using a problem transformation method and a attribute selection algorithm, in some cases the algorithm reached a success rate greater than 99 %. However the algorithm in almost all cases had a better specificity but as already said it might reduce the cost for the health systems as it shows a path to the diagnose avoiding expenses with unnecessary exams, and also reduce the time that it takes for the doctor do diagnose the real cause of the condition.

As a future work, a benchmark of different classifiers could be done in order to discover which one is the one that fits the best in the Chronic Pelvic Pain diagnose problem, also a benchmark of different attribute selection algorithms probably could improve the classification accuracy.

References

1. ACOG: ACOG Practice Bulletin No. 51. Chronic pelvic pain. Obstetrics & Gynecology. vol. 103, 589–605 (2004)
2. Howard, F.M.: Chronic pelvic pain. Obstet. Gynecol. **101**, 594–611 (2003)
3. Blyth, F.M., March, L.M., Brnabic, A.J., Cousins, M.J.: Chronic pain and frequent use of health care. Pain **111**, 51–58 (2004)
4. Tolley, E.A., Headley, A.S.: Meta-analyses: what they can and cannot tell us about clinical research. Cur. Opin. Clin. Nutr. Met. Care. **8**, 177–181 (2005)
5. Nilsson, N.J.: Introduction to Machine Learning: An Early Draft of a Proposed TextBook. Stanford University (1997)
6. Mitchell, T.M.: Machine Learning. McGraw-Hill Science/Engineering/Math (1997)
7. Haykin, S.: Neural Networks: A Comprehensive Foundation. Prentice Hall (1998)
8. John, G.H., Langley, P.: Estimating continuous distributions in Bayesian classifiers. In: Proceedings of the Eleventh Conference on Uncertainty in Artificial Intelligence, pp. 338–345. Morgan Kaufmann Publishers (1995)
9. Michie, D., Spiegelhalter, D.J., Taylor, C.C.: Machine learning, neural and statistical classification. Ellis Horwood (1994)
10. Tsoumakas, G., Katakis, I.: Multi-label classification: an overview. Int. J. Data Warehouse. Min. **3**, 1–13 (2007)
11. Carvalho, A., Freitas, A.A.: A tutorial on multi-label classification techniques. Found. Comput. Intell. **5**, 177–195 (2009)
12. Boutell, M.R., Luo, J., Shen, X., Brown, C.M.: Learning multi-label scene classification. Pattern Recogn. **37**, 1757–1771 (2004)
13. Li, T., Ogihara, M.: Detecting emotion in music. In: Proceedings of the International Symposium on Music Information Retrieval (2003)
14. Hall, M.A.: Correlation-based Feature Selection for Machine Learning (Doctoral thesis). University of Waikato, Hamilton (1999)
15. Lachenbruch, P.A., Mickey, M.R.: Estimation of error rates in discriminant analysis. Technometrics **10**, 1–12 (1968)
16. Hall, M.A., Frank, E., Holmes, G., Pfahringer, B., Reutemann, P., Witten, I.H.: The WEKA data mining software: an update. SIGKDD Explor. **11**(1), 10–18 (2009)

Use of Emerging 3D Printing and Modeling Technologies in the Health Domain

A Systematic Literature Review

Carolina Ávila[1], Gustavo López[1(✉)], Gabriela Marín[1], Lisbeth Salazar[2],
Zaray Miranda[2], Jessica González[2], and Brian Brenes[2]

[1] Research Center for ICT, University of Costa Rica, San José, Costa Rica
{carolina.avilaarias,gustavo.lopez_h,gabriela.marin}@ucr.ac.cr
[2] School of Medicine, University of Costa Rica, San José, Costa Rica
{lizbeth.salazar,zaray.mirandachacon,
jessica.gonzalez_f}@ucr.ac.cr, brianbreness@gmail.com

Abstract. Three-Dimensional (3D) technologies emerged from the technological advances in manufacturing required to produce physical versions of
digital models. The most attractive feature of 3D technologies is that virtual
models are easy to mold, and custom-made items can be physically produced.
Health domains are areas in which 3D technologies have been applied, and
several studies have been conducted assessing the usefulness of such technologies in those domains. In this paper we present the results of a Systematic
Literature Review (SLR) on the applications of 3D technologies in the health
domain. Discussion from the revision of 33 papers is presented. The main
finding of this SLR is that none of the available research papers are focused on
computer science related areas (i.e., all papers are published by doctors or
researchers in Medicine). Moreover, all the included papers were published in
journals specialized in Medicine. Therefore, they do not delve in the computational conclusions of the studies. In this article, we identified significant
research gaps (from the computational perspective), as well as new ideas are
being proposed on the future of 3D technologies in health.

Keywords: 3D printing · Health education · Health training · 3D technologies
medical applications

1 Introduction

3D technologies, associated with science and technology, include but are not limited to:
3D computer generated graphics applied in several domains (e.g., video games, television, films, and projections), 3D rendering, 3D modeling, 3D scanning (i.e., digitalizing
physical objects) and 3D printing (i.e., creating solid objects from a digital model).

One application domain for 3D technologies is health. Great medical advances have
been seen in the past years. The application of 3D technologies revolutionized and
boosted these advances, by facilitating the replication of body parts. The main

© Springer International Publishing AG 2016
C.R. García et al. (Eds.): UCAmI 2016, Part I, LNCS 10069, pp. 86–98, 2016.
DOI: 10.1007/978-3-319-48746-5_10

applications of 3D technologies in the medical domain are: surgical planning, prosthesis creation, implanted structure, and medical education, among others.

This paper presents a Systematic Literature Review (SLR) of 3D printing and modeling technologies applied in the health domain. This review was conducted in the scope of a research project that seeks to determine the possibility of anatomical 3d models with sufficient accuracy to be used in medical education programs.

The main problem that medical education programs find is that human bones are not easy to obtain. They are supplied for students to manipulate, but only within the laboratory facilities, since they cannot be freely used outside restricted areas due to biohazardous concerns [1].

Given the difficulty of obtaining anatomical parts, their high social costs, difficulties for their preservation and the associated biological risks; techniques have been developed in different countries in order to provide exact bones replicas.

One of this techniques is bone replication through 3D technologies. In this process, real bones serve as templates initially using clay, fiberglass, silicone and polyester resin, generating bone replicas, with similar characteristics to the originals. The rapid evolution of 3D technologies, especially 3D scanning and printing allows the reproduction of bones using such technologies.

The conceptual framework behind 3D scanning is to take an object and create a 3D model of the object. A 3D model is a digital representation of a physical object. 3D scanning equipment exists to capture and transform the dimensions of the physical object into 3D digital models.

3D printing is the process of making three dimensional solid objects from a digital model. The creation of a 3D printed object is achieved using an additive process. In it, successive layers of a material are laid down until the entire object is created. Each of the material layers can be seen as a thinly sliced horizontal cross-section of the original physical object or of the 3D model.

3D printing is evolving at an extremely rapid pace as specialists are beginning to utilize 3D printing in more advanced ways for medical applications. Patients can experience improved quality of their care through 3D printed implants and prosthetics. In bio-printing, layers of living cells are deposited onto a gel medium and slowly built up to form three dimensional structures.

Similar efforts to the one presented in this paper have been conducted; however, all of them are focused on the medical perspective of the issue (i.e., the medical applications). We describe the main advances in including 3D technologies in health domains, reported in literature, from a computational perspective. Moreover, we identify significant research gaps, as well as new ideas are being proposed on the future of 3D technologies in health.

The remaining of this paper is structured as follows: Sect. 2 delves on related works (i.e., systematic literature reviews conducted by health specialists), Sects. 3 and 4 present our SLR methodology and results, Sect. 5 discusses our findings, and Sect. 6 concludes this research paper.

2   Related Work

As we mentioned before, all the SLR on the application of 3D technologies in health domains, found in the academic repositories searched, are focused from the medical perspective. Also, all of them have been conducted by health specialists, rather than technocrats. This section summarizes the results presented in those health focused systematic literature reviews.

In 2015, Malik et al. [2], presented a review of 3D printing in surgery, they described three categories of applications: anatomic models (54.8 %), surgical instruments (12.9 %), and implants and prostheses (20.4 %), and multiple fields (11.8 %) from a total of 93 papers. Their search included: MEDLINE, EMBASE, and PsycINFO databases and PubMed search engine. All these databases are focused on medical advances.

Also during 2015, AlAli et al. [3] published another SLR, which was conducted in PubMed and Web of science. Results show benefits of 3D technologies in surgical applications; however, authors state that longer follow-up and more trials are needed to assess the real impact of these technologies.

In 2016, Martelli et al. [4] also conducted a SLR, again this review used medical references. Authors found preoperative planning, and time saved in the operating room to be the most important advantages of 3D printing applied in surgery. Also in 2016, Vakharia, Vakharia and Hill [5] published another SLR. In this research authors focus on cranial neurosurgery. This SLR searched in PubMed, OVID MEDLINE, Embase, and Cochrane databases. Preoperative applications are the main advantage reported. Moreover, detailing techniques are applied on 3D printed pieces to provide a more realistic representation. Other SLR were revised [6, 7], however, their results were not relevant for this research. It is interesting to note that related SLR has been conducted in the past 3 years, showing how relevant this topic is for the health specialists.

3   Literature Review Methodology

We performed a Systematic Literature Review in electronic databases during April and May 2016. Searched databases included: Access Medicine[1], ACM Digital Library[2], IEEE Digital Library[3] and, Springer Link[4]. Searches were performed using relevant keywords to increase the possibility of relevant work identification maximization. Limits were defined on language and publication date. Only papers written in English and published between 2000 and 2016 were considered, as to assess the current state of the art

The first screening process (i.e., (title and abstract review) included only papers that referenced the use of 3D technologies. Then, a second screening process was performed (i.e., full text review).

---

[1] http://accessmedicine.mhmedical.com/.

[2] http://dl.acm.org/.

[3] http://ieeexplore.ieee.org/.

[4] http://link.springer.com/.

Three keywords were used to conduct this SLR: (1) "3D Printing", (2) "Anatomy", and (3) "Anatomy teaching". Table 1 shows the results of the screening processes in comparison to the amount of papers, separated by database.

Table 1. Amount of papers identified and included in this SLR divided by electronic databases. Each consulted page grouped 20 papers.

Data Base	Total	1st review	2nd review	Consulted Pages	% included
Access Medicine	1	0	0	1/1	0 %
ACM	60	2	0	4/4	0 %
IEEE	157	5	0	7/7	0 %
Science Direct	500	33	16	15/20	48,5 %
Springer	1,112	28	17	20/56	51.5 %
TOTAL	**1830**	**68**	**33**	**47/88**	**100 %**

The main question driving this research is: How much work has been done (reported in scientific papers) from a computational perspective to include 3D printing in health domains?

All databases were consulted were ordered by relevance to the query string. Consulted pages, mentioned in Table 1, refer to the number of pages (over the total number of pages) that were consulted until three consecutive pages did not present any paper included for further review (i.e., significance was too low to show relevant papers).

3.1 Data Extraction

Data extraction was conducted systematically. Each primary study was revised and title, application context, publication year, models reproduced and forum were gathered. Table 2 lists the 33 papers included in this SLR.

After a first reading of every article retrieved, 2 researchers (1st and 2nd authors) drew up a list of categories and regrouped included studies. This categorization was performed both for application context, and model type.

An extensive analysis of the gathered papers was conducted to determine the best way in which the results of this SLR could be addressed. The revised paper went through a data extraction process to determine from which countries the papers came from (using affiliation data to extrapolate the geographical location), the area of expertise of the authors (using affiliation keywords), publication year, application context (from a list of predetermined possibilities), and the model type (i.e., parts of the body that were being reproduced).

Table 2. Primary studies selected. (**Model types:** C: Cardiovascular, M: Musculoeskeletal, N: Nervous, H&I: Hemic and Immune, D: Digestive, R: Respiratory, E: Endocrine, U: Urogenital) (**Application Contexts:** Educ: Education, SP&T: Surgery planning and training, ID: Implant design)

Year	Application Context	Model Type	Journal	Reference
2008	Educ.	C	Int. J. Comput. Assist. Radiol. Surg.	[8]
2009	Educ.	C	Int. J. Comput. Assist. Radiol. Surg.	[9]
2014	SP&T, Educ.	R	J. of cardiothoracic and vascular anesthesia	[10]
	SP&T	C	J. of Cranio-Maxillofacial Surgery	[11]
	ID	M	J. of Surgical Education	[12]
	Educ.	R	J. of Surgical Education	[13]
	SP&T, Educ.	M, N	World Neurosurgery	[14]
	SP&T	C	J. of Cardiovascular Magnetic Resonance	[15]
	SP&T, Educ.	C, N	J. of Otolaryngology Surgery	[16]
2015	Educ.	C	American Journal of Otolaryngology	[17]
	ID	M	Clinical Radiology	[18]
	Educ.	M	Int.J. of Pediatric Otorhinolaryngology	[19]
	SP&T	U	Quaternary International journal	[20]
	SP&T	M	Urology	[21]
	SP&T	C	World Neurosurgery	[22]
	SP&T	M	World Neurosurgery	[23]
	ID, Research	M	3D Printing in Medicine	[24]
	Educ.	C M	3D Printing in Medicine	[25]
	Research	M	J. of Cardiovascular Magnetic Resonance	[26]
	Educ.	C, E, R	J. of Orthopedic Science	[27]
	SP&T, Educ.	U	Medical and Biological Engin. and Comp.	[28]
	SP&T	N	Medical Science Educator	[29]
	SP&T	M, N	Surgical and Radiologic Anatomy	[30]
2016	SP&T	R	J. of Surgical Education	[31]
	SP&T	N	J. of Surgical Education	[32]
	SP&T	M	World Neurosurgery	[33]
	SP&T	H&I, E	World Neurosurgery	[34]
	Educ.	D	Child's Nervous System	[35]
	SP&T, Educ.	C, E	Child's Nervous System	[36]
	SP&T	H&I	Indian J. of Surgery	[37]
	Educ.	U	Surgical endoscopy	[38]
	Educ.	N	World J. of Surgery	[39]
	SP&T	N, M	World J. of Urology	[40]

The main description of the papers included in Table 2 is grouped in Sect. 4.1. In this section the included papers are summarized by year of publication, application contexts, parts of the body being reproduced, area of knowledge of the authors and country.

4 Systematic Literature Review Results

4.1 Included Papers Summary

In this section we examine the process conducted in order to determine the inclusion of the different papers incorporated in the present SLR. A strong trend can be seen in the amount of papers published reporting the application of 3D technologies in health domains. The amount of published papers doubled from 2014 to 2015.

In the first 5 months of 2015, more than 70 % of the amount of papers published in 2015 had already been released. Figure 1 shows the results regarding the amount of papers published by year.

Four major application contexts were discovered during our SLR: Surgery planning and training, education, implant design and research. Figure 2 shows the percentage of papers in each category. These results are calculated from33 papers; however, the baseline is 39, since several papers were categorized in more than one category.

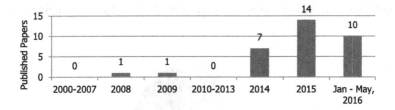

Fig. 1. Number of included papers published by year

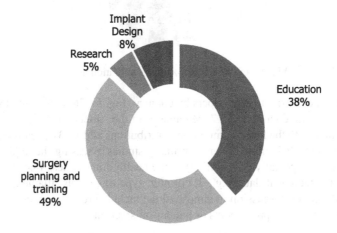

Fig. 2. Percentage of included papers by application contexts

Applications based on 7 human body systems were found in our SLR. Figure 3 shows the percentage of papers in each category. This result is calculated from 33 papers; however, the baseline is 40, since several papers were categorized in more than one category.

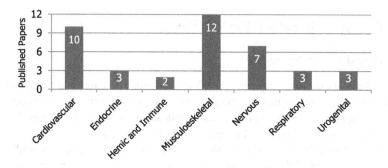

Fig. 3. Number of included papers by addressed human body system

Considering author's affiliations (Fig. 4), 54 % are from medicine or related areas, 37 % from engineering related areas and 9 % from other areas. Even though there is a significant participation of experts in engineering, the results presented in the papers are focused on medical applications. This is a reflect of the journal in which these papers were published, as most of them are focused on medicine rather than engineering.

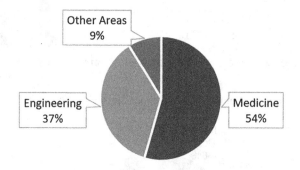

Fig. 4. Distribution of author's affiliation areas

Reviewing the distribution of papers by country (Fig. 5), 26.92 % came from countries of the European continent, 55.77 % came from the American continent, being the USA the country with the largest amount of contributions and 17.31 % came from Asia. Even though our SLR included over 30 primary studies assessing the applicability of 3D technologies (especially 3D printing) in the health domain, less than 5 % of these papers included technical data (e.g., 3D printer, type of models, filament or printing materials). Moreover, discussion in almost all the included research papers focused on health issues, medical improvements or patient satisfaction.

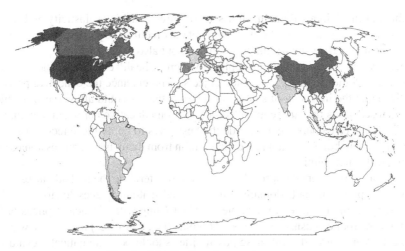

Fig. 5. Distribution of papers by country.

5 Discussion

In this section, we present our efforts to draw technological conclusions from the 33 papers included in this SLR. As we mentioned before, all the included papers were published in health-related journals. Moreover, all papers were written by health specialists from different countries.

The use of 3D technologies for health applications began using visualizing techniques [8, 9]. Since then, health specialists have been applying technological tools to support education and professional activities. Problems that are still unsolved include scanning technology deficiencies, and calibration and accuracy issues.

An issue frequently associated with the novelty of 3D technologies is its "high" cost [10, 13]. From a technological perspective, we believe that 3D technology costs will eventually drop as the technology advances. However, transdisciplinary studies must be conducted to assure that those advances are applicable in health domains.

Delving in this transdisciplinary approach, some health specialists stated that technical expertise is required to tailor virtual models [17]. Furthermore, those specialists believe that 3D technologies understanding and technical skills will be incorporated in their professional practices (i.e., they will be learning how to use 3D technologies, instead of technical people applying it for them) [20].

Health specialists are applying 3D printed objects to confirm conclusions drawn from 2D images [11]. This approach also presents a problem, the time required to print a virtual model, or worst print a mold or template, to create physical representations of those 2D images. Printing time is a technical issue that needs to be addressed in order to use 3D technologies, not only in health domains but in general.

Health specialists have also started to define metrics for accuracy of 3D printed models [18]. This type of works can be used to measure technological improvements. Also from the technological perspective, algorithms are required to automatically polish and refine virtual models gathered from physical objects.

In the transdisciplinary domain, efforts are required to achieve elasticity of different densities and soft tissues [37]. This work will not only require the participation of people with technical expertise and health professionals, but also experts in arts.

Currently, 3D printed models are applied to improve health education. The inclusion of other technologies to these 3D printed objects could enhance the educative process. We believe that the inclusion of sensors or micro actuators could allow the simulation of different scenarios that are required for a hands-on educative approach. Again, it is not in the hands of technocrats to decide the best ways to apply these technologies in the health domain, but, without direct collaboration from them, health professionals will not come with such solutions.

Finally, an experimental approach is required to determine the real advances in 3D technologies applied in health domains. From original anatomic pieces, to virtual models generated by scanning those physical pieces. Continuing with physical replicas of the original piece produced using 3D printers or molds (i.e., templates) to create new physical objects. We believe that all those possibilities should be systematically evaluated to really assess the applicability of 3D technologies in health domains.

6 Conclusions

In order to forge the present review, five different databases were consulted for references: Access Medicine, ACM, IEEE, Science Direct and Springer which provided a total of 1830 results, 1761 of those were discarded based on its title and abstract, resulting on 33 remaining papers being included on the review. Our review focused on technological conclusions that could be drawn from health-related publications.

Along the development process of the current paper, some of the most fundamental advantages and disadvantages for the uses of 3D models in the medical field came into focus. The advantages are directly related with patient wellbeing or an easing of medical education. On the other hand, disadvantages are commonly referred to technical limitations or the necessity of further studies.

Although different technologies have emerged, still today, the practice carried out in corpses is one of the most important means of anatomy and procedure teaching, as well as surgery training for medical students. Even though the difficulties associated to this method still exist: the high social costs, the preservation difficulties, the associated biological risks as well as the laboratory-only environment requirement. Therefore, the need for alternate methods, which might be more affordable, not only economically but socially as well as more accessible beyond a controlled environment, is clearly latent.

Thus, seeking for developing technologies whose applications might contribute to solving the need for 3D models in the medical field is still a valuable research field. Furthermore, the combination of 3D technologies with small sensors or actuators could provide simulations of real environments that are nowadays inaccessible for medical training.

For example, plastic bones, which were amongst some of the initial alternatives for the 3D models problems, were said to have some deficiencies quality-wise such as lack of cavities, texture, and a plastic feel to it. This led to a different practice, in which actual bones were used as a template to create models using materials like clay, fiberglass, silicone, polyester resin and others, to create these new representations. The method improved the quality of the resultant model as well as its dimensional accuracy which is crucial, given the model's applications.

3D printed bones or replicas created using 3D printed molds are valuable. But they will be even more valuable if features were added to replicate not only their appearance but also their behavior in certain circumstances. 3D technologies applied in the health domain have improved the learning curve for complex procedures, diagnosis ability, preoperative planning, patient education and more. These results have been achieved with the participation of medical or health specialists. The incursion of transdisciplinary teams could boost these results.

Nevertheless, the 3D printing method could also involve some aspects that might be seen as disadvantages, such as the investment required for the acquisition of the proper equipment and the amount of time and human resources required for the creation of every finished piece. Efforts are still required to provide 3D printed replicas with soft tissue or other anatomical components. This work will not be possible without art experts.

Another arising issue in regard of fundamental resources is the technical expertise required to tailor virtual models. Due to this consideration, 3D technologies understanding has strong potential to be incorporated in their practice which would allow them to develop the necessary tools for obtaining data abstraction, models, and others, essential to achieve a finished piece.

Acknowledgements. This project was partially funded by VINV at UCR. Grant No. 834-B6-076.

References

1. Quijano Blanco, Y., Rodríguez, M.F.C., Peralta R.K., Cortés C.S.: Polyester resin bone replica, as didactic tool for anatomy learning. Rev. U.D.C.A Actual. Divulg. Científica. **15**(2), 275–281 (2012)
2. Malik, H.H., Darwood, A.R.J., Shaunak, S., Kulatilake, P., El-Hilly, A.A., Mulki, O., Baskaradas, A.: Three-dimensional printing in surgery: a review of current surgical applications. J. Surg. Res. **199**, 512–522 (2015)
3. AlAli, A.B., Griffin, M.F., Butler, P.E.: Three-dimensional printing surgical applications. Eplasty **15**, e37 (2015)
4. Martelli, N., Serrano, C., Van Den Brink, H., Pineau, J., Prognon, P., Borget, I., El Batti, S.: Advantages and disadvantages of 3-dimensional printing in surgery: A systematic review. Surg. (United States) **159**, 1485–1500 (2016)
5. Vakharia, V.N., Vakharia, N.N., Hill, C.S.: Review of 3-dimensional printing on cranial neurosurgery simulation training. World Neurosurg. **88**, 188–198 (2016)
6. Marro, A., Bandukwala, T., Mak, W.: Three-dimensional printing and medical imaging: a review of the methods and applications. Curr. Probl. Diagn. Radiol. **45**, 2–9 (2016)

7. Banoriya, D., Purohit, R., Dwivedi, R.K.: Modern trends in rapid prototyping for biomedical applications. Mater. Today Proc. **2**, 3409–3418 (2015)
8. Vázquez, P.P., Götzelmann, T., Hartmann, K., Nürnberger, A., Vázquez, P.P., Tzelmann, G.T., Hartmann, K., Rnberger, A.: An interactive 3D framework for anatomical education. Int. J. Comput. Assist. Radiol. Surg. **3**, 511–524 (2008)
9. Seitel, M., Maier-Hein, L., Seitel, A., Franz, A.M., Kenngott, H., De Simone, R., Wolf, I., Meinzer, H.P.: RepliExplore: Coupling physical and virtual anatomy models. Int. J. Comput. Assist. Radiol. Surg. **4**, 417–424 (2009)
10. Bustamante, S., Bose, S., Bishop, P., Klatte, R., Norris, F.: Novel application of rapid prototyping for simulation of bronchoscopic anatomy. J. Cardiothorac. Vasc. Anesth. **28**, 1122–1125 (2014)
11. Schrot, J., Pietila, T., Sahu, A.: State of the art: 3D printing for creating compliant patient-specific congenital heart defect models. J. Cardiovasc. Magn. Reson. **16**, W19 (2014)
12. Jardini, A.L., Larosa, M.A., Filho, R.M., Zavaglia, C.A.D.C., Bernardes, L.F., Lambert, C.S., Calderoni, D.R., Kharmandayan, P.: Cranial reconstruction: 3D biomodel and custom-built implant created using additive manufacturing. J. Cranio-Maxillofacial Surg. **42**, 1877–1884 (2014)
13. Hochman, J.B., Unger, B., Kraut, J., Pisa, J., Hombach-Klonisch, S.: Gesture-controlled interactive three dimensional anatomy: a novel teaching tool in head and neck surgery. J. Otolaryngol. - head neck Surg. **43**, 38 (2014)
14. Waran, V., Narayanan, V., Karuppiah, R., Pancharatnam, D., Chandran, H., Raman, R., Rahman, Z.A.A., Owen, S.L.F., Aziz, T.Z.: Injecting realism in surgical training - Initial simulation experience with custom 3D models. J. Surg. Educ. **71**, 193–197 (2014)
15. Watson, R.A.: A low-cost surgical application of additive fabrication. J. Surg. Educ. **71**, 14–17 (2014)
16. Rubino, P.A., Bottan, J.S., Houssay, A., Salas López, E., Bustamante, J., Chiarullo, M., Lambre, J.: Three-dimensional imaging as a teaching method in anterior circulation aneurysm surgery. World Neurosurg. **82**, E467–E474 (2014)
17. Giannopoulos, A.A., Chepelev, L., Sheikh, A., Wang, A., Dang, W., Akyuz, E., Hong, C., Wake, N., Pietila, T., Dydynski, P.B., Mitsouras, D., Rybicki, F.J.: 3D printed ventricular septal defect patch: a primer for the 2015 Radiological Society of North America (RSNA) hands-on course in 3D printing. 3D Print. Med. **1**, 1–20 (2015)
18. Cai, T., Rybicki, F.J., Giannopoulos, A.A., Schultz, K., Kumamaru, K.K., Liacouras, P., Demehri, S., Shu Small, K.M., Mitsouras, D.: The residual STL volume as a metric to evaluate accuracy and reproducibility of anatomic models for 3D printing: application in the validation of 3D-printable models of maxillofacial bone from reduced radiation dose CT images. 3D Print. Med. **1**, 1–19 (2015)
19. Cohen, J., Reyes, S.A.: Creation of a 3D Printed Temporal Bone Model from Clinical CT Data. Am. J. Otolaryngol. **36**, 1–6 (2015)
20. Wake, N., Chandarana, H., Huang, W.C., Taneja, S.S., Rosenkrantz, A.B.: Application of anatomically accurate, patient-specific 3D printed models from MRI data in urological oncology. Clin. Radiol. **71**, 3–7 (2015)
21. Rose, A.S., Webster, C.E., Harrysson, O.L.A., Formeister, E.J., Rawal, R.B., Iseli, C.E.: Pre-operative simulation of pediatric mastoid surgery with 3D-printed temporal bone models. Int. J. Pediatr. Otorhinolaryngol. **79**, 740–744 (2015)
22. Valverde, I., Gomez, G., Suarez-mejias, C., Hosseinpour, A., Hazekamp, M., Roest, A., Vazquez-jimenez, J.F., El-rassi, I., Uribe, S., Gomez-cia, T.: 3D printed cardiovascular models for surgical planning in complex congenital heart diseases. J. Cardiovasc. Magn. Reson. **17**, P196 (2015)

23. Li, C., Yang, M., Xie, Y., Chen, Z., Wang, C., Bai, Y., Zhu, X., Li, M.: Application of the polystyrene model made by 3-D printing rapid prototyping technology for operation planning in revision lumbar discectomy. J. Orthop. Sci. **20**, 475–480 (2015)

24. Sutradhar, A., Park, J., Carrau, D., Nguyen, T.H., Miller, M.J., Paulino, G.H.: Designing patient-specific 3D printed craniofacial implants using a novel topology optimization method. Med. Biol. Eng. Comput. **54**, 1–13 (2015)

25. Fredieu, J.R., Kerbo, J., Herron, M., Klatte, R., Cooke, M.: Anatomical models: a digital revolution. Med. Sci. Educ. **25**, 183–194 (2015)

26. Mitsopoulou, V., Michailidis, D., Theodorou, E., Isidorou, S., Roussiakis, S., Vasilopoulos, T., Polydoras, S., Kaisarlis, G., Spitas, V., Stathopoulou, E., Provatidis, C., Theodorou, G.: Digitizing, modelling and 3D printing of skeletal digital models of Palaeoloxodon tiliensis (Tilos, Dodecanese, Greece). Quat. Int. **379**, 4–13 (2015)

27. Fasel, J.H.D., Aguiar, D., Kiss-Bodolay, D., Montet, X., Kalangos, A., Stimec, B.V., Ratib, O.: Adapting anatomy teaching to surgical trends: a combination of classical dissection, medical imaging, and 3D-printing technologies. Surg. Radiol. Anat. **38**, 361–367 (2016)

28. Knoedler, M., Feibus, A.H., Lange, A., Maddox, M.M., Ledet, E., Thomas, R., Silberstein, J.L.: Individualized physical 3-dimensional kidney tumor models constructed from 3-dimensional printers result in improved trainee anatomic understanding. Urology **85**, 1257–1261 (2015)

29. Mashiko, T., Otani, K., Kawano, R., Konno, T., Kaneko, N., Ito, Y., Watanabe, E.: Development of three-dimensional hollow elastic model for cerebral aneurysm clipping simulation enabling rapid and low cost prototyping. World Neurosurg. **83**, 351–361 (2015)

30. Ryan, J.R., Chen, T., Nakaji, P., Frakes, D.H., Gonzalez, L.F.: Ventriculostomy simulation using patient-specific ventricular anatomy, 3D printing, and hydrogel casting. World Neurosurg. **84**, 1333–1339 (2015)

31. Wen, G., Cong, Z.X., Liu, K.D., Tang, C., Zhong, C., Li, L., Dai, X.J., Ma, C.: A practical 3D printed simulator for endoscopic endonasal transsphenoidal surgery to improve basic operational skills. Child's Nerv. Syst. **32**, 1–8 (2016)

32. Rehder, R., Abd-El-Barr, M., Hooten, K., Weinstock, P., Madsen, J.R., Cohen, A.R.: The role of simulation in neurosurgery. Child's Nerv. Syst. **32**, 43–54 (2016)

33. Singhal, A.J., Shetty, V., Bhagavan, K.R., Ragothaman, A., Shetty, V., Koneru, G., Agarwala, M.: Improved surgery planning using 3-D printing: a case study. Indian J. Surg. **78**, 100–104 (2016)

34. Zheng, Y.-X., Yu, D.-F., Zhao, J.-G., Wu, Y.-L., Zheng, B.: 3D printout models vs. 3D-rendered images: which is better for preoperative planning? J. Surg. Educ. **73**, 518–523 (2016)

35. Kong, X., Nie, L., Zhang, H., Wang, Z., Ye, Q., Tang, L., Li, J., Huang, W.: Do three-dimensional visualization and three-dimensional printing improve hepatic segment anatomy teaching? a randomized controlled study. J. Surg. Educ. **73**, 264–269 (2016)

36. Pietrabissa, A., Marconi, S., Peri, A., Pugliese, L., Cavazzi, E., Vinci, A., Botti, M., Auricchio, F.: From CT scanning to 3-D printing technology for the preoperative planning in laparoscopic splenectomy. Surg. Endosc. **30**, 366–371 (2016)

37. Krauel, L., Fenollosa, F., Riaza, L., Pérez, M., Tarrado, X., Morales, A., Gomà, J., Mora, J.: Use of 3D prototypes for complex surgical oncologic cases. World J. Surg. **40**, 889–894 (2016)

38. Bernhard, J.C., Isotani, S., Matsugasumi, T., Duddalwar, V., Hung, A.J., Suer, E., Baco, E., Satkunasivam, R., Djaladat, H., Metcalfe, C., Hu, B., Wong, K., Park, D., Nguyen, M., Hwang, D., Bazargani, S.T., de Castro Abreu, A.L., Aron, M., Ukimura, O., Gill, I.S.: Personalized 3D printed model of kidney and tumor anatomy: a useful tool for patient education. World J. Urol. **34**, 337–345 (2016)

39. Ploch, C.C., Mansi, C.S.S.A., Jayamohan, J., Kuhl, E.: Using 3D printing to create personalized brain models for neurosurgical training and preoperative planning. World Neurosurg. **91**, 1–7 (2016)
40. Ryan, J.R., Almefty, K.K., Nakaji, P., Frakes, D.H.: Cerebral aneurysm clipping surgery simulation using patient-specific 3d printing and silicone casting. World Neurosurg. **88**, 175–181 (2016)

Specifying How to Motivate People in Computer Assisted Rehabilitation

Víctor López-Jaquero[✉] and Francisco Montero

LoUISE Research Group, Computing Systems Department,
University of Castilla-La Mancha, 02071 Albacete, Spain
{victor,fmontero}@dsi.uclm.es

Abstract. The growing interest in computer assisted rehabilitation to alleviate the lack of enough facilities and specialists to cope with current demand for rehabilitation, especially related to the ageing of population, has pushed forward challenges and innovation related to the design and development of such systems. One of the aspects present in rehabilitation is motivation. Motivation is not essential in rehabilitation, but has been proven a useful factor to increase the efficiency of a rehabilitation process. In this paper we discuss the concept of motivation by providing a model that aims at supporting the design of the characteristics of motivation. Influence Awareness model is introduced as a vehicle to provide the patient with the information required to influence her behavior to improve her motivation towards rehabilitation in a computer assisted environment. Moreover, this Influence Awareness is integrated into a modelling language that enables the specification of the tasks to be accomplished during rehabilitation. Lastly, these concepts are exemplified in a case study.

Keywords: Influence · Awareness · Rehabilitation · Task model · CSRML

1 Introduction

It is well-known the growing interest in the development of e-health solutions, because of the on-going ageing of population. This ageing has introduced the need to find solutions that can cope with the increasing number of persons that require assistance from the healthcare system, but also as a solution to support a better healthcare assistance. This healthcare assistance can be oriented to improve the well-being of population as well, for instance by supporting some tele-healthcare assistance so as to prevent the patients with some mobility problems from going to the hospital.

This situation leads to the search of proper solutions that range from the assistive robot technology initiative in Japan [1] to the different initiatives in both Europe and the USA. To put this phenomenon into figures, the European Commission estimates a growth from 7.6 to 17.6 billion Euros already by 2017 in the global e-Health market [2]. Among these initiatives for e-Health we can found many topics included into the rehabilitation spectrum. Rehabilitation is closely related to population ageing as well, since many diseases that require rehabilitation are more usual in older people.

© Springer International Publishing AG 2016
C.R. García et al. (Eds.): UCAmI 2016, Part I, LNCS 10069, pp. 99–110, 2016.
DOI: 10.1007/978-3-319-48746-5_11

Health at the times of Internet, or e-Health, is the second most popular topic on the Web and it has an enormous potential in terms of quality, efficiency, and cost of health-care systems, it could bring transformational changes in medical research and practice, given that it is technically mature. And despite that, all the attempts to extend very successful pilot projects to a general framework have not met the promised results or they have failed to a large extent. Additional characteristics must be considered in order to design and develop this kind of high interactive applications properly and guarantee its success.

In this work, we focus our interest on motivation, a key factor in the success or failure of an interactive system. In order to achieve this characteristic our proposal integrates human-centered design and influence techniques. Thus, we are aimed at providing a mean for the designers and developers of rehabilitation activities to be able to incorporate into their developments those aspects related to motivation, relying on a solid foundation.

This paper is structured like this: after this introduction we discussed some issues related to the motivation in the e-Health domain. Next, we describe the design approach proposed to design e-Health systems. The details about how motivation can be modelled and the awareness interpretation created follow. Afterwards, a case study to illustrate the approach is explained. Some hints about how the specification could be implemented are provided next. The paper is rounded up with some conclusions and future work.

2   Motivation in the e-Health Domain

Although making rehabilitation activities easy to do is critical for its success, there is more to it than just that. How do you ensure that people experience exactly what you want them to experience? The answer is by increasing motivation.

Motivation is considered a key factor, which influences people's ability to use, learn or to make decisions, among other things. There has been much research related to this subject, with important implications for rehabilitation and, therefore, it would be impossible to ignore such an area for e-Health domain.

Specialists in rehabilitation and e-Health systems need to motivate, persuade, and in general, influence patients constantly. A definition of these terms can be found in [3]. Motivation is "the general desire or willingness to do something", while persuasion is "a process designed to change the attitude or behavior of a person or group from their current view to a view that the persuader wants them to hold". Lastly, influencing is "the power to affect a person or course of events without undertaking any direct action and to be a compelling force on the behavior of others".

There are different theories that elaborate on motivation and these related terms, and that have proposed different frameworks or models to describe them. In this sense two of the most widely used are the theory of Influence [3, 4] and the Self-Determination Theory [5].

Cialdini in [4] describes how someone can be influenced relying on six different psychological principles, namely: reciprocity, scarcity, authority, consistency, liking and consensus. Moreover, these principles have been empirically validated [3].

Section 4.1 includes a discussion of these principles.

On the other hand, Self-Determination Theory (SDT) relies on three principles: competence, relatedness and autonomy. Competence principle says that the motivation of a person is increased whenever that person feels competent for the action being performed. Relatedness says that the feeling of belongingness and connectedness with others also has an influence in improving motivation. Lastly, autonomy principle says that a person is more motivated when he feels has some autonomy and therefore has the locus of causality. These principles have been also empirically validated.

It's also important to highlight that in SDT there is distinction between intrinsic motivation and extrinsic motivation. Intrinsic motivation is the "prototypic manifestation of the human tendency toward learning and creativity", while extrinsic motivation "refers to the performance of an activity in order to attain some separable outcome and, thus, contrasts with intrinsic motivation, which refers to doing an activity for the inherent satisfaction of the activity itself" [5].

In this paper, we focus on the six principles by Cialdini, since currently it is the theory we have been using in out developments, but SDT adds some extra dimension to influence motivation that can complement those offered by Cialdini's principles.

These principles will be reviewed and integrated with the concept of Awareness [6] to provide a tool for designers to guide the inclusion of motivation aspects in their designs.

3   Designing e-Health System

In e-Health systems older people or patients interact with a platform and they must understand some new information that is essential to their rehabilitation. Sometimes, it can be challenging to motivate these people during their rehabilitation process. You may feel as if the patients are only participating because they have to, not because they want to. Patients may approach the rehabilitation as routine and compulsory. Because human behavior is complex and people are naturally curious it is important to design assisted rehabilitation that motives the patients.

Knowing what motivates people, what satisfies humans in terms of design and how it influences the rehabilitation process, enables the design of an effective e-Health design. Motivation itself is a broad subject. There are different motivation theories that have been developed by scientists and psychologists that try to explain ways to motivate patients and older people. They seek to explain motivation and how it affects the rehabilitation process [7].

Even though different development approaches can be used to develop rehabilitation systems, we support the use of the Model-Based User Development approach. Model-Based User Interface Development (Mb-UID) is one approach that aims at coping with the challenges of the interactive systems and at decreasing the effort needed to develop UIs while ensuring UI quality. The purpose of Model-Based Design [8] is to identify high-level models that allow designers to specify and analyze interactive applications from a semantic oriented level, rather than just starting immediately to address the implementation level. This enables focusing on the more important aspects without being immediately confused by myriad of implementation details, and then to use tools that generate an implementation consistent with the high-level choices made during modelling.

Among the typical models involved in Mb-UID are: the task model, the domain model and the context of use mode. It promotes a user-centered development lifecycle. The task model is especially relevant in this paper, since our approach starts with a design of the motivation that is embedded in this model. Task models are useful when designing and developing interactive systems. They describe the steps to be carried out to perform a users' goals, together with their temporal relationships (e.g., T2 cannot be executed until T1 is finished). In our context, these activities and tasks are related to the rehabilitation process.

There are different specification languages for task modeling. In our proposal, CSRML (Collaborative Systems Requirements Modeling Language) [9] will be used as the task modelling language. This language is a Goal-Oriented and i*-inspired Requirements Engineering Language that enables the specification of CSCW (Computer Supported Cooperative Work) systems. By using CSRML, a whole CSCW can be modeled: tasks (individual, collaboration, coordination and communication tasks), goals, participants, resources and awareness needs.

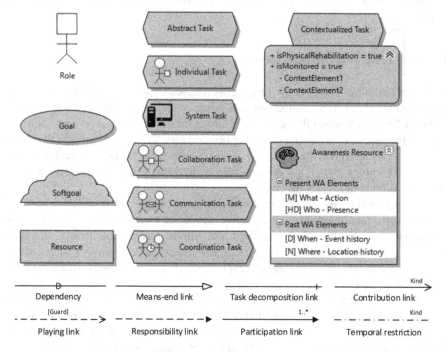

Fig. 1. Elements of the CSRML.

Figure 1 shows the elements and relationships defined on CSRML. Different kinds of tasks can be specified with these elements and several types of relationships can be defined between those elements. Another important element in the CSRML language are the resources and the awareness resources, these elements are useful to specify and design for motivation. For a whole specification of the language please refer to [9].

4   Designing Motivation in e-Health Systems

As stated in [10], motivation is not essential to patient rehabilitation, but in most cases results in better outcomes. Therefore, if we plan to create a good rehabilitation system, neglecting the design of how motivation will be delivered to the patient can result in a worse design, of even discourage the patient from using it. Thus, we find that the design of those aspects related to motivation in rehabilitation cannot be left to the imagination of the application designer without explicit guidance.

Motivating a person can be achieved by using different approaches. One of them is by using influence [3] to motivate the user to do something, and therefore improving the willingness the user has with regard behave in a specific way. In our case, in the domain of e-Health what we are pursuing is influence the patients to foster their willingness to perform their rehabilitation duties.

Influence emerges from social interaction, for instance, a person is more willing to something if he learns other people has already done that. This social dimension of interaction is closely related to awareness. Dourish and Belloti defined awareness as the "understanding of the activities of others, which provides a context for your own activity" [6]. In this sense, different types of awareness can provide the information required to influence a person by supplying the right information at the right time. Among the different types of awareness, Workspace Awareness [11] was chosen as the foundation of this approach, since it is probably the approach that covers more features of interaction and it is widely validated. Not any information can be used to use influence to motivate people, but on the contrary, just specific information has been proved to be useful for this purpose. Therefore, we must select what information can be used to provide the different types of influence.

In this paper we are relying of the six influence principles enumerated by Cialdini [3], but other theories can be merged to provide a richer view. Cialdini principles are widely used, and they are also concrete enough to be specified and shared between the stakeholders (developers, specialists, etc.).

4.1   Designing Influence Awareness

In this section we describe those awareness elements that have been derived from the influence principles of Cialdini. Moreover, how each element of this type of awareness is used will be described in depth. The explanation will be split according to the six principles (Table 1).

Reciprocity. People feels like they are in debt with someone that gave them something. Since reciprocity is directly related to what people has received from other persons, two different elements were identified. On the one hand, the object that was given (*Reciprocity Item*) to the user to foster reciprocity must be specified. On the other hand, the identity of the person that gave (*Reciprocity Identity*) the object should also be specified. Thus, we will be able to influence a person by reminding him what was given to him, and who did. Please, note that there is also a time component playing a role in this awareness elements. That is, similarly to what Gutwin proposes for Workspace awareness we include a temporal dimension as well. This is interesting to describe when the object we plan to use to produce the reprocity effect was given. Maybe this object was given to the person we want to influence in the past, right now or will be given in the future. Thus, suppose we want to influence a person to share the knowledge she gets in a learning platform. We could provide her with awareness about what knowledge has been share with here by other students in her group, so she feels more attracted to the idea of sharing what she has just learn with them, and thus boost learning in a collaborative learning environment.

Scarcity. We tend to prefer those things which are scarce, because of our fear of losing the potential benefits of the scarce element if it becomes unavailable. Therefore, if we would like to use scarcity to influence a person we should make that person aware of the object which is scarce (*Scarce Item*), the amount of items of that object left (*Availability*), who else owns that object (*Owners*) and the benefits that we lose in we don't get the item (*Benefits*). Depending on the item whose scarcity we want to highlight, it is also interesting introducing the time dimension in the specification. That is, we could say that an item was scarce in the *past*, or that it is scarce currently (*present*) or even that it will be scarce in the *future*. Furthermore, the *Availability* and the *Owners* of the scarce item could be different depending on the time dimension. For instance, to influence the motivation of students you could say that there are only two pass with honors grades available per year. Thus, by using scarcity awareness we could say provide information about the scarce item (pass with honors), the *Availability* in the past was 2, and in the present could be 1 (because one student already got one). In this case the *Availability* in the future is not relevant. Lastly, by using the *Owners* element of scarcity we could provide awareness about who already got one pass with honors (if any). This last *Owners* element can also be used to show relevant persons that got pass with honors grade in the past to increase more the influence. Additionally, we could provide also awareness about the *Benefits* by showing the student that if they get the pass with honors degree they will be included in the Hall of Fame of students.

Authority. People in general usually respects authority. E.g., we are more willing to do what someone in uniform tells us. If we plan to use authority to influence someone's behavior, we should provide awareness that help to reinforce this authority. Authority can be reinforced by providing the *Ranks* of a person. These *ranks* can be a degree in something, a diploma, the position held in an organization, etc. Depending on the situation, and the goal of influence, the designer should decide which *ranks* are more relevant to show the authority of the person trying to influence someone's behavior. Another source of authority is *Recommendations*. We are willing to listen to someone having good recommendations. Lastly, *Experience* provides a mean to express how knowledgeable a person is. Again, the time dimension can be introduced to express that the *rank*, the *recommendations*, or the *Experience* were in the past, the present of the future.

For instance, is not the same saying that a person has a *rank* of degree in physiotherapy for one year than for 20 years (*Experience*). We tend to play attention to people with more experience even though we don't know whether this experience was good or bad. The authority of this physiotherapist could be reinforced by proving awareness about who recommends this professional as found in many on-line buying websites. It is usual in these on-line buying websites that the recommendations can be order according to time dimension.

Consistency. For us is easier to make commitments if we make them voluntarily and if this commitment is public. Therefore, if we want to use consistency principle of influence we can offer awareness about what *Commitments* we made and also about how those *Commitments* were made publicly available (*Publicity*). Again, the time dimension can play an important role to show when these commitments were made. For instance, if a person has to walk for 45 min each day, a reminder can be used to reinforce the commitment and also we can provide awareness about in which social networks this commitment has been shared. Thus, we are showing how public this commitment is and showing that people now about that commitment.

Liking. It's easier for us to do what people alike us do. To comply with this principle, we aim at providing awareness about who is similar to us (*Similarities*), who makes compliments to us (*Supporters*) and who collaborates with us (*Collaborators*). Time dimension is relevant here as well, since it is interesting knowing when they made the compliments or when they collaborated with the person being influenced. For instance, when if we want to apply liking principle is would be possible to offer awareness about what likings we share (musical styles, sports teams, etc.) (*Similarities*), how many times I have made compliments by forwarding or liking one of his publications in a social network (*Supporters*) and how many times we have made an activity together (for instance attending together an event) (*Collaborators*). By providing these awareness elements we are showing the strength of our links and the person will be more predisposed to be influenced.

Consensus. It is very common to do what other people do. In this principle we want to influence the behavior by providing feedback about what other people does, did in past or will do (*Someone else's Tasks*). Therefore, time dimension is again relevant in this principle. If we would like a person to walk for 45 min every day we can show awareness about who else already did that, is doing it or will do it.

At first, we could think that including every single element of influence awareness would be the best solution to improve motivation. Nevertheless, this is not true, since overloading the user with information will result in the user ignoring most of the information because of the high cognitive load of the user interface. Therefore, for each situation we should choose only those influence awareness elements we find relevant to the situation and the target audience.

Table 1. Overview of the influence awareness elements.

Concern	Element	Description
Reciprocity	*Reciprocity Item*	What items were given to expect reciprocity?
	Reciprocity Identity	Who gave the items for reciprocity?
Scarcity	*Scarce Item*	What items are scarce?
	Availability	What is the availability of the scarce items?
	Owners	Who is already an owner of a scarce item?
	Benefits	What benefits are expected from the scarce item?
Authority	*Ranks*	What degrees, diplomas, position are relevant to reflect authority?
	Recommendations	Who recommends the person trying to influence someone?
	Experience	What experience has the person influencing?
Consistency	*Commitments*	What commitments has the user?
	Publicity	Where have been made public those commitments?
Liking	*Similarities*	What are the similarities between the user and the influencer?
	Supporters	Who makes compliments to the person influenced?
	Collaborators	Who collaborates with the person influenced?
Consensus	*Someone else's Tasks*	What related task have been made o are being made o will be made by someone else?

4.2 A Case Study: Including Influence Awareness in an Upper Limb Rehabilitation Activity

In this section we present a case study where influence awareness is illustrated in a rehabilitation exercise. This rehabilitation exercise is taken from [12], where different rehabilitation activities for elder people are described. In the activity chosen, the patient is asked to move her arms until she reaches a specific position to perform the so called *Upper Limb Rehabilitation* (ULR). This activity is aimed at strengthening the arms of the patient, therefore she is asked to perform the movements a number of repetitions (between 3 and 8 times). In our setup, this activity is performed in an environment where a Microsoft Kinect is used to monitor the motion and positioning of the arms of the patient [13].

Figure 2 depicts a task model specified by using CSRML language [9] that describes this rehabilitation exercise together with the awareness resources provided to improve the user experience. The task model has been pruned for the sake of understandability. The root of the model is *Upper Limb Rehabilitation (ULR)*. This task is decomposed into *Start ULR*, *Execute ULR* and *Stop ULR*. *Start ULR* represents the initial positioning of the patient to start the rehabilitation exercise. *Execute ULR* is used to represent the execution of the exercise and *Stop ULR* represents when the user stops the exercise. Please, note how they are connected by using temporal operators. *Execute ULR* can't be performed by the user until *Start ULR* is finished. *Stop ULR* is related to *Execute ULR* by using the *disabling* operator. It means that whenever *Stop ULR* task is executed the other two tasks are disabled, and therefore the execution of the exercise is finished. On the other hand, *Start ULR* is further decomposed into *Good Seated Posture* and *Hold Arms Straight*. It describes that the user should start the exercise both seated and with arms straight. *Execute ULR* is further decomposed into *Move UL* and *Cancel ULR*. Lastly, *Move UL* is decomposed into *Move Left Arm* and *Move Right Arm*. These last two task represent the actual move of both arms to do the exercise. Since the exercise should be made between 3 and 8 times, the user is allowed to cancel the exercise when it has already been performed 3 times by using the optional (denoted by *[]*) task *Cancel ULR*.

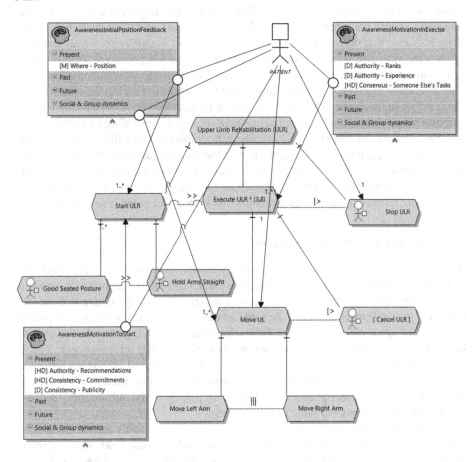

Fig. 2. A task model specification including influence awareness.

In the task model there is a single role, namely *PATIENT*. This role represents the patient who will perform the exercise. Therefore, the patient is the role responsible for making the rehabilitation tasks properly. In this case, two different awareness resources are included. These awareness resources are aimed at improving the user experience by providing valuable information that will help the user be aware of surrounding information that the designer found relevant. At the top left corner *AwarenessInitial*

PositionFeedback is found. This resource is provided to the user for two different tasks: *Start URL* and *Move UL*. Both tasks require the user to be aware of her position. Thus, for the user to be able to know whether the initial position has been achieved or how well is doing an exercise, we provide the user with awareness information about the position of her body at any time. Moreover, two awareness resources are used to improve the motivation of the patient. On the one hand, in the left bottom corner *AwarenessMotivationToStart* is an awareness resources aimed at improving the motivation of the patient to start the exercise. Three awareness elements have been included: *Ranks*, *Experience* and *Someone else's tasks*. Thus, we would like to influence the patient behavior towards the rehabilitation by showing the *Rank* and the *Experience* of the physiotherapist that designed the rehabilitation activity (*Authority* principle) and also by showing who else is performing this exercise (*Consensus* principle). Additionally, at the top right corner of the task model we can find *AwarenessMotivationInExercise*. This awareness resource is aimed at improving the motivation during the execution of the exercise. In this sense, we have chosen three influence awareness elements for this purpose: *Recommendations*, *Commitments* and *Publicity*. By providing awareness about who has recommended this exercise (*Authority* principle) we are telling the patient that this exercise is appropriate, with the backup of the recommendations of other patients. On the contrary, with *Commitments* and *Publicity* (*Consistency* principle) we want to reinforce the commitment to finish the exercise of the patient, by reminding her the commitment she made and that other people know about her commitment as well.

4.3   Implementing Influence Awareness

After the designer has modelled the influence awareness to be used to increase the motivation in the exercise, it is time to implement it. There is no one-to-one mapping between an awareness element and the way it is presented to the user. On the contrary, there is a myriad of possibilities to represent the same awareness element. For instance, focusing on reprocity in an e-commerce website, if we want to help to persuade the user to subscribe to a service in our website we can show on the profile information on the top right corner the cost of all the free services he has already enjoyed. To further influence the user to subscribe to our service scarcity principle could be used by showing the limited number of subscriptions available (*Scarce Item* is the subscription and the number of subscriptions available is *Availability*).

In the previous example the presentation chosen has been mostly textual, but graphical hints can convey meaningful information faster and more efficiently in many situations. For instance, in our rehabilitation example for the presentation of the rank, we can provide awareness about the authority of the person that designed the activity by showing an avatar with the typical medical white coat. In this way we are showing the authority of the avatar that is telling the patient to do an exercise in a graphical an implicit manner.

As aforementioned there are plenty of possibilities to represent the awareness influence elements chosen. Choosing one or another can depend on the target platform, but mostly on the target user we want to influence.

5   Conclusions and Future Work

Motivation can play an important role for patients during rehabilitation activities. One of the tools therapist have to improve this motivation is by influencing the behavior of the patient towards the rehabilitation. To achieve this influence different theories can be used. Similarly, in the context of computer assisted rehabilitation this influence can also be used to foster motivation during the rehabilitation. This influence during rehabilitation can be realized by providing awareness about those elements from the surrounding environment that promote and influence in patients' motivation.

In this work an awareness definition is introduced, namely Influence Awareness, aimed at providing an underlying foundation to provide this kind of awareness when the designer needs to model how he can influence someone. This awareness interpretation emerges for the empirically tested influence principles enunciated by Cialdini [3]. Moreover, this awareness interpretation is integrated into CSRML, a modelling language that has been proved useful in the design of rehabilitation systems [14]. By using this influence awareness interpretation, the designer of the application can more easily choose which elements related to each influence principles contribute to improve the motivation of the user and can also inspire the designer in those changes available to achieve the motivation. When talking about influence, the reader should not forget the ethical issues that can raise, for example, by using these influence awareness elements to provide false information.

Even though this awareness interpretation already helps the designer in knowing and understanding some plausible means to influence someone's behavior, some additional tools can be devised to further guide influence to motivate. For instance, it would be nice to have a set of predefined widgets that provided an implementation for each awareness element, as it already exists for workspace awareness [15].

The use of different profiles would be also advisable when providing this influence awareness, because probably neither the same awareness elements nor the same presentation will be equally effective, for example, for children and elder persons.

Future work will integrate and clarify the value of further dynamic adaptation by integrating Influence Awareness into the ISATINE adaptation framework [16] as well. Also some other motivation theories will be integrated into the approach, e.g. SDT.

Acknowledgements. This work has been funded by the Spanish Ministry of Economy and Competitiveness and by FEDER funds from the EU under the grants insPIre (TIN2016-79100-R) and HA-SYMBIOSIS (TIN2015-72931-EXP).

References

1. Maverick, T.: Japan's Tech Solution for Its Aging Population. http://www.wallstreet daily.com/2015/07/11/japan-healthcare-robots/
2. European Commission: eHealth and Ageing. https://ec.europa.eu/digital-single-market/en/ ehealth-and-ageing
3. Cialdini, R.B.: Influence: The Psychology of Persuasion. Morrow, New York (1993)
4. Cialdini, R.B.: Harnessing the science of persuasion. Hardvard Bus. Rev. **79**, 72–81 (2001)

5. Ryan, R.M., Deci, E.L.: Self-determination theory and the facilitation of intrinsic motivation, social development, and well-being. Am. Psychol. **55**, 68–78 (2000)
6. Dourish, P., Bellotti, V.: Awareness and coordination in shared workspaces. In: ACM Conference on Computer-Supported Cooperative Work (CSCW 1992), pp. 107–114. ACM Press, Toronto, Canada (1992)
7. Maclean, N., Pound, P.: A critical review of the concept of patient motivation in the literature on physical rehabilitation. Soc. Sci. Med. **50**, 495–506 (2000)
8. W3C Working Group: Introduction to Model-Based User Interfaces. https://www.w3.org/TR/mbui-intro/
9. Teruel, M.A., Navarro, E., López-Jaquero, V., Montero, F., González, P.: CSRML: a goal-oriented approach to model requirements for collaborative systems. In: Jeusfeld, M., Delcambre, L., Ling, T.-W. (eds.) ER 2011. LNCS, vol. 6998, pp. 33–46. Springer, Heidelberg (2011). doi:10.1007/978-3-642-24606-7_4
10. Pickrell, M., Bongers, B., van den Hoven, E.: Understanding persuasion and motivation in interactive stroke rehabilitation. In: MacTavish, T., Basapur, S. (eds.) PERSUASIVE 2015. LNCS, vol. 9072, pp. 15–26. Springer, Heidelberg (2015)
11. Gutwin, C., Greenberg, S.: A descriptive framework of workspace awareness for real-time groupware. Comput. Support. Coop. Work **11**, 411–446 (2002)
12. Best-Martini, E., Jones-DiGenova, K.A.: Exercise for Frail Elders. Human Kinetics, Champaign (2014)
13. Oliver, M., Montero, F., Molina, J.P., González, P., Fernández-Caballero, A.: Multi-camera systems for rehabilitation therapies: a study of the precision of Microsoft Kinect sensors. Front. Inf. Technol. Electron. Eng. **17**, 348–364 (2016)
14. Teruel, M.A., Rodríguez, A.C., Simarro, F.M., Navarro, E., López-Jaquero, V., González, P.: An alternative to W3C task model for post-WIMP. In: 9th International Conference Ubiquitous Computing and Ambient Intelligence. Sensing, Processing, and Using Environmental Information (UCAmI 2015), pp. 297–308 (2015)
15. Roseman, M., Greenberg, S.: Building real-time groupware with GroupKit, a groupware toolkit. ACM Trans. Comput. Interact. **3**, 66–106 (1996)
16. López-Jaquero, V., Vanderdonckt, J., Montero, F., González, P.: Towards an extended model of user interface adaptation: the isatine framework. In: Gulliksen, J., Harning, M.B., van der Veer, G.C., Wesson, J. (eds.) EIS 2007. LNCS, vol. 4940, pp. 374–392. Springer, Heidelberg (2008)

Real Time Gait Analysis Using RGB Camera

Mario Nieto-Hidalgo[✉] and Juan Manuel García-Chamizo

Department of Computing Technology, University of Alicante,
Campus San Vicente del Raspeig, Alicante, Spain
{mnieto,juanma}@dtic.ua.es
http://www.dtic.ua.es

Abstract. In this paper we propose a vision based gait analysis approach that work under real time constraints. We propose the use of a multiresolution pyramid image representation that allows to provide suboptimal responses if the deadline is reached. The impact of each suboptimal response is analysed showing that although there is an impact in the quality of the output, the gait analysis algorithm still provides satisfactory results. In addition, the adjustment to time constraints of the proposed approach is also analysed showing suitability for real time constraints.

Keywords: Real time · Gait analysis · RGB camera · Background subtraction

1 Introduction

Vision based gait analysis is the focus of our project. We aim at developing a low cost, non-invasive system to obtain the parameters of human gait. We are focusing in the gait of elderly people with the objective of early detection of frailty and dementia syndromes. This is supported by several studies that link the degeneration of gait with those syndromes [3,12–14].

Although we focus in the gait of elderly people, our approach could be applied to other population sectors (children, athletes...) for rehabilitation or identification of deviations from standard patterns.

The use of computer vision to analyse gait provides an objective external measure of kinematic parameters unlinking the results from the dynamic approach where there are physiological and emotional influences that could compromise the objectivity of the output.

Computer vision demands a high computational power that makes it difficult to work in low cost devices under time constraints, however, it is convenient to advance in this matter so every geriatrics could make use of these kind of solutions. In this paper, we propose a real-time approach for our previous work [6,7] in which a method for vision based gait analysis that uses only RGB camera is presented.

This method performs background subtraction to obtain the silhouette of the subject and then obtains the heel and toe of each foot. A processing based

© Springer International Publishing AG 2016
C.R. García et al. (Eds.): UCAmI 2016, Part I, LNCS 10069, pp. 111–120, 2016.
DOI: 10.1007/978-3-319-48746-5_12

on gradient analysis extracts the heel strike (HS) and toe off (TO), which are
the spatio-temporal parameters used in gait analysis. Finally, the obtained features are processed by a classifier that determines whether the subject presents
abnormal gait patterns or not.

Now that the extraction of spatio-temporal parameters and classification has
been sufficiently resolved, we focus in providing real time capabilities that could
provide a greater variety of applications. With real time capabilities, not only
the method could be used to analyse gait, but also to provide feedback to the
subject which is precisely the evolution of our project.

1.1   Related Works

Most of the vision based systems proposed can work at real time only for specific computational power, i.e., if the device that perform the computation is not
sufficiently faster then the system cannot work under time constraints. These
approaches are sufficient when they are executed in specific hardware and do
not require scalability. However they cannot be executed in lower computational
performance hardware due to their inability to reach the deadline in time. A
proper real time application should adapt to the available computational power,
providing a suboptimal response if the deadline is reached before finishing the
processing. A way to obtain a suboptimal response in our case is the multiresolution pyramid.

The pyramid approach has been widely used in computer vision and computer
graphics. The simplest pyramid approach consists in iteratively computing copies
of lower resolution of the original image. An example of this is the mipmap used
in computer graphics for texture filtering. A multiresolution texture is computed
at loading time, then the appropriate resolution is selected depending on the
distance at which the texture has to be rendered [15].

According to Lindeberg [4,5], pyramids, wavelets and multi-grid methods
were the precursors of the scale space theory developed in image processing,
computer vision and signal analysis. Space scale theory deals with multi-scale
representation of images (or signals). This states that when building a multi-
scale representation image, each subsequent downsampling should constitute a
simplification of previous level and should not add artefacts due to the smoothing
method used. Therefore, the requirement for a kernel is linearity and spatial
shift invariance. A kernel that fulfil these premises is the Gaussian kernel and
its derivatives.

There are two main approaches for pyramid representation: Gaussian Pyramid and Laplacian Pyramid. In the former, each level of the pyramid is first
processed with a gaussian smoothing and then downsampled to 1/2 size, the
process is repeated for the number of levels required. In the latter, in each level,
a difference of the blurred image of previous level is stored, except the smallest level in which the image is only blurred. The objective is to have different
scaled convolution versions of the same image in an efficient way. The orientation
invariant approach is called Steerable Pyramid [2].

There are many applications of these approaches. Some of these applications are image compression, detail manipulation, computer graphics... [1,8].

A method for hallucinating high resolution faces from low resolution ones using Steerable Pyramid is proposed in [11]. Strengert et al. proposed the construction of pyramid based filters using the built in bilineal filtering capabilities of Graphics Processing Units (GPU) [10]. An edge aware image processing method using Laplacian Pyramid is proposed by Paris et al. [9]. Yadav et al. [16] present a method based on Gaussian Pyramid to classify microscopic images of hardwood species.

2   Real Time Background Subtraction

In most vision based applications, background subtraction is the initial step followed by noise reduction techniques like morphological operations. Those techniques often reduce the resolution of the silhouette. This resolution downgrade is accepted because the benefits of a de-noised silhouette are greater than those of a high resolution one. Most of the applications do not even require high resolution silhouettes. Assuming this, the first step in order to reduce the computation time of a background subtraction algorithm would be reducing the input image resolution. However, even if the silhouette resolution is not critical, a higher resolution could be beneficial in some cases and usually provides better results. We performed some experiments to test the impact of different resolutions in our gait analysis system. Results of this experiment are shown in Sect. 3.

In our approach the silhouette extraction phase using Mixture of Gaussians [17] is the most computationally expensive task. With Full HD resolution, 90 % of the time is consumed there. This task takes around 90 ms to complete using an Intel Core i7 2630QM CPU at 2.00 GHz and 8 GB RAM DDR3.

For our approach to work under time constraints, we need to redesign this critical phase so it can provide a fast suboptimal response that can be iteratively improved depending on the available time.

2.1   Iterative Multiresolution Processing in Real Time

What we propose is an Iterative Multiresolution Processing in Real Time (IMPReTi) approach that provides increasingly higher resolution silhouettes as long as there is time remaining.

IMPReTi First Approach. The first step is to create a multiresolution image of the original, to do so we proceed creating a mipmap of the input image. The mipmap is organized following the order shown in Fig. 1 using the Algorithm 1. This organization ensures that the first obtained silhouette will be the lower resolution one providing also some steps of some of the next resolutions. However, this also increases the memory and time needed by 50 % (considering a linear algorithm) to complete the maximum resolution. The usable space required is only 1/3 bigger than the original image since the sum $1/4 + 1/16 + 1/64 + \cdots +$

$1/2^{2n}$ converges to $1/3$. The mipmap approach [15] achieve this $1/3$ increase in space by splitting the RGB channels of the image as shown in Fig. 2. This however will require a modification in the background subtraction algorithm to work with this specific layout.

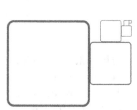

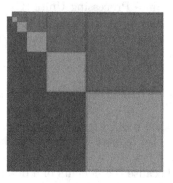

Fig. 1. Mipmaps generated. Overall image size increased by $1/2$.

Fig. 2. RGB optimized mipmap. Overall image size increased by $1/3$.

Algorithm 1. MipMap organization

$lastRect \leftarrow Rect(0, 0, src.width, src.height)$
$lastImage \leftarrow src$
$dst(lastRect) \leftarrow src$
for $i < numMipMaps$ **do**
    $Resize(lastImage, 0.5)$
    if $i mod 2 = 0$ **then**
        $lastRect.x \leftarrow lastRect.x + lastRect.width0$
        if i = numMipMaps -1 **then**   ▷ The smallest resolution must be put on top
        so it is processed first
        $lastRect.y \leftarrow 0$
    else
        $lastRect.y \leftarrow lastRect.y + lastRect.height * 0.25$
    end if
    else
        $lastRect.x \leftarrow lastRect.x + lastRect.width * 0.25$
        $lastRect.y \leftarrow 0$
    end if
    $dst(lastRect) \leftarrow lastImage$
end for

Algorithm 2 shows the procedure to work in real time using the mipmap image.

Algorithm 2. Real-time iterative background subtraction first approach

---
for $i < m$ **do**
  $ProcessLine(i)$
  if *timeexceeded* **then**
    break
  end if
end for
$Result \leftarrow GetMaxResolutionCompleted(i)$ ▷ Depending on the number of lines
  processed obtain the maximum resolution completed

This approach could provide good results with linear or less complexity algorithms. However, as the size of the image is increased a 50 % (being a 19 % empty) it will significantly increase the processing time required to even compute the lower resolution.

IMPReTi Second Approach. Another solution is to compute separately each resolution, starting with the lowest and iteratively increasing it as long as there is time remaining. We proceed creating different resolution images like in the previous method, however we do not combine them. Then the real time algorithm will be as shown in Algorithm 3. The advantage of this approach is that it only increases the total time and space in a 1/3 rather than a 1/2 like the previous approach (assuming the initialization time of the background subtraction algorithm is minimum and linear complexity) achieving the same spatial increase as the RGB mipmap. As downside, in this approach, each resolution is processed independently so a previously computed resolution do not provide anything to next resolution computation.

Algorithm 3. Real-time iterative background subtraction second approach

---
$time \leftarrow 0$
for $i < numResolutions$ **do**
  $lastTime \leftarrow CalcTime(Process(resolution[i]))$
  $time \leftarrow time + lastTime$
  if $time + PredictNextResolutionTime(lastTime) > frameTime$ **then**
    break
  end if
end for

We propose the use of lower resolution computed to remove noise. To do so we average all the computed resolutions and keep as silhouette only the pixels with value greater than a threshold. This threshold can be empirically adjusted to reduce more or less noise.

Being independent each resolution, multiprocessing techniques could be added to process each in parallel, in which case the algorithm will be as shown in Algorithm 4.

Algorithm 4. Real-time iterative background subtraction second approach in parallel

---

for $i < numResolutions$ **do**
    $StartThread(Process(resolution[i]))$
end for
$Wait(frameTime)$
$CancelUnfinishedThreads()$ ▷ This function should keep in mind that at least one
    resolution has to be completed.

Another alternative would be to use the times from the previous frames computed to estimate the maximum resolution that can be computed in the required time and compute only that. The first frames are processed exactly like shown in Algorithms 3 or 4 and then, when a sufficient amount of frames computed could provide an accurate estimation of the required time for each resolution, use the estimator to only compute the maximum resolution possible.

3 Results and Discussion

The first experiment performed was aimed at determining how the resolution of the silhouette affect the final output of the heel strike and toe off detection. We tested four different resolutions (1920×1080, 960×540, 480×270, 240×135 pixels respectively). The silhouette output of each resolution is shown in Fig. 3. We compared the output of the second filter method described in [7].

Fig. 3. Silhouettes computed in each resolution. From left to right: 1080, 540, 270, 135 pixels height.

Figure 4 shows the Root Mean Square Error (RMSE) of the heel strike and toe off detection compared to a manual marking, as described in [6,7], for each resolution. There is practically no difference between 1080 and 540 resolutions in terms of accuracy.

Figure 5 shows the amount of undetected cases for each resolution. In this case, 1080 shows the best results closely follow by 540.

Finally, Fig. 6 shows the processing time required for each resolution as well as the frames per second (FPS) allowed with that amount of time. The processing time increases linearly along with the resolution size, this was as expected since the complexity of the background subtraction algorithm used was linear (number of pixels in the image). This chart shows the greatest differences between each resolution. Therefore it is precisely time the parameter that establishes which resolution to use.

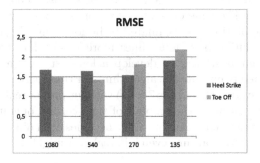

Fig. 4. RMSE result of the heel strike and toe off detection algorithm for each resolution.

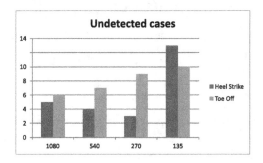

Fig. 5. Amount of undetected cases of heel strike and toe off for each resolution

The second experiment checked the real-time suitability of the Algorithm 3. The IMPReTi algorithm was executed with four different FPS constraints: 15,

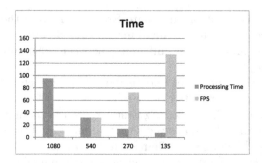

Fig. 6. Processing time in milliseconds and FPS required for silhouette extraction phase for each resolution.

30, 60 and 120; that means the deadline was 66.67 ms, 33.33 ms, 16.67 ms and 8.33 ms respectively. The time estimator was computed as shown in Eq. 1. The time of the next resolution was estimated to be four times bigger than the last since the next resolution have four times more pixels than the previous one. The objective of our project is to develop a low-cost system with a minimal infrastructure needed to execute the algorithm. For that reason we used a general purpose operating system (Windows 7 × 64) without proper real time capabilities where is difficult to estimate the amount of time certain operation will take to complete. If we add multicore capabilities it becomes even difficult. Therefore we decided to use the theoretical time even if in reality it might be different. A 4 level

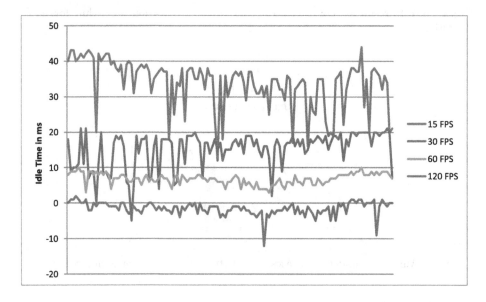

Fig. 7. Graph showing the idle time for each frame with different time constraints. A negative value means that the time constraint is exceeded.

pyramid (1920×1080, 960×540, 480×270, 240×135 pixels) was used and we considered the time between the task was completed (the algorithm determines that the next pyramid level cannot be computed) and the deadline as a measure of adjustment to time constraint. If that measure is zero or positive, that means the algorithm adjusted successfully to the time constraint, otherwise it did not.

$$elapsedTime + lastTime \times 4 < deadline \qquad (1)$$

Figure 7 shows the adjustment to the deadline performed by the algorithm with each FPS constraint. The graph represents the idle time for each frame processed, i.e., the remaining time between completing the task and the deadline is reached. As shown in the graph, 120 FPS is the limit at which the algorithm can work with the tested hardware. The reason is that the minimum time required for computing the smaller resolution is greater or equal to the time constraint. Improvements can be made by adding more pyramid levels but smaller resolutions could compromise the accuracy of the results. The graph also shows a great variability in processing time, that is due to the use of a general purpose operating system without proper real time capabilities.

4 Conclusion

The gait analysis algorithm proposed in [6,7] was executed with different input image resolutions to test the impact in the final result. Results of the different resolution execution show that, although small differences, it is desirable to use a bigger resolution. The bigger the resolution the better the results, however the time also increases. Therefore there is an inverse relation between the quality of the output and the required time to obtain it. Working with time constraints, it might not be possible to compute the higher resolution, and there is where the benefits of the IMPReTi algorithm appear as it iteratively process resolutions from smaller to bigger until the deadline is reached. The IMPReTi algorithm proposed was tested with different time constraints and a 4-level pyramid. Results show that the time constraints are maintained except in the case of 120 FPS where the processing time of the smallest resolution is sometimes bigger than the time constraint.

Acknowledgements. This research is part of the FRASE MINECO project (TIN2013-47152-C3-2-R) funded by the Ministry of Economy and Competitiveness of Spain.

References

1. Adelson, E.H., Anderson, C.H., Bergen, J.R., Burt, P.J., Ogden, J.M.: Pyramid methods in image processing. RCA Eng. **29**(6), 33–41 (1984)
2. Freeman, W.T., Adelson, E.H.: The design and use of steerable filters. IEEE Trans. Pattern Anal. Mach. Intell. **13**(9), 891 (1991)

3. Fried, L.P., Tangen, C.M., Walston, J., Newman, A.B., Hirsch, C., Gottdiener, J., Seeman, T., Tracy, R., Kop, W.J., Burke, G., et al.: Frailty in older adults evidence for a phenotype. J. Gerontol. Ser. A: Bio. Sci. Med. Sci. **56**(3), M146–M157 (2001)
4. Lindeberg, T.: Scale-space theory: a basic tool for analyzing structures at different scales. J. Appl. Stat. **21**(1–2), 225–270 (1994)
5. Lindeberg, T.: Scale-Space Theory in Computer Vision, vol. 256. Springer Science & Business Media, New York (2013)
6. Nieto-Hidalgo, M., Ferrández-Pastor, F.J., Valdivieso-Sarabia, R.J., Mora-Pascual, J., García-Chamizo, J.M.: Vision based extraction of dynamic gait features focused on feet movement using RGB camera. In: Bravo, J., Hervás, R., Villarreal, V. (eds.) AmIHEALTH 2015. LNCS, vol. 9456, pp. 155–166. Springer, Heidelberg (2015). doi:10.1007/978-3-319-26508-7_16
7. Nieto-Hidalgo, M., Ferrández-Pastor, F.J., Valdivieso-Sarabia, R.J., Mora-Pascual, J., García-Chamizo, J.M.: A vision based proposal for classification of normal and abnormal gait using RGB camera. J. Biomed. Inf. **63**, 82–89 (2016)
8. Ogden, J.M., Adelson, E.H., Bergen, J.R., Burt, P.J.: Pyramid-based computer graphics. RCA Eng. **30**(5), 4–15 (1985)
9. Paris, S., Hasinoff, S.W., Kautz, J.: Local laplacian filters: edge-aware image processing with a laplacian pyramid. Commun. ACM **58**(3), 81–91 (2015)
10. Strengert, M., Kraus, M., Ertl, T.: Pyramid methods in gpu-based image processing. In: Proceedings Vision, Modeling, and Visualization 2006, pp. 169–176 (2006)
11. Su, C., Zhuang, Y., Huang, L., Wu, F.: Steerable pyramid-based face hallucination. Pattern Recogn. **38**(6), 813–824 (2005)
12. Verghese, J., Lipton, R.B., Hall, C.B., Kuslansky, G., Katz, M.J., Buschke, H.: Abnormality of gait as a predictor of non-alzheimer's dementia. N. Engl. J. Med. **347**(22), 1761–1768 (2002)
13. Waite, L., Grayson, D., Piguet, O., Creasey, H., Bennett, H., Broe, G.: Gait slowing as a predictor of incident dementia: 6-year longitudinal data from the sydney older persons study. J. Neurol. Sci. **229**, 89–93 (2005)
14. Waltson, J., Fried, L.: Frailty and the old man. Med. Clin. North Am. **83**(5), 1173–1194 (1999)
15. Williams, L.: Pyramidal parametrics. In: ACM Siggraph Computer Graphics, vol. 17, pp. 1–11. ACM (1983)
16. Yadav, A.R., Anand, R., Dewal, M., Gupta, S.: Gaussian image pyramid based texture features for classification of microscopic images of hardwood species. Optik-Int. J. Light Electron Opt. **126**(24), 5570–5578 (2015)
17. Zivkovic, Z., Heijden, F.: Efficient adaptive density estimation per image pixel for the task of background subtraction. Pattern Recogn. Lett. **27**(7), 773–780 (2006)

Towards an Awareness Interpretation
for Physical and Cognitive Rehabilitation Systems

Miguel A. Teruel[✉], Elena Navarro, and Pascual González

LoUISE Research Group, Computing Systems Department,
University of Castilla – La Mancha, Albacete, Spain
miguel@dsi.uclm.es, {elena.navarro,pascual.gonzalez}@uclm.es

Abstract. When collaborating remotely, being aware of other participants (their actions, locations, status, etc.) is paramount to achieve a proper collaboration. This issue is magnified when talking about rehabilitation systems, whose users may require additional specific awareness information, due to their cognitive or physical disabilities. Moreover, because of these disabilities, this awareness may be provided by using specific feedback stimuli. This constituted the main motivation of this work: the development of an awareness interpretation for collaborative cognitive and physical therapies. With this aim, an awareness interpretation already applied to the collaborative games field has been modified and extended to make it suitable for these systems. Furthermore, in order to put this interpretation into practice, a case study based on an association image-writing rehabilitation pattern is presented illustrating how this cognitive rehabilitation task has been extended with collaborative features and enriched with awareness information.

Keywords: Awareness · Collaboration · Virtual rehabilitation rooms · Physical rehabilitation · Cognitive rehabilitation · Case study

1 Introduction

Although there is no a widely accepted definition of eHealth [1], there certainly is a consensus about both its meaning and its usefulness in the short and long term. Basically, eHealth environments promote the synergy of health care and technology to provide patients and practitioners with proper solutions according to their specific needs. These needs have been categorized into three main areas [2]: (1) storing, managing, and transmission of data; (2) clinical decision support; and (3) facilitating care from a distance. Among these areas, the third one, also known as *tele-rehabilitation* [3], has special interest as it helps to move healthcare from hospitals and care centres to patients' home exploiting computing technologies, telecommunications, etc. This results into important benefits from the point of view of both patients and policymakers. First, patients with mobility problems are not dependent on their relatives to move to hospital for their rehabilitation but they can do it just at home. Second, policymakers are able to offer rehabilitation to more patients at reasonable costs [4].

When developing tele-rehabilitation systems there are several technological challenges that must be addressed. First of all, they should be designed to provide specialists

© Springer International Publishing AG 2016
C.R. García et al. (Eds.): UCAmI 2016, Part I, LNCS 10069, pp. 121–132, 2016.
DOI: 10.1007/978-3-319-48746-5_13

with facilities to design *bespoke therapies*, that is, therapies adapted to the patients' abilities, disabilities and needs. This has led us to develop a tool [5] that enables therapists to design bespoke therapies which is part of Vi-SMARt, a system whose final aim is to provide support for physical and cognitive rehabilitation [6–9]. These therapies, once designed, are executed, monitored and adapted thanks to a fuzzy inference system that has been integrated into Vi-SMARt [10].

Second, and equally important, the fact that patient is at home may hamper its interaction and, thus, the outcome of the rehabilitation process unless specific facilities are considered in the design of the tele-rehabilitation systems. These systems should be able not only to monitor patient's status to detect stress or any other kind of discomfort but also they should provide him with the *feedback* necessary to conduct his therapy. The design of this feedback can be specially challenging when developing *virtual rehabilitation rooms*, one of the main features of Vi-SMARt [7], where they can collaborate, cooperate and communicate for the achievement of both personal goals and group goals. These virtual rehabilitation rooms are being integrated into Vi-SMARt because different studies, such as [11], have highlighted the importance of collaboration with other peers as a facilitator of the rehabilitation.

If we considered those virtual rooms just as usual CSCW systems, then patients should be provided with *awareness* [12] information, that is, they must know who is in the virtual room, what the collaborators are doing, where they are, how and when certain action happened, who did it, etc. However, they are not usual CSCW systems, but systems whose users have their abilities hampered by some kind of trauma, congenital problem, etc. These systems are also technology-demanding, as these virtual rooms have virtual reality interfaces, haptic devices, auditory devices, etc. Therefore, Awareness Interpretations defined up to now should be adapted to consider the special needs of this domain. This is the main aim of this work, to define an awareness interpretation for developing Physical and Cognitive Rehabilitation systems. This awareness interpretation has been distilled thanks to our experience of developing rehabilitation systems during the latest years in different domains such as Acquired Brain Injury [6, 13, 14], Children with Special Education Needs [15] or Gerontechnology [10], as well as of working with CSCW systems [16, 17].

This paper has been structured as follows. After this introduction, Sect. 2 describes the related work in the area. Then, Sect. 3 describes our proposal, an awareness interpretation for physical and cognitive rehabilitation systems. Section 4 presents by means of a case study how this proposal can be put into practice. Finally, the drawn conclusions and our future work are described in Sect. 5.

2 Related Works

Over the last years several proposals, commercial [18, 19] and academic [10, 20–22] ones, have been developed to offer new ways to carry out physical and cognitive rehabilitation therapies, allowing patients to perform these activities not only in specialized centers but also at home, making use of tele-rehabilitation systems. Although all these systems have been created to be managed by different patients, in general these solutions have been designed to implement specific therapies [20]. Anyhow, there are some solutions where the therapists can adapt some features to the patient's skills [23, 24] or create their own therapies from scratch [10].

Some collaborative features have been already included in these systems. For instance, they provide therapists with facilities to control the therapy execution, to connect collaboratively with the patient while he is carrying out his rehabilitation task. However, although in the commercial solutions it is frequent to use some collaborative feature, such as video-conference [25] to facilitate the communication between therapists and patients, it is not so frequent to find systems that exploit 3D tele-immersive feedback [26] as part of the rehabilitation process. Moreover, only few proposals [5, 10] have been designed as collaborative environments that enable several specialist to collaborate in the design of a therapy. It is uncommon to find proposals that enable several patients to collaborate while they carry out a specific therapy. For instance, as far as we know only TANGO [27] offers this feature but patients must be located at the same physical space.

As we have already highlighted, tele-rehabilitation systems are collaborative in nature. Therefore, it is evident that relevant concepts used in the design of CSCW systems should be also analyzed when they are developed. One of the main CSCW concepts is *awareness* that has been defined in the computer collaboration field as "the up-to-the-moment understanding of another person's interaction within a shared workspace" [12]. There are multiple awareness interpretations [17], being the most well-known interpretations Collaboration Awareness, Situation Awareness, Workspace Awareness, Context Awareness, Social Awareness and so on. In a previous work [17], they were analyzed and it was concluded that it is not possible to cover all the features of modern complex collaborative systems by using just only one of them. For this reason, we carry out a thematic analysis [17] to define a novel awareness definition, Gamespace Awareness that integrates the main of the previous proposals in order to provide guidance in the specification of the awareness of one of the most complex collaborative systems: collaborative video-games. Therefore, in this work we use this novel awareness definition to evaluate its relevance in the design of another complex domain: Physical and Cognitive Rehabilitation Systems.

3   Awareness Interpretation for Physical and Cognitive Rehabilitation Systems

This section presents the awareness interpretation defined in order to deal with the awareness needs of tele-rehabilitation systems for physical and cognitive therapies. This interpretation has been developed by adapting Gamespace Awareness [17] to make it suitable for our target systems. Due to space constraints, in this article we focus just on the present awareness elements, which are paramount for providing patients with real-time awareness of what is happening during a rehabilitation session. Therefore, the other elements of Gamespace Awareness related to future, past, etc., will be adapted for our target systems in a future work.

The elements that this awareness interpretation identifies are shown in Table 1. They are categorized into four different categories, depending on what awareness information they are providing. More specifically, they deal with *who* is participating, *what* and *where* they do anything, and *how* to do it. Along with these awareness elements, a set of questions have been defined aimed at helping designers to identify the awareness needs of a rehabilitation system. As an example, consider a remote physical rehabilitation system whose patients work collaboratively. In order to collaborate, they should be aware of *who* is available in the rehabilitation session with, *what* the other patients are doing to coordinate their actions, *where* they are located in their own space and *how* to interact with remote patients. This awareness information, which could be considered obvious in a non-remote and non-computer-assisted rehabilitation systems, is crucial when dealing with remote collaboration. Therefore, one of the goals of this awareness interpretation is to make remote rehabilitation as understandable and fruitful as local rehabilitation.

As Table 1 shows, for each awareness element it has been also identified which feedback stimuli should be used to provide participants with the desired awareness. That is, *visual* (by using a computer screen or a virtual reality headset), *aural* (by emitting sound or audio messages) or *haptic* (by receiving vibrations on different parts of the body). Moreover, the possibility of providing awareness information through different stimuli is paramount when dealing with disabled people. For instance, if a deaf user is being rehabilitated, audio messages must be replaced by screen notifications or haptic signals. It is worth noting that not all awareness elements could be provided properly by using every stimulus. For instance, making the participants aware of the login of a new user in the system (element *Identity*) by using haptic feedback make no sense since it would require to codify each new participant ID as a different haptic stimulus. This could be overwhelming for users and difficult to implement as the number of users increases. However, providing this awareness information by using an audio message (e.g. "John is now online") could be easily understandable by most of the participants.

Moreover, Table 1 also provides some examples of how to implement each awareness element, i.e. how to gather such awareness information and how to provide participants with it. As an example, the *Status* element, which is related to the participant's physical and emotional status could be gathered by using either a biometric sensor to obtain biometric data such a heat rate or skin conductance [28], or a camera along with an emotional analysis software to analyze participants' emotions [29]. Besides, this awareness information could be provided by using different stimuli. For instance, if what we want to make a participant aware of the other participant physical status by a measurements of the heart rate, this awareness information could be provided by using the three considered stimuli. First, visual stimuli can be easily used by presenting animated heartbeats on the screen to represent the heart rate of the remote participant. Second, aural stimuli can also be considered and implemented by playing heartbeats thought audio. Finally, it could be possible to use haptic stimuli as well, thus emulating heartbeats by using haptic impulses that the participant will feel on a specific part of his/her body.

Table 1. Awareness elements for physical and cognitive Rehabilitation

Category	Awareness element	Specific questions	Recommended feedback stimuli[a]			Implementation examples	
			V	A	H	Gathering	Providing
Who	Presence	Is anyone in the system?	X	X	X	Motion sensing	Notification of participant login
	Identity	Who is participating? Who does this avatar belong to? Who is available to collaborate with?	X	X		Face recognition	Recognized participant ID
	Authorship	Who is doing that?	X	X		Motion sensing	Notification of current action's authorship
What	Task	What are they doing? What is the difficulty of this task?	X	X	X	Motion sensing	Visualization, hearing and haptic feedback of remote action
	Intention	What goal is that task part of?	X	X		Manual input	Notification of current goal
	Object	What object are they working on? What object can I work with?	X	X		Motion sensing with object recognition	Visual notification of currently-used objects
	Status	What are the participants' status? What are their feelings? What is the objects' status?	X	X	X	Biometric sensor/ emotion detection	Visualization, hearing and haptic feedback of participant's status and feelings
	Disabilities	What are the participant disabilities? What are they not able to do because of such disabilities?	X	X		Manual input	Visual warnings of disabled participants
	Perception	What are the other participants perceiving? (Looking, touching, hearing…)	X	X	X	Head-mounted camera with mic and motion sensing	Visualization, hearing and haptic feedback of other participants' perception
Where	Location	Where are the participants/ avatars participating? Is it a physical or virtual location?	X			Motion sensing/GPS	Map locations
	Gaze	Where are the participants looking at?	X			Eye tracking	Visualization of other participants gaze
	Reach	Where can the participants/ avatars reach?	X			Motion detection	Visualization of reach area
	Position	Where is an object? How near is it?	X	X	X	Object and proximity detection	Visualization, hearing and haptic feedback of position and nearness of objects
How	Device	How do I use a certain device to interact?	X	X		Hardware detection/ Manual input	Audio and video instructions

[a](V)isual, (A)ural, (H)aptic

4   Case Study

Once the awareness interpretation has been presented, it will be exemplified in this section by means of a case study based on a physical-cognitive collaborative rehabilitation exercise. This rehabilitation exercise is offered as a game whose two users play collaboratively yet remotely. The interaction with the exercise is done by using a motion sensing device that translates the participants' movements into avatars movements. Figure 1 shows an example of how a rehabilitation systems of this type could be. It can be seen a motion sensing device such as Microsoft Kinect [26] to gather the participants' movements as well as a high definition camera to record the users' face and analyze interpret their emotional status using a specific software [29]. Moreover, a head-mounted eye-tracking device (e.g. Tobii Pro Glasses 2 [30]) could gather the participants gaze and a wristband (e.g. Apple Watch [31]) will both measure their heart rate and provide them with haptic stimuli.

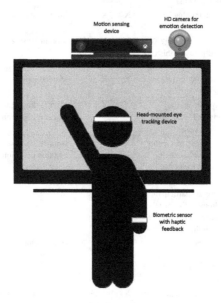

Fig. 1. Participants' hardware environment

Regarding cognitive rehabilitation exercise it is really an *association image-writing* rehabilitation pattern. This was defined in [6] to improve patients' front executive capability. The participants' avatar will be located in a virtual scenario in which different virtual coins will have images and words on it. The implementation of the rehabilitation pattern consists in requesting participants to find and touch a virtual coin related to a specific concept. For instance, if the system request to find and touch the "fruit" coin, one participant will have to touch the coin with the image of a pear on it meanwhile the other one do so with the coin shown the word "pear". Figure 2 illustrates two different avatars, blue and red, will touching the requested coins collaboratively.

Fig. 2. Prototype of participants' user interface (Color figure online)

Besides, as far as physical rehabilitation in concerned, the therapist will be able to place the virtual-world coins' in different places to encourage the participants' movements. As an example, if a participant needs and upper limb therapy, the therapist could locate the coins in a high position, so that the participant will have to lift his arm in order to touch such coin. Moreover, the size of the virtual world could be customizable according to the displacement requirements of the therapy to be performed.

Furthermore, the therapist will have a different view of the system to monitor the therapy execution, thus enabling her to see each participant view, as well as the participants themselves (Fig. 3). Such view will also provide the therapist with the participants' heart rate, their gaze (gathered by means of a head-mounted eye tracking device), as well as with their emotional status (obtained by using a facial analysis software).

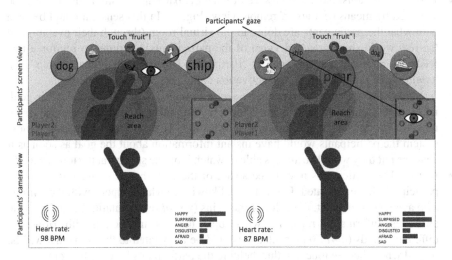

Fig. 3. Prototype of therapist's user interface

In order to exemplify how the awareness interpretation presented in Sect. 3 could be used in the design of such rehabilitation exercise, in the following it is explained how several awareness elements could be implemented and presented to the participants for the recommended feedback stimuli of Table 1:

- *Presence*: Participants have to be aware of the presence of a new participant with who to collaborate. Following the suggested implementation described in Table 1, the exercise could be implemented according to the following requirements: when a motion sensing device detects a new participant, the system will provide the already-connected participant (if any) with a *haptic* stimuli indicating the presence of a team-mate with whom to perform the rehabilitation session. Therefore, it would not be necessary that a logged-in participant is continuously looking at the screen to know whether there is another user in the virtual rehabilitation room, being warned with a vibration on his wrist when the session is ready. However, this awareness information could also be provided by means of *visual* or *aural* signal indicating a new log-in into the system.
- *Identity*: Participants have to be aware of who is the participant related to an avatar. Similarly for this awareness element, a *visual* list of participants (bottom-left corner of Fig. 2) could associate the avatars' color with the identity of the participant. More-over, when a new participant logs in into the system, the *aural* message "the player [participant name] is ready" will be played.
- *Authorship*: Participants have to be aware of who activated a coin in the virtual world. The requirement would be: the color of such coin (*visual* representation) could change to match the color of the participant's avatar. Figure 2 shows that the pear (image) coin has been touched by the blue player, meanwhile the other pear (text) coin was touched by the red player. Alternatively, an *aural* message indicating who activated that coin will be emitted.
- *Task*: The therapist have to be aware of what the participants are doing. It could be achieved by means of a *visual* remote view (Fig. 3). In this sense, it could be seen both what the participants are doing in the virtual room (through their avatars) and the real world (real streamed video of the participants). In order to reinforce this feedback, an *aural* message such as "Participant 1 has activated the dog coin" or a *haptic* signal representing a coin activation could be sent to the participants.
- *Intention*: The participants have to be aware of their goals. For example, this goal, i.e. the coin they will have to touch, could be communicated by means of both a *visual* message on the screen and an *aural* notification. Thank to this double awareness system the participants would have instant information about the goal as soon as it changes but they would be always able to watch it on the screen (at the top of Fig. 2).
- *Object*: The participants have to be aware of the coin that he as well as the other participants have activated. For instance, likewise to what happens with the *author-ship* awareness element, the color of the coins (*visual* representation) could provide awareness information regarding what object they are interacting with. However, different sounds (*aural* representation) could be associated to the coins that will be played when that are touched, thus helping the participants to identify them.
- *Status*: The therapist has to be aware of both the participants' heart rate and emotional status. To implement this awareness element, the participants' heart rate and emotional status could be presented in a *visual* manner to the therapist who would be able to interrupt the session or adjust if needed. For instance, if one participant's

heart rate was considerably high or he was in a bad emotional state, the therapist could interrupt the session and adapted according to the participant's needs. Instead, the heartbeats of a participants could be coded into *aural* beats or *haptic* vibrations aimed at making the therapist aware of a participant's heartrate.

- *Disabilities*: The system have to be aware of any participant's disabilities in order to avoid and/or adapt provided stimuli. Prior to beginning a session, the therapist will indicate whether any participant have disabilities in order for the system to be configured. For instance, if a participant is deaf, audio messages will be presented by using *visual* closed captions. Besides, blind participants may interact with the system by receiving *aural* messages about the coins' location. Moreover, if a participant is unable to walk, all the coins will be located within the participant's reach area.

- *Perception*: Related to the *task* element, the therapist have to be aware of what the participants are seeing thanks to a remote *visual* view of their screens. Moreover, she may also listen to the *aural* messages of the session and be aware that a participant has received *haptic* feedback (vibration symbols on the bottom part of Fig. 3 can be taken of an example of the implementation of this awareness element).

- *Location*: The participants have to be aware of their locations. The patient will know such location by looking at a *visual* map of the scenario (bottom-right corner of Fig. 2). Moreover, by looking at this map, he may obtain information about the position of the other participants. It is worth noting that this map may represent the participants as circles with the same color than the participants' avatars.

- *Gaze*: The therapist has to be aware of where the participants are looking at, aiming at detecting cognitive problems. For instance, the therapist may see the point of the screen where the participants are looking at on the therapist's view in a *visual* manner (eye icons on Fig. 3). Therefore, if a participant was constantly looking at a screen point where no coin or participant were present, a cognitive issue could be identified.

- *Reach*: The therapist has to be aware of what the participants' can reach. For example, the therapist may see on her screen a *visual* representation of each participants' reach area, which may be generated based on their previous movements. Therefore, the therapist will analyze if the physical rehabilitation process has been successful by measuring a possible enlargement of such reach areas (i.e. the participants are able to reach further with their limbs than before starting the rehabilitation process).

- *Position*: Participants have to be aware of the position of the coins. Just as it has happened with the *location* element, thank to which the participants may see their locations, participants may know the position of the elements by using this *visual* map (bottom-right corner of Fig. 2). Thanks to this awareness feature, the participants could be aware of the presence of coins positioned behind them that cannot be seen in a 3D third-person view. For a more detailed analysis of the difference between location and position, please refer to [17]. To reinforce this feedback, the concept of nearness to the coin could be represented as *aural* messages with a variable pitch or increasingly the *haptic* signal depending of such nearness.

- *Device*: Participants have to be aware of how to interact with the system. For instance, the interaction with the system in this case study will be performed by means of the motion sensing device. Therefore, if the system detects that a participant was not aware what he has to do, a *visual* or *aural* message would be displayed or played, respectively, thus informing such participant about how to interact.

Thanks to the implementation of these awareness elements, the participant of a rehabilitation system like the one presented at the beginning of this section will be able to interact with it, collaborating with remote participants, as well as enabling the therapist to monitor and adapt the therapies.

5   Conclusions and Future Work

Awareness information is paramount to achieve a proper collaboration while interacting with remote participants. This issue is magnified when dealing with rehabilitation systems, whose participants suffer from any cognitive or physical disability. This turns the awareness information into a crucial element to provide patients with a proper rehabilitation process. In order to guide in the identification of such awareness requirements when developing cognitive and physical rehabilitation systems, we have adapted an already existing awareness interpretation, namely Gamespace Awareness [17]. It was developed to deal with the awareness requirements of collaborative games. However, in this work we have adapted it to make it suitable for rehabilitation systems featuring ambient intelligence facilities. This new interpretation comprises 14 awareness elements (classified into 5 different categories) that will provide both patients and therapists with the awareness information required to facilitate collaborative and remote rehabilitation. Moreover, along with this collection of elements, this interpretation provides a series of questions aiming at helping designers of new rehabilitation systems to identify their awareness requirements. Furthermore, we also provide recommendation of which feedback stimuli could be used to provide each awareness element (visual, aural or haptic), as well as implementation examples for gathering and providing each one.

In order to exemplify the awareness interpretation created for this target system, a case study has been presented. It describes two participants while performing a collaborative physical and cognitive rehabilitation exercise. The interaction with the system is performed by means of motion sensing devices that translate the participants' movements into avatars' movements in the virtual world. Moreover, biometric devices and emotional analysis is used to make the therapist aware of the patients' physical and emotional status.

This awareness interpretation deal with the most relevant elements of a remote real-time collaborative system, which are those related to the present. However, as a future work, it is planned to broaden this interpretation with a whole new set of elements related to the past, future and social aspects. Therefore, they will enable the therapist to make a comprehensive analysis of the therapies performed (past) as well as they will improve the participants' performance by enabling them to prepare their actions (future). Moreover, more participant will be able to participate in collaborative therapies by including social awareness elements. Finally, once the interpretation has been enriched with the aforementioned elements, a proper evaluation will be performed using a real rehabilitation system in order to assess the suitability of the awareness interpretation in a real scenario in order to evaluate out proposal properly.

Acknowledgements. This research has been funded by the Spanish Ministry of Economy and Competitiveness and by the FEDER funds of the EU under the projects grants TIN2016-79100-R and TIN2015-72931-EXP. It has also been funded by Spanish Ministry of Education, Culture and Sports with the FPU scholarship (AP2010-0259).

References

1. Oh, H., Rizo, C., Enkin, M., Jadad, A., Powell, J., Pagliari, C.: What is ehealth (3): a systematic review of published definitions. J. Med. Internet Res. **7**, e1 (2005)
2. Black, A.D., Car, J., Pagliari, C., Anandan, C., Cresswell, K., Bokun, T., McKinstry, B., Procter, R., Majeed, A., Sheikh, A.: The impact of ehealth on the quality and safety of health care: a systematic overview. PLoS Med. **8**, e1000387 (2011)
3. Brennan, D.M., Mawson, S., Brownsell, S.: Telerehabilitation: enabling the remote delivery of healthcare, rehabilitation, and self management. Stud. Health Technol. Inform. **145**, 231–248 (2009)
4. European Commission Information Society and Media: ICT for Health and i2010: Transforming the European Healthcare Landscape Towards a Strategy for ICT for Health. European Comission, Luxembourg (2006)
5. Rodrıguez, A.C., Roda, C., Montero, F., González, P., Navarro, E.: A collaborative system for designing tele-therapies. In: Pecchia, L., Chen, L.L., Nugent, C., Bravo, J. (eds.) IWAAL 2014. LNCS, vol. 8868, pp. 377–385. Springer, Heidelberg (2014)
6. Montero, F., López-Jaquero, V., Navarro, E., Sánchez, E.: Computer-aided relearning activity patterns for people with acquired brain injury. Comput. Educ. **57**, 1149–1159 (2011)
7. Roda, C., Rodriguez, A.C., Lopez-Jaquero, V., Navarro, E., Gonzalez, P.: A multi-agent system for acquired brain injury rehabilitation in ambient intelligence environments. Neurocomputing (2016, in press)
8. Gascueña, J.M., Navarro, E., Fernández-Sotos, P., Fernández-Caballero, A., Pavón, J.: IDK and ICARO to develop multi-agent systems in support of ambient intelligence. J. Intell. Fuzzy Syst. **28**, 3–15 (2015)
9. Oliver, M., González, P., Montero, F., Molina, J.P., Fernández-Caballero, A.: Smart computer-assisted cognitive rehabilitation for the ageing population. In: Lindgren, H., De Paz, J.F., Novais, P., Fernández-Caballero, A., Yoe, H., Ramirez, A.J., Villarrubia, G. (eds.) Ambient Intelligence-Software and Applications – 7th International Symposium on Ambient Intelligence (ISAm I 2016). Advances in Intelligent Systems and Computing, vol. 476, pp. 197–205. Springer, Heidelberg (2016)
10. Rodríguez, A.C., Roda, C., Montero, F., González, P., Navarro, E.: An interactive fuzzy inference system for teletherapy of older people. Cognit. Comput. **8**, 318–335 (2016)
11. Doig, E., Fleming, J., Kuipers, P.: Achieving optimal functional outcomes in community-based rehabilitation following acquired brain injury: a qualitative investigation of therapists' perspectives. Br. J. Occup. Ther. **71**, 360–370 (2008)
12. Gutwin, C., Greenberg, S.: A descriptive framework of workspace awareness for real-time groupware. Comput. Support. Coop. Work **11**, 411–446 (2002)
13. Navarro, E., López-Jaquero, V., Montero, F.: HABITAT: a web supported treatment for acquired brain injured. In: IEEE International Conference on Eighth Advanced Learning Technologies (ICALT 2008), pp. 464–466 (2008)
14. Krynicki, K., Jaen, J., Navarro, E.: An ACO-based personalized learning technique in support of people with acquired brain injury. Appl. Soft Comput. **47**, 316–331 (2016)

15. Rubio, G., Navarro, E., Montero, F.: APADYT: a multimedia application for SEN learners. Multimed. Tools Appl. **71**, 1771–1802 (2014)
16. Teruel, M.A., Navarro, E., López-Jaquero, V., Montero, F., Jaen, J., González, P.: Analyzing the understandability of requirements engineering languages for CSCW systems: a family of experiments. Inf. Softw. Technol. **54**, 1215–1228 (2012)
17. Teruel, M.A., Navarro, E., González, P., López-Jaquero, V., Montero, F.: Applying thematic analysis to define an awareness interpretation for collaborative computer games. Inf. Softw. Technol. **74**, 17–44 (2016)
18. Brontes Processing: SeeMe Rehabilitation. http://www.virtual-reality-rehabilitation.com/products/seeme/what-is-seeme
19. Virtualrehab. http://www.virtualrehab.info/support/
20. Dimbwadyo-Terrer, I., de los Reyes-Guzman, A., Bernal-Sahun, A., Lopez-Montaegudo, P., Trincado-Alonso, F., Polonio-Lopez, B., Gil-Agudo, A.: Virtual reality system toyra: a new tool to assess and treatment for upper limb motor impairment in patients with spinal cord injury. In: Pons, J.L., Torricelli, D., Pajaro, M. (eds.) Converging Clinical and Engineering Research on Neurorehabilitation. Biosystems & Biorobotics, vol. 1, pp. 853–858. Springer, Heidelberg (2013)
21. Tong, R.K.Y., Hang, C.H., Chong, L.K.W., Lam, N.K.F.: KineLabs 3D motion software platform using kinect. In: 2012 International Conference on Computerized Healthcare (ICCH), pp. 164–165 (2012)
22. Oliver, M., Molina, J.P., Montero, F., González, P., Fernández-Caballero, A.: Wireless multisensory interaction in an intelligent rehabilitation environment. In: Ramos, C., Novais, P., Nihan, C.E., Rodriguez, J.M.C. (eds.) Ambient Intelligence - Software and Applications: 5th Int Symposium on Ambient Intelligence (ISAMI). Advances in Intelligent Systems and Computing, vol. 291, pp. 193–200. Springer, Heidelberg (2014)
23. Pirovano, M., Mainetti, R., Baud-Bovy, G., Lanzi, P.L., Borghese, N.A.: Self-adaptive games for rehabilitation at home. In: 2012 IEEE Conference on Computational Intelligence and Games (CIG), pp. 179–186. (2012)
24. Chang, Y.-J., Chen, S.-F., Huang, J.-D.: A kinect-based system for physical rehabilitation: a pilot study for young adults with motor disabilities. Res. Dev. Disabil. **32**, 2566–2570 (2011)
25. Brennan, D.M., Georgeadis, A.C., Baron, C.R., Barker, L.M.: The effect of videoconference-based telerehabilitation on story retelling performance by brain-injured subjects and its implications for remote speech-language therapy. Telemed. J. E. Health **10**, 147–154 (2004)
26. Kurillo, G., Han, J.J., Nicorici, A., Bajcsy, R.: Tele-MFAsT: kinect-based tele-medicine tool for remote motion and function assessment. In: Studies in Health Technology and Informatics, pp. 215–221. IOS Press (2014)
27. González, C.S., Toledo, P., Padrón, M., Santos, E., Cairos, M.: TANGO:H: creating active educational games for hospitalized children. In: Casillas, J., Martinez-Lopez, F.J., Vicari, R., De la Prieta, F. (eds.) Management Intelligent Systems, pp. 135–142. Springer, Heidelberg (2013)
28. Cusveller, J., Gerritsen, C., de Man, J.: Evoking and measuring arousal in game settings. In: Göbel, S., Wiemeyer, J. (eds.) GameDays 2014. LNCS, vol. 8395, pp. 165–174. Springer, Heidelberg (2014)
29. Joho, H., Jose, J.M., Valenti, R., Sebe, N.: Exploiting facial expressions for affective video summarisation. In: ACM International Conference on Image and Video Retrieval (CIVR 2009), pp. 31:1–31:8 (2009)
30. Tobii A.B.: Tobii Pro Glasses 2. http://www.tobiipro.com/product-listing/tobii-pro-glasses-2/
31. Apple Inc.: Apple Watch. http://www.apple.com/watch/

Early Detection of Hypoglycemia Events Based on Biometric Sensors Prototyped on FPGAs

Soledad Escolar[1]([✉]), Manuel J. Abaldea[2], Julio D. Dondo[2], Fernando Rincón[2], and Juan Carlos López[2]

[1] Institute of Technology and Information Systems, Ciudad Real, Spain
soledad.escolar@uclm.es
[2] School of Computing Science, University of Castilla-La Mancha, Ciudad Real, Spain
{manueljose.abaldea,juliodaniel.dondo,
fernando.rincon,juancarlos.lopez}@uclm.es

Abstract. Diabetes is a chronic disease that requires continuous medical care and patient self-monitoring processes. The control of the glucose level in blood is a task that the patient needs to perform to prevent hypoglycemia episodes. Early detection of hypoglycemia is a very important element for preventing multi-organ failure. The incorporation of other biomedical parameters monitoring, combined with glucose levels can help to early detect and prevent those episodes. At this respect, several e-health platforms have been developed for monitoring and processing vital signals related to diabetes events. In this paper we evaluate a couple of these platforms and we introduce an algorithm to analyze the data of glucose, in order to anticipate the moment of an hypoglycemia episode. The proposed algorithm contemplates the information of several biomedical sensors, and it is based on the analysis of the gradient of the glucose curve, producing an estimation of the expected time to achieve a given threshold. Besides, the proposed algorithm allows to analyze the correlations of the monitored multi-signals information with diabetes related events. The algorithm was developed to be implemented on an FPGA-based SoC and was evaluated by simulation. The results obtained are very promising and can be scalable to further signals processing.

Keywords: E-health platforms · FPGAs · Biometric sensors · Continuous Glucose Monitoring · Diabetes

1 Introduction

The International Diabetes Federation estimates that 387 million people worldwide suffered from diabetes in 2012 and it is expected an increase of 215 million people more by 2035 [1]. Diabetes is a chronic illness that occurs when the pancreas is no longer able to produce insulin (or not enough amount), an hormone that acts letting glucose that we obtained through the ingestion of carbohydrates, to pass from the blood towards the cells in the body to produce energy. Consequently, the diabetic patient presents abnormally raised glucose levels in

© Springer International Publishing AG 2016
C.R. García et al. (Eds.): UCAmI 2016, Part I, LNCS 10069, pp. 133–145, 2016.
DOI: 10.1007/978-3-319-48746-5_14

blood that, in absence of an effective treatment, may produce important damages to various organs or even the death.

The control of its glucose level in blood is a basic task that a diabetic patient needs to perform several times per day in order to help adjusting the amount of insulin to be injected. The most basic way consists in piercing the skin (normally a finger) using an electronic device called glucometer that extracts a small blood sample and then applies to a chemically active disposable test-strip, able to read the concentration of glucose. However, according to [7], this approach presents limitations with regard to the accuracy and specificity as well as the need of sticking several times per day. Advances in microelectronics enable the Continuous Glucose Monitoring (CGM) [12], a technique that determines glucose levels in the interstitial fluid on a continuous basis. To this end, a glucose sensor is implanted under the skin of the patient for a few days, normally between 3 and 7 days. This sensor normally operates by transmitting every a few minutes the average of the concentration of glucose of the samples towards a nearby non-implanted receiver, which displays on a small screen both the actual measurement and the curve of glucose levels along the time to see rising and falling trends. In order to describe more precisely the current clinical state of the diabetic patient and to be able to anticipate diseases as are the hypoglycemias and hyperglycemias (values abnormally low and high of glucose, respectively), the monitoring of additional parameters is being progressively incorporated. As described in [2], the heart rate variability combined with the monitoring of the glucose levels may increase the time of forecasting of hypoglycemias, yielding a lead time of 22 min as compared to the CGM device. The work presented in [6] reveals significant inverse changes of the ECG parameters (e.g. QT, PR, RT and TpTe intervals) upon the occurrence of an hypoglycemic process. Therefore, the real-time processing of more and more signals, corresponding to vital signals whose values are altered in presence of hypo- and hyperglycemia events such as the heart rate, sweeting, and blood pressure, could increase the time interval given by the moment of detection of the event and the moment of its potential occurrence. It is important to stress that such time of anticipation could result critical for implementing the medical actuation required to avoid the risk. Given the potentially high number of signals to be processed and the importance of the processing time, FPGAs are very adequate for the execution of real-time medical applications where the analysis and study of signal patterns behavior are necessary. The internal structure of FPGAs allows parallelizing the execution of several algorithms using simultaneous instantiation of the corresponding component, feature that is very useful to analyze the correlation of events produced in a determined signal, in correspondence with the behavior of the rest of them. Besides, FPGAs allow to develop customizable high speed data acquisition systems to create multi-signals processing systems.

In this work we evaluate a couple of commercial e-health platforms that enable the continuous monitoring of vital parameters. e-health platforms integrate several biometric sensors, a microcontroller, and some sort of communication radio to transmit the readings towards an external receiver. By using biometric sensors, we propose an algorithm for improving the detection of hypo-glycemias and we implement it on an FPGA with the purpose of comparing its performance against alternative e-health platforms and evaluating its suitabil-ity for implementing medical algorithms. The rest of the paper is organized as follows. After reviewing the related work we describe in Sect. 3 the medical para-meters to be monitored in presence of diabetes and in Sect. 4 we propose and algorithm for hypoglycemias detection. Section 5 shows the results of testing two e-health platforms and the evaluation of the proposed algorithm on an FPGA. Finally, in Sect. 6 we draw the conclusions and future research work.

2   Related Work

CGM enables to predict the risk of hypo- and hyperglycemia and to adjust better the administration of insulin [4]. However, most of the current CGM devices are invasive (since they require accessing blood or interstitial fluid), expensive, they require still calibration by finger sticks (several times per day) for optimal glucose sensor accuracy, and their lifespan is limited to just a few days. Three examples of certified, still invasive CGM sensors currently used by diabetic patients are *ipro*, *abbot*, and G4/G5 Dexcom series. *ipro* kit is composed of a sensor implanted under the skin and an *ipro recorder* that receives and stores the readings of the sensor. A reading is sent from the sensor towards the receiver each 5 min, which represents 288 daily readings. The *ipro recorder* is not able to communicate with a smartphone; instead of that, after as much 6 days, the sensor must be removed and replaced, and data must be downloaded from the recorder for its interpretation. The *abbot* system comprises a CGM sensor and a reader device able to scan the sensor when located at distances from 1 up to 4 cm. This CGM sensor measures the glucose level each 15 min, which represents 96 daily readings. In turn, the glucose sensors series from Dexcom are especially indicated for children from 2 years. The novelty of this system regarding to the previous ones, is that the sensor is able to transmit each reading via Bluetooth towards a smartphone, which enables also its visualization. The next generation of CGM includes a small pump of insulin that is connected to a needle subcutaneously implanted under skin; this mechanism is able to supply insulin upon the clicking of a button, at discrete time to reduce the glucose concentration or continuously to maintain the basal rate [3], based on the readings from the glucose sensor.

The research in microelectronics and MEMS technology is focused on pro-viding still continuous monitoring but through pain-free, non-invasive devices that avoid the necessity of piercing the skin. This technique is known as Non-invasive Glucose Monitoring. The main weakness of non-invasive sensors is their accuracy, which is still far from achieving the precision level of finger sticks. In the last few years have appeared non-invasive devices to measure the glucose levels, as GlucoTrack, that provides a sensor that clips to the patient's ear lobe and uses an algorithm to compute the glucose level, or Glucowise, which may be positioned between the thumb and forefinger or at the earlobe. Wearable com-puting also enables the continuous monitoring of parameters related to health and physical activities. Wearable computing is intended to be continuously available, observable, and controllable by the user, but does not need its attention and do not constraint its movements [5]. Wearable computers are implicit to the body, they are worn (not carried) comfortably on our clothes or as watches, glasses or lens, and are aimed at sensing both vital signals as environmental parameters through multiple sensors. In this sense, the next generation of non-invasive glucometers trends to be devices worn, able to continuously read the glucose level and communicate the readings wirelessly towards a smartphone or computer. A first prototype of these devices are iWatch (Apple) and Google's smart contact lens. Continuing at the experimental level, open e-health platforms are proliferating as an effective mean mainly oriented to assist developers and researchers in the evaluation of innovative algorithms for predicting, detecting, and tracking illnesses. They are not conceived for the monitoring of critical patients since they do generally not have medical certifications. An e-health platform enables the body monitoring through a rich set of biomedical sensors, as well as providing the capabilities of processing, storing, and communication. e-health Sensor Shield [8] is a PCB designed to connect nine sensors: patient position (accelerometer), glucometer (invasive), body temperature, blood pressure (sphygmomanometer), pulse and oxygen in blood, airflow (breathing), sweating via galvanic skin response (GSR), electrocardiogram (ECG), and electromyography (EMG). This shield can be connected to both Arduino and Raspberry PI platforms, which provide capabilities of processing and transmission of data (e.g. Wi-Fi, GPRS, Bluetooth, 802.15.4). The medical information collected can be used to monitor in real time the state of a patient and for medical diagnosis, yielding a large set of different medical applications. A limitation of the e-health Sensor Shield is that not all sensors can work together. The BioMedical Development Kit [10] from BITalino, is an easy-to-use and low-cost toolkit to learn and prototype applications using body signals. This consists of a PCB with a microcontroller, Bluetooth 2.0, a Li-Po Battery 320 mAh, a LED actuator and ECG, EMG, Electrodermal Activity, accelerometer and light sensors, all of them can be connected to the board through USB ports.

On the other hand, the inherent parallelism to FPGA architectures results very appealing for the implementation of data-intensive medical applications. For example, the work presented in [9] implements on an FPGA a discrete-time inverse neural controller to regulate the glucose level in diabetic patients, thus providing a first step to develop an artificial pancreas.

3   Early Detection of Hypoglycemias

The system that we are proposing has as a primary goal the early detection of hypoglycemias. Our proposal applies to diabetic patients subject to a therapy consisting in the continuous monitoring of their glucose level in blood (glycemia), which is the most relevant evidence for the diabetic. In our system model, the diabetic patient monitors its glycemia by means of a CGM device, which measures the glucose level in blood in a continuous basis. In particular, the values of glycemia before and two hours after breakfast, lunch, and dinner are especially relevant. The evidence that reports on if the patient is controlling its glycemia well is the glycosylated hemoglobin (also known as HbA_{1c}), that represents the average glycemia during the last 90–120 days and that is obtained through a blood test in the laboratory. In addition to this, some diabetic patients present risk factors for the illness as are the hypertension and the overweight. Hypertension is controlled through blood pressure tests, which deliver two values p_1, p_2, where p_1 is the systolic pressure (the pressure when the heart beats) and p_2 is the diastolic pressure (the pressure when the heart muscle is resting between beats and refilling with blood). In turn, the existence of overweight is determined by means of the Body Mass Index (BMI), that represents the relative size of an individual and it is computed as $BMI = \frac{weight}{height^2}$, where $weight$ is expressed in kilograms and $height$ in meters. It follows that the lifestyle, particularly diet and practice of sports, impact on BMI. Diet is a critical part of the treatment of any diabetic patient with overweight, intended to take care of the ingestion of calories, fats, and carbohydrates, including the uniform distribution of calories among meals. Physical exercise is indicated in most of the cases but mainly in presence of overweight. The heart rate provides the number of contractions of the heart per minute, and it increases with the intensity of the exercise. To this regard, during the physical activity of the patient, it would be useful to monitor its heart rate variability to avoid that it exceeds the maximum heart rate (HR_{max}), which can be computed by taking into account the gender and the age of the patient according to the Haskell and Fox's equation: $HR_{max} = 220\text{-age}$ (in men) or $HR_{max} = 226\text{-age}$ (in women). Note that HR_{max} is the theoretical maximum heart rate that can be achieved without harming the health under optimal physical conditions. Note also that exercise usually lowers blood glucose level; therefore, the monitoring of the glucose level during the physical activity is key for hypoglycemias detection.

We consider two symptoms more that generally accompany the first stages of hypoglycemia: sweating and trembling. Sweating occurs all over the body but mainly in face and hands, and it may be associated to an increase of the body temperature, which should be also monitored. A sort of slight trembling may appear in fingers and hands, and it is generally only observed by the person that experiences it without being visible to other persons. There exist many other symptoms associated to the early stages of hypoglycemia such as hunger, weakness and fatigue, headache or impaired vision. For our purpose, we have focused on those parameters associated to hypoglycemias that can be measured through the e-health platforms that we have available in our laboratory. Table 1 presents the values of reference and imbalances for the parameters considered.

4   Algorithm for Hypoglycemias Detection

Let us consider an e-health platform for the continuous monitoring of glucose in conjunction with the monitoring of heart rate, blood pressure, temperature, position, sweating, and trembling. Thus, the platform integrates $n = 7$ sensors

Table 1. Normal and altered values for some vital parameters related to diabetes.

Parameter	Normal values	Abnormal values	Observations
Glycemia	$70 - 100$ mg/dl	–	No diabetes (fasting)
	<140 mg/dl	–	No diabetes (after eating)
	$100 - 125$ mg/dl	–	Pre-diabetes (fasting)
	$140 - 199$ mg/dl	–	Pre-diabetes (after eating)
	–	≥ 126 mg/dl	Diabetes (fasting)
	–	≥ 200 mg/dl	Diabetes (after eating)
	–	≤ 70 mg/dl	Hypoglycemia
	–	≥ 200 mg/dl	Hyperglycemia
HbA_{1c}	$4 - 6\%$	–	–
	–	$\geq 6.5\%$	Bad control of glycemia
BMI	$18.0 - 24.9$	–	No overweight
	–	$25.0 - 29.9$	Overweight
	–	≥ 30.0	Obesity
HR	$\leq (60 - 80\%)HR_{max}$	$> HR_{max}$	–
p_1	$90 - 119$ mm Hg	–	Systolic Pressure
	–	$140 - 159$ mm Hg	Stage 1 Hypertension
	–	$160 - 179$ mm Hg	Stage 2 Hypertension
p_2	$60 - 79$ mm Hg	–	Diastolic Pressure
	–	$140 - 159$ mm Hg	Stage 1 Hypertension
	–	$160 - 179$ mm Hg	Stage 2 Hypertension

named $s_0, \ldots, s_6$, each one is sampling a vital sign at a suitable periodicity: s_0 is a CGM sensor, s_1 is a heart rate sensor, s_2 is a tensiometer that measures the blood pressure (systolic and diastolic), s_3 is a body temperature sensor, s_4 is an accelerometer that detects the patient's position (fowler's, prone, supine, and recumbent) and that is useful to detect falls, s_5 is a GSR sensor that measures the electrical conductance of the skin, which varies with its moisture level and s_6 is an EMG sensor, which measures the muscle activation via the electric potential. All these sensors are available in the e-health platforms described in Sect. 2. We also consider the age, the gender, and the weight and height of the patient as fixed parameters which, therefore, do not need to be continuously monitored through a sensor; similarly, HbA_{1c} is a parameter that could be estimated by computing the average of the values of glucose.

Each sensor is provided with a sampling frequency f_i, which corresponds to the rate of readings taken by sensor i, initially defined as $f_i = 300$ s $\forall i \in [0, n)$. These frequencies could be adjusted depending on the variability of their values along a day and the necessity of register them for diagnosis purposes. Each sensor is also provided with a maximum threshold denoted as $\max_i$. By taking the series of readings from the sensors along the time as an input, we propose an

---

Algorithm 1. Hypoglycemias Detection Algorithm

Require: v_i is the reading of sensor i at time t, $f_i = 300$ is the sampling frequency
$\forall i \in [0,6]$; $\max_i$ is the threshold for sensor i $\forall i \in [1,6]$
Require: $\min_0 = 70$ is the minimum threshold for s_0; α is the maximum angle
Ensure: T: the estimated anticipation time of a potential hypoglycemia
  $G = 0$ *%initial value of glucose*
  $F = f_0$ *% the frequency for sampling the glucose sensor*
  $threshold = \min_0 \times 1.25$ *% a threshold for the glucose value*
  loop
    % At each sampling period
    if$(G == 0)$ **then** $G = v_0$; break;
    $m = \frac{G - v_0}{f_0}$; $\theta = \arctan(m)$; $T = \frac{f_0 \times (v_0 - \min_0)}{G - v_0}$; $G = v_0$
    case 0: $(\theta < \alpha)$
      break;   *% Normal state*
    case 1: $(\theta < \alpha) \wedge (v_0 \leq threshold)$
      initiate sampling $s_1 \ldots s_6$ *% Low glucose*
      if $(v_i \geq \max_i), 1 \leq i < n$ **then return** T   *% Alert hypoglycemia*
    case 2: $(\theta \geq \alpha)$
      $f_0 = \frac{F}{3}$ *% Pre-hypoglycemia state*
      initiate sampling $s_1 \ldots s_6$
      loop
        $m = \frac{G - v_0}{f_0}$; $\theta = \arctan(m)$; $T = \frac{f_0 \times (v_0 - \min_0)}{G - v_0}$; $G = v_0$
        if$(\theta \geq \alpha)$ **then** $f_0 = \frac{F}{3}$
        if$(\theta < \alpha) \wedge (m > 0)$**then** $f_0 = \frac{F}{2}$ *% Risk factors state*
        if $(m \leq 0)$ **then** $F = f_0$; stop sampling $s_1 \ldots s_6$; break
        if $(v_i \geq \max_i), 1 \geq i < n$ **then return** T   *% Alert hypoglycemia*
      end loop
  end loop

---

algorithm for analyzing the data of glucose in order to anticipate the moment of time of the occurrence of an hypoglycemia event. This analysis is based on the computation of the slope of the curve drawn by the glucose level in blood along the time. At each sampling period, a value of each sensor denoted as v_i is obtained, for all $i \in [0,n)$. Let us also define $v_0(t)$ as the glucose reading at time t and α as the maximum angle drawn for the segment $\overrightarrow{AB}$ ($A = v_0(t)$, $B = v_0(t+1)$) with the horizontal axis. Thus, for any two consecutive readings $v_0(t)$ and $v_0(t+1)$ the slope of the curve is $m = \frac{dv_0}{dt} = \frac{v_0(t) - v_0(t-1)}{t - (t-1)}$ and by using simple geometry its angle is $\theta = \arctan m$. The slope is positive (ascending) iff $m > 0$ and it is negative (descending) iff $m < 0$. If $\theta < \alpha$ (θ, α are expressed in degrees) the slope of the curve is under the threshold and glucose keeps within the normal levels; otherwise, the slope of the curve is above the threshold and, therefore, glucose level is falling more quickly than recommended. Note that it could be still possible a descending slope while $\theta < \alpha$ holds, so glucose is falling but not dramatically for our purpose. The pseudo-code is shown in Algorithm 1.

    The algorithm enters into a loop that starts to sample only the glucose sensor s_0 each f_0 and keeps in this state until two possible events occur: (1) v_0 drops under a threshold defined slightly above $min_0 = 70 \, mg/dl$ (which is the minimum value of glucose to be considered hypoglycemia) and (2) the angle θ is larger or equal than the maximum angle α. In both cases, the glucose level is descending with the time (in the second case it falls at a faster pace than in the first case), so in both cases the algorithm starts sampling the rest of sensors $s_1 \ldots s_6$ to monitor the symptoms of a possible hypoglycemia. In the first case, if some value v_i exceeds the allowed threshold (i.e. $v_i > max_i, i \in [1, n)$) then, an alert is generated to warn the medical team about a potential hypoglycemia and the algorithm returns the estimated time T to achieve min_0 while the slope m is kept. The second case occurs when two consecutive values of glucose form an angle $\theta \geq \alpha$, which means that is dropping quickly. The algorithm adjusts the sampling frequency for the glucose sensor to $f_0 = \frac{f_0}{3}$ in order to be able to anticipate the risk detection. As in the first case, if some value v_i exceeds the allowed threshold an alert is immediately generated. Otherwise, if the slope is still lower than 0 but at slower pace ($\theta < \alpha$) then the reading frequency for the glucose sensor is updated to $f_0 = \frac{f_0}{2}$. Under the event of a glucose value larger than the previous one, i.e. drawing an ascending slope ($m \geq 0$), the algorithm returns to the initial state. Figure 1 represents the different cases described above.

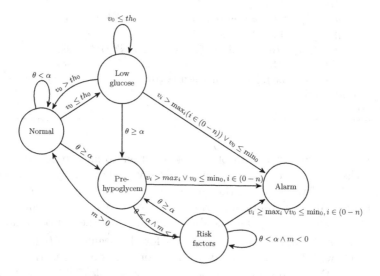

Fig. 1. State transition diagram for the cases considered in Algorithm 1.

5   Evaluation

This section presents the evaluation of our approach. We first test the e-health sensor shield and BITalino platforms in order to compare the results that are obtained from equivalent sensors in both platforms. Second, we evaluate by simulation our algorithm on an FPGA-based SoC. For the work presented here a development platform based on SmartFusion II FPGA with Arduino compatibility has been used. This compatibility allows to connect the sensing platform to the FPGA to perform the required computation. Although the evaluated platforms are based on a microprocessor such Arduino, ARM, the incorporation of reconfigurable logic allows to develop hardware versions of different algorithms for signals processing that could require improved computational performance. The next subsections describe the evaluation method and results.

5.1   Testing E-health Sensor Shield and BITalino Platforms

We have written a program to collect data from the sensors in e-health Sensor Shield connected to Arduino. This program enters into a loop where in each iteration the pulseoximeter, temperature, GSR, accelerometer, and airflow sensors are sequentially read. Since ECG and EMG sensors cannot be used simultaneously, we proceed to implement different versions of the program, one to read ECG signal and the other one to read the EMG signal. The glucometer and the sphygmomanometer devices can neither work together; they are not sampled as a result of the invocation of a program's function but instead they work autonomously and just transmit data to Arduino (number of measures stored in the device, and date and time associated to each value of glucose/blood pressure sample) when they are requested via the appropriate reading function. Thus, in each loop iteration we ask for new measures of glucose/blood pressure to avoid overflow the output buffer. Accelerometer and blood pressure sensors were sampled only once since they do not (or almost not) suffer variations along the time frame. Glycemia was not monitored in this experiment (see next subsection for details). The test demonstrated that the ECG, temperature, oxygen saturation, and blood pressure sensors seem working accurately for purposes of non-critical monitoring. Additionally, since EMG sensor measures the muscle intensity, the test proved that the highest values coincide with some action done by the carrier of the sensor. GSR conductance voltage and airflow values should be compared against another reliable device. However, the position sensor revealed incorrect

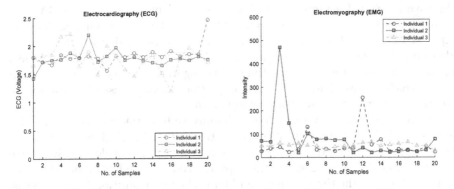

Fig. 2. ECG (on the left) and EMG (on the right) samples obtained from Arduino.

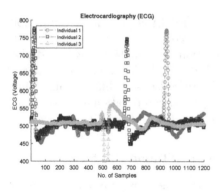 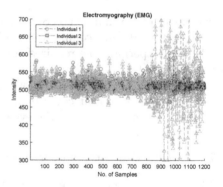

Fig. 3. ECG (on the left) and EMG (on the right) samples obtained from BITalino.

results in most of the samples as it is also stated in [8]. The average time taken by each loop iteration is 318.8 ms. In turn, BITalino provides a software that makes most of the work for us, letting to sample the sensors and visualize the results in a real-time via a user-friendly interface on the PC or smartphone. The sampling program executes on Arduino and BITalino platforms during a time frame of 10 min and by using a sampling period of 30 s, which means that 20 readings per sensor and per individual were collected. The tests were developed with help of three healthy volunteers in seated position.

As an example, we show in Fig. 2 the values of ECG and EMG collected on the Arduino platform. ECG parameters are, according to [6], altered in presence of hypoglycemia. ECG and EMG results for the same persons obtained from BITalino platform are presented in Fig. 3. As observed, the sampling frequency of this platform is much higher than the provided by Arduino. Both platforms may potentially support an algorithm for hypoglycemia detection based on the continuous monitoring of ECG parameters together with the glucose levels.

5.2 Simulation of the Algorithm on an FPGA

We have developed a prototype in VHDL to be deployed on any FPGA. Our prototype uses two data bus for input/output standard communication and an input signal for each sensor $s_0, \ldots, s_6$. Our prototype is able to simulate the algorithm described in Sect. 4 by taking the CGM input data from real patients. In our simulations, the execution time of the algorithm is 6 cycles (in the worst case), which means that the simulated platform (SmartFusionII) working at 100 MHz delivers a time of approximately 60 ms.

In order to make more realistic simulations we have taken the data of CGM of three diabetic patients described in [11] that suffered hypoglycemia episodes. For our purpose we fix $\alpha = [-5, -8]$ (note that a negative angle corresponds to a $360° + \alpha$ angle). Table 2 shows the expected time T in minutes and the slope m for each one of the three patients and for each state transition (i.e. each slope variation) before achieving the minimum value (70 mg/dl). Figure 4 shows the best results for patient 1 (left), patient 2 (center) and patient 3 (right). The axis x is showing the number of samples and the axis y represents the glucose levels. Figures on the left and on the right correspond to transitions from Normal to Low state, that occurs when the threshold 88 mg/dl (e.g. 1.25 % of 70 mg/dl) is achieved (red line), while the figure in the middle shows the case when the algorithm transits from Normal to Pre-hypoglycemia state because $\theta \geq \alpha$, that occurs for glucose levels under 70 mg/dl (blue line). Times are provided when the threshold is achieved (figures on the left and right) or when $\theta \geq \alpha$ (figure in the middle). The best case occurs if in the moment of detection the glucose is far from the threshold and θ is slightly above α.

Table 2. Estimated time (T) in minutes for an hypoglycemia episode and gradient (m) of the curve for different values of α.

	$\alpha = -5$		$\alpha = -6$		$\alpha = -7$		$\alpha = -8$	
	T	m	T	m	T	m	T	m
Patient 1	9.4	−0.3	28.3	−0.3	28.3	−0.3	28.3	−0.3
	1.4	−0.9	1.4	−0.9	1.4	−0.9	1.4	−0.9
Patient 2	23.9	−0.9	23.9	−0.9	23.0	−0.9	23.9	−0.9
	700	−0.3	700	−0.3	700	−0.3	700	−0.3
Patient 3	95	−0.1	95	−0.1	95	−0.1	95	−0.1
	30	−0.1	30	−0.1	30	−0.1	30	−0.1

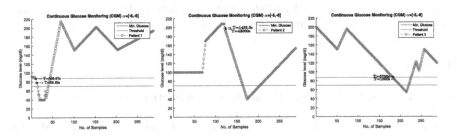

Fig. 4. CGM curves and estimated time for hypoglycemia for different values of α. (Color figure online)

6   Conclusions

The continuous monitoring of variables associated to medical disorders by means of biometric sensors, integrated into e-health platforms and into wearable devices, enables the design of algorithms able to detect the potential occurrence of risk events based on the correlation of data series collected from the sensors. Anticipating the early detection of risks is of utmost importance to increase the time to implement medical actions that avoid critical situations. Precisely with this motivation we have firstly tested two commercial e-health platforms (e-health Shield Sensor/Arduino and BITalino) to show their suitability and weaknesses for biomedical signal monitoring and data acquisition for medical applications. Secondly, we have proposed an algorithm for early detection of hypoglycemias that in this first stage was simulated on an FPGA, in order to investigate how can be implemented taking into account the correlation of the signals obtained with the aforementioned platforms. The algorithm is based on the analysis of the gradient of the glucose curve and estimates the expected time to achieve a given threshold. The simulation takes as input the glucose levels of diabetic patients that suffered hypoglycemias. The results show that our algorithm may effectively predict their hypoglycemias episodes anticipating the time of its occurrence (from several minutes to hours depending on the gradient considered). The execution time of our algorithm on an FPGA is several orders of magnitude lower than the time delivered by Arduino.

As future works we plan to improve the anticipation time of our algorithm by investigating the correlation of the data series collected from other sensors (e.g. heart rate, ECG, sweating) with regard to the glucose levels, since they are measuring recognized symptoms of hypoglycemia. We also plan a more exhaustive evaluation that takes as input data obtained from real diabetic patients and covers a wider spectrum for the values α and θ.

Acknowledgments. This work has been funded by the Programme for Research and Innovation of University of Castilla-La Mancha, co-financed by the European Social Fund (Resolution of 25 August 2014) and by the Spanish Ministry of Economy and Competitiveness under project REBECCA (TEC2014-58036-C4-1-R) and the Regional Government of Castilla-La Mancha under project SAND (PEII_2014_046_P).

References

1. Annual Report 2012: International Diabetes Federation (2012). http://www.idf. org
2. Cichosz, S.L., Frystyk, J., Hejlesen, O.K., Lise, T., Jesper, F.: A novel algorithm for prediction and detection of hypoglycemia based on continuous glucose monitoring and heart rate variability in patients with typpe 1 diabetes. J. Diab. Sci. Technol. **8**(4), 731–737 (2014)
3. Halvorson, M., Carpenter, S., Kaiserman, K., Kaufman, F.R.: A pilot trial in pediatrics with the sensor-augmented pump: combining real-time continuous glucose monitoring with the insulin pump. J. Pediatr. **150**(1), 103–105 (2007)
4. Guillod, L., Comte-Perret, S., Monbaron, D., Gaillard, R.C., Ruiz, J.: Nocturnal hypoglycaemias in type 1 diabetic patients: what can we learn with continuous glucose monitoring? Diabetes Metab. **5**(33), 360–365 (2007)
5. Mann, S.: Wearable Computing as Means for Personal Empowerment. IEEE Computer Society Press, Fairfax (1998)

6. Nguyen, L.L., Su, S., Nguyen, H.T.: Identification of hypoglycemia and hyperglycemia in typpe 1 diabetic patients using ecg parameters. In: 2012 Annual International Conference of the IEEE Engineering in Medicine and Biology Society, pp. 2716–2719, August 2012
7. Olansky, L., Kennedy, L.: Finger-stick glucose monitoring. Diabetes Care **33**(4), 948–949 (2010). http://dx.doi.org/10.2337/dc10-0077
8. Rakay, R., Visnovsky, M., Galajdova, A., Simsik, D.: Testing properties of e-health system based on arduino. J. Autom. Control **3**(3), 122–126 (2015)
9. Romero-Aragon, J.C., Sanchez, E.N., Alanis, A.Y.: Glucose level regulation for diabetes mellitus typpe 1 patients using fpga neural inverse optimal control. In: 2014 IEEE Symposium on Computational Intelligence in Control and Automation (CICA), pp. 1–7, December 2014
10. da Silva, H.P., Guerreiro, J., Loureno, A., Fred, A., Martins, R.: Bitalino: a novel hardware framework for physiological computing. In: Proceedings of the International Conference on Physiological Computing Systems, pp. 246–253 (2014)
11. Tomasello, A.: Incidencia de Hipoglucemias en DM2 mayores de 60 años medidas a través de monitoreo glucémico continuo y su relación con estilo de vida y tratamiento de Diabetes. Ph.D. thesis, Fundación H.A. Barceló (2014)
12. Vashist, S.K.: Continuous glucose monitoring systems: a review. Diagnostics **3**(4), 385–412 (2013). http://www.mdpi.com/2075-4418/3/4/385

Management of the Hypertension: An Architecture Based on BPM Integration

Javier Ramírez-Navarro[✉], Virgilio Gilart-Iglesias, Antonio Soriano-Paya,
Daniel Ruiz-Fernandez[✉], Diego Marcos-Jorquera, and Victor Vives-Boix

Department of Computer Technology, University of Alicante, Alicante, Spain
{jramirez,vgilart,asoriano,druiz,dmarcos,vvives}@dtic.ua.es

Abstract. Hypertension affects eight out of ten adult population over 65 years. Healthcare processes require interdisciplinary cooperation and coordination between medical teams, clinical process and patients. The lack of patients' empowerment and adherence to treatment makes it necessary to integrate patients, data collecting devices and the clinical process together. The use of Business Process Management (BPM) paradigm and their associated technologies as an integrating tool throughout the clinical process of coordinating the data collected hypertension patients through the devices, the clinical process and the needs of the medical equipment is proposed.

Keywords: Architecture device · Business Process Management · Hypertension · Chronic disease management

1 Introduction

High blood pressure (hypertension), is considered a risk for cardiovascular disease and has high prevalence in population [1]. It is also the commonest chronic disorder seen in primary care, with around one in eight of all people receiving antihypertensive treatment. Experts of the Spanish Society of Hypertension-Spanish League for the Fight Against Hypertension Arterial [2] estimate that 588 million people could be hypertensive in 2025. In Spain, this condition affects about 40 % of the adult population, a percentage that increases to 85 % when it comes to over 65 years. In addition, it is noteworthy that among those under 18 years the prevalence is between 3.5 % and 5 % and that children/ young hypertensives have increased cardiovascular risk in adulthood.

Despite its importance, the processes related to treatment have some weaknesses along the clinical process and patient's treatment like cultural norms, insufficient attention to health education and a lack of referral to registered dietitians, economic disincentives to healthier lifestyles and so on. These barriers to prevention of hypertension continue to impede progress [3]. Another problem found is the low level compliance with prescribed medical interventions by patients making health spending increases year after year [4].

Furthermore, patients believe that long-term antihypertensive drugs are not good for the body and sometimes they left medical treatment because they feel well. Some

C.R. García et al. (Eds.): UCAmI 2016, Part I, LNCS 10069, pp. 146–155, 2016.
DOI: 10.1007/978-3-319-48746-5_15

patients don't worry about their hypertension and symptoms are often associated with familiar symptoms as if the absence of them meant that blood pressure was controlled. There is also a lack of information provided directly from health professionals and patients often acquire that information from other sources like TV programs or magazines. Another weakness is the big gap between patients and physicians relationship. Most of the time of consultation, treatment are focused on medical prescription or general information instead of patient's own perception and sensations about their illness [5].

As the treatment of other chronic diseases, telemedicine has become an integral part of healthcare [6] and specifically telemonitoring allows remote data transmission from patient's home to health center. This new way of bringing medical care to the patient, has proved to be beneficial for empowering patients, influencing their attitudes and behaviors, increasing adherence to treatment and improving their medical condition [7].

There are some research in which devices like blood pressure device, smart wrist band or any wearable activities devices are connected to mobile apps in order to check some parameters like blood pressure, physical activities and so. All of them aim control health status of people but most of them have lack of integration with clinical process and they work standalone.

Healthcare processes require interdisciplinary cooperation and coordination, not only in organizational process oriented to communications between medical teams (doctors, nurses) but medical treatment process which are linked to patients. It is very important to use standard protocols like HL7 (Health Level 7) or DICOM (Digital and Communications in Medicine) to allow inter-organizational communications. Nevertheless, there is still a lack of functional integration due to disparate systems [8].

During decades, in other areas such as manufacturing and business, other strategies and paradigms have been developed for the continuous improvement of both, the processes oriented to client's satisfaction and process execution, involving models of great success and study. Business Process Management (BPM) is one of the most recent strategies of process management and also the one that has a significant impact. It is focused on the continuous improvement of business processes using information technology as one of its main principles in processes execution [9]. So far, in health issues, it has only been applied to the improvement of administrative processes.

The proposal and novelty of this paper focuses on a comprehensive redesign of the clinical process of hypertension, integrating telemedicine with a flexible, dynamic and agile business process management applied to clinical process. We use an integration of devices oriented to control hypertension through a mobile application and connected with a BPM model to the hypertension clinical process, in order to reduce the problems associated to the current clinical process, with the specific goal of improving the patient's empowerment and adherence to treatment while reducing the costs and errors associated to that process. More specifically, we focus on the redesign of the current treatment and monitoring process by implementing a new paradigm for the management of hypertension.

In this sense, in the following section we study the state of the art of the related research. Then, in Sect. 3 there is an analysis of the different guidelines which describe the Hypertension clinical process and its weakness in treatment and monitoring area. In Sect. 4 we propose an architecture system of devices used by patients to control some issues related to lifestyle, physical condition and blood pressure in order to integrate them through the clinical process which is modelled by the standard Business Process Model Notation (BPMN). Finally, in Sect. 5, the conclusions of this paper together with the future work are presented.

2   State of the Art

Nowadays, there are many factors to consider in order to monitor hypertension [10]. Measuring blood pressure is one of the major factors in current studies and techniques are based. The remote measurement of blood pressure through various devices connected to a smart device, is a current trend that benefits most patients. A large number of studies have reported improved blood pressure using mobile health (mHealth) solutions. In [11] they use a phone-based reminder application for patients who are using two prescriptions medications. This application works standalone without any integration with the clinical process. In [12] they tele-monitored blood pressure using a mobile device, and both patients and physicians were informed about data but the system was focused just on alerts not in the clinical process itself. That system do not inform about how to neutralize those alerts.

In order to improve patient's empowerment and their physical activities, there are some wearable devices which track people activities and can be used to measure their data. In [13] a smart wristband is used to empower patients to achieve their health goals, but the data collected is not integrated in the patient's clinical process.

There are some systems available on the market that collect and transmit the data using different ways. Among all existing wireless technologies today, Bluetooth and RFID technologies are most common used ones because they are user-friendly and not limited by patients' appliances [6]. Such technologies are available in many current devices (phones, tablets). Data transmission between devices and service portal server is usually achieved through a landline broadband or cellular network and security is ensured by encryption protocols (S-HTTP or S-FTP). The following Table 1 represents a summary of the most common devices used by people in order to improve their healthcare and lifestyle oriented to hypertension.

If we talk about management clinical process, current models focus on process-oriented IT technologies which have failed in meeting the requirements to integrate process support, information management and knowledge management. Current workflow management systems offer a promising approach for implementing site-specific, organizational processes, but there are still lots of features missing [8]. They still do not have the ability to cope flexibility, agility and continuous improvement required to optimize clinical processes.

BPM offers many of the features required in current clinical processes. This technology brings from concept, flexibility, availability and agility that are needed for both data and equipment physicians and patients are fully integrated in clinical processes [14, 15].

Table 1. Devices used to control hypertension parameters.

Brand	Model	Communication	App	Price	Modality	Device
Withings	Wireless blood pressure monitor	Bluetooth	- Mobile - Web - Cloud	130 €	Closed system	Blood pressure
A&D medicals	UA-767PBT-Ci	Bluetooth	- Mobile - PC - Web cloud	157 €	Closed system	Blood pressure
Angel sensor	m1	Bluetooth RFID/NFC	Mobile	99 $	Open system	Activity wristband
Xiaomi	My Band	Bluetooth	Mobile	27,99 $	Closed system	Activity wristband
Medisana	BS 440	Bluetooth	- Mobile - Web cloud	89 €	Closed system	Scales
A&D medicals	AD-6121A	Bluetooth	- mobile - pc - web cloud	520 €	Closed system	Scales

3   Hypertension Clinical Process

This section will deal with the discovery stage of the Hypertension clinical process and will have the goal of understanding and knowing thoroughly how such disease is currently managed (AS_IS process), what tasks are performed, who is responsible, and what roles are involved in them, in order to later analyze the weaknesses.

This study is based on the analysis of different medical guidelines, both worldwide the United Kingdom [10], United States [16] as an example of guides studied.

From the study it is gathered that, although all the guidelines define a group of common tasks, each of them establishes a series of subtasks or specific procedures according to the environment where the implementation is developed (geographic location, primary care centers, hospitals, etc.), which shows a lack of a *de facto* standard.

Besides, all these guidelines are presented as procedures (oriented to the development of the task itself) much more than as processes, which are centered in the patients and in how to add value to satisfy their needs.

The current Hypertension process involves several human teams participating in the different tasks, which implies the need of adequate coordination among them in order to avoid problems which could affect the patients.

When a person is diagnosed with hypertension, begins the treatment and monitoring process in order to control its blood pressure. That person has to be classified according to its symptoms. It involves some questionnaires, physical explorations and the physician takes blood pressure from time to time depending on the severity of their illness. It is possible that the patient has to initiate a drug treatment which is supervised regularly. All this treatment and monitoring process requires the patient to go to health center in person. The following Fig. 1 shows the hypertension clinical process as is.

Nowadays, the Hypertension clinical process in primary care centers has a large number of inefficiencies and weaknesses which, on the one hand, make the process have a higher cost for both, the patient and the health system, and, therefore, society. On the other hand, in most cases such weaknesses directly affect the patient's quality of life,

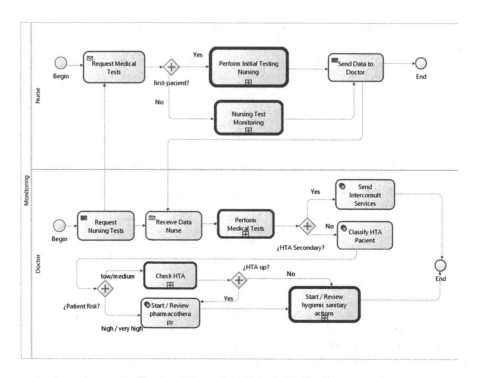

Fig. 1. Hypertension clinical process as is

empowerment and adherence to treatment and, therefore, cause dissatisfaction in the patient [5].

The goal of this section is to identify in which part of the process problems are produced and their causes, and, later, to set up a more efficient redesign of the process that reduces and focuses on the improvement of patient's quality of life and satisfaction. In order to do so, we have analyzed different studies which have allowed us to identify such problems and their possible causes.

One of the problems found is patients sometimes suffer from 'white coat' symptom which makes the securities are not real and have to be retested.

The lack of empowerment by patients in their treatment is another problem. They have no enough information about their illness and most of the times don't feel that they are really controlled. They just go from time to time to have a check at the primary health center and the physicians just prescribe the drugs avoiding other important aspects of them like how do they feel about their condition, changes in their lifestyles and so on.

Another problem detected in the time between one visit and another. The health teams just check the patient's health status when they come to the health center which often occurs after several months. Most of the times physicians and nurses don't know what happened between this period of time.

4 Proposed Architecture

Once the clinical process has been analyzed and its problems and weaknesses have been detected, we are going to describe the redesign and modeling the Hypertension treatment and monitoring subprocess. It is in this subprocess where most deficiencies are detected, which implies an additional cost, as well as a patient's lower satisfaction.

The treatment and monitoring subprocess comprises the patient's clinical evaluation, the blood pressure test, and other optional complementary tests each time they go to the primary health center.

Our proposal includes the full integration of measurement devices, smart devices, medical equipment and patients in the hypertension clinical process modelled by BPM.

First of all, measurement devices like blood pressure device, smart band and scale collect data from patients automatically. This devices have their own operating interface, easy to use by patients. Once the data is collected, it is sent to a smart device like a smart mobile or tablet through Bluetooth or Wifi communication.

The smart devices have their own application which format the data in a standard way and can be shown to the patient to ensure the measurement is all right. These applications also guide the patient in the control and compliance objectives stipulated in its clinical process.

The information contained in the smart devices can follow two paths depending on whether it is a private or open application. Normally when patients use private applications, information is sent to a private cloud following the A1 path as shown in Fig. 2. The data center where the clinical process is running get the useful data by querying the private cloud following the A2 path.

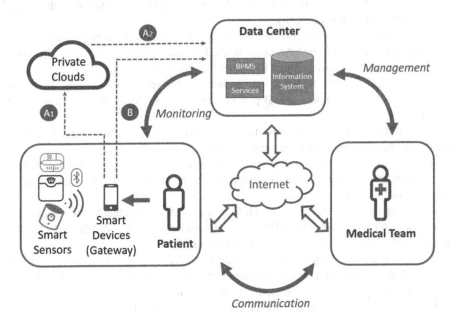

Fig. 2. Architecture device integration process

On the other hand, if patients use open applications, the information stored in the smart devices can be sent automatically to the data center avoiding private communication protocols. This solution is shown in Fig. 2 in the B path.

Once the data is stored in the data center, is automatically included into the clinical process. The clinical process is modelled by BPMN (Business Process Management Notation) and is implemented by a BPMS (Business Process Management Software).

In this way, the information is always available to all agents involved in the clinical process through an Internet connection. This allows monitoring of the patient in a personalized way, in addition to include changes in the clinical process in a more flexible, faster and more automated way. Thus, it gives a better response to changes in the patient personal monitoring in hypertension. Communication between patient and doctor also improves with this strategy since abnormalities are detected earlier and changes in treatment may be consulted by the patient in their smart device immediately. The following figure shows the architecture device integration process.

More specifically, our proposal involves using three devices that are connected to clinical process. These three devices collect information provided by the user in their day to day aspects such as weight, blood pressure and physical activity automatically.

It has been particularly used the MiBand wristband activity device to collect all relevant information from the patient's physical activity. The ease of use of this device is a factor to consider because the age of patients with hypertension is high and are often unfamiliar with technology. The wristband collects activities parameters automatically and send them to the smart device app through Bluetooth communication.

In order to collect blood pressure data we used the UA-767PBT-Ci blood pressure device from A&D Medical which it is clinically validated with ISO 13485:2003. This device is also very easy to use and sends the same way the information to the smart device via Bluetooth automatically.

Weight loss is another factor that positively affect control of hypertension, so we used the AD-6121A Scale from A&D Medicals. Just as the previous two devices it sends the data to the smart device through the Bluetooth communication.

Once the data from these devices are gathered in the smart device application, it is sent data directly to the portal (via B path) to integrate into the clinical process of the patient.

The format of the data to be sent to the platform would follow the standard HL7 specific for medical electronic communications.

As the patient data are sensitive data, it is necessary for communication between mobile platform and travel safely. In this way a layer of SSL-based secure communication would be used.

As part of the integrated process solution of clinical hypertension it has also redesigned the clinical process using BPMN. To implement the proposed solution, it is used an open BMP software called Bonita BPM Solution.

The patient no longer has to complete questionnaires in primary health centers and nurses and doctors do not have to be present in performing them. These are the patients themselves who previously completed the questionnaires and send them via the mobile application, so that the medical team has data automatically. This way you can use the time a patient is treated in physician's office to evaluate other aspects of hypertension. The following Fig. 3 shows the redesigned hypertension clinical process.

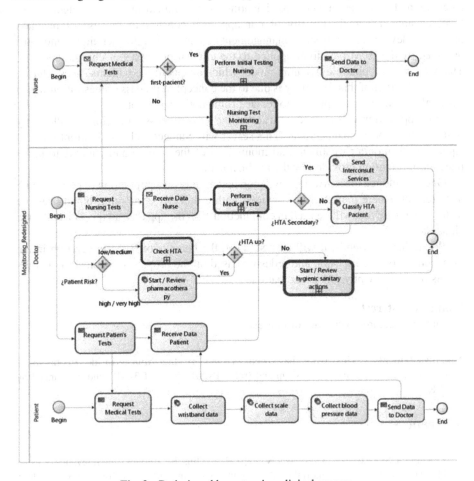

Fig. 3. Redesigned hypertension clinical process

5   Conclusions

As a consequence of a higher human life expectancy, the advances in medicine and in medical treatments have achieved that a high percentage of people may live longer, turning potentially deadly diseases into chronic diseases. Currently, national health systems bear a higher economic and management load derived from these chronic diseases, which imply high health expenditure.

The inefficiency problems in clinical processes of chronic diseases, and the lack of integration among medical staff, families and the process itself, are goals to be reached through the implementation of a BPM strategy.

Our proposal has focused on the application of a BPM strategy to the Hypertension clinical process, proposing a comprehensive management framework which coordinates, globally, all the elements participating in the clinical process management of Hypertension. The main novelty of our approach consists in the use of business processes, devices integration, IT management strategies, and the techniques and tools provided by the BPM paradigm applied to the clinical processes of chronic diseases. This way, we can obtain a dynamic model which adapts to the patients' needs during their disease. Part of this flexibility is due to the concept of process orchestration which easily allows, as a jigsaw puzzle, to replace some options with others.

This application will connect to a server business processes developed with Pretty Software for process management. This server will connect both the different medical equipment to monitor treatment and monitoring of the disease and patients to know relevant information provided by the medical teams.

Once developed the software, it will conduct a study on a population of patients with hypertension where they will be provided with a bracelet of activity, blood pressure meter and a scale that will be used in conjunction with the app to send the data collected along day.

When this track ends, it will be a study of the benefits of BPM integration in the management of hypertension and redesign based on the proposed architecture and the results obtained by physicians and patient.

Conflict of Interest
The authors declare no conflict of interest.

Acknowledgments. This work has been granted by the Ministerio de Economía y Competitividad of the Spanish Government (ref. TIN2014-53067-C3-1-R) and cofinanced by FEDER.

References

1. Lewington, S., Clarke, R., Qizilbash, N., Peto, R., Collins, R.: Age-specific relevance of usual blood pressure to vascular mortality: A meta-analysis of individual data for one million adults in 61 prospective studies. Lancet **360**, 1903–1913 (2002)
2. SEH-LELHA. http://www.seh-lelha.org/. Accessed 17 May 2016
3. Whelton, P.K., He, J., Appel, L.J., Cutler, J.A., Havas, S., Kotchen, T.A., Roccella, E.J., Stout, R., Vallbona, C., Winston, M.C., Karimbakas, J.: Primary prevention of hypertension: clinical and public health advisory from The National High Blood Pressure Education Program. JAMA **288**, 1882–1888 (2002)
4. Vermeire, E., Hearnshaw, H., Van Royen, P., Denekens, J.: Patient adherence to treatment: Three decades of research. a comprehensive review. J. Clin. Pharm. Ther. **26**, 331–342 (2001)
5. Gascon, J.J.: Why hypertensive patients do not comply with the treatment: Results from a qualitative study. Fam. Pract. **21**, 125–130 (2004)
6. Omboni, S., Ferrari, R.: The role of telemedicine in hypertension management: focus on blood pressure telemonitoring. Curr. Hypertens. Rep. **17**, 21 (2015)
7. AbuDagga, A., Resnick, H.E., Alwan, M.: Impact of blood pressure telemonitoring on hypertension outcomes: a literature review. Telemed. e-Health. **16**, 830–838 (2010)

8. Lenz, R., Reichert, M.: IT support for healthcare processes - premises, challenges, perspectives. Data Knowl. Eng. **61**, 39–58 (2007)

9. Smith, H., Fingar, P.: Business Process Management: The Third Wave. Meghan-Kiffer Press (2003)

10. Hypertension in adults: diagnosis and management. https://www.nice.org.uk/guidance/cg127/chapter/1-guidance. Accessed 20 May 2016

11. Patel, S., Jacobus-Kantor, L., Marshall, L., Ritchie, C., Kaplinski, M., Khurana, P.S., Katz, R.J.: Mobilizing your medications: an automated medication reminder application for mobile phones and hypertension medication adherence in a high-risk urban population. J. Diabetes Sci. Technol. **7**, 630–639 (2013)

12. Logan, A.G., McIsaac, W.J., Tisler, A., Irvine, M.J., Saunders, A., Dunai, A., Rizo, C.A., Feig, D.S., Hamill, M., Trudel, M., Cafazzo, J.A.: Mobile phone-based remote patient monitoring system for management of hypertension in diabetic patients. Am. J. Hypertens. **20**, 942–948 (2007)

13. Nelson, E.C., Verhagen, T., Noordzij, M.L.: Health empowerment through activity trackers: An empirical smart wristband study. Comput. Human Behav. **62**, 364–374 (2016)

14. Benyoucef, M., Kuziemsky, C., Rad, A.A., Elsabbahi, A.: Modeling healthcare processes as service orchestrations and choreographies. Bus. Process Manag. J. **17**, 568–597 (2011)

15. Bertolini, M., Bevilacqua, M., Ciarapica, F.E., Giacchetta, G.: Business process re-engineering in healthcare management: a case study. Bus. Process Manag. J. **17**, 42–66 (2011)

16. James, P.A., Oparil, S., Carter, B.L., Cushman, W.C., Dennison-Himmelfarb, C., Handler, J., Lackland, D.T., LeFevre, M.L., MacKenzie, T.D., Ogedegbe, O., Smith, S.C., Svetkey, L.P., Taler, S.J., Townsend, R.R., Wright, J.T., Narva, A.S., Ortiz, E.: 2014 evidence-based guideline for the management of high blood pressure in adults. JAMA **1097**, 1–14 (2013)

Change Point Detection Using Multivariate Exponentially Weighted Moving Average (MEWMA) for Optimal Parameter in Online Activity Monitoring

Naveed Khan[1(✉)], Sally McClean[1], Shuai Zhang[2], and Chris Nugent[2]

[1] School of Computing and Information Engineering,
Ulster University, Coleraine, UK
khan-n5@email.ulster.ac.uk, si.mcclean@ulster.ac.uk
[2] School of Computing and Mathematics, Ulster University, Jordanstown, UK
{s.zhang, cd.nugent}@ulster.ac.uk

Abstract. In recent years, wearable sensors are integrating frequently and rapidly into our daily life day by day. Such smart sensors have attracted a lot of interest due to their small sizes and reasonable computational power. For example, body worn sensors are widely used to monitor daily life activities and identify meaningful events. Hence, the capability to detect, adapt and respond to change performs a key role in various domains. A change in activities is signaled by a change in the data distribution within a time window. This change marks the start of a transition from an ongoing activity to a new one. In this paper, we evaluate the proposed algorithm's scalability on identifying multiple changes in different user activities from real sensor data collected from various subjects. The Genetic algorithm (GA) is used to identify the optimal parameter set for Multivariate Exponentially Weighted Moving Average (MEWMA) approach to detect change points in sensor data. Results have been evaluated using a real dataset of 8 different activities for five different users with a high accuracy from 99.2 % to 99.95 % and G-means from 67.26 % to 83.20 %.

Keywords: Multiple change points · Activity monitoring · Genetic algorithm · Accelerometer

1 Introduction

In the current era, the world is changing very fast in almost every aspects of life. Hence, the capability to detect, adapt and respond to change performs a key role in all aspects of life. The number of real world problems such as fault detection and diagnosis (monitoring) [1], quality control [2], natural catastrophic event prediction like earthquakes [3] and monitoring of context aware systems requires sequential detection of a change in the process. Activity monitoring is a key element of context aware systems. The primary use of such system within healthcare is to detect daily life activities and to monitor these over time. Body movement can be captured through wearable sensors such as accelerometers, gyrometers etc. to detect different transitions of movement from one

© Springer International Publishing AG 2016
C.R. García et al. (Eds.): UCAmI 2016, Part I, LNCS 10069, pp. 156–165, 2016.
DOI: 10.1007/978-3-319-48746-5_16

activity to another for activities such as walk, sit, stand, and run. The key issue is often the detection of abrupt change points from one activity level to another in real time systems [4]. Such abrupt change points can be very fast with respect to the sampling period of measurement. In real time system, online change detection algorithms are used to observe, monitor and evaluate data as soon as it becomes available. The objective of an online change detection algorithm is to detect a change in a sequence of random observations from a probability distribution. Also, online change detection algorithms are generally required to be fast and minimize false alarms. In activity monitoring such automatic change point detection is still a challenging task for researchers. The sensor data arrives continuously as sequential and fast data streams. Therefore, the algorithm should be lightweight to detect changes in sensor data and work efficiently under resource limited constraints [5]. Such in-time response can be useful in various scenarios such as to generate real world datasets or observing patient vital signs for example heart rate against various activities [6]. The detection problem can be evaluated on the basis of relative time constants of the process to be monitored on the sampling data. Moreover, the probability distribution over past and present intervals of time series data can be compared using change point detection techniques. However, specific strategy use in different techniques for detection of a particular change point to prompt an alarm as two distributions becomes significantly different [7].

In this paper, we evaluate our proposed technique Multivariate Exponentially Weighted Moving Average (MEWMA) on detecting multiple changes in activities on data collected from real sensor for various subjects on a number of different activities. In [8], we tuned different parameters of MEWMA manually to detect the change point between two user activities. However, in current work, we evaluate the algorithm for detecting multiple changes in user activities for various subjects. Also, the MEWMA incorporates an appropriate fitness function using a GA to automatically identify the optimal set of parameters for detecting multiple changes in the sensor data. The various parameters such as λ, window size and significance value are evaluated using genetic algorithm to find the optimal parameter set for MEWMA. The performance of the extracted optimal parameter for accurate change point detection were analyzed using different metric measures like accuracy, specificity, precision, sensitivity and G-Means. The remainder of this paper is structured as follows: in Sect. 2 Related work is presented. In Sect. 3 we provide an overview of our proposed approach and the experimental setup with results presented in Sect. 4. Finally, Conclusion and Future Work are presented in Sect. 5.

2 Related Work

In a real time scenario, the data is evolve continuously over time and can be analyzed adequately and appropriately as it become available. Nowadays, smart devices are used more frequently for online data collection in various domains. However, online data learning and evaluation of such data create considerable challenges for associated learning algorithms. Moreover, accurate change detection and in-time decision making from observed data is still an important problem that needs to be addressed. A numbers of algorithms have been discussed in the literature to detect changes in health sensor data. The Hidden Markov Models (HMM) have been used in [9] to detect change in streaming data. In this approach, an appropriate threshold value has been used for automated change detection. In the first step, the interrelationship is formed between two data streams through a time-invariant sequence of linear dynamic model. In the second step, the estimated parameters are modelled using HMM to evaluate the likelihood ratios for the new parameters. Finally, a change is flagged if the likelihood ratio is less than the given threshold. This technique requires quick probability estimation in two consecutive windows to detect changes in streaming data which comes from different distribution. The authors [10] have used a semiparametric log-likelihood criterion (SPLL) to detect change in multivariate streaming data. Additionally, the two well-known criterion Kullback-Leibler (K-L) distances and Hotelling's T-square have also been used together with SPLL. The experiments were performed on 30 real datasets for detecting change. The results have shown that SPLL performs better than K-L and Hotelling's T-square on both normalized and un-normalized data. A reactive clustering algorithm have been proposed in [11] to detect change in multivariate streaming data. The two overlapping windows were used to identify the change. The first window used a reference window to form a cluster and the second window used to capture the new incoming data. The distance between the incoming data and centre of the cluster is then calculated, and if it is greater, the new data point considered as a change. A drawback of this technique is the proper selection of window size according to the corresponding data. Moreover, the feature space, hypersphere and hypersphere radius have been used in support vector change point detection (SVCPD) algorithm [12] to identify the location and to detect change in the data stream. The advantage of SVCPD algorithm is to monitor and analyze each data point, and also compare the distance with current hypersphere models to accurately classify change points in the data stream. The authors have used Cumulative Sum Control Chart (CUSUM) [13] to monitor and detect small shifts in cardiovascular events using the process mean. Also, a number of primary methods have been used such as a process control approach, biometric methods and an online recognition approaches to analyze and evaluate physiological monitoring. Such multivariate analyses are crucial to investigate because the problem involves more than one variable which are correlated and observed simultaneously. Moreover, numerous parameter tuning has also been used to improve monitoring and detection of changes in user activity. Optimization is used for tuning input parameters to find the best solution from all feasible solutions. In the literature, the Genetic algorithm (GA) [14] has been used extensively for optimization problems to find and identify the optimum solution. The analysis of the literature review reflects that most algorithms requires prior knowledge of the characteristics of change points and the data stream's underlying distribution(s) which can be ineffective for our target application.

3 The Proposed Approach

3.1 Multivariate Exponentially Weighted Moving Average (MEWMA) Change Point Detection Algorithm

The Multivariate Exponentially Weighted Moving Average (MEWMA) is a statistical control method to monitor simultaneously two or more correlated variables and also provide sensitive detection of small and moderate shifts in time series data. The MEWMA statistic incorporates information of all prior data including historical and current observation with a user-defined weighted factor [15, 16]. Moreover, MEWMA can be used to detect shift of any size in the process. The MEWMA has achieved better performance to detect small and moderate changes than other multivariate control chart like the T-Square control chart [17]. It is described by the following equation.

$$\mathbf{Z}_i = \Lambda \mathbf{X}_i + (1 - \Lambda)\mathbf{Z}_{i-1} \qquad i = 1, 2, 3 \ldots n \qquad (1)$$

where $\mathbf{Z}_i$ is the ith MEWMA vector, Λ is the diagonal matrix with elements λ_i for $i = 1, \ldots, p$ where p is the number of dimensions and $0 < \lambda_i \leq 1$, and $\mathbf{X}_i$ is the ith input observation vector, $i = 1, 2, 3 \ldots n$. The out-of-control signal is defined in Eq. 2.

$$\mathbf{T}_i^2 = \mathbf{z}_i' \Sigma_i^{-1} \mathbf{z}_i < h \qquad (2)$$

where $\sum_i$ is the variance covariance matrix of $\mathbf{Z}_i$ and h (>0), chosen to achieve a specified in-control signal. The analysis of MEWMA is used to evaluate and monitor simultaneously two or more correlated variables and the inter-relationship among these variables. In multivariate analysis, the data points $\mathbf{x}_1, \mathbf{x}_2, \mathbf{x}_3 \ldots \mathbf{x}_n$ is a subsequence of a data stream where n is the length of the subsequence. The data points in the data stream may be from various distributions, for example, $\mathbf{x}_1, \mathbf{x}_2, \mathbf{x}_3 \ldots \mathbf{x}_{i-1}$ and $\mathbf{x}_1, \mathbf{x}_{i+1} \ldots \mathbf{x}_n$ can be from distributions D1 and D2 respectively. The algorithm's objective is to find and evaluate the location of the change points i in the time series data. MEWMA is applied to each data stream to calculate the exponentially weighted moving average of multivariate input observations in order to evaluate and find the location for change points. In our experiments, we incorporate sliding windows to perform sequential analysis of input data incremented by one within each window. Likewise, the MEWMA vector is calculated using input vectors and is represented by $\mathbf{Z}_i$ as shown in Eq. 1. Moreover, in order to find the T-squared, the variance-covariance matrix of $\mathbf{Z}_i$ is calculated recursively and is represented by $\sum_i$ as shown in Eq. 2. However, the significance value is used to classify the confidence of the entire window.

3.2 Genetic Algorithms

The Genetic Algorithm (GA) is a well-known heuristic search algorithm that inspired by the process of evolution in nature. The GA starts with a random number of variables that intelligently exploit the random search of individual solutions to solve the optimization problems. The GA searches to identify the fittest value among the individuals over successive generation of solutions [14]. Optimization is used for tuning input parameters to find the best solution form all feasible solutions. The GA used fitness function to find the optimal solution for a system. In the current scenario of our proposed work, the different combination of the three variables, namely λ, window size and significance value, is used to identify a single point in the population. The individual solutions "evolve" over consecutive generation to find the optimal solution. The fitness function is used in each iteration by the GA to evaluate the quality of all the proposed solutions to the problem in the current population. The fitness function evaluates how good a single solution in a population. The fitness function is the core component of a GA, which identifies the optimal fitness value after evaluating each individual in the population. In our fitness function, we initialize the population of vectors whose elements contains the λ value, window size and significance value. Here, our fitness function is chosen as G-means with a given range of input values. G-means is used as the measure to find the ratio and overall efficiency of an activity by combining sensitivity and specificity. It is defined as follows:

$$G\_means_{max} = max_{(\lambda, win\_size, sig\_value)}(G\_means_{MEWMA}) \tag{3}$$

where, λ ranges from 0.1 to 1 for each activity with corresponding significance values of 0.05, 0.01, 0.025, 0.005 and window sizes of 1 s, 2 s, 3 s, 4 s, 5 s and 6 s.

The following GA parameters are used in our experiments to maximize our fitness function and identify the optimal parameter set with maximum accuracy as shown in Table 1.

Table 1. GA Parameters

Parameters	GA
Population size	50
Selection	Stochastic uniform
Crossover rate	0.8
Mutation	Gaussian
Crossover	Heuristic
Generations	200

Our proposed model used Eq. 3 as the fitness function by initializing upper and lower bounds of the three parameters to find the maximum G-means with the optimal parameter set. After exploration with different GA parameter setting, the optimal GA parameter settings were chosen as shown in Table 1. These GA parameters are then used to maximize our fitness function and return the optimal best parameters with maximum G-Means.

4   Experimental Setup

A real accelerometer dataset was used to perform quantitative evaluation of change detection algorithm in human activity. The data set was collected from 5 participants consists of 3 males and 2 females. The shimmer sensing platform [18] integrated with three-axis accelerometer was used to collect the data. Each participant wore an accelerometer on the right ankle to collect the data from the accelerometer signals for various activities with a sample frequency of 102.4 Hz. The sampling rate is chosen by the Shimmer sensing platform. Also, the storage is supported by the Shimmer sensing platform and the data is transferred periodically to the computer via Bluetooth communication protocol. The change points detection and the evaluation were implemented in Matlab. To facilitate future work, additional shimmers were also placed on the participants' sternum and lower limb to facilitate evaluation and analysis of the optimal sensor placement for detecting changes in human activity.

The total eight activities were performed by each participant as presented in Table 2.

Table 2. Overview of activities in dataset

Activity Seq.	Label	Type	Description
1	Sit	Static	Sit for 5 min (m)
2	Sleep	Static	Lie on sofa for 5 m
3	Stand	Static	Standing still for 5 m
4	Stand to walk	Transitional	Stand for 10 s and walk for 5 s
5	Walk	Dynamic	Walk on treadmill at constant speed of 5 m
6	Run	Dynamic	Run on treadmill at constant speed of 5 m
7	Watch TV	Static	Sit on sofa for 5 m
8	Vacuum	Dynamic	Vacuum for 5 m

Each activity was carried out in the predefined order above with a rest period of one minute observed between each activity. The different activities were classified as either static, representing that each participant was asked to remain comfortably still such that small natural movements were allowed, or dynamic representing purposeful human movement. The change points were manually labelled in a controlled environment by a human expert. Moreover, if a participant was unable to complete the tasks in succession they were allowed to rest with the start and end time recorded and the relevant sensor data subsequently removed from the dataset. The resultant dataset contains a continuous data stream of approximately 35 min for each participant with the activities performed according to the order in Table 2. There are 7 labelled changes for each participant as a result of the change of activities.

4.1 Results Evaluation

This section evaluates the performance of the MEWMA for change detection where GA was applied on the real dataset to identify the optimal parameter set. The MEWMA algorithm is applied and the calculated vector is used to detect changes in the data stream. The different performance measures such as accuracy, precision, sensitivity and specificity and G-means were used to evaluate change point detection in activity monitoring. The detected change point is classified as true if in the data the index i, $i \in \{z - (f/4), \ldots \ldots z + (f/4)\}$ where f is the sampling frequency in Hz and z indicates the index of manually label change in the data stream. The target of our proposed approach is to find and detect the primary change point in different activities such as sit, stand, walk, sleep, run, vacuum and watching TV as shown in Fig. 1.

The x, y and z acceleration magnitude is calculated form input observation and used as input to MEWMA. The different parameters of MEWMA were analyzed initially; λ (0.1 to 1), window size (1 s, 2 s, 3 s, 4 s, 5 s. 6 s) and significance values (0.005, 0.01, 0.025, 0.05) in order to evaluate and find the accurate change point. Moreover, following this, in offline mode, the GA is used to find the optimal parameter set for MEWMA.

The positive and negative detection is defined as; true positive (TP) is the correctly classified change points, false positive (FP) is non-transitional point but algorithm detect it as a change. The True negative (TN) is the non-transitional points and not labelled as change while false negative (FN) is the transitional change points missed by detection algorithm. The real dataset example of subject 3 for change detection using MEWMA for different activities are shown in Fig. 1.

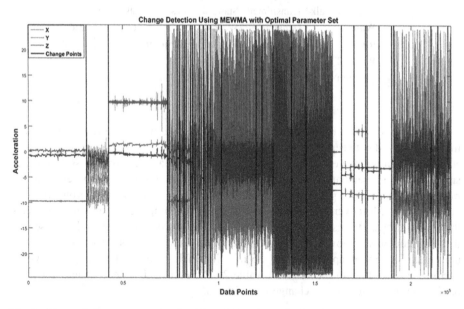

Fig. 1. The real dataset example of subject 3 for change point detection using MEWMA in different activities. The vertical black lines identify change points detected by our algorithm.

Table 3 presents the results of the model performances and the best combination of optimal parameter set (λ, window sizes and significance values) for MEWMA using the GA for 5 subjects performing 8 different activities. The values presented here are the optimal values derived from the GA that optimize our fitness function.

The accuracy, precision, specificity, sensitivity and G-means metrics were used for evaluation of optimal parameter selection for MEWMA algorithm. The accuracy is the ratio of correctly classified data point over the total data points. However, the precision is the ratio of true positive over true positive plus false positive.

The highest accuracy achieved is about 99.2 % to 99.5 % of window size (3 s, 4 s and 5 s), λ (0.6 & 0.7) and $p = 0.05$ for the optimal parameter set using GA of all subjects with 8 different activities. However, the maximum precision range from 20 % to 33 % for the same optimal set of parameters as presented in Table 3. The reason for low precision is due to the high number of occurrences of false alarms as our algorithm is very sensitive and detects possible change points even if they are small. Likewise, the specificity and sensitivity are used to find and measure the proportion of correctly classified negative and positive detection in the data.

The highest specificity and sensitivity achieved is about 91.50 % to 97.50 % and 55 % to 71 % of window size (3 s, 4 s and 5 s), λ (0.6 & 0.7) and p = 0.05 for the optimal parameter set using GA as presented in Table 3. The specificity is used to identify the performance of an algorithm with regard to accurate prediction. The results show that our proposed approach achieved higher specificity and made accurate prediction. However, the sensitivity was dropped slightly because our algorithm missed few true change points which were classified as false negative. Moreover, G-means is the combination of sensitivity and specificity and is used to find the ratio of positive and negative accuracy of the data and calculated using Eq. 4.

$$\sqrt{sensitivity \times specificity} = \sqrt{\frac{TP}{TP+FN} \times \frac{TN}{TN+FP}} \tag{4}$$

The highest G-means achieved is about 67.26 % to 83.20 % of the window size (3 s, 4 s and 5 s) and $p = 0.05$ for the optimal parameter set using GA as presented in Table 3. The G-means are used as fitness functions for the GA to find the optimal parameter set for MEWMA algorithm.

Table 3. MEWMA optimal parameter set using GA for 5 different subjects on real dataset

Optimal Parameters by GA				Model Performances				
Participants	Win Size	Significance value	λ	Accuracy %	Precision %	Specificity %	Sensitivity %	G-Means %
Subject1	3 s	0.05	0.7	99.92	25	91.50	55	70.94
Subject2	4 s		0.7	99.94	20	90.50	50	67.26
Subject3	5 s		0.6	99.95	33	97.50	71	83.20
Subject4	4 s		0.6	99.94	30	96.25	62	77.25
Subject5	5 s		0.7	99.95	28	95.75	57	73.90

Overall, we have achieved good results for different metrics except for the low precision. Our focus is to find the change points so our proposed approach detects every potential change point which can cause a relatively large number of false alarms resulting in low precision. This might not be a major issue for us but we still plan to address it further in future work. This issue of low precision is partly due to the class imbalance problem in our dataset, which we plan to explore in our future work via the online Bagging and Boosting algorithm [19]. Hopefully such an approach can improve the precision while maintaining the good performance on our performance metrics.

5 Conclusion

The GA is used to identify an optimal parameter set for MEWMA to successfully detect multiple change points in different user activities. The different parameters of MEWMA are optimized using the GA to find the maximum G-means and identify the optimal parameter set for each subject's activities. The optimal parameter set has achieved good results for most performance metric considered. The potential of the algorithm is to adjust the individual changes and learn through time irrespective of the individual patterns. The collection of data is expansive and time consuming. Moreover, the real data is used in our experiments and trying to evaluate the prototype of the algorithm that gives the promising results which opens up opportunities to be tested on more subjects. In the future we will explore the low precision problem and try to improve it. Also, the class imbalance problem will also be analyzed for the existing dataset. Moreover, different datasets will be used for evaluation with multiple change points.

References

1. Fabien Meinguet, E.S., Kestelyn, X., Mollet, Y., Gyselinck, J.: Change-detection algorithm for short-circuit fault detection in closed-loop AC drives. IET Electr. Power Appl. **8**, 165–177 (2014)
2. Evan, R.H.W., Brooks, B., Thomas, V.A., Blinn, C.E., Coulston, J.W.: On-the-Fly massively multitemporal change detection using statistical quality control charts and landsat data. IEEE Trans. Geosci. Remote Sens. **52**, 3316–3332 (2014)
3. Brunner, D., Bruzzone, L., Lemoine, G.: Change detection for earthquake damage assessment in built-up areas using very high resolution optical and SAR imagery. In: 2010 IEEE International Geoscience and Remote Sensing Symposium (IGARSS) 2010, pp. 3210–3213 (2010)
4. Basseville, M., Nikiforov, I.V.: Detection of Abrupt Changes: Theory and Application, vol. 104. Prentice Hall, Englewood Cliffs (1993)
5. Gama, J., Gaber, M.M.: Learning from Data Streams: Processing Techniques in Sensor Networks, vol. 21. Springer, New York (2007)
6. Cleland, I., Han, M., Nugent, C., Lee, H., Zhang, S., McClean, S., Lee, S.: Mobile based prompted labeling of large scale activity data. In: Nugent, C., Coronato, A., Bravo, J. (eds.) IWAAL 2013. LNCS, vol. 8277, pp. 9–17. Springer, Heidelberg (2013)
7. Darkhovski, B.S.: Nonparametric methods in change-point problems: a general approach and some concrete algorithms. In: Carlstein, E., Muller, H.-G., Siegmund, D. (eds.) Change-point Problems, vol. 23, pp. 99–107. Institute of Mathematical Statistics, Hayward (1994)

8. Khan, N., McClean, S., Zhang, S., Nugent, C.: Parameter optimization for online change detection in activity monitoring using multivariate exponentially weighted moving average (MEWMA). In: Ubiquitous Computing and Ambient Intelligence. Sensing, Processing, and Using Environmental Information, pp. 50–59 (2015)

9. Alippi, C., Ntalampiras, S., Roveri, M.: An HMM-based change detection method for intelligent embedded sensors. In: The 2012 International Joint Conference on Neural Networks (IJCNN), pp. 1–7 (2012)

10. Kuncheva, L.I.: Change detection in streaming multivariate data using likelihood detectors. IEEE Trans. Knowl. Data Eng. **25**, 1175–1180 (2013)

11. Tran, D.-H.: Automated Change Detection and Reactive Clustering in Multivariate Streaming Data, arXiv preprint arXiv:1311.0505 (2013)

12. Vlasveld, R.: Temporal Segmentation using Support Vector Machines in the context of Human Activity Recognition, pp. 1–85 (2014)

13. Zhang, S., Galway, L., McClean, S., Scotney, B., Finlay, D., Nugent, C.D.: Deriving relationships between physiological change and activities of daily living using wearable sensors. In: Par, G., Morrow, P. (eds.) S-CUBE 2010. LNICST, vol. 57, pp. 235–250. Springer, Heidelberg (2011)

14. McCall, J.: Genetic algorithms for modelling and optimisation. J. Comput. Appl. Math. **184**, 205–222 (2005)

15. Khoo, M.B.: An extension for the univariate exponentially weighted moving average control chart. Matematika **20**, 43–48 (2004)

16. Pan, X., Jarrett, J.E.: The Multivariate EWMA model and health care monitoring. Int. J. Econ. Manage. Sci. **3**, 176 (2014)

17. Hotelling, H.: Multivariate quality control. Techniques of statistical analysis (1947)

18. Shimmer: Shimmer Wearable Sensing Technology. http://www.shimmersensing.com/. Accessed April 2016

19. Wang, S., Minku, L.L., Yao, X.: A learning framework for online class imbalance learning. In: 2013 IEEE Symposium on Computational Intelligence and Ensemble Learning (CIEL), pp. 36–45 (2013)

Improving Learning Tasks for Mentally Handicapped People Using AmI Environments Based on Cyber-Physical Systems

Diego Martín[1(✉)], Borja Bordel[1], Ramón Alcarria[2], Álvaro Sánchez-Picot[1], Diego Sánchez de Rivera[1], and Tomás Robles[1]

[1] ETSI Telecommunications, Technical University of Madrid,
Av. Complutense 30, 28040 Madrid, Spain
{diego.martin.de.andres,tomas.robles}@upm.es, bbordel@dit.upm.es,
alvaro.spicot@gmail.com, diego.sanchezderiveracordoba@gmail.com
[2] ETSI Topography, Geodetics and Cartography, Technical University of Madrid,
Camino de la Arboleda s/n, 28031 Madrid, Spain
ramon.alcarria@upm.es

Abstract. In this research work it is presented a preliminary prototype for an ambient intelligence scenario based on cyber-physical systems for improving learning tasks. The system proposed is composed of a cyber-glove, a worktable (both with RFID and NFC detection zones) and a AmI software application for modeling and workflow guidance. The authors carried out a case study where 12 mentally handicapped people and 3 trainers were involved executing workflows creation and performing and controlling tasks. The results obtained indicate that this kind of solutions are feasible, but due to the problem complexity and to the fact that the proposed solution is a preliminary version, we have found many issues to be solved in next versions. This research helped us to uncover these issues and design a better system.

Keywords: Task learning · Ambient intelligence · Mentally handicapped · Cyber-physical systems · Cyber-glove · Worktable · ehealth

1 Introduction

In this paper we present an ambient intelligence (AmI) system based on cyber-physical systems for tracking tasks. The CPS presented in this research work are a cyber-glove, a worktable and a AmI software for creating and control workflows, whose tasks involve actions about the cyber-glove and the worktable. This system is framed in a research project funded by a grant from Madrid Autonomous Community called SEMOLA. Currently this research project is in a preliminary phase so the developments done are also at a exploratory stage. The whole system is called LAoCA, an acronym from "Learning Architecture over CPS and AmI".

© Springer International Publishing AG 2016
C.R. García et al. (Eds.): UCAmI 2016, Part I, LNCS 10069, pp. 166–177, 2016.
DOI: 10.1007/978-3-319-48746-5_17

In order to guide this research work three research questions were stated:

- **RQ1:** Can an AmI environment for CPS traceability facilitate learning for mentally handicapped people?
- **RQ2:** Does it improve control over the performed tasks?
- **RQ3:** Is LAoCA accepted by the final users?

A case study was carried out by the authors in order to validate the environment and the solution proposed in this paper; where twelve mentally handicapped people with Down syndrome from the one of the most important foundations for mentally handicapped people in Spain, were involved. The validation consisted of studying the improvement of participants' learning capabilities, analyzing the system's control of the tasks performed using the cyber-glove and the worktable and a survey about the final user acceptance of the system.

The results obtained are very promising confirming that the proposed solution is feasible, but as it is a preliminary version. This first validation allowed us to find weaknesses in the proposal with the aim of improving it, in following versions and improve the design validation for future experiments.

2   Related Work

As mentioned by Bordel [3], this research work assumed the fact that CPS paradigm fits perfectly with traceability solutions. The proposal of this research work consists of movements traceability using a cyber-glove, a worktable and a workflow software. In this section a brief review of the related work is presented where three research areas regarding to traceability systems were studied. These research areas are:

Automated Industrial Processes. The use of control systems in manufacturing and energy automation systems increased on recent years. E.g. the German Engineering Federation calculated the ratio of the cost of control software with regarding to the cost of machinery, and the ratio has doubled from 20 % to 40 % in a decade [21] The International Electrotechnical Commission (IEC) [7] and Automation Research Corporation (ARC) [1] advisory group described automation products as heterogeneous solutions based on proprietary technologies which difficultly may be integrated each other (excluding certain proposals such as OPC - Object Linking and Embedding for Process Control [18]). The approach presented in this research work was designed as a complete and integrated solution including all the requirements needed for automated industrial processes; allowing a reduction in the system's complexity, and therefore, reducing the investment. The automated industrial systems require experienced workers in software engineering and industrial processes able to program low-level languages as PLC [9,23]. Therefore, to avoid low-level programming systems and enable the domain experts to implement ideas in such systems; it will be a requirement for the proposal presented, the use of visual systems for programming, such as end-user development systems or prosumer systems. [15–17] Embedded devices designed for traceability solutions environments normally used a fixed network architecture model; making it impossible to monitor workers, reorganize the machine distribution or change devices easily [4,8].

Cyber-physical Systems. One of the most important requirements of the proposal presented in this paper is to collect data in real-time efficiently; including adaptation capabilities. Since 2010, a new theoretical framework appear for this kind of systems: tne "cyber-physical systems" (CPS) [12]. In this proposal, CPSs are understood as several elements with communication capabilities for real-time processing. The research challenges of this work are related to computing problems with devices with low resources [22] (although the research about CPS has moved to vertical issues such as communications, networking, data services, pattern recognition and decision making). In this field it's necessary to take into account the reference architecture by the National Institute of Standards and Technology (NIST); proposing that cyber-physical Systems or 'smart' systems are co-engineered interacting networks of physical and computational components. [20] This proposal offers a new standard for commercial products based on CPS.

Learning systems based on CPS. In the last five years, the CPS paradigms have been applied to many different fields, form traceability solutions and industrial systems to pervasive computing solutions. Among all these proposals, learning systems are one of the most remarkable. In particular, several works try to infer the Activities of Daily Living [10] performed by users using a sort of RFID-enabled cyber-glove [14] (possibly complemented with additional sensors such as accelerometers [2]). The applications of these systems are mainly focused on occupational therapy [6] for neurological patients; childrens control, augmented reality [11] and behavioral therapy [5]; and accessibility (such as the system SignAloud proposed by the MIT [13]).

3   LAoCA - Learning Architecture over CPS and AmI

In this section we present a preliminary development framed within a research project called SEMOLA (2016–2019), funded by a grant from Madrid Autonomous Community. Among the many specific objectives of the SEMOLA project we developed a prototype to test the technology to support people with intellectual disabilities in their personal development, taking timely remedial actions and anticipating problems that can be found. Thus, we will generate enough knowledge for the upcoming project phases, such as lessons learned, best practices, etc.

Our *LAoCA* (Learning Architecture over CPS and AmI) prototype is composed of three elements: a cyber-glove, a worktable for tracing the items and an AmI software aplications for creating, managing workflows and also controlling the actions performed with the whole system. All components are connected by means of a Bluetooth network with star topology, acting the AmI application as central element. Bluetooth 3.0 technology allows creating ad hoc networks with a valuable data rate (until 3Mbps), which perfectly fit with the real-time requirements of **LAoCA**. In the next sub-setion we are reviewing in detail each cited component.

3.1 Cyber-Glove

Figure 1 shows the prototype of the cyber-glove proposed in this research paper. It is made of cloth and it has a compartment where all the necessary electronics for its operation are stored (see Fig. 2). This compartment can be positioned below or above the wrist in order to facilitate hand movements. The main functionality of the cyber-glove is to be a device capable of identifying objects tagged with RFID or NFC wirelessly and having communication capabilities with the software that controls and manages the movements. In summary, the cyber-glove may detect any object touched or taken by users and send the information immediately to the management software. The cyber-glove may also detect the moment when the user releases the object (if he held it) informing to he management software. The cyber-glove cannot detect two or more objects touched at the same time.

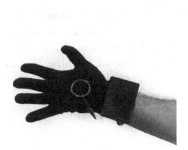

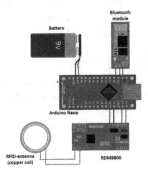

Fig. 1. Cyber-glove   **Fig. 2.** Cyber-glove electronics schema

The electronics of the cyber-glove consists of several elements as seen in Fig. 2: an Arduino Nano for data processing, a RDM8800 NFC chip for reading the RFID and NFC elements, a HC-06 Bluetooth module for communicating with the control program, a coil in the palm that works as antenna for reading RFID and NFC elements, and a battery.

3.2 Worktable

In this section we present a worktable made of plastic with four detection zones as seen in Fig. 3. The main purpose for which the worktable was designed is to identify objects (tagged with RFID or NFC) placed in the four detection

Fig. 3. Worktable with four detection zones and NFC tags.

zones and transmit that information wirelessly in real time to the control program. It also may detect the moment when an object previously placed over the worktable is removed. The worktable also includes some actuators in order to interact with the users and inform them about the execution of the planned tasks (see Sect. 3.3). The electronics of the worktable are composed by: four printed coils working as antennas which sense the four detection areas; four RDM8800 RFID and NFC readers (one for each detection area); five Arduinos Nano, four dedicated to manage the four antennas and the last one acting as main microcontroller in the system; a bluetooth module for its communication with the control software: four green LEDs (one for each detection zone) used to illuminate the detection surface and additional three LEDs indicators (actuators) for showing its operation and giving some feedback to the user. The surface LEDs are used to describe the task to be performed at an earlier stage of training. Figure 4 shows an inside view of the worktable, while Fig. 5 shows the electronic schema of the worktable.

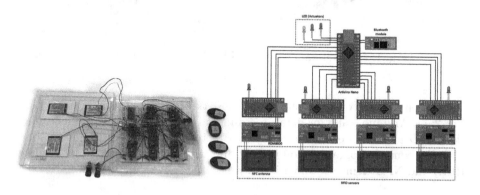

Fig. 4. Electronics inside the worktable   **Fig. 5.** Worktable electronics schema

3.3   Workflow Creation and Control Software

The workflow creation and control software is an ambient intelligent tool for creating and managing workflows made of different tasks (such as position control or state monitor manage) involving the tagged objects with RFID and NFC through the cyber-glove and the worktable. The different tasks are related by means of some "transitions" which are triggered if the associated condition is fulfilled.

This software has two main features: (a) it models the workflow of the task intended to execute, using a *prosumer* interface that allows a user with no programming experience to model the tasks and (b) it also executes the control workflows previously created in order to supervise and analyze the actions performed by a user who is working with the cyber-glove and the worktable.

For workflow creation, the AmI tool includes a graphic environment where users may compose their own workflows using different predesigned modules. In respect to the second functionality (workflow control), the software permanently is hearing for the information from the cyber-glove and/or the worktable. It evaluates the notifications and triggers the proper transitions (if any exists). Every workflow should include a "fatal error tasks" to which the workflow moves if the execution fails. Besides, a "sucessfully finished task" would be advisable to be included. In Fig. 6 we present an example workflow, indicating the described desiderable structure.

Additionally, the AmI software transmits towards the worktable information about the workflow evolution. Then, the worktable can show that information (using the actuators -LEDs-) to the users (for example, if the workflow finshes with a fatal error, a red RED will be turn on).

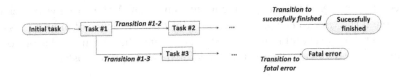

Fig. 6. Example workflow

4   Experimental Validation

This research work has been guided by three research questions presented in the introduction. We designed and performed a case study where twelve mentally handicapped people performed some tasks, defined and supervised by three trainers from a Foundation committed to people with intellectual disabilities. The validation presented in this research work is a preliminary action framed in the early years of development of a the SEMOLA project. Our goal is to test the feasibility of LAoCA; and with the results obtained, improve it with a new deployment at the Foundation and extend the experimentation with more people involved. The researchers did not influence participants using the prosumer environment. This approach is appropriate to replicate the experiment in similar contexts.

4.1   Context

The authors of this research work (hereafter, experts) designed, executed, and assessed the case study, whose research areas are cyber-physical systems, ambient intelligence, knowledge management, etc.

Twelve mentally handicapped people from the Foundation (hereafter, participants) participated in the experimentation performing 4 tasks each, and three trainers from the same foundation helped in training the participants in some tasks using the software for workflow modeling of LAoCA.

4.2   Planning

The experimentation plan was executed in four phases:

- *Training phase*: Trainers received some instructions about the use and operation of the CPS presented in the paper with the aim to train the participants about the use of the cyber-glove and to perform some tasks with it. The training sessions consisted of a one-hour lecture at the beginning of the experimental validation given by one of the experts.
- *Tasks performing*: The participants executed four different tasks, two of them were done using LAoCA and the other two without it. At the beginning of each task, the system showed the sequence of movements through the LEDs of the detection surface. For the experiment without LAoCA the coach was in charge to explain the task to the participants. A task is a sequence of movements over the worktable of several tagged objects. Following the recommendations of the trainers, for this experimentation we defined two types of tasks:

1. Task composed of five movements of only one tagged object
2. Task composed of three movements of each two tagged objects

All the tasks were randomly generated.

-*Data evaluation phase*: In this phase the trainers were asked about the participants' impressions about the use of the system by the experts. They also helped to asses 48 tasks performed by the participants.

4.3   Data Collection

The data gathered to answer *RQ1* were obtained from the software that guided the tasks and the notes taken by the experts during the *"Tasks performing phase"*. We measured the number of errors made by the participants. For example a wrong movement or moving the wrong object is considered an error. The data collected to address *RQ2* was obtained from the control software and workflow guidance of LAoCA and the perception from the trainers; at first, a survey was considered to ask the trainers, but due to the small number of them we opted for oral interviews. The information to answer *RQ3* was obtained through surveys filled by the trainers after evaluating each participant.

5 Result

In this section we present the results obtained from the case study. The data and information will be presented trying to answer the three research questions:

Can an AmI environment for CPS traceability facilitate learning for mentally handicapped people? In this section we compare the results from the validation phase where the participants learnt 4 tasks; two of them using our proposal and the other two learnt by the standard way with the help of the trainer and without the use of our proposal. Figure 7 shows the number or total errors for the tasks guided with LAoCA and without it. The median number of errors using LAoCA is 1.58 while the median of errors without it is 2.04. The values are very close, so we carried out a Mann-Whitney-U test in order to check whether the participants perform less errors by using LAoCA. The test was negative ($\rho > 0.05$) and we can not confirm that hypothesis. The first impression from Fig. 7 is that using LAoCA, the number of errors are reduced, but the median of both sets is very close.

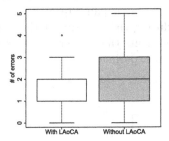
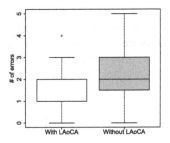

Fig. 7. Errors for all tasks   **Fig. 8.** Errors for tasks type 2

However, we performed a further study analyzing the results for each type of task. During the execution of the experiment and analyzing the data obtained, we realized that the task two, despite being more complex, the participants obtained better results compared with the same type of task without using LAoCA. Figure 8 shows two boxplots with the results only for the task type two. In this case the median for the case of using LAoCa was 1.42 instead of 2.33 from the other case; we performed another Mann-Whitney-U test in order to confirm the hypothesis and the result was positive ($\rho < 0.05$).

But looking at Figs. 7 and 8, the samples for the errors using LAoCA in both cases (all the tasks' types and only type 2) are quite similar, the difference is the samples for the errors performed without using LAoCA. So, we can state that errors increase when not using LAoCA.

Does it improve control over the performed tasks? To answer this research question we have received the opinion of the trainers who helped us to carry out the experimentation of this research. Although we only had the information provided by three trainers his opinion has been very valuable. In their opinion the greatest contribution of this system is the possibility of tracing object movements on the worktable and the ability of recording, analyzing and, even though it is not the focus of this research project, that information can be served over the Internet in real time. Therefore, and in the opinion of trainers, LAoCA enables control and tracking capabilities; but as demonstrated by experimentation, it must be improved. These future improvements, further LAoCA versions and experiments will be discussed in next section.

Is LAoCA accepted by the final users? This section describes the analysis of the satisfaction perceived by the users. In this experiments we had two kinds of users: participants and trainers. Participants were asked by trainers on two questions on the use of LAoCA: satisfaction and stress; while trainers were asked about satisfaction and relevance. The results of the trainers were not representative, as we had the cooperation of only three people; although they showed great satisfaction in its use. Figure 9 shows that the overall evaluation of the participants for satisfaction was positive, with a mean value of 4.2; but nevertheless there were high scores for the stress measurements. According to the opinions of their trainers, this is because the participants reacted badly to the pressure of the experimentation because during the experiment there were five people unknown to them. For future experiments the trainers suggested us to become familiar with them before running an experiment.

Fig. 9. Satisfaction evaluation

6   Discussion and Future Work

This paper presents a development and a preliminary experimentation done in one of the most important foundations for mentally handicapped people in Spain;

these works are framed in a project called SEMOLA funded by a grant from Madrid Autonomous Community. The development, called LAoCA, is composed of three main elements: a cyber-glove, a worktable and a software for modeling and executing workflows. LAoCA is an AmI development based on CPS techniques. A case study was carried out with the participation of twelve mentally handicapped people and their trainers in order to give answers to the research questions presented in this work; and we are going to use them in order to guide this section:

Can an AmI environment for CPS traceability facilitate learning for mentally handicapped people? As seen on previous section, some of the learning tasks were improved, particularly, those most difficult since two objects and six movements come into play. While the other tasks did not suffer any significant improvement. Using a classical training participants had trouble completing the most complex tasks, however, using LAoCA they performed less errors. For this reason, we can assume that an AmI system based on CPS techniques can be useful for learning tasks for mentally handicapped people.

However, we have found very important problems to be solved. LAoCA is a prototype and it was developed as such, meaning that the graphical interface is not very usable for the participants. The tagged objects selected for the experiment were in fact laboratory instruments for testing as seen in Figs. 3, 4 and 10. The trainers remarked these facts at the beginning of experimentation. In order to improve the results and as a proposal from trainers, for the following versions of LAoCA we will develop more visually attractive objects or we will use familiar objects. The same applies to the worktable whose detection areas are named from A to D, identification not very adequate for participants. We suggest converting the detection surface into something more visual, using projections on the surface, a smart blackboard or e-ink displays. Therefore the main objective for the new version of LAoCA is to turn it into something more attractive and realistic.

Fig. 10. Example of one tagged object

Does it improve control over the performed tasks? Trainers concluded that the worktable is a good solution for control tasks and traceability. But we did not get enough data in the research presented in this article. That is why for future experiments we must find more trainers to help us conclude firmest statements. For example, trainers suggested us the design of a new kind of tasks: the specific tasks. In this research we have worked with abstract tasks i.e. "Move object 2 from position A to C". Specific tasks are concerned with everyday tasks such as: "leave the toothbrush on the glass"; this suggestion is close to the work of Philipose [19]. This new perspective means a qualitative sensorization and communication challenge.

Is LAoCA accepted by the final users? Results suggested that these techniques are valid for traceability scenarios with mentally handicapped people. We had a problem with subjective measurement of stress coming from a lack of familiarity with the participants. For future experiments we propose two solutions: The first one is to create a familiar atmosphere with participants and the second consists to introduce new sensors to measure stress, blood pressure, sweat, etc. With these new sensors we could know if the participant is suffering stress and we could stop the experimentation. Another suggestion from the trainers consists of selecting for the study people with the same level of mental disability, to obtain less dispersed data. This research work was not focused on the behavior of trainers, for that reason we propose to analyze the ability of trainers to model tasks with software to create workflows in LAoCA.

The main objective of LAoCA is to trace the movements of RFID and NFC tagged objects over the worktable and the cyber-glove. After running the experiment, we have noticed that it involves a lot of randomness due to the human behavior, especially if we are dealing with people with mental disabilities. For that reason, erroneous measurements, mistakes and false events can occur. We proposed to add more cybernetic devices and sensors (such as biometric sensors) for measurement in order to obtain better values. This will happen for future developments and versions of LAoCA. With more information provided by these new devices and using proper algorithm we expect more accurate measurements.

Acknowledgement. The research leading to these results has received funding from the Ministry of Economy and Competitiveness through SEMOLA project (TEC2015-68284- R)

References

1. ACR Advisory Group: Automation and software expenditures. for discrete industries (2015). http://www.arcweb.com/market-studies/pages/automation-expenditures-for-discrete-industries.aspx
2. Atallah, L., Lo, B., King, R., Yang, G.Z.: Sensor positioning for activity recognition using wearable accelerometers. Biomed. Circuits Syst. IEEE Trans. 5(4), 320–329 (2011)
3. Bordel Sánchez, B., Alcarria, R., Martín, D., Robles, T.: Tf4sm: A framework for developing traceability solutions in small manufacturing companies. Sensors 15(11), 29478–29510 (2015)
4. Erl, T.: Service-Oriented Architecture (SOA): Concepts, Technology, and Design. Prentice Hall, Upper Saddle River (2005)
5. Escobedo, L., Ibarra, C., Hernandez, J., Alvelais, M., Tentori, M.: Smart objects to support the discrimination training of children with autism. Pers. Ubiquit. Comput. 18(6), 1485–1497 (2014)

6. Hallam, J., Whiteley, V.: Interactive therapy gloves: reconnecting partners after a stroke. In: CHI 2011 Extended Abstracts on Human Factors in Computing Systems, pp. 989–994. ACM (2011)

7. International Electrotechnical Commission: ANSI/ISA-95.00.01-2010 (IEC 62264-1 Mod) Enterprise-Control System Integration - Part 1: Models and Terminology.ANSI/ISA (2010)

8. Jammes, F., Smit, H.: Service-oriented paradigms in industrial automation. Ind. Inform. IEEE Trans. 1(1), 62–70 (2005)

9. Jimenez, M., Rosique, F., Sanchez, P., Alvarez, B., Iborra, A.: Habitation: a domain-specific language for home automation. Softw. IEEE 26(4), 30–38 (2009)

10. Katz, S., Ford, A.B., Moskowitz, R.W., Jackson, B.A., Jaffe, M.W.: Studies of illness in the aged: the index of adl: a standardized measure of biological and psychosocial function. Jama 185(12), 914–919 (1963)

11. Konkel, M., Leung, V., Ullmer, B., Hu, C.: Tagaboo: a collaborative children's game based upon wearable rfid technology. Pers. Ubiquit. Comput. 8(5), 382–384 (2004)

12. Lee, E.A.: The past, present and future of cyber-physical systems: A focus on models. Sensors 15(3), 4837–4869 (2015)

13. Lemelson MIT: Signaloud: Gloves that transliterate sign language into text and speech (2016). https://www.youtube.com/watch?v=l01sdzJHCCM

14. Majoros, A.E., Fredgren, B.C., Davies, P.R., Kalinowski, R.D.: Data interface process with rfid data reader glove (Jul 9 2013), uS Patent 8,482,412

15. Martin, D., Alcarria, R., Robles, T., Morales, A.: A systematic approach for service prosumerization in iot scenarios. In: 2013 Seventh International Conference on Innovative Mobile and Internet Services in Ubiquitous Computing (IMIS), pp. 494–499. IEEE (2013)

16. Martín, D., Alcarria, R., Sánchez-Picot, Á., Robles, T.: An ambient intelligence framework for end-user service provisioning in a hospital pharmacy: a case study. J. Med. Syst. 39(10), 1–10 (2015)

17. Martín, D., Alcarria, R., Sánchez-Picot, A., Robles, T., Sánchez de Rivera, D.: A four-leaf clover shape methodology for prosumer service developments. In: Hervás, R., Lee, S., Nugent, C., Bravo, J. (eds.) UCAmI 2014. LNCS, vol. 8867, pp. 488–495. Springer, Heidelberg (2014)

18. OPC Fundation: Opc 2.1 standard (1996). https://opcfoundation.org/

19. Philipose, M., Fishkin, K.P., Perkowitz, M., Patterson, D.J., Fox, D., Kautz, H., Hähnel, D.: Inferring activities from interactions with objects. Pervasive Comput. IEEE 3(4), 50–57 (2004)

20. National Institute of Standards & Technology: Cps public working group presentation (2015). http://www.nist.gov/el/upload/CPS-PWG-Kickoff-Webinar-Presentation-FINAL.PDF

21. Stetter, R.: Software im maschinenbau-lästiges anhängsel oder chance zur marktführerschaft? (2011). http://www.software-kompetenz.de/servlet/is/21700/Stetter-SW_im_Maschinenbau.pdf

22. Sánchez De Rivera, D., Alcarria, R., Martín, D., Bordel, B., Robles, T.: An autonomous information device with e-paper display for personal environments. In: 2016 IEEE International Conference on Consumer Electronics (ICCE), pp. 139–140. IEEE (2016)

23. Thramboulidis, K., Zoupas, A.: Real-time java in control and automation: a model driven development approach. In: 10th IEEE Conference on Emerging Technologies and Factory Automation, 2005. ETFA 2005. vol. 1, pp. 8-46. IEEE (2005)

Towards Personalised Training of Machine Learning Algorithms for Food Image Classification Using a Smartphone Camera

Patrick McAllister[1], Huiru Zheng[1(✉)], Raymond Bond[1], and Anne Moorhead[2]

[1] School of Computing and Mathematics, Ulster University,
Newtownabbey, Northern Ireland
mcallister-p2@email.ulster.ac.uk, {h.zheng,rb.bond}@ulster.ac.uk
[2] School of Communication, Ulster University, Newtownabbey, Northern Ireland
a.moorhead@ulster.ac.uk

Abstract. This work is related to the development of a personalised machine learning algorithm that is able to classify food images for food logging. The algorithm would be personalised as it would allow users to decided what food items the model will be able to classify. This novel concept introduces the idea of promoting dietary monitoring through classifying food images for food logging by personalising a machine learning algorithm. The food image classification algorithm will be trained based on specific types of foods decided by the user (most popular foods, food types e.g. vegetarian). This would mean that the classification algorithm would not have to be trained using a wide variety of foods which may lead to low accuracy rate but only a small number of foods chosen by the user. To test the concept, a range of experiments were completed using 30 different food types. Each food category contained 100 images. To train a classification algorithm, features were extracted from each food type, features such as SURF, LAB colour features, SFTA, and Local Binary Patterns were used. A number of classification algorithms were used in these experiments; Nave Bayes, SMO, Neural Networks, and Random Forest. The highest accuracy achieved in this work was 69.43 % accuracy using Bag-of-Features (BoF) Colour, BoF-SURF, SFTA, and LBP using a Neural Network.

Keywords: Obesity · Machine learning · Classification · Food logging · Photographs

1 Introduction

Obesity is increasing globally [1] and is the cause of many chronic conditions such as diabetes, heart disease, hypertension, and some cancers [2]. Within the UK, 61 % of adults are classified as either obese or overweight. Within the period from 1993 to 2013 obesity levels in men increased from 13.2 % to 26 % and 16.4 % to 23.8 % for women [3]. The main cause of obesity is a result of a high fat/calorie

© Springer International Publishing AG 2016
C.R. García et al. (Eds.): UCAmI 2016, Part I, LNCS 10069, pp. 178–190, 2016.
DOI: 10.1007/978-3-319-48746-5_18

diet and when the energy is not burned off through physical activitiese, then the excess energy will be stored as fat around the body [2].

The high prevalence of obesity also puts an economic burden on governments and health institutions around the world [3–5]. Information Communication Technologies (ICT) have been developed to allow individuals to self-manage their diet. There is a plethora of Smartphone applications available that allows users to document their energy intake. These applications allow the user to search for a food item and to determine the energy intake, however this can be cumbersome and time consuming for the user since they are required to navigate through numerous drop down menus to identify the correct food item [6]. A convenient approach would be to take photograph of a meal using a Smartphone camera and use the touch screen to draw around the food portion which can be automatically classified using computer vision methods. The amount of calories in a food item can also be estimated by taking in account the geometric area of the food portion, which can correlated with the amount of calories. The food item's area can be calculated using reference such as a coin in the photograph or a shape (area of reference shape is known to the user). Work has been completed in this area by using a reference point to determine portion size [7]). The food portion classification would then be used to search for the calorie content and portion size.

This paper focuses on using computer vision methods to extract features from a food image dataset and then used to train machine learning models to classify food items within the images. The rationale for the work presented in this paper is to inform the development of a personalised classification model that is tailored to the user's food selection. Much of the research completed in this area [10–12] use a multitude of classification models to classify a large range of food categories. Moreover, these models result in inaccuracies due to the large number of food classes the model can classify, this can be seen as wasteful since many of these food classes are not needed within an individuals diet. For example, a user may be vegetarian and would only be interested in using a system that is able to classify a selection of vegetables or meals that would be in their diet. We envisage that a user would select these foods and submit their selections to a cloud service where a classification model would be trained using features extracted from the chosen food categories. The personalised classification model would be downloaded onto the users device. The work presented in this paper uses a smaller number of food categories that are hypothetically selected by the user to classify food items. This system is described in Fig. 2. This work will consist of a range of experiments using a food image dataset (representing foods from typical food groups) and using feature combination and classification techniques to predict the food type. The remainder of this paper will discuss related work in this area; the methods used in the experiment which relate to feature detection and descriptors; the machine learning classification techniques used and the statistical methods used for evaluation.

2   Related Work

Much research has been conducted that use computer vision techniques for classifying objects in images. In [8] a classification technique using Random Forests was trained to mine images for discriminative parts (e.g. super-pixels). The discriminative components that were identified were then shared in order to improve accuracy. A challenging food image dataset was also constructed in [8]. This dataset is described as challenging as most of the images may contain multiple items and food types within each image. The dataset provided consisted of 101 food categories with 1000 images in each food category. The research presented in [8] also used Bag-of-Features (BoF), Histogram of Oriented Gradients (HOG), and LAB colour values were used. An accuracy of 50.76 % was achieved when using this dataset [8]. In [9] food texture and local gradient features were used to identify and classify food categories for dietary assessment. The texture and local gradient features used were entropy-based categorization and fractal dimension estimation (EFD), Gabor-based image decomposition and fractal dimension estimation (GFD), and the third descriptor is based on the spatial relationship of gradient orientations (GOSDM). GOSDM is obtained by finding out of the occurrence rate of pairs of gradient orientations of neighbourhood scales. The number of food categories used in this work is 46. The food items used in this experiment were segmented from the scene from feature extraction. Results from this work show that EFD with Neural Network achieved 79.2 %, GFD with Neural Network achieved 72.2 %, and also GOSDM with Neural Network achieved 65.3 % [9]. Also in [13] a real time food classification system was developed that utilises bounding boxes as an adjunct to segment the food area within an image in order to classify the region. In [13] two types of features were utilised; (1) BoF with a colour histogram and (2) a HOG patch and colour patch descriptor with Fisher-vector representation. As a result, the classification model [21] achieved 79 % accuracy for the top 5 categories. The work presented

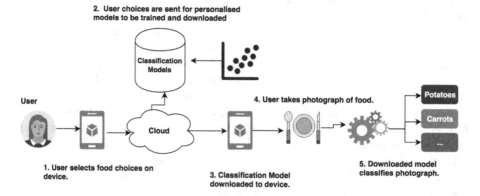

Fig. 1. Diagram describing proposed system that would allow users to download classification models.

in this paper seeks to explore the use of conventional machine learning classifiers for non-segmented food images to inform the development of a user tailored
classification model.

3   Aim and Objectives

The aim of this work is to classify different images of foods using a combination
of feature types with different machine learning algorithms. The number of food
classes used in the image dataset for this work is 30. We also used different
machine learning algorithms classifying the food items. This work will combine
global and local features to classify images of food. To achieve this aim, a number
of objectives need to be completed; (1) an image dataset would need to be
collected consisting of different food categories, (2) different types of feature
descriptors need to be extracted and represented as feature vectors for each image
in the image dataset, (3) a number of supervised classifiers need to be used and
evaluated using 10-fold cross validation. The extracted feature vectors will then
be encoded into the classifiers. The final objective is (5) which involves evaluation
metrics to assess the performance of each classifier and feature combination, and
in turn to determine the best classifier and feature combination.

4   Methodology

4.1   Image Dataset

There has been much research dedicated to constructing food image datasets
for the purpose of research computer vision classification methods [10–12]. The
images used in this work was taken from [10]. Thirty food item types was used
for this work.

4.2   Feature Selection

This section will discuss feature types used in this work. The feature types
used in this work will consist of global and local features. LAB colour space
statistics will be extracted from the image dataset and a standard bag-of-features
(BoF) method will be applied to the extracted colour features to create a visual
dictionary. Local features will also be extracted from the image dataset; Speed-
Up-Robust-Features (SURF) will be used to extract features from the food image
dataset. Again a BoF model will be applied to the SURF features to create a
visual vocabulary to classify images. Segmented Fractal Textual Analysis (SFTA)
and Local Binary Patterns (LBP) will also be used in this work. This section
will give a brief overview of these methods.

4.3   Bag of Features

Bag-of-features (BoF) or bag-of-visual words (BoVW) is a technique that is used to describe an image through a series of visual word occurrences using a visual dictionary. A vector is then produced after using a feature extraction method which represents features in an image. The vector is created through using an interest point extractor and then applying a descriptor such as SURF or SIFT to represent or describe the area around these points. BoF technique uses a code book or a visual dictionary that is created using features extracted from the training image set. Each visual word in the visual dictionary represents patches in a visual dictionary. An image can be classified by counting the amount of visual word occurrences that are present in the visual dictionary. The results feature vector can then be quantified using a histogram to represent the number of visual word occurrences in an image.

4.4   Speeded-Up-Robust-Features (SURF)

In this work, SURF feature descriptor was used. SURF is based on using a Hessian matrix to determining interest points. BLOB (large binary object) elements, used in SURF algorithm, are detected at a location where the determinant of Hessian is at maximum. The determinant of Hessian can also be used to for scale selection [14]. The following Eq. (1) defines the Hessian matrix at point X in an image.

$$H(x,\sigma) = \begin{bmatrix} L_{xx}(x,\sigma) & L_{xy}(x,\sigma) \\ L_{xy}(x,\sigma) & L_{yy}(x,\sigma) \end{bmatrix} \tag{1}$$

$L_{xx}(x,\sigma)$, $L_{xy}(x,\sigma)$ and $L_{yy}(x,\sigma)$ represent the convolution of the Gaussian second order derivative in image I at point x [4]. The SURF algorithm uses Hessian matrix and integral images to allow for quicker calculations. Convolutions are accelerated using the integral images method. In an integral image, a location represents the sum of all pixels in an image within a certain region. This is described in (2) [14].

$$I(x,y) = i(x,y) + I(x-1,y) + I(x,y-1) - I(x-1,y-1) \tag{2}$$

(x,y) represents a point in a rectangular region. The remaining points I(x−1,y), I(x,y−1) and (1,1) represent the remaining points in the rectangular region. This process only requires three operations to compute the value of the region [14]. In this work, a grid feature detection method was used. An 15×15 pixel grid was placed across each image and the SURF features were extracted from the locations where each horizontal and vertical grid connected. Features at these points were extracted at different scales to promote scale invariance.

4.5   Segmentation Based Fractal Textual Analysis (SFTA)

SFTA is a feature extraction method that is able to extract texture information from an image [15]. The algorithm accepts an input image and the images are then decomposd into multiple binary images using a Two-Threshold Binary Decomposition (TTBD) method.

$$I_b(x,y) = \begin{cases} 1 & if\ t_l < I(x,y) \le t_u \\ 0, & otherwise \end{cases} \tag{3}$$

where $I(x,y)$ is a set of binary images. Binary images are computed by using thresholds from T and using the Two-threshold segmentation as described in (1) [15]. t_l and t_u represent a pair of upper and lower thresholds. Pairs of thresholds are applied to the input image to obtain a set of binary images. The reason for applying pairs of thresholds to obtain binary images is to ensure that objects in the input images are segmented. The binary images that are outputted from the TTBD method can be described as a sub set of binary images that would have been outputted using a single threshold algorithm. SFTA feature vector is constructed using the binary images by extracting the pixel count (size), gray level and boundaries fractal dimension [15]. These measurements are used to describe object boundaries in each input image. The SFTA feature vector size is directly related to the number of binary images generated using the TTBD algorithm, for example if eight images were computed after using the TTBD algorithm on an input image, the SFTA feature vector would be 8×3 (3 being the number of measurements extracted from the binary images: size, fractal dimension, and mean gray level).

4.6 LAB Colour Space

Global colour features were extracted from the food image dataset and used within a BoF model to create a visual dictionary to classify test images. Lab colour space is described as a 3 axis colour system; L representing lightness and A and B representing colour dimensions [16]. There are several advantages to using LAB colour space as a method to represent colour in images; it provides a precise means of representing colour and LAB is device independent and also LAB colour space can easily be quantified to compare images. [16]. In this work, RGB images are converted to LAB colour space. The image is divided in 16×16 pixel blocks and the average value of each block is computed. The image is then scaled down in order to compute the average LAB colour value over the entire image. The average LAB values are then stored in a matrix and normalised. The location from where the colour feature was extracted and appended to the feature.

4.7 Local Binary Patterns (LBP)

Local Binary Patterns (LBP) is a visual descriptor that has been used for texture classification. To create an LBP vector the following method is used, firstly, the area in question is divided into a number of the cells. The cells in the area are measured 3×3 pixels usually. The center pixel in the cell is compared with its neighbours. If the center pixels value is greater than the neighbour, then the neighbouring pixel is assigned as 0 or if the neighbouring pixel value is greater than the center pixel then it is assigned 1. After this process is completed, a binary sequence is then computed for each pixel within the cell. The binary sequence is computed to reveal an LBP code. A histogram is then generated to statistically measure the occurrence of LBP codes in an image. This histogram can then be used to classify an image [17].

4.8   Classifiers

In this work a range of classifiers were used to assess the performance using the extracted features types extracted. Table 1 is a list of the machine learning classifiers used in this work.

Table 1. Summary of classifiers and parameters used in this work.

Machine learning classifiers	Parameters used
Naive Bayes (NB)	Weka default parameters
SMO [19]	Polynomial Kernel
Neural Network (NN) [24]	1 layer, 100 neurons, 1000 iterations
Random Forest Tree (RF) [18]	300 trees

4.9   Evaluation and Statistical Analysis

Metrics were used to evaluate the performance of the machine learning algorithms. Ten-fold cross validation was used to accurately calculate the performance metrics. The output of the 10-fold cross validation included the kappa statistic for each experiment. This also included the mean percentage accuracy rate (number of correct classifications) as computed from each of the folds. Cohens Kappa was used to measure the agreement between the predicted class and the actual class for each food image. Initial experiments consisted of increasing the visual word count in the BoF model using 500 increments. This was done for BOF-SURF and BoF-colour. This was to find out other optimum visual word count for each classifier by using percentage accuracy as a measurement. The highest accuracy achieved for each classifier (using the 500 visual word increments) would be combined with the remained feature sets extracted from the image dataset. The labelled feature set combinations were extracted to a CSV file format using Matlab (R2016a) [22] and the Weka Analysis (v3.7.13) [23] platform was used to train machine learning algorithms using the features extracted.

5   Results

Experiments were completed using the image dataset described in Sect. 4. The image dataset consisted of images with other food items and other objects in them i.e. noise and unrelated food items. Various combinations of BoF-SURF and BoF-Colour were fused together with SFTA and LBP features to achieve the highest result. Table 2 shows the percentage accuracy of increasing the visual words using BoF-SURF and BoF-colour features in a BoF model using for each machine learning classifier.

Results from the visual word experiments show the percentage accuracy achieved for each classifier. The results from these experiments were incorporated into future classification tests. Future experiments were carried out by combining feature types for each machine learning algorithms. SURF and colour visual words that achieved the highest accuracy were combined together for each

Table 2. Results from increasing the visual word count by 500 for SURF and colour features using BOF method. SMO classifier (SMO) and Naive Bayes (NB) was used in these experiments.(^{a} denotes highest accuracy achieved).

Visual Words	SMO SURF	SMO Colour	NB SURF	NB Colour
500	46.30	34.67	22.73	19.20
1000	48.17	33.43	23.87	21.37
1500	48.87	34.00	24.67	21.83
2000	50.17	34.73	25.13	22.90
2500	50.27^a	35.67	25.63	24.00
3000	50.27	36.43	25.47	24.40
3500	49.90	35.60	26.40^a	24.53
4000	49.70	35.87	25.70	24.67
4500	49.50	36.57^a	25.17	24.73
5000	49.47	35.80	25.23	25.37^a

Table 3. Initial results from increasing the visual word count by 500 for SURF and colour features using BOF method. Neural Network (NN) and Random Forest (RF) classifier were used in these experiments. (^{a} denotes highest accuracy achieved).

Visual Words	NN SURF	NN Colour	RF SURF	RF Colour
500	49.80	38.67^a	36.43^a	40.87^a
1000	52.37	37.93	35.47	40.27
1500	54.43	37.00	34.93	38.40
2000	54.33	36.33	35.07	38.23
2500	55.70	36.83	34.13	38.00
3000	54.47	35.53	33.90	38.03
3500	55.53	36.87	33.90	37.83
4000	56.33^a	36.70	33.27	37.07
4500	55.97	36.37	32.80	37.33
5000	55.90	36.66	33.40	36.23

Table 4. Results from combining features together. (^{a} denotes highest accuracy achieved).

Classifier	Colour+ SURF	SURF+Colour SFTA	SURF+Colour+ SFTA+LBP	SURF+LBP
SMO	61.9	63.23	64.57	52.1
Naive Bayes	33.63	33.7	34.00	28.26
Neural Network	67.00^a	68.73^a	69.43^a	60.03^a
Random Forest	48.90	50.30	48.07	37.63

Table 5. Further results combining different feature types together. (^{a} denotes highest accuracy achieved).

Classifier	SURF+SFTA	Colour+SFTA
SMO	53.8	40.53
Naive Bayes	27.1	25.56
Neural Network	59.26^a	44.43^a
Random Forest	40.33	43.53

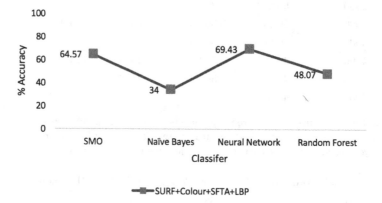

Fig. 2. Diagram showing final results from combining features across different machine learning classifiers.

classifier e.g. SURF and colour features that achieved the highest accuracy for SMO were combined. Figure 2 shows the results of using feature combinations trained using the machine learning classification algorithms. The results from the 10-fold cross validation show that Neural Network trained with BoF-Colour, BoF-SURF, SFTA, and LBP feature combination achieved the highest accuracy with 69.43 %. From the combination feature results, Neural Network achieved the highest accuracy in all feature combination experiments (Table 4).

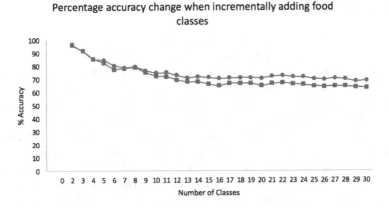

Fig. 3. Diagram describing the change in percentage accuracy when incrementally adding food classes to an image dataset. For this experiment SMO classifier was used with BoF-SURF, BoF-colour, and SFTA.

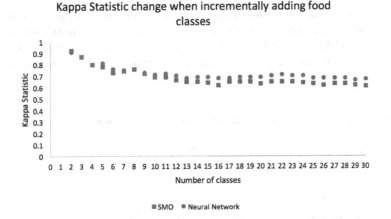

Fig. 4. describing the change in Cohen's Kappa when incrementally adding food classes to an image dataset. SMO classifier was used with BoF-SURF, BoF-colour, and SFTA

Further experiments were conducted to depict the decline in accuracy when incrementally increasing the number of classes. Cohen's Kappa was noted from each experiment to measure the performance of each iteration. Figures 3 and 4 shows the results from these experiments. Figure 3 is a graph showing the percentage accuracy change when food classes were adding incrementally to the dataset. Figure 4 is a graph that depicts the Kappa Statistic change when classes were incrementally added.

6   Discussion

This work uses a feature combination approach to train several machine learning models. The motivation for this work was to inform the development of a personalised machine learning model approach to classify food images. Relating to Fig. 1, the user would be able to select their favourite foods for classification to predict the food meal in the image. The performance of this work was assessed using a 10-fold cross validation approach and results show that Neural Network trained with BoF SURF, BoF colour, SFTA, and LBP achieves the highest accuracy with 69.43 % accuracy. Neural Network consistently achieved higher accuracy across all feature combinations, and Nave Bayes achieved the lowest accuracy in each feature combination test. Table 6 is a comparison table from other works completed along with the accuracy and feature types, this shows that the results achieved in this work is comparable with other results achieved in this area. It is important to note that the images used in this work were not segmented but the entire image was used for feature selection. From the experiments, it is revealed that a reasonable degree of accuracy can be achieved through classifying non-segmented meal images. This could be increased by segmenting the meals to promote feature selection accuracy and ultimately classification accuracy. This work shows that there is potential to utilise conventional based feature extraction and machine learning classifiers to classify entire food meal images with reasonable accuracy however more comparative research is needed to compare further feature extraction methods (CNN feature extraction) (Table 6).

Table 6. Table showing highest accuracy achieved in other work in food classification.

Method	% Accuracy
SVM + mixture of global and local features [20]	0.861 (average across all tests, 39 classes)
BoF/Fisher-Vector [21]	79.2 % (top 5 classes)
Random Forest for component mining [8]	50.76 (101 classes)
Texture Features + Neural Networks [9]	79.2 % (segmented food images, 46 classes)
Neural Network (this paper)	69.43 % (30 classes, unsegmented images)

7   Future Work and Conclusion

Several limitations have been identified in this work. Some of the images used in this work for each category include other objects or food items are present in the image. Certain non-food features may be selected and used in the training of the machine learning process, which can result in a number of misclassifications. Future work will be to address this issue by creating an image dataset using food images that focus in on the food item and texture directly and to ensure that no other non-food items or other food items are present in the scene. In future work, the food items would be segmented from the image and then feature types would be extracted from the segmented image. This would improve the algorithms accuracy by allowing relevant interest points to be selected. The number of images in this work was 100 per category, which can be considered to be a low number in comparison to other works. Future work would address this issue by increasing the amount of images in each category and ensure that these images do not contain any other food or non-food item. As a result, the increase in training data for each food category should also increase the accuracy of the algorithm. Other machine learning models would also be considered in future work; further analysis could be undertaken by changing different parameters for each model used, e.g. changing the number of layers in neural network structure along with the amount of neurons or changing kernels used in SMO classifier. Other machine learnings could be applied to the image dataset such as Self-Organizing Maps (SOM) or utilise multi-class classifier approaches and document the performance of these techniques (one vs one, one vs rest). For feature extraction, other feature types could be used such as Gabor Filters to extract textual information from the dataset. Research would also focus on developing an hierarchical classification approach to classify food type and then pinpoint exact food item.

References

1. DHSSPSNI, Health Survey Northern Ireland, First Results 2013/2014 (2013–2014)
2. Nhs.uk, "Obesity, NHS Choices", Nhs.uk (2016). www.nhs.uk/Conditions/Obesity/Pages/Introduction.aspx. Accessed 15 Jun 2016
3. Noo.org.uk "About Obesity: Public Health England" (2016). www.noo.org.uk/NOO_about_obesity/adult_obesity/UK_prevalence_and_trends
4. Scarborough, P., Bhatnagar, P., Wickramasinghe, K., Allender, S., Foster, C., Rayner, M.: The economic burden of ill health due to diet, physical inactivity, smoking, alcohol and obesity in the UK: an update to 2006–07 NHS costs. J. Public Health 33(4), 527–535 (2011)
5. Noo.org.uk, "Economics of obesity: Public Health England Obesity Knowledge and Intelligence team", Noo.org.uk (2016). www.noo.org.uk/NOO_about_obesity/economics. Accessed 15 Jun 2016
6. MyFitnessPal, C.: M. LLc, "Calorie Counter & Diet Tracker by MyFitnessPal on the App. Store", App. Store (2016). itunes.apple.com/gb/app/calorie-counter-diet-tracker/id341232718?mt=8. Accessed 15 Jun 2016
7. McAllister, P., et al.: Semi-automated system for predicting calories in photographs of meals. In: IEEE International Conference on Engineering, Technology and Innovation/International Technology Management Conference (ICE/ITMC). IEEE (2015)
8. Bossard, L., Guillaumin, M., Van Gool, L.: Food-101 – mining discriminative components with random forests. In: Fleet, D., Pajdla, T., Schiele, B., Tuytelaars, T. (eds.) ECCV 2014, Part VI. LNCS, vol. 8694, pp. 446–461. Springer, Heidelberg (2014)

9. Bosch, M., et. al.: Food texture descriptors based on fractal and local gradient information. In: 19th European Signal Processing Conference, pp. 764–768. IEEE (2011)

10. Farinella, G.M., Allegra, D., Stanco, F.: A benchmark dataset to study the representation of food images. In: ECCV European Conference in Computer Vision. Zurich, Workshop Assistive Computer Vision and Robotics (2014)

11. Joutou, T., Yanai, K.: A food image recognition system with multiple kernel learning. In: 16th IEEE International Conference on Image Processing (ICIP), pp. 285–288. IEEE (2009)

12. Kawano, Y., Yanai, K.: Foodcam-256: a large-scalereal-time mobile food recognition system employing high-dimensional features and compression of classifier weights. In: Proceedings of the ACM International Conference on Multimedia, ser. MM 14, pp. 761–762 (2014)

13. Hartigan, J.A., Manchek, A.W.: Algorithm AS 136: a k-means clustering algorithm. J. Roy. Stat. Soc.: Ser. C (Appl. Stat.) **28**(1), 100–108 (1979)

14. Bay, H., Tuytelaars, T., Van Gool, L.: SURF: speeded up robust features. In: Leonardis, A., Bischof, H., Pinz, A. (eds.) ECCV 2006, Part I. LNCS, vol. 3951, pp. 404–417. Springer, Heidelberg (2006)

15. Costa, A.F., Humpire-Mamani, G., Traina, A.J.M.: An efficient algorithm for fractal analysis of textures. In: 25th SIBGRAPI Conference on Graphics, Patterns and Images (SIBGRAPI). IEEE (2012)

16. "Lab Color - MATLAB", Uk.mathworks.com (2016). http://uk.mathworks.com/discovery/lab-color.html. Accessed 15 Jun 2016

17. Ojala, T., Pietikinen, M., Harwood, D.: Performance evaluation of texture measures with classification based on Kullback discrimination of distributions. In: Proceedings of the 12th IAPR International Conference on Pattern Recognition (ICPPR 1994), vol. 1, pp. 582–585 (1994)

18. Breiman, L.: Random forests. Mach. Learn. **45**(1), 5–32 (2001)

19. Platt, J.C.: Sequential Minimal Optimization: a fast algorithm for training support vector machines. In: Advances Kernel Methods, pp. 185–208 (1998)

20. Bosch, M., Zhu, F., Khanna, N., Boushey, C.J., Delp, E.J.: Combining global and local features for food identification in dietary assessment. In: Proceedings - International Conference on Image Processing, ICIP, pp. 1789–1792 (2011)

21. Kawano, Y., Yanai, K.: FoodCam: a real-time mobile food recognition system employing fisher vector. In: Gurrin, C., Hopfgartner, F., Hurst, W., Johansen, H., Lee, H., O'Connor, N. (eds.) MMM 2014, Part II. LNCS, vol. 8326, pp. 369–373. Springer, Heidelberg (2014)

22. MATLAB - MathWorks: Matlab.co.uk (2016). http://matlab.co.uk. Accessed 15 Jun 2016

23. Weka 3 - Data Mining with Open Source Machine Learning Software in Java. Cs.waikato.ac.nz (2016). http://www.cs.waikato.ac.nz/ml/weka/. Accessed 15 Jun 2016

24. (Convolutional) Neural Network, "amten/NeuralNetwork", GitHub (2016). https://github.com/amten/NeuralNetwork. Accessed 15 Sep 2016

Interoperability in Electronic Health Records Through the Mediation of Ubiquitous User Model

Ma. Lourdes Martínez-Villaseñor[1(✉)], Luis Miralles-Pechuan[1],
and Miguel González-Mendoza[2]

[1] Universidad Panamericana Campus México,
Augusto Rodin 498, Col. Insurgentes-Mixcoac, México, D.F., Mexico
{lmartine,lmiralles}@up.edu.mx
[2] Tecnológico de Monterrey, Campus Estado de México, Edo., México, Mexico
mgonza@itesm.mx

Abstract. The paradigm of healthcare systems has change from isolated proprietary health records to patient-centric solutions in which government, hospitals
and clinics, general practitioners and other stakeholders must cooperate in order
to provide improved health services. Enabling interoperability to share heterogeneous medical and administrative information in a secure environment is an
issue addressed worldwide. Standards help though are not enough to provide the
right information at the right time and place. In this paper we proposed to leverage
the interoperability between standards through the mediation of a ubiquitous user
model and an automatic process of concept alignment.

Keywords: Personal health records interoperability · Electronic · Health records
interoperability · Ubiquitous user modeling

1 Introduction

Healthcare systems have been changing in the last decades to a more patient-centric
model. It is urgent that information about patient profile, medical history, problems
progress, tests, treatments and other related records are no longer gathered in separated
silos. The focus of healthcare must be the patient needs and values; patient has to be in
control of his/her information. It is important that all parties cooperate and share information in order to provide right information, to the right person, at the right time and
place [1]. Healthcare is moving towards "solutions which support a continuous medical
process and (i) include multiple healthcare professionals and institutions, (ii) utilize
ubiquitous computing healthcare environments and (iii) embrace technological
advances, typical of the domain of today's pervasive software applications" [2].

It is incredible that in the digital age, handwritten documents remain prevalent
throughout most of the health sector, in spite of all efforts to automate and share electronic health information among general practitioners, patients and other stakeholders.

Many efforts have been made to automate medical information developing Electronic Healthcare Records (EHRs) and standards to enable sharing and reusing information amongst healthcare software systems. Nevertheless, health care information is

© Springer International Publishing AG 2016
C.R. García et al. (Eds.): UCAmI 2016, Part I, LNCS 10069, pp. 191–200, 2016.
DOI: 10.1007/978-3-319-48746-5_19

very complex and therefore interoperability between health systems is hard. Hospital medical records are extremely varied. Millions of different formats and forms are used to capture patient's personal, social, family and medical history. Patient's care involves documents of different nature: treatments, tests, progress notes, referrals, imaging, medical charts, and nursing notes just to mention a few. Communication is also many to many given that the doctor communicates with different specialists, patients go to multitude of doctors, treatment services, administrative parties and agents.

Healthcare systems and EHRs have been developed worldwide. Health care information is stored in different proprietary formats, and this information is managed in multiple types of hardware and software solutions for diverse business processes. Medical information is stored in structured formats including databases, and unstructured documents. This differences result in a severe interoperability problems [3].

Interoperability between EHR is important to deliver more effective and efficient patient care assisting the retrieval and processing of clinical information about patients from and to different health systems. Duplicate testing and prescribing can be reduced [3]. Standards can contribute to exchange medical information in a safe, secure and reliable manner.

Several international standards development organizations have been working towards enabling healthcare interoperability. Multiple efforts to address EHR interoperability problems are focus in developing international standards [1, 3]. One of the main problems is that there are too many standards and the adoption of each one of them entails enormous efforts. Standards are also not static; they are constantly evolving in content and structure [2]. There are just a few success cases like MedCom [4].

As in other domains, there are syntactic and semantic heterogeneities added to heterogeneities in hardware and software and purpose. Gibbons et al. [5] define interoperability in three categories technical, semantic, and process interoperability in healthcare systems.

Despite of all efforts done by governments, standards organizations and different stakeholders involved in healthcare sector, interoperability between EHRs is still an open issue.

In this paper, we present a small effort to enable interoperability between EHRs through the mediation of our ubiquitous user model [6, 7]. Our framework could help as a mediator between different health systems. Information from different applications could be shared and reused with our user profile.

The rest of the paper is organized as follows. State of the art efforts towards EHR interoperability are presented in Sect. 2. An overview of our framework for ubiquitous user model interoperability is described in Sect. 3. In Sect. 4, we present an application scenario of interoperability in EHR through the mediation of ubiquitous user model. Experiments and results are shown in Sect. 5. We conclude and outline future work in Sect. 5.

2   Electronic Health Records Interoperability

In this section we reviewed the most prominent standards, which address the interoperability problems in order to share information across healthcare systems.

The major International Organizations for Standardization providing standard solutions for EHR interoperability are: International Organization for Standardization [8], European Committee for Standardization [9], Health Level Seven [10] accredited by American National Standards Institute [11], and Digital Imaging and Communications Medicine [12].

The International Organization for Standardization (ISO) established ISO's Technical Committee ISO/TC 215, which deals with health informatics. This committee introduces several standards. One of them, ISO/TR 20514 defines the structure and context of an EHR offering a basic-generic EHR. ISO 13606-reference model was published to enhance EHR communication [8].

Health Informatics of the European Committee for Standardization (CEN/TC 251) presented a reference model, an archetype interchange specification, reference archetypes and term lists, security features, and exchange models. CEN/ISO 13606 is a European norm approved also by ISO to achieve semantic interoperability in EHR communication. It defines a Dual Model architecture: Reference Model for EHR representation, and archetypes to provide semantic meaning to the Reference Model structure [9].

Health Level Seven (HL7) term is used as a name for the organization, and as a set of messaging standards. HL7 are successful messaging standards that support two messaging protocols: HL7 Version 2 and HL7 Version 3 [10]. HL7 Version 3 proposed the Clinical Document Architecture (CDA) for exchanging documents across healthcare systems. There are areas of harmonization between standards: "HL7CDA and CEN 13606 Reference Models and CEN/openEHR archetypes with HL7 Templates. The OpenEHR Reference Model uses the CEN13606 Reference Model, which in turn is used in HL7CDA" [2].

Regarding DIACOM is known as de facto standard for medical image communication [2, 3] . DIACOM standards introduced data structures and services to enable the exchange of medical images and related information across vendors. They presented two EHR standards: Web Access to DICOM Persistent Objects (WADO), and DICOM Structured Reporting.

An industry initiative Integrating the Healthcare Enterprise (IHE) encourages the coordinate use of existing standards like DICOM and HL7. They propose storing health documents in a XML repository to facilitate sharing and reusing of EHR information.

Dossia proposed a personal health record (PHR) management systems in 2006 [13]. Major technology players, Google and Microsoft have also tried to contribute with personal health record (PHR) management systems [14]. Google Health offered the users a Web-based system to manage health information in 2008 but they retired in 2012 for lack of adoption. Microsoft HealthVault [15] was introduced in October of 2007 and is still active as a personal health record management system. These initiatives didn't achieve the expected user adoption [14].

In this section, we only write a summary of the major standards, but in real-world there are many more. These standards are dynamic and it is difficult to cope with complex descriptions and documentation. There is a large number of conflicts between them. It is clear that given the great amount of standards, there is no healthcare standard winner. None of them provides a sufficient plug-and-play standard 'n' '0'. There is no one-size fit all patient record.

Another less explored element to address EHR interoperability is using mapping and alignment tools for exposing, sharing and reusing healthcare information of different EHR repositories and data providers [16]. We propose a solution using mapping and schema alignments to enable EHR interoperability in the following sections.

3   Overview of a Framework for Ubiquitous User Model Interoperability

In a multi-application, multi-device ubiquitous environment, user profile information is scattered in distributed user models. When trying to integrate all this valuable user information, it is important to take into account that highly autonomous profile suppliers and consumers are participating in the interoperability process. This means, first of all, that providers are free to decide what data to store, how to describe the data, set of constrains on the data, and associate an interpretation [14]. Providers also decide what data to share, policies and means of how to share it. Consumers of profile information want to decide when join and leave the system as well. Consumers have also their ways to describe and interpret data. Therefore mechanisms of interoperability must be provided that require the least intervention and effort of the ubiquitous user modeling stakeholders in order to enable interoperability respecting the providers' and consumers' autonomy. These conditions stand in learning environments. The user or learner information representation must be machine-readable, and flexible to allow the integration of information of new providers.

In previous works [6, 7] we presented a framework for ubiquitous user interoperability. The proposed framework enables the interoperability between profile suppliers and consumers with a mixed approach that consists in central ubiquitous user model ontology to provide formal representation of the user profile and a process of concept alignment to automatically discover the semantic mappings between the user models.

The central ubiquitous user model interoperability ontology (U2MIO) is a flexible representation of a ubiquitous user model to cope with the dynamicity of a distributed multi-application environment that provides mediation between profile suppliers and consumers. U2MIO can evolve over time to adapt the representation to the changing multi-application environment. The dynamic user profile structure ontology is based in Simple Knowledge Organization for the Web (SKOS) [17].

The process of concept alignment is briefly described below. This process automatically discovers the semantic mapping between the concepts of profile suppliers and consumers and the U2MIO ontology in order to interpret the information from heterogeneous sources, and integrate them into a ubiquitous user model. This process is crucial for the construction and maintenance of the ubiquitous user model; it enables interoperability and allows the evolution in time of the U2MIO ontology. We proposed a two-tier matching strategy for the process of concept alignment in a hybrid integration system to provide mediation between heterogeneous sources. This architecture and the process of concept alignment facilitate the participation of new stakeholders in the interoperability process.

3.1   Ubiquitous User Model Interoperability Ontology

The Ubiquitous User Modeling Interoperability Ontology (U2MIO) represents a flexible user model profile that evolves during time according to the recommendations of the concept alignment. The ontology reuses SKOS ontology designing a central concept scheme for the ubiquitous user model and one concept scheme for each profile supplier or consumer. Semantic mapping relations between each stakeholder's concept scheme concepts and the central user model concept scheme concepts are determined by the process of concept alignment. Semantic relations are set with SKOS properties. This representation supports interoperability overcoming semantic differences and enables the participation of new stakeholders in the interoperability process without effort of the profile information provider or consumer. Figure 1 shows the interrelations between profile stakeholders and the ubiquitous user model concept.

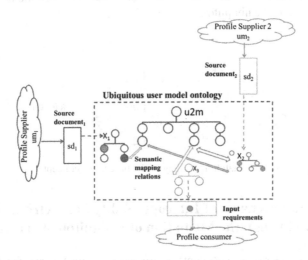

Fig. 1.   Interrelations between profile stakeholders and ubiquitous user model.

3.2   Process of Concept Alignment

Our ubiquitous user modeling framework deals with the profile suppliers' transfer mechanisms and recollects source documents *(sd)* in XML, JSON or RDF. If the source is new to the system, a corresponding skos:ConceptScheme *(X)* is designed and added to U2MIO. The process of concept alignment is based in a two-tier matching strategy (Fig. 2). First an element level matching step finds a set of concept candidates for alignment for each concept in the source concept scheme. This task is performed combining three types of similarity measures: (a) String similarity based in Dice [18] (b) A simple distance of longest substring c) semantic similarity based on WordNet [19]. From this step in which we analyze the word similarity between each concept in the source with all concepts in ubiquitous user model concept schema *(u2 m)*, we find a set of best suited concepts for alignment (or one best suited concept) in the target *(u2 m)*. Next, the method looks for structure similarity. The goal in the structure level matching step is to disambiguate the meaning of the word analyzing its context, this means analyzing the structure and meaning of the neighbor concepts in the same source document. In this step, the similarity between the neighbor concepts in the source and the neighbors of the best suited concept(s) in the target are calculated. After this step, a set of IF THEN rules are applied to determine one-to-one semantic mappings and recommendations of concept and collection additions. The process of concept alignment shown in Fig. 2 roughly describes the inputs and outputs of each phase. A concept scheme is defined as (C, H_C, V_C) where C is a set of concepts arranged in a subsumption hierarchy H_C. V_C is the set of corresponding concept values. C_s is the set of concept labels extracted from the source document. C_T is the set of concept labels extracted from the target (ubiquitous user model scheme), and C_{bT} is the set of concepts that are best suited for alignment. R_0 (C_s, C_{Tb}) are the highest relations obtained from the element level matching phase and $R(C_s, C_T)$ are the final semantic mapping relations found between the concepts of the source document and the ubiquitous user model (target).

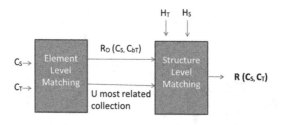

Fig. 2. Two-tier matching stat, egy of the process of concept alignment

4   Application Scenario of Interoperability in Electronic Health Records Through the Mediation of Ubiquitous User Model

There are many standards of EHRs content, structures and mechanisms for the exchange, Nevertheless as we described in Sect. 2, many health systems model their own personal health record or adopt one standard that is not interoperable with other standards used by other health agents, providers or consumers of EHR information. Some personal health record (PHR) management systems have own APIs and web services to enable populating or extracting profile information. Standards and transfer mechanism can change anytime. Prior agreement between stakeholders implies adherence and adoption or/and manual or semiautomatic mapping to enable interoperability.

In this section we propose two experiments in order to establish a proof of concept of two use cases:

(1)   Interoperability between EHRs through the mediation of ubiquitous user model
(2)   EHR enrichment reusing Facebook information

4.1 Evaluation Metrics

In order to measure the efficiency and effectiveness of the matching/mapping systems, different metrics have been proposed in the literature [22].

In this work, the evaluation of the process of concept alignment is focused in:

- The human effort required by the mapping designer to verify the correctness of the mappings, which is quantified with the metric and partially measures the efficiency of the process.
- The quality of the generated mappings quantifying the proximity of the results generated by the process of concept alignment to those expected with four known metrics: precision, recall, f-measure and fall-out .With these metrics a partial measure of the effectiveness of the process is performed.

These metrics are based on the notions of true positives (TP), false positives (FP), true negatives (TN) and false negatives (FN).

A human expert provided a list of expected matches for the proof of concept example and evaluated the outcomes, deciding if the semantic mapping relations found were correct and recommendations make sense. Exact match relations correctly found by the process, and good recommendations for concept or collection addition were considered as *TP*. Wrong exact matches were listed as *FP*. When a relevant exact match was not found by the process, a concept was improperly discarded or a wrong recommendation was made, it was registered as *FN*. Properly discarded concepts were recorded as *TN*.

4.2 Experiments

Case 1: Interoperability between EHRs through the mediation of ubiquitous user model. We used FHIR (Fast Healthcare Interoperability Resources) Specification, Patient-example.xml [20] to enhance our Ubiquitous user model interoperability ontology. Next we suppose that the patient wants to use Microsoft HealthVault personal health record (PHR) management system, so in order to enable interoperability between both standards, we performed a process of concept alignment with the Basic Demographic Information [21]. The true errors (FP and FN) were generated due to the ambiguity of used label in both sides. Code, text, value, name are frequently used in a schema hindering the semantic matching.

The results of the process of concept alignment between HL7 schema and Basic HealthVault PHR are presented in the confusion matrix of table. Even though the Basic profile only has 8 concepts, the semantic meaning of the concepts are difficult to interpret given the level of granularity, especially of country concept (Table 1).

Birth year is detailed alone for example. In HL7 gender is associated with "patient" and in Basic HealthVault PHR with "basic". These schema associations change the outcome of the system adding the concept to the most related collection instead of defining an exact match. The decision is reasonable given that in other cases the alignment is correct, for example *spouse* or *contact* gender. The only exact match found was incorrect. Labels where the same (code_value) but the meaning was completely different.

Table 1. Resulting confusion matrix of the matching process between HL7 and Basic MHVault

Case 1		Expected matches	
HL7 vs Basic MHV		positive	negative
Process of concept alignment	positive	TP=4	FP=2
outcome	negative	FN=1	TN=1

Case2: EHR enrichment reusing Facebook information. The ubiquitous user model interoperability ontology contained already information about Facebook User profile. We considered the case of EHR enrichment reusing Facebook information to populate Basic Demographic Information.

Table 2 presents the confusion matrix resulting of aligning Basic HealthVault PHR and the ubiquitous user model enhanced with Facebook profile. The results are perfect when you only consider if the semantic relations found were correct, and the system's recommendation make sense to a human evaluator. Although the system made good decisions, no exact match could be found. Two concepts were discarded correctly, this is no matching was possible.

Table 2. Resulting confusion matrix of the matching process between Facebook and Basic MHVault

Case 2		Expected matches	
Facebook vs Basic MHV		positive	negative
Process of	positive	TP=6	FP=0
concept alignment outcome	negative	FN=0	TN=2

4.3 Results

The efficiency and effectiveness of the process of concept alignment for case scenario 1 and case scenario 2, are shown in Table 3. The results of effectiveness show that recall results exceed our needs (medium recall), but our requirements for high precision were not fulfilled in case 1. The same weight was given to precision and recall in order to calculate F-measure and case 1 results are only fair. The greater the overall, less human effort is needed to correct the automatic mapping. In case 1, the automatic process of schema matching was not worth the effort to correct it.

Table 3. Efficiency and effectiveness measuring results

		Case 1	Case 2
Measure	Metric	HL7 vs Basic MHV	Facebook vs Basic MHV
Quality of generated mappings (Effectiveness)	Precision	67%	100%
	Recall	80%	100%
	Fall-out	67%	0%
	F-measure	73%	100%
Human Effort (Efficiency)	Overall	40%	100%

5 Conclusions and Future Work

The paradigm of healthcare systems has change from isolated proprietary health records to patient-centric solutions in which government, hospitals and clinics, general practitioners and other stakeholders must cooperate in order to provide improved health services. Enabling interoperability to share heterogeneous medical and administrative information in a secure environment is an issue addressed worldwide. Standards help though are not enough to provide the right information at the right time and place. In this paper we proposed to leverage the interoperability between standards through the mediation of a ubiquitous user model and an automatic process of concept alignment. Although results prove that the process is making sense in the schema matching decisions, in many cases semantic interoperability is hard and the human effort to mend ambiguities is too much. Nevertheless, automatic schema mapping can be improved and in some cases eases the load of finding consensus between EHRs.

For future work, we are trying to implement fuzzy logic to deal with semantic uncertainties.

References

1. Benson, T.: Principles of health interoperability HL7 and SNOMED. Springer, Heidelberg (2012)
2. Begoyan, A.: An overview of interoperability standards for electronic health records. In: USA: Society for Design and Process Science (2007)
3. Eichelberg, M., Aden, T., Riesmeier, J., Dogac, A., Laleci, G.B.: A survey and analysis of electronic healthcare record standards. ACM Comput. Surv. (Csur) 37(4), 277–315 (2005)
4. Saranummi, N.: Regional health economies and ICT services: the picnic experience. IOS Press (2005)
5. Gibbons P, et al.: Coming to terms: Scoping interoperability for health care (2007)
6. Martinez-Villaseñor, M.D.L., Gonzalez-Mendoza, M., Hernandez-Gress, N.: Towards a ubiquitous user model for profile sharing and reuse. Sensors 12(10), 13249–13283 (2012)
7. Martinez-Villaseñor, M.D.L.: Design and implementation of a framework for ubiquitous user model interoperability. Tesis Doctoral. Ph.D. Thesis, Instituto Tecnológico y de Estudios Superiores de Monterrey, Estado de México, México (2013)
8. ISO International Standards (2016). www.iso.org

9. The EN 13606 Association, The CEN/ISO EN 13606 standard (2015). http://www.en13606.org/the-ceniso-en13606-standard, June 14, 2016
10. HL7. EHR System Functional Model: "A Major Development Towards Consensus on Electronic Health Record System Functionality", A White Paper. Health Level Seven, Inc. (2004)
11. America National Standards Institute (ANSI) (2016). http://www.ansi.org, June 15, 2016
12. Digital Imaging and Communications Medicine (DICOM) (2016). http://dicom.nema.org/, June 15, 2016
13. Dossia consortium (2014). http://www.dossia.org, June 14, 2016
14. Spil, T., Klein, R.: The personal health future. Health Policy Technol. 4(2), 131–136 (2015)
15. Microsoft, Microsoft HealthVault (2016). www.healthvault.com, June 14, 2016
16. Perakis, K., Bouras, T., Ntalaperas, D., Hasapis, P., Georgousopoulos, C., Sahay, R., Usurelu, D.: Advancing patient record safety and EHR semantic interoperability. In: 2013 IEEE International Conference on En Systems, Man, and Cybernetics (SMC), pp. 3251–3257. IEEE (2013)
17. Miles, A., Matthews, B., Wilson, M., Brickley, D.: SKOS core: simple knowledge organisation for the web. In: International Conference on Dublin Core and Metadata Applications, pp. pp. 3–10 (2005)
18. Dice, L.R.: Measures of the amount of ecologic association between species. Ecology 26(3), 297–302 (1945)
19. Fellbaum, C.: WordNet and wordnets (2005)
20. FHIR (Fast Healthcare Interoperability Resources) Specification, Patient-example.xml. https://www.hl7.org/fhir/patient-example.xml.html, last updated: Sat, Oct 24, 2015 07:43 + 1100, consulted: June, 15th, 2016
21. Microsoft, Basic demographic information example. https://developer.healthvault.com/DataTypes/Overview?TypeId=3b3e6b16-eb69-483c-8d7e-dfe116ae6092, last updated: 2014, consulted: June, 15th, 2016
22. Bellahsene, Z., Bonifati, A., Duchateau, F., Velegrakis, Y.: On evaluating schema matching and mapping. In: Bellahsene, Z., Bonifati, A., Rahm, R. (eds.) schema matching and mapping, pp. 253–291. Springer, Heidelberg (2011)

Component-Based Model for On-Device Pre-processing in Mobile Phone Sensing Campaigns

Iván R. Félix, Luis A. Castro$^{(\boxtimes)}$, Luis-Felipe Rodríguez, and Erica C. Ruíz

Sonora Institute of Technology (ITSON), Ciudad Obregón, Mexico
rogelio.felix@gmail.com, luis.castro@acm.org,
{luis.rodriguez,erica.ruiz}@itson.edu.mx

Abstract. In mobile sensing, modern phones allow researchers obtain the information about the participants and their surroundings in a precise, unobtrusive, unbiased, and timely way. However, obtaining this information is just the first step of the research work, concentrating, processing, and giving meaning to the collected data also require a considerable amount of effort. In this work, we present a platform that addresses the aforementioned activities by providing a means to obtain data through sensors of a mobile phone and process those data in the mobile phone, prior to sending them to an online repository.

Keywords: Mobile phone sensing · Sensing platform · Data processing

1 Introduction

When doing research, acquiring data from experiments or fieldwork could take a considerable amount of effort depending on what is needed. Mobile phones have become one of the preferred tools to collect data about users' behavior and their surroundings through sensing campaigns[1]. Mobile phones have been used in different research areas. For instance in health, they have promoted wellbeing [1, 2], and monitored the quality of the sleep [3]; in psychology to gather personality traits [4]; in urbanity to help create maps of noise pollution [4], map potholes or problematic traffic areas [5], and finally, in human computer interaction to create better ways to interact with the smartphone [6, 7]. However, the aforementioned works have one common feature: they developed a mobile software tool to fulfill a specific task in mind. These developed tools can hardly be reused in a different sensing campaign without modifying their very essence.

There are some works that have aimed at enabling researchers to obtain data from mobile phones without developing a software tool from scratch. One of them is AndWellness [8], with the idea in mind of obtaining data from end users through surveys that are launched based on a schedule or on a reduced set of events that AndWellness

---

[1] A sensing campaign is a planned enterprise for collecting data from end users, typically through a research protocol. A sensing campaign defines what data are to be captured and when. That is, what sensors are needed, how and when these sensors will be used, and if there are going to be some processing of the collected data in the mobile device.

© Springer International Publishing AG 2016
C.R. García et al. (Eds.): UCAmI 2016, Part I, LNCS 10069, pp. 201–206, 2016.
DOI: 10.1007/978-3-319-48746-5_20

is able to detect. Another one is MyExperience [9], which presented a more elaborated architecture, on which you can select from a set of available sensors to obtain data, monitor the gathered data by triggers to detect particulars events, and take actions based on detected events. Also, Funf [10] is a framework that ease the development of sensing tools by providing pre-programed routines that allows a developer to easily access a sensor or send the collected data to remote repositories.

In this work, we propose a component-based model for a research kit in mobile sensing, which facilitates on-device analytics. This model can increase users' privacy and the overall performance of a sensing campaign by sending processed data through the network. We next present the problem statement.

2   Problem Statement

Thus far, most current software for sensing campaigns place particular emphasis on collecting raw data from sensors for server-side processing or offline analysis in the lab. However, it is desirable to have on-device analytics for several reasons. One of them is privacy, since data can be pre-processed in the mobile phone of the participant and send processed data to the server; thus anonymizing and transforming data that can be used for identifying end users (e.g., user voice). Another reason is that some data can take considerable time to send over the network (e.g., audio files), so it may be better to process audio in the mobile phone and send only relevant features of the audio signal or the output of an on-device classification algorithm (e.g., decision tree).

Having software (or a mobile phone app) that collects unprocessed sensor data only can have some advantages such as requiring minimal changes in the mobile phone app source code, thus reducing the number of updates needed. On the flip side, having on-device analytics means that there are several algorithms embedded in the mobile phone app for pre-processing, filtering, or classifying data before is sent to a central repository. Incorporating new on-device algorithms means that the app needs to be updated every now and then. Moreover, incorporating new algorithms means that there has to be a knowledgeable programmer with enough familiarity with the code to add new algorithms into the platform. In the end, having numerous algorithms incorporated for on-device analytics can result in a large-sized app that needs to be updated frequently. This, by all means, can be impractical for software maintenance and for the end user participating in the campaign. This latter has caused some end users to drop out from participating in a sensing campaign [11, 12].

3   InCense Platform: Components-Based Model

This work draws on a mobile phone sensing platform called InCense [13, 14]. The InCense platform spans beyond a traditional software tool for collecting data during a sensing campaign. InCense was conceived as a means wherein researchers interested in analyzing behavior data from populations could create sensing campaigns. As mentioned, in this work, we propose a component-based model for a research kit in mobile sensing, which facilitates on-device analytics. This model relies on on-device analytics for data pre-processing, and providing a high-level, open way to incorporate new processing components into the mobile phone sensing platform. The component-based model is based on the idea of having loosely-coupled components within the mobile phone app. In doing so, the components can be individually and remotely updated without directly modifying the mobile phone app source code.

Components are the most variable aspect of sensing campaigns due to the peculiarities of each sensing campaign and, therefore, the elements in which developers are most likely to partake. For this reason, we abstracted the complexity of creating new components into InCense by providing a Web-based platform for creating new components. That is, programmers of new components do not need to know the internal composition of the InCense platform for creating new components. Instead, through this component-based model, components are added to the mobile app at runtime.

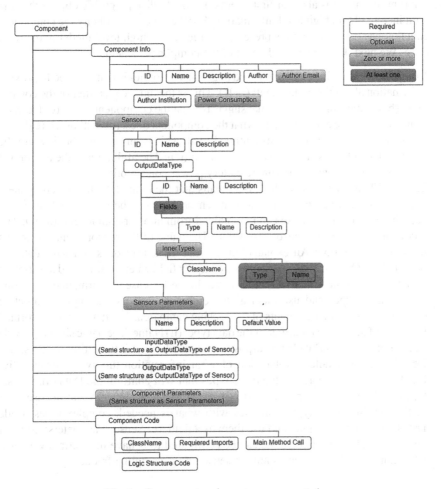

Fig. 1. Components schema tree representation

3.1 Architectural Model

The architectural model represents the main elements that integrate the platform and the most important actions these elements can perform. Each of them is briefly described: (1) InCense RESTful Web Services: Their main role is to provide a place where to manage, search, and generate components, and also a place where to store the collected data. (2) The Web Client: This is a Web user interface that presents a Web-based form that helps the developer write a component. (3) Android Client: The client (i.e., mobile phone app) is in charge of executing the sensing campaigns.

3.2 Component Schema

This schema is used to establish the elements of a component required for generating a package that can be seamlessly integrated into the InCense client (i.e., mobile phone app) at runtime, and it is also our first attempt to standardize pluggable objects that can be combined to obtain high level information. For the sake of simplicity the component schema that has been designed is presented in Fig. 1 as a high level model in the form of a tree. We next describe each element of the component schema.

1. Component Info. This element is used to group a set of fields that are used to provide information about the component: (a) ID: This is the unique identifier of the component. (b) Name: This is a name that suggests what the component is for. (c) Description: An extensive explanation of what the component does. (d) Author: Here should be entered the author name. (e) Author Email: This is an optional field where the email of the author is stored. (f) Author Institution: The affiliation of the author. (g) Power Consumption: Approximate battery power consumption.
2. Sensor. When a sensor is included, it means that the input data that the component will receive, will be obtained from that sensor. This can be an optional, since the data the component will use can be obtained from another component. (a) ID: The unique identifier of the sensor. (b) Name: The name of the sensor is entered in this field. (c) Description: An explanation of what the sensor does and what data are obtained. (d) OutputDataType: This is a complex field where a structured description of the format of the sensor output is stored. In the InCense platform, one can create custom DataTypes and use them as the output of sensors and input / output of components and other elements of the sensing campaign. The data types are formed by: (i) ID: The unique identifier of the data type; (ii) Name: The name should provide an idea of what this DataType purpose is, and the kind of information it stores; (iii) Description: A detailed explanation of what information this type contains; (iv) Fields: It represents each of the basic types that will conform the DataType (basic types could be int, char, float, string, etc.); (v) InnerTypes: In case none of the existing basic types complies with what is needed, complex types inside DataType can be declared, and use them as a field. (e) Sensor Parameters: Some of the sensors of the mobile phone can be configured to behave in a certain way, and what can be configured varies among sensors (e.g. sampling frequency).

3. InputDataType. This element of the schema uses a defined resource as the one stated in the OutputDataType element of the sensor. It is used to define the data that can be received by the component.
4. OutputDataType. This also uses a defined resource as the OutputDataType element of the sensor. With this the output data of the component is defined.
5. Component Parameters: Components can also be parameterized to customize their behavior, just like sensors.
6. Component code. Here, the algorithm that will process the data is defined. All the code must be created as a Java class with all the required functions declared inside the class: (a) Class Name: Stores a suggested name of the class. (b) Required Imports: All the external libraries that are required by the component class must be stated in this field. Available libraries are existing Java and Android SDK's libraries. (c) Main Method Call: Is the method that will be called, so the component performs its processing task. (d) Logic Structure Code: All auxiliary functions, properties and variables required by this component, are declared in this section.

3.3   InCense RESTful Web Services

InCense platform provide several RESTful Web services that complement the data gathering process by providing services that allow developers and researchers to upload the collected data, create custom data types and components, download components and search for components that might help developers avoid extra work. There is a Web user interface to define DataTypes in order to create compatible types that will allow the communication of data between campaign elements, and will let components have enough information to execute their processing and inferences. There is a Web user interface for components too. Through this user interface, developers can express data needed to create a component as defined by the schema.

3.4   InCense Client

The InCense client (i.e., mobile phone app) has been modified so it can take advantage of the RESTful Web services offered by the platform. The InCense client receives the sensing campaign, and makes sure it has all the components needed for on-device processing. If not, it retrieves them from the RESTful Web services and incorporates them onto the client at runtime, in a transparent fashion.

4   Conclusions

In this work, we stated that researchers have created two types of sensing applications: (a) One type that is designed and focused on a single kind of task; (b) Another type of sensing apps seeking abstract common tasks of data sensing and ease the creation of sensing campaigns by lowering the technical knowledge required. Afterwards, we presented the InCense platform, a service that seeks to fulfill the purpose of the second type of sensing application in a very comprehensive manner. Finally, we presented the component-based model that integrates with the InCense platform.

Acknowledgements. This work was partially funded by National Council for Science and Technology in Mexico (CONACYT), and the Sonora Institute of Technology (ITSON).

References

1. Consolvo, S., et al.: Activity sensing in the wild: a field trial of ubifit garden. In: Proceedings of the SIGCHI Conference on Human Factors in Computing Systems. ACM (2008)
2. Lane, N.D., et al.: Bewell: Sensing sleep, physical activities and social interactions to promote wellbeing. Mobile Netw. Appl. **19**(3), 345–359 (2014)
3. Chen, Z., et al.: Unobtrusive sleep monitoring using smartphones. In: 2013 7th International Conference on Pervasive Computing Technologies for Healthcare (PervasiveHealth). IEEE (2013)
4. Chittaranjan, G., Blom, J., Gatica-Perez, D.: Who's who with big-five: Analyzing and classifying personality traits with smartphones. In: 2011 15th Annual International Symposium on Wearable Computers (ISWC). IEEE (2011)
5. Mohan, P., Padmanabhan, V.N., Ramjee, R.: Nericell: rich monitoring of road and traffic conditions using mobile smartphones. In: Proceedings of the 6th ACM Conference on Embedded Network Sensor Systems. ACM (2008)
6. Campbell, A., et al.: NeuroPhone: brain-mobile phone interface using a wireless EEG headset. In: Proceedings of the second ACM SIGCOMM Workshop on Networking, Systems, and Applications on Mobile Handhelds. ACM (2010)
7. Miluzzo, E., Wang, T., Campbell, A.T.: EyePhone: activating mobile phones with your eyes. In: Proceedings of the second ACM SIGCOMM Workshop on Networking, Systems, and Applications on Mobile Handhelds. ACM (2010)
8. Hicks, J., et al.: AndWellness: an open mobile system for activity and experience sampling. In: Wireless Health 2010. ACM (2010)
9. Froehlich, J., et al.: MyExperience: a system for in situ tracing and capturing of user feedback on mobile phones. In: Proceedings of the 5th International Conference on Mobile Systems, Applications and Services. ACM (2007)
10. Xue, Q.L., et al.: Life-space constriction, development of frailty, and the competing risk of mortality: the women's health and aging study I. Am. J. Epidemiol. **167**, 240–248 (2008)
11. Gao, H., et al.: A survey of incentive mechanisms for participatory sensing. IEEE Commun. Surv. Tutorials **17**(2), 918–943 (2015)
12. Restuccia, F., Das, S.K., Payton, J.: Incentive Mechanisms for Participatory Sensing: Survey and Research Challenges (2015). arXiv preprint arXiv:1502.07687
13. Perez, M., Castro, L., Favela, J.: Incense: A research kit to facilitate behavioral data gathering from populations of mobile phone users. In: Proceedings UCAmI, Cancun, Mexico, pp. 25–34 (2011)
14. Castro, L.A., et al.: Behavioral data gathering for assessing functional status and health in older adults using mobile phones. Pers. Ubiquit. Comput. **19**(2), 379–391 (2015)

m^k-sense: An Extensible Platform to Conduct Multi-institutional Mobile Sensing Campaigns

Netzahualcóyotl Hernández[1(✉)], Bert Arnrich[2], Jesús Favela[1], Remzi Gökhan[2],
Cem Ersoy[2], Burcu Demiray[3], and Jesús Fontecha[4]

[1] Computer Science Department, CICESE Research Center, Ensenada, Mexico
{netzahdzc,favela}@cicese.mx
[2] Computer Engineering Department, Boğaziçi University, Istanbul, Turkey
{bert.arnrich,gokhan.yavuz,ersoy}@boun.edu.tr
[3] Psychology Department, University of Zürich, Zurich, Switzerland
b.demiray@psychologie.uzh.ch
[4] Computer Science Department, University of Castilla-La Mancha, Ciudad Real, Spain
jesus.fontecha@uclm.es

Abstract. Mobile sensing has become a growing area of research in pervasive healthcare. In this paper we present m^k-sense, an open framework for mobile sensing on smartphones. m^k-sense is an initiative to reduce the efforts of researchers involved in multi-institutional sensing campaign. It is designed to facilitate the collaboration of researchers that run simultaneous data collection efforts in different locations. We illustrate the use of m^k-sense with two cross-cultural studies conducted in four different countries (Turkey, Mexico, Switzerland, and Spain) with a total of 77 participants. In this paper, we describe the challenges and experience of conducting research *in the wild* by using m^k-sense as sensing platform. Finally, we present how the conducted studies influenced the design decisions of m^k-sense, including features, and tools to monitor data gathering in real-time.

Keywords: Mobile devices · Smartphones · Sensing campaign · Data management application

1 Introduction

Mobile phones are becoming pervasive worldwide. It has been estimated that there is an average of almost 2 mobile devices per user. Mobile phones have become the fastest-selling gadgets, outselling computers four to one [1]. Moreover, Google announced it had hit over 1.4 billion monthly active users on the Android platform [2], with a tendency to further increase.

The proliferation of smartphones enables the gathering of user information from devices that are geographically scattered. This phenomenon gives researchers the opportunity to expand their understanding in many fields. For instance, Silva, T.H. *et al.*, explored the potential of participatory sensing derived from location sharing systems (*e.g.*, Foursquare) to understand human dynamics of cities [3]. Eagle, N. *et al.*, used smartphones' Bluetooth as a proximity sensor, frequency of applications, and call

© Springer International Publishing AG 2016
C.R. García et al. (Eds.): UCAmI 2016, Part I, LNCS 10069, pp. 207–216, 2016.
DOI: 10.1007/978-3-319-48746-5_21

records to recognize social patterns in the daily-life user activity, to infer relationships, and to identify socially significant locations [4].

Extracting collective information holds the potential to help us understand the dynamics of society, as well as to predict collective phenomena such the spread of an infectious disease. Examples are the observation of the spatiotemporal movements of millions of people during disease outbreaks [5], and the rapid detection of an unusual respiratory illness in a remote village [6].

There already exist sensing platforms to support data collection using smartphones. For instance, PRISM (Platform for Remote Sensing using Smartphones) allows to personalize a sensing application by its flexible use of pre-defined modules [7]; PHONELAB provides a manageable interface to initiate a sensing campaign with no coding involved [8]; MyExperience combines sensor and questionnaire collection of data among other functions [9]; FUNF consists of an open source framework to collect sensor data remotely and it provides services to define technical configuration at low level [10]. However, these studies have already tackled important aspects on a sensing campaign (*i.e.*, scalability, no technical knowledge required, and variety on features such as sensor collection and surveys), few efforts have focused on providing a monitor service to supervise completeness of data along sensing campaigns, which is important in terms of quality and quantity of samples being collected.

2 The Concept of m^k-sense as a Platform

m^k-sense is an initiative to reduce the efforts of researchers involved in multi-institutional sensing campaign. As a general view, m^k-sense implements a client-side application able to setup automatically based on server-side requests. It allows researchers to conduct simultaneous campaigns with minimal configuration effort. Thus, researchers could focus on their studies and gather data instead of investing resources in developing specific software.

In this paper, we describe m^k-sense, an extension of the open source framework Funf to collect data through mobile devices, and to manage the collaboration of multiple researchers involved in studies with the same approach. We present overviews of two studies conducted in naturalistic conditions in which we used our earliest version of the m^k-sense. We elaborate on how previous experiences influence the design of our final version of m^k-sense. We conclude with lessons learned, challenges, experience, and future work.

3 m^k-sense

3.1 Principles

m^k-sense was designed based on the following principles:

- **Approach centered.** It is aimed at allowing researchers to focus on the analysis of the data rather than investing effort and resources on developing the sensing system. Thus, operating m^k-sense requires minimal technical knowledge.

– **Modular study-packages.** It is based on the concept of packing, allowing researchers to create several studies simultaneously. Each package is treated independently, but managed with the same Graphical User Interface (GUI) environment.
– **Creation of mobile phone campaign.** Due to the purpose of the platform, after installing m^k-sense on a smartphone, participants are allowed to register themselves to any study-package available, as well as receive updates automatically, remotely and effortlessly.

3.2 Architecture

m^k-sense consists of a three-layer client-server architecture. The data-layer stores information about user devices, survey questions and responses, and sensor data in a relational database. The presentation-layer consists of a Graphical User Interface (GUI) that enables required services to create study-packages and to monitor data completeness. These two layers are executed in the server. Finally, the business-layer manages surveys and sensors, and temporarily keeps data in the client (*i.e.*, smartphone) before it can be sent to the server.

As shown in Fig. 1, once the sensing application is installed on the smartphone, the user receives a sequence of surveys per day set up at random times (Fig. 1-a), while the smartphone constantly collects data through the sensors using Funf (Fig. 1-b). Both sensor and survey data are temporarily stored on the smartphone, waiting to be sent opportunistically by a wireless connection to the server. Batches of data are sent periodically to the server-side (Fig. 1-c). The server collects data and stores them in databases in a way that allows researchers to have an overview about the current study by providing a view of data completeness in real time (Fig. 1-d).

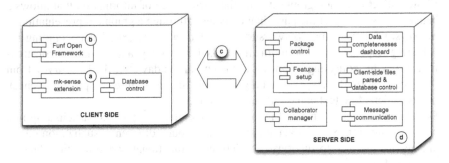

Fig. 1. m^k-sense data collection architecture.

Client. The client consists of an Android-based extensible framework designed to collect smartphone probes. It flexibility allows devices to be configured via server synchronization of all supported sensors from 3 different categories: (1) Sensor: accelerometer, Bluetooth devices, proximity and light sensor, gyroscope, WiFi scan, location, (2) Mobile phone: OS information, browser search history, cell towers, contact list, hardware information, on/off screen-event, phone-call logs, applications used, battery information, SMS history, running applications, and (3) Voluntary input: survey answers as self-report information, audio recording, and photo images.

Once m^k-sense is installed on the smartphone, data probes are collected in the background. Data is temporarily stored on the device as SQLite[1] files, waiting to be sent periodically to the server; opportunistically and unobtrusively by WiFi connections.

Server. The server consists of a web system developed using the Laravel[2] framework and MVC (Model View Controller) architecture. The server constantly listens to requests from the smartphones to store data remotely. When data are successfully sent to the server, these files are deleted from the smartphone in order to release memory space on the mobile device. Meanwhile, the data received on the server are parsed and stored into a MySQL[3] database. This is done by two different processes, so data are available to be monitored in real-time once received.

3.3   Additional Features

m^k-sense provides four additional features that distinguishes it from most sensing platforms: (1) audio recording is privacy-preserving, (2) photo collection, (3) questionnaires as surveys and its triggering function, and (4) dashboard.

- **Audio recording.** Audio data are a rich source of information, which allows, for example, to detect whether someone is having a conversation. On the other hand, most people do not accept audio recordings due to privacy reasons. In order to overcome this tradeoff, a privacy preserving way of audio recording was implemented. For each audio recording, the user can decide whether the recording is uploaded for further processing or deleted.
- **Photo collection.** Photographs are another rich source of information that allows a better understanding of the participant's context through a graphic representation.
- **Surveys.** m^k-sense supports two survey mechanisms: (1) experience sampling for gathering responses at random time intervals during a day, and (2) daily reconstruction survey for collecting responses at the end of the day after the last survey from the first category. Both types of surveys can consist of a mixture of input types: check boxes, sliders, free text entry and audio message.
- **Dashboard.** It is implemented in order to track the smartphones participating in a specific campaign. Sensor data are monitored through different visualization mechanisms, for instance to supervise accelerometer functionality and location data, as shown in Fig. 2.

To recognize data collection problems in a timely manner, a data completeness visualization is available. For instance, Fig. 3 shows accelerometer data collected for 9 days, segmented by hours; where the brightest intensity represents less data and the darkest intensity represents the highest amount of data collected in a period of time. It

---

[1] https://www.sqlite.org/.
[2] https://laravel.com/.
[3] https://www.mysql.com/.

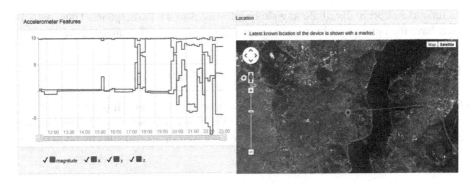

Fig. 2. Accelerometer (left) and location (right) visualizations available through dashboard.

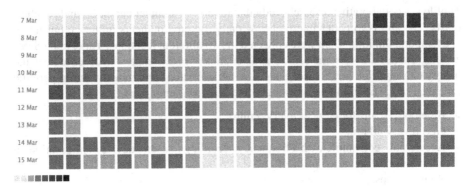

Fig. 3. Data completeness visualization of accelerometer data. Each line corresponds to one day and each square corresponds to one hour. Color-coding indicates the amount of data collected: bright color indicates no/less data; dark color stands for high amount of data. (Color figure online)

can be observed that data collection started in the evening of March 7th. In the afternoon of March 15th, no location data was collected for 3 h. Afterwards, the data connection problem was solved and data collection resumed. Similarly, on March 13rd and 14th data was missed for one hour each day.

If the researcher detects a problem with data collection during the sensing campaign, he or she can inform the participant by sending a message. Messages are sent as notifications directly to the participants' smartphone. Alternatively, the system can be configured to send these messages automatically once a condition is detected.

3.4   Study-Package Structure

A study package follows the idea consists of the idea of enclosing a resource in a single virtual location to keep information well organized and easy to handle when performing any maintenance operation to respective data.

A package can be created by defining a list of sensors to be enabled in the study, a set of rules to define duty cycles, and triggering conditions. Study packages are automatically updated in every smartphone that has previously installed m^k-sense, reducing the time and effort to distribute any study campaigns to the participants. Thus, participants have the option to subscribe or unsubscribe from a set of available campaigns.

4   Conducting Multi-site Sensing Campaigns

As a proof of concept of the m^k-sense framework, we present multi-institutional sensing campaigns: (1) Thought and Life Logging (Tholilo) [11], and (2) a 21-day sensing campaign on walkability. Both projects were deployed in several sites using the *beta-version* of the m^k-sense platform.

4.1   Thought and Life Logging (Tholilo)

Tholilo is a collaborative research study that involves computer engineers and psychologists. The aim is to better interpret how daily life environments influence our mood and temporal thinking. Data were collected in two different locations: Turkey and Switzerland. Table 1 shows some basic characteristics of both samples. In order to keep the battery consumption low, sensor data were not collected continuously, but in periodic time intervals. The following sensor configuration was employed:

- Bluetooth (scans for devices every 5 min),
- GPS (every 30 min),
- Accelerometer (sample with a frequency according to user's device configuration on intervals of 10 s every 5 min),
- Running apps,
- Screen on/off states.

Table 1. Sample characteristics.

	Group A	Group B
No. of participants	6	6
City, Country	Zürich, Switzerland	Istanbul, Turkey
Size of the city	Medium (396 k)	Large (14 M)
Density of population	4.5 k/km^2	2.6 k/km^2
Gender	(1 male; 5 female)	(1 male; 5 female)
Average age (S.D)	33.16 (14.40)	23.33 (1.5)

Each participant was asked to complete a survey 7 times a day at random time points. Right before each notification, a one-minute audio sample was recorded in the privacy-preserving format explained earlier. Surveys focused on collecting data on momentary feelings and thoughts based on an already standardized protocol. Data were collected during a 10-day period.

The users carried their smartphones as usual, no special instructions were given to operate the system. We conducted the study with two different groups of participants. A total of 12 volunteers participated. The inclusion criteria were that the user had to own an Android smartphone and to know how to operate it. A total of 265 surveys were collected during 10 days of the study (105 from Group A and 160 from Group B). Please refer to [11] for a more detailed description of data analysis.

4.2 21-Day Sensing Campaign on Walkability

The Walkability study is an initiative to explore the possibility of automatically evaluating how friendly an area is for walking. The concept of walkability includes issues such as infrastructure and physical access (*e.g.*, sidewalks, street layout), the existence of places of interest to visit (*e.g.*, market, schools, retail, recreation spaces, transit stops), and proximity to home.

The study was conducted with people who work or study at a university and thus recorded data in the surroundings of their campus. The study was replicated in three different countries. Table 2 shows some basic characteristics of the participants. In order to keep battery consumption low, sensor data were collected in periodic time intervals similar to the Tholilo study. Unlike the Tholilo study, in this sensing campaign we increased accelerometer's sample intervals, so we have a more detailed data to infer if the person is walking. The following sensor configuration was employed:

- GPS (every 30 min),
- Accelerometer (sample with a frequency according to user's device configuration on intervals of 20 s every 5 min).

Table 2. Sample characteristics.

	Group AA	Group BB	Group CC
No. of participants	29	21	15
City, Country	Ensenada, Mexico	Istanbul, Turkey	Toledo & Castille-La Mancha, Spain
Size of the city	Medium (500 k)	Large (14 M)	Small (84 k) & Large (2 M)
Density of population	9/km^2	2.6 k/km^2	362/km^2 & 27/km^2
Gender	(15 male; 14 female)	(17 male; 4 female)	(4 male; 9 female)
Average age (S.D.)	28.48 (5.79)	23.24 (3.62)	28.42 (9.08)

Each participant received a survey under two conditions: (1) automatically triggered by detecting that the participant had walked for 5 min continuously, or (2) on demand. Surveys focused on evaluating walkable areas and pedestrian experience. Data were collected during a 21-day period with an optional extension of 7 days.

Participants carried their smartphones as usual. We replicated the study by providing the same training protocol and directions to three different groups of participants. A total of 65 volunteers participated in the study. Each user owned and regularly used an Android smartphone. A total of approximately 500 surveys were completed during the study.

At the time of this writing, the collected data from the study "Walkability: a 21-day sensing camping", has not been yet analyzed in full detail.

5 Lessons Learned and Discussion

Over the course of 10 to 21 days, with 77 users participating in two different studies, we have observed four main aspects related to the following issues: User-experience, technical mobile phone aspects, monitoring data, and replication of studies.

User-experience: Our main challenges developing a platform to be deployed on the user's personal mobile phone were the heterogeneity of OS version and library/services available. Across the studies, we deployed several updates to fix on-the-fly issues that did not show in our pilot test. This aspect is challenging when talking about mobile phones because users tend to rely on mobile phones for critical communication functions, such as emergency calls. Thus, we should guarantee that participants enable automatic updates-mechanism in their smartphones, so we could provide them unexpected updates along the study.

Technical mobile phone aspects: Several cases showed heterogeneous software resources and functionalities available on participants' mobiles devices due to either OS version or device model/brand. A few common examples are:

- **Google Cloud Messaging (GCM):** not all devices had enabled this service which offers to send messages to users through push notifications function.
- **Acceleration frequency:** devices have a different acceleration frequency limited by hardware sensor or set up by the user through configuration preferences.
- **Linear acceleration:** not all devices might provide this service due sensor requirements.
- **Timestamp issue:** timestamp values seems to be retrieved differently from device to device. For instance, some devices populate timestamp with nanoseconds while other use seconds (Unix time). Some sensor's model/brands include an offset to all timestamp. Others, use boot time as base for their timestamp.

We found this aspect to be important since one of the motivations of the sensing campaigns was to create open datasets accessible to the research community in an effort to provide a resource for the analysis on behavior recognition. Thus, there is a need to address the issue of data quality in heterogeneous datasets.

Monitoring data: To supervise data completeness during the campaigns, we assigned a single researcher to monitor data completeness. If a lack of data was identified, he communicated with the remote collaborator to establish communication with respective participants. In order to facilitate effort and coordination among researchers involved in multi-institutional campaigns, a controlled access to monitor data completeness is required for each collaborator. Thus, we considered expanding m^k-sense with a multi-level privilege section.

Replication of studies: We prepared a study protocol and closely provided support to the collaborators. Due to the effort invested when supervising campaigns remotely, we have considered to extend the current platform version with a protocol module, so we are able to tackle two main aspects: sequence of tasks and feedback among collaborators to share experiences and unexpected participant reactions that might vary from country to country. In addition, two aspects we had to deal with were the differences in time zones (among countries and when traveling within the country) and the different survey languages for the different samples (*i.e.*, Spanish, Turkish, English). Thus, we collect time zone data from participant's smartphones, as well as based on geographic location. Finally, the respective client-side GUI resource was validated for 3 native speakers from each country involved in the study. The common language we used to coordinate was English.

6 Conclusion and Future Work

We introduced m^k-sense, a research initiative to facilitate the deployment and supervision of multi-institutional sensing campaigns. Principles of the platform were based on an approach-centered design, modulation by study-package, and creation of mobile phone campaigns. The architecture consists of a three-layer client-server model. The main contributions of m^k-sense consisted of (1) the package-study feature, (2) data completeness monitor in real-time, and (3) a graphical interface to manage sensing campaigns. Altogether, contributions focused on reducing the barrier of technical concepts for non-technical researchers, so that they could focus on analyzing data rather than investing time developing a sensing platform from scratch.

We conducted two multicultural sensing campaigns in four different countries (*i.e.*, Turkey, Mexico, Switzerland, and Spain): (1) Thought and Life Logging, and (2) a 21-day sensing campaign on walkability. A total of 12 and 65 participants collaborated in the studies. Along these campaigns we faced four relevant aspects:

- **User-experience:** users tend to rely on mobile phones for critical communication functions, like emergency calls, thus, a mechanism to guarantee uninterrupted support during sensing campaigns was included in the protocol, nevertheless, we would like to guarantee it programmatically into the m^k-sense application.
- **Technical mobile phone aspects:** due the heterogeneity and diversity of smartphones among participants, we will address a new mechanism when collecting data to guarantee high quality in heterogeneous datasets.
- **Monitoring data:** to improve coordination among multiple collaborators involved in a sensing campaign, we consider it important to include a multilevel privilege section in further versions.
- **Replication of study:** to ensure that a campaign's protocol is appropriately attended, we consider it is important to extend the current version with a new module to keep control of times and sequence of tasks, in which collaborators are able to create a personal schedule of activities, as well as provide/get feedback in real-time from the experience from collaborators in different locations.

Regarding technical aspects, we will consider migrating our current database core to MongoDB[4] since in recent years it has shown a high reliability and better performance when working with largest amount of data.

---

[4] https://www.mongodb.com/.

Additionally we aim at developing an iOS[5] version of the client-side to facilitate recruitment process when designing a sensing platform. Thus, we would aim to cover a broader sample of potential participation of smartphone users and increase the sample of data collected.

Acknowledgment. We thank the participants of the two sensing campaigns described in the paper for contributing their time and effort in making them successful. This work was partially funded by (1) the Co-Funded Brain Circulation Scheme Project "Pervasive Healthcare: Towards Computational Networked Life Science" (TÜBİTAK Co-Circ 2236, Grant agreement number: 112C005) supported by TÜBİTAK and EC FP7 Marie Curie Action COFUND and (2) the EC FP7 Marie Curie Action "UBIHEALTH - Exchange of Excellence in Ubiquitous Computing Technologies to Address Healthcare Challenges" (Project number 316337).

References

1. The Economist. Planet of the phones, February 2015. http://goo.gl/qoX2cc
2. TC Media. Google announces 1.4 billion Android activations, September 2015. http://goo.gl/buxpwO
3. Silva, T.H., Vaz de Melo, P.O.S., Almeida, J.M., Salles, J., Loureiro, A.A.F.: Revealing the city that we cannot see. ACM Trans. Internet Technol. **14**, 1–23 (2014)
4. Eagle, N., (Sandy) Pentland, A.: Reality mining: sensing complex social systems. Pers. Ubiquitous Comput. **10**, 255–268 (2005)
5. Bengtsson, L., Lu, X., Thorson, A., Garfield, R., von Schreeb, J.: Improved response to disasters and outbreaks by tracking population movements with mobile phone network data: a post-earthquake geospatial study in Haiti. PLoS Med. **8**, e1001083 (2011)
6. Brownstein, J.S., Freifeld, C.C., Madoff, L.C.: Digital disease detection–harnessing the Web for public health surveillance. N. Engl. J. Med. **360**, 2153–2155, 2157 (2009)
7. Das, T., Mohan, P., Padmanabhan, V.N., Ramjee, R., Sharma, A.: PRISM: platform for remote sensing using smartphones. In: Proceeding of 8th International Conference Mobile Systems, Applications, and Services, MobiSys 2010, pp. 63–76 (2010)
8. Nandugudi, A., Maiti, A., Ki, T., Bulut, F., Demirbas, M., Kosar, T., Qiao, C., Ko, S.Y., Challen, G.: PhoneLab: a large programmable smartphone testbed. In: Proceedings of First International Workshop on Sensing and Big Data Mining, pp. 1–6 (2013)
9. Froehlich, J., Chen, M.Y., Consolvo, S., Harrison, B., Landay, J.A.: MyExperience: a system for in situ tracing and capturing of user feedback on mobile phones. In: Proceedings of the 5th International Conference on Mobile Systems, Applications and Services, pp. 57–70. ACM, New York (2007)
10. Aharony, N., Gardner, A., Sumter, C., Pentland, A.: Funf: Open Sensing Framework (2011). http://funf.media.mit.edu
11. Hernández, N., et al.: Thought and life logging: a pilot study. In: García-Chamizo, J.M., Fortino, G., Ochoa, S.F. (eds.) UCAmI 2015. LNCS, vol. 9454, pp. 26–36. Springer, Heidelberg (2015). doi:10.1007/978-3-319-26401-1_3

---

[5] http://www.apple.com/ios/.

Distributed Big Data Techniques
for Health Sensor Information Processing

Diego Gachet[✉], María de la Luz Morales, Manuel de Buenaga,
Enrique Puertas, and Rafael Muñoz

Universidad Europea de Madrid, 28670 Villaviciosa de Odón, Spain
{diego.gachet,mariadelaluz.morales,buenaga,
enrique.puertas,rafael.munoz}@universidadeuropea.es

Abstract. Recent advances in wireless sensors technology applied to e-health allow the development of "personal medicine" concept, whose main goal is to identify specific therapies that make safe and effective individualized treatment of patients based, for example, in health status remote monitoring. Also the existence of multiple sensor devices in Hospital Units like ICUs (Intensive Care Units) constitute a big source of data, increasing the volume of health information to be analyzed in order to detect or predict abnormal situations in patients. In order to process this huge volume of information it is necessary to use Big Data and IoT technologies. In this paper, we present a general approach for sensor's information processing and analysis based on Big Data concepts and to describe the use of common tools and techniques for storing, filtering and processing data coming from sensors in an ICU using a distributed architecture based on cloud computing. The proposed system has been developed around Big Data paradigms using bio-signals sensors information and machine learning algorithms for prediction of outcomes.

Keywords: Internet of things · Cloud computing · ICU · Sensors, Big Data

1 Introduction

The intensive care units (ICUs) are responsible for the treatment of extremely ill patients, who need continuous monitoring of their status and vital constants. Nowadays, a very high number of heterogeneous medical and bio-signal sensors are commonly used in that units at hospitals, and the information provided by them can be used for example to develop methods for patient-specific events prediction or in-hospital mortality. Most of the data generated at ICUs are wasted mainly due to complicated process of storing, sharing and processing this huge volume of information. Actually, the rate of generation of clinical data at ICUs has surpassed the capacity for effective storing and analysis using current computational techniques [1]. At the other hand, ubiquitous monitoring of ICU patients presents many opportunities but also great challenges from the point of view of data processing and analysis. At first, most of the information required to diagnose, treat and discharge a patient is present in modern ICUs databases but those are in a variety

© Springer International Publishing AG 2016
C.R. García et al. (Eds.): UCAmI 2016, Part I, LNCS 10069, pp. 217–227, 2016.
DOI: 10.1007/978-3-319-48746-5_22

of heterogeneous formats, including lab results, clinical observations, images, free text evolution notes, continuous waveforms and more.

Considering that sensors used in ICUs can provide precise, heterogeneous and continuous information about clinical condition of a patient, as for example the heart rate, mean arterial blood pressure, diastolic arterial blood pressure, systolic arterial blood pressure, etc., the use of this information can be used in an intelligent data analysis framework for providing detection of abnormal events in the health status of patients or also for predicting unknown situations like nosocomial infections or mortality probabilities, also helping health professionals in doing medical diagnosis in advance, and finally achieve Predictive, Preventive and Personalized Medicine (PPM) [2]. Preventive and Personalized medicine is a concept in health care that allows to predict patient's predisposition to diseases based on data analysis from heterogeneous data sources as medical records, bio-signal sensor information coming for example from wearable devices or in-hospital devices, evolution notes, or even social media, etc., and then to provide relevant information for healthcare professionals in order to take preventive measures. The reminder of this paper is structured as follows. Section 2 introduces the use of Big Data technologies in health care and sensor information processing. Section 3 describes distributed data processing using Spark framework. Section 4 describes the preliminary results and conclusions and finally Sect. 5 presents the future work.

2   Big Data Processing of Health Sensor Information

2.1   Big Data and Health Care

The use of Big Data techniques and technologies are increasingly in the health sector. The amount of structured and non-structured data stored in Hospital's units as well as the proliferation of wearable devices constitutes the perfect scenario where the five V's that identify the Big Data paradigm can be used (Volume, Velocity, Variety, Veracity and Value). The traditional storing, preprocessing and analytical methods are not able to handle this amount of data. In addition, storing and retrieving Big Data need a more complex infrastructure. By using these technologies, we were able to store and process these datasets with the help of distributed systems implemented on cloud infrastructures, public or private, where parts of the data are stored in different locations, connected by networks and brought together by software layers. Recent advances in Big Data technology as, for example, Spark [3], enable us to analyze the data in both off-line and real-time i.e. the data stream is not even stored in a database dealing with the high velocity at which the data are produced. Variety refers to the different types of data that are generated and used for different purposed such analytics, recommendation engines, etc.

Over past years, the data generated and the tools and techniques developed was dedicated to work on structured data that fits into tables or relational databases, and information was obtained using query languages like SQL. However, the data generated in Hospitals, as for example evolution notes, laboratory analysis, images, sensor data, etc. are unstructured and therefore need Big Data tools to easily be stored into new style tables or databases i.e. the so called NoSQL databases. Other complexity factor which it is necessary to take in account is the recent appearance in the health sector of a huge collection of portable wireless devices (pulse-oximeters), electrocardiograph, blood pressure apparatus, etc., it is not possible to obtain valuable information from combining this kind of different sources of information without using Big Data techniques that provide reliable and different analysis methods for heterogeneous data types [4].

As the volume and complexity of data increases, novel and innovative solutions are needed on a technological level. Processing and analyzing big sensorial and multimodal data require enormous computational and storage power; therefore, new architectures emerged like Map-Reduce [5]. In 2004, Google published a paper explaining the MapReduce algorithm, a new model that allows running distributed programs on large amounts of data using commodity hardware. Apache Hadoop [6], is an open-source solution that implements the Map-Reduce algorithm proposed by Google. It is a framework for storing and processing big data in a distributed way, allowing the use of low-cost massive data storage and faster processing. Hadoop has allowed researchers to explore new ways to get value from data in many domains like healthcare. Big Data can improve services with a more efficient processing of electronical medical record, genomics research, or promoting healthy life [7].

Hadoop and its ecosystem gain high popularity over the years, but processing data from disk made it inefficient for many data analysis applications that often require iteration, which is not easily performed in MapReduce [8]. In order to solve these limitations, Spark, a distributing computing framework, was developed allowing in-memory and iterative computation. The programming mode in Spark is based on driver program that run the user's main function and executes parallel operations in a cluster, the main abstractions provided by Spark are called Resilient Distributed Datasets (RDD) [9], which store data in-memory and can be operated in parallel. RDDs can be understood as read-only distributed shared memory, Spark has been shown to outperform Hadoop by up to two orders of magnitude in many cases. MLlib [10] is the machine learning library for Spark covering a broad range of learning algorithms including regression models. Users accustomed to programing in R or Python languages can use a lightweight front-end to a Spark system using a well-defined API, making the learning curve easy and increasing the popularity of R and Python as data science programming languages.

The online (streaming) processing is particularly important in the analysis of the data captured by continuous monitoring in ICU. Continuous ICU monitoring is a powerful tool for evaluating vital function in obtunded and comatose critically ill patients. The online processing of that ICU data can used for example to assist healthcare professionals in decision-making. However, such online analysis is a major task because of the volume of data generated during continuous monitoring and the need for near real-time interpretation of a patient's ICU patterns. Big data tools reduce the tremendous time burdens that accompany analysis of the complete ICU data stream, and allow bedside personnel and non-expert staff to potentially to recognize significant changes in a timely fashion.

In the batch (off-line) processing, the data are collected over a period and are processed by lots, following the work line of physionet challenge. This kind of processing handles large volumes of information, but they have a high latency, which generates a wait until you can see the results. Therefore, it is important for ICU the online analysis. In this work, we use stored data (offline data) as the Physionet Challenge 2012, but we use online (streaming) analysis in order to make our model more suited to the needs of the ICU.

2.2 Health Sensor Information Processing

One of the most important aspects when dealing with health monitoring, is how the data from sensors and medical devices are processed and analyzed. The first thing we think is the goal, that is, we need to establish what we want to do before thinking about how we are going to achieve it. Health data mining approaches are similar to standard data mining procedures, and are performed basically in five stages [11].

- Data Acquisition and Preprocessing. The three most important data sources are experimental data, public datasets, and simulated data. In the first scenario, data is usually gathered from a set of in-hospitals or wearable devices that are monitoring a group of test users. Public datasets are those that have been made publicly available in sites like UCI ML Repository or Kaggle.com. When data is gathered from many heterogeneous wearable devices or sources, a normalization of data step is required. Data preprocessing involves data cleaning for removing noise and data interpolation for mitigate the effects of missing values. Data cleaning is a common step in machine learning applications, and it becomes critical in medical environments because the data is collected for enhancing patient care, not to facilitate numerical or statistical analysis, it is especially true when we are analyzing evolution notes, where is common to find manuscript annotations or comments for a particular situation. In the case of signal analysis, it is absolutely necessary to recognize true measurements from noisy observations, data corruption and the analysis of values out the normal range are also common tasks to be performed before data analysis.
- Data Transformation. When there are a big number of attributes, dimensionality reduction is a required step because it improves efficiency and reduces overfitting. There are usually two ways to do this task: feature selection and feature extraction [12]. In data transformation, the data are transformed or consolidated into forms appropriate for mining including strategies as for example smoothing, include techniques as binning, regression, and clustering or attribute construction (or feature construction), where new attributes are constructed and added from the given set of attributes to help a posterior data analysis stage, or aggregation, where summary or aggregation operations are applied to the data. Also it is possible to apply operations like normalization, where the attribute data are scaled to fall within a smaller range for example $-1, 1$. At this point it is possible to apply discretization where the raw values of a numeric attribute are replaced by intervals or conceptual labels that can be grouped to form a concept hierarchy.
- Modeling. This stage, applies knowledge discovery algorithms to identify patterns in the data or predict some variables, at this point we can apply several algorithms as for example Rule Induction Learners, Decision Trees, Probabilistic Learners, Support Vector Machines (SVM), Hidden Markov Models (HMM), etc.
- Evaluation. The effectiveness of learning algorithms systems is measured in terms of the number of correct and wrong decisions. Some of the metrics used for evaluating

the modes are recall and precision. Recall is defined as the proportion of class members assigned to a category by a classifier. Precision is defined as the proportion of correctly assigned documents to a category.

3   Distributed Data Processing Using Spark

Spark allows faster in-memory computations through above mentioned Resilient Distributed Datasets objects (RDD) that can be constructed from files, shared file systems for example HDFS, parallel operations, transform on existing RDD etc. The usage of RDDs is an important technique to realize parallel computing not only outside but also inside of a slave node. A slave node only needs to maintain some partitions of the training data set. Instead of handling the original whole data set, every slave node can focus on its partitions simultaneously. This mechanism achieves parallelism if the number of partitions is enough. Spark provides two types of parallel operations on RDDs: transformations and actions. Transformations, including operations like map and filter, create a new RDD from the existing one. Actions, such as reduce or collect, conduct computations on an RDD and return the result to the driver program. The Spark core system is a computational engine that is responsible for: scheduling, distributing and monitoring jobs across different nodes. A workflow for a typical machine learning distributed processing task is shown in Fig. 1, starting with data acquisition and preprocessing stages before to use the Spark core and MLIB for model building, training and prediction.

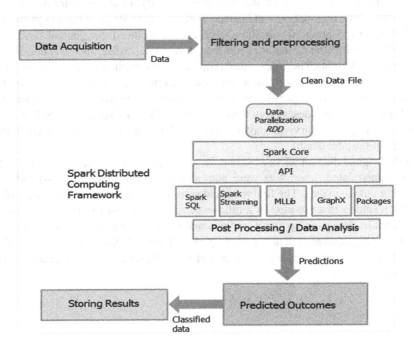

Fig. 1. Distributed data processing with Spark

3.1 Cardiovascular Data from ICU

Normally the data obtained at ICUs are stored in databases provided by the hardware and software companies responsible for the equipment used at ICU, so it is difficult to obtain historical data because of limitations when acquiring storing technologies that depends on the manufacturer. Other common problems include the anonymization of information, removing any reference to personal data according with the directives of national laws about personal and health related information. Fortunately, some initiatives have appeared providing open access to ICU data to researchers. The most important project releasing of data in critical care is the PhysioBank component of PhysioNet [13] and, in particular, the Multiparameter Intelligent Monitoring in Intensive Care II (MIMIC-II) database [14]. PhysioNet is a resource for freely available physiologic signals, which was collected during patient's stay in critical care units. MIMIC-II is a large open clinical database that provides anonymized patient records for over 30.000 patients.

As a use case for data processing and analytics, in this paper we use real data set (Training set A) obtained from Physionet Computing in Cardiology Challenge 2012: Predicting Mortality of ICU Patients [15]. The origin of data is hospital medical information systems for Intensive Care Unit (ICU) patients with ICU stays lasting at least 48 h. The dataset consisted of four thousand records (text files) corresponding to the four thousand ICU stays (patients), and each record was composed of up to 37 time series variables (such as Heart Rate, Weight, pH, SysABP, DiasABP, Urine,…) which could be observed once, more than once, or not at all in some cases (not at all records), and could be recorded at regular intervals (hourly, daily) or at irregular intervals. The time stamps of the measurement indicated the elapsed time since admission to the ICU. In addition to the previous variables, each record included six general descriptors collected at the time the patient was admitted in ICU (RecordID, Age, Gender, Height, ICUType, and Weight). These descriptors appeared at the beginning of each record (time 00:00). In correspondence with those data, the outcomes were a file composed by four thousand rows, where each row contained six outcome-related descriptors for each record (patient). These descriptors were: RecordID, SAPS-I score [16], SOFA score, Length of stay (days), Survival (days) and In-hospital death (0 indicated survival and 1 indicated in-hospital death).

In the original data set all valid values for general descriptors, time series variables, and outcome-related descriptors were non-negative (≥ 0). A value of -1 indicated missing or unknown data. The four thousand records of individual patients were joined together resulting in a file next to 2 million of rows (1885594 rows). This amount of data cannot be processed by many conventional analysis tools. In order to process and analyze this big amount of data, we used Spark with their Python language API and the MLlib library to perform a predictive model from the cardiovascular data described previously.

3.2   Predictive Modelling with MLlib

The aim of the model is to predict in-hospital mortality (0: survival, or 1: in-hospital death) of each patient from the corresponding variables and descriptors. The first step for building a predictive model about the patient's mortality in ICU is to perform data formatting and pre-processing. The text file of 1885594 rows (and four columns: RecordID, Time, Variable, Value), which contained the complete time series variables of the four thousand patients, was saved as a "data frame". This allowed us to process big data with high speed. In order to get static variables, that is, in order to work with a unique value for each time series variable, for each patient (record) we calculated the median of the measurements for each variable.

Then, we generated a structure with the (37) variables as columns, and the 4000 patients (RecordID) as the rows. We also added 8 columns corresponding to the following general and outcomes-related descriptors: RecordID, Age, Gender, Height, ICUType, SAPS.I, SOFA and InHospitalDeath.

Before using these data for the logistic regression model, we carried out a data pre-processing step, that consisted of:

- Replacing invalid physiological values with valid values in the descriptor Height (for example, height value of 13 cm probably corresponds to 130 cm).
- Assigning NA (Not Acknowledge) to both outlier and invalid values of the following variables: pH, NISysABP, NI DiasABP, DiasABP, MAP (for example, a value of 0 in NISysABP);
- Replacing -1 with NA from missing or unknown data (which were indicated with -1 in the original dataset).

A preliminary statistics processing of data set do not show any special relation between any particular variable and the outcome (In.hospital_death), Fig. 2 shows the frequency distribution for the Age variable for both values of In.hospital_death. Similar analysis performed for the others independent variables show similar results.

Logistic regression is a common analysis technique for situations with binary outcome data [17]. This method has been employed by several participants of the Physionet Challenge 2012 to produce predictions of the binary variable "InHospitalDeath" [18]. Logistic regression (LR) is a widely used linear classifier for modeling the probability p of a dependent binary variable given a vector of independent variables X. This model is defined as follows:

$$\log\left(\frac{p}{1-p}\right) = \theta_0 + \theta_1 x_1 + \theta_2 x_2 + \ldots + \theta_n x_n \tag{1}$$

Where p is the probability of the event of interest occurs. In our case, it would be the probability that the patient dies in the hospital (the variable "InHospitalDeath" is 1 in this case). θj with $j = , \ldots, n$, represent the weights of the corresponding dependent variable, *while $p/(1-p)$* is called the odds ratio. The θj parameters of the model can be interpreted as changes in log odds or the results can be interpreted in terms of probabilities. Interpretability, scalability and good predictive performance made logistic regression a widely used classifier in the medical domain.

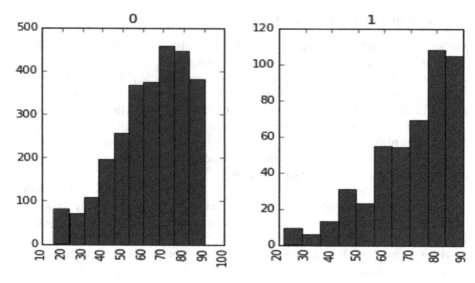

Fig. 2. Frequency distributions (axe y) for Age variable (x axe) related with outcome (above figure)

In this work, we used the same method to predict survival or in-hospital death using the Machine Learning MLlib from Spark. The logistic regression was performed using the function *LogisticRegressionWithLBFGS* that train a classification model for Multinomial/Binary Logistic Regression, using Limited-memory Broyden–Fletcher–Goldfarb–Shanno algorithm for parameter estimation included in the package *pyspark.mllib.classification* of MLlib.

The dependent variable of the model was InHospitalDeath and the independent variables will be the rest of the columns (pre-processed variables and descriptors) previously presented. Due to the logistic model in Spark does not perform well with the missing observations, we only used as independent variables the variables or descriptors in which missing data were present in less than 10 % of patients. In addition, we deleted the rows (patients) with missing data in any column (796 of 4000 rows). We applied repeatedly the model in order to select the more significant variables, and only the variables with a statistical significance level ($p < 0.001$) were included in the final model.

The p-values of the tests are calculated using chi-squared distribution. For training the logistic regression model we used the 60 % of the patients (training dataset, 1922 patients) and the remaining 40 % (testing dataset, 1282) was used to test the model. The variables finally considered for inclusion in the logistic regression model are: BUN Blood urea nitrogen; Glucosa Serum glucose; HCT Hematocrit; HR Heart rate; Mg Serum magnesium; Temp Temperature; Urine.Sum. Table 1 shows the three first row of data set used for training.

Finally, we used the function "predict" included in Spark to predict the probability of death of the testing dataset patients using the final model obtained with the training dataset patients. The predicted outcome is a value between 0 and 1. In order to get a binary outcome, that is, to predict survival (0) or in-hospital death (1), we assigned 0 to

Table 1. First rows of clean data set for training

	Age	HR	Temp	GCS	HCT	BUN	Mg	Glucose	Urine.Sum	In.hosiptal_death
0	76	80	37,45	15	28,8	18	2,1	125,5	26,74	0
1	44	85,5	37,85	5	28,7	3	1,8	141	29,1	0
2	68	74	36,4	15	36,8	20	2,1	117	17,375	0

the predicted value when the probability predicted was lower than 0.5, and in otherwise, we assigned 1 to the predicted value. For model evaluation we take into account the official metric used for Physionet Challenge 2012, score 1 (s1), defined as the minimum value between Sensitivity (S_e) and Positive Predictivity (P^+):

$$S_e = \frac{TP}{TP + FN} \tag{2}$$

$$P^+ = \frac{TP}{TP + FP} \tag{3}$$

TP is the number of true positives, FP is the number of false positives and FN is the number of false negatives. True positive indicates that the model predicts 1 when InHospitalDeath is 1, false positive indicates that the model predicts 1 when InHospitalDeath is 0, and false negative indicates that the model predicts 0 when InHospitalDeath is 1. Therefore, the Se value quantifies the fraction of in-hospital deaths that are predicted, and p^+ quantifies the fraction of correct predictions of in-hospital deaths.

4   Preliminary Results and Conclusions

The efficacy of the model was determined by calculating the s1 score (see Sect. 3.2). We obtained a fraction of correct predictions of in-hospital deaths, P^+ of 0.46. The fraction of in-hospital deaths that are predicted, Se, was 0.12. Therefore, the score s1 obtained by our model was of 0.12. Our fraction of correct predictions, i.e., P^+, was similar to the s1 value obtained by the winners of Challenge 2012 [19], also using SetA (Physionet Challenge 2012). The winners of Challenge 2012 reported the s1 value but not both sensitivity (Se) and positive predictivity (P+) values. Therefore, it is not a strict comparison but illustrative.

We can conclude that the fraction of correct predictions of in-hospital deaths predicted by our model is relatively good (in the same order than the fraction of in-hospital deaths that are predicted by the challenge winners). However, the fraction of in-hospital deaths predicted by our model was smaller. A possible cause is that many variables (22 physiological variables) were not taken into account by the model due to frequent missing data. However, frequent missing data does not imply a minor relation between the variables and the patient death. An information gain analysis performed between the median of each variable and the in-hospital death variable (results not shown) revealed that variables which were in the variable group with longer weights, i.e., the variables better related with the death of the patient (such as PaCo2, Bilirubin, Albumin and AST) were rejected by high missing observations. Also, in the model the threshold of probability was set to 0.5. It is possible that other values would lead to a better prediction of our model.

Other aspects that could affect to the results of our model are the diverse population with a wide variety of life-threatening conditions, with frequent missing and occasionally incorrectly recorded observations. Whatever the cause, our logistic regression model can be improved, however, the aim of this work was not to get the best model, but carry out a distributed Big Data Spark implementation of a predictive model based on cardiovascular data. In this environment, our classifier executed in 0.132 s and trained in 2.198 s, i.e., our architecture presents a very good efficiency.

Therefore, the methodology proposed in this research using the MLlib regression package can be used for analyzing other biomedical datasets. Spark and in particular, MLlib has a rich set of algorithms and tools that can help to analyze and visualize complex datasets, and it lets researchers to deal with Big Data, providing libraries and functions for cleaning and analyzing large volumes of data produced by medical devices and sensors.

5   Future Work

We have designed a solution based on Spark easily adaptable to Big Data processing. We have tested the architecture for a dataset of size 8 MB. As future work we planning to test it with larger biomedical datasets, and to analyze the architecture in terms of efficiency.

Acknowledgments.   This work is still being developed with funds granted by the Spanish Ministry of Economy and Competitiveness under project iPHealth (TIN-2013-47153-C3-1).

References

1. Ghassemi, M., Celi, L.A., Stone, D.J.: State of the art review: the data revolution in critical care. Crit Care (2015). http://ccforum.com/content/19/1/118
2. Golubnitschaja, O., Kinkorova, J., Costigliola, V.: Predictive, Preventive and Personalised Medicine as the hardcore of "Horizon 2020": EPMA position paper. EPMA J. 5(1), 6 (2014). doi:10.1186/1878-5085-5-6. PMID: 24708704
3. Zaharia, M., Chowdhury, M., Franklin, M.J., Shenker, S., Stoica, I.: Spark: cluster computing with working sets. In: Proceedings of the 2nd USENIX conference on Hot topics in cloud computing (2010)
4. Sagiroglu, S., Sinanc, D.: Big data: a review. In: International Conference on Collaboration Technologies and Systems (CTS), pp. 42–47. IEEE (2013)
5. Dean, J., Ghemawat, S.: MapReduce: simplified data processing on large clusters. Commun. ACM 51(1), 107–113 (2008)
6. White, T.: Hadoop: The definitive guide, 2nd edn. O'Reilly Media, Sebastopol (2010)
7. Gachet Páez, D., Buenaga, M., Puertas, E., Villalba, M.T., Muñoz Gil, R.: Big Data processing using wearable devices for wellbeing and healthy activities promotion. In: Cleland, I., Guerrero, L., Bravo, J. (ed.) IWAAL 2015, vol. 9455. LNCS, pp. 196–205. Springer, Switzerland (2015)

8. Dean, J., Ghemawat, S.: MapReduce: simplified data processing on large clusters. Commun. ACM **51**(1), 107–113 (2008)
9. Zaharia, M., Chowdhury, M., Das, T., Dave, A., Ma, J., McCauley, M., Franklin, M.J., Shenker, S., Stoica, I.: Resilient distributed datasets: a fault-tolerant abstraction for in-memory cluster computing. In: Proceedings of the 9th USENIX Conference on Networked Systems Design and Implementation (2012)
10. http://spark.apache.org/docs/1.0.0/mllib-guide.html
11. Sow, D.M., Turaga, D.S.: Schmidt: mining of sensor data in healthcare: a survey. In: Aggarwal, C.C. (ed.) Managing and mining sensor data, pp. 459–504. Springer, Berlin (2013)
12. Apiletti, D., Baralis, E., Bruno, G., Cerquitelli, T.: Real-time analysis of physiological data to support medical applications. Trans. Info. Tech. Biomed. **13**, 313–321 (2009)
13. Goldberger, A., Amaral, L., Glass, L.: PhysioBank, PhysioToolkit, PhysioNet: components of a new research resource for complex physiologic signals. Circulation **101**(23), e215–e220 (2000)
14. Saeed, M., Lieu, C., Raber, G., Mark, R.G.: MIMIC II: a massive temporal ICU patient database to support research in intelligent patient monitoring. Comput. Cardiol. **29**, 641–644 (2002)
15. Physionet 2012 Cardiovascular Challenge. http://physionet.org/challenge/2012/
16. Le Gall, J.R., Loirat, P., Alperovitch, A., Glaser, P., Granthil, C., Mathieu, D., Mercier, P., Thomas, R., Villers, D.: A simplified acute physiology score for ICU patients. Crit. Care Med. **12**(11), 975–977 (1984)
17. Hosmer, D.W.: Lemeshow S Applied Logistic Regression, 2nd edn. John, New York (2000)
18. Vairavan, S., Eshelman, L., Haider, S., Flowers, A., Seiver, A.: Prediction of mortality in an intensive care unit using logistic regression and Hidden Markov Model. Comput Cardiol **39**, 393–396 (2012)
19. Johnson, A.E.W., Dunkley, N., Mayaud, L., Tsanas, A., Kramer, A.A., Clifford, G.D.: Patient specific predictions in the intensive care unit using a Bayesian ensemble. Comput. Cardiol. **39**, 249–252 (2012)

Android Application to Monitor Physiological Sensor Signals Simultaneously

David González-Ortega[✉], Francisco Javier Díaz-Pernas, Amine Khadmaoui,
Mario Martínez-Zarzuela, and Míriam Antón-Rodríguez

Department of Signal Theory, Communications and Telematics Engineering,
Telecommunications Engineering School, University of Valladolid, Valladolid, Spain
{davgon,pacper,marmar,mirant}@tel.uva.es, amine.khd@gmail.com

Abstract. In this paper, we present an Android application to control and monitor the physiological sensors from the Shimmer platform, which include ECG (Electrocardiogram), EMG (Electromyogram), and GSR (Galvanic Skin Response) modules and accelerometer, magnetometer, and gyroscope. The application can configure, select, receive, and represent graphically and store the signals from the sensors. Experimental results with two Android devices were carried out. The ECG, EMG, GSR, and gyroscope sensors were monitored simultaneously at a sampling rate of 10.2 Hz. The application can be applied to many different users such as patients with chronic diseases, athletes, or drivers.

Keywords: Physiological sensors · Mobile application · Android · ECG · EMG · GSR · Gyroscope

1 Introduction

Mobile devices are increasingly present in our everyday life. With such widespread use of these devices, there is a huge demand for applications to address the need of millions of users in many fields such as education, health, business, commerce, and entertainment. Android and iOS are the leaders in mobile operating systems. Between them, Android is the most adopted platform, is growing faster and is the platform with the largest number of apps available for download in its app store (Google Play) with 2.3 million apps comparing to the 2 million apps in the Apple App Store [1]. Besides, Android users are very receptive to new applications so that this platform stands out as the best option to develop a mobile application.

Physiological sensors have gained a lot of importance for the assessment of the human functional state [2]. The biomedical signals are important not only for traditional applications such as medical diagnosis and subsequent therapy, but also for continuous monitoring of physiological information. Mobile health applications interacting with small and non-intrusive wireless physiological sensors can monitor ECG, EMG, respiration rate, and body temperature of a patient for a long term without the need to be hospitalized [3–5].

Physiological sensors from the Shimmer platform include ECG, EMG, GSR, accelerometer, magnetometer, and gyroscope. They are small and light devices that can obtain

© Springer International Publishing AG 2016
C.R. García et al. (Eds.): UCAmI 2016, Part I, LNCS 10069, pp. 228–233, 2016.
DOI: 10.1007/978-3-319-48746-5_23

accurate data for biomedical research [6–8]. Real-time data extracted from the sensors can be used to monitor a patient with chronic diseases, an athlete performance, or any person doing an activity that requires a particular physical and emotional state such as driving.

In this paper, we present an Android health application to control the Shimmer sensors through a Bluetooth connection monitoring their signals simultaneously and storing them in different files as a function of the sensors and the monitored user. These files can be sent by e-mail or shared with other Android applications such as Dropbox or Google Drive.

The rest of the paper is organized as follows. Section 2 presents the physiological sensors from the Shimmer platform that are controlled by the application. Afterwards, Sect. 3 explains the developed Android application. Section 4 details the obtained experimental results and finally Sect. 5 draws the main conclusions about the presented application.

2 Physiological Sensors from the Shimmer Platform

The Shimmer platform [9] provides a set of physiological sensors that can measure different human body parameters suitable for biomedical research. The signals are transmitted through a Bluetooth connection to a PC or a mobile device using an appropriate application.

The Shimmer sensors are small and compact and weigh around 20 g. These features make them suitable to be placed in the human body regions suitable to obtain the required parameters. All the sensors are controlled by an MSP430 microprocessor with 16-bit RISC architecture, which has a low power consumption especially in inactivity periods. The mainboard of the sensors have a 3-axis accelerometer with a range of ± 2 g., ± 4 g., ± 8 g., or ± 16 g. They have two radio modules based on the standards 802.15 or Bluetooth with Mitsumi WML-C46 N CSR design and 802.15.4. Both modules can work simultaneously and stay disconnected in inactivity periods to reduce the power consumption. The CC2420 transceiver is used in the 802.15.4 module. Apart from the signal of the accelerometer, each sensor includes in its basic unit another module to extract physiological parameters such as ECG, EMG, GSR, or 9DOF (9 Degrees of Freedom).

The ECG module can obtain the electrical activity of the heart. To that aim, four electrodes connected to the ECG module have to be placed strategically around the rib cage. Thus, the electrical activity of the heart beats is registered. ECG is a main tool in cardiology, very important for the diagnosis and monitoring of cardiovascular diseases.

The EMG module can obtain the electrical activity related to the muscular contractions. It can be used to evaluate the nerve conduction, the muscular response in an injured tissue, the activation level, and the biomechanics of the human motion. Its electrodes have to be carefully placed to obtain correct values. The positive and negative poles have to be placed in parallel to the muscle fiber. The reference electrode has to be placed in an electrically neutral region of the body as far as possible from the monitored muscle.

The GSR module can obtain the electrical signal caused by the changes in the skin resistance. Figure 1(a) shows it. The emotional state of a person determines such changes. The two electrodes have to be placed in two fingers of one hand as shown in the Fig. 1(b).

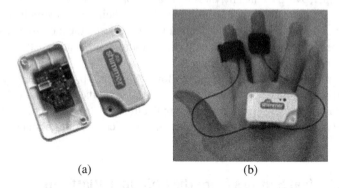

(a)   (b)

Fig. 1. (a) Shimmer GSR module; (b) Placing of the electrodes of the GSR sensor.

The 9DOF module combines a gyroscope with a magnetometer and is a powerful solution to the kinematic detection. This module, together with the accelerometer incorporated in the mainboard of the sensors, can provide a static and dynamic orientation of inertial measurement and thus becomes a complex motion sensor. The gyroscope obtains the speed in the changes of the orientation, measured in degrees per second, with respect to the 3 axes. The accelerometer, magnetometer, and gyroscope have to be calibrated to obtain accurate data.

3   Android Application for the Shimmer Sensors

To develop the application, the Shimmer Android Instrument Driver Library (version 2.1) was used. On the other hand, a set of classes have been developed to interact with the Shimmer sensors, with the Bluetooth functionality, and with the storage memory to save the data in the corresponding files. The Shimmer library allows to communicate with the Shimmer sensors through the SPP (Serial Port Profile) protocol. Android has used this protocol since the version 2.0 (API 5) for the Bluetooth communication.

The Shimmer class in the Shimmer library provides, among other things, the interaction with the sensors, allowing to set up the sampling rate, change the range of the accelerometer, enable or disable some modules of the sensors, and connect several sensors simultaneously to an Android device using several instances of the Shimmer class. This class is based on the Bluetooth interface provided by Android to set the connection with the particular sensor through the SPP. This protocol is in charge of emulating a connection through serial cable with the wireless Bluetooth technology. Each sensor connected with the application is represented through a Shimmer object (instance of the Shimmer class).

The application is structured in three activities: MainActivity, ManageFiles, and ManageDevices. The first activity deals with the Bluetooth settings. It allows to check the current state of the Bluetooth connection, change that state, search the close Bluetooth devices, and select them for a later communication. The second activity manages the previously saved files. These files have the data stored in past sessions organized as a function of the user. The files can be shared with other applications such as e-mail or storage cloud. The third activity is in charge of detecting the state of the Shimmer sensors, communicating with them, and the signal representation and data storage.

The GUI (Graphical User Interface) of the application utilizes both the widget subclass (View class) and the layout subclass (Viewgroup class). The widgets are objects already developed that make programming easier and are directly included to the user interface, e.g. text fields and buttons. The layouts allow to contain the included widgets in an organized way, i.e. provide layout architectures, such as Linear, Tabular, and Relative. The GUI has four screens. Figure 2(a) shows the first screen (Bluetooth settings). It has different sections. The first section has the title and a menu button with only one option "Manage files", which allows to access the activity that is in charge of the file where the sensor data in the previous executions have been saved. The second section is a layout of the state of the Bluetooth that allows to change that state. The third section is a button that allows to search for close Bluetooth devices. The fourth section has a list of found Bluetooth devices. Finally, the fifth section "Manage Devices" has a button to access the next activity to manage the selected devices. Figure 2(b) shows the second screen (File management). Figure 2(c) shows the third screen where the sensors are managed. Its first section has a menu button to select among the following options: "Start all" to set all the sensors in the transmission state, "Streaming" to begin the transmission of the sensors, "Disconnect all" to disconnect all the connected sensors, and "Go home" to return to the first activity. Figure 2(d) shows the fourth screen where graphics can be seen with the online data obtained from the connected sensors.

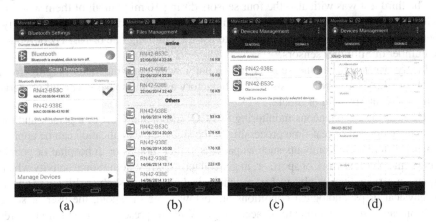

Fig. 2. Four screens of the GUI of the application.

The application needs some classes to work although they do not belong to any activity such as GraphView, DataLogging, Tools, and mySharedPrefs. Graph View creates a view corresponding to a graph with the axes defined as a function of the signal represented in them. Its method setData receives an array with samples of a signal and goes across them representing each sample of the corresponding signal. DataLogging creates the files in the corresponding user folders, writes the header of the files and then the received data. Tools provides the operations that can be applied to the sensors as a function of their state. mySharedPrefs stores the configuration of the sensors, recovers it and makes the same operations for each property of that configuration individually.

4   Experimental Results

The application has been tested with two Android devices (version 2.3 of the Android operating system) and with different number of sensors, sampling rates, and signals to obtain in each sensor. The two Android devices were the Samsung Galaxy SCL (i9003) and the Motorola Moto G (XT1032). The former has a 1 GHz 32-bit Single Core Processor and 478 MB LPDDR RAM and the latter has a 1.2 GHz 32-bit Quad Core Processor and 1 GB LPDDR2 RAM. The aim of using two different devices was to study the constraints of the application as a function of the device performance.

The first test was the simplest and consists of using the ECG, EMG, gyroscope, and GSR sensors with a sampling rate of 10.2 Hz, 10 min duration, and synchronized transmission. The application worked correctly in both devices without any interruption, delay, or block. As a result, it was proved that the application can communicate, represent, and store data from the 4 different sensors in a synchronized way.

The second test was with the aforementioned four sensors during 10 min but with a sampling rate of 50.2 Hz for the ECG and EMG sensors and a different sampling rate of 10.2 Hz for the gyroscope and the GSR sensors. While the Galaxy SCL device suffered from several blocks before closing the application abruptly, the Motorola Moto G was able to end the test.

The third test was with also the four sensors during 10 min but all of them working with a sampling rate of 50.2 Hz in a synchronized way. Neither device worked properly. Therefore, with these devices is necessary to use the sampling rate of 10.2 Hz or reduce the number of Shimmer sensors.

Lastly, we tested all the sensors individually with sampling rates ranging from 10.2 Hz to 128 Hz. All these tests were satisfactory as all the sensors worked properly without any interruption or block.

Through the simultaneous monitoring of ECG, EMG, and GSR of a person and the future development of real-time processing of the signals, the application can be applied to many different environments such as patients at their homes or in hospital or people doing some physical work or sport, or, in general terms, while doing some activity which requires a certain level of physical or psychological conditions such as driving. Thus, if the physical or psychological conditions are below some threshold, the user or some clinician can be sent a warning to act accordingly. With the present and the future features of the application and the improvements of newer versions of the physiological sensors in terms of autonomy and size, the application can address requirements of an Ambient Intelligent system such as transparency to the user, ubiquity, and responsiveness.

5   Conclusions

In this paper, an Android mobile application for the control of the physiological sensors from the Shimmer platform and the monitoring of their signal is presented. The application is compatible with the 2.3 and later versions of the Android operating system.

The connection with the sensors is transparent to the user. The application receives the sensor signals, represents them graphically and stored them in files for later analysis. It is able to use four sensors simultaneously in two low-cost Android devices at a sampling rate of 10.2 Hz so that a health monitoring can be fulfilled in many interesting environments. For instance, drivers can be monitored on route and the stored data can be used later to analyse the physical and emotional state of the driver as the ECG, EMG, and GSR sensors can be used to that aim. The gyroscope can be placed on the steering wheel to obtain the angular speed.

The application can be extended so that a real-time processing of the signals can be made to alert the user as soon as some data imply an abnormal physical or emotional state. For instance, this functionality can alert a driver when the level of attention and drowsiness are not suitable for a safe driving. The potential benefits of mobile applications with these functionality in our lives are great and numerous.

Acknowledgements.   This work was partially supported by the National Department of Traffic (belonging to the Interior Ministry) under project SPIP2015-01801.

References

1. Statista. http://www.statista.com/statistics/276623/number-of-apps-available-in-leading-app-stores/
2. Kaniusas, E.: Biomedical Signals and Sensors I. Springer-Verlag, Heidelberg (2012)
3. Xia, H., Asif, I., Zhao, X.: Cloud-ECG for real time ECG monitoring and analysis. Comput. Methods Programs Biomed. **110**(3), 253–259 (2013)
4. Liu, L., Chen, X., Lu, Z., Cao, S., Wu, D., Zhang, X.: Development of an EMG-ACC-based upper limb rehabilitation training system. IEEE Tran. Neural Syst. Rehabil. Eng. doi:10.1109/TNSRE.2016.2560906
5. Lou, D., Chen, X., Zhao, Z., Xuan, Y., Xu, Z., Jin, H., Guo, X., Fang, Z.: A wireless health monitoring system based on android operating system. IERI Procedia **4**, 208–215 (2013)
6. Burns, A., Greene, B.R., McGrath, M.J., O'Shea, T.J., Kuris, B., Ayer, S.M., Stroiescu, F., Cionca, V.: SHIMMER™ – a wireless sensor platform for noninvasive biomedical research. IEEE Sensors J. **10**(9), 1527–1534 (2010)
7. Dao, T.T., Tannous, H., Pouletaut, P., Gamet, D., Istrate, D., Ho Ba Tho, M.C.: Interactive and connected rehabilitation systems for E-Health. IRBM, doi:http://dx.doi.org/10.1016/j.irbm.2016.02.003
8. Abbate, S., Avvenuti, M., Bonatesta, F., Cola, G., Corsini, P., Vecchio, A.: A smartphone-based fall detection system. Pervasive Mobile Comput. **8**, 883–899 (2012)
9. Shimmer sensing. http://www.shimmersensing.com

Monitoring Chronic Pain: Comparing Wearable and Mobile Interfaces

Iyubanit Rodríguez$^{(\boxtimes)}$, Carolina Fuentes$^{(\boxtimes)}$, Valeria Herskovic$^{(\boxtimes)}$, and Mauricio Campos$^{(\boxtimes)}$

Pontificia Universidad Católica de Chile, Santiago, Chile
{iyubanit,cjfuentes,vherskovic}@uc.cl, macampos@med.puc.cl

Abstract. Technologies to monitor patients are convenient for patients and can reduce health costs. Chronic pain is a pain that lasts more than 3 months and affects the welfare of patients. Pain is subjective and there are applications to self-report pain, but their adherence rates are low. The purpose of this article is the understanding of the characteristics of technology that helps the adoption of these systems. We have implemented two solutions (mobile application and wearable device), in order to compare them to measure the rate of user acceptance, and also to get feedback about fundamental features of interfaces to report pain levels. To evaluate the two solutions we conducted interviews with 12 people. The results showed that when given the choice between both devices, 67% of the users preferred the wearable device over the mobile application, and 16.5% preferred the mobile application over the wearable device. We also found that a device for reporting pain must be specific to this purpose, aesthetically pleasing and allow users to report easily and at the right time.

1 Introduction

Patient monitoring is technology to manage, control and treat patients while collecting information remotely [1]. These technologies are becoming widespread: they are more convenient for patients and can potentially reduce health care costs [2]. The information that is collected by these systems is sent to healthcare professionals, who receive a medical report in real-time and can improve the patient's diagnosis and treatment [3].

Chronic pain is pain that lasts more than 3–6 months and adversely affects patients' wellbeing [4]. Pain may also interfere with daily activities and affect health, employment and life [5]. Pain is subjective, so the only way to evaluate it successfully is to ask the patient [6], which is usually done during a doctor's appointment. There are several pain measurement scales [7] suited to different types of patients. This work proposes remote monitoring for patients with pain, in order to understand the patients' pain levels during longer time periods. We propose two types of interfaces for pain monitoring: a mobile application and a wearable device. Our research questions are the following ones:

© Springer International Publishing AG 2016
C.R. García et al. (Eds.): UCAmI 2016, Part I, LNCS 10069, pp. 234–245, 2016.
DOI: 10.1007/978-3-319-48746-5_24

1. Which is more appropriate (has a higher rate of user acceptance) for monitoring pain: a wearable interface or a mobile application?
2. Which characteristics, or features, of the interface, are critical for users to be able to report their pain levels?

This paper is organized as follows. First, we discuss related work, considering self-report of pain and technologies to report pain. Then, we describe the design and characteristics of our prototypes. Section 4 describes our methodology, then Sect. 5 describes the results and their discussion. Finally, Sect. 6 presents our conclusions and discusses possible avenues of future work.

2   Related Work

This section presents the related work: first, we discuss how pain is reported. Then, we review literature about self-report technologies and then we discuss interfaces for the self-report of pain.

2.1   Pain Measurement

Several scales, aimed at different target users, exist to report pain (Fig. 1). The visual analog scale (VAS) is easy to use for patients with a small amount of training [8]. However, elderly people with cognitive impairment or mobility problems may have trouble using it and it can not be administered over the phone [8]. The scale of faces (WBS) is suitable for use by children and elderly people [9]. The numerical scale (NRS) can deliver results graphically and verbally [10]. The NRS scales and descriptive scale (VRS) are best suited for patients with dementia [11]. For people who can not use one of these scales, for example pre-verbal children, observation and opinion of their relatives or caregivers can be used [11].

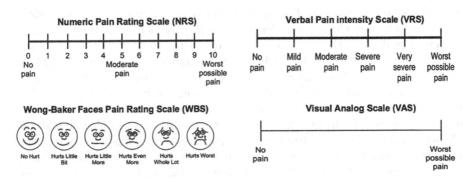

Fig. 1. Types of scales for measuring pain. Adapted from [7,12].

Physicians usually use on of the previous scales to ask patients about their pain during their appointment. This may be problematic, as pain is then evaluated mainly during the clinic visit [13], and not in a real scenario. Additionally, pain is usually registered on paper, which can cause information loss and difficulties in analyzing and searching for data [14].

2.2 Technology for Pain Monitoring

A system for patients to report pain from anywhere, at any time, can be used to monitor the evolution of pain levels [15]. Self-reporting can help patients become more aware of the characteristics of their pain, e.g. its intensity, patterns, triggers and location [16], and be more engaged in the self-management activity [17].

Several applications allow people to report episodes of pain at any time [18]. One mobile application displays a human figure and asks the user to indicate the position, intensity and type of pain he/she feels [19,20]. Another application also incorporates virtual reality [14]. Researchers have also proposed tangible technology that allows users to easily record their pain [15]. These types of applications allow new avenues of patient-doctor interaction [14] and patients feel confidence that their diagrams will be interpreted correctly, while doctors consider the diagrams and text descriptions complete and relevant [19].

Adherence rates for these applications are often low [21]. Besides, some tools are burdensome [17] or not portable. Additionally, in most cases, healthcare professionals have not been involved in the design of mobile applications for pain management [22]. In the case of this study, a healthcare professional is part of the research team, providing his insight about issues regarding pain and self-reporting. For these reasons, we believe that understanding the characteristics of technology that help adherence and adoption, as well as designing a device with the information gathered from the healthcare perspective, is crucial to developing systems that are useful for patients with pain.

2.3 User Preferences for Wearable Devices

Several researchers have studied users' preferences regarding wearable devices. Six group of factors affect wearables' acceptability, namely: that they fulfill fundamental needs, that they are useful and easy to use, their effect on social interaction, physical effects of the device, and demographic characteristics [23]. A recent survey found that the most important characteristics of wearable interfaces are those regarding functionality, form factor, and interaction design, while characteristics such as sharing are not priorities for users [24]. The acceptability of medical wearables in healthcare settings has also been studied. For example, following the discharge from an intensive care unit, patients using wearable monitors removed them because of e.g. discomfort and irritation, feeling unwell and overwhelmed [25]. We aim to contribute to this literature, comparing the acceptability of wearable and mobile devices in remote pain monitoring.

3   Design of Self-reporting Interfaces

We designed and implemented a wearable device and a mobile application to self-report pain. Both of these technological solutions use a simple VRS scale

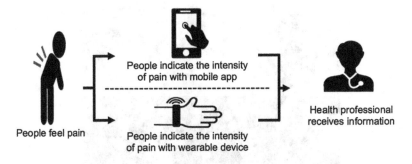

Fig. 2. Scheme for self-reported pain

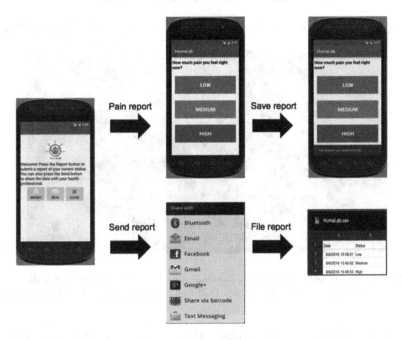

Fig. 3. Mobile app to self-report pain (*painApp*)

with three levels of intensity (Low, Medium and High). When the user feels pain during his/her daily life, he/she may report pain intensity by using the application. This information can be shared, e.g. sent to health professionals (see Fig. 2).

3.1 *PainApp*: A Mobile Application to Report Pain

We implemented PainApp, a simple Android application that asks users about their pain level and stores the information in a database. The information can then be sent through email, bluetooth, social networks, etc. (Fig. 3). The application

Fig. 4. *B-pain.* Above: inside view, below: outside view. (Color figure online)

Fig. 5. B-pain: (a) person uses the wearable on the wrist. (b) person indicates the intensity of pain by pressing the button (red light for feedback). (Color figure online)

was designed considering older adults as the target users, as they more often suffer from pain. For this reason, we used considerations such as high color contrast, simplicity, large font, tactile interaction and explicit messages [26, 27].

3.2 *B-pain*: A Wearable Device to Report Pain

We implemented B-pain, a wearable device (worn on the body, e.g. embedded in clothing or accessories [28]). B-pain was designed to be worn as a bracelet, and it implements the same scale as the previous application: a VRS scale with three levels of intensity (Low, Medium and High). *B-pain* was implemented using Lily-Pad Arduino USB (electronic card based on the microcontroller Atmega32U4), blue, yellow and red LEDs, conductive fabric to create buttons, thread and a 110mAh battery. Figure 4 shows some components of the bracelet and the completed prototype.

When a person feels pain during the day, he/she can report the intensity of pain by pressing one of three buttons (green = low, yellow = medium and red = high) and receive feedback through the LED light (see Fig. 5).

4   Methodology

We used a qualitative methodology for data collection: we applied semi-structured interviews. Each interview lasted about 15 min. To evaluate the solutions the participants interacted with the mobile application and wearable device and then we collected four types of information:

- Questionnaire results regarding digital skills (based on DIGCOMP [29]).
- Results from a usability evaluation using SUS (System Usability Scale) [30].
- Questionnaire results regarding usability of the wearable device.
- Audio recordings from the interviews.

4.1   Participants

Our participants were 12 undergraduate students from different specialities (6 women and 6 men). The average age of participants was 26 with a standard deviation of 5.4. All participants have *above basic* digital skills.

4.2   Assessment Tools

- DIGCOMP is a standardized instrument to measure digital competences, where users are categorized into one of four possible groups, according to their digital skill levels: *none, low, basic* or *above basic* [29].
- System usability scale (SUS) is a quick way to measure the overall usability of the system [30]. In this scale, scores below 60 indicate poor usability, while scores over 80 indicate very good usability [31].

4.3   Experiment

We performed semi-structured interviews with 12 participants in total during May 2016. To avoid bias, half of the participants interacted with the mobile application first and the wearable device second, and the other half performed the opposite process. Each interview had the following structure:

1. One researcher gave a brief introduction about the study and its purpose.
2. The participant read a scenario describing a person with pain (a college student who after a car accident is suffering from chronic back pain).
3. The first interface was explained.
4. The participant was given time to interact with the first interface.
5. The researcher asked questions about the interface, using a predefined question set to guide the discussion.
6. Steps 3–5 were repeated with the second interface
7. The researcher asked questions comparing the two interfaces.
8. Finally, participants completed the DIGCOMP test, SUS questionnaire and user experience survey (see Fig. 6).

Fig. 6. Evaluation of prototypes.

4.4   Analysis

Interviews were recorded and transcribed. Subsequently, each interview was assigned a code (P1 to P12). We used thematic analysis to code and analyze the data [32]. Some quotes from participants are provided in the results (translated from Spanish).

5   Results

5.1   Which Is More Appropriate for Monitoring Pain: A Wearable Interface or a Mobile Application?

67 % of participants found the wearable device (B-pain) was more simple, while only 16.5 % found the mobile application simpler (and 16.5 % found that both technologies are equally simple). P4:*"the bracelet, because it's easy and fast. If I feel pain I just need to push a button, while with the cellphone I have to turn it on, open the application, and then report pain"*. 75 % of participants believed that the wearable device allows users to report pain at the right time, whereas the mobile application does not, because the user is delayed by opening his/her smartphone and finding the app.

When participants imagined suffering from some kind of chronic pain, 67 % indicated that they would prefer to use the wearable device. P1: *"The wearable device is easy to use, does not bother me and would not be difficult to use."*

Regarding the digital skills necessary to use each interface, 41.6 % of participants believed the mobile application requires some knowledge about how to use a smartphone, while 33 % believed the wearable device only requires a brief initial explanation about how to use it.

However, users not only found differences between both prototypes; they also believed the two prototypes could complement each other in different situations. P8: *"Maybe the bracelet and the app should be linked, and instead of mailing the data it could be sent to the app...".* For example, the bracelet could be easier to use in some situations (e.g. driving) while the mobile application would be more appropriate in others (e.g. gala dinner). P6: *"I have the phone nearby but wouldn't use it in the kitchen or car, while in the car it is easier to press the button and in other cases I would use my cellphone".*

5.2   Which characteristics, or features, of the wearable interface, are critical for users to be able to report their pain levels?

The B-pain device had a SUS score of 87, which represents good usability. Table 1 displays the average score (in a 5-point Likert scale) for each of the questions in the user experience questionnaire given at the end of the experiment. Most questions have very good scores, and the issues of "comfortable to use" and "response time is slow," have a greater dispersion. We also analyzed the semi-structured interviews, usability and results using thematic analysis, and present our insights below.

Table 1. Results of user experience questions for B-pain device

Statement[a]	Average	Standard deviation
1. The bracelet is comfortable to use	4,00	1,00
2. The bracelet is heavy to carry	1,08	0,28
3. Bracelet elements are messy	1,17	0,37
4. Response time is slow	2,00	1,22
5. The bracelet is intuitive to use	4,58	0,86

[a] Scale: 1 (strongly disagree) to 5 (strongly agree) for each question.

Low Cognitive Load. B-pain requires a low cognitive load from the users. The device is simple to understand as it resembles a traffic light and it only has one functionality. P12: *"I liked the colors, they are traffic light colors, and everyone is familiar with them.".* One user did mention that this device might not work for colorblind users, so it is important to complement the interface with, e.g. words or textures, that can help users with disabilities or other conditions use them.

Anytime/Anywhere Availability. The bracelet is easily available at all times facilitating access to self-report. We call this anytime-anywhere availability *"when you need it, you have it"(WYNIYHI)..* P1: *"you are always carrying it, while you may have left your cellphone far away and not have it on hand to report pain at that exact moment".*

Materials. It is important to consider the type of material with which the wearable device is designed. Materials can cause problems for users, e.g. allergies. We found the current material of the prototype (felt) is not appropriate, and that future versions must consider the aesthetics and functionality of the bracelet materials. P3: *"I'd be scared to drop it in the water... I don't know what it's made of or whether it would give me allergies or something like that... and if you want to go to a party this could be aesthetically unpleasant."*

The feedback given to the user should be clear and at the right time, so that the user is aware that the actions have been properly completed. P6: *"It is difficult to use outside because the light is too small to know whether it is working or not".*

Self-reflection. Reporting pain through a device is useful not only to share information with medical personnel, but also for users to be able to reflect on their own pain. P2: *"I like that it makes me aware of pain ... and I can have an answer, it is received by a doctor or a group of persons with pain and I can feel understood or that someone knows about this pain."*

5.3 Discussion

We found that the wearable device had a higher acceptance for monitoring pain than a mobile device. Surprisingly, the fact that users would have to carry an additional device (the bracelet) did not hinder acceptance. As in previous studies e.g. [23,24], the functionality of the wearable device greatly affected its acceptance - since the reason for wearing the device was an important problem such as chrnoic pain. We also found, similarly to previous studies, that the physical format of the device is an important aspect.

We also focus our attention on the fact that the wearable device presents a low cognitive load, even to users who are unfamiliar with technology. This could be a clear benefit of the wearable. However, the mobile application is easily replicable, able to be installed and disseminated easily through e.g. application stores. This could result in wider adoption than the wearable device, which requires hardware. Although this hardware is inexpensive, it does represent a cost and requires effort to manufacture (as well as solving technical problems such as malfunctions and battery life). There is, therefore, a trade-off between the usability of the wearable and the difficulty in replicating and maintaining it.

Our proposal and preliminary evaluation present some limitations that we would like to acknowledge. First, the participants were all people without pain and all of them undergraduate students with above basic digital skills. It is possible that they are more open to trying new technology and positive towards novel interfaces such as wearables. Second, these prototypes were tested during a short period of time. Longer evaluation is need to truly assess adoption and usability. Nevertheless, the evaluation was a first step to identify concerns about the design of a wearable device to report pain before evaluating with patients that suffer chronic pain. Third, the interface is an overly simplistic view of the problem of chronic pain. For example, there are only three buttons to self-report pain in the wearable device, which is simple to understand by users; however, they do not take into account intermediate levels of pain. To improve the adoption, it is necessary to give users a greater choice of pain intensity levels, but without making the design more complex. P2: *"It may be missing more options, pain is not only physical it can also be emotional, spiritual and there are many types of pain, this only involves a general concept of pain."*

6 Conclusion

This paper presented a comparative study of two prototypes that allow users to self-report pain during their daily lives, allowing medical workers to monitor their pain: (1) a simple mobile application and (2) a bracelet. Both prototypes use a simple 3-level pain scale (low, medium, or high). We evaluated our prototypes with 12 participants, who were more favorable towards the wearable device.

The next steps in this research are to perform interviews and co-design sessions with patients who suffer from chronic pain, therapists and clinical teams, to create a second version of the wearable device. From our study, we believe a useful device such as a wristwatch can be used to incorporate pain reporting mechanisms. Furthermore, we will conduct long-term testing with users to deeply understand their perceptions towards a wearable device to report pain.

Acknowledgments. This proyect was supported partially by CONICYT-PCHA/ Doctorado Nacional/13-21130661, 2014-63140077, CONICIT and MICIT Costa Rica PhD scholarship grant, Universidad de Costa Rica and Fondecyt Proyect (Chile), grant: 1150365.

References

1. Ryu, S.: mHealth: new horizons for health through mobile technologies: based on the findings of the second global survey on eHealth. Healthc Inform. Res. (2012)
2. Field, M.J., Grigsby, J.: Telemedicine and remote patient monitoring. JAMA **288**(4), 423–425 (2002)
3. Alahmadi, A., Soh, B.: A smart approach towards a mobile e-health monitoring system architecture. In: 2011 International Conference on Research and Innovation in Information Systems, pp. 1–5, November 2011
4. ACPA. Glossary @ONLINE (2016)
5. Gureje, O., Von Korff, M., Simon, G.E., Gater, R.: Persistent pain and well-being: a world health organization study in primary care. JAMA **280**(2), 147–151 (1998)
6. McCaffrey, M., Beebe, A.: Giving narcotics for pain. Nursing **19**(10), 161–165 (1989)
7. NIPC. Pain assessment scales @ONLINE (2001)
8. Hawker, G.A., Mian, S., Kendzerska, T., French, M.: Measures of adult pain: visual analog scale for pain (VAS pain), numeric rating scale for pain (NRS pain), McGill pain questionnaire (MPQ), short-form McGill pain questionnaire (SF-MPQ), chronic pain grade scale (CPGS), short form-36 bodily pain scale (SF-36 BPS), and measure of intermittent and constant osteoarthritis pain (ICOAP). Arthritis Care Res. **63**(S11), S240–S252 (2011)

9. Jackson, D., Horn, S., Kersten, P., Turner-Stokes, L.: Development of a pictorial scale of pain intensity for patients with communication impairments: initial validation in a general population. Clin. Med. **6**, 580–585 (2006)

10. Williamson, A., Hoggart, B.: Pain: a review of three commonly used pain rating scales. Issues Clin. Nurs. **14**, 798–804 (2005)

11. Horgas, A.L.: Assessing pain in older adults with dementia @ONLINE (2012)

12. Garra, G., Singer, A.J., Taira, B.R., Chohan, J., Cardoz, H., Chisena, E., Thode, H.C.: Validation of the wong-baker faces pain rating scale in pediatric emergency department patients. Acad. Emerg. Med. **17**(1), 50–54 (2010)

13. Chhikara, A., Rice, A.S.C., McGregor, A.H., Bello, F.: In-house monitoring of low back pain related disability (impaired). In: 30th Annual International Conference of the IEEE Engineering in Medicine and Biology Society, EMBS 2008, pp. 4507–4510, August 2008

14. Spyridonis, F., Hansen, J., Gronli, T., Ghinea, G.: Paindroid: an android-based virtual reality application for pain assessment. Multimedia Tools Appl. **72**(1), 191–206 (2014)

15. Alakarppa, I., Riekki, J., Koukkula, R.: Pervasive pain monitoring system: user experiences and adoption requirements in the hospital and home environments. In: 3rd International Conference on Pervasive Computing Technologies for Healthcare, PervasiveHealth 2009, pp. 1–8, April 2009

16. Rini, C., Williams, D.A., Broderick, J., Keefe, F.: Meeting them where they are: using the internet to deliver behavioral medicine interventions for pain. Transl. Behav. Med. **2**(1), 82–92 (2012)

17. MacLeod, H., Tang, A., Carpendale, S.: Personal informatics in chronic illness management. In: Proceedings of Graphics Interface, GI 2013, pp. 149–156. Canadian Information Processing Society, Toronto (2013)

18. Huang, Y., Zheng, H., Nugent, C., McCullagh, P., Black, N., Vowles, K.E., McCracken, L.: Feature selection and classification in supporting report-based self-management for people with chronic pain. IEEE Trans. Inf. Technol. Biomed. **15**(1), 54–61 (2011)

19. Jang, A., MacLean, D.L., Heer, J.: Bodydiagrams: Improving communication of pain symptoms through drawing. In: Proceedings of the SIGCHI Conference on Human Factors in Computing Systems, CHI 2014, pp. 1153–1162. ACM, New York (2014)

20. Serif, T., Ghinea, G., Frank, A.O.: Visualizing pain data for wheelchair users: a ubiquitous approach. J. Mob. Multimed. **1**(2), 161–177 (2005)

21. Rosser, B.A., Vowles, K.E., Keogh, E., Eccleston, C., Mountain, G.A.: Technologically-assisted behaviour change: a systematic review of studies of novel technologies for the management of chronic illness. J. Telemedicine Telecare **15**(7), 327–338 (2009)

22. Rosser, B.A., Eccleston, C.: Smartphone application for pain management. J. Telemedicine Telecare **17**(6), 308–320 (2011)

23. Gimhae, G.-N.: Six human factors to acceptability of wearable computers. Int. J. Multimedia Ubiquitous Eng. **8**(3) (2013)

24. Rantakari, J., Inget, V., Colley, A., Häkkilä, J : Charting design preferences on wellness wearables. In: Proceedings of the 7th Augmented Human International Conference 2016, AH 2016, pp. 28:1–28:4. ACM, New York (2016)

25. Jeffs, E., Vollam, S., Young, J.D., Horsington, L., Lynch, B., Watkinson, P.J.: Wearable monitors for patients following discharge from an intensive care unit: practical lessons learnt from an observational study. J. Advanced Nurs. (2016)

26. Iglesias, R., de Segura, N.G., Iturburu, M.: The elderly interacting with a digital agenda through an rfid pen and a touch screen. In: Proceedings of the 1st ACM SIGMM International Workshop on Media Studies and Implementations That Help Improving Access to Disabled Users, MSIADU 2009, pp. 63–70. ACM, New York (2009)
27. Ferron, M., Mana, N., Mich, O.: Mobile for older adults: towards designing multimodal interaction. In: Proceedings of the 14th International Conference on Mobile and Ubiquitous Multimedia, MUM 2015, pp. 373–378. ACM, New York (2015)
28. Motti, V., Kohn, S., Caine, K.: Wearable Computing: a Human-centered View of Key Concepts, Application Domains, and Quality Factors. In: Proceedings of the 16th International Conference on Human-Computer Interaction with Mobile Devices & Services, pp. 563–564, Toronto (2014)
29. Ferrari, A.: Digital competence in practice: An analysis of frameworks. Technical report, Research Centre of the European Commission (2012)
30. Brooke, J.: Sus-a quick and dirty usability scale. Usability Eval. Indus. **189**(194), 4–7 (1996)
31. Tullis, T., Albert, W.: Measuring the User Experience: Collecting, Analyzing, and Presenting Usability Metrics. Morgan Kaufmann Publishers Inc., San Francisco (2008)
32. Braun, V., Clarke, V.: Using thematic analysis in psychology. Qual. Res. Psychol. **3**(2), 77101 (2006)

Development a Mobile System Based on the Harris-Benedict Equation to Indicate the Caloric Intake

Vladimir Villarreal[✉] and Manuel Otero

GITCE Research Lab, Technological University of Panama, Chiriquí, Panama
{vladimir.villarreal,manuel.otero}@utp.ac.pa

Abstract. This project is focused on the design and development of a mobile application that records the daily food intake for a person, and the caloric based-content indicates that it is the amount of calories consumed. To perform the calculation of Basal Metabolic Rate (BMR) Harris Benedict equation is used, this method of calculation is based on age, sex, height and weight. The estimated value is multiplied by a number corresponding to the level of activity of the individual. The resulting number is the recommended kilo calories to maintain current body weight daily intake. The system will have two modules, one is that which manages the data capture and delivery for storage. This in turn consists of a mobile application with a simple user interface where you can enter data and prepares to send them to the storage service. In addition, the App can view the recorded data and display it on the screen data queries.

Keywords: Object-relational model · Framework · E-health · Calories intake · Harris benedict equation

1 Introduction

In recent years we have witnessed the great technological advances and the importance in the lives of each of us. Devices such as computers, Smart TVs and mobiles phones are three of the electronic devices that we use today [1], but there is one in particular that has become more important for their application in different areas: The *Smartphones*. These devices have some utilities such as GPS, camera, music player, beyond its *hardware* capabilities usefulness is enhanced by the large number of application that exist to solve different types of problems in different areas such as education, social service, Health.

The application development had tremendous growth at present and this is due to what is to become indispensable technology today. Following the trend in the health area there is also a lot of applications available to solve problems related to health [2], these applications are designed to improve the lifestyle of people and the quality of health. In addition, such tools have open space in the hospital and clinical field, because the portable that are electronic tablets and mobiles phones, some hospitals have chosen to use these new technologies and *Apps* in clinical practice [3].

© Springer International Publishing AG 2016
C.R. García et al. (Eds.): UCAmI 2016, Part I, LNCS 10069, pp. 246–254, 2016.
DOI: 10.1007/978-3-319-48746-5_25

Following this technological trend in the field of Health we focus our work on the design and development of an application for the weight control patient through calories intake that will allow us to keep a count of calories burned, to regulate excessive caloric intake also allow us to create a tool that can be applied to future work related to weight control.

In this project we propose to generate develop a tool to help reduce obesity rates that increase each day, through an application on *Android* can store the calories that a person consumes daily. Based on a set time the person can see how much caloric intake leads, this food-based and so can see keep records enabling its caloric intake. To set the limit of calories that a certain person can consume we will build on the Harris-Benedict equation. This application will be able to help people to have better food and improve the quality of life through a balanced diet according to their age, weight, sex, height and level of physical activity.

2 Weight Control Based on the Harris-Benedict Equation

Weight control is an issue of high public health priority for the growing number of people who are overweight/obesity and the negative impact it has on health, as it has been linked to an increased risk of cardiovascular disease, hypertension, some cancers, diabetes, arthritis, digestive diseases, respiratory diseases, hyperuricemia, psychological problems, etc.

The ideal treatment of overweight and obesity is prevention, but once instituted disease, low calories diet will be the first step in treatment. In addition, therapeutic intervention should be aimed at achieving changes in eating habits of the person, increased physical activity, behavioural support, and in those cases where it is necessary, you can expect drug delivery [3]. There are two factors that determine the need for calories and these are:

- The Basal Metabolic Rate (BMR): is the energy needed to maintain basic physiological functions of your body at rest.
- Physical activity level: these are the calories per day needed to meet the level of physical activity, can be estimated based on your body weight [4].

The BMR varies depending on genetics, age, sex, height, body composition and physical activity level. There are many behavioural, environmental and genetic factors have been shown to affect the body weight of a person. The calories balance over time is the key to weight control.

The Calorie Balance refers to the relationship between calories consumed from food and drink and the calories expended [5] in the normal functions of the body and through physical activity.

Calories consumed must equal the calories expended for a person to maintain the same body weight. Consuming more calories than are expended will lead to weight gain [6].

If you consume less calories expended will result in weight loss. This can be achieved over time by eating fewer calories, be more active or best of all a combination of the two.

People cannot control the calories expended in metabolic processes, but they can control what they eat and drink, as well as the amount of calories that are used in physical activity [6].

2.1 TMB Calculation Methods

Harris-Benedict equation is a method used to calculate the basal metabolic rate (BMR) [7]. The calculation is based on age, sex and height. The estimated value of BMR is multiplied by a number that corresponds to the activity level of the individual. The resulting number is the recommended amount of calories to maintain current body weight daily intake. The Harris-Benedict equation can be used to help weight loss by reducing the number of kilocalories intake below the estimated intake conservation.

2.2 Mapping Techniques Object-Relational Data for MBR Methods

The technique Object-Relational Mapping for the acronym in ORM it basically allows us to convert data between incompatible systems as a relational data and object-oriented design [8] offering many benefits as obtained from the two types of systems.

For the part of relational systems that are flexible and robust systems for managing data [9] and side object-oriented that the business logic is implemented directly in the programming language, using design patterns design, improved maintenance and code reuse.

Hibernate [10] is a solution of object-relational mapping (ORM) for JAVA. It is open source. It is a powerful, high performance object-relational persistence system and a consultation service for any Java application. The advantages of using Hibernate are:

- It is responsible for mapping Java classes to database tables using XML files and without writing any line of code.
- It provides simple APIs to store and retrieve Java objects directly from and to the database.
- It does not require an application server to operate.
- Manipulate complex associations of objects of the database.
- It provides simple query data.

3   Mobile Application Design: LowCalories

For the design and development of this project we use an iteration development mechanism with one first iteration, the target for the first iteration in the functionality needed to count caloric intake was used. Throughout this section the components that will define the system, has two modules:

Module 1: It is responsible for data acquisition and sending for data storage. This consists of a mobile application with a simple user interface where you can enter data and prepares to send them to the storage service. In addition, the application can view the recorded data and display it on the screen data queries.

Module 2: A compounded Web Service set of drivers that allow sending and query data from the mobile application. Storage Services receive and prepare the data for later storage in the database, which will receive as parameters. All data sent or consulted be transferred using the *HTTP* protocol. The stored data to be consulted is returned as *JSON*. In the request we store data on a remote server, all communication process is done via the *HTTP* protocol. In Fig. 1 the network diagram in which the initial prototype will be based is presented.

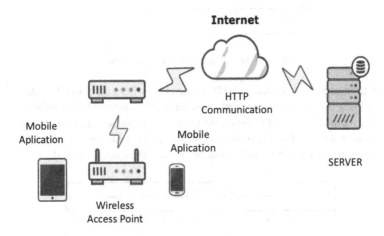

Fig. 1. Network diagram for application development.

This section presents the diagrams of the entities involved in the process of records, processing and data query by a user caloric intake daily. The diagrams show the attributes of the entities, the relationship between entities and function possess. With this model we seek to present the main architecture of the system in order to express their functionality. The system design was performed by applying a methodology object-oriented design of seeking to create a scalable model for future work, implementing the reuse of classes.

In Fig. 2 the entities that compound the process of caloric intake by a user, which comprises the following classes are presented:

- **User:** This class contains detailed information of the user name, age, sex and others. In addition to manage the consumption process and get the daily consumption of added functions implementing patient and get consumer consumption.
- **Intake:** This class encapsulates the process of adding the details of consumption, which is to store a detailed log of food consumed, the amount (units) and consumed weight (grams).

- **Food:** This class has the properties of food such as name, description and approximate calories in a gram of food.

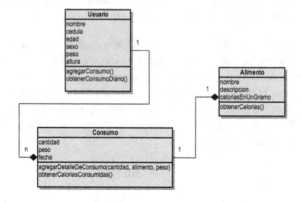

Fig. 2. Class diagram of the application.

The method used for calculating BMR is the Harris-Benedict, based on the equation algorithm which is contained in the *caloriasDiariasRecomendadas( )* method as shown in Fig. 3, this method requires the parameters was developed sex, age, height and activity level of the user, to calculate the limit of calories you should consume the patient, once the calculation performed the result is returned and subsequently stored.

TMBCalculadora
caloriasDiariasRecomendadas(sexo, peso, estatura, edad, nivelActividad)

Fig. 3. Calculator basal metabolic rate.

After defining the logical structure of the system, the next step was the creation of design of the user interface, as the system was defined in the previous section in its first iteration consists of four classes, this user interface is where the user enters the data and it also allows you to display the stored record.

The design was done with the objective that was easy to use by the user through a simple and intuitive design. As a result of this four *mockup* which are the four interfaces that were generated graphic component of the application:

BMR Calculator: From this interface (Fig. 4a) can perform the calculation of the calories you should consume a user to perform the calculation all data will be required.

List of food: This interface can display the name and an image of each food registered for this prototype a fixed number of food is defined as shown in Fig. 4b, the system in its first iteration will not allow register new foods. Once you have selected one of the foods the screen is displayed with full detail food.

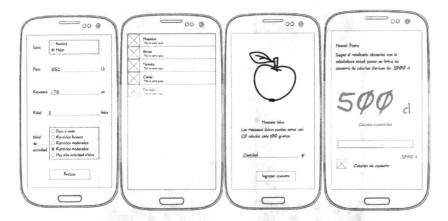

Fig. 4. a. BMR calculator, b. Food List, c. Income calories consumed and d. Detail calories intake.

Income consumption: This interface shows a complete detail of food the calories, food name and an image as shown in Fig. 4c, also this screen contains a text field where you can enter the amount (units) consumed, the data is recorded and stored to bring the count of the calories consumed.

Detail calorie intake: This interface (Fig. 4d) shows the amount of calories consumed by the data recorded on the registration screen consumption also limit calories you should consume shown as calculated with the calculator BMR.

4   Development of the Application

The entire development process was carried out of the development environment Android Studio. This powerful development tools have a large number of alternatives to create interfaces on for the Android platform, this tool provide means for us to carry out the generation screens for our application.

In Fig. 5 the interfaces of the *LowCalories* application is shown in the image on the left screen is shown for calculating the TMB and the image on the right navigation menu where all three options are samples which is shown tell the application to finish the job.

In the previous section related to the creation of the user interface it was shown. It should be noted that the data are entered in the application screen will not be stored on the device, so the system does not have functions for internal storage, the application was developed to store all data on a server database through a Web Service.

The of the mobile application development consisted only of user interfaces. Upon completion of the stage of development of the interface for data capture worked with the communication mechanism with web services for processing and storage.

Then communication between the data capture interface and Web Services is managed through the REST communication mechanism. The project is designed as an architecture type client-server that allows us to separate the user interface server. This separation means that, for example, customers do not have to do with data storage, which

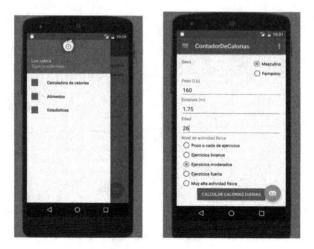

Fig. 5. LowCalories applications.

remains internal to each server, so the client code portability is improved. The server is not worried about the state of the user interface which simplifies the task server and allows more scalable platforms. The main advantage of this architecture is that servers and clients can also be replaced and developed independently, as long as the interface between them is not altered. The REST data transfer for this project is done via the *HTTP* protocol communication and through consultation (GET, POST and PUT) query, creation and modification of resources of the database is done. Additionally, REST allows the implementation of *JSON* for sending and receiving data, this is achieved by adding to the body of the query data in *JSON* format.

In Fig. 6 it is shown as is separating the user interface logic. This allows for future jobs can be generated client application on other platforms, for example, a Web application or an application of IOS re-used logic stored in the Web Services.

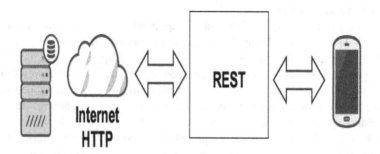

Fig. 6. Communication diagram REST.

For the generation of necessary services to manage sent or accessed data from the mobile application, we use the *Spring-MVC* framework, which allowed us to develop the paradigm *Model-View-Controller*. The managing data from Web Services consist of three steps:

Send data capture everything from the screen: In this step, a number of drivers using the *HTTP* methods for consultation, creation and modification of resources were created. HTTP methods allow the capture of the requests from the mobile application.

Interpret the data and represented as objects: Once captured the data, which are sent in *JSON* format through a *REST* query we continue with the next step to interpret the data that comes a format plain text and convert into an object, for them a tool that lets it was used manipulate data in *JSON* format, then these data are used to generate objects.

Generate object relational mapping to store data: Once define the objects it is necessary the implementation of a mechanism for the object-relational mapping. The tool used is Hibernate which allows us to store our objects in a relational database.

5   Conclusions

In this work, we wanted to expand our field of vision on the application for weight control where we carry out a series of situations that spend millions of users today worldwide due to their poor diet or lack of guidance by eating their food.

Our work is a contribution to the problem of poor nutrition in many cases can lead to overweight or no good nutrition. In the development of this project we take this issue as a starting point to make our application, we understand that weight management is a high priority problem in public health.

Today, much of the population is overweight/obesity and the negative impact it has on health has increased user risk of cardiovascular disease, hypertension, certain cancers or silent disease called diabetes.

It is important that the user to control the percent of body fat by applying for appropriate guidance for each food you choose in the same and maintained within the limits established for that purpose, it is essential in addition to diet physical training that the calculator use for the control of your weight.

In conclusion no diet can be effective and correct if not totally customized, made and controlled by a nutritionist conduct a thorough the user *kinanthropometric* study. The application after completing the diagnosis always sends a warning message to the users that the is manipulated.

Acknowledgments. The first author is member of the National Research Investigator award (SNI) from the SENACYT as a National Research I and the second author is an Engineer in Computer Systems of the Technological University of Panama.

References

1. Garzon, J.: (2014, 26 de diciembre). El futuro de las tabletas y la evolución de las computadoras (2015). http://www.cnet.com/es/noticias/futuro-tabletas-evolucion-computadoras-2015/
2. Ortega, R.Mª., Requejo, A.Mª.: Control de peso de forma saludable. Editorial Dirección General de Salud Pública y Alimentación
3. Universidad de California: Calories Counter (2005). www.snac.ucla.edu
4. Hill, J.O., Wyatt, H.R., Peters, J.C.: Energy Balance and Obesity. Circulation **126**(1), 126–132 (2012). http://doi.org/10.1161/CIRCULATIONAHA.111.087213
5. Balancing Calories to Manage Weight, Dietary Guidelines for Americans (2010)
6. The Harris Benedict equation re-evaluated: resting energy requirements and the body cell mass
7. Benedict, H.: Formula for women and men (2014). http://gottasport.com/weight-loss/71/harris-benedict-formula-for-women-and-men.html
8. Le Vie, Jr., D.: Writing Software Requirements Specifications (SRS). http://techwhirl.com/writing-software-requirements-specifications/
9. Hibernate. Application layer agnostic validation, 9 April 2011. http://hibernate.org/validator/
10. University of Olso. Object-Relational Mapping (ORM) and Hibernate (2007). https://www.uio.no/studier/emner/matnat/ifi/INF5750/h07/undervisningsmateriale/object-relational_mapping_and_hibernate.pdf

Process Support for Continuous, Distributed, Multi-party Healthcare Processes - Applying Workflow Modelling to an Anticoagulation Monitoring Protocol

Ian McChesney[✉]

School of Computing and Mathematics, Ulster University, Newtownabbey, Northern Ireland, UK
ir.mcchesney@ulster.ac.uk

Abstract. Workflow management has been shown to be a promising approach to the support of a range of healthcare processes, with tools available for their formal specification, analysis and implementation. To further illustrate its relevance, we apply a workflow modelling approach to the specification and analysis of an anticoagulation monitoring protocol, illustrating a Petri Net-based solution using YAWL and Coloured Petri Nets. The selected scenario is representative of healthcare processes which have not been extensively considered for workflow solutions in the past – namely highly distributed, multi-party activities executing over an extended period of time. In presenting a workflow analysis for such a case, we identify challenges in supporting these types of primary and community care-based processes and identify possible areas in which workflow solutions could be extended to address their particular process requirements.

Keywords: Workflow modelling · Petri nets · Healthcare processes · Community care

1 Introduction

In this paper we focus on workflow modelling as one approach to designing and enabling healthcare processes. Workflow modelling seeks to understand organizational tasks holistically, viewing workflows as a set of interrelated tasks typically crossing internal and external organizational boundaries to form a complete system of connected activities and people. For this reason, workflow modelling has found relevance in the analysis and support of a range of healthcare processes, for example [1–3].

A trend in healthcare over the past say 15 years [4] has been the move towards preventative treatments in primary care and through community care processes – processes which can be understood as continuous, distributed, multi-party workflow systems. In this paper we review workflow modelling approaches for this type of process and describe, as an illustrative example, a simple workflow modelling solution based on Petri Nets for an anticoagulation monitoring protocol. In so doing, we illustrate the value of workflow modelling for process understanding, simulation and implementation, and identify some important characteristics of primary and community care processes which merit further investigation for process support.

© Springer International Publishing AG 2016
C.R. García et al. (Eds.): UCAmI 2016, Part I, LNCS 10069, pp. 255–266, 2016.
DOI: 10.1007/978-3-319-48746-5_26

The remainder of the paper is organized as follows: In Sect. 2 we review workflow modelling techniques as they have been applied to healthcare processes. Section 3 introduces the case study of an anticoagulation management protocol. Section 4 describes the modelling approach adopted and presents a YAWL (Yet Another Workflow Language) [5] and CPN (Coloured Petri Nets) [6] representation of the case study. Section 5 presents some observations arising from our models and in Sect. 6 conclusions are drawn.

2   Related Work

The original application of workflow management techniques to clinical workflow is attributed to Dadam et al. [7], who noted the tension between the need for formal modelling of critical processes while allowing for flexibility and ad-hoc variation in their implementation. In a review of work since then, Gooch and Roudsari [3] identify the key challenges in the implementation of information systems to support an "idealized clinical workflow". They emphasize the need to support adaptive care pathways – adapting to both clinical and organizational changes. The need for adaptive processes are both an opportunity and a challenge for workflow management solutions.

Workflow modelling and workflow management systems are concerned with the understanding of organizational tasks as a whole to achieve some business or organizational objective. Work Systems Theory [8, 9] provides a framework which reinforces the notion of organizational processes as a work system. It makes two important distinctions; first that the customer (or in our case patient) is preeminent in understanding the purpose of any workflow and second, that the development of a workflow system cannot be understood as a one-off processes, but is a system which is in a cycle of initiation, development, implementation and operation & maintenance.

A full review of workflow modelling approaches as applied in healthcare is beyond the scope of this paper. By way of summary, there are approaches which are concerned with one or a combination of (a) "modelling for understanding", involving construction of models to aid communication between system developer and stakeholders, for example [10, 11], (b) "modelling for simulation", seeking to construct a workflow model of the healthcare process with a view to its analysis through visualization and performance analysis, for example [12, 13], and (c) "modelling for implementation", concerned with the enablement of a workflow system through a workflow engine, for example [14, 15].

3   Case Study Overview

Workflow modelling in healthcare has tended to focus on intra-organization processes, such as acute care in a hospital or processing of patients in an accident and emergency department [16–18]. In this paper we examine a primary and community care process concerned with the ongoing monitoring and management of patients undergoing anticoagulation treatment for either prevention of disease or as therapy for an ongoing condition [19, 20].

The case study is representative of those healthcare processes which we describe as continuous, distributed, multi-party processes. Continuous in the sense of executing over an extended period of time, sometimes indefinitely until some significant event occurs. Distributed in the sense that they are located across multiple physical locations, with different activities possibly taking places at different locations (e.g. health clinic, pharmacy, home) and multi-party in that the process is undertaken by a group of participants, typically physically dispersed, whose actions must be coordinated for a successful workflow.

Overview of an Anticoagulant Monitoring Process. The process is concerned with patients who are referred from secondary care (hospital) to primary care (their local General Practitioner – GP) for the purpose of anticoagulation treatment and monitoring. This is achieved through GP consultation, patient education, dosage specification and adjustment, regular blood tests for INR (international normalized ratio) measurement (either in clinic or domiciliary) and periodic review.

Referral from secondary care and treatment initiation: Patients are referred to primary care from secondary care using an agreed transfer process. This process includes the transfer of documentation and patient record details for existing and new patients.

Medication and monitoring: On receipt of the prescription by the patient's preferred pharmacy, delivered either in person by the patient or directly from the GP Practice, the pharmacy will dispense the tablets. Along with the dosage instruction, the patient is then able to begin treatment. A characteristic of anticoagulation treatment is regular INR monitoring, typically 8–12 weeks, which may lead to a change in dosage.

Dosage adjustment: The dosage regime (whether changed or unchanged) will be formally notified to the patient. There is a detailed protocol for how this is to be achieved depending on whether the patient is told directly by telephone or through a carer, whether they are living in a care home, and whether a monitored dosage system is in use.

Discontinuation: Any decision to discontinue will be based on a formal consultation with the GP.

4   Modelling Approach

We follow and extend Jorgensen et al.'s approach [21] for modelling a healthcare workflow system. This approach is consistent with recommendations [22] to use of a variety of modelling and diagram types when developing healthcare systems - in early stages, choice of model should be determined by the usability of the notation for communication between modeller and stakeholder. We describe and adapt the four stages as below:

4.1 Informal Description

The means through which a healthcare process will initially be described will vary depending on context. In our case, the starting point is a text-based description of the anticoagulation monitoring process setting out tasks, participants and supporting documents.

4.2 Workflow Requirements Model

YAWL is both a language and environment for the modelling and implementation of workflow systems. It adopts a state-based modelling approach based on the ideas of Petri Nets and a comprehensive set of workflow patterns. Control flow in a workflow system is modelled using tasks, conditions (implicit or explicit) and flow relations. These are used to form an "extended workflow net"; a set of these nets can be organized hierarchically to form a workflow specification.

Figure 1 shows the top level workflow net for the anticoagulant monitoring case. This uses a subset of the YAWL notation which is fully described in [5]. The focus of the notation is on control flow, in this case from the perspective of the patient as they "flow" or "move" through the system. YAWL also provides support for the modelling of workflow data and resources.

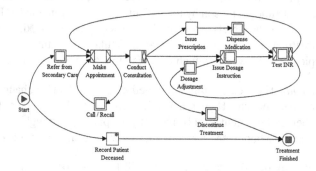

Fig. 1. Top level workflow net for anticoagulant monitoring

The first task in the workflow is *Refer from Secondary Care*. This is shown as a composite task, indicating that it consists of further detail which is described in a separate extended workflow net which may in turn consist of atomic or composite tasks. *Make Appointment* is modelled as an atomic task which may take be triggered by three possible inputs: a referral from secondary care, as a result of the call/recall procedure (when a patient does not attend for an appointment), or based on the outcome of an INR test result. Since any one appointment will be due to only one of these preconditions, the task is modelled as an XOR-join task. If a patient attends their appointment, the *Conduct Consultation* task can then take place, otherwise the *Call/Recall* task is invoked. *Make Appointment* is modelled as an XOR-split task, ensuring that only one of the two outcomes is possible.

Conduct Consultation is an example or an OR-split task, whereby the thread of control can be passed to one or more of the outgoing arcs. In this case, the possible outcomes are (re)issue of a prescription, set up and issue of dosage instruction or discontinuation of treatment. This is not an XOR condition as the *Issue Prescription* and *Issue Dosage Instruction* tasks may both be necessary.

The remainder of the workflow net and notation can be interpreted by the reader. One point to note is the *Record Patient Deceased* task. YAWL permits the specification of cancellations sets. These are tasks which may be associated with some form of cancellation event which, on execution, causes the set of tasks associated with it to be terminated.

4.3 Workflow Specification Model

Coloured Petri Nets is a formal, graphical language for the modelling and analysis of any type of concurrent system. It combines the key concepts of Petri Nets (places/transitions), tokens with data values and the ability to programmatically describe system behaviour and data using the programming language CPN ML [6]. Workflows expressed in YAWL can be easily translated to their CPN equivalent. Further, as a formal representation, CPNs can be executed using environments such as CPN Tools [23], enabling their verification and simulation. In this way, CPNs are suitable for checking workflow requirements, constructing a formal specification of the system and conducting simulation and performance analysis.

We use Coloured Workflow Nets (CWNs) to assemble the specification model for anticoagulant monitoring workflow. CWNs are Coloured Petri Nets with restrictions on their data types to enforce specification of tasks from the perspective of the workflow system [24]. The CWN is a visually more complex representation than the YAWL model. State is explicitly represented and places, transitions and arcs are annotated with rules (expressed in CPN ML) which control the specific behaviour of the system. The following subsections describe aspects of the anticoagulant monitoring CWN in more detail. We assume the reader is familiar with the basic concepts of Petri Nets.

Modelling for Understanding - Control Flow. Workflow patterns described in YAWL can be mapped directly to a CPN representation. Figure 2 shows the CWN elements for modelling referral from secondary care.

This segment models a <u>sequential workflow</u>. Place *start* represents the point at which referral from secondary care begins. In this example, there are patients awaiting referral (p101, p102, p104). The firing of the *Refer from Secondary Care* transition represents a patient referral being handled. This transition uses a hospital *admin* resource, as specified by the *has_role* function on the transition. When the task is complete, the referred patient *p* is moved through the system, as represented by the place *Referred Patients*. Also on completion of the *Refer from Secondary Care* transition, the *admin* resource is released back to the resource pool – modelled as a CPN fusion place.

As an example of <u>synchronization</u>, the AND-join *Test INR* (from Fig. 1) is represented in CPN as shown in Fig. 3 (resources are omitted for readability). In Fig. 4 we can see a case of <u>simple merge</u> where the YAWL XOR-join for *Make Appt* is modelled.

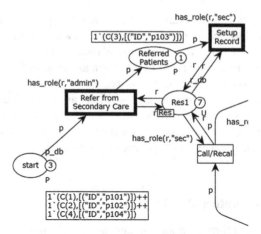

Fig. 2. CWN segment for referral from secondary care. Bold borders show enabled transitions.

There are three possible workflow sequences which can require an appointment to be made: referral from secondary care (transition *Setup Record*), a requirement for a review appointment (transition *Set up Review*), or if a patient is being identified through the call/recall procedure (transition *Call/Recall*). The CWN is showing that the *Make Appt* task requires action (for p103) and the *Call/Recall* task requires action (for p102). There is a CPN ML function *attends* associated with the *Make Appt* transition, modelling whether a patient will attend their appointment:

```
fun attends() = uniform(0.0, 1.0) <= 0.8;
```

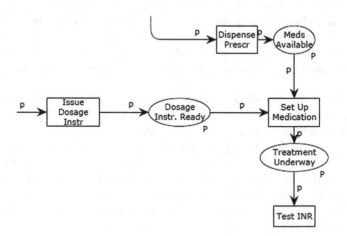

Fig. 3. CPN representation of an AND-join – Test INR

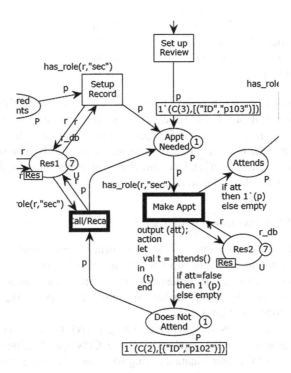

Fig. 4. CPN representation of an XOR-join - Make Appt

Modelling for Simulation. Having established that the CWN correctly reflects the required workflow functionality, it can be extended with timing properties to enable simulation and performance analysis. This can help answer questions such as: how many INR tests are likely to be conducted per month? How many review appointments can be expected per month? How much time do we expect to spend on call/recall appointments?

CPN ML functions can be used to simulate workflow behaviour. The *attends* function (Fig. 4) has already been highlighted to model the frequency with which appointments are kept. The probability distribution can be changed to reflect different simulation scenarios. Additional functions are used in this model to simulate the need for patient review and discontinuation of treatment. The CWN can also simulate the referral of new patients from secondary care into the system (see e.g. [25] for approach).

To illustrate the possibilities through simulation, we consider a version of the CWN which simulates the handling of 80 referrals over a period of time. We assume that a patient is referred randomly every 14–28 days. We make other assumptions for simulation purposes regarding how long certain tasks take to complete, for example, 2 days to complete the referral paperwork, 1 day to set up an appointment, 2 days to generate a repeat prescription. From this position, we can establish some performance statistics through simulation such as:

Observation	Count
Number Of Patient Reviews	669
Instances of SetUpMedication	4290
Model time (days)	3666

Model time is in days, so 3666 days represents 131 months (effectively an 11 year cycle for the throughput of 80 patients undergoing anticoagulation treatment). Under these assumptions we have on average 5.12 patient reviews per month and 32.75 medication setups per month. We can similarly simulate a more steady state scenario where say 80 patients are "in the system" and then simulate system performance during a period when a further 10 referrals are received.

4.4   Workflow Implementation with YAWL

The purpose of the CPN representation is to confirm a correct understanding of the system, to enable simulation, and to allow for a range of different types of performance analysis. CPN is not suitable for implementation or enablement as a live workflow system. There are numerous options for how this might be achieved. Here we illustrate how the YAWL system facilitates this.

In the same way that a CPN version of an existing YAWL workflow net can be easily constructed, similarly the YAWL equivalent of the CPN specification model can be constructed. With the CWN representation having articulated the resource requirements of the workflow, these resources can also be mapped directly into the YAWL Environment.

The YAWL system enables execution of a workflow net as a workflow case. In addition to the control-flow aspect of the workflow, as specified visually in the YAWL Editor, the YAWL environment permits the specification of data associated with the

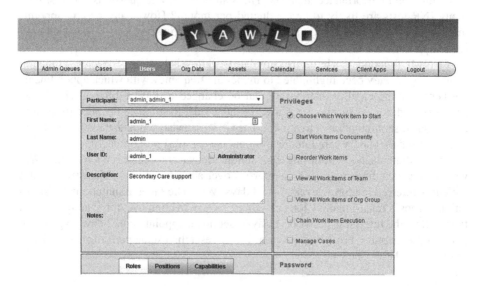

Fig. 5. Setting up users in the workflow system

workflow and resources to enact the workflow. For example, referral of a patient from secondary care is achieved via a Referral Form (this is identified in the sub-net associated with referral from secondary care). In YAWL, this can be specified as a data object associated with the *Refer From Secondary Care* task using the built-in complex datatype *YDocumentType*.

Organizational structures can be specified in the YAWL system terms of roles, capabilities, positions and organization groups. For each role, individual users of the workflow system can be specified, along with their privileges and their place within the organizational structure (Fig. 5).

When a case is executing, the YAWL Environment, using the workflow specification, manages the execution flow in terms of, for example, work items currently awaiting execution. Depending on their configuration, work items can be allocated to a resource manually or automatically. The significance to note is that, having translated the CWN into YAWL, the workflow execution is based on a formally verified CPN model of the workflow requirements.

5 Observations

As noted above, we have selected our case study as representative of healthcare processes which are continuous, distributed and multi-party. We present a number of observations regarding the modelling of such processes. Strengths of the workflow approach for this type of scenario include:

- the workflow model is patient centered. Process and state is modelled from the perspective of the patient as they "move" through the system. This supports the notions of Work Systems Theory in which the "customer" is central to the process. The model seeks to ensure the patient does not "get lost" in the system, that every action performed on a patient case has achievable preconditions and postconditions.
- our approach begins and ends with YAWL. This addresses the need for modelling which can be used in stakeholder communication and the need for a model which is executable. This also supports the notion of a workflow system as being in a cycle of evolution rather than a one-off project - the notation used for "modelling for understanding" is also the notation for implementation, supporting cyclical evaluation and improvement.
- workflow exceptions can be modelled through the suite of workflow patterns supported by YAWL and CPN. Functional accuracy and correctness can be verified in the CPN model before translation to YAWL for implementation.
- though the example above presents a flat CPN, a hierarchical model can be developed reflecting the hierarchy in the domain and the original YAWL specification. This enables a loose coupling of different workflow components, facilitating the management of complexity.
- an executable workflow model enables process awareness. For example, the YAWL workflow engine ensures that each participants' obligations and next steps can be explicitly modelled and notified to them.

– in simulation mode (CWN) or execution mode (YAWL system), the model can generate event logs of actual process. This enables the application of process mining for process enforcement and process enhancement [26].

Characteristics of this type of process which present challenges from a modelling perspective include the following:

– in such multi-party and distributed processes, message exchange is a key coordination mechanism. When an unexpected event occurs (for example, the pharmacy will not have the required medication for 24 h), how do we model who should be informed?
– how can the correct level of support be provided to participants who are typically working in different organizations or healthcare teams? In establishing the desired level of coordination, there are many choices to be made in terms of control and flexibility. We note Cabitza and Simone's alpha-level taxonomy as providing a useful framework for conceptualizing this problem [27].
– resources modelled in CWNs and YAWL are static, yet real-world processes typically have different participants moving in and out of the workflow (for example, personnel in care support teams, locum GPs). How is resource allocation to be managed to ensure continuity of the workflow and continuity of care?
– there is no explicit workflow concept of location awareness. For example, can workflow efficiencies be achieved where multiple executing instances identify similar tasks in the same geographical areas such as domiciliary INR testing or replenishment of supplies?
– how are the coordination mechanisms which are necessary between participants to be supported? For example, can process awareness best be supported in a distributed fashion or centrally though control from the workflow owner, for example GP surgery.

6   Conclusions

Modelling, analyzing and implementing a continuous, distributed, multi-party healthcare processes with complex coordination requirements has been presented through an approach using established Petri Net and workflow technologies. We have argued that such a workflow approach is patient centric, and addresses the requirement of a mixed modelling notation which supports a process cycle of ongoing improvement.

By illustrating how YAWL and CPN can be used for this, we have highlighted process characteristics which can be modelled in this way, be it modelling for understanding, for analysis or for implementation. Further work will require refinement of model parameters to reflect different healthcare process scenarios for realistic performance modelling purposes.

Primary care, community care and home care processes present many challenges in ensuring their efficient operation. We have shown how existing tools for workflow modelling and management are sufficiently expressive to capture much of these. However, there are many technical opportunities for further work, for example [28, 29], to deliver process enhancement for this class of healthcare process.

References

1. Schadow, G., Russler, D.C., McDonald, C.J.: Conceptual alignment of electronic health record data with guideline and workflow knowledge. Int. J. Med. Inform. **64**(2), 259–274 (2001)
2. Fox, J., Black, E., Chronakis, I, Dunlop, R, Patkar, V., South, M., Thomson, R.: From guidelines to careflows: modelling and supporting complex clinical processes. In: ten Teije, A., Miksch, S., Lucas, P. (eds.) Computer-Based Medical Guidelines and Protocols: A Primer and Current Trends, 139, pp. 44–62. IOS Press, Amsterdam (2008)
3. Gooch, P., Roudsari, A.: Computerization of workflows, guidelines, and care pathways: a review of implementation challenges for process-oriented health information systems. J. Am. Med. Inform. Assoc. **18**(6), 738–748 (2011)
4. Genet, N., Boerma, W., Kroneman, M., Hutchinson, A., Saltman, R.B. (eds): Home Care Across Europe - Current Structure and Future Challenges. European Observatory on Health Systems and Policies, London (2013)
5. van der Aalst, W.M., Ter Hofstede, A.H.: YAWL: yet another workflow language. Inf. Syst. **30**(4), 245–275 (2005)
6. Jensen, K., Kristensen, L.M., Wells, L.: Coloured Petri Nets and CPN Tools for modelling and validation of concurrent systems. Int. J. Softw. Tools Technol. Transfer **9**(3–4), 213–254 (2007)
7. Dadam, P., Reichert, M., Kuhn, K.: Clinical workflows – the killer application for process-oriented information systems?. In: Abramowicz, W., Orlowska, M.E. (eds.) BIS 2000, pp. 36–59. Springer, London (2000)
8. Alter, S.: Using work system theory to link managerial and technical perspectives on BPM. In: 2013 IEEE International Conference on Business Informatics, pp. 222–227. IEEE Press, New York (2013)
9. Alter, S.: Work system theory: overview of core concepts, extensions, and challenges for the future. J. Assoc. Inf. Syst. **14**(2), 72 (2013)
10. Fanti, M.P., Mininel, S., Ukovich, W., Vatta, F.: Modelling alarm management workflow in healthcare according to IHE framework by coloured Petri Nets. Eng. Appl. Artif. Intell. **25**(4), 728–733 (2012)
11. Ruiz, F., Garcia, F., Calahorra, L., Llorente, C., Gonçalves, L., Daniel, C., Blobel, B.: Business process modeling in healthcare. Stud. Health Technol. Inform. **179**, 75–87 (2012)
12. Jansen-Vullers, M.H., Reijers, H.A.: Business process redesign at a mental healthcare institute: a coloured petri net approach. In: Proceedings of the Sixth Workshop and Tutorial on Practical Use of Coloured Petri Nets and the CPN Tools (PB-576), pp. 21–38 (2005)
13. Elnahrawy, E., Martin, R.P.: Studying the utility of tracking systems in improving healthcare workflow. In: 8th IEEE International Conference on Pervasive Computing and Communications Workshops (PERCOM Workshops), pp. 310–315. IEEE Press, New York (2010)
14. van der Aalst, W.M.P., Aldred, L., Dumas, M., ter Hofstede, A.H.M.: Design and implementation of the YAWL System. In: Persson, A., Stirna, J. (eds.) CAiSE 2004. LNCS, vol. 3084, pp. 142–159. Springer, Heidelberg (2004)
15. Mans, R., van der Aalst, W., Russell, N., Moleman, A., Bakker, P., Jaspers, M.: YAWL4Healthcare. In: Hofstede, A.H., van der Aalst, W.M., Adams, M., Russell, N. (eds.) Modern Business Process Automation, pp. 543–565. Springer, Heidelberg (2010)
16. Vanberkel, P.T., Boucherie, R.J., Hans, E.W., Hurink, J.L., Litvak, N.: A survey of health care models that encompass multiple departments. University of Twente, Enschede (2009). http://www.math.utwente.nl/publications/

17. Rohleder, T.R., Lewkonia, P., Bischak, D.P., Duffy, P., Hendijani, R.: Using simulation modeling to improve patient flow at an outpatient orthopedic clinic. Health Care Manage. Sci. **14**(2), 135–145 (2011)

18. Ortiz Barrios, M.A., Escorcia Caballero, J., Sánchez Sánchez, F.: A methodology for the creation of integrated service networks in outpatient internal medicine. In: Bravo, J., Hervás, R., Villarreal, V. (eds.) AmIHEALTH 2015. LNCS, vol. 9456, pp. 247–257. Springer, Heidelberg (2015). doi:10.1007/978-3-319-26508-7_24

19. Blann, A.D., Fitzmaurice, D.A., Lip, G.Y.: Anticoagulation in hospitals and general practice. Br. Med. J. **326**(7381), 153 (2003)

20. Keeling, D., Baglin, T., Tait, C., Watson, H., Perry, D., Baglin, C., Kitchen, S., Makris, M.: Guidelines on oral anticoagulation with warfarin–fourth edition. Br. J. Haematol. **154**(3), 311–324 (2011)

21. Jørgensen, J.B., Lassen, K.B., van der Aalst, W.M.: From task descriptions via colored petri nets towards an implementation of a new electronic patient record workflow system. Int. J. Softw. Tools Technol. Transfer **10**(1), 15–28 (2008)

22. Jun, G.T., Ward, J., Morris, Z., Clarkson, J.: Health care process modelling: which method when? Int. J. Qual. Health Care **21**(3), 214–224 (2009)

23. CPN Tools, http://cpntools.org/

24. Aalst, W.M.P., Jørgensen, J.B., Lassen, K.B.: Let's go all the way: from requirements via colored workflow nets to a BPEL implementation of a new bank system. In: Meersman, R., Tari, Z. (eds.) OTM 2005. LNCS, vol. 3760, pp. 22–39. Springer, Heidelberg (2005). doi: 10.1007/11575771_5

25. Jensen, K., Kristensen, L.M.: Coloured Petri Nets: Modelling and Validation of Concurrent Systems. Springer, Heidelberg (2009)

26. van der Aalst, W.M.: Process Mining: Discovery, Conformance and Enhancement of Business Processes. Springer, Heidelberg (2011)

27. Cabitza, F., Simone, C.: Computational coordination mechanisms: a tale of a struggle for flexibility. Comput. Support. Coop. Work **22**(4–6), 475–529 (2013)

28. Toutain, F., Le Huérou, E., Beaufils, E.: On webco interoperability. In: Proceedings of the 1st Workshop on All-Web Real-Time Systems Article 5, 6 p. ACM, New York (2015)

29. Tolkiehn, G., Lebedev, M., Makariti, A.: MyWebRTC, a free do-it-yourself kit for secure real-time internet-communication. In: Information Technologies in Innovation Business Conference (ITIB 2015), pp. 81–84. IEEE Press, New York (2015)

The Use of Gamification Techniques in a Clinical Setting for the Collection of Longitudinal Kinematic Data

Andrew Ennis[1(✉)], Ian Cleland[1], Chris Nugent[1], Laura Finney[2],
David Trainor[3], and Aidan Bennett[4]

[1] Computer Science Research Institute and School of Computing and Mathematics,
University of Ulster, Newtownabbey, Co. Antrim BT37 0QB, Northern Ireland, UK
{a.ennis,i.cleland,cd.nugent}@ulster.ac.uk
[2] Leckey, 19C Ballinderry Road, Lisburn BT28 2SA, Northern Ireland, UK
laura.finney@leckey.com
[3] Sentireal, Queens University of Belfast Northern Ireland Science Park,
Queens Road, Queens Island, Belfast BT3 9DT, Northern Ireland, UK
david.trainor@sentireal.com
[4] Data Analytics Labs Ltd., Scottish Provident Building, 7 Donegall Square West,
Belfast BT1 6JH, Northern Ireland, UK
aidanbennett@dataanalyticslabs.com

Abstract. Children with physical impairments, ranging from impaired mobility to very limited mobility, often require mobility aids to compensate for these difficulties. These impairments can adversely affect the child to varying degrees and have an impact on their health and wellbeing. It is estimated that 30 %–40 % of medical interventions have no reported evidence base and another 20 % of interventions delivered are ineffective. Clinicians are under increasing pressure to provide evidence of the effectiveness of prescribed treatments and products. Therefor there is a need to provide clinicians with empirical data that evidences practice and provides a quantified assessment of treatment efficacy through data gathering in both real-time and longitudinally, combined with data analytics to further develop treatment strategies. This paper presents a system to assist and enable clinicians to analyze and asses the effectiveness and usage of prescribed treatments for physically impaired children. The system achieves this through the use of a gamified data collection app and a web portal to analyze and present summarized measures of gait.

Keywords: Gamification · Step counting · Postural aids · Mobility

1 Introduction

Children with physical impairments may suffer from limitations in walking, ranging from impaired to no walking. Often they require mobility aids or wheelchairs to compensate for these difficulties [1]. Physical impairments can to varying degrees, adversely affect the physical, cognitive and sensory development of a child, with adverse impacts on health and wellbeing [1]. These impacts can be influenced by a number of

© Springer International Publishing AG 2016
C.R. García et al. (Eds.): UCAmI 2016, Part I, LNCS 10069, pp. 267–273, 2016.
DOI: 10.1007/978-3-319-48746-5_27

factors, such as; body structure and function, daily activities of personal care, participation in home, school, work and family issues and other personal factors [1, 2]. Reductions in muscular strength, difficulties in coordination, and alterations in the gross and fine motor movements are the most common limitations caused by physical motor disabilities [3]. On many occasions, limitations of motor impairments require the use of assistive devices, such as wheelchairs and postural aids and these form a large part of standard care for children with physical disabilities [4]. Such devices can increase a child's independence, participation and quality of life by improving their mobility [5]. It is estimated that 30 %–40 % of medical interventions have no reported evidence base and another 20 % of interventions delivered are ineffective, unnecessary, or cause harm [4]. Currently within the pediatric rehabilitation sector clinicians are under increasing pressure to provide evidence of the effectiveness of treatments and products prescribed for children they are referred. Due to the nature of the pediatric special needs market there is little published research into the effectiveness of mobility and postural aids [4]. Clinicians are under increasing pressure to provide this evidence, however, the role of a clinician is to diagnose and assess impairment in the patient, not the performance of the mechanism or device that delivers this improvement. Nevertheless, by increasing knowledge in the areas of intervention and clinical research the potential exists to achieve system-wide improvements in health care quality and health outcomes. There is therefore a real need to provide clinicians with empirical data that evidences practice [4]. Therefore a quantitative way of assessing treatment efficacy, through data gathered in real-time and collated longitudinally, combined with data analytics to provide summary information to clinicians, parents and users is essential to manage and further develop treatment strategies [6].

The most commonly used devices to improve the standing position of children are mobility supports and adaptive seating, that provide more autonomy and diminish dependence [3]. Most of the research studies evaluating gait have focused on gross motor skills and analysis of the degree of movement, however, have not examined the quality of movement in terms of kinematics and geometry of the movement [3].

2   Implementation

We consulted with three experts in pediatric physiotherapy who provided us with an insight into the clinical needs of treating a child with walking impairments. With this clinical expertise, combined with a review of the literature, it was possible to identify areas on which to focus the platform. These namely being a gamified data collection app, based on the detection of step counts and a web portal aimed at clinicians to allow the review of the child's progress and clinical parameters of gait.

In order to facilitate the data gathering and presentation, we developed a platform that enabled the collection of accelerometer data, which is uploaded to a cloud backend. This allows clinicians to view, analyze and summarize the data. The collected and analyzed data will allow a clinician to better determine the effectiveness of a given treatment. This was highlighted as an issue in both the literature review and engagement with clinicians. We gamified the data collection app in order to improve engagement of the child with the solution which in turn increases the amount of accelerometer data generated by the child. The mobile app connects to a Shimmer (Shimmer 3, Shimmer research, Dublin) device via Bluetooth, as shown in Fig. 1A, to collect the accelerometer data. Shimmer is a well know platform within the connected health and assisted living research domains and offers a range of onboard sensing technologies, such as 3-axis accelerometer, digital magnetometer, gyro and pressure sensor [7, 8]. The Shimmer platform also has the capability of optional expansion modules that enable ECG, EMG and GSR [7]. When in use, the Shimmer device is attached to the child, either on the feet or lower back, or it may be integrated within the walker itself.

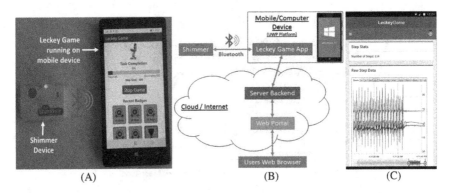

Fig. 1. (A) Shimmer device and Leckey Game app running on mobile phone. (B) System architecture. (C) Web portal displayed in web browser of a mobile smart phone.

The mobile app was developed on top of UWP (Universal Windows Platform) in C#. This allowed the app to be deployed to a wide range of computing devices, ranging from a smartphone to Raspberry Pi 3, or laptop/desktop computer. Figure 1A shows the app running on a Windows mobile. The system architecture can be seen in Fig. 1B and the web portal running in a smartphone browser can be seen in Fig. 1C.

2.1 Gamification

In order to gamify the app, we selected step counts as the metric used for the game, because steps are a commonly used metric within health promotion [9]. The objective of the game is to complete a set amount of steps per day, which is determined by the clinician. Currently, for testing purposes, we have the step achievement badges set at 5 step increments. This can, however, be set by the clinician to give a personalized target and will vary depending on the child's abilities. When an achievement badge is unlocked a notification is displayed to the user to alert them and encourage them to keep progressing. A new achievement badge is then displayed in the "Recent Badges" section, as can be seen on the mobile device in Fig. 1A.

2.2 Step Counting Algorithm

For the gamification of the app, it is necessary to calculate step counts locally on the device, in real-time. This also enables the game to run on the mobile device without the need to connect to external services and therefore does not consume mobile data.

An example of two walking steps of the left foot, from an un-impaired adult is shown in Fig. 2. The first step in the figure has been annotated to show the various points of the foot step.

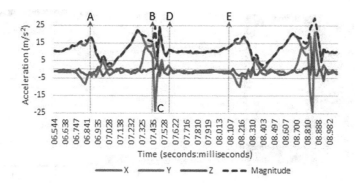

Fig. 2. Graph showing accelerometer data of 2 steps of the left foot, of an un-impaired adult. A: toe off. A to B: foot swing. C: heal strike. D to E: Left foot stationary, right foot moving.

To detect a step, we use an algorithm that analyses the x, y, z from the 3-axis accelerometer data to determine if the accelerations match a step profile. The algorithm we use is based on the algorithm proposed by [10] which detects peaks that are above a dynamic threshold. The first step in the algorithm is to calculate the magnitude for every x, y, z data point, as shown in the equation below. This means the Shimmer device can be orientation free and still reliably detect steps.

$$Mag = x^2 + y^2 + z^2$$

We then take a sliding window, containing 50 samples, and calculate the maximum, minimum and average, of the sliding window, and continuously update them every 50 samples, as shown in Fig. 3. The average is used as the dynamic threshold and is dynamic because it is updated every 50 samples.

We define that a step has been taken when a new magnitude point is less than the old magnitude point, e.g. a negative slope, when it crosses the threshold. Figure 3 shows a sample of step data from an un-impaired adult, along with the calculated maximum, minimum and dynamic threshold.

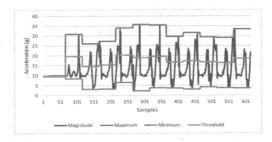

Fig. 3. Graph showing magnitude and the calculated max, min of the sliding window, updated every 50 samples. The graph also shows the calculated threshold of the sliding window, updated every 50 samples.

3 Results

Initial testing of the step counting algorithm and data collection app was carried out on two un-impaired adults from the research team without a postural aid and then subsequently while using a postural aid (enlarged for adults and built by Leckey). The test consisted of wearing the Shimmer device on the left outer ankle and walking around the perimeter of a defined rectangle. The size was determined by the limited open area available to test in. the participant was instructed to place the shimmer device in any orientation and this was not constrained. The participants walked 100 steps of the left foot. This was counted with a tally counter by an observer and the observer stopped the participant once 100 steps was achieved. Our reason for selecting 100 steps, is that a child with impaired walking is likely to take less steps than a non-impaired child. Hence our algorithm must detect as many of the steps as possible to be a viable metric for gamification purposes.

When 100 steps were taken without the postural aid, both participants' step counts were very close, being only 2 steps over the ground truth measured by the observer, as shown in Table 1. Nevertheless, when using the postural aid, the number of step counts significantly varied from the ground truth (Table 1). For participant 1 this was up to 25 steps over the ground truth. Participant 2 was closer to the ground truth, being only 5 steps over the ground truth.

Table 1. Two evaluations from two participant for both no postural aid and with a postural aid. P1 being participant 1 and P2 being participant 2.

	Ground Truth	Evaluation 1	Evaluation 2
P1 – No postural aid	100	101	102
P2 – No postural aid	100	101	100
P1 – with postural aid	100	116	125
P2 – with postural aid	100	101	105

Figure 4 shows the first 5 s of step accelerometer data without a postural aid (A) and with a postural aid (B). It is evident from the Figure that the step pattern is similar, however, with the postural aid (B) the steps are less pronounced and have a weaker magnitude.

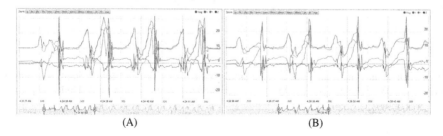

(A)   (B)

Fig. 4. Graph A showing first 5 s of unfiltered walking data without a postural aid. Graph B shows first 5 s of unfiltered walking data with a postural aid, from the same participant with the Shimmer located in the same position and orientation.

4   Conclusions

The results demonstrate that, when the postural aid was used the algorithm over counted the number of steps. This is because the accelerometer magnitude was less pronounced and therefore the dynamic threshold was lower, hence more minor step movements were counted as a step. Based on these results it appears the step counting algorithm is too sensitive when dealing with less defined footsteps. Due to this issue a normal step counting algorithm will not work very accurately. A solution maybe to independently run step detection on each axis, along with the magnitude and then using an assigned weighting on each axis to determine if a step has been taken. The weightings will be dynamically applied based on the amount of acceleration change during the sliding window. The step detection algorithm can also be modified to detect both peaks of the footstep profile and not just the heal strike, signifying the end of the step. As step count is only used for gamifying in the data collection app, being out by several steps is not critical, as the raw 3-axis accelerometer data is what is critical to the clinician. This is analyzed by our backend system to determine other data metrics to provide an information summary to the clinician.

Future work will involve a larger study with child participants to better determine the accuracy of the step counting algorithm for children. We will also further develop the web portal to implement more summary information of gait (cadence, cycle times, stride length, trunk control and balance) to enable clinicians to better understand the usage and effectiveness of the prescribed treatment.

Acknowledgments. Invest Northern Ireland is acknowledged for supporting this project under the Competence Centre Programs Grant RD0513853 – Connected Health Innovation Centre.

References

1. Casey, J., McKeown, L., McDonald, R., Martin, S.: Wheelchairs for children under 12 with physical impairments. Cochrane Database Syst. Rev. Issue 10. Art. No. CD010154 (2012). doi:10.1002/14651858.CD010154
2. International Classification of Functioning, Disability, and Health: Children & Youth Version: ICF-CY. World Health Organization (2007)
3. Montero, S.M., Gómez-Conesa, A.: Technical devices in children with motor disabilities: a review. Disabil. Rehabil. Assist. Technol. 9(1), 3–11 (2014)
4. Novak, I., Mcintyre, S., Morgan, C., Campbell, L., Dark, L., Morton, N., Stumbles, E., Wilson, S.A., Goldsmith, S.: A systematic review of interventions for children with cerebral palsy: state of the evidence. Dev. Med. Child Neurol. 55(10), 885–910 (2013)
5. Gough, M.: Continuous postural management and the prevention of deformity in children with cerebral palsy: an appraisal. Dev. Med. Child Neurol. 51(2), 105–110 (2009)
6. Patel, S., Park, H., Bonato, P., Chan, L., Rodgers, M.: A review of wearable sensors and systems with application in rehabilitation. J. Neuroeng. Rehabil. 9(12), 1–17 (2012)
7. Shimmer: Shimmer3. http://www.shimmersensing.com/shop/shimmer3. Accessed: 06 June 2016
8. Burns, A., Greene, B.R., McGrath, M.J., O'Shea, T.J., Kuris, B., Ayer, S.M., Stroiescu, F., Cionca, V.: SHIMMER - a wireless sensor platform for noninvasive biomedical research. IEEE Sens. J. 10(9), 1527–1534 (2010)
9. Maher, C., Crettenden, A., Evans, K., Thiessen, M., Toohey, M., Dollman, J.: A pedometer based physical activity self-management program for children and adolescents with physical disability - design and methods of the StepUp study. BMC Pediatr. 14, 31 (2014)
10. Zhao, N.: Full-featured pedometer design realized with 3-axis digital accelerometer. Analog Dialogue 44(2), 1–5 (2010)

Reducing Appointment Lead-Time in an Outpatient Department of Gynecology and Obstetrics Through Discrete-Event Simulation: A Case Study

Miguel Angel Ortiz[1(✉)], Sally McClean[2], Chris D. Nugent[3], and Anyeliz Castillo[1]

[1] Department of Industrial Engineering, Universidad de la Costa CUC, Barranquilla, Colombia
{mortizl, acastill20}@cuc.edu.co
[2] School of Computing and Information Engineering, University of Ulster, Coleraine, County Londonderry BT52 1SA, UK
si.mcclean@ulster.ac.uk
[3] School of Computing and Mathematics, University of Ulster, Coleraine, UK
cd.nugent@ulster.ac.uk

Abstract. Appointment lead-time is a critical variable in outpatient clinic services. In Gynecology and Obstetrics departments, longer appointment lead times are associated with lower patient satisfaction, the use of more complex healthcare services, development of long-term and severe complications and the increase of fetal, infant and maternal mortality rates. This paper aims to define and evaluate improvement alternatives through the use of Discrete-event simulation (DES). First, input data analysis is performed. Second, the simulation model is created; then, performance metrics are calculated and analyzed. Finally, improvement scenarios are designed and assessed. A case study of a mixed-patient type environment (Perinatology and Gynecobstetrics) in an outpatient department has been explored to verify the effectiveness of the proposed approach. Statistical analysis evidence that appointment lead times could be significantly reduced in both Perinatology and Gynecobstetrics appointments based on the proposed approaches in this paper.

Keywords: Appointment lead-time · Discrete event simulation · Outpatient department · Healthcare · Gynecology · Obstetrics

1 Introduction

The problem presented in this paper reflects the concern relating the period of time that patients currently have to wait to be seen by physicians in outpatient departments. Long appointment lead times are not uncommon in these units [1] and could become a significant problem in the future as demands on healthcare services continue to rise. Long waiting times cause patient dissatisfaction and can also have negative effects on patient's health [2]. Lead time has also been denoted as the factor which has the highest

© Springer International Publishing AG 2016
C.R. García et al. (Eds.): UCAmI 2016, Part I, LNCS 10069, pp. 274–285, 2016.
DOI: 10.1007/978-3-319-48746-5_28

association with patient non-attendance of clinical appointments [3]. This has resulted in a greater emphasis on preventative medicine by researchers and practitioners who work in this field [4]. To provide an efficient solution to the problem of lead time requires that the complex internal interactions of departments must be fully known and understood to ensure focused and effective decisions can be made moving forward [5]. This has the potential for the efficient use of medical resources and patient´s timely access to quality care [6]. Appointment scheduling impacts upon patient waiting times in outpatient services and is subject to certain constraints associated with the overall operational capacity of the system. Although, several studies have concluded that physician's time is more valuable than a patient's time [7–10], this is no longer valid in today´s view of healthcare, waiting time has been recognized as being critical to satisfaction (CTS) which determines how patients select healthcare provider of choice.

In the outpatient departments of Gynecology and Obstetrics, time represents an important factor for pregnant women. It becomes even more important for those who require perinatology consultation due to high risk pregnancy. It must be appreciated that extended waiting times could lead to an increase of fetal, infant and maternal mortality rates. Treatment costs with increased waiting times are also affected in these departments; pregnant women with diverse pathologies could develop more severe complications due to periods of extended delay and result in requirement of complex services like emergency care, hospitalization and intensive care [11, 12].

In response to this situation, this study proposes a methodological approach to reduce the appointment lead-time in the outpatients´ departments of Gynecology and Obstetrics. The framework considered involves using process diagramming, input data analysis, discrete-event simulation (DES), output data analysis and design/evaluation of improvement scenarios. This research will provide a methodological tool based on DES for the field of Gynecology and Obstetrics; which will represent a significant offering for society.

The remainder of this paper is organized as follows: in Sect. 2, a brief literature review relating improvement strategies for reduced appointment lead times in departments of Gynecology and Obstetrics is presented; Sect. 3 illustrates the proposed methodology; Sect. 4 describes and analyses the results of a case study from the hospital sector. Finally, Sect. 5 presents the conclusions and future work from the study.

2 Strategies to Reduce Appointment Lead Times in Outpatient Departments: A Brief Literature Review

Several researchers have considered different strategies to reduce appointment lead times in outpatient departments. Harper & Gamlin used a detailed simulation model of an Ear, Nose and Throat (ENT) outpatient department. This strategy allowed managers to examine different appointment schedules and their effect on the clinic. The results provided evidence that alternative appointment schedules could drastically reduce patient waiting times without need for extra doctors and support personnel [13]. Elkhuizen et al. developed a simulation model to determine the capacity required in appointments management of hospitals. The added value of this model was the possibility of considering variations in demand for different weekdays and a realistic schedule for doctor's consultations [14]. Wijewickrama performed a simulation analysis for reducing queues in a mixed-patients' outpatient department. In this work, two improvement scenarios were designed and assessed, however, neither of them was found as being a feasible solution for the healthcare system under study [1]. Santibáñez *et al.* used simulation approaches to analyze the simultaneous impact of operations, scheduling, resource allocation on patient wait time, clinic overtime and resource utilization. As a result, a proposed revised configuration of services achieved a reduction of up to 70 % in patient wait times and 25 % in physical space requirements with the same appointment volume [15]. Finally, Gillespie *et al.* [16] provided a framework based on discrete-event simulation to model stroke care and evaluate the impact of discharge queues. The findings from the work evidenced that the availability of suitable data could represent a restriction upon modeling healthcare services.

A number of the aforementioned works addressed the problem of lead-times through a six sigma methodology [12–17]. There is a marked trend towards the use of DES solutions in an effort to the reduction of appointment lead-times in outpatient departments. In this paper, a DES technique is proposed to address problems associated with lead-times. This has been complemented by the usage of six sigma indicators to illustrate the current performance of the real system and evaluate the effectiveness of the proposed improvement scenarios.

3 Methodology

For an effective implementation of DES techniques in healthcare systems, it is necessary to guarantee that the structure, details and assumptions of the simulation model are clearly shown and that the results and predictions validated to be statistically comparable with the real world [18, 19]. If the model does not represent the real system, the current status of the system cannot be properly analyzed and therefore improvement scenarios cannot be suitably designed. An approach comprised of 5 phases has been proposed to address this problem (refer to Fig. 1). This framework has been developed with the foresight to be replicated in a wide range of healthcare systems and can be used without limitations of complexity or size.

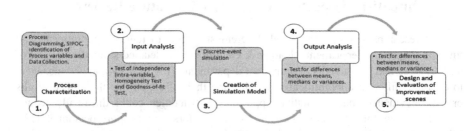

Fig. 1. Methodological approach to reduce appointment lead-time in outpatient departments

- **Phase 1 (Process Characterization)**: One of the key features to make the simulation model comparable or statistically equivalent to the real system is a suitable characterization of the process being considered. In this phase, a process diagram should be defined to identify the main components (sub-processes) of the system; existing interactions and sequence. Information about service times, installed capacity, schedules, time between arrivals, entities per arrival, process constraints, failures and other variables must be also collected for a correct process model.
- **Phase 2 (Input analysis):** After collecting illustrative information about the system as outlined in Phase 1, input analysis of the data is performed through three statistical techniques: Test of Independence (intra-variable), Homogeneity Test and Goodness-of-fit Test. The test of independence (intra-variable) evaluates if the data sequence of a variable is random. If so, it is concluded that the variable is not linked to a dependence factor and can be represented by a probability distribution. The Homogeneity Test is used to determine whether several populations are statistical homogeneous (one probability distribution) or must be represented by two or more probability distributions. The Goodness-of-fit Test measures how well do the observed data correspond to a specific distribution and which parameters can represent them the best.
- **Phase 3 (Creation of simulation model):** With the results of Phase 1 and Phase 2, the real healthcare system can be modeled through process simulation software. The animation provided by the software supported engagement with the decision maker and reinforces related model validation [16]. This also calculates metrics with which overall performance can be assessed from repeated iterations of the model. With the aid of the model, it will be easier to forecast the impact of changes in patient waiting times, resource utilization, complex relationships and other process variables. Moreover, its results allow managers to design improvement scenarios and reconfigure existing systems without changing the present system.
- **Phase 4 (Output analysis):** A hypothesis test is performed to prove whether the simulation model correctly characterizes the real-world system. Tests for differences between means, medians or variances can be used in this phase. If the p-value is greater than alpha ($\alpha = 0.05$), then the simulation model is deemed to give a sufficiently accurate representation of the real performance of the healthcare system; if not, some refinement must be made on the model until it is sufficiently close to reality.
- **Phase 5 (Design and Evaluation of improvement scenarios):** As a final step, decision makers should design improvement scenarios to be validated in a simulation model created in the previous phase. The results of each scenario must be statistically compared with the current performance to validate if the proposed strategies provide improved outputs. Statistical techniques used in Phase 4 are also recommended in this stage.

4 An Illustrative Example: Modeling the Outpatient Department of Gynecology and Obstetrics

Using the proposed approach described in the previous section, a case study of an outpatient department of Gynecology and Obstetrics from hospital sector has been explored. The model describes the journey of pregnant women from appointment scheduling to consultation. This journey has been divided into a number of phases and pathways according to the results of Phase 1 as shown below:

4.1 Process Characterization

The outpatient department of Gynecology and Obstetrics is based on a 1-year (2015) prospective dataset extracted from the User Information System (USI) of a colombian hospital and consisted of all pregnant and non-pregnant women admitted between January 1st and December 31st in this department. USI is used by the hospital to manage patient registration, appointment scheduling, billing and consultation. The purpose of this system is to reduce errors during registering and scheduling patients, monitor appointment lead-time, analyse patient satisfaction and improve the resource utilization [20, 21]. Patients are women between the ages of 16 and 43 years old. For the purpose of this study, all the patients of the hospital have been categorized into 5 appointment types: first-time, control, gynecology, perinatology and other. The first four correspond to the department of Gynecology and Obstetrics, while the last type represents the rest of appointments registered by the hospital that are different from Gynecology and Obstetrics. Specifically, *first-time appointments* are assigned when the patient (pregnant woman) who has not previously had an appointment with a gynecobstetrics doctor and has not started a perinatal control. *Control appointments* are given to those pregnant women who are under a perinatal control and have already had appointments with a gynecobstetrics doctor. *Gynecology appointments* are scheduled for women who require for medical intervention and *Perinatology appointments* are assigned for women who have been considered as being high-risk pregnancy.

Patients or their families can go to the hospital (OUTPATIENT DEPARTMENT) to request an appointment or can request it by telephone. In this hospital, 66.66 % of the appointments are requested in the hospital directly and the rest are made by telephone. The OUTPATIENT DEPARTMENT provides 2 servers (Server 1, Server 2) to schedule the appointments requested in the hospital directly and 1 server (Server 3) to schedule appointments that are demanded by phone (refer to schedules in Table 1).

Table 1. Schedules for servers in scheduling department

Server	Opening hours
1	8:00 am–12:00 m and 1:00 pm–5:00 pm
2	8:00 am–1:00 pm and 2:00 pm–5:00 pm
3	8:00 am–12:00 pm and 1:00 pm–5:00 pm

First-time, *control* and *gynecology appointments* are allocated to 8 gynecologists and *perinatology appointments* are assigned to 1 perinatologist. The current schedules of these doctors are described in Table 2. "M" means that the gynecologist or perinatologist treats patients from 8 am to 12 m and "A" means that the gynecologist or perinatologist treats patients from 1 pm to 5 pm.

Table 2. Schedules of Perinatologist and Gynecologists

Resource – Doctor	Schedule				
	Mon	Tue	Wed	Thu	Fri
Gynecologist 1	M	M		M	
Gynecologist 2				M	
Gynecologist 3			M		
Gynecologist 4		M		M	M
Gynecologist 5		A		A	A
Gynecologist 6	M				
Gynecologist 7		M–A	M		
Gynecologist 8					M
Perinatologist				Mª	M–A

ªPerinatology extends their shift until 2 pm

Table 3. Schedules for servers in billing department

Server	Opening hours
b1	8:00 am–12:00 m and 1:00 pm–5:00 pm
b2	8.00 am–1:00 pm and 2:00 pm–5:00 pm

Patients must go to the BILLING DEPARTMENT before being attended by the corresponding doctor. The BILLING DEPARTMENT has two servers (Server b1, Server b2). The schedules of the servers are described in Table 3 while Fig. 2 illustrates the patient flows, sub-processes and different pathways in the department of Gynecology and Obstetrics.

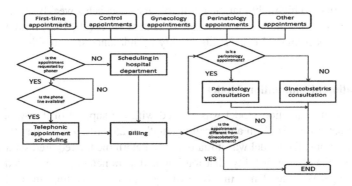

Fig. 2. A flow diagram for the department of Gynecology and Obstetrics

4.2 Input Analysis

Process variables from the healthcare system in study were identified and the relevant data collected: time between arrivals for each appointment type, failures; and service times for scheduling department (both telephonic and personalized), billing department and perinatology/gynecobstetrics consultation. Tests of intra-variable independence were carried out evidencing p-values greater than $\alpha = 0.05$, which means that data sequence of each variable is random and could be represented by a probability distribution.

Homogeneity tests were performed for each dataset. With p-values greater than $\alpha = 0.05$, all datasets were found to be homogeneous and each variable can be characterized by one probability distribution.

Finally, Goodness-of-fit tests were implemented and specific probability distributions and parameters were determined for each process variable. Tables 4 and 5 summarize the findings of the statistical technique deployed.

Table 4. Probability distributions for time between arrivals in each appointment type

Appointment type	Time between arrivals
First-time	EXPO (45,4374) min
Control	EXPO (48.6743) min
Perinatology	EXPO (163,202) min
Gynecology	EXPO (15.893) min
Other appointments	EXPO (52.9995) min

Table 5. Probability distributions of consultation times for each appointment type

Appointment type	Consultation times
First-time	UNIF (45,63) min
Control	N (35, 5.7) min
Perinatology	UNIF (63, 90) min
Gynecology	UNIF (20, 36) min

It is important to highlight that the perinatologist cancels his weekly agenda once in a month. All the gynecologists become late (Lateness $\sim$ N (30, 10.5) min) every day. In addition, Gynecologist 2 cancels his weekly agenda once in a month.

4.3 Creation of Simulation Model

A discrete-event simulation model was created with the support of the Arena 14.0 ® software (refer to Fig. 3). With a replication length of 25 days, 9 h per day (work shift) and 10 replications; the model was initially run to determine the required sample size to suitably describe the probability distribution and parameters of Weighted Waiting Time, Average Waiting Time in Gynecology, Average Waiting in Perinatology, Maximum Waiting Time in Gynecology, Maximum Waiting Time in Perinatology and

GYNECOBSTETRICS DEPARTMENT

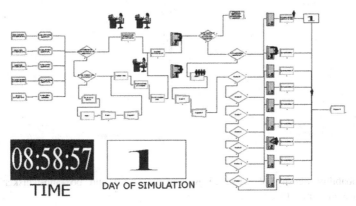

Fig. 3. Simulation model for Gynecobstetrics department

Resource Utilization. After running the simulation model, the necessary sample size was calculated as 39 with ±1 h of error and 95 % confidence level.

4.4 Output Analysis

After running the simulation model according to the sample size established in the previous phase (n = 39), a test for differences between medians (Mann-Whitney Wilcoxon W-Test) was carried out to prove that the simulation model was statistically comparable with the real-world system. Since the P-value (0.5119) was greater than 0.05, there was not a statistically significant difference between the medians of the simulation model and the real system at the 95.0 % confidence level. This means that the simulation model represents the real performance of the department under study.

Key performance indexes were also calculated and graphed to evidence the current performance of the system. First, Fig. 4 (left side) describes the Weighted Waiting Time in Gynecology and Obstetrics Department, its normal distribution parameters and government target (8 days as maximum). In this case, the sigma level is equal to -1.24 which illustrates a poor performance process. This is confirmed upon determining that 996928 out of 1000000 will be assigned with waiting time greater than 8 days. Considering maximum waiting times of Gynecobstetrics and Perinatology by Box-and-whisker plots in Fig. 4 (right side), it can be viewed that Gynecobstetrics make higher contributions to Weighted Waiting Time than Perinatology. Nonetheless, Maximum waiting times in Perinatology are represented by 95 % confidence interval [5.22; 13.05] days; which increases the risk of perinatal, fetal and maternal mortality. It is also useful to note that resource utilization in Gynecobstetrics (3.18) and resource utilization in Perinatology (1.78) are greater than 1; therefore, queues in this system are out of control and waiting times will tend to be greater with the passing of time.

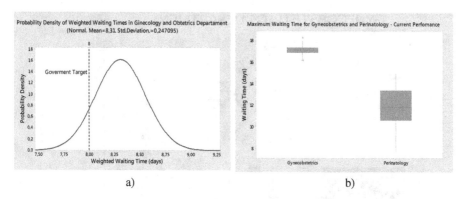

Fig. 4. Probability density of weighted waiting times (a) and box-and-whisker plot for maximum waiting times (b)

4.5   Design and Evaluation of Improvement Scenarios

Three improvement scenarios have been proposed with the aid of the director and medical staff from the hospital for department of Gynecology and Obstetrics:

– **First scenario**

• Hire gynecologist 2 for Monday and Wednesday mornings
• Hire gynecologist 6 for Wednesday mornings.
• Hire gynecologist 8 for Monday and Wednesday mornings.
• Assign perinatologist outpatient functions during Monday mornings and replace his hospitalization functions with 1 gynecologist from the hospital staff.

– **Second scenario**

Establish a sanction policy (financial) where cancellations of medical agendas could be eliminated as it happens with Gynecologist 2 and Perinatologist.

– **Third scenario**

• Dismiss Gynecologist 2, Gynecologist 3, Gynecologist 6 and Gynecologist 8.
• Hire gynecologist 1 for Wednesday and Friday mornings.
• Hire gynecologist 4 for Monday and Wednesday mornings.
• Hire gynecologist 5 for Monday and Wednesday afternoons.
• Hire gynecologist 7 for Thursday and Friday mornings.
• Assign perinatologist outpatient functions during Monday mornings as Scenario 1

Considering comparisons (Fig. 5) between the current state and proposed scenarios in terms of maximum waiting time for Perinatology, p-values were significantly lower than 0.05 (0.000013401, 4.10464E−9 and 0.00000814919 for scenarios 1, 2 and 3 respectively) which indicates that assigning perinatologist outpatient functions during Monday mornings or establishing financial sanctions due to cancellations of weekly

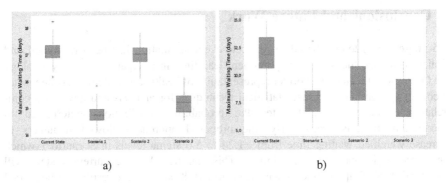

Fig. 5. Comparison between current state and proposed scenarios 1, 2, 3 in terms of maximum waiting time for Gynecobstetrics (a) and Perinatology (b)

medical agenda are both operationally beneficial. Nevertheless, Scenarios 1 and 3 provide improved performance compared with Scenario 2. As for Gynecobstetrics, p-values were also meaningfully lower than 0.05 (5.97455E−8, 0.00520282 and 3.56715E−8 for scenarios 1, 2 and 3 respectively). This means that new scheduling configurations and sanction policy are both operationally favorable for patients who request first-time, control or gynecology appointments. Nevertheless, Scenario 1 could be considered as the optimal solution. Weighted waiting time measures have been also considered to compare the effectiveness of the proposed scenarios with respect to the real performance of the system in study (Fig. 6). Results demonstrate that the sigma level increased from −1.24 to 5.0 in Scenario 1 with 233 defective appointments out of 1.000.000. In Scenario 2, the sigma level improved from −1.24 to −0.46 with 975002 defective appointments per 1.000.000. Finally, in Scenario 3, the index increased from −1.24 to 2.91 with PPM (parts per million) = 79270.

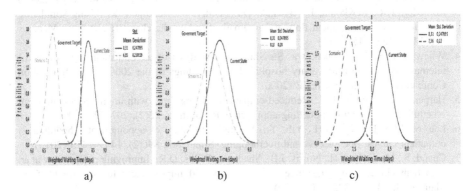

Fig. 6. Comparison between current state and scenario 1 (a), scenario 2 (b) and scenario (c) in terms of weighted waiting time

5 Conclusions and Future Work

A 5-phase methodology based on discrete-event simulation has been presented and applied to reduce the average appointment lead-time in a department of Gynecology and Obstetrics. To ensure a correct representation of healthcare systems, it is necessary to collect appropriate data, use statistical techniques for analysis and develop a comprehensible model that integrates the probability distributions determined in Goodness-of-fit tests. Particularly, the proposed approach allowed managers to decrease weighted waiting time from -1.24 to 5.0 sigma levels in Scenario 1 which represents an increase of 6.24 sigmas. This signifies that the current system will scheduled 996655 appointments with lead time ≤ 8 days. These results are beneficial for pregnant women who will have a minor risk of perinatal, fetal or maternal mortality. Benefits were also evidenced in both Perinatology and Gynecobstetrics consultations in terms of reduced maximum waiting times.

This framework has been designed with the aim of supporting decision making in healthcare systems. It also permits evaluating the potential impact of implementing different improvement scenarios without altering the real-world system. Nonetheless, we consider this research has meaningful potential to be extended by incorporating interactions with hospitalization, emergency and intensive care departments as future work. With this, more detailed scenarios can be established to achieve better results for both hospitals and patients.

References

1. Wijewickrama, A.K.: Simulation analysis for reducing queues in mixed-patients' outpatient department. Int. J. Simul. Model. 5(2), 56–68 (2006)
2. Giachetti, R.E.: A simulation study of interventions to reduce appointment lead-time and patient no-show rate. In: 2008 Winter Simulation Conference, pp. 1463–1468. IEEE (2008)
3. Rohleder, T.R., Lewkonia, P., Bischak, D.P., Duffy, P., Hendijani, R.: Using simulation modeling to improve patient flow at an outpatient orthopedic clinic. Health Care Manage. Sci. 14(2), 135–145 (2011)
4. Wijewickrama, A.A., Takakuwa, S.: Simulation analysis of an outpatient department of internal medicine in a university hospital. In: Proceedings of the 2006 Winter Simulation Conference, pp. 425–432. IEEE (2006)
5. Harper, P.R., Gamlin, H.M.: Reduced outpatient waiting times with improved appointment scheduling: a simulation modelling approach. OR Spectrum 25(2), 207–222 (2003)
6. Lee, S., Min, D., Ryu, J.H., Yih, Y.: A simulation study of appointment scheduling in outpatient clinics: open access and overbooking. Simulation 89(12), 1459–1473 (2013)
7. Chand, S., Moskowitz, H., Norris, J.B., Shade, S., Willis, D.R.: Improving patient flow at an outpatient clinic: study of sources of variability and improvement factors. Health Care Manage. Sci. 12(3), 325–340 (2009)
8. Rohleder, T.R., Lewkonia, P., Bischak, D.P., Duffy, P., Hendijani, R.: Using simulation modeling to improve patient flow at an outpatient orthopedic clinic. Health Care Manage. Sci. 14(2), 135–145 (2011)

9. Cao, W., Wan, Y., Tu, H., Shang, F., Liu, D., Tan, Z., Xu, Y.: A web-based appointment system to reduce waiting for outpatients: a retrospective study. BMC Health Serv. Res. **11** (1), 1–5 (2011)

10. Qu, X., Peng, Y., Kong, N., Shi, J.: A two-phase approach to scheduling multi-category outpatient appointments–a case study of a women's clinic. Health care Manage. Sci. **16**(3), 197–216 (2013)

11. Barrios, M.A.O., Caballero, J.E., Sanchez, F.S.: A methodology for the creation of integrated service networks in outpatient internal medicine. In: Bravo, J., Hervas, R., Villarreal, V. (eds.) AmIHEALTH 2015. LNCS, vol. 9456, pp. 247–257. Springer, Heidelberg (2015). doi:10.1007/978-3-319-26508-7_24

12. Barrios, M.A.O., Jimenez, H.F.: Reduction of average lead time in outpatient service of obstetrics through six sigma methodology. In: Bravo, J., Hervas, R., Villarreal, V. (eds.) AmIHEALTH 2015. LNCS, vol. 9456, pp. 293–302. Springer, Heidelberg (2015). doi:10. 1007/978-3-319-26508-7_29

13. Harper, P.R., Gamlin, H.M.: Reduced outpatient waiting times with improved appointment scheduling: a simulation modelling approach. OR Spectrum **25**(2), 207–222 (2003)

14. Elkhuizen, S.G., Das, S.F., Bakker, P.J.M., Hontelez, J.A.M.: Using computer simulation to reduce access time for outpatient departments. Qual. Safety Health Care **16**(5), 382–386 (2007)

15. Santibáñez, P., Chow, V.S., French, J., Puterman, M.L., Tyldesley, S.: Reducing patient wait times and improving resource utilization at British Columbia Cancer Agency's ambulatory care unit through simulation. Health Care Manage. Sci. **12**(4), 392–407 (2009)

16. Gillespie, J., McClean, S., Garg, L., Barton, M., Scotney, B., Fullerton, K.: A multi-phase DES modelling framework for patient-centred care. J. Oper. Res. Soc. (2016)

17. Gijo, E.V., Antony, J.: Reducing patient waiting time in outpatient department using lean six sigma methodology. Qual. Reliab. Eng. Int. **30**(8), 1481–1491 (2014)

18. Eddy, D.M., Hollingworth, W., Caro, J.J., Tsevat, J., McDonald, K.M., Wong, J.B.: Model transparency and validation: a report of the ISPOR-SMDM modeling good research practices task force-7. Value Health **15**, 843–850 (2012)

19. McClean, S.I., Barton, M., Garg, L., Fullerton, K.: Combining Markov models and discrete event simulation to plan stroke patient care. Trans. Model. Comput. Sci. **21**(4), 25 (2011)

20. Jun, J.B., Jacobson, S.H., Swisher, J.R.: Application of discrete-event simulation in health care clinics: a survey. J. Oper. Res. Soc. **50**(2), 109–123 (1999)

21. Herazo-Padilla, N., Montoya-Torres, J.R., Munoz-Villamizar, A., Nieto Isaza, S., Ramirez Polo, L.: Coupling ant colony optimization and discrete-event simulation to solve a stochastic location-routing problem. In: 2013 Simulations Conference (WSC), pp. 3352–3362. IEEE (2013)

Employing UNICEF Open Source Software Tools in mHealth Projects in Nicaragua

Pritpal Singh[✉]

Department of Electrical and Computer Engineering, Villanova University, Villanova, PA, USA
pritpal.singh@villanova.edu

Abstract. The United Nations Children's Fund (UNICEF) is a UN organization whose charter is to protect and improve the lives of children around the world. Maternal and child health are health-related areas where UNICEF has developed innovative Information and Communication Technology (ICT) solutions in the general domain of mHealth in which text messages have been used to address particular health issues. We have used two UNICEF open source software packages, Rapid SMS and Rapid Pro, in tele-health projects in Nicaragua. In this paper we describe the implementation of these projects and the relative advantages/ disadvantages of using these two software tools in implementing our solutions.

Keywords: mhealth · Open source software · UNICEF

1 Introduction and Background

The Nicaraguan government provides a free national health care system to its citizens as a right to its people. However, there are many parts of North Central Nicaragua that are remote, rural, mountainous and difficult to access because of the limited road infrastructure in these regions. The geography along the Atlantic Coast of Nicaragua includes many rivers and so many people reside on islands separated by rivers and transport to these communities is by boat. The inhabitants of these island communities are sparsely distributed and are again difficult to reach. In both of these geographical regions access to health care service is limited because of a shortage of health care professionals (doctors and nurses) in these areas, and because of a lack of transportation infrastructure. Over the last six years, we have been developing telehealth systems to improve access to health care in these regions [1]. In North Central Nicaragua, we have primarily worked in the communities surrounding the town of Waslala. Our original partner in this project was the Catholic Parish in Waslala that delivered social as well as spiritual services to the surrounding communities. However, this was superseded by partnering with an NGO, Asociacion Desarollo Integral y Sostenibilidad (ADIS), because the Catholic Parish discontinued its support for health programs in these communities. Both of these programs were run in parallel to the Ministry of Health's National Health Service using a volunteer network of community health workers (CHWs). Our more recent work has involved working with the Regional Government of the Southern Atlantic and Caribbean region, an autonomously governed region. Two pilot projects in this geographical region

C.R. García et al. (Eds.): UCAmI 2016, Part I, LNCS 10069, pp. 286–293, 2016.
DOI: 10.1007/978-3-319-48746-5_29

have been sponsored by UNICEF and are located on the islands of Laguna de Perlas and El Bluff. In the Waslala region, we employed an older software tool, Rapid SMS, and in the pilot projects in Laguna de Perlas and El Bluff we have been developing applications around the more recently developed software tool, Rapid Pro. In this paper we will describe the implementation methods for the two systems and provide a comparison of the two approaches.

2 Waslala Telehealth System Overview

Figure 1 shows an overview of the telehealth system used in both the Waslala system and the Laguna de Perlas and El Bluff systems. The system design was previously described in reference [2]. The system design philosophy emphasized hardware reliability and low power consumption. For that reason we chose a Dell PC with an ultra-small form factor, 10 GB hard drive and a power supply with high efficiency. In terms of software selection, our approach had to be based on Open Source Software to maintain low system cost. The Linux operating system and MySQL database software were selected for the Waslala system. The Laguna de Perlas/El Bluff system also used the Linux operating system but could use the built-in database that comes with Rapid Pro. Besides being free (and thus saving substantial licensing costs), these software components are also more immune to computer viruses (saving costs on anti-virus software). The cell system connectivity was provided by a rugged industrial grade modem connected to the serial port of the computer for the Waslala system. To avoid having to be tied to a particular service provider, several different Linux-compatible modems that were not dependent on a particular service provider (such as Claro in Nicaragua) were evaluated. Furthermore, the modems had to be compatible with the GSM phone frequencies used in Nicaragua. We chose the "MultiModem GSM/GPRS Wireless Modem" for the Rapid SMS-based system. For the system based on Rapid Pro, a low cost Android phone was used for sending and receiving text messages from the computer server.

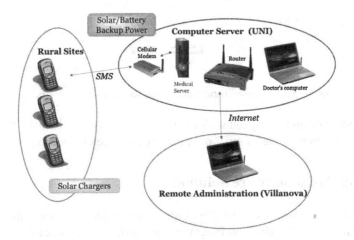

Fig. 1. Waslala telehealth system block diagram

The software structure for the Waslala telehealth system was built around the open source software tool, Rapid SMS [3]. This software package was developed by UNICEF to enable programmers to develop software applications incorporating the sending and receiving of text messages for data collection, remote monitoring, reporting and educational purposes. RapidSMS is based on Django, the popular "Web Framework" Python interface. It provides tools for GSM modems that allow SMS messages to be sent and received, and for these messages to be analyzed and stored in a relational database. RapidSMS also facilitates the creation of a "web-GUI" for visualizing and managing information. RapidSMS also allows the addition of new applications to process incoming messages, post replies, and extend the user interface. The application we developed contained several formats for managing the health information. The data was organized into fields in an electronic health record system in an easy-to-read format for review by health care professionals. The interface enables the rapid identification of relevant and necessary information to illuminate potential health problems.

A screenshot of a patient record in the Rapid SMS environment is shown in Fig. 2.

Fig. 2. Screen shot of patient data in the Rapid SMS environment

The GSM modem is equipped with a SIM card and interfaces with the Rapid SMS software application through a serial port, sending and receiving messages.

3   Cloud-Based Software Solution

To improve the stability and scalability of the system, we have explored the option of migrating to an API (Application Programming Interface) web-based system to send and receive SMS messages. This approach reduces the reliance on the physical location of the computer server and enables the project development environment to take place in the "cloud", see Fig. 3. There are several platforms that offer APIs to send and receive SMS messages via the Internet. One example is Moonshado [4], a mobile solution which allows local connection through the Claro network in Nicaragua. A second example is Chat Salud [5], which also offers a Cloud-based solution.

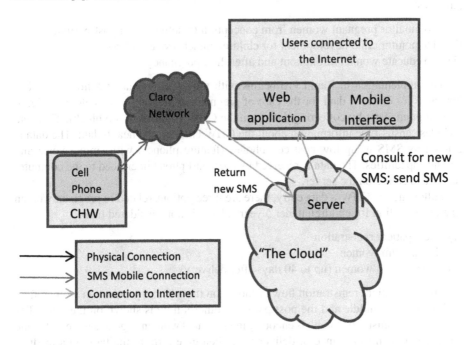

Fig. 3. Block diagram of the proposed system incorporating "Cloud Computing"

In 2015, UNICEF released an updated and substantially enhanced version of its Rapid SMS software, Rapid Pro [6]. This software leveraged development efforts of another product, "TextIt". Rapid Pro is also a cloud-based solution, that allows for a more robust and scalable solution than is available through Rapid SMS. Furthermore, the Rapid Pro solution is designed to be built without programming expertise using an interactive GUI interface. A Rapid Pro deployment toolkit has been developed which takes the developer through a series of activities to clarify exactly what the program is to be designed to do. The charts used in the Deployment Toolkit may be translated into a block diagram flow that can be constructed through the GUI interface to establish the program code for the application. The easiest way to implement the application is by interfacing through an Android phone, rather than through a modem, to provide the cloud connectivity and may be used even in environments with sporadic connections to the Internet.

Another important feature of Rapid Pro is its data analytics capability. Since the data is stored in the Cloud, extensive data may be stored and charts and trend lines may be easily established as data is accumulated. We chose to use Rapid Pro for the Laguna de Perlas and El Bluff telehealth system deployments.

4   Pilot Telehealth Project in Laguna de Perlas/El Bluff

4.1   Flowchart of Program

The UNICEF-sponsored telehealth project in Laguna de Perlas and El Bluff has three purposes:

(1) To monitor pregnant women from conception to delivery and post-partum
(2) To monitor child development for children under 5 years of age
(3) To educate women throughout and after their pregnancy

The implentation in Rapid Pro begins with the development of a flowchart. The flowchart for entering data for the case of pregnant women is shown below in Fig. 4. The program starts by collecting data from the CHW (right hand top block). This data includes census-type information about the CHW entering the health data. The data is entered by SMS using low cost cell phones (feature phones) with simple voice and texting capabilities. The data is received by the smart phone interfaced to the computer server and stored on the server.

Following the CHW's data entry, there are three options related to pregnant women (the fourth option for children under 5 years of age is not considered here):

(1) New patient registration
(2) Pre-partum women
(3) Post-partum women (up to 40 days after delivery)

The new patient registration flow is shown on the left, the pre-partum women flow is shown in the middle and the post-partum mother's flow is shown on the right. The Nicaraguan Ministry of Health is encouraging pregnant women to go to a maternal home about one month in advance of delivery and then give birth to the baby in a medical clinic adjacent to the maternal home rather than in the communities. There is an optional path in case women give birth to the babies in their communities.

This entire flow can be simulated in a simulator in the Rapid Pro environment to verify that the responses to the questions texted out lead to correct flows in the flowchart. Once the flow is verified in the simulator, the code can be ported to a live application. Instructions can be added to send out text messages to the CHWs to enter data (e.g. CHW or patient registration data) or receive messages to response questions (e.g. did the mother go to the maternal home?). The resulting text responses are stored in a data-base in the cloud.

The data can then be analyzed using Data Analytics tools available in Rapid Pro. For example, the number of pregnant women from different communities who have gone to the maternal home may be tracked. The information collected and displayed can then be used to inform health care interventions based on evidence collected from the field.

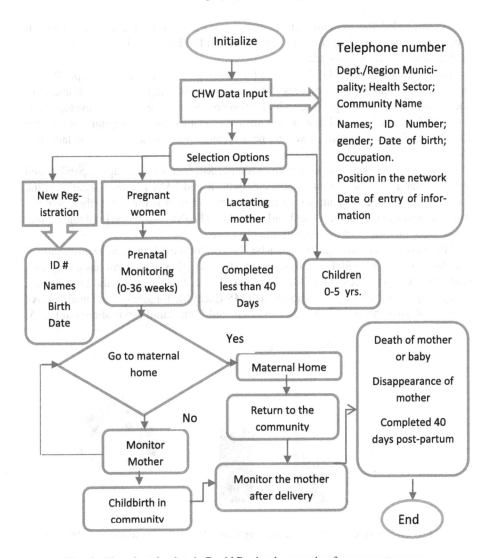

Fig. 4. Flowchart for data in Rapid Pro implementation for pregnant women

5   Comparison of Rapid SMS and Rapid Pro Implementations

There are very significant differences in working with Rapid SMS compared to working with Rapid Pro. The Rapid SMS tool can be easily accessed by anyone through a website and downloaded onto a local server. On the other hand, our experience has been that to access the Rapid Pro software, one has to access it through a UNICEF country office account. This can be a challenge if one does not have a connection with a UNICEF country office which has a Rapid Pro account.

The Rapid SMS software can interface to a modem with a SIM card connected to the serial port of a computer for sending and receiving text messages. On the other hand, the recommended way to communicate with Rapid Pro is through an Android phone. It is possible to use a modem for interfacing to Rapid Pro but it needs significant config-uration setup to accomplish that.

The Simulator tool and GUI interface for building the applications in Rapid Pro are easy to use, particularly for engineers with limited programming experience. Rapid SMS does require significant experience with Python programming in order to develop appli-cations. The Simulator tool also allows for easy verification of program flow so that errors in the logical program flow may be detected before the application is launched live.

A major advantage of Rapid Pro over Rapid SMS is its data storage capability and hence, scalability. Since the data collected with Rapid SMS is stored locally on the computer server, the amount of data that may be collected is limited to the computer server's memory size. On the other hand, with Rapid Pro's cloud-based implementation, hundreds of thousands of data entries may be stored.

The data entries from Rapid SMS can be stored in form fields that can be programmed into, for example, a MySQL database. As mentioned earlier, Rapid Pro has a very well developed data analytics capability. Data may be accessed through the built-in data storage application or may be exported to a MS Excel file for storage and analysis. An example of a dashboard display that can be created from Rapid Pro is shown in Fig. 5.

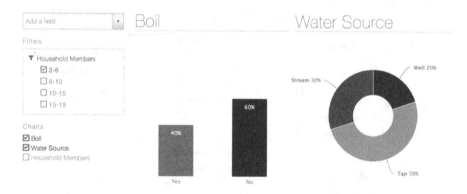

Fig. 5. Example dashboard data display from a Rapid Pro implementation [6]

As can be seen, the data may be visualized in the form of tables, graphs and charts, all through the built-in data analytics tools available through the Rapid Pro platform.

There are many other features in Rapid Pro, such as campaigns that may be run, messages can be accessed using a mailbox-type of interface, etc. [see ref. 6]. Details of these features are not included here.

6   Summary

In this paper we have described two different UNICEF open source software platforms, Rapid SMS and Rapid Pro that have been used to implement telehealth projects in Nicaragua. Rapid SMS is a tool built on the Django framework and implemented in

Python code. It requires knowledge of programming and can be directly interfaced to a computer using a simple modem. However, it has no data analytics capability and has limited scalability. Rapid Pro, on the other hand, is a cloud-based solution and uses a low-cost Android smartphone to connect to the server. It is designed to be used by people without programming expertise through a simple GUI interface. It offers very good data analytics and data visualization features. However, accessing and using Rapid Pro can be more challenging logistically and may require funds to support the Cloud-based data storage features. Both approaches do offer open source means of building applications in which SMS data can be used to collect health data and to support education and monitoring of patients.

Acknowledgements. The author wishes to thank Peter Shaw and Melvin Mendoza for software development and Dr. Rafael Amador of UNICEF Nicaragua for guidance in developing the application for Laguna de Perlas and El Bluff.

References

1. Singh, P., Kulkarni, S., Keech, E., McDermott-Levy, R., Klingler, J.: Progress on making healthcare more accessible to rural communities in Waslala, Nicaragua, using low-cost telecommunications. In: IEEE Global Humanitarian Technology Conference, Seattle, WA, October 30–November 1, 2011 (2011)
2. Singh, P., Moncada, M., Beyer, J., Shaw, P.: Improving quality of life in isolated communities in the RAAN, Waslala, through the application of telecommunication technologies at low cost. In: Proceedings of IEEE Concapan XXXII Conference, Managua, Nicaragua, November 14–16, 2012 (2012)
3. Rapid SMS website. https://www.rapidsms.org/. Accessed 13 Sep 2016
4. https://github.com/moonshado/moonshado-sms. Accessed 13 Sep 2016
5. http://www.mobilemamaalliance.org/sites/default/files/Spotlight-Chatsalud.pdf. Accessed 13 Sep 2016
6. https://community.rapidpro.io/. Accessed 13 Sep 2016

Using Computer Simulation to Improve Patient Flow at an Outpatient Internal Medicine Department

Miguel A. Ortiz[1(✉)] and Pedro López-Meza[2]

[1] Department of Industrial Engineering, Universidad de la Costa CUC, Barranquilla, Colombia
`mortiz1@cuc.edu.co`
[2] Department of Industrial Engineering, Institución Universitaria ITSA, Soledad, Colombia
`plopezmeza@itsa.edu.co`

Abstract. This paper presents the use of discrete-event simulation to support process improvements at an outpatient internal medicine department. This department is significantly effective upon treating patients; however, patient waiting times tend to be longer and consequently patient satisfaction rates continue to decrease. With the aid of this technique, 3 improvement scenarios proposed by medical and administrative staff from this department were designed and simulated including changes related to installed capacity and an emphasis on physicians keeping to the schedule. Statistical analysis of output data evidenced which scenarios resulted in poor performance (statistically equal or higher waiting times) and which strategies caused lower waiting times. In this case, Scenario 3 was selected as the best improvement choice with 71.28 % and 19.28 % reduction in average waiting time and standard deviation respectively. With this approach, inefficient strategies can be avoided and real improvement alternatives can be identified.

Keywords: Discrete event simulation · Process improvement · Internal medicine · Patient waiting time · Healthcare

1 Introduction

A substantial waiting time for patients who request for outpatient services is represented by the interval between patient´s need for special treatment, well known as *referral date* and actual date of treatment or *outpatient clinic date*. This delay - *appointment lead time* - results in more patient dissatisfaction than generated when patients arrive to the outpatient department and wait until physicians call them for treatment [1, 2]. This may represent a weighty number of patients who decline to attend their appointment because of the expectation of long appointment lead times [3].

Specifically, outpatient internal medicine departments are in charge of identifying risk individual factors related to those diseases that affect diverse organs or systems simultaneously; and also treating patients with pluripathology. Both situations tend to be more frequent due to the progressive aging of population. In this way, delayed diagnosis or interventions related to internal medicine could bring about the development of more severe complications in patient´s health and more complex healthcare services

© Springer International Publishing AG 2016
C.R. García et al. (Eds.): UCAmI 2016, Part I, LNCS 10069, pp. 294–299, 2016.
DOI: 10.1007/978-3-319-48746-5_30

such as hospitalization, surgery, intensive care and emergency care could be required [4]. Nonetheless, outpatient internal medicine departments are composed by complex structures; reason why the day-to-day planning of these departments become in a challenging task and should be supported in computational intelligence techniques [5].

In an effort to address this problem, this paper presents a computer discrete-event simulation (DES) approach whose primary aim is to define and evaluate improvement alternatives for the reduction of appointment lead times in outpatient internal medicine departments. This paper also aims to demonstrate how inefficient strategies can be discarded without implementing them on real healthcare systems; in this way, extra charges and negative operational effects can be avoided for both patients and healthcare providers [6].

The remainder of this paper is organized as follows: in Sect. 2 a brief literature review is presented; Sect. 3 presents a case study in an outpatient internal department from hospital sector. Analysis and discussion on results are also described in this section. Finally, Sect. 4 presents concluding remarks and future work.

2   Related Work

There is clear evidence that the research community has focused on using computational simulation techniques to reduce patient waiting times in outpatient departments. Wijewickrama used simulation analysis to reduce queues in mixed-patient´s outpatient department. During this process, Wijewickrama explored bottlenecks in consultation rooms and evaluated four appointment scheduling rules and their possible combinations [7]. This author also applied DES simulation in an outpatient department of Internal Medicine in Japan to reduce patient waiting times before doctor's calling for treatment. In the simulation model, doctor schedule mixes (DSMs) and diverse appointment schedules (Ass) were examined. Conclusions of this work evidenced meaningful reduction of patient waiting time by combining one DSM found via an optimization program with some ASs [5].

Harper & Gamlin presented a specific simulation model of an ENT clinic that was created in Simul8. In this study, different appointment schedules were tested and it was concluded that waiting times may be meaningfully reduced in that clinic by improved appointment schedules and better management of the schedule [6]. Similar work was developed by Giachetti et al. who described a simulation model to design the appointment system of a dermatology clinic. In this clinic, patients arrive at the same time in a day to reduce physician´s idle time, which is suitable when the clinic cannot predict no-shows. Recommendations of this work express that it would be better to implement a policy in which patients can ask for an appointment in the morning and be seen the same day [8].

Several case studies were designed for specific hospitals and clinics as exposed by Takakuwa & Katagiri where simulation models represented outpatient departments with all patient pathways, human resources and service times [9]; meanwhile, other authors like Kuljis et al. focused on generic methodologies to model outpatient departments.

In their work, they proposed CLINSIM approach with successful implementation in 20 clinics located in UK [10].

Even though these studies have exposed different solutions to reduce waiting times in different outpatient departments, a little effort has been reported considering the need of minimizing appointment lead times. Therefore, this paper aims to contribute to this research field by supporting healthcare decision making in these departments with the aid of computational simulation techniques. In this way, guidance is provided for both practitioners and researchers who work in this area.

3   A Case Study: Outpatient Department of Internal Medicine

A case study of an outpatient department of internal medicine from hospital sector is presented to explore the validity and effectiveness of the proposed approach. This department operates from 8.0 to 17.0 during weekdays with two different types of patient appointments: first-time and control.

First-time appointments are assigned for patients who request outpatient internal medicine services for first time. In these appointments, internists spend time getting to know the patients and checking out their medical history to establish suitable treatments. Furthermore, control appointments are scheduled to monitor the progression of patient 's health and effectiveness of prescribed treatments.

Medical consultation in internal medicine are in charge of 3 internists who have different working hours. Internist 1 attends patients on Monday, Tuesday and Thursday from 10.30 to 14.0; while Internist 2 treats them on Tuesday and Wednesday in the same time as Internist 1. Finally, Internist 3 is available for consultation on Friday at the same period as the rest of internists. In this process, - *appointment lead time* – is a critical to satisfaction and is regulated by the Government. The upper specification limit for this indicator has been established as 8 days/appointment on average.

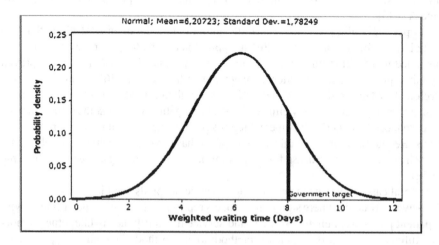

Fig. 1. Current performance of the outpatient department of internal medicine in terms of appointment lead-time

A simulation model was designed with the support of Arena 14.0 ® software to improve the current performance of the outpatient department. With a p-value equal to 0.3957 (higher than 0.05), it was validated that simulation model is statistically equivalent to the real system. After this, current appointment lead time was measured. On average, a patient has to wait 6.2 days with a standard deviation of 1.78 (refer to Fig. 1b). This means there is a probability of 15.6 % that a patient waits for more than 8 days before being treated by an internist of this department. In an effort to address this problem, 3 improvements scenarios were designed by medical staff from the department and assessed through the simulation model without implementing them on the real system (Figs. 2a, b, c). This is to avoid possible negative affectations of poor-performance strategies and their related extra charges.

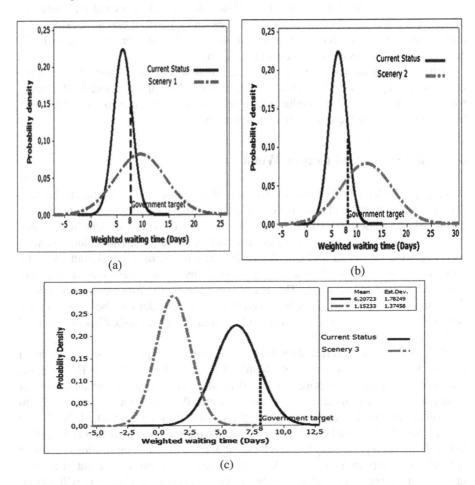

(a)

(b)

(c)

Fig. 2. Comparative analysis for appointment lead time between current state and Scenario 1 (a) Current state and Scenario 2 (b) Current state and Scenario 3 (c)

Scenario 1 proposes eliminating the cancellations of medical agenda through a sanctions policy where each cancelled appointment represents financial penalties for the internist. Meanwhile, Scenario 2 suggests increasing the installed capacity of Internist 2 through an extension of his opening hours (from 8.0 to 14.0) on Tuesdays and Wednesdays. Finally, Scenario 3 recommends setting Tuesdays, Wednesdays and Fridays for Internist 3 in the same time proposed in Scenario 2. After simulating these scenarios, results evidence that appointment lead times of Scenarios 1 and 3 are statistically different compared to those in current system with a p-value $= 0$ in both cases. Specifically, appointment lead times in Scenario 1 are statistically higher than those in real-world system; nonetheless, these waiting times in Scenario 3 are statistically lower compared to those in current outpatient department of internal medicine (Average appointment lead time $= 1.15$ days, standard deviation $= 1.37$ days and probability of overpassing upper specification limit $= 0$ %) reason by which it can be considered as the best improvement choice. In addition, it was concluded that Scenario 2 is statistically equal to real-world system with a p-value $= 0.388$.

With regard to the maximum appointment lead time, Scenario 1 and Scenario 2 are both statistically equal to the current system with P-values of 0.305 and 0.509 respectively. Nevertheless, with a p-value $= 0$, it was proved that Scenario 3 is statistically lower compared with the initial situation of the system.

4 Conclusions and Future Work

In this paper we have proved the effectiveness of computational simulation techniques to reduce appointment lead times in an outpatient internal medicine department. Results evidenced that, under the existing system, 15 % of the appointments scheduled in this department will have an appointment lead time higher than 8 days. Thus, 3 improvement scenarios were simulated and evaluated with the support of medical staff from the hospital; nonetheless, 2 of the scenarios were identified as inefficient and consequently discarded as potential solutions. This is relevant upon considering the negative operational and financial effects if implemented in real-world system for both patients and healthcare providers. This was further evidenced through the application of statistical analysis.

The simulation model created for this case study provided quick insight into the extra capacity needed for this department and influence of sanctions policy. In this case, the proposed penalty policy did not cause a positive effect on waiting time; while the impact of increased installed capacity was proved as statistically significant in Scenario 3. With this scenario, the probability of overpassing upper specification limit established by the Government (8 days) can be reduced to 0 %; which represents a significant contribution to healthcare upon preventing the development of more severe complications in patient ′s health. This approach can be implemented in any outpatient department of internal medicine; although it can be also extended to other specialties. Future work will include financial analysis on each improvement scenario with the purpose of strongly supporting healthcare decision making and developing optimal combinatorial approaches with significant results [11].

References

1. Günal, M.M., Pidd, M.: Discrete event simulation for performance modelling in health care: a review of the literature. J. Simul. **4**(1), 42–51 (2010)
2. McCarthy, K., McGee, H.M., O'Boyle, C.A.: Outpatient clinic waiting times and non-attendance as indicators of quality. Psychol. Health Med. **5**(3), 287–293 (2000)
3. Blizzard, R.: Patient satisfaction starts in the waiting room. Gallup Poll News Service (2009)
4. Barrios, M.A.O., Caballero, J.E., Sánchez, F.S.: A methodology for the creation of integrated service networks in outpatient internal medicine. In: Bravo, J., Hervás, R., Villarreal, V. (eds.) AmIHEALTH 2015. LNCS, vol. 9456, pp. 247–257. Springer, Heidelberg (2015)
5. Wijewickrama, A., Takakuwa, S.: Simulation analysis of appointment scheduling in an outpatient department of internal medicine. In: Proceedings of the Winter Simulation Conference, pp. 2264–2273. IEEE (2005)
6. Harper, P.R., Gamlin, H.M.: Reduced outpatient waiting times with improved appointment scheduling: a simulation modelling approach. OR Spectr. **25**(2), 207–222 (2003)
7. Wijewickrama, A.K.: Simulation analysis for reducing queues in mixed-patients' outpatient department. Int. J. Simul. Model. **5**(2), 56–68 (2006)
8. Giachetti, R.E., Centeno, E.A., Centeno, M.A., Sundaram, R.: Assessing the viability of an open access policy in an outpatient clinic: a discrete-event and continuous simulation modeling approach. In: Proceedings of the 37th Conference on Winter Simulation, pp. 2246–2255. Winter Simulation Conference (2005)
9. Takakuwa, S., Katagiri, D.: Modeling of patient flows in a large-scale outpatient hospital ward by making use of electronic medical records. In: 2007 Winter Simulation Conference, pp. 1523–1531. IEEE (2007)
10. Kuljis, J., Paul, R.J., Chen, C.: Visualization and simulation: two sides of the same coin? Simulation **77**(3–4), 141–152 (2001)
11. Herazo-Padilla, N., Montoya-Torres, J.R., Munoz-Villamizar, A., Nieto Isaza, S., Ramirez Polo, L.: Coupling ant colony optimization and discrete-event simulation to solve a stochastic location-routing problem. In: 2013 Simulations Conference (WSC), pp. 3352–3362. IEEE (2013)

A Proposal for Long-Term Gait Monitoring in Assisted Living Environments Based on an Inertial Sensor Infrastructure

Iván González$^{(\boxtimes)}$, Jesús Fontecha, Ramón Hervás,
Mercedes Naranjo, and José Bravo

University of Castilla-La Mancha, 13071 Ciudad Real, Spain
{Ivan.GDiaz,Jesus.Fontecha,Ramon.HLucas,
Mercedes.Naranjo,Jose.Bravo}@uclm.es

Abstract. Clinical gait analysis provides an evaluation tool that allows clinicians to characterize person's locomotion at a particular time. There are currently specialized systems to detect gait events and compute spatio-temporal parameters of human gait, which are accurate and redundant. These systems are expensive and are limited to controlled settings with gait evaluations widely spaced in terms of time. As alternative, a proposal for long-term gait monitoring in Assisted Living Environments based on an infrastructure of wireless inertial sensors is presented. Specifically, heel-strike events will be identified in multiple elders in a rest home and throughout the day. A small wearable device composed of a single inertial measurement unit will be placed at the back of each elder, on the thoracic zone, capturing trunk accelerations and orientations which will enable the demarcation of heel-strike events and the computation of temporal gait parameters. This proposal attempts to contribute to the development of a less intrusive and reachable alternative for long-term gait monitoring of multiple residents, which has been poorly investigated.

Keywords: Gait analysis · Long-term gait monitoring · IoT · Assisted Living Environment · Heel-strike estimation · Trunk accelerations

1 Introduction

Until recently, gait analysis has been typically focused on controlled gait trials inside specialized laboratories in physical performance, where it is possible to estimate gait parameters that are accurate and redundant. These laboratories use systems for 3-D motion capture as the Vicon motion capture system (Vicon Motion Systems Ltd., Oxford, UK) or pressure sensorized mats as the GAITRite electronic walkway (CIR Systems Inc., PA, USA) which provide excellent gait event estimations. Specifically, spatio-temporal gait parameters such as the step/stride time and the step/stride length are derived from these estimated gait events and summarized through several measures of dispersion, commonly used to characterize person's locomotion at a particular time.

© Springer International Publishing AG 2016
C.R. García et al. (Eds.): UCAmI 2016, Part I, LNCS 10069, pp. 300–305, 2016.
DOI: 10.1007/978-3-319-48746-5_31

Nonetheless, despite the accuracy achieved by these controlled gait trials to describe the subject's gait condition in a clinical setting, there are a number of constraints that limit their uses and the scope outside the laboratories. In this sense, long-term gait monitoring makes possible to analyze the inherent gait variability over time which is a crucial aspect for diagnosing and monitoring the clinical course of specific disabilities or diseases [1,2]. Changes over time in the gait patterns have a potential use as specific predictive markers of frailty syndrome [3], the onset of cognitive decline [4] and neurodegenerative diseases such as Parkinson [5] and Dementia [6], among others. From this standpoint, these kind of gait evaluations in specialized laboratories are obviously limited over time due to the cost of equipment and the hard deployment of these technologies in a real-life scenario. Therefore, the frequency between gait trials may not be good enough for capturing gait variability with the required time resolution. Laboratory settings are usually not representative of a realistic living environment and the subjects who are undergoing the gait trials often present different gait patterns modifying their walking pace due to the fact they can feel conditioned by the clinician supervision and the gait analysis tools. Against this background, there is a need for affordable technologies suitable for gait monitoring that can be deployed in Assisted Living Environments and characterize gait during daily activities, reducing the stress involved in clinical evaluations. These solutions should provide enough gait data to achieve long-term monitoring and to identify patterns of evolution in the gait dynamics. The study of these patterns may be useful in quantifying pathologic and age-related alterations in the locomotor control system and in augmenting objective measurement of mobility conditions, providing sound elements to the experts to diagnose early stages of specific diseases, such as the ones mentioned before. In addition, long-term gait analysis helps to document improvements in response to therapeutic interventions and determine the medication utility [7].

In this paper, a proposal for long-term gait monitoring in Assisted Living Environments is presented. An inertial sensor infrastructure will enable the automatic demarcation of gait events. Specifically, heel-strike (HS) events will be identified in multiple elders in a rest home and throughout the day. A small wearable device composed of a single Inertial Measurement Unit (IMU) will be placed at the back of each elder, on the thoracic zone. Each wearable will acquire raw data from trunk acceleration and orientation of each person and will send it to a dedicated server (broker) in the local area network, through its wireless transmitter. The broker will be responsible for managing multiple publication requests from all the wearables in the network, forwarding them to a special client node where data interpolation is conducted to ensure a uniform sampling rate. Other preprocessing operations will be performed at this point, prior to the demarcation of HS events and the computation of derived temporal gait parameters for each of the elders.

2   Related Work

The ability to demarcate the timing of gait events using the signals acquired from a single IMU has been an increasing interest in designing wearable systems for gait analysis. Just the fact that a single device can provide some of these gait events is potentially interesting because it reduces the number of sensors attached to the body, i.e. two devices mounted on lower limbs may be avoided if the aim is to detect only HS events. Furthermore, these systems for gait monitoring using a single IMU provide measurements of trunk accelerations and trunk orientations, which are also well suited to estimate other gait related features, such as balance [8] or the automated detection of turns during the gait [9].

An inverted pendulum model is used in [10] to identify HS events from subjects walking on a treadmill. A tri-axial accelerometer positioned over the second sacral vertebra enables the acquisition of antero-posterior acceleration which is low-pass filtered with a 4th order Butterworth filter (first stage of filtering), and filtered again using a cut-off frequency of 2 Hz (based upon the expected maximum step rate). HS events occur when the sign of the antero-posterior acceleration changes from positive to negative (zero-crossing). A refinement of this method is also provided using the peak in acceleration preceding the zero-crossing to estimate the HS event. Both approaches are validated by comparison to ground reaction forces with a significant improvement in the last one (in terms of error in estimation). The peak detection method from [10] is adapted in [11] for estimating HS events in older adults. In this occasion, temporal gait parameters are compared to those estimated using a GAITRite electronic walkway. Interclass correlation coefficients (ICC) for step durations ranging from 0.81 to 0.88 are obtained.

Zero-crossing technique is also present in [12], Mansfield et al. acquire data from accelerations perpendicular to the lumbar spine (antero-posterior axis). The gravity component is compensated by estimating the tilt of the accelerometer during an initial standing position. After a 2 Hz low-pass filter, HS events are segmented when the slope of the signal changes from negative to positive. The system is compared to a footswitch device.

In [13] we propose a system to estimate HS events and to compute derived temporal gait parameters by using the built-in IMU integrated in a mobile phone. The device is positioned over the second lumbar vertebra, clipped to a customized belt. Trunk accelerations are acquired during several gait tests. Signals from the acceleration magnitude and the vertical acceleration are smoothed through scale-space filters. Cut-off points between filtered signals as a result of convolving with varying levels of Gaussian filters and other robust features against temporal variation and noise are used to identify peaks that correspond to gait events in the antero-posterior acceleration. For the proposal presented here, the algorithm used by the system in [13] is reconfigured to identify peaks that correspond to HS events from trunk acceleration signals acquired using the wearable devices. Minor adjustments are required since the IMU is now located at the thoracic zone instead of the lumbar zone. Finally, It should be pointed out that, to the best of our knowledge, there are not similar approaches reported in the literature focused on monitoring the gait of multiple persons in rest homes and throughout the day.

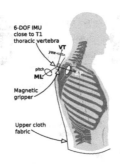

Fig. 1. IMU attached using the magnetic grip system. The vertical (VT), antero-posterior (AP), medio-lateral (ML) axes and the Euler angles are displayed.

3 Details of the Proposal for Long-Term Gait Monitoring

The proposal consists of an infrastructure of wearable devices (sensorization layer), where each of the nodes is attached to the upper cloth of one elder, close to the T1 thoracic vertebra. A two-piece magnetic gripper is used for clamping, as shown in the diagram in Fig. 1. Each wearable device is equipped with a small 802.11 wireless transmitter ESP826612E (Espressif Systems Inc., Shanghai, China), which integrates a 32-bit RISC Tensilica Xtensa LX106 micro-controller that enables I^2C communication[1] with a single InvenSense MPU-6050 6-DOF IMU[2] (InvenSense Inc., CA, USA). This setup allows us to acquire trunk accelerations and orientations for each of the elders and transmit them to a dedicated server (broker) using the MQTT [3] messaging protocol, commonly implemented in Internet of Things (IoT) networks for managing sensor data transmissions. An overview of the approach is shown in Fig. 2.

A special client is subscribed to the "`sensors/imu_raw_data/#`" topic, receiving raw data from trunk accelerations and orientations at a 100 Hz uniform sample rate, after an interpolation process. This client (in the intelligence layer) provides reasoning capabilities to discriminate walking forward from other low-level activities, such as idling, going upstairs, going downstairs, rotating on the subject's axis and running. A Gaussian Naive Bayes (GNB) classifier similar to the one proposed in [14] enables the low-level activity clustering. In this case, the feature vector is composed of time domain and spectral features derived from trunk accelerations and orientations (e.g., sum of acceleration magnitude below 25 percentile, peak frequency in vertical acceleration below 5 Hz, etc.)

From those periods of activity identified as "walking forward periods", a straightness analysis procedure, considering the changes in yaw rotation, is conducted to identify turns or changes of direction which are required to properly segment the straight paths inside the gait trajectory.

---

[1] Inter-Integrated Circuit data serial bus.

[2] 6-Degrees of Freedom IMU (3-axis accelerometer and 3-axis gyroscope).

[3] MQTT (*Message Queuing Telemetry Transport*). It is a lightweight transport protocol based on publication/subscription policies to defined messages, known as *topics*.

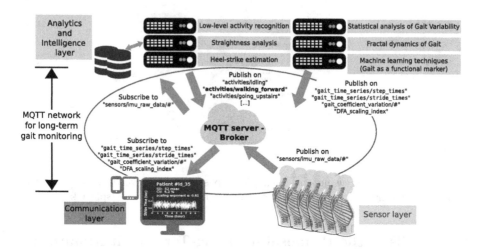

Fig. 2. Proposal for long-term gait monitoring in residential environments.

Raw data produced while walking through each of these segmented straight paths feeds the modified version of the algorithm in [13] to estimate HS events[4]. Gait parameter time series derived from HS events, such as step/stride time series are published on the "gait_time_series/#" topic. Different kind of clients, such as mobile phones or computers may subscribe to this topic to communicate this information to patients, relatives and clinicians (communication layer). Furthermore, reasoning capabilities at this data processing level can help to characterize person's locomotion over time, either based on a statistical analysis, by using machine learning techniques, or with more novel approaches such as fractal dynamics to analyze long-range correlations in stride interval fluctuations [7].

4   Conclusion

The proposal is oriented to support the design of less intrusive and reachable alternatives for long-term gait monitoring of multiple persons in an Assisted Living Environment. Such a settlement, has been poorly investigated in the area of gait analysis and it has potential use to concurrently characterize the locomotion of multiple residents during their daily activities. This approach allows us to go beyond separate gait evaluations and analyze the gait variability over longer periods. The research described in this paper is in progress, we have developed some prototypes of the wearable device integrating the ESP826612E and the MPU-6050 IMU and tested them at the thoracic zone, sending raw data through the network to the MQTT client node where interpolation and low-level activity clustering have been implemented. The classifier requires further

---

[4] Gait parameter estimation in clinical settings generally uses straight paths because turns or changes in the gait trajectory distort the measurements.

evaluations before continuing with the straightness analysis and the heel-strike estimation.

Acknowledgements. This work is supported by the FRASE MINECO project (TIN2013-47152-C3-1-R) and the Plan Propio de Investigación from Castilla-La Mancha University.

References

1. Brach, J.S., Perera, S., Studenski, S., Newman, A.B.: The reliability and validity of measures of gait variability in community-dwelling older adults. Arch. Phys. Med. Rehabil. **89**(12), 2293–2296 (2008)
2. Hausdorff, J.M.: Gait variability: methods, modeling and meaning. J. NeuroEng. Rehabil. **2**, 19 (2005)
3. Fontecha, J., Navarro, F.J., Hervas, R., Bravo, J.: Elderly frailty detection by using accelerometer-enabled smartphones and clinical information records. J. Pers. Ubiquit. Comput. **17**(6), 1073–1083 (2013)
4. Camicioli, R., Howieson, D., Oken, G., Sexton, G., Kaye, J.: Motor slowing precedes cognitive impairment in the oldest old. Neurology **50**(5), 1496–1498 (1998)
5. Moore, S.T., MacDougall, H.G., Gracies, J.M., Cohen, H.S., Ondo, W.G.: Long-term monitoring of gait in Parkinson's disease. Gait Posture **26**(2), 200–207 (2007)
6. Verghese, J., Lipton, R.B., Hall, C.B.: Abnormality of gait as a predictor of non-Alzheimers dementia. N. Engl J. Med. **347**(22), 1761–1768 (2002)
7. Hausdorff, J.M.: Gait dynamics, fractals and falls: finding meaning in the stride-to-stride fluctuations of human walking. Hum. Mov. Sci. **26**, 555–589 (2007)
8. Grimpampi, E., Bonnet, B., Taviani, A., Mazzà, C.: Estimate of lower trunk angles in pathological gait using gyroscope data. Gait Posture **38**, 523–527 (2013)
9. Novak, D., Goršič, M., Podobnik, J., Munih, M.: Toward real-time automated detection of turns during gait using wearable inertial measurement units. Sensors **10**, 18800–18822 (2014)
10. Zijlstra, W., Hof, A.: Assessment of spatio-temporal gait parameters from trunk accelerations during human walking. Gait Posture **18**(2), 1–10 (2003)
11. Hartmann, A., Luzi, S., Murer, K., De Bie, R.A., De Bruin, E.D.: Concurrent validity of a trunk tri-axial accelerometer system for gait analysis in older adults. Gait Posture **29**(3), 444–448 (2009)
12. Mansfield, A., Lyons, G.M.: The use of accelerometry to detect heel contact events for use as a sensor in FES assisted walking. Med. Eng. Phys. **25**(10), 879–885 (2003)
13. González, I., Fontecha, J., Hervás, R., Bravo, J.: Estimation of temporal gait events from a single accelerometer through scale-space filtering. J. Med. Syst. (accepted) (published in 2016)
14. González, I., Fontecha, J., Hervás, R., Bravo, J.: An ambulatory system for gait monitoring based on wireless sensorized insoles. Sensors **15**(7), 16589–16613 (2015)

Analysis of EEG Frequency Bands During Typical Mechanics of Platform-Videogames

Tania Mondéjar[1,3](✉), Ramón Hervás[1], José Miguel Latorre[2],
Iván González Diaz[1], and José Bravo[1]

[1] Department of Technologies and Information Systems, University of Castilla-La Mancha,
Paseo de La Universidad 4, Ciudad Real, Spain
{ramon.hlucas,Ivan.GDiaz,jose.bravo}@uclm.es
[2] Department of Pshychology, University of Castilla-La Mancha, Almansa, 14, Albacete, Spain
Jose.Latorre@uclm.es
[3] esmile, Psychology for Children and Adolescents, Calle Toledo 79,1ºE, Ciudad Real, Spain
Tania.mondejar@esmile.es

Abstract. In this paper, it has been analysed the responses, in terms of cognitive activation through EEG, to specific external stimuli. It has been developed a videogame, as a particular kind of serious games from health, which promotes the exercise of cognitive abilities. The participants were ten healthy children between 7 to 12 years old, selected because of their developmental age. Mechanics included in the videogame have been evaluated and related to the processing of new information and user response in preliminary works. The hypothesis of the current work refers to how specific mechanics that are involved in platform-videogames cause activation in the electroencephalogram waves according to cognitive processes such as short-time memory, attention and concentration. It has been analyzed through the magnitude of EEG frequency bands. The results are consistent by showing a differential activation during several game mechanics. With these results we can conclude that the videogame promotes activation and exercise in areas related to the mentioned cognitive skills when the participants are playing the videogame mainly during particular mechanics.

Keywords: Serious games · Pervasive health · Health games · Cognitive skills · Computational neurosciences · Cognitive rehabilitation · EEG

1 Introduction

In this work, we were focused on studying brain activity on the cortical surface to observe waves activation based on particular stimulus in terms of platform videogame mechanics. This paper contributes to the area of serious games for health. Serious games typically deal with the integration of educative goals with game mechanics based on well-known tests to enhance and generalize learning to become significant [1], apart from helping to discover and use information instead of just memorizing it [2]. Regarding the health area, videogames are becoming a successful tool to teach and train in areas such as chronic diseases and disability.

C.R. García et al. (Eds.): UCAmI 2016, Part I, LNCS 10069, pp. 306–317, 2016.
DOI: 10.1007/978-3-319-48746-5_32

In a preliminary work, we analysed which game mechanics develop cognitive skills related to executive function [3]. These findings guided the development of a particular platform-based videogame named *Api's Adventures*. This videogame has been used in the present proposal to evaluate changes in brain-waves frequency to infer cognitive process during the use of the mentioned videogame.

Attending to the neurophysiological perspective, it is possible to determinate the response by external stimulus through the electrophysiological changes. Specifically in this work we were focused on cortical changes while playing videogames, particularly during five kinds of game mechanics [3] that will be described in Sect. 4.

The paper is organized as follows: Sect. 2 explains the neuropsychological fundamentals of this work; Sect. 3 explores related work on the same area of our study. We reviewed the background and related proposals, highlighting the differences and similarities between these works and our proposal. Section 4 describes the developed videogame and explains the different elements and related mechanics involved on it. Next Sect. (5) is the core of the paper that presents the overall experiment that has been conducted, including the target population, the method, the work hypothesis, the different experiment stages, the used materials, and the experiment results (Sect. 6). Finally, Sect. 7 concludes the paper.

2   Neuropsychological Fundamentals

The electrical activation in brain has a topographical classification where we can observe changes originated from external perception. These variants in reactivity of different rhythms and brain zones allow us to infer cognitive process such as memory, attention and concentration.

In psychological evaluation the most applied technique to evaluate cognitive process is the standard paper–based tests. Particularly, for attentional process, tools like d2 [4], for concentration and *EDHA* [5] for attention deficit disorder and hyperactivity (ADHD) or Wechsler Memory Scale IV [6] for working memory, are being used.

Nowadays we are living a big change by means of the general use of new technology in this evaluation context. For example, not only we can evaluate cognitive skills in a point of time using technology, but also we can infer long-time cognitive process during the execution on determined tasks. This paper contributes with a new step inferring cognitive processes through videogames by means of analysing mainly alpha and beta waves through electroencephalography (EEG).

There are some researches that suggested a causal relationship between playing action videogames and improvements in attentional skills [7]. This enhancement is based on the named neuronal plasticity. This ability of brain consists in a particular way to adapt and regenerate or reorganize the nervous tissue in response a specific stimulation. Through the registration by electroencephalogram, we can observe that subjects underwent cognitive training showing changes in brain structures [8] in favour of improved neural efficiency when performing certain tasks [9].

Also it is very important to consider the close relation between attention and memory, specifically in games that require a global cognitive process. Some psychological models consider the relationship between attention and memory what explains short-term memory and working memory as emerging from an interaction between attention and long-term memory [10]. For this reason in our study it has been taken into account short-term memory related to theta rhythm and occipital zone.

3   Related Work

There are studies that relate cognitive abilities with commercial games such as those focused on attention using the Tetris game [11], and the proposal centred on decision making with The Sims 2 [12]. Other examples seek to improve attention problems related to Autism [13]. Further studies deal with offering feedback to the user such as Wang et al. [14], who proposes a nonlinear fractal dimension based approach to neuro-feedback implementation targeting EEG-based serious games designs, and Camerião et al. [15] whose works are centred on cognitive rehabilitation.

Industry of videogames is growing interest for serious games encouraging the creation of this type of games with different goals. For example, 'RESET'[1] aims to provide a new approach in order to evaluate the attention, executive functioning and memory in patients diagnosed with Acquired Brain Injury or other disorders like ADHD, (Autism Spectrum Disorders); Treasures of Bell Island[2] can monitor changes in attention, memory and executive function in students; The game 'Braingame Brian' [16] is a serious game that aims to improve the executive functions and working memory of children with ADHD aged between 8 to 12 years old. Finally, Plan-IT Commander [17] highlights efficacy in cognitive process.

From our point of view we contribute to the rise of this form of entertainment based on a scientific perspective offering not only the game itself, but evidence of enhancements at cognitive level.

4   Api's Adventures Videogame Design

Api's Adventures is a 2D platform videogame developed using Unity[3]. Platform videogames involve to guide the main character (Api) to run, jump and shoot over enemies and obstacles. The game has side-scrolling movements and is divided into 10 stages with incremental difficulty. Each stage includes new and harder elements to improve the progressive learning and improvement of needed skills in the game. *Api's Adventures* also includes an endless running mode in which users can test how much time are able to keep Api alive and how many obstacles and enemies can face. The endless mode has been developed to evaluate long-term improvement of cognitive skills in the future. In this experiment we only used the stages mode to assess cognitive skills during each kind of mechanic.

---

[1] http://www.bluemarblegameco.com/products/reset/.
[2] http://www.bluemarblegameco.com/products/treasure-of-bell-island/.
[3] https://unity3d.com/.

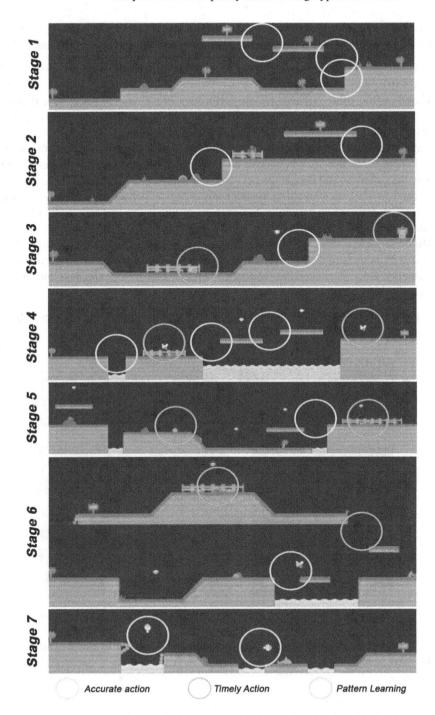

Fig. 1. First seven stages of the Api's Adventures videogame showing three kinds of mechanics (Color figure online)

The different elements in the game correspond to the five main mechanics previously identified [3]. Following we describe the game elements of each kind of mechanic:

- Accurate action (yellow circles): Api has to face obstacles through movements and jumps in a precise and careful way.
- Timely action (blue circles): player performs a movement or jump in a defined moment that is determined by obstacles or enemies in simple movements (vertical or horizontal). The most important thing is the timing.
- Pattern learning (red circle): the player has to learn the movement pattern of obstacles and enemies. In this case the player challenge is not the timing but understanding how the pattern is and decide the best moment and way to overtake it.
- Logical puzzles: the player has to understand a logical behaviour of elements in the game to go forward. In particular, there are doors with levers that follow certain logic that player has to understand to open the doors.
- Mimic sequence: this mechanic has been implemented in the final boss level. The boss is immune until the users mimic a sequence of actions shown in the game screen explicitly. Once mimicked the sequence, the player can damage the boss during few seconds.

Figures 1 and 2 show the 10 stages of *Api's Adventures* identifying the elements of the game that correspond to the five mentioned mechanics.

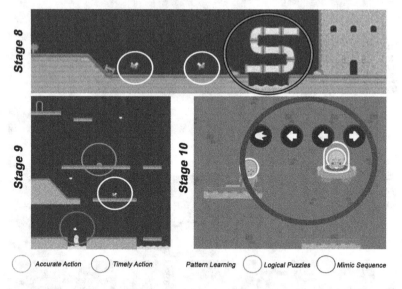

Fig. 2. Last three stages of Api's Adventures videogame that include the five kinds of mechanics. (Color figure online)

5   Experiment: Analysis Based on EEG Data

5.1   Population

The experiment was conducted with one particular cohort: healthy preadolescents aged between 7–12 years old (n = 10, boys = 5, girls = 5). The participants and their parents were informed about the scope and goals of this research and about the collected data. They received and signed the information sheet and the consent form.

5.2   Method

This experiment has followed an empirical method to gather evidences in terms of EEG data that was analysed quantitatively. The formulated hypothesis that guides this experiment is: *Typical mechanics involved in platform-videogames cause activation in electroencephalogram waves according to the cognitive processes short-term memory, attention and concentration.*

The followed protocol can be summarized as follows: (1) participants were kindly informed about what an EEG device is and what kind of data it can collect; (2) participants were required to wear the EEG headset, ensuring their comfort and confidence, (3) the psychologist explained what was happening on the researcher screen (EEG data visualization software) where participants could observe their brain activity; (4) the psychologist gave instructions about the activity to perform: they had just to play the videogame, and (5) participants performed the proposed activity with no interruptions due to the researcher observation neither EEG monitoring. Participants played and wore the EEG headset for approximately 20 min. The experiment was recorded using a video camera (having concern of preserving participant anonymity) and the EEG dataset were generated. Once all data was collected, the next stage was the manual segmentation, processing and analysis to support (or not) the declared hypothesis (Fig. 3).

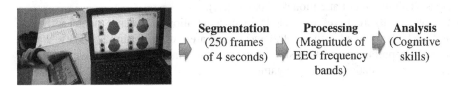

| Segmentation | Processing | Analysis |
| (250 frames of 4 seconds) | (Magnitude of EEG frequency bands) | (Cognitive skills) |

Fig. 3. Summary of the experiment steps

5.3   Materials

For the development of this work, the main materials were the developed *Api's Adventures* videogame and the Emotiv Epoc + neuroheadset to analyse brain activity.

Emotiv EPOC + neuroheadset features 14 EEG channels plus two reference chanels offering positioning for accurate spatial resolution. These channels include eight frontal electrodes (named AF3, F7, F3, and FC5 at the left hemisphere, and FC6, F4, F8, and AF4 at the right hemisphere). The rest of electrodes are: two temporal electrodes (T7 & T8), two occipital electrodes (O1 & O2), and two parietal electrodes (P7 and P8). The EEG headset uses a sequential sampling method at a rate of 128 samples per second. In order to analyse the EEG dataset, we used the Xavier TechBench Software^{TM} to collect and visualize the EEG signals.

In general, the Emotiv EPOC + device is able to record EEG data in a satisfactory manner. There are several studies that evidence the significant worse performance of this device compared with professional medical devices. However, some of the studies remark the validity of this device for non-critical proposes, such as for games [18]. The level of precision is not a strict requirement in our study because it is not necessary to collect highly accurate brain activity. The experiment lies in estimate attention metrics based on brain bandwidths. In this case, the device performs with an acceptable level of accuracy. Moreover, the election of this device is also because it is easy to use with children during the experiment time and it has a rapid calibration that is required for laboratory studies.

5.4 Data Computation: Frequency Analysis of EEG Waves

This section explains how EEG collected data was computed, obtaining the associated results.

Firstly, for a better understanding of brain activity we need to explain the four different cerebral wave bands and their connection with cognitive processes:

- Delta waves (δ) are related to sleep stages or abnormal brain activity so they have been not analysed in this work.
- Theta waves (θ) are mainly located in the temporal parietal area of the brain. They are produced by emotional stress, especially frustration or disappointment, and this activity seems to be connected to creativity, memory recall, emotions, and sensations [19].
- Alpha waves (α) are present during waking, on posterior regions of the head, usually with larger amplitude on the occipital areas [20]. And synchrony between cortical areas as a function of attentional demands [21].
- Beta waves (β) are waves associated with concentration and intense mental activities and are better defined in the central and frontal areas of the brain [22]. These waves are very important in our study since they are a direct indicator of cognitive activation in executive function during the game.

In the frequency term, it is known that alpha band frequency range has been associated with attention [23]. The same way beta activity is most evident in the frontal cortex and is connected to some cognitive processes like decision-making, problem solving, and information processing [24]. Taking this idea as a starting point and observed the most activation in the different electrodes we process to analyse these two values in a particular moment during the game.

Oscillations have an impact on information processing that is proportional to their magnitude [25]. Based on this affirmation we analyse the data in several steps. First of all we watched the video recorded during the experiment and we identified the specific time in which each subject performed each game mechanic. It provided us 250 segments of 4 s (25 segments per person).

The next steps were the computation of each segment. Raw data from each of the 14 electrodes in the neuroheadset is acquired at a 128 Hz uniform sample rate and stored for further off-line processing. Such task consists in windowing each of the EEG channels using sliding windows of size 128 samples (1 s). The Fast Fourier Transform (FFT) is applied to get the spectral representation of each windowed frame. An array of 128 positions, also known as "FTT bins", is obtained as a result of the transformation. Each FFT bin encloses a range of frequencies that can be computed using the Formula 1:

$$FFTbin_{width} = \frac{Fs}{N} \tag{1}$$

where **Fs** represents the sample rate (128 Hz) and **N** the total number of bins or FFT size (128). Therefore, in this particular case, the FFT bin width is equal to 1 Hz. According to the Nyquist-Shanon sampling theorem, a 128 Hz sample rate ensures a faithful representation of the spectral domain up to 64 Hz. Nonetheless, the cognitive waves range up to 30 Hz (Beta waves). Once spectral representation of each windowed frame is obtained (128 complex numbers), the FFT magnitude is required. The cognitive waves are computed as the mean value of the magnitudes within the FFT bins enclosed by each of these parameters.

6 Results

The results were obtained after analyzing and computing the previously mentioned segments of 4 s of time where subjects performed the identified mechanics. We analysised the magnitude of beta, alpha and theta frequency bands in specific electrodes that are reference areas for cognitive activity (frontal, parietal and occipital lobe). We can see the behavior of these frequencies during games mechanic. The analysis has been focused on the general response in frequency bands based on the external stimuli (mechanic) and, particularly, frequencies related to memory, attention and concentration. In general, we can observe the activation in both hemispheres in frontal lobe and in some point in occipital areas (related to memory tasks). Thus, beta waves are related with the frontal area (electrodes O2 and FC6) of the brain is activated in situations of analysis of information, motivated by necessities in terms of the particular mechanics (e.g. logical puzzles that entail more concentration). In those moments where players failed to pass a mechanic, we can observe a peak of theta waves, associated with frustration.

Deeping on each kind of mechanic, the cognitive related activity can be summarized as follows:

- Accurate action: In this case, the magnitude-based analysis did not result on a particular pattern; there is a general activation from the beginning to the end of the mechanic in beta waves that are linked with concentration.
- Timely action (Fig. 4): This mechanic entails a characteristic pattern. This mechanic involves a timely action in a precise moment. It is need a general coordination of brain processes that increase at the moment of executing the action and it keep active after that due to the induced alert state, as we can see mainly in medium and posterior brain electrodes (FC6, P7, O2).

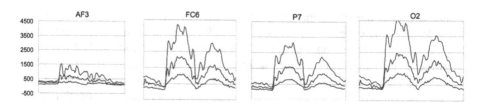

Fig. 4. Recurrent pattern in timely action mechanic (alpha: blue line; beta: red line; theta: green line) (Color figure online)

- Pattern learning: Again there is no an identified pattern during this mechanic. However, it can be observed a prominent activation on the frontal area (AF3 and FC6) due to the needed understanding of patterns in the game, a process closely related to executive functioning.
- Logical puzzles (Fig. 5): During this mechanic we can distinguish a initial period of high level of attention and concentration needed to understand the challenge (puzzle). Where the user understand the game behaviour, the user carry out the action to face the challenge and there is an activation in terms of alpha band in middle areas (FC6 and O2)

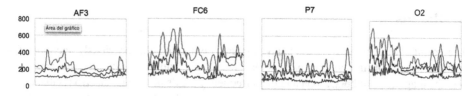

Fig. 5. Recurrent pattern in logical puzzles mechanic (alpha: blue line; beta: red line; theta: green line) (Color figure online)

- Mimic sequences involve low general activation at the beginning during the pre-processing stage when users are memorizing the sequence of action. After that, it happens a rise on the waves magnitude when they are mimicking the sequence mainly in the occipital area where the memorizing processes occur (Fig. 6).

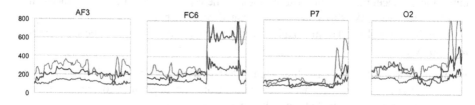

Fig. 6. Recurrent pattern in mimic sequences mechanic (alpha: blue line; beta: red line; theta: green line) (Color figure online)

7   Conclusions

The conclusions of this work have two different and complementary lines. On the one hand, the usability of the developed game was evaluated. For this goal, we use a specific questionnaire called SUS [26]. We got 80 % of positive user opinions remarking that it is easy and fun. Also the participants think that they felt confortable playing it. Another question was if the game is consistent and the history line has sense, what got positive results. Some participants said that it is necessary to train to play the game successfully. In the experiment we did not give any instruction to observe if it is intuitive enough. Attending the observation and the SUS questionnaire results, the game is intuitive but some mechanics need further explanation ingame (particularly, logical puzzle). This questionnaire is very important to ensure user motivation. If they like the game, it is more probably that they expend time playing it, and consequently, training some cognitive skills.

On the other hand, we can conclude our main hypothesis is accepted based on the results as we evidenced before. In this work we focused on particular abilities: short-time memory, attention and concentration. With this quantitative analysis it is possible to correlate higher magnitudes on frequency bands with particular game mechanics. In general, we evidenced greater significance in terms of activation in the two types of waves: beta and alpha. It is necessary to remark that theta waves are also important in this process because they are related to the frustration when the mechanic is failed. Also, theta rhythm appears during focus act or mental tasks or meditative concentration in neurotypical subjects [19]. Certainly there is activation at cognitive level while playing the *Api's Adventures* videogame. Particularly, the results show EEG frequency band prominence according to memory, attention and concentration being more present in specific mechanics such as: mimic sequences (more activation in occipital area O2), timely action (higher magnitude in frequency band because of cognitive requirements) and logical puzzle (activation in middle and posterior area related to alpha rhythm). Accurate actions show a relevant presence of beta waves, which are related to concentration without any recurrent patterns. Finally, the mechanic pattern learning activates the frontal area closely related to executive functioning.

The future work will be focused on including population with other characteristic such as disabilities and attention disorders to analyse their EEG activation while playing the *Api's Adventures* videogame and to test explicit patterns of activation, and changes at cognitive level during long-term experiments.

The findings of this paper encourage us to continue this research line because it is possible to change and improve the way of exercising abilities trough platform-based videogame. At the same time, it is an innovative form to treat people with cognitive deficits and as complement to increase the cognitive development.

Acknowledgments. This work was conducted in the context of UBIHEALTH project under International Research Staff Exchange Schema (MC-IRSES 316337). We want to thank, especially children who have helped us playing and appreciating our game. Also we want to thanks the parents to support and collaborated in our investigation. Finally, many thanks to Rodrigo Marin for developing such amazing videogame.

References

1. Shapi'i, A., Mat Zin, N.A., Elaklouk, A.M.: A game system for cognitive rehabilitation. In: BioMed Research International (2015)
2. Sourina, O., Wang, Q., Nguyen, M.K.: EEG-based "Serious" games and monitoring tools for pain management. Stud. Health Technol. Inform. **163**, 606–610 (2011)
3. Mondéjar, T., Hervás, R., Gutierrez, C., Johnson, E., Latorre, J.M.: Correlation between videogame mechanics and executive functions through EEG analysis. J. Biomed. Inform. **63**, 131–140 (2015)
4. Brickenkamp, R., Zillmer, E.: Test de Atención d2. TEA (2002)
5. Farré I Riba, A., Narbona, J.: EDHA. Escala para la Evaluación del trastorno por déficit de atención con hiperactividad. TEA edn. Madrid (2013)
6. Wechsler, D.: Wechsler memory scale. Psychological Corporation Wechsler memory scale, San Antonio (1945)
7. Green, C.S., Bavelier, D.: Action video game modifies visual selective attention. Nature **423**, 534–537 (2003)
8. Olesen, J., Westerberg, H., Klingberg, T.: Increased prefrontal and parietal activity after training of working memory. Nat. Neurosci. **7**, 75–79 (2003)
9. Brehmer Y., Westerberg H., Backman L.: Working-memory training in younger and older adults: training gains, transfer, and maintenance. Training-Induced Cogn. Neural Plasticity, **72** (2012)
10. Cowan, N.: Evolving conceptions of memory storage, selective attention, and their mutual constraints within the human information-processing system. Psychol. Bull. **104**, 163–191 (1988)
11. Green, C.S., Bavelier, D.: Action video game modifies visual selective attention. Nature **423**, 534–537 (2003)
12. Green, C.S., Pouget, A., Bavelier, D.: A general mechanism for learning with action video games: improved probabilistic inference. Biol. **20**, 1573–15792 (2010)
13. Cowan, J.D., Markham, L.: EEG biofeedback for the attention problems of autism: a case study. In 25th the Annual Meeting of the Association for applied Psychophysiology and Biofeedback, pp. 287–287 (1994)
14. Wang, Q., Sourina, O., Nguyen, M.K.: Fractal dimension based neurofeedback in serious games. Visual Comput. **27**, 299–309 (2011)
15. Cameirão, M.S., Badia, S.B., Zimmerli, L., Duarte Oller, E., Verschure, M.J.: A virtual reality system for motor and cognitive neurorehabilitation. Challenges Assistive Technol. **20**, 393–397 (2007)
16. Prins, P.J., Brink, E.T., Dovis, S., Ponsioen, A., Geurts, H.M., De Vries, M., Van Der Oord, S.: "Braingame Brian": toward an executive function training program with game elements for children with ADHD and cognitive control problems. Games Health: Res. Dev. Clin. Appl. **2**, 44–49 (2013)
17. Bul, K.C.M., Franken, I.H.A., Van der Oord, s., Kato, Danckaerts, M., Vreeke, L.J., Willems, A., Van Oers, H.J.J., Van den Heuvel, R., Van Slagmaat, R., Maras, A.: Development and user satisfaction of "Plan-It Commander," a serious game for children with ADHD. Games Health Res. Dev. Clin. Appl. **4** (2005)
18. Goel, V., Grafman, J.: Are the frontal lobes implicated in "planning" functions? Interpreting data from the Tower of Hanoi. Neuropsychological **33**, 623–642 (1995)
19. Aftanas, L.I., Golocheikine, S.A.: Human anterior and frontal midline theta and lower alpha reflect emotionally positive state and internalized attention: high-resolution EEG investigation of meditation. Neurosci. Lett. **310**, 57–60 (2001)

20. Nowack, W.J.: Neocortical dynamics and human EEG rhythms. Neurology **45**, 1793 (1995)
21. Saalmann, Y.B., Pinsk, M.A., Wang, L., Li, X., Kastner, S.: The pulvinar regulates information transmission between cortical areas based on attention demands. Science **337**, 753–756 (2012)
22. Zhang, Y., Chen, Y., Bressler, S.L., Ding, M.: Response preparation and inhibition: the role of the cortical sensorimotor beta rhythm. Neuroscience **156**, 238–246 (2008)
23. Adrian E., Matthews B.: The Berger rhythm: potential changes from the occipital lobes in man. Brain: a journal of neurology. 57, 355–385 (1934)
24. Ray, W.J., Cole, H.W.: EEG alpha activity reflects attentional demands, and beta activity reflects emotional and cognitive processes. Science **228**, 750–752 (1985)
25. Compston A.: The Berger rhythm: potential changes from the occipital lobes in man. Brain: a journal of neurology. 133, 3–6 (2010)
26. Bangor, A., Kortum, P.T., Miller, J.T.: An empirical evaluation of the system usability scale. Int. J. Hum.-Comput. Interact. **24**, 574–594 (2008)

Human-Computer Interaction

From Paper to Play - Design and Validation of a Smartphone Based Cognitive Fatigue Assessment Application

Edward Price[1(✉)], George Moore[1], Leo Galway[1], and Mark Linden[2]

[1] School of Computing and Mathematics, Ulster University, Coleraine, UK
price-e@email.ulster.ac.uk, {g.moore,l.galway}@ulster.ac.uk
[2] School of Nursing and Midwifery, Queens University Belfast, Belfast, UK
m.linden@qub.ac.uk

Abstract. This paper investigates the user experience design of a smartphone application for the objective assessment of cognitive fatigue. This is as an alternative to using an established paper questionnaire that offers subjective self-assessment. Taking a multidisciplinary approach, challenges relating to the usability and the efficacy of the smartphone assessment tool were explored. Furthermore, to enable validation of the proposed new approach, challenges relating to how best to deliver the traditionally paper-based questionnaire on a smartphone display, while retaining the validity of the measure it affords, had to be addressed. Results show that the smartphone based cognitive testing methods was comparable to outcomes from the pre validated mobile based Mental Fatigue Scale. Participant feedback showed that the smartphone-based approach offered a more acceptable and engaging user experience, while retaining the ability to accurately measure cognitive fatigue.

Keywords: Mobile · Questionnaire adaptation · Cognitive tests · Fatigue evaluation · Self-assessment

1 Introduction

Fatigue can be defined as "the awareness of a decreased capacity for physical and/or mental activity due to an imbalance in the availability, utilization, and/or restoration of (physiological or psychological) resources needed to perform activity" [1]. Fatigue is often caused by a lack of sleep, stress, or a cognitive deficiency. Cognitive fatigue is a common symptom that may occur after an Acquired Brain Injury (ABI), and can have a very detrimental effect on a person's ability to conduct activities of daily living. Measuring cognitive fatigue is considered problematic due to the absence of biological markers and a lack of standardized tests. This results in an absence of available technology-based solutions [22]. Consequently, episodes of fatigue can potentially be misinterpreted.

This paper investigates the user experience design of a smartphone application for the objective assessment of cognitive fatigue. This is as an alternative to using an established paper questionnaire that offers subjective self-assessment. Taking a

© Springer International Publishing AG 2016
C.R. García et al. (Eds.): UCAmI 2016, Part I, LNCS 10069, pp. 321–332, 2016.
DOI: 10.1007/978-3-319-48746-5_33

multidisciplinary approach, challenges relating to the usability and the efficacy of the smartphone application assessment approach were explored. It also aimed to validate its use on a smartphone alongside objective methods that would previously have been deployed using large screen-based devices. Furthermore, it anticipates the collaborative use, or eventual replacement, of traditional self-assessment methods with pervasive computing approaches. Self-assessment of fatigue most frequently takes place within a clinical environment, which doesn't necessarily facilitate the convenient and timely self-reporting of fatigue during everyday life. However, tests such as the Psychomotor Vigilance Task and Spatial Span Task can be adapted for mobile devices, which, in turn, could be utilized to provide more effective and accurate fatigue assessment. Results show that the mobile-based approach offered a more acceptable and engaging user experience, while retaining the ability to accurately measure cognitive fatigue.

The remainder of this paper provides an overview of the background and related work in this area. This is followed by discussion of the application design utilized for the research conducted within this paper, which indicates how relevant research has been used to inform the design of the related smartphone application. The results from a preliminary study using the application will be subsequently presented, and finally, concluding remarks and future work will be discussed.

2   Related Work

2.1   Subjective Assessment

Traditional methods of subjective assessment in the area of cognitive fatigue have utilized self-assessment questionnaires as a way of measuring an individual's perceived level of fatigue. There have been a number of specific self-assessment questionnaires designed to target cognitive ability and its relation to fatigue, including the Visual Analogue Scale for Fatigue [18], Fatigue Severity Scale [15] and the Mental Fatigue Scale (MFS) [13]. All of these scales use a visual analogue representation of targeted questions in order to aid a participant in self-evaluation. Moreover, the validity of such scales has been evaluated and shown to be effective in their assessment capabilities [16]. However, as no medical standard for fatigue measurement currently exists, different scales are available depending on whether or not the physical or emotional aspect is being evaluated.

The MFS is the first scale that has been adapted to assess fatigue irrespective of the underlying neurological condition. Similar to the previous scales, this scale takes the form of a self-assessing questionnaire, which consists of 15 questions specifically aimed at covering the main symptoms that occur after a brain injury, including cognitive symptoms, sleep deprivation and duration, and other common effects [11]. Questions do not focus specifically on any particular area so that a wider understanding of fatigue can be garnered. In addition, the scale has been shown to be invariant to age, gender and educational profile [2]. Johansson measured the effectiveness of the MFS against a series of neuropsychological tests in order to prove its validity [12]. The tests used were; digit symbol-coding from the The Wechsler Adult Intelligence Scale (WAIS)-III [21], measuring information processing speed; the digit span from the WAIS-III, measuring attention and working memory [21]; verbal fluency test [19] and Trail Making Test (TMT) A and B [17], measuring visual scanning, divided attention and motor speed.

As self-assessment is a key approach to monitoring fatigue, it has great potential to be adapted and deployed onto mobile platforms. Within the research literature, Swendeman et al. [20] carried out a study into the validity of self-reporting via a smartphone. They evaluated behavioral and emotional self-reports daily over a 6-week period. Daily completion rates of surveys were reported to be 50 %, with 70 % of participants completing three follow up surveys after the 6-week period. Adherence to the daily assessment was observed to be low, which was attributed to errors in data that subsequently had to be excluded from the evaluation results. It may indicate the monotonous nature of self-assessment for participants, regardless of medium, which subsequently highlights the overall need for a more engaging approach.

2.2 Objective Assessment

The WAIS was originally designed to measure intelligence but has since been adopted by neuroscientists in order to evaluate cognitive performance of brain-damaged individuals in terms of processing speed, reaction and memory [2, 12].

Van Dongen [6] defined three computerized methods for assessing fatigue after chronic sleep restriction: (1) a mental arithmetic test to assess cognitive throughput; (2) a sustained reaction time test; (3) a digit-symbol substitution task to assess memory. The experiment yielded convergent findings of sleep dose-response effects on all three cognitive performance functions. Specifically, sleep periods limited to four hours and six hours per night progressively eroded the effectiveness of psychomotor vigilance performance, working memory performance and cognitive throughout performance, thus providing evidence for the adverse effects of chronic sleep restriction and fatigue on cognitive function. While many technology-based approaches exist that are capable of assessing fatigue within a clinical environment, it is important to also develop mobile based methods, which would potentially facilitate assessent outside of the clinical environment.

The Psychomotor Vigilance Task (PVT) was originally designed for a static computer-based evaluation, however, it is one of the few tests that has been modified for use on mobile platforms. Work by Kay [14] and Gartenberg [8] investigated how effective short duration mobile tests would be, in conjunction with the usability issues that arise. They concluded that mobile-based variations were just as effective as desktop-based assessment, thus highlighting the adaptability of the underlying cognitive tasks. However, the assessments employed only focused on measuring vigilance as an evaluation of alertness and would have benefited from additional measurements such as working memory and throughput.

The Spatial Span Task used by Johansson, taken from the WAIS, measures the same cognitive attention and working memory ability as the Digit-Symbol Coding Task defined by Van Dongen as a metric to measure fatigue [6]. The key difference between the two tasks lies in the simplicity of the Spatial Span Task, which proves easier for individuals with to actively engage in. Furthermore, its simplicity further supports development and deployment on a mobile platform.

Johansson [9] compared the ability of a mental fatigue questionnaire with cognitive tests in order to determine if there is a direct correlation in their ability to subjectively and objectively measure fatigue. The neuropsychological tests employed included Digit Symbol-Coding Task, Digit Span Task, Spatial Span Task [19] and Trail Making Tests [17]. Accordingly, these tests were employed to measure processing speed attention, working memory, verbal fluency and reading speed. It was concluded that subjective mental fatigue mainly correlates with objectively measured information processing speed [9].

3   Methodology

This research employed a multi-disciplinary, iterative approach to systematically inform and evaluate each aspect of the smartphone application. Experts from the field of acquired brain injuries, psychology and interaction design were involved in informing initial design decisions and function of the application, alongside user pilot studies. This permitted the design and development of the smartphone application to be informed by clinical theory and practice, as well as commercial design theory and user opinion. This iterative design process is overviewed in Fig. 1.

Fig. 1. Iterative design process

The designed smartphone application utilized a variation of the MFS for use on a small screen. To ensure impartiality, the original paper design of the questionnaire has been utilized for the mobile variation employed, including the visual design of the questions, the sequencing of questions, and numbering of the scale. Its validity has previously been assessed alongside a series of neuropsychological tests [10]. Consequently, it was chosen for adoption in the smartphone application discussed herein, together with three different cognitive tests: (1) the Spatial Span Task from WAIS; (2) the PVT; (3) Serial Addition/Subtraction Task. Correspondingly, the cognitive tests selected require sufficient cognition to evaluate multiple different areas of affect, including memory, attention, speed of processing and cognitive throughput.

3.1   Expert Review

The initial phase of the design process was focused on clinical consultation and expert knowledge in order to inform the workflow of the application. Ordering of tests was considered as a crucial step, as retaining user attention while they might be cognitively fatigued is a difficult challenge. Consequently, through clinical expertise, ordering of tasks was based on the perceived level of task difficulty in conjunction with the perceived level of user enjoyment for individual tasks. As such, more difficult tasks were sequenced earlier, whereas more engaging tasks were sequenced later, in order to retain attention and engagement as the tasks become increasingly more stimulating. In addition, providing a 'fun' task after a 'boring' task gives the user an incentive to continue, which may be potentially helpful under fatigued circumstances. Subsequently, the ordering of the task as presented by the application is MFS, Spatial Span Task, PVT and Serial Addition/Subtraction Task. The overall application test takes no more than 10 min to complete, with the duration selected to ensure better user engagement as longer time on tasks can lead to a level of degradation in participation and a lower level of perceived effort. Expert review was carried on alongside the next stage of focus group testing.

3.2   Focus Group Pilot Study

Next, the initial version of the proposed smartphone application was delivered to a small group of participants (n = 5), recruited from the Ulster University, in order to investigate how information design and visual design choices made during expert review might affect the usability of the application. This was also an important stage as it permitted evaluation of the difficulty of each of the cognitive tests; if they were too complex they would be difficult for users to follow, however, by contrast, if they were too simplistic, they might not produce enough variability in the results obtained for conducting an effective degree of data analysis. For increased usability the application included an instructional screen before each of the cognitive tests. This was included to help users understand the nature and goal of the tests and to reduce the number of mistakes that were recorded by users during the pilot study.

Designing a smartphone application approach to a paper-based questionnaire produces many design and usability challenges. Careful consideration is needed though each stage of the iterative design process in order to take into account both expert opinion as well as user feedback. The Mental Fatigue Scale has 15 questions, each with 7 possible response options. On a paper-based format, it is easy to present all of this information on a page, however, on testing with a small-screen based mobile device, the original format of the questionnaire proved to be too complex and a modified approach was required. Consequently, each question and response option was given its own screen; this permitted the user to focus on just one question before having to think or be over-loaded with new information. In addition, it also removed the need to make use of a long scrolling screen for questions, which would potentially lead to misunderstanding of the current question. Figure 2 illustrates one of the question screens for the modified questionnaire; each question is presented and the user response must be obtained before moving on to the presentation of the next question. In order to improve accessibility, feedback from the pilot study showed that response options should have an indicator to highlight user selections, which was added to the final version of the smartphone application. Through the pilot study, feedback and clinical expertise, the MFS component of the application was modified to more closely follow the design and functionality of Apple's ResearchKit [23, 24] survey delivery design. This included use of simplistic design, visual layout of questions and answer format.

Fig. 2. Example question screen

Second stage of the overall application was the delivery of the Spatial Span Task. This was initially designed with a 5 × 5 grid layout, however, feedback from the pilot study indicated the proposed layout was too complex for the size of the screen, which resulted in making each square more difficult to select on touch-screen devices. In addition, iOS Human Interface Guidelines recommend any touch-screen element that is to be pressed should be 44 × 44 pixels, so the grid was subsequently reduced to 4 × 4 squares to accommodate this, as illustrated in Fig. 3a. The Spatial Span Task employs a limit of 90 s for the user to complete as many sequences as possible, so a countdown timer was added to the top-right of the screen in order to inform the user of the remaining time during the test. Due to the possible, varied lengths of the current sequence to be reproduced by the user, a progress bar was also included at the bottom of the screen in order to provide additional visual feedback to the user. Similar to the modified design of the MFS, this section of the application also followed the design principles used in Apple's ResearchKit [23, 24] Spatial Memory Task with only a few small adjustments in an effort to simplify the overall task for users. As a result, the grid design used is somewhat more simplistic than that used by Apple in attempts to reduce the on-screen complexity and potential for distraction. The addition of a sequence progress bar also provides real-time feedback to users for improved usability.

The PVT requires participants to react, as quickly as possible, 15 times to an on screen prompt. Initial design reviews showed that having a just a single prompt appear in the same position on screen allowed participants to preempt when to tap the stimulus. As preempting a response breaks the reactive nature of the test, and would not give an accurate indication of a user's fatigue levels, it was decided that a varying stimuli was needed. This was realized by splitting the screen in half and randomizing which side produced a stimulus in order to eradicate the preemptive responses in the task, as shown in Fig. 3b. Early or preemptive reactions resulted in a red screen stating the error. Correct reactions display the reaction time on screen, by way of providing feedback of task completion to the participant. This task differs from the reaction time task provided by

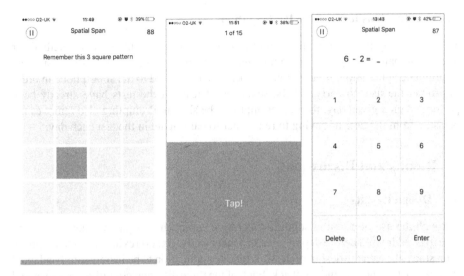

Fig. 3. a. Spatial span task **b.** PVT, **c.** Serial Addition/Subtraction

Apple's ResearchKit in two main ways. Firstly, our approach has a varying stimulus in an attempt to minimize preemptive responses. Also, the input modality is different, as in the ResearchKit version the user is required to shake the device in response to a stimulus. However, in testing this approach it was found that it resulted in a higher rate of errors than a finger press, and so for the final application the finger press was chosen to be included.

The final test delivered by the smartphone application was the Serial Addition/ Subtraction Task. Through the iterative user centered development approach employed, feedback from user experience expert highlighted the layout of the keyboard, as illustrated in Fig. 3c as a potential concern. During the pilot study, some participants viewed the keypad as being the incorrect orientation for a calculator-based interaction as they are traditionally laid out with the number sequence 1–2–3 on the bottom row. However, most participants considered the number layout shown in Fig. 3c as a more familiar keypad, similar to that used for smartphone calling applications, which are used more regularly than keyboard number pads with a calculator layout. Consequently, it was decided that layout would be used instead of the reverse calculator button layout.

All acquired data collected during assessments is stored internally by the smartphone application once a test is completed and is subsequently transmitted for external storage on a secure server that hosts a back-end database. Storing the acquired data on the device allows for instances when there is little or no network connectivity available, thereby preventing potential loss of test responses. In such cases, when network connectivity is restored the test data is transmitted to the back-end server. This is good practice for alleviating frustration on the user's part, which could be caused by any lost data and having to retake a test.

3.3 Notifications to Promote Participation

Task prompting has been widely employed as an effective compensatory method for memory impairments [4, 5]. To help increase participation with daily testing using the smartphone application, notifications are periodically issued to the smartphone in order to prompt the user to carry out the sequence of tests. If the tests have already been performed on a given day, then no prompt will be shown. Prompting also removes the pressure from the user of having to remember to participate in the test each day.

4 Results and Discussion

4.1 Design Results

Through the use of a multidisciplinary iterative approach, design considerations were able to be addressed before deployment in a main study. Expert review and a focus group pilot study allowed the design of the smartphone application to be incrementally adapted in response to concerns and feedback. Each of the three different cognitive tests received significant design revision after scrutiny from clinical expertise and user feedback. The Spatial Span Tasks grid size was reduced to 4×4 in response to user feedback and results which showed that a 5×5 grid was too complex to process and didn't give a wide enough variability in results. Though user testing in the pilot study it was shown that the initial design of the PVT task allowed participants to preempt the prompt and so this was addressed by varying the location of the stimuli on screen. This increased the reactive nature of the test which give a better measurement of a participants speed of processing. Finally, the keyboard layout of the Serial Addition/Subtraction Task was addressed through expert review as it was initially thought that the layout might been seen by participants as upside down for a calculator based task. User feedback from the pilot study indicated that this wasn't the case and that the layout provided was familiar due to its being the same orientation that is used for smartphone calling applications.

4.2 Study Results

Immediately after the study had been completed users were required to complete a System Usability Scale questionnaire [3]. This is one of the most widely used usability questionnaires and was chosen in this case as it is technology independent, being able to assess the usability of a wide range of software types, including smartphone applications. Additionally, participants were also asked to freely write what they found the most and least enjoyable aspects of the smartphone application. Participants (n = 21) were recruited to participate over a two-week period. The mean age of participants recruited was 22 years (SD = 4). Consequently, 81 individual testing instances were recorded. Significantly, due to the independent nature of each set of data resulting from a test run by a participant, all resulting statistical analysis was able to consider each set of results as an independent data point.

After the study was carried out, 81 % of participants took part in the follow up usability questionnaires. From the System Usability Scale, the overall application received and average score of 74, indicating an above average rating for its ease of use. Through the open comments it was seen that the biggest drawback of the application was the MFS and its perceived tedious nature. Results from this evaluation indicated that the primary reason for non-adherence was the MFS, which was considered as "boring" and "strenuous" in terms of having to answer multiple questions. By comparison, the cognitive tests were perceived to be "fun" and "enjoyable". The questionnaire also took the longest out of all four tasks to complete. The shortcomings of the application were predominantly focused on the questionnaire rather than its overall ease of use.

Overall daily adherence by participants was 24 %. Daily reminders were issued at 15:00 and resulted in a participant adherence rate of 23 % within the first two hours of receiving the reminder; this indicates that a large proportion of application use was in direct response to the daily reminders.

Analysis of the results obtained from the study indicates that the PVT, which is measured to 1/100 s, has the strongest correlation with the MFS, measuring 0.293 with a significance of 0.008. Figure 4 shows this positive liner correlation in data. This correlation may indicate that from a usability perspective the MFS could be replaced by the PVT and still produce accurate fatigue analysis in a more user friendly manner. This concurs with the results from previous studies into reaction times, showing that PVT is accurate at determining the occurrence of mental fatigue. By comparison, the Spatial Span Task had a correlation to the MFS of –0.141, with significance of 0.209, and the Serial Addition/Subtraction Task was found to have a correlation to the MFS of -0.016, with significance of 0.884. Subsequently, both the Spatial Span Task and Serial Addition-Subtraction Task do not provide a strong correlation with the MFS. However, the correlation analysis would indicate PVT's potential to assess mental fatigue using a mobile device, as it is able to determine the current level of mental fatigue. A higher correlation of 0.342 for the MFS and PVT is observed when outliers were removed on the basis of inaccurate subjective-assessment, e.g. assessment scores were abnormally

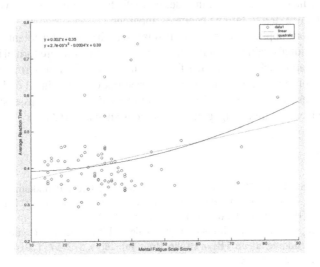

Fig. 4. MFS vs PVT Data plot with linear correlation

high or low when compared to testing scores, in conjunction with a simplistic pattern of responses observed (i.e. all responses were the lowest or highest possible choices). When further investigated, the majority of these outliers occurred by participants who reported that they arose in instances where the participants did not want to fill in the questionnaire and only wanted to take part in the other more engaging tasks. This would suggest that a questionnaire can be successfully adapted onto a mobile device, however, it doesn't guarantee that users will correctly engage with it, which could still potentially lead to a higher error rates in the scoring of results obtained from the questionnaire. On the other hand, the PVT showed promise as a potentially accurate and engaging way of assessing fatigue on a mobile device; participants were happier to engage with this task and it produced a correlative response to the validated MFS.

5   Conclusion and Future Work

The user experience design and efficacy of the proposed smartphone based cognitive fatigue objective assessment application have validated, through the use of an iterative multidisciplinary design methodology. However, a number of areas for improvement remain. User feedback indicated that carrying out the MFS was one of the least enjoyable parts of the overall process, which potentially reduces engagement in the process. As the use of PVT has been shown to provide similar assessment of mental fatigue, future work can exclude the use of MFS. Subsequently, this could further increase user participation rates, which, in turn, may potentially increase the accuracy of the mental fatigue evaluation. All three of the tasks employed resulted in positive user feedback, with some participants even indicating that they would like personal scores as it would further encourage them to participate more frequently. Consequently, by introducing a competitive aspect to the cognitive games, user effort and daily participation rates would potentially improve. Future work may additionally permit the availability of real-time data for relevant medical professionals, in order that effective and timely intervention could be arranged if any extreme fatigue becomes apparent.

The smartphone application presented in this research provides a potentially effective tool for the individual evaluation of fatigue levels in situations where formal intervention and assessment approaches are neither feasible, nor available. Furthermore, the smartphone application permits evaluation to be carried out on a continual daily basis. The study also proves that tradition self-assessment methods of fatigue assessment can be accurately replaced by more engaging test methods such as a PVT.

References

1. Aaronson, L.S., Teel, C.S., Cassmeyer, V., Neuberger, G.B., Pallikkathayil, L., Pierce, A.W.J., Press, A.N., Williams, P.D.: Defining and measuring fatigue. J. Nurs. Scholarsh. **31**(1), 45–50 (1999). http://doi.org/10.1016/j.apmr.2013.02.026
2. Johansson, B., Ronnback, L.: Mental fatigue scale and its relation to cognitive, social and emotional functioning after a TBI or stroke. Brain Inj. **28**(1), 572–573 (2014). http://doi.org/10.4172/2329-9096.1000182

3. Brooke, J.: SUS-A quick and dirty usability scale. Usability evaluation in industry **189**(194), 4–7 (1996)
4. Chang, Y.-J., Chen, S.-F., Chou, L.-D.: A feasibility study of enhancing independent task performance for people with cognitive impairments through use of a handheld location-based prompting system. IEEE Trans. Inf. Technol. Biomed. **16**(6), 1157–1163 (2012). http://doi.org/10.1109/TITB.2012.2198484. A publication of the IEEE Engineering in Medicine and Biology Society
5. Das, B., Thomas, B.L., Seelye, A.M., Cook, D.J., Holder, L.B., Schmitter-Edgecombe, M.:Context-aware prompting from your smart phone. In: IEEE Consumer Communications and Networking Conference (CCNC), pp. 56–57 (2012). http://doi.org/10.1109/CCNC.2012.6181049
6. Van Dongen, H.P., Maislin, G., Mullington, J.M., Dinges, D.F.: The cumulative cost of additional wakefulness: dose-response effects on neurobehavioral functions and sleep physiology from chronic sleep restriction and total. Sleep, **26**(2) 117–126 (2003). http://www.med.upenn.edu/uep/user_documents/VanDongen_etal_Sleep_26_2_2003.pdf. Accessed 19 Nov 2014
7. Engström, A.-L.L., Lexell, J., Lund, M.L.: Difficulties in using everyday technology after acquired brain injury: a qualitative analysisScandinavian J. Occupational Therapy, **173**, 233–243 (2010). http://doi.org/10.3109/11038120903191806
8. Gartenberg, D., McGarry, R.: Development of a Neuroergonomic application to evaluate arousal. In: Advances in Understanding Human Performance, pp. 6378–6387 (2012). http://books.google.com/books?hl=en&lr=&id=Plqeq0FmkIYC&oi=fnd&pg=PA239&dq=Development+of+a+Neuroergonomic+Application+to+Evaluate+Arousal&ots=s0N2Ln1UjT&sig=VCNgcFs-Wq4W3pf8kfpZTR-gJQg. Accessed 3 Dec 2014
9. Johansson, B., Berglund, P., Rönnbäck, L.: Mental fatigue and impaired information processing after mild and moderate traumatic brain injury. Brain Injury: [BI], **23**, 13–14: 1027–1040 (2009). http://doi.org/10.3109/02699050903421099
10. Johansson, B., Bjuhr, H., Rönnbäck, L.: Evaluation of an advanced mindfulness program following a mindfulness-based stress reduction program for participants suffering from mental fatigue after acquired brain injury. Mindfulness (2013). http://doi.org/10.1007/s12671-013-0249-z
11. Johansson, B., Rönnbäck, L.: Mental Fatigue; A Common Long Term Consequence After a Brain Injury (2009)
12. Johansson, B., Rönnbäck, L.: Mental Fatigue and Cognitive Impairment after an Almost Neurological Recovered Stroke. In: ISRN Psychiatry 2012, pp. 1–7 (2012). http://doi.org/10.5402/2012/686425
13. Johansson, B., Starmark, A., Berglund, P., Rödholm, M., Rönnbäck, L.: A self-assessment questionnaire for mental fatigue and related symptoms after neurological disorders and injuries (2009). http://informahealthcare.com/doi/abs/10.3109/02699050903452961. Accessed 12 May 2015
14. Kay, M., Rector, K: PVT-touch: adapting a reaction time test for touchscreen devices. In: PervasiveHealth 2013, pp. 248–251 (2013). http://ieeexplore.ieee.org/xpls/abs_all.jsp?arnumber=6563934. Accessed 3 Dec 2014
15. Krupp, L.B., LaRocca, N.G., Muir-Nash, J., Steinberg, A.D.: The fatigue severity scale: application to patients with multiple sclerosis and systemic lupus erythematosus. Arch. Neurology **46**(10), 1121–1123 (1989)
16. Lee, K.A., Hicks, G., Nino-Murcia, G.: Validity and reliability of a scale to assess fatigue. Psychiatry research **36**(3), 291–298 (1991)

17. Reitan, R.M., Wolfson, D.: The Halstead-Reitan neuropsychological test battery: Theory and clinical interpretation. Reitan Neuropsychology (1985)

18. Shahid, A., Wilkinson, K., Marcu, S., Shapiro, C.M.: Visual analogue scale to evaluate fatigue severity (VAS-F). In: Shahid, A., Wilkinson, K., Marcu, S., Shapiro, C.M. (eds.) STOP, THAT and One Hundred Other Sleep Scales SE – 100, pp. 399–402. Springer, New York (2012). http://doi.org/10.1007/978-1-4419-9893-4_100

19. Sue Baron, I.: Delis-Kaplan executive function system. Child Neuropsychology **10**, 147–152 (2004)

20. Dallas Swendeman, W., Comulada, S., Ramanathan, N., Lazar, M., Estrin, D.: Reliability and validity of daily self-monitoring by smartphone application for health-related quality-of-life, antiretroviral adherence, substance use, and sexual behaviors among people living with HIV. AIDS Behav. **19**(2), 330–340 (2014). http://doi.org/10.1007/s10461-014-0923-8

21. Wechsler, D.: Wechsler Adult Intelligence Scale, 4th edn. NCS Pearson, San Antonio (2008)

22. Ziino, C., Ponsford, J.: Measurement and prediction of subjective fatigue following traumatic brain injury. J. Int. Neuropsychol. Soc. **11**(04), 416–425 (2005). http://journals.cambridge.org/abstract_S1355617705050472. Accessed 12 Nov 2014

23. ResearchKit Reference. http://researchkit.org/docs/index.html. Accessed 9 Feb 2016

24. iOS Human Interface Guidelines: Research Apps. http://researchkit.org/hig/index.html. Accessed 9 Feb 2016

Supporting User Awareness Using Smart Device-Based Notifications

Gustavo López[✉] and Luis A. Guerrero

University of Costa Rica (UCR), San José, Costa Rica
{gustavo.lopez_h,luis.guerreroblanco}@ucr.ac.cr

Abstract. This paper provides an overview of a doctoral research project which focuses in developing a framework to allow smart device-based notifications to provide user awareness. Notifications are mechanisms by which the user's attention is driven to specific tasks or events. Notifications should provide a balance between intrusiveness and value in order to avoid annoyed users. The results reported in this paper include 50 % of the overall results expected for the project. The first step was to conduct a systematic literature review assessing the use of smart devices to deliver notifications, the second step was the development of a framework to allow notification coordination among smart devices and the third result is a laboratory case study assessing the framework. Future work includes two case studies in real scenarios and further analysis of usage patterns identified during this research.

Keywords: Notification · User experience · Smart devices · Interruption · Human attention

1 Introduction

In times of increasing amounts of information, human attention is becoming a bottleneck [1]. A large number of ubiquitous devices and services seek human attention through notifications. The goal of such notifications is to provide user awareness; however, the amount and type of notifications can be distractive which can negatively affect task performance [2].

Humans have the biological ability to selectively perceive stimuli and recall gathered information from those stimuli as short term memory [3]. However, the use of technological devices to force the attention of a user in a particular piece of data is overriding such abilities.

Notifications are often generated by social networks and collaborative systems, and there are social expectations towards the timely response of such notifications. Paying attention and responding properly to all those notifications is becoming stressful to the users [4]. Some users are ignoring notifications; consequently, missing crucial information and becoming less efficient in their tasks, just by the fact that the amount of notifications is too high.

© Springer International Publishing AG 2016
C.R. García et al. (Eds.): UCAmI 2016, Part I, LNCS 10069, pp. 333–340, 2016.
DOI: 10.1007/978-3-319-48746-5_34

The research proposal described in this paper focuses on solving the **problem** caused by the overload of notifications received by users. The **scope** of this research is limited to the use of smart device-based notifications. Smart devices are electronic apparatus that can somehow interact with people and/or each other (e.g., smartphones, smart watches, smart bands, smart keychains, home and work appliances).

The main **research question** of this project is: How can smart devices be used as notification mechanism in an effective and efficient way? This work is **relevant** for the smart device development community, because their products will have an added value. Users of smart devices will benefit from the success of this research as they will be provided with less intrusive and more valuable notifications through their smart devices.

Moreover, the timing of this project is **justified** by the transition to the era of the Internet of Things in which handling incoming notifications and delivering them opportunely is a key issue [5, 6].

The rest of this paper is structured as follows: Sect. 2 describes the methodology followed in this research project, Sect. 3 describes the preliminary results and discussion and Sect. 4 summarizes the research project, its progress status and future work.

2 Research Methodology

This research project aims to handle notifications in an efficient way delivering them through smart devices. To achieve that goal, smart devices must comply with certain characteristics to assure compatibility. The main characteristics required for smart devices were described in a framework for designing, developing and evaluating augmented objects [7]. The features defined in such framework assure technical compatibility with this proposal.

To gather information about the use of smart devices to deliver notifications, a systematic literature review was conducted following Kitchenham's procedures for performing systematic reviews [8]. Research published in the last 10 years in ACM Digital Library, IEEE Digital Library, and Springer Publishing databases were included. The review results are under revision for publication [9]. The systematic review was driven by the following research question: Are there any reported collaborative tools that use ubiquitous mechanism to provide awareness in the collaborative domain?

The review results showed that traditional interfaces are still the main notification mechanism used (i.e., graphical notification in PC applications or mobile notifications). However, smart devices (e.g., lamps, vibro-tactile belt, ad-hoc notified) are also being used to deliver notifications. This results confirms the necessity of a framework to effectively manage notifications through smart devices.

A first approach for a smart device-based notification framework was developed with the experience and lessons learned of several research projects [10]. This framework consists of 3 layers: application, communication and user interaction. The user interaction layer gathers the smart devices available in the context of a user and uses them to deliver notifications and gather information.

In order to evaluate the framework a set of smart devices were developed [11] and combined with other devices available.

Given the number of smart devices that will be available in the nearby future, the selection of the "best" smart device to deliver a notification is not a trivial process. Therefore, the necessity of a system capable of deciding in which way a notification should be delivered was included in this research. A preliminary approach to this issue was proposed, implemented, evaluated and discussed [12]. Moreover, a smart device structure model was proposed to increase the compatibility of the framework proposed in this research with other devices available.

Even though this research focuses on delivering notifications through smart devices, a two-way communication is normally required (i.e., users should be able to provide feedback to the system using smart devices). An approach to achieve this goal was described and evaluated [13].

3   Results

The question driving this research is: How can smart devices be used as notification mechanism in an effective and efficient way? The first approach to answer this question was to assess the use of smart devices as notification mechanisms. From the extensive search (i.e., Systematic Literature Review) only 63 papers were found addressing the use of some kind of interface to deliver notifications. Approximately half of those papers reported the use of traditional interfaces as notification mechanisms. One third of the papers reported the use of mobile devices to deliver information to users. Public displays were the third most used interaction mechanisms. Finally, only 6 % of the reviewed papers used non-traditional (e.g., light display, smart devices and wearable technology) to deliver notifications.

This results are consistent with the authors expectations. Most of the work being applied in this field is being conducted by manufacturers and not researchers. Therefore, a limited amount of results are being published in peer reviewed conferences or journals. Table 1 show the summary of papers found in the published research.

Table 1. SLR summary by type of evaluation and application context

Type of evaluation	% of papers	Context	% of papers
Not Specified	42%	Work	34,9%
Case Study	19,2%	Social	18%
Preliminary Study (Lab)	14,4%	Health	14,4%
Usability	8,4%	Education	12%
Example	6%	Various	10,7%
Experiment	6%	Emergency management	6%
Heuristics	1,3%	Geographical	2%
Empirical Evaluation	1,3%	Security	1%
Performance Evaluation	1,3%	Smart Home	1%

Figure 1 shows which mechanisms were used to gather information and to notify the users. The main conclusion that can be drawn from Fig. 1 is that traditional interfaces is still the most used mechanisms followed by mobile devices, and public displays.

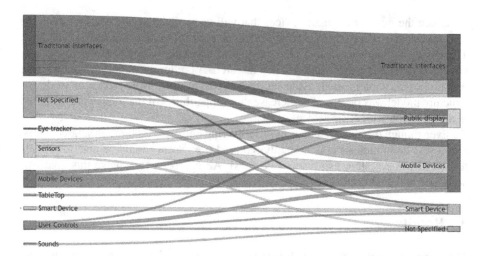

Fig. 1. SLR data-gathering (left) and information providing mechanisms (right).

Up to this point the information gathered was sufficient to carry a case study in a particular context. In order to assess the applicability of the proposed framework in a laboratory setting. The results of this case study were satisfactory for the research collaborators (i.e., functional testing was performed and results were acceptable).

To conduct the case study, the proposed framework was implemented. Two servers were required one executing the coordination system and one that offered and consumed web services to and from smart devices. These two servers were virtualized to allow scalability and replicability.

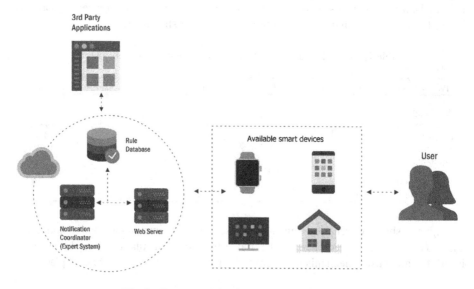

Fig. 2. Framework implementation architecture

The user interaction layer of the framework consists of all available smart devices. This layer allows direct communication with the users. Event tough this layer was designed to allow notification delivery through smart devices, it also allows data gathering from the user.

Figure 2 shows the overall implementation architecture. In Fig. 2 the user interaction layer is represented by all available smart devices in a user context at a given time.

The communication layer is based on web services (Web Server in Fig. 2). Moreover, this layer represents the communication protocol that finally allows smart device coordination through effective communication with the notification coordinator and third party applications.

The last layer (application) models the intelligence that allows smart device coordination. This layer contains both the notification coordinator (expert system) and 3rd party applications. This connection with third party applications is essential since most of the notifications are generated by them.

This framework proposal allows coordination by centralizing notifications and delivering them in an effective manner at an opportune moment. This results could not be achieved if each system delivers notifications independently to the user.

The notification coordinator has an internal structure that allows dynamic coordination and distribution of notification across smart devices. Figure 3 show the notification coordinator internal design.

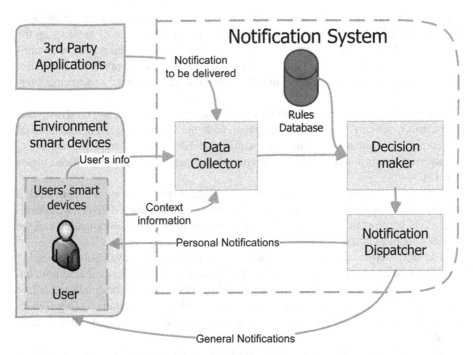

Fig. 3. Notification coordinator design

During the implementation of the system, the necessity of user feedback was identified. This could improve the effectiveness of delivered notifications by adding new rules or rearranging delivery priorities. To allow this feedback, the system provides a survey that assess the way in which a notification was delivered with the final user. This feedback mechanism produces additional work for the final user, however, we expect the benefits to be enough in order to promote users to answer the survey.

Moreover, once the system stabilizes for a particular user, the feedback mechanism would not be necessary, unless new smart devices are added to the user context and the user could disable this feature.

The management efforts to maintain this framework up and running are high. Moreover, the adoption of standards in the development of smart devices is a requirement for this project to be massively adopted. Similar research proposals were found in the literature reviews performed before the beginning of this project. However, they worked on independent parts of the framework proposed in this paper. The combination of those parts is unique and has not been addressed.

The topic of notification delivery through smart devices is a hot topic and several workshops are being conducted to promote research in this area [14, 15].

4   Summary and Future Work

The research project described in this paper is, in opinion of the authors at 50 % of progress according with the goals originally stated. Authors proposed as first step the conduction of a systematic literature review to assess the use of smart devices as notification delivery mechanisms. This review showed that the amount of notification delivered through smart devices is very small (at least in projects reported in academic literature).

Even though the review showed that smart devices are not commonly used to deliver notifications, several workshops collocated with the most recognized international conferences in Human Computer Interaction and Ubiquitous Computing are being conducted assessing notification management using smart devices and related topics [14, 15].

With the results of the literature review and the experiences of previous work a preliminary framework to manage smart device-based notification delivery was developed. This framework was evaluated with a case study in a laboratory setting and the results were promising.

The next step in this project would be to conduct formal evaluations assessing usability, efficiency, effectiveness and user satisfaction of smart device-based notifications in specific domains. At least two case studies are expected to be conducted in two different domains. The results are going to be measured both quantitatively (e.g., reduction in the amount of notifications, response time, reduction of interruption) and qualitatively (user satisfaction).

Moreover, a separation of the components of the framework should be considered in the evaluation. Since most smart devices are only being introduced to the users, assessing the framework with those devices could compromise the findings of this research. This issue is still being discussed by the authors to avoid bias in the framework evaluation results due to external factors.

The evaluation of this project is expected to be conducted in a different country that the one in which the initial case study was conducted. Moreover, the facilities to replicate would be considered in order to allow multiple researchers to run similar evaluations with different smart devices in different contexts. Therefore, allowing a more extensive evaluation of the framework.

The main **contribution** of this doctoral project is a framework that eases the management of notification using a centralized services and delivers notifications through smart devices in an opportune moment and in a proper way (i.e., considering the user's cognitive load).

Acknowledgment. The advisor for this project is Dr. Luis A. Guerrero. This work is conduced as a research project at CITIC and ECCI both at UCR. Grant No. 834-B6-178. This work is also supported by MICITT and CONICIT, institutions of the Costa Rican government.

References

1. Okoshi, T., Nozaki, H., Nakazawa, J., Tokuda, H., Ramos, J., Dey, A.K.: Towards attention-aware adaptive notification on smart phones. Pervasive Mob. Comput. **26**, 17–34 (2016)
2. Borst, J.P., Taatgen, N.A., van Rijn, H.: What makes interruptions disruptive?: a process-model account of the effects of the problem state bottleneck on task interruption and resumption. In: Proceedings of the 33rd Annual ACM Conference on Human Factors in Computing Systems, pp. 2971–2980. ACM, New York (2015)
3. Charlton, B.G.: Evolution and the cognitive neuroscience of awareness, consciousness and language. In: Psychiatry and the Human Condition (2000)
4. Pielot, M., Rello, L.: The do not disturb challenge: a day without notifications. In: Proceedings of the 33rd Annual ACM Conference Extended Abstracts on Human Factors in Computing Systems, pp. 1761–1766. ACM, New York (2015)
5. Pejovic, V., Musolesi, M.: InterruptMe: designing intelligent prompting mechanisms for pervasive applications. In: Proceedings of the 2014 ACM International Joint Conference on Pervasive and Ubiquitous Computing, pp. 897–908. ACM, New York (2014)
6. Pielot, M., de Oliveira, R., Kwak, H., Oliver, N.: Didn't you see my message?: predicting attentiveness to mobile instant messages. In: Proceedings of the 32nd Annual ACM Conference on Human Factors in Computing Systems, pp. 3319–3328. ACM, New York (2014)
7. López, G., López, M., Guerrero, L.A., Bravo, J.: Human-objects interaction: a framework for designing, developing and evaluating augmented objects. Int. J. Hum. Comput. Interact. **30**, 787–801 (2014)
8. Kitchenham, B.: Procedures for performing systematic reviews, Keele University. Technical Report TR/SE-0401, Department of Computer Science. Keele University, United Kingdom (2004)
9. López, G., Guerrero, L.A.: Interaction mechanisms for collaborative systems a systematic literature review. In: Computer-Supported Cooperative Work and Social Computing. ACM, Portland (2017, in press)

10. López, G., Guerrero, L.A.: Ubiquitous notification mechanism to provide user awareness. In: Rebelo, F., Soares, M. (eds.) Advances in Ergonomics in Design. Advances in Intelligent Systems and Computing, vol. 485, pp. 689–700. Springer, Heidelberg (2016)
11. Brenes, J.A., López, G., Guerrero, L.A.: Development and evaluation of augmented object prototypes for notifications in collaborative writing environments. In: Nunes, I.L. (ed.) Advances in Human Factors and System Interactions. Advances in Intelligent Systems and Computing, vol. 497, pp. 301–312. Springer, Heidelberg (2017)
12. López, G., Guzman, M., Marín, G., Guerrero, L.A.: Towards smart notifications - an adaptive approach using smart devices. In: International Conference on Ubiquitous Computing and Ambient Intelligence. Springer (2016, in press)
13. López, G., Quesada, L., Guerrero, L.A.: Gesture and speech as mechanism to interact with smart devices. J. Ambient Intell. Human. Comput. (2016, in press)
14. Voit, A., Henze, N., Poppinga, B., Gehring, S., Weber, D., Okoshi, T., Böhmer, M., Pejovic, V.: UbiTtention: Smart & Ambient Notification and Attention Management. In: Workshop in Conjunction with UbiComp 2016. http://projects.hcilab.org/ubittention/
15. Weber, D., Poppinga, B., Shirazi, A.S., Pielot, M., Gehring, S., Okoshi, T., Henze, N.: Smarttention, please! intelligent attention management on mobile devices. In: Workshop in Conjunction with MobileHCI 2016. http://mhci16.smarttention.com/

Sensing Affective States
Using Facial Expression Analysis

Anas Samara[✉], Leo Galway, Raymond Bond, and Hui Wang

School of Computing and Mathematics, Ulster University, Belfast BT37 0QB, UK
samara-a@email.ulster.ac.uk, {l.galway,rb.bond,h.wang}@ulster.ac.uk

Abstract. An important factor for the next generation of Human Computer Interaction is the implementation of an interaction model that automatically reasons in context of the users goals, attitudes, affective characteristics and capabilities, and adapts the system accordingly. Although various techniques have been proposed for automatically detecting affective states using facial expression, this is still a research challenge in terms of classification accuracy. This paper investigates an extensible automatic affective state detection approach via the analysis of facial expressions from digital photographs. The main contribution of this study can be summarised in two points. Firstly, utilising facial point distance vectors within the representation of facial expressions is shown to be more accurate and robust in comparison to using standard Cartesian coordinates. Secondly, employing a two-stage Support Vector Machine-based classification model, entitled Hierarchical *Parallelised Binary Support Vector Machines* (HPBSVM), is shown to improve classification performance over other machine learning techniques. The resulting classification model has been evaluated using two different facial expression datasets (namely CKPLUS and KDEF), yielding accuracy rates of 96.9 % and 96.2 % over each dataset respectively.

Keywords: User modelling · Facial expression · Emotion detection · Affective computing · Human Computer Interaction

1 Introduction

Affective state detection in the context of Human-Computer Interaction (HCI) is important for intelligent adaptation and interaction, which are defining features of next generation user interfaces. Consequently, there are several studies that focus on detecting different sets of emotions [9]. However, within the domain of Affective Computing, there is no agreement on a definitive set of human emotions to recognise. Hence, several research efforts have defined different sets of labels that are domain and application specific. For example, Ekman and Friesen [8] revealed six emotions that can be inferred from facial expressions, including *surprise, fear, happiness, sadness, anger* and *disgust*. Whereas in Shan et al. [29], a different set of emotions were detected including *anger, anxiety, boredom, disgust, joy, puzzlement* and *surprise*, using facial expression as one of the inputs

© Springer International Publishing AG 2016
C.R. García et al. (Eds.): UCAmI 2016, Part I, LNCS 10069, pp. 341–352, 2016.
DOI: 10.1007/978-3-319-48746-5_35

in their system. By contrast, Busso et al. [5] only labelled four emotions, which included *sadness, anger* and *happiness*, along with a *neutral* state, using facial expression as one of the inputs.

Posner et al. proposed a model of affective states, entitled the Circumplex Model of Affect (CMA), which states that instead of defining labels as discrete emotions, an affective state is a result of two neurophysiological dimensions: (1) the Pleasant-Unpleasant continuum, known as the *valence* axis; (2) the Activation-Deactivation continuum, which is known as the *arousal* axis [27]. Furthermore, in [31] three classes were defined for both arousal and valence, with the arousal classes containing the states *calm, medium aroused* and *activated*, and the valence classes containing the states *unpleasant, neutral* and *pleasant*. Other studies, such as the work carried out in [15], used two approaches to model affective expressions; the first model, referred to as *Pronounce Level*, uses three categories to classify facial expressions according to how much they are pronounced: No (*neutral*), Low (*angry, disgust, fear* and *sad*) and High (*happy* and *surprise*). The second model, referred to as the *Facial Expression Change Rate*, represents how often the detected facial expressions changed from one category to another, which subsequently indicates the level of affect within the content of a video clip.

This paper proposes a facial feature representation that utilises distances among facial landmark points rather than using standard location coordinates. Moreover, it presents a combination of Support Vector Machine models that evaluate a state in two cascaded stages of hierarchical parallelised binary classifiers, where a single classifier is used for each target class. The structure of the paper is as follows: background research on user state perception and facial expression analysis is presented in Sect. 2. Section 3 describes the method and the techniques used within this paper, together with a brief description of the datasets used in the experiments, which are subsequently presented in Sect. 4. Section 5 discusses the results, including comparison with related work. Finally, Sect. 6 presents a summary and concludes with a discussion of future work.

2 Background

2.1 User State Perception

The perception of the users state is a key component in Adaptive-HCI [25, 32]. Therefore, researchers investigate techniques to detect and predict the users affective states whilst the user interacts with a computer system. Many studies have focused on building annotated and robust datasets in order to develop computerised models for the automatic prediction of states of human emotion. For example, Afzal et al. [1] used emotional videos to induce different emotions that were subsequently detected from facial expressions. Furthermore, in [2], Ahn and Picard showed that visual-based inputs are used to predict customer's desires by analysing the state shown in the facial expression of subjects during a beverage tasting experiment. Other studies have explored the use of facial expression within a learning context using pedagogical agents and tutoring systems [34] using action units listed in the Facial Action Coding System (FACS) framework [10].

2.2 Facial Expression as Input Modality

Facial expressions are considered as one of the most relevant features that can provide an indication about a users emotional state [1,12]. Furthermore, they are considered instrumental in revealing mental states and clues to the user's feelings [3]. Facial expressions are generated from the movements of facial muscles, which can be produced unconsciously [33]. Within the research literature, facial gestures are detected by analysing features from different regions of the face, primarily the mouth, nose, eyes, eyebrows, and forehead [3]. Consequently, extracting features from human faces is fully dependent on locating these regions. In other words, imprecise estimation of these points will substantially impair the accurate detection of corresponding affective states.

2.3 Geometric-Based Facial Feature Detection

Geometric-based techniques extract features from local regions of interest and then generate a representation based on facial geometrical properties [14,30]. In other words, geometric-based techniques for facial expression analysis are based on locating the facial points (referred to as *fiducial points*) and determining the location and the shape of associated facial components including the eyebrows, eyes, nose, lips and mouth. Asthana and Zafeiriou developed a tool that serves as a geometric-based technique, entitled *Chehra*, which is a facial landmark detector based on discriminative facial deformable models, trained using a cascade of linear regressions [4]. As shown in Fig. 1, the *Chehra* detector locates 49 facial landmark points as follows: [1–10] eyebrows, [1–19] nose, [20–31] eyes, [32–43] mouth outer lips, and [44–49] mouth inner lips.

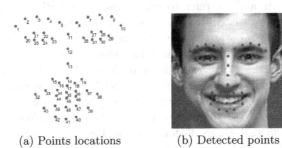

(a) Points locations   (b) Detected points

Fig. 1. The 49 facial landmark points detected on a sample face

2.4   Affective State Modelling Techniques

Within the research literature, several machine learning methods have been used for facial expression classification. For example, McDuff et al. used Support Vector Machine (SVM) and Bayesian classifiers to recognise user stress state where facial expression is one of the inputs [23]. Moreover, Oliver built a real-time recognition system that tracks lips and facial expressions in order to detect a set of emotions using Hidden Markov Models (HMM) [24]. By contrast, Kapoor et al. [16] utilised facial expressions together with other input modalities to predict frustration using a range of classification techniques including SVM, Gaussian Process, and K-Nearest Neighbour (KNN). Additionally, the use of facial expression features with Bayesian classifier to determine affective scenes while watching videos was also proposed by Joho et al. [15]. Nevertheless, existing research is limited in terms of the number of states detected and the application targeted. Therefore, the aim of this study is to extend previous work in order to provide a classification mechanism that is extensible over a number affective states, taking into account classification accuracy.

3   Methodology

The study presented within this paper exploited two different benchmark datasets to measure efficiencies and validate different techniques and approaches to user affective state modelling. Firstly, the Cohn-Kanade Plus dataset (CKPLUS) was used, which is an extension of the version released in 2000, and is deemed a benchmark for automatic facial expression analysis and detection [20]. CKPLUS is comprised of 593 sequences taken from 123 subjects. The labelling process was carried out using the FACS coding system, and only 327 sequences meet the criteria to be labelled as a specific emotion. The sequences were divided into seven groups: *angry* (45), *contempt* (18), *disgust* (59), *fear* (25), *happy* (69), *sadness* (28), and *surprise* (83). This dataset is used throughout the experiments and we refer to the dataset as CKPLUS-7 as it includes 7 classes of affective state. Moreover, as sequences in the CKPLUS dataset are captured from a neutral state as the first frame is followed by sequences until the peak frame, therefore, an additional 112 images were annotated as *neutral*. This modification makes it a slightly different dataset from the CKPLUS dataset and we refer to this in our experiments as CKPLUS-8 as it contains 8 classes of affective state. Secondly, the Karolinska Directed Emotional Faces dataset (KDEF) [21], which consists of 4900 pictures captured from 70 subjects (equally divided between 35 males and 35 females), and each subject acted seven different affective states, which include: *afraid, angry, disgusted, happy, neutral, sad* and *surprised*. Each facial expression was captured in two sessions from 5 different angles: full left, half left, straight, half right, and full right. However, the KDEF dataset was filtered to use only images that are relevant within the HCI context, which only involved the frontal view where the user faces towards the camera. Therefore, the filtered KDEF dataset subsequently used for testing and modelling techniques and expressions classification contains only 980 images (7 states x 70 subjects x 2 sessions).

3.1 Distance-Based Facial Feature Descriptors

Facial points can be directly used as Cartesian coordinates for machine learning. Subsequently, using 49 coordinates will produce a vector of 98-dimentional features. However, this approach is not sufficiently robust enough to permit recognition of states from facial expressions not provided in the training data. This is due to the fact that the constellation of these points varies among the myriad of facial shapes that comprise different facial morphologies [28]. Therefore, researchers have attempted to find alternative descriptors. Martinez proposed a shape-based model, which defines *configural features* that represent intra-facial component distances, in particular, the vertical distances between eyebrows and mouth [22]. Consequently, in this study we propose to use a complementary representation based on finding the separation between all facial landmark points. Subsequently, the *Euclidian distance* metric for two points $p_1 = (x_1, y_1)$ and $p_2 = (x_2, y_2)$ is given as:

$$d_{1,2} = \sqrt{(x_2 - x_1)^2 + (y_2 - y_1)^2}$$

To facilitate classifier training using distances among facial points requires the production of a feature vector that represents the Euclidean distances between all points, as illustrated in Fig. 2. As a result, combinations of 49 coordinates C_2^{49} will produce a vector of 1176-dimensional features.

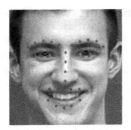   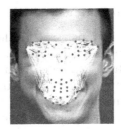

(a) Detected points   (b) Linked points

Fig. 2. Lines connecting detected points

3.2 Classification Techniques

Extracted facial features will be exploited with machine learning techniques that support pattern recognition in order to build an efficient predictive model that can envision an approximation of the affective state of a user derived from facial expression analysis. Within this study the Weka API implementation was

Table 1. Snapshot of the intermediate dataset generated by binary classifiers during the first stage, which is subsequently used to train the final aggregator classifier

Afraid/Others	Angry/Others	Disgust/Others	Happy/Others	Sadness/Others	Surprise/Others	Final State
Afraid	Others	Others	Others	Sadness	Others	Afraid
Others	Others	Disgust	Others	Others	Surprise	Surprise
Others	Others	Others	Happy	Others	Others	Happy

used for the purpose of the exploration and to ascertain the accuracy of various machine learning methods. Specifically, the following techniques were used: (1) SimpleLogistic, implemented by Landwehr et al., in which classification is applied using a stage-wise fitting process to build logistic regression models [18]; (2) a Logistic Regression Tree (LMT) classifier, which comprises classification trees with logistic regression functions at the leaves; (3) Multi-Layer Perceptron, which uses back-propagation to train a neural network consisting of multiple layers of nodes built from the sigmoid logistic function; (4) Support Vector Machine, which is widely used in data analysis and binary/multiclass classification. SVM tries to find an optimal hyperplane that separates labelled training data categories with the maximum margin. Two variations of SVM have been tested in this study: (a) Sequential Minimal Optimization (SMO), proposed by Platt [26]; and (b) C-Support Vector Classification (C-SVC) with linear kernel, which is available in the LIBSVM library developed at National Taiwan University that can be deployed in Weka [6,11]. For the purpose of the experiments conducted, along with analysis of the associated results, we hereafter refer to the use of the C-SVC variation as SVM.

3.3   Hierarchal Parallelised Binary Support Vector Machines

In this work we also propose a classification framework involving a hierarchy of classifiers that operates in two stages. During the first stage, binary SVM models are constructed from annotated data, with one model employed for each affective state within the dataset. Furthermore, during the second stage, a multiclass SVM model is constructed to predict the state based on the decisions from all of the binary SVM models. This classification framework is presented in Fig. 3. As depicted in Table 1, a snapshot of the intermediate dataset after the first stage is shown, which has been generated by executing the aforementioned parallelised classifiers. Subsequently, the length of the intermediate vectors equals the number of binary classifiers utilised in the first stage. Thereafter, this intermediate dataset is used to train the second stage classifier (i.e. the aggregation classifier), which eventually gives the final decision on the detected affective state.

Accordingly, the output of each classifier from the first stage represents a feature in the fabricated intermediate vector, which will be utilised as an input vector to the second stage. Consequently, the intermediate dataset resulting from the first stage is represented using a smaller set of features. Moreover, when we look at the values of the data they are more consistent with small variance. Subsequently, these facilitate more efficient and accurate classification during

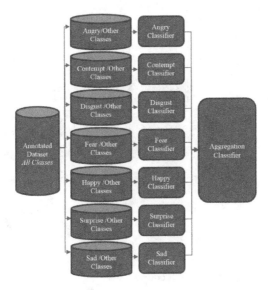

Fig. 3. Hierarchal parallelised binary support vector machines for automatic affective state detection

the second stage. By considering the whole system, the hierarchal classification structure improves efficiency through decomposition of the overall problem into smaller decisions that are made by specialised classifiers, which are trained differently in order to distinguish one class from others. As a result, the whole system benefits from the advantages of making some features more discriminative for specific classes and eventually combining the individual results [17].

4   Results

In the study presented in this paper a number of experiments were performed to probe different machine learning techniques for analysing features populated from facial expressions. Consequently, unimodal prediction models were constructed for the five techniques previous discussed in Sect. 3.2 that exploit facial input modality to automatically model affective states. Furthermore, a two-stage SVM-based classification technique, outlined in Sect. 3.3, was investigated in conjunction with a distance-based approach to facial feature representation. All experiments carried out use the 10-fold cross validation technique. Additionally, a 95 % confidence interval of classification results has been used in order to show the lower and upper limits along with the statistical significance of the results obtained.

4.1   Classification Using Unimodal Prediction Models

Extracted facial features from the set of images provided in the datasets were input to the set of prescribed machine learning algorithms using Weka, with the

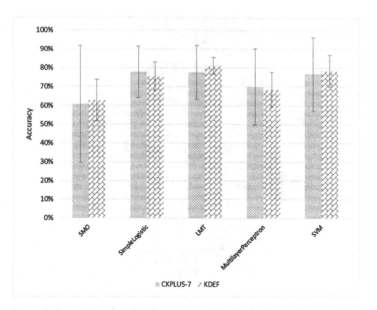

Fig. 4. Automatic facial expression classification accuracy of different machine learning techniques on CKPLUS-7 and KDEF datasets together with lower and upper bounds using a 95 % confidence interval

aim of measuring the resulting classification performance and to provide a comparison among the different classifiers. Subsequently, the classification accuracies obtained, along with the corresponding lower and upper bounds are depicted in Fig. 4. An interesting observation from the results shown in Fig. 4 is that some techniques outperform others, depending on the target dataset, yet SVM provides comparable performance on both the CKPLUS-7 and KDEF datasets. Therefore, SVM has been selected as the base component for use in further investigations.

4.2 Utilising a Distance-Based Facial Feature Representation

From a statistical analysis point of view, reducing the standard deviation indicates that the data is more clustered around the mean, which subsequently conveys the data is more consistent, thus potentially improves the result of classification process. Correspondingly, by calculating the average of standard deviation of all features across all instances we obtained 15.2 and 21.5 for distance-based features, and 32.6 and 40.7 for Cartesian coordinate features, for the CKPLUS-8 and KDEF datasets respectively. Subsequently, it implies that distance-based features contain less variation across all instances.

4.3   Classification Using Hierarchal SVM Model

As previously described in Sect. 3.3, the hierarchal model composed of two cascaded processes. First, a set of binary classifiers are executed in parallel, where each classifier is committed to detect one affective state. Therefore, the number of binary classifiers in this stage equals the number of emotional labels contained within the original dataset. For the purpose of validating any improvement achieved by the hierarchal model, we carried out experiments on the three datasets (CKPLUS-7, CKPLUS-8, and KDEF) using both normal and hierarchal SVM-based models. The results obtained are illustrated in Fig. 5. In terms of accuracy, as given in Fig. 5, the hierarchal model achieves 96.9 % while the normal model achieves 82.9 % for CKPLUS-7. Moreover, the hierarchal model achieves 95.7 %, while the normal model achieves 78.4 % for CKPLUS-8. Lastly, the hierarchal model achieves 96.2 % for KDEF, whereas the normal model achieves 81.8 %.

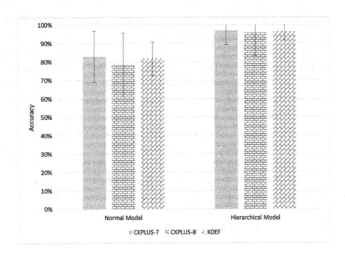

Fig. 5. Automatic facial expression classification accuracy, using normal and hierarchal models, on CKPLUS-7, CKPLUS-8 and KDEF datasets; together with lower and upper bounds using a 95 % confidence interval

5   Discussion

With regard to the hierarchal models advantages over other models given in the literature; based on our knowledge, the best recognition accuracy for CKPLUS-7 is 91.2 % using SVM applied on Histogram of Oriented Gradients (HOG) descriptor published in [19]. Furthermore, in the study reported in [13] an accuracy of 97.35 % was achieved using SVM applied on geometric features. However, their results are not necessarily directly comparable as only six classes (without contempt) of the CKPLUS dataset were used. In addition, the later study only

Table 2. Confusion matrix, precision, and recall of affective recognition for CKPLUS-7

	Anger	Contempt	Happy	Sadness	Surprise	Disgust	Fear	Recall
Anger	45	0	0	0	0	0	0	1.00
Contempt	0	17	0	1	0	0	0	0.94
Happy	1	0	61	6	0	1	0	0.88
Sadness	0	0	0	28	0	0	0	1.00
Surprise	0	0	0	1	82	0	0	0.99
Disgust	0	0	0	0	0	59	0	1.00
Fear	0	0	0	0	0	0	25	1.00
Precision	0.98	1.00	1.00	0.78	1.00	0.98	1.00	

adopted 5-fold cross validation. For the KDEF dataset, as reported in [7], the highest accuracy achieved was 89 % using the face reader software, which deploy Active Appearance Model (AAM) descriptors to train artificial neural network.

Table 2 presents the confusion matrix together with values for precision and recall for the classification results obtained from the experiments carried out using the hierarchal model applied to the CKPLUS-7. Accordingly, it seems that the precision of detecting states such as *happy* and *surprise* is comparably better than detecting other states such as *fear*, *anger*, *sadness*, and *disgust*. Interestingly, our results agree with facial expressions pronounce level model proposed by Joho et al. that *happy* and *surprise* states are high pronounced expressions, while *angry*, *disgust*, *fear* and *sad* are low pronounced [15]. Similarly, many instances had been misclassified to be *contempt*, which are actually *angry*, or *neutral* in CKPLUS-8 experiment. Likewise, 15 *sad* instances had been misclassified to *afraid* in KDEF experiment. This is potentially due to the similarity in the geometric shape of facial expressions for these states, which makes these states difficult for automatic recognition.

6 Conclusion and Future Works

Recognising affective states using automatic facial expression analysis is an intriguing research challenge. In this study we have explored different datasets across different machine learning models for the purpose of automatic affective state detection. However, the use of a feature representation that makes use of Euclidean distances between fiducial points, along with the use of Hierarchical Parallelised Binary Support Vector Machines yielded a considerable improvement in affective state classification. Further progress can be applied to use other modalities to complement classification weaknesses in distinguishing states such as *angry*, *disgust* and *fear*. Moreover, many challenges remain in applying such systems within a mobile context, which typically suffer from non-posed facial expression analysis and low quality image capture.

References

1. Afzal, S., Sezgin, T.M., Gao, Y., Robinson, P.: Perception of emotional expressions in different representations using facial feature points. In: Proceedings - 2009 3rd International Conference on Affective Computing and Intelligent Interaction and Workshops, ACII 2009 (2009)
2. Ahn, H.I., Picard, R.W.: Measuring affective-cognitive experience and predicting market success. IEEE Trans. Affect. Comput. **5**(2), 173–186 (2014)
3. Çınar Akakın, H., Sankur, B.: Spatiotemporal-boosted DCT features for head and face gesture analysis. In: Salah, A.A., Gevers, T., Sebe, N., Vinciarelli, A. (eds.) HBU 2010. LNCS, vol. 6219, pp. 64–74. Springer, Heidelberg (2010)
4. Asthana, A., Zafeiriou, S., Cheng, S., Pantic, M.: Incremental face alignment in the wild. In: Proceedings of the IEEE Computer Society Conference on Computer Vision and Pattern Recognition, pp. 1859–1866 (2014)
5. Busso, C., Deng, Z., Yildirim, S., Bulut, M.: Analysis of emotion recognition using facial expressions, speech and multimodal information. In: Proceedings of the 6th International Conference on Multimodal interfaces, pp. 205–211 (2004)
6. Chang, C.C., Lin, C.J.: LIBSVM - A Library for Support Vector Machines (2001), http://www.csie.ntu.edu.tw/~cjlin/libsvm/
7. Den Uyl, M.J., Van Kuilenburg, H.: The FaceReader: online facial expression recognition. Proc. Measuring Behav. **30**, 589–590 (2005)
8. Ekman, P., Friesen, W.V.: Constants across cultures in the face and emotion. J. Pers. Soc. Psychol. **17**(2), 124–129 (1971)
9. Ekman, P.: What scientists who study emotion agree about. Perspect. Psychol. Sci. **11**(1), 31–34 (2016)
10. Ekman, P., Friesen, W.V., Hager, J.C.: Facial Action Coding System - Investigator's Guide (2002)
11. EL-Manzalawy, Y.: WLSVM (2005), http://www.cs.iastate.edu/~yasser/wlsvm/
12. Fragopanagos, N., Taylor, J.G.: Emotion recognition in human-computer interaction. Neural Netw. Official J. Int. Neural Netw. Soc. **18**(4), 389–405 (2005)
13. Ghimire, D., Lee, J.: Geometric feature-based facial expression recognition in image sequences using multi-class AdaBoost and support vector machines. Sensors (Basel, Switzerland) **13**, 7714–7734 (2013)
14. Jiang, B., Valstar, M.F., Pantic, M.: Action unit detection using sparse appearance descriptors in space-time video volumes. In: 2011 IEEE International Conference on Automatic Face and Gesture Recognition and Workshops, FG 2011, pp. 314–321 (2011)
15. Joho, H., Jose, J.M., Valenti, R., Sebe, N.: Exploiting facial expressions for affective video summarisation. In: CIVR 2009, p. 1 (2009)
16. Kapoor, A., Burleson, W., Picard, R.W.: Automatic prediction of frustration. Int. J. Hum. Comput. Stud. **65**(8), 724–736 (2007)
17. Koller, D., Sahami, M.: Hierarchically classifying documents using very few words. In: Proceedings of the Fourteenth International Conference on Machine Learning, pp. 170–178 (1997)
18. Landwehr, N., Hall, M., Frank, E.: Logistic model trees. Mach. Learn. **59**(1–2), 161–205 (2005)
19. Liew, C.F., Yairi, T.: Facial expression recognition and analysis: a comparison study of feature descriptors. IPSJ Trans. Comput. Vis. Appl. **7**, 104–120 (2015)

20. Lucey, P., Cohn, J.F., Kanade, T., Saragih, J., Ambadar, Z., Matthews, I.: The extended Cohn-Kanade dataset (CK+): a complete dataset for action unit and emotion-specified expression. In: 2010 IEEE Computer Society Conference on Computer Vision and Pattern Recognition - Workshops, CVPRW 2010, pp. 94–101 (2010)

21. Lundqvist, D., Flykt, A., Ohman, A.: The Karolinska directed emotional faces (KDEF). CD ROM from Department of Clinical Neuroscience, Psychology section, Karolinska Institutet, pp. 91–630 (1998)

22. Martinez, A.M.: Deciphering the face. In: IEEE Computer Society Conference on Computer Vision and Pattern Recognition Workshops (2011)

23. McDuff, D., Gontarek, S., Picard, R.: Remote measurement of cognitive stress via heart rate variability. In: 36th Annual International Conference of the IEEE Engineering in Medicine and Biology Society (EMBC), pp. 2957–2960. IEEE (2014)

24. Oliver, N.: LAFTER: a real-time face and lips tracker with facial expression recognition. In: CVPR, vol. 33, pp. 1369–1382 (1997)

25. Picard, R.W.: Affective Computing. MIT Press, Cambridge (2000)

26. Platt, J.C.: Fast training of support vector machines using sequential minimal optimization. In: Advances in Kernel Methods, pp. 185–208 (1998)

27. Posner, J., Russell, J.A., Peterson, B.S.: The circumplex model of affect: an integrative approach to affective neuroscience, cognitive development, and psychopathology. Dev. Psychopathol. **17**, 715–734 (2005)

28. Salah, a., Sebe, N., Gevers, T.: Communication and automatic interpretation of affect from facial expressions. Affective Computing and Interaction, pp. 157–183 (2009)

29. Shan, C., Gong, S., McOwan, P.W.: Beyond facial expressions: learning human emotion from body gestures. In: Procedings of the British Machine Vision Conference 2007, pp. 43.1-43.10 (2007)

30. Shan, C., Gong, S., McOwan, P.W.: Facial expression recognition based on Local Binary Patterns: a comprehensive study. Image Vis. Comput. **27**(6), 803–816 (2009)

31. Soleymani, M., Pantic, M., Pun, T.: Multimodal emotion recognition in response to videos. IEEE Trans. Affect. Comput. **3**, 211–223 (2012)

32. Sullivan, J.W., Tyler, S.W.: Intelligent User Interfaces. ACM Press Series. ACM Press, New York (1991)

33. Vega, K., Arrieta, A., Esteves, F., Fuks, H.: FX e-Makeup for muscle based interaction. In: Marcus, A. (ed.) DUXU 2014. LNCS, vol. 8519, pp. 643–652. Springer, Heidelberg (2014). doi:10.1007/978-3-319-07635-5_61

34. Whitehill, J., Bartlett, M., Movellan, J.: Automatic facial expression recognition for intelligent tutoring systems. In: 2008 IEEE Computer Society Conference on Computer Vision and Pattern Recognition Workshops, pp. 1–6 (2008)

Alternative Reality: An Augmented Daily Urban World Inserting Virtual Scenes Temporally

Fumiko Ishizawa and Tatsuo Nakajima^(✉)

Department of Computer Science and Engineering, Waseda University, Tokyo, Japan
{f.ishizawa,tatsuo}@dcl.cs.waseda.ac.jp

Abstract. In this paper, we propose a new design strategy for integrating fictionality into the real world named *Alternative Reality, which* makes it possible to connect the daily urban world with the virtual world from a temporal aspect to influence humans to adopt better lifestyles. The worlds also can be seamlessly integrated because the virtual world consists of real landscapes, objects and persons. This means that it may be possible to enhance the real world by showing fictional events among real events: people experience the enhanced hybrid world as in the real world rather than in a fictional world such as a movie. To demonstrate the design strategy of *Alternative Reality*, we have developed two case studies. The first case study investigates whether a user can sense the improbable behavior of a moving object as realistic, where the user can interact with the object. The second case study investigates whether a user can experience fictional occurrences in the virtual world as they are experienced in the real world. In both case studies, a user wears a head-mounted display to increase the immersion in the hybrid world created by *Alternative Reality*, in which the virtual world is created by capturing the real world with a 360-degree camera. The insights of the experiments with the case studies show that *Alternative Reality* effectively augments the real world without losing touch with reality.

Keywords: Embedding fictionality · Virtual reality · Augmented reality · Head mounted display · Behavior changes

1 Introduction

Augmented reality (AR) technologies have become popular for developing a variety of entertainment services. AR is typically used to spatially present virtual images or textual information superimposed on the real world either to help people make better decisions or to present remarkable expressions [1]. The potential power of AR makes it possible to change the semiotic meaning of the real world, strongly influencing human attitudes and behavior to adopt a better lifestyle, thus solving common social problems such as environmental sustainability. Typical AR approaches can simply integrate computer-generated virtual images into the real world. The images typically present invisible information that cannot be seen by a user in the real world. Although it is possible to show fictional images to enhance the meaning of the real world, this approach limits the potential power because only some pieces of real-world objects can be enhanced.

© Springer International Publishing AG 2016
C.R. García et al. (Eds.): UCAmI 2016, Part I, LNCS 10069, pp. 353–364, 2016.
DOI: 10.1007/978-3-319-48746-5_36

In contrast, current virtual reality (VR) technologies make it possible to create a new fictional (but realistic) virtual world by using 3D models of real persons, objects and landscapes in the real world; it is possible to present fictional events in the virtual world because believe that the events actually happened in the real world.

This paper proposes a new design strategy named *Alternative Reality,* which overcomes the drawbacks of AR techniques by integrating VR techniques; a new type of ambient intelligence experience can be offered. Although a user watches the real world, some scenes of the real world may be temporally replaced in favor of virtual scenes that are actually represented as the virtual world for a short period; however, he/she is not aware of the inserted virtual world and feels that the fictionality in the virtual world actually occurs in the real world because real landscapes, persons and objects are used to construct the virtual world.

Because the hybrid real world can be represented abstractly, remarkably, or ironically as fictional virtual scenes through framing to either simplify or exaggerate essential concepts in our daily lives, people easily notice important concepts that are relevant to achieving an ideal, sustainable society through fictionality [17]. Accordingly, this approach can be used to overcome serious social problems through human behavior change [21].

In *Alternative Reality*, a user wears a head-mounted display (HMD) and the virtual world watched by the user consists of real landscapes and real persons constructed as a 360-degree video movie; thus, the user can interactively navigate the virtual world. Because the virtual world is seamlessly integrated with and temporally connected to the real world, a user feels that fictional events in the virtual world are performed in the real world even though the virtual-world events are not real. This approach provides a novel method of enhancing the meaning of the real world to develop advanced ambient intelligence experiences, thereby integrating the transmedia storytelling approach to incorporate fictionality into the real world [8].

In this paper, after presenting an overview of *Alternative Reality*, we introduce its basic concept. To demonstrate the feasibility of the concept, we have developed two case studies in which fictional events occur in a real location. The first case study investigates whether a user can believe that the improbable behavior of a moving object is realistic, where the user can interact with the object. The second case study investigates whether a user can experience fictional occurrences in the virtual world as in the real world. In both case studies, a user wears an HMD to increase the immersions of the hybrid world created by *Alternative Reality*, in which the virtual world is created by capturing the real world with a 360-degree camera. We conducted user studies to extract insights that would help us investigate the feasibility of the *Alternative Reality* concept, even though the current work is still at a preliminary stage. The insights of the experiments with the case studies show that *Alternative Reality* effectively augments the real world without losing sight of reality.

2   A Framework for Augmenting Real World Through Inserting Virtual Scenes Temporally

There are several ways to incorporate fictionality into the real world. One typical approach is to use live action role playing (LARP) [12] or alternative reality games (ARG) [10]. During LARP, players play fictional roles based on a pervasive role-playing concept [11] and a game master to control the gap between fiction and reality. ARG adopts a concept named transmedia storytelling [18], using multiple media to incorporate fictional stories into the real world. These approaches are promising, but the approach requires a rigorous plan that requires a long time to reduce the gap between fiction and reality. Augmented reality and virtual reality technologies offer another possibility to incorporate fictionality into the real world. For example, in [14, 22], by using head-mounted displays, a user immersively changes the meaning of the real world to alter his or her attitude and behavior.

In *Alternative Reality*, a user watches a sequence of scenes on an HMD. As shown in Fig. 1, the sequence consists of several scenes. Some scenes are captured from present scenes in the real world (Real Scenes in Fig. 1). The scenes are recorded by a 360-degree camera, and shown on the HMD in real time.[1] However, some scenes in the sequence are not real; the scenes might be actually constructed through VR techniques and are fictional (Virtual Scenes in Fig. 1). Additionally, in the virtual scenes, several events might not occur in the real world as it is now. In particular, Fig. 1 presents that there are two persons in the room. One person watches the room through an HMD. Real scene A or C is a video that captures the room as it is in the present. Virtual scene B or D is a video that captured the room in the past. The person who wears an HMD watches the virtual scenes and he/she can feel that the other person is in front of him/her. However, in the real world, the person is actually behind him/her.

Typically, the scenes are constructed using the 3D models of real persons, objects and landscapes in advance, but some real persons who might not be actually present now can appear. One of the important requirements of *Alternative Reality* is that a user feels that these real and virtual scenes are continuous and thus is unaware of the boundary between the two scenes. The magic circle is defined as the boundary between the real world and the virtual world [15]. If a user is not aware of a magic circle between the worlds developed by *Alternative Reality*, the user cannot notice that the virtual world generated by *Alternative Reality* is not real. Therefore, he/she feels that the virtual scenes actually happen in the real world. The most important issue in realizing immersion blurs the magic circle. The use of an HMD offers a better immersive experience by showing a video stream that captures the real world and then replacing some real components in the video stream with fictional components [16].

Several previous investigations used a 3D model composed from real scenes. For example, in [2], a user interacts with the 3D model of a building to learn routes inside

---

[1] In the first experiment, a camera is deployed behind a user, and only the center of the captured image is trimmed and shown on his/her HMD. When the user tilts his/her head, the trimmed area shown on the HMD moves in accordance with the movement of the head. This approach simulates a 360-degree movie.

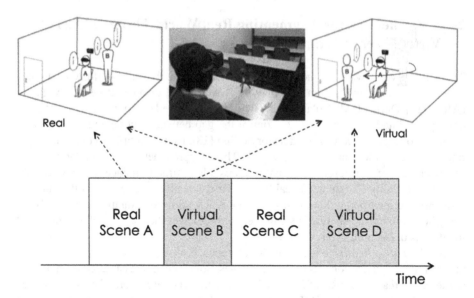

Fig. 1. A timeline model of alternative reality

the building. The user can learn the real routes in the real town in the virtual world. *Alternative Reality* similarly uses the virtual world composed from real persons and landscapes, but the virtual world may contain probable events in the possible future that either might not actually occur in the real world or are fictional events. The events and the stories created from them are perceived as an experience in the real world. By integrating possible future or fictional events into real events, a user can accept the events as his/her own real, present experience; thus, the presented stories can influence the user's future behavior [7].

Here, we show two typical examples of the benefits of adopting the *Alternative Reality* concept:

- Pervasive Game: Pervasive games enable us to play games in the real world [12]. Extending a user's experience from the pervasive game's world to the hybrid (real and virtual) world would be easier with *Alternative Reality*.
- Overcoming Social Problems: Behavior changes are essential to overcome various social problems [6, 26]. *Alternative Reality* enables an awareness of social problems such as environmental or health issues because people notice more easily the effect of the future events shown as *Alternative Reality*.

In this paper, we focus on the feasibility of the *Alternative Reality* approach to influencing human behavior and extract some useful insights to develop services based on *Alternative Reality*.

3   Case Studies

The current case studies demonstrate the feasibility of *Alternative Reality*, for which we have developed movies that connect real and virtual scenes. In the case-study experiments, we presented the movies to participants by wearing HMDs and interacting with the 360-degree movies by moving the participants' heads. Although the case studies did not present the full potential of *Alternative Reality*, we can still extract useful insights and potential pitfalls to guide our approach towards the next step.

3.1   Interactive Improbable Object

"Interactive Improbable Objects" has been developed as a first case study, which is a movie in which a moving object with which a user can interact behaves in an improbable way. A user watches the movie through an HMD (Oculus Rift[2]). This experiment investigates whether a user believes an object's improbable behavior to be realistic when the object reflects his/her interaction.

In the *"Interactive Improbable Objects"* experiment, participants watched the movie as scenes taking place before them in the present. Because the movie is captured with a 360-degree camera (BublCam[3]) from the participants' locations and they watched it through HMDs, they can feel the movie as though it is the present real world. In the movie, virtual scenes show a moving object, but that object's movement usually is not natural in the real world. However, the object does return feedback with the participant's interaction. For example, when he/she asks a question of the object, it stops to listen to him/her and turns its head toward him/her. The movie is captured in advance as time-lapse imaging and is shown with 15 fps. Figure 2 shows some of the time-lapse images in the movie. An object moves from left to right (left scenes in Fig. 2). When a user asks the object a question, the object stops to listen to the user's voice and turns its head to him/her (right scenes in Fig. 2). When a participant speaks to the object, as shown in the right-hand scenes of Fig. 2, the object reacts to his/her voice.

Eleven participants participated in the experiment and were the subject of semi-structured interviews. In the interviews, we asked participants whether they feel the moving objects to be strange. In addition, we asked whether the movement becomes realistic by allowing them to interact with the object.

Most of participants said that at first, the object's unexpected movement amazed them; however, they gradually felt that the movement was realistic and that they experienced no uncomfortable feeling related to the improbably moving object. Moreover, some of them said, *"The object was like a machine because it was moving regularly"*. However, once they interacted with the object, most of participants said that it looked like a living thing. Offering interaction with an artificial object makes it believable as a living thing with its own will.

One design issue that is important for increasing the reality of an improbable object is the fact that people usually predict how to move the object based on either their

---

[2] https://www.oculus.com/.
[3] http://www.bublcam.com/.

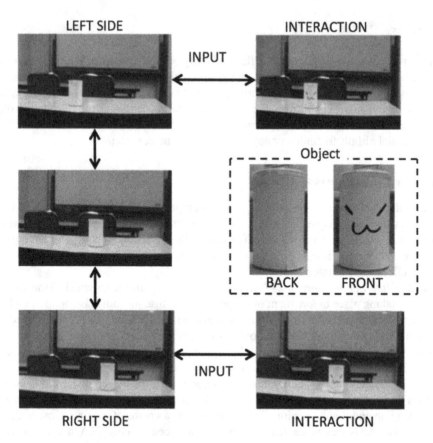

Fig. 2. Interactive improbable object

technological predictions or past experiences. For example, we can easily predict the movement of an object that has wheels or whose shape is like a humanoid robot. From the results of the experiment, the movement also becomes acceptable when it obeys physical laws. In the case study, if the object moves with a simple harmonic motion, a participant feels the movement as though the object is a living thing; however, he/she could find the movement unnatural or mechanical if it moves with uniformly linear motion.

To achieve interaction with an object as a living thing, its latency in returning feedback is also important. When there is a time lag before the object's head turns when a participant asks a question, the participant will not feel that the object is truly a living thing.

3.2   Fictional Future

"*Fictional Future*" has been developed as a second case study that is a movie containing both present and possible future occurrences to demonstrate the *Alternative Reality* concept. The case study is performed by real persons whom know well each other and in real locations known to the participants such that the users believe that these occurrences are real. This case study is similar to the one developed to demonstrate the feasibility of the Substitutional Reality (SR) system [25].

In the *"Fictional Future"* experiment, a participant watched three movies that were merged into one movie through an HMD similar to *"Interactive Improbable Objects"*. The first movie is a real-time captured movie that shows the current real location in detail. The second and the third movies are constructed based on the *Alternative Reality* concept and the scenes in the movies are scenes performed in the past as a possible future. The second movie was performed by an experimenter and captured the scene of the experimenter and participant entering the room. The third movie was performed by the experimenter and consisted of possible future occurrences, such as gratefully giving money, which the experimenter believes has happened. Figure 3 shows the screenshots of the second and third movies. In Fig. 3, the first photo shows the second movie where a participant and an experimenter entered a room as a past event, the second photo shows third movie where the lady moved ahead as a possible future event. Finally, the third photo presents the third movie where the lady explained the occurrences as a possible future event. After watching the merged movie, when the participant removed the HMD, the experimenter performed the same activities performed in the third movie. Thus, a participant watches the same scene shown in the third movie.

Eleven participants participated in the *"Fictional Future"* experiment, and we conducted semi-structured interviews with the participants. In the interviews, we asked participants whether they feel that the possible future in *"Fictional Future"* actually happened in the real world. If their answers were positive, we also asked them why they felt that the potential future depicted represented reality.

Some of them said, *"After taking off the HMD, when I was viewing the scenes shown in the third movie, I felt déjà vu to be seeing the same scenes again."* This means that the participants experienced the merged movie made by the *Alternative Reality* concept as real scenes and that after they removed their HMDs, they felt that they had seen the scene before. Additionally, some participants said, *"I felt and expected that the activities in the future movie would happen because the activities are desirable and make me happy"*. Similarly, after the experiment, a participant asked, *"Can I get some money?"* This is because we explained the concept of money given in gratitude in the third movie; this comment means that the participant believed in the possible future presented in the third movie.

One interesting finding of the experiments is that people tend to think that the performed events are real if the activities are common or desirable. This enables us to believe that the events occur in the real world as it is right now. Additionally, the realistic landscape is a key to making the depicted events realistic. However, of course, it is important to ensure a sense of the reality of the virtual scenes. If a user loses a sense of that reality, the user confuses what happens in his/her present life and is aware of the "magic circle" boundary because he/she may feel that even real scenes are not real. A user also tends to remember remarkable situations. When a participant feels déjà vu in the experiment, it is typical that these events, such as putting a doll on a desk, touching a doll, or leaving a room, are noticed.

Fig. 3. Fictional Future

3.3 Design Implication

One important design issue implicated by *Alternative Reality* is whether a user feels that virtual scenes represent reality. As shown in [7], increasing visual reality is not the only way to make a user sense reality. The feasibility studies described in this section present some evidence that even events that did not actually occur in the real world can be incorporated into the real world without losing reality. More specifically, the results from the first case study demonstrate the feasibility of an unrealistic fictional event that can offer very strong stimuli for designing advanced, pervasive games. However, our current participants may be the most accustomed to virtual content such as animations or movies making improbable objects feel realistic. For example, one participant said, *"I have seen this movement in some movies"*. Conversely, another participant from a foreign country said, *"In my country, a moving object by itself is thought as something like a ghost"*. He also said that the experience was scary and uncomfortable. We need to design fictionality in *Alternative Reality* according to a user's experiences and culture.

As shown in [17], fictionality has a powerful persuasive effect to overcome serious social problems. *Alternative Reality* offers powerful persuasiveness through immersively incorporated fictionality. More specifically, as shown in [13], the persuasive power of fictionality can be increased by presenting it as transmedia storytelling. The second case study demonstrated how to insert virtual scenes so that they would not lose their reality. The virtual scenes may be portions of transmedia stories that can teach people the importance of overcoming their problems. Persuasiveness designed as digital rhetoric is a promising direction for offering abstractions to design the enhancement of meaning in the real world [20]; the abstraction can be used to design virtual scenes that influence human attitude and behavior more easily.

4   Related Work

Augmented reality techniques can be used to enhance existing artifacts. For example, [27] describes several augmented reality games that are enhanced versions of traditional physical games. Specifically, *Augmented Go* [9] demonstrates a promising approach to maintaining the advantages of the physicality of the board game while adding virtuality. *Virtual Aquarium* [13] shows a virtual fish tank in which the movement of the fish reflects a user's tooth-brushing behavior. *Enhanced TCG* [23] enhances our real world by replacing a real-world component with a fictional component for changing the semiotic meaning of the real world.

Most recently, digital marketing and social media practitioners have referred to this approach as *gamification*. The addition of *badges* and *leaderboards* is a typical approach to achieving gamification [3]. The idea is to use game mechanics, such as those in online games, to make a task entertaining, thus encouraging people to conscientiously complete target goals. In [5], gamification is defined from a service-marketing perspective as follows: "*A process of enhancing a service with affordances for gameful experience to support user's overall value.*" In traditional gamification, a set of game mechanics is widely adopted for motivating human behavior; however, incorporating game mechanics into the real world is not easy. Thus, simple mechanics such as badges, leaderboards and points are typically used.

When attempting to solve serious social problems such as sustainability issues, health issues, and happiness [6, 26], guiding people's attitudes and behaviors is an important design issue. Enhancing the semiotic meaning of the real world through incorporated virtuality is a powerful technique for altering people's attitudes and behaviors [19]. As shown in [24], procedural rhetoric is a promising theoretical foundation to increase persuasiveness by making the enhanced real world meaningful.

Several case studies use augmented reality technologies to enhance the meaning of the real world, thus influencing people's behavior. For example, in [22], the authors propose a service to both implicitly influence people's satisfaction while drinking a beverage and to control beverage consumption by creating a volume perception illusion using augmented reality technologies. The system proposed in [14] realizes a method for modifying perceptions of satiety and controlling nutritional intake by changing the apparent size of food with augmented reality technologies.

In [4], Dunne and Raby use design to offer new forms of expression for complex and critical issues; these forms of expression are grounded in the most abstract, speculative and future-focused considerations. Critical questions about emerging technology in everyday situations have presented preferable futures as opposed to predicting the future. They call this design approach *Speculative Design*. The approach taken in *Alternative Reality* can be considered an example of *Speculative Design* because the aim is to investigate whether a user feels as though he/she is watching a future scene when the scene uses only components that exist in the real world.

Some works produced by Sputniko! are similar to *Alternative Reality*. For example, popular works such as *Crowbot Jenny* and *Menstruation Machine, Takashi's Take* use only existing persons, landscapes and prototype artifacts to create futuristic movies (http://sputniko.com/works/). Although they are similar to science fiction movies or fantasy dramas, these movies do not use unrealistic artifacts; instead, they present influences and debates by introducing emerging new technologies in our real lives. However, these art works traditionally do not offer the artists' explicit interpretations; instead, interpretation is open for audiences. Thus, audiences may feel that art is boring because they cannot understand its meaning.

5   Conclusion

In this paper, we proposed *Alternative Reality*, which enables us to change the meaning of the daily urban world by inserting fictional virtual scenes among real scenes. The virtual scenes are constructed from real-world components so that a user believes that the virtual scenes actually take place in the real world. to demonstrate the design strategy of *Alternative Reality*, we have developed two case studies. The first case study investigates whether a user can feel that the improbable behavior of a moving object is realistic, where the user can interact with the object. The second case study investigates whether a user can experience fictional events in the virtual world as they are experienced in the real world. We extracted some insights that can be used to develop future services based on *Alternative Reality*.

As future directions, we consider the following two issues. The first issue is to discuss the relationship among similar frameworks, particularly the *gameful digital-rhetoric framework* [21] and the *value-based analysis framework* [19]. We need to discuss how these frameworks are mutually related, along with possibilities to integrate these frameworks into a more generalized framework. The second issue is to explore the possibility of using advanced ubiquitous computing technologies for designing methods of persuasion. Sensing technologies enable us to develop persuasive methods that are customized for each person. Moreover, advanced wearable technologies may change the perceived meaning of the real world. The studied technologies allow us to develop more effective persuasive methods. We also need to discuss how procedural rhetoric concept is related to persuasive methods that are enhanced through ubiquitous computing technologies.

In the next step, we will try to develop and evaluate a new prototype service based on the *Alternative Reality* concept. This service will present a long fictional scene to a user, where the scene embeds several persuasive messages ambiently. We like to evaluate whether he/she feels that the scene occurs in the real world and how the scene influences the user's behavior changes when the user watches the scene. The new service will show the essential persuasive power of *Alternative Reality* and indicates the potentiality that the current case studies could not clarify.

References

1. Azuma, R.T.: A survey of augmented reality. Presence **6**(4), 355–385 (1997)
2. Bailey, J.H., Knerr, B.W., Witmer, B.G.: Virtual Spaces and real world places: transfer of route knowledge. Int. J. Hum Comput. Stud. **45**(4), 307–321 (1996)
3. Deterding, S., Dixon, D., Khaled, R., Nacke, N.: From game design elements to gamefulness: defining "Ramification". In: Proceedings of the 15th International Academic MindTrek Conference: Envisioning Future Media Environments (2011)
4. Dunne, A., Raby, F.: Speculative Everything: Design, Fiction, and Social Dreaming. MIT Press, Cambridge (2013)
5. Huotari, K., Hamari, J.: Defining gamification – a service marketing perspective. In: Proceedings of the 16th International Academic Mindtrek Conference, pp. 17–22 (2012)
6. Institute of Government: MINDSPACE: Influencing Behavior through Public Policy, CabinetOffice (2010)
7. Ishizawa, F., Takahashi, M., Irie, K., Sakamoto, M., Nakajima, T.: Analyzing augmented real spaces gamifed through fictionality. In: Proceedings of the 13th International Conference on Advances in Mobile Computing and Multimedia (2015)
8. Ishizawa, F., Sakamoto, M., Nakajima, T.: A service design framework for designing alternative reality experiences. DCL Technical Report DCL-2016-2. Waseda University (2016)
9. Iwata, T., Yamabe, T., Nakajima, T.: Augmented reality go: extending traditional game play with interactive self-learning support. In: Proceedings of the 17th IEEE Conference on Embedded and Real-time Computing Systems and Applications, pp. 105–114 (2011)
10. McGonigal, J.: Reality Is Broken: Why Games Make Us Better and How They Can Change the World. Penguin Press, New York (2011)
11. Montola, M.: Tangible pleasures of pervasive role-playing. In: Proceedings of International Conference on DiGRA 2007 (2007)
12. Montola, M., Stemros, J., Waern, A.: Pervasive Games - Theory and Design. Morgan Kaufmann, San Francisco (2009)
13. Nakajima, T., Lehdonvirta, V.: Designing motivation in persuasive ambient mirrors. Pers. Ubiquit. Comput. **17**(1), 107–126 (2013)
14. Narumi, T., Ban, Y., Kajinami, T., Tanikawa, T., Hirose, M.: Augmented perception of satiety: controlling food consumption by changing apparent size of food with augmented reality. In: Proceedings of the Conference on Human Factors in Computing Systems (2012)
15. Nieuwdorp, E.: The pervasive interface: tracing the magic circle. In: Proceedings of DiGRA 2005 Conference: Changing Views – Worlds in Play (2005)
16. Rolland, J., Biocca, F., Hamza-Lup, F., Yanggang, H., Martins, R.: Development of head-mounted projection displays for distributed, collaborative, augmented reality applications. Presence Teleoperators Virtual Environ. **14**(5), 528–549 (2005)

17. Sakamoto, M., Nakajima, T.: Gamifying intelligent daily environments through introducing fictionality. Int. J. Hybrid Inf. Technol. **7**(4), 259–276 (2014)
18. Sakamoto, M., Nakajima, T.: Incorporating fictionality into the real world with transmedia storytelling. In: Marcus, A. (ed.) DUXU 2015. LNCS, vol. 9186, pp. 654–665. Springer, Heidelberg (2015)
19. Sakamoto, M., Nakajima, T., Alexandrova, T.: Enhancing values through virtuality for intelligent artifacts that influence human attitude and behavior. Multimedia Tools Appl. **74**(24), 11537–11568 (2015)
20. Sakamoto, M., Nakajima, T.: In search of the right design abstraction for designing persuasive affordance towards a flourished society. In: Proceeding of the 9th International Conference on Design and Semantics of Form and Movement (2015)
21. Sakamoto, M., Nakajima, T., Akioka, S.: Gamifying collective human behavior with gameful digital rhetoric. Multimedia Tools Appl. (2016). doi:10.1007/s11042-016-3665-y
22. Suzuki, E., Narumi, T., Sakurai, S., Tanikawa, T., Hirose, M.: Illusion cup: interactive controlling of beverage consumption based on an illusion of volume perception. In: Proceedings of the 5th Augmented Human International Conference (2014)
23. Takahashi, M., Irie, K., Sakamoto, M., Nakajima, T.: Incorporating fictionality into the real space: a case of enhanced TCG. In: Proceedings of the 2015 ACM International JoinConference on Pervasive and Ubiquitous Computing and Proceedings of the 2015 ACM International Symposium on Wearable Computers (2015)
24. Treanor, M., Schweizer, B., Bogost, I., Mateas, M.: Proceduralist readings: how to find meaning in games with graphical logics. In: Proceedings of Foundations of Digital Games (2011)
25. Wakisama, S., Fujii, N., Suzuki, K.: Substitutional Reality System: A Novel Experimental Platform for Experiencing Alternative Reality, Scientific Reports (2012). doi:10.1038/srep00459
26. Wolfe, A.K., Malone, E.L., Heerwagen, J., Dion, J.: Behavioral Change and Building Performance: Strategies for Significant, Persistent, and Measurable Institutional Change, US Department of Energy (2014)
27. Yamabe, T., Nakajima, T.: Playful training with augmented reality games: case studies toward reality-oriented system design. Multimedia Tools Appl. **62**(1), 259–286 (2013)

Designing an End-User Augmented Reality Editor for Cultural Practitioners

Marco Romano[✉], Ignacio Aedo, and Paloma Díaz

Information Technology Department, Universidad Carlos III de Madrid, Madrid, Spain
{mromano,pdp}@inf.uc3m.es, aedo@ia.uc3m.es

Abstract. Nowadays, the rapid spread of new technologies has certainly revolutionized the way how people communicate and access information. Cultural practitioners deal with this issue endlessly and look to the new technologies as an opportunity to enhance their results in terms of exhibit experience and expressiveness. Such technology adoption needs to come along with the development of tools that make it possible for cultural practitioners to freely develop their ideas. The design of such tools for a specific category of users requires a deep knowledge of that category in order to establish appropriate usability requirements. In this paper we present a participatory design process aimed at defining solutions to support cultural practitioners in developing augmented reality applications for the specific cultural domain.

Keywords: Augmented reality · Mobile devices · Participatory design · System usability · End-user

1 Introduction

Nowadays, modern technologies are always more and more present and essential in our daily activities. Such increased exposure to the technology can cause some challenges especially to younger people. Indeed, they not only will have developed a habit to use technology to look for information and to interact with others, but also they might have developed different ways of learning [1]. For such reasons there is a growing interest in making the culture "enjoyable" to this new kind of users. A quick adoption of the technology is general notable in cultural sites (CSs) that are progressively enhanced with augmented and virtual reality systems. The use of augmented reality (AR) systems in CSs is not a particularly recent practice. Back in 1999, Brogni et al. [2] tried to envision the future of AR systems in CSs based on some kind of wearable or mobile devices. Nowadays, despite the expectations raised by devices supporting AR, such as large see-through screens or holograms, the most common solutions are mobile devices. Indeed, these devices are generally technically feasible and affordable as explained in [3], where authors integrate common smartphones in contextualized objects to create full interactive AR systems for museums and archeological sites. Another example is given by Veenhof and Skwarek in 2010 who organized an uninvited AR art exhibition at the

C.R. García et al. (Eds.): UCAmI 2016, Part I, LNCS 10069, pp. 365–371, 2016.
DOI: 10.1007/978-3-319-48746-5_37

MoMA[1] NYC. Visitors were invited to use their phones to discover several hidden digital artworks in the museum's rooms. A last example is Casa Batlló[2] (Spain), where visitors can experience a virtual and augmented visit using a provided smartphone.

However, as explained in [4], to integrate these technologies in specific domains and efficiently support users, their growth needs to come along with the development of authoring tools. This is because it is paramount to include cultural practitioners into the design of cultural applications [5]. End-user programmers, indeed, are those users who program to support some goal in their own domains of expertise [6]. Moreover, end-user development is an essential activity rather than a luxury because it is impossible to design artefacts for all the problems that occur at use time [7].

Companies are trying to meet the needs of non-programmer end-users proposing generic solutions. Augment[3], Layar[4], Aurasma[5], Wikitude[6] are some examples allowing users to produce their own AR mobile applications. Users can upload to a web application their artworks, associate them to a pattern or to an image to augment and then download the AR application for their mobile platform. However, all these applications are designed for generic users without considering specific needs or abilities. Moreover, they allow to create applications using a regular computer, this entails users will be able to experiment their work just in a second step and maybe in a different context. This can be annoying and may cause usability problems.

Given this context, the goal of our research is to lay the foundations for developing AR end-user programming (EUP) tools to support cultural practitioners. We take in mind that such EUP tools must not divert the professional objectives; they have to bridge the technological gap and allow practitioners to focus especially on their own domains of expertise.

2   Designing an AR EUP Editor for Cultural Practitioners

With a view to understand how to support end-users in the AR domain, we adopted a participatory approach [8] where stakeholders were involved in the elicitation and analysis of the requirements of potential technological solutions. During this process, interviews and field work were conducted. In particular, we conducted three interviews: one with an architectural and environmental engineering researcher who works in the digital reconstruction of ancient buildings; a second with an artist who likes to experiment several technologies for her exhibitions and, a third interview with the technological manager (TM) of an Italian IT start up. Below we report some of the most relevant considerations.

The first interviewee told us about the experience in developing an AR system to make people better envision ancient eras of a modern city: "*Even if our research group*

---

[1] www.moma.org.
[2] www.casabatllo.es/en/visit/videoguide.
[3] www.augment.com.
[4] www.layar.com.
[5] studio.aurasma.com.
[6] studio.wikitude.com.

has basic programming skills and we bought a AR framework to make it easier, developing the system is a really time-consuming task while we are supposed to be mainly focused on other aspects". Also the artist, gave a similar consideration. She stated, on the one hand, that modern technologies are a little limiting, because often requires specific technical knowledge and, on the other, a strong push to the expressiveness. However, artists not only often cannot afford for IT practitioners' services, but also need to individually manage the technology to bend it to the own necessities. This is rarely possible and move the artists' focus far from their specific domain of expertise. The last interview with the TM gave us a different point of view. The development of such systems is a non-trivial task for potential clients. Indeed, they not only need IT practitioners to develop a software system but need also to prepare digital content. Then, they have to work in close contact with developers and learn how to express their ideas, provide material and also understand some technical problems.

Starting from the field study we started our brainstorming activities to envision ways to allow end-users to develop their own AR applications. Such activities led us to elicit an initial set of requirements: (1) an AR editor must provide an approach based on visual interaction. The end-users can be from disparate extractions, just some of them possess some basic programming knowledge and generally consider programming a costly and extra activity (2) The physical space of the exhibit must be considered as an integrating part of the AR creation. Therefore, the editor must provide users with functionalities supporting the mobility, such as taking pictures of the objects to be augmented and previewing the final result directly in situ. (3) The EUP system is ubiquitous. The exhibit is prepared by a creator through a EUP tool and will be explored by other stakeholders, which are the visitors. The visitor experience will depend on different factors including the devices used to explore the exhibit. They can be with different screen sizes, such as tablets, smartphones or wearable. Moreover, the devices choice depends also on the available financial recourses. Therefore, the system must be able to deploy the AR experiences on different hardware platforms and automatically synchronize them in a way transparent to the users. (4) The system must be able to manage different media, the digital content that can be superimposed to the reality is heterogeneous.

2.1 Prototype

In order to develop our EUP AR editor, we took into account all the requirements produced during the field study. First of all, the system will exploit common and cheap technologies such as regular mobile devices running Android. Then, it will allow users to produce their digital content in the way they prefer, using the same mobile device or their computer. Finally, it automatizes complex tasks such as content synchronization between different devices. The solution is distributed on two main applications: one for tablets and one for smartphones. The former allows creators to work directly in situ and develop their own AR exhibit. The smartphone application is a merely viewer of the AR exhibit. Figure 1 shows the architecture of the system.

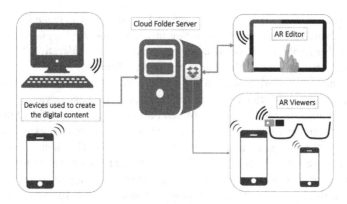

Fig. 1. The system architecture. The cloud server synchronizes the content with the editor. The AR exhibits produced by the editor are synchronized with the AR viewer devices

The tablet application is based on a 10 inched screen Samsung tablet equipped with Android 5.1.1W. It integrates the Wikitude 5.1.4 framework that allows to easily recognize images through the phone camera and to superimpose digital elements on them. The editor allows to create an AR exhibit that is a collection of AR elements specific for a selection of exhibited objects. Figure 2 shows its workflow.

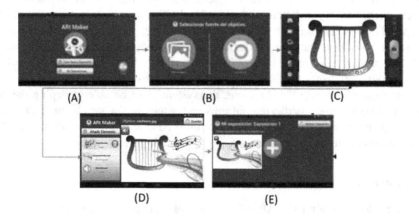

Fig. 2. The AR editor workflow

First, users have to create or modify an exhibit (fig. A). For each exhibit they can add several targets to be augmented. The targets can be loaded from the internal mobile gallery or the users can take a picture through the application (fig. B, C). This is to allow creators to work directly in situ. Then, users can drag and drop digital elements on the target image (fig. D). The elements are synchronized with the cloud storage Dropbox through the Core API[7]. The editor accepts disparate type of files. There is no limit to the number of digital elements that can be added to a single target. Then, users can save the

---

[7] www.dropbox.com/developers-v1/core.

AR object and add a new one (fig. E). When the users are satisfied of their exhibit they can save it and check the result. The second application is designed for running on any android device with small or larger screens, it is also able to run on android AR glasses such as Google Glass. The application is a simple AR viewer. It automatically synchronizes the AR exhibits through the shared folder and allows to select between different existing exhibits. The idea is that the exhibition organization provides visitors with the smartphones instead of the typical audio guides and the deployment process is totally transparent for the creators (Fig. 3).

Fig. 3. The harp is the target image of the AR while the other images are the AR content

2.2 Evaluation

A usability pilot study was carried out to understand the potential of the editor prototype. The goal was to evaluate the quality of the interaction in terms of ease to use and user satisfaction. In the first part of the study we involved four usability experts to carry out a usability walkthrough. The second part was a prototype review with the artist who participated during the field study.

Regarding the walkthrough, we asked to the three experts to evaluate the usability of the developed prototype. The experts were informed about the profiles of the potential stakeholders and then introduced to an exhibit scenario; a curator building an AR exhibit for a history museum using the prototype. Finally, we showed them the application, let them to explore it and required to follow each step to create an exhibit. All the multimedia content was already synchronized and ready to use. This is because we wanted to analyse just the aspect strictly related to the prototype, while producing the content is related to the different competences of each user. They pointed out just a few usability issues and, apart from them, all the experts stated that the system interfaces are well structured. Then they were asked about their general opinion on the application. One said "*It is so easy that even my grandmother could use it*". Another added "*The synchronization of the content among all the devices, can be considered a value-added for these kinds of users who can be annoying by dealing with technical problems*". Finally, "*The choice of using mobile technologies can be winning considering that nowadays people tend to be more and more expert of mobile technologies even ignoring traditional desktop technologies*".

In the second part, we prepared a prototype review to get feedback from a real potential stakeholder. The artist was led through the different steps for creating a complete AR exhibit. For each step she was let free to comment and make questions. She stated: "*it is so easy that even children can use it and produce their AR stories. Actually, there are many different applications for such tool*". Moreover, she appreciated the inner workings of the system. She highlighted the importance for artists to use their habitual software environment to create the digital elements and said "*The tablet application looks like a portable bridge between my favourite software and the AR*". Finally, she stated there is a lack of customization. Indeed, she would like visitors can interact with some virtual elements or even directly with the artist through them.

3   Conclusions

In this paper we presented the participatory design approach we followed to develop an EUP AR editor. The prototype allows cultural practitioners without specific technical competences to get the benefits of an AR system as to enhance their products, their expressiveness and the experience of their visitors.

In the next future, we plan to collaborate with different cultural practitioners to experiment our solution in real contexts. Indeed, currently the editor is being experiment in Alicante (Spain) for the creation of an artistic AR exhibit. Finally, from the point of view of the development we are planning to integrate new features to allow the creators to receive real-time feedback from the visitors and interact with them.

Acknowledgement. This work is supported by the project CREAx grant funded by the Spanish Ministry of Economy and Competitiveness (TIN2014-56534-R).

References

1. Bennett, S., Maton, K., Kervin, L.: The 'digital natives' debate: a critical review of the evidence. Br. J. Educ. Technol. **39**(5), 775–786 (2008)
2. Brogni, B.A., Avizzano, C.A., Evangelista, C., Bergamasco, M.: Technological approach for cultural heritage: augmented reality. In: 8th IEEE International Workshop on Robot and Human Interaction (RO-MAN 1999), Pisa, pp. 206–212 (1999)
3. Romano, M., Díaz, P., Ignacio, A., D'Agostino, P.: Augmenting smart objects for cultural heritage: a usability experiment. In: Paolis, L.T., Mongelli, A. (eds.) Augmented Reality, Virtual Reality, and Computer Graphics. LNCS, vol. 9769, pp. 186–204. Springer, Heidelberg (2016)
4. Bellucci, A., Romano, M., Aedo, I., Díaz, P.: Software support for multitouch interaction: the end-user programming perspective. IEEE Pervasive Comput. **15**(1), 78–86 (2016)
5. Ardito, C., Costabile, M.F., Desolda, G., Matera, M., Piccinno, A., Picozzi, M.: Composition of situational interactive spaces by end users: a case for cultural heritage. In: Proceedings of the 7th Nordic Conference on Human-Computer Interaction: Making Sense Through Design, pp. 79–88. ACM (2012)

6. Ko, A.J., Abraham, R., Beckwith, L., et al.: The state of the art in end-user software engineering. ACM Comput. Surv. **43**(3), 21 (2011)
7. Fischer, G.: End-user development: from creating technologies to transforming cultures. In: Burnett, M., Mørch, A., Redmiles, D., Dittrich, Y. (eds.) IS-EUD 2013. LNCS, vol. 7897, pp. 217–222. Springer, Heidelberg (2013)
8. Sanders, E.B.N., Stappers, P.J.: Co-creation and the new landscapes of design. Co Des. **4**(1), 5–18 (2008)

Towards Smart Notifications - An Adaptive Approach Using Smart Devices

Gustavo López$^{(\boxtimes)}$, Marcelo Guzmán, Gabriela Marín,
and Luis A. Guerrero

Universidad de Costa Rica, San José, Costa Rica
{gustavo.lopez_h, adrian.guzman, gabriela.marin,
luis.guerreroblanco}@ucr.ac.cr

Abstract. The use of smart devices is increasing rapidly; this trend is changing the paradigm in which notifications are delivered to users. Smart devices are important to provide user awareness. However, their use must be controlled and human perception should be considered to avoid information overload. In this paper, we present a dynamic mechanism to coordinate the distribution of notification across smart devices. This personalized notification mechanism uses an inference engine and a set of rules to generate notification alternatives and select the "best" one. A continuous refinement approach is also used to improve notification delivery. Our system was evaluated and the baseline rules were established by 11 expert users. The main results show that in some scenarios, the notification mechanism selection converged quickly and results are promising. However, further work is required to provide not only personalized but integrated (i.e., more than one device at the time) notification management.

Keywords: Personalized notification management · User awareness · Smart devices · Information overload · Human perception · Ambient intelligence · Rule-based decision making

1 Introduction

Human computer interaction methods have changed drastically over the last three decades. The information era, mobile technologies, wearable, and ubiquitous computing are just four examples of the breakthroughs and trends that exemplify this accelerated change rate [1].

Currently, smart devices are used to promote ubiquitous computing. Smart devices are objects equipped with sensing (i.e., data gathering) or actuating (i.e., information providing) capabilities [2]. These capabilities enable a wide range of applications (e.g., home, building, and factory automation and monitoring, health management systems, energy and transportation management) [3].

Data gathering refers to the constant and unbiased monitoring of the actions or the context characteristics in which a user performs his tasks. Information providing refers to the act of proactively informing the user about something he is supposed to know.

Smart device-based notifications can be used to inform about incoming messages, announce upcoming events, highlight changes or provide information important for the

© Springer International Publishing AG 2016
C.R. García et al. (Eds.): UCAmI 2016, Part I, LNCS 10069, pp. 372–384, 2016.
DOI: 10.1007/978-3-319-48746-5_38

user's tasks, or in general, increase situational awareness. Clearly, the implementation of smart device-based notifications can be disruptive and intrusive. Therefore, a balance must be established to avoid negative effects on the daily activities of a user.

Ubiquitous devices and services allow continuous communication with the users transforming human attention in a bottleneck. Therefore, ubiquitous notifications can become too disruptive and intrusive. To avoid this issue a coordination and distribution mechanism must be implemented, assuring effective delivery of notifications and reducing redundancies.

This paper presents a dynamic mechanism that allows coordination and distribution of notifications across smart devices. This mechanism works within a framework that also considers data gathering smart devices. A rule-based inference engine allows users to establish parameters and continuous feedback improves notification delivery effectiveness (i.e., reduce possible negative effects of intrusive notifications). The main contribution of this research is a generic (i.e., non-corporate or technology associated) and adaptive holistic management of smart device-based notifications.

2 Background

This section provides a definition of smart devices, notifications and user awareness. **Smart devices** are electronic apparatus that can somehow interact with people and/or each other [4]. Many smart devices are available commercially and the purchase rate is growing rapidly. An industrial trend has been to sell smart devices with multiple capabilities (i.e., manufacturers are embedding multiple computational accessories in the same device to provide them with more capabilities).

Awareness is defined as the consciousness that a user has. This consciousness is provided when the attention of a user is captured by an event and stored in his memory. Humans have the biological ability to selectively perceive stimuli and recall gathered information from those stimuli as short term memory [5].

A way in which computational devices focus the attention of users in one particular event is through notifications. According to the Oxford Dictionary of English, the term **notification** refers to the action of informing someone about something [6]. Different mechanisms have been used to deliver notifications to the users through technological applications and devices (e.g., pop-up messages in a PC screen, emergency alerts connected via Internet).

The amount of information delivered to users has increased at a fast rate, in the past years and this has become a bottleneck for human attention [7]. Furthermore, currently users are adapting to those notifications and starting to ignore them. Moreover, the same notification mechanisms are being used to inform users of heterogeneous data (i.e., mobile phones notify or social network updates, incoming text messages and emails, among others).

In the era of the Internet of Things (IoT) handling incoming notifications is a priority. Researchers are focusing on how to deliver notifications at opportune moments [8–10]. Notifications may come from multiple sources including other users, systems or even triggered by computational capabilities embedded in their context.

The next section describes a system proposal that addresses the delivery of notifications through smart devices. Moreover, the system uses two main types of notifications (i.e., personal and contextual) to allow categorization of notifications. The system architecture allows third party applications to deliver notifications in an ordered way to users, reducing the cognitive load that separate notifications might require.

3   System Overview

The distribution of notification among different devices is not a trivial task. Moreover, selecting a proper device and an opportune moment to deliver a notification requires a large amount of coordination and information. The architecture proposed in this section builds on a framework that defines a set of characteristics that each smart device must possess [11]. Figure 1 shows basic architectural diagram of the system that implements an adaptive approach to deliver notifications through smart devices.

In the architecture, two types of information sources are considered: user related and context information. **User information** is data that identifies the user. This type of information is collected from **user's smart devices** (i.e., objects that the user carries and are for personal use). User's smart devices have the highest possibility to be seen by the user. However, they are also the most intrusive ones. Therefore, notifications provided by user's smart devices should be carefully selected.

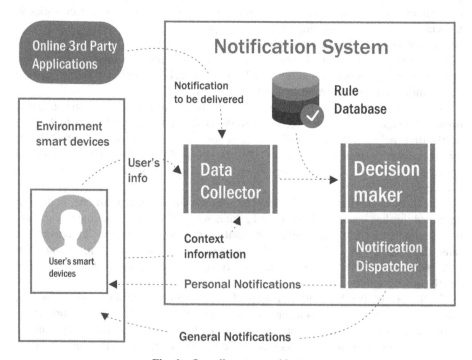

Fig. 1. Overall system architecture

The **context information** is collected from non-personal devices. This type of information is gathered from **environment smart devices**. These devices can be used or shared with several people, for instance a Smart TV at the living room, Amazon Echo in the kitchen, Smart Radio in the car, and smart lighting switches at the entrance of the user's home.

Two types of notifications (personal and general) are also considered. **Personal notifications** are only delivered through user's smart devices. Examples of content and messages considered personals are bank statements, medical records, videos, and images from sources defined as personal by the user.

General notifications deliver content that does not compromise the user's privacy if delivered publicly. This type of notification is intended to inform users of events that impact their daily activities. Examples of these notifications could be traffic or weather reports, among others.

The system architecture provides a framework to deliver notifications. However, such notifications proceed from multiple sources. **Third party applications** are modeled as those applications that require notifications to be delivered to a user. These applications include online services delivering content and messages to the user (e.g., weather conditions, stock exchange, traffic reports, emergencies, natural disasters, monitors or sensors installed in cars, stores or homes).

A **data collector** is responsible of getting the information from third parties and respond to their notification requests. All notifications have specific characteristics including: privacy, sense of urgency, and type.

Once the data collector has all the required information it transmits it to the **decision maker module** to define (using an inference engine and rules previously defined) the "best" alternative to deliver the notification. The decision maker module is the core of the system, being responsible for all the decisions: every time it receives a notification to be delivered, it uses the data collector's information to decide in which way the user should be notified. Figure 2 models the decision process.

The system is powered from two sources, content and data from third party applications and smart devices the user has registered. Data is collected by a module which main function is to review each request and identify the next steps or an action to take. If there is an action to be made, the problem is reviewed to generate possible alternatives.

Possible alternatives are generated using the target, the notification type, the privacy characteristics and the sense of urgency. After evaluating these aspects, set of rules are ready to be evaluated by the inference system, which contains a knowledge base to provide advice alternatives to deliver the content.

The selected alternative is implemented by the **notification dispatcher**. The results are evaluated both automatically (if feedback is required, the system stores the time required to get it) and using a user query to ask if the notifications delivered were good. This process allows continuous improvement of the rule database and notification delivery improvement over time. To allow the inclusion of smart devices into the proposed architecture a data model was developed.

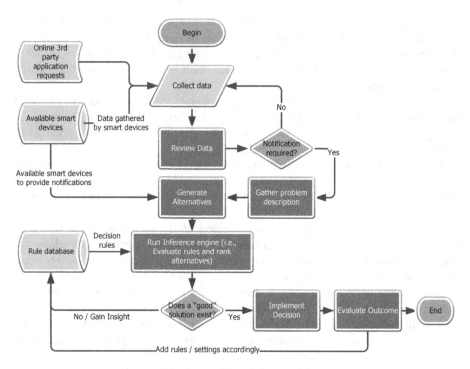

Fig. 2. Decision maker model

3.1   Smart Device Structure Model

An adaptive framework that delivers notifications should be able to allow users to add new smart devices. However, a structured way to describe smart devices was required. This model is essential to manage the heterogeneity of resources and to effectively apply them in different contexts.

The smart device structure model represents smart devices as static values, while the dynamic ones can be obtained by invoking the appropriate operations on their services. Our model is divided in four main categories:

- **Type:** Represents the type of smart device. It contains: an identifying tag (allowing device categorization), and an ID which allows its unique identification.
- **Characteristics:** Defines the physical characteristics of the including but not limited to: operative system, name, version, if it is public or private, if it can provide feedback, if it can be moved or it is mobile.
- **Services:** Contains the list of services provided by the smart device. Every service has a name, a description, and a type (sensing or actuating).
- **Location:** Represents the position of the device. It can be absolute (i.e., specifying the latitude and longitude), or relative (i.e., through the use of tags such as "city name", "building name", "room number"). Depending on the moving capabilities of the object, the location could either be a characteristic or a service.

3.2 Data Transmission

For data transmission, a JSON (JavaScript Object Notation) text format is used because it is lightweight. JSON considerably reduces network traffic compared to XML [12], which is very important for wireless applications and smart devices that use low battery power. All data transmission is carried through web services ready to receive and provide data in this manner.

3.3 Use Example

A usage example might be: It's Monday morning and Steven (user) is ready to go to the office. He has a scheduled meeting at 11am. This meeting was saved in his Google calendar (third party application). Steven gets a reminder at 8 a.m. in his smart watch (user's smart device) about the meeting. This reminder was programmed by Steven himself when he set the meeting in his calendar.

Soon before Steven departures, the traffic system (third party application) reports repairs in progress on the route Steven will use according to Waze (third party application). Since the time estimated to get to his office allows him to get on time, the notification is not urgent. Therefore, he will be notified as soon as he gets in his car in the car's screen (environment smart device). During the meeting, a package is delivered to Steven's home, in this case to avoid distractions the system delivers the notification in Steven's work PC. This notification is delivered through an app installed in Steven's PC and it is displayed as an icon without being intrusive. This is because the notification is not urgent.

4 Evaluation Procedure

This section details the way in which the framework was implemented and evaluated. This evaluation did not consider connectivity issues between smart devices, nor smart device specific functionality.

4.1 Setup

Complying with the smart device structure model, each device provides information of its location. In this evaluation relative locations were used. Locations included: house, house – kitchen, house – TV room, car, office, and street (i.e., on the go).

The data collector implementations considered five types of content for each notification: simple text, audio, video, image, and link.

Four levels of sense of urgency were defined: informative (i.e., can be deferred), warning (i.e., information is delivered but requires feedback), alarm (i.e., information is delivered and immediate feedback is required), and critical alarm (i.e., does not only require immediate feedback, but also, user should be forced to stop other activities). This list was defined by two experts in decision making support systems.

Table 1. Location of each available smart device

Smart Device	House	Kitchen	TV Room	Car	Office	On the go
Smart phone	*	*	*	*	*	*
Smart TV			*			
Personal Tablet	*	*	*	*		*
Work PC					*	
Smart Fridge	*	*				
Amazon Echo	*	*				
Car's screen				*		

Table 2. Smart device and its type of message delivery capabilities

Smart Device	Simple text	Audio	Video	Image	Link	Allows feedback
Smart phone	*	*	*	*	*	*
Smart TV	*	*	*	*	*	*
Personal Tablet	*	*	*	*	*	*
Work PC	*	*	*	*	*	*
Smart Fridge	*	*		*		*
Amazon Echo	*	*				*
Car's screen	*	*		*	*	*

Table 3. Smart devices and associated sense of urgency

Smart Device	Informative	Warning	Alarm	Critical Alarm
Smart phone	*	*	*	*
Smart TV	*	*		
Personal Tablet	*	*	*	
Work PC	*	*		*
Smart Fridge	*			
Amazon Echo	*			
Car's screen	*	*		*

Tables 1, 2 and 3 show the characteristics of each smart device. Table 1 shows the location of each smart device, Table 2 the types of messages that the smart device can deliver and other features, and Table 3 the sense of urgency that each smart device provides. This last characteristic could be immediately mapped with the level of intrusiveness of each object and its privacy characteristics.

The characteristics of each object, its location and message delivery capabilities were defined by the authors, based on previous interaction with these smart objects. The sense of urgency preference was established by our expert group.

4.2   Implementation

To implement the decision maker module CLIPS was used. CLIPS is an expert system tool, designed to facilitate the development of software to model human knowledge or expertise. CLIPS shell provides the basic elements of an expert system: (1) Fact-list, and instance-list: Global memory for data, (2) Knowledge- database: Contains all the rules, the rule-database, (3) Inference engine: Controls overall execution of rules.

The following pseudocode shows some rules used for the system to consider the best device for delivering a message in our knowledge database

- (rule (if the user is at "home-tv-room") (then best place for delivery is home-tv-room with possibility 70 and best place for delivery is home-kitchen with possibility 40 and best place for delivery is home with possibility 10))
- (rule (if is "a personal message") (then the desired feature is a personal device with a possibility 60)).

4.3   Rule Baseline

To establish the baseline rules of the system, a series of scenarios were evaluated with expert users to determine which one of the available devices they would choose in each one (i.e., original decisions were defined by expert users).

The expert group was composed by 11 users (4 experts in human-computer interaction, 3 expert decision makers, and 4 computer scientists). Moreover the group was divided 45 % men and 55 % women. The age distribution was: 36 % between 20 and 30, 28 % between 30 and 40, 18 % between 40 and 50, and 18 % between 50 and 60.

Each expert was asked for a decision in 21 different scenarios. The results were averaged and smart devices were weighted accordingly and included in the initial set of rules. In some scenarios 100 % of the experts gave the same response.

The expert users were presented with the following scenario: the user is in his office, and he receives a message indication that he just got paid. The expert users selected from the available devices, and the results were: Smartphone (36.3 %) and Work PC (63.6 %). Other scenario was: There is a collision on the route the user usually uses to go home, and he is in his office. Responses were: Smartphone (36.3 %), Work PC (27.2 %), and Car's screen (36.3 %).

Three of the 21 scenarios got a response of 100 % for one specific smart device. 16 out of the 21 scenarios got two candidates to deliver the notification. In all these scenarios the smartphone was one of the candidates. This result might be caused by the extensive use of smartphones for notifications. Two out of the 21 scenarios got 3 candidate smart devices. No scenarios got more than 3 candidate smart devices.

5   Results

Another set of scenarios were evaluated in the system, with similar characteristics with the ones originally programmed. Table 4 shows the results of 7 test scenarios with office as location. Results shown in Table 4 are significant as work related messages are delivered through work devices, and personal affairs are prioritized to be delivered through the personal smartphone. However, in some cases the difference between devices is not significant.

Table 4. Evaluation results using "office" as location

Message related to	Sense of urgency	Message Type	Results		
Home security	Critical alarm	Image	Work PC (6.4)	Smartphone (3.6)	
Personal affairs	Alarm	Link	Smartphone (8.2)	Work PC (1.8)	
	Alarm	Text	Smartphone (5.4)	Work PC (4.5)	
	Informative	Text	Smartphone (8.2)	Amazon Echo (0.9)	Work PC (0.9)
Traffic	Warning	Link	Car's screen (3.6)	Smartphone (3.6)	Work PC (2.8)
Work	Informative	Text	Work PC (6.4)	Smartphone (3.6)	
	Alarm	Text	Work PC (6.4)	Smart watch (2.7)	Smartphone (0.9)

Other significant result shows that traffic related messages are delivered through the car's screen, and time related messages also consider the Smart watch as a possibility (i.e., the last scenario is a meeting reminder and the Smart watch is a candidate object, however Work PC is prioritized used to deliver work related messages). The only scenario in which work devices are used to deliver messages not related to work is in the case of the critical alarm that requires immediate attention form the user. In this case, the first scenario represents the house alarm triggered by an intruder.

The scenario changes when the location is the user's car (Table 5). In this case if the message has a high sense of urgency, or it is traffic related, it should be delivered through the car's screen, otherwise the smartphone is preferred to deliver the message. Other set of evaluations were performed using house as location. Table 6 shows the results of this evaluation.

Some scenarios in which a notification made no sense (i.e., the user is in his house, and a traffic report is affecting his common route between work and house) were included to determine the response of experts. In this scenario, 7 out of the 11 experts stated that a notification was not necessary; the remaining 4 responses were Smartphone (2), Car's screen (1) and Smart Fridge (1).

Table 5. Evaluation results using "car" as location

Message related to	Sense of urgency	Message Type	Results	
Home security	Critical alarm	Image	Car's screen (10)	
Personal affairs	Warning	Text	Smartphone (6.4)	Car's screen (3.6)
	Informative	Text	Smartphone (5.4)	Car's screen (4.5)
Traffic	Informative	Text	Car's screen (10)	

Table 6. Evaluation results using "house" as location. In all scenarios message type was "Text"

Disappearing	Disappearing	Disappearing	Disappearing		
TV room	Leisure	Warning	Smart TV (10)		
	Personal affairs	Alarm	Smart TV (5.5)	Smartphone (4.5)	
	Work	Informative	Smartphone (6.4)	Smart TV (1.8)	Work PC (1.8)
Kitchen	Personal affairs	Informative	Smart Fridge (6.4)	Smartphone (2.7)	
Not provided	Personal affairs	Alarm	Smartphone (9.2)	Smart Watch (0.9)	Smart TV (0.9)

6 Discussion

This paper presented a system developed to coordinate the distribution of notification across smart devices. Current trends in notification delivery use the same device (smartphone) without considering the type of notification, its content or any of the other characteristics described in this paper.

The distribution of notifications was developed selecting the "best" candidate to deliver a particular notification. However, a combination of smart devices can be used in some contexts. The evaluation conducted and reported in this paper shows reasonable responses. This was expected, once a set of characteristics are defined the way in which a notification should be delivered becomes apparent. However, a framework is required to allow the distribution and delivery of such notifications.

To allow the inclusion of smart devices into the framework, a smart device structure model was proposed and web service-based communications were used. The main contribution of this paper is a model that can manage notifications across different smart devices and platforms.

Eleven experts were involved in this research. They defined the set of initial rules to evaluate the system. Once the system was implemented patterns in the system results emerged. Those patterns were validated with the users and responses were confirmed (i.e., the system response was the one the user expected). The emergence of patterns with this preliminary evaluation led authors to believe that once the system is released and massively used, user's feedback could be used to determine types of users and create predetermined preferences. However, the main advantage of the system is its adaptability both to the notification characteristics and the user preferences.

The proposed decision maker model uses continuous feedback and learning capabilities to improve decisions. Automatic reviews of the feedback time are used to determine how long the user took to see the message. Moreover, until the user decides not to provide more responses, a survey is used to determine if the notifications were acceptable. This characteristic is an extra task to the user: however, they could not respond and the system will stop requesting feedback. The proposed survey is only a yes no question, if the answer is positive, smart devices used get a plus in their electability percentages, otherwise these percentages are reduced (i.e., if the adequate object was not selected, the selected one gets its possibilities to be selected reduced, in the specific scenario).

One of the main difficulties that this research faced was the lack of experience that participants had with smart devices. In some scenarios the participants were not able to imagine how a notification could be delivered though a smart device since they are not working with such devices every day. Moreover, some of the participants were so fixed up in the idea of notifications being delivered through the smart phone that thinking of other possibilities was not an easy task.

This paper provides evidence of the difficulties that smart devices will face in the nearby future. Most users are getting used to receive notifications through their smart phones. However, the emergence of the IoT and smart devices will change this perspective drastically and a framework like the one proposed in this paper could allow a better use of the possibilities that smart devices will provide for notification delivery.

7 Conclusions

Human interruption management is very important. Currently, notifications are being delivered to users in an indiscriminately way and their effectivity in tasks is being affected due to constant interruptions. This problematic could expand significantly once smart devices are adopted by users. Nowadays, smart devices manufacturers are developing smart devices with multiple capabilities. Therefore, it is not enough to select among the available smart devices to deliver a message. To allow useful notifications for each smart device, the correct way to provide the notification must be established.

In this paper a framework that allows an adaptive use of smart devices to deliver notifications was described. The adaptive characteristic is given by the possibility of the system to change the way in which a particular notification is delivered, depending on the context or personal characteristics of the user. Moreover, since smart devices have more than one mechanism that allow the delivery of the notification, the system could also adapt the way in which a particular smart device delivers a notification.

Managing interruptions and notifications adaptively is not an easy task. The level of intrusiveness in each notification should be considered, otherwise, results could be negative (i.e., user's attention could be lost). Moreover, sometimes even if the "best" smart device and the "best" way in which that device will deliver the notification are selected, is not enough.

Smartphones are currently the main notification mechanism. This might be due to the extensive use of such devices to indiscriminately deliver notifications. Further refinement will be required to determine if users decide whether this mechanism continues to be used in the nearby future.

In this paper only a set of smart devices were considered as possibilities to deliver notifications (e.g., smart phone, smart watch, refrigerator, automobile, smart TV, Amazon Echo). In future researches, more smart devices should be considered. However, the framework proposed in this paper will be able to include more smart devices as long as they comply with the minimum characteristics described in the smart devices structure model and they offer their functionalities through web services.

Future work will require to implement the ability of using a combination of smart devices to deliver a notification. Finally, a larger set of representative users should be considered to determine the way in which meaningful feedback would be provided in other scenarios. Moreover, a test of this framework in real scenarios (i.e., not laboratory case studies) will be required to assess its applicability. Only in real scenarios notification and interruption reduction could be assessed, and the effects of this reduction can be properly measured.

Acknowledgments. This work was partially supported by *Centro de Investigaciones en Tecnologías de la Información y Comunicación* (CITIC), *Escuela de Ciencias de la Computación e Informática* (ECCI) both at *Universidad de Costa Rica*. Grant No. 834-B6-178. This work was also supported by MICITT and by CONICIT of the Government of Costa Rica.

References

1. Jacko, J.A.: Human-Computer Interaction Handbook: Fundamentals, Evolving Technologies, and Emerging Applications, 3rd edn. CRC Press Inc., Boca Raton (2012)
2. Vasseur, J.-P., Dunkels, A.: Interconnecting Smart Objects with IP: The Next Internet. Morgan Kaufmann Publishers Inc., San Francisco (2010)
3. Fortino, G., Guerrieri, A., Russo, W., Savaglio, C.: Middlewares for Smart Objects and Smart Environments: Overview and Comparison. In: Fortino, G., Trunfio, P. (eds.) Internet of Things Based on Smart Objects: Technology, Middleware and Applications, pp. 1–27. Springer International Publishing, Heidelberg (2014)
4. Poslad, S.: Ubiquitous Computing: Smart Devices, Environments and Interactions. Wiley Publishing, Inc., New Jersey, United States (2009)
5. Charlton, B.G.: Evolution and the cognitive neuroscience of awareness, consciousness and language. Psychiatry Hum. Cond. **13**(1), 34–42 (2000). Oxford, United Kingdom
6. Oxford Dictionaries: Oxford Dictionary of English. Oxford University Press (2010)

7. Okoshi, T., Nozaki, H., Nakazawa, J., Tokuda, H., Ramos, J., Dey, A.K.: Towards attention-aware adaptive notification on smart phones. Pervasive Mob. Comput. **26**, 17–34 (2016)
8. Pielot, M., de Oliveira, R., Kwak, H., Oliver, N.: Didn'T you see my message?: predicting attentiveness to mobile instant messages. In: Proceedings of the 32Nd Annual ACM Conference on Human Factors in Computing Systems, pp. 3319–3328. ACM, New York (2014)
9. Poppinga, B., Heuten, W., Boll, S.: Sensor-based identification of opportune moments for triggering notifications. IEEE Pervasive Comput. **13**, 22–29 (2014)
10. Okoshi, T., Ramos, J., Nozaki, H., Nakazawa, J., Dey, A.K., Tokuda, H.: Reducing users' perceived mental effort due to interruptive notifications in multi-device mobile environments. In: Proceedings of the 2015 ACM International Joint Conference on Pervasive and Ubiquitous Computing, pp. 475–486. ACM, New York (2015)
11. López, G., López, M., Guerrero, L.A., Bravo, J.: Human-objects interaction: a framework for designing, developing and evaluating augmented objects. Int. J. Hum. Comput. Interact. **30**, 787–801 (2014)
12. Drossos, N., Mavrommati, I., Kameas, A.: Towards ubiquitous computing applications composed from functionally autonomous hybrid artifacts. Disappearing Comput. **4500**, 161–181 (2007)

Methods to Observe and Evaluate Interactions with Everyday Context-Aware Objects

Manuel Portela$^{(\boxtimes)}$ and Carlos Granell-Canut

Universitat Jaume I, Castellon de la Plana, Spain
{portela,carlos.granell}@uji.es

Abstract. The Smart Cities discourse intends to envision the future of cities. It is mostly orientated towards an efficient and optimal management of citys resources to enhance peoples life. Our relation with the city environment is changing since connected objects are incorporated in the city bridging the physical with the virtual world. With new opportunities of engaging citizens in new relations within the city, what we present is a multidisciplinary framework for observing those interactions. It combines different methods from Computer Sciences, Social Sciences and Design, to evaluate the assemblages in the urban space with the idea to understand the benefits of affective and empathic relations in long-term interactions with software enabled objects. While this framework will be tested in different experiments, the ultimate aim is to provide knowledge and insightful support for designing future objects for the urban space that enhance the experience of people's everyday life.

Keywords: Smart cities · Conversational agents · Affective relations · Context-awareness · HCI · Empathy · Urban computing · Socio-technical assemblages

1 Introduction

The concept of Smart Cities itself is a future desire that fuels the development of new technologies. Leveraged by new data processing capacities (e.g. Machine Learning (ML), Cloud computing, Artificial Intelligence) along with the advent of Ubiquitous Computing and IoT, companies and governments are trying to take advantage of these technological advances to design and deploy Smart Cities solutions to solve the biggest issues facing cities today (e.g. mobility, transport, environment).

Beyond the immediate benefits and consequences of novel technologies in cities, the discussion turns interesting when envisioning the possibilities of implementing new relations between people and urban objects mediated by technology. From a social sciences and design standpoint, the ecosystem of technologies in Smart Cities initiatives brings unexplored opportunities to evaluate possible constraints in societies and communities, being the latter as novel and important as the technology advancement itself.

© Springer International Publishing AG 2016
C.R. García et al. (Eds.): UCAmI 2016, Part I, LNCS 10069, pp. 385–392, 2016.
DOI: 10.1007/978-3-319-48746-5_39

Urban space can be seen as an interrelated and dynamic web of infrastructures, territories, and interactions between objects and living creatures. Nevertheless, a great proportion of smart cities projects pay no or little attention to the construction of relations between society and technology as an assemblage [1] leaving the social and cognitive perception as an external effect rather than an integrative part of its construction and its relation with the space. Our concern in this research is to study how to relate these issues, which are unveiled at different scales, to build an exploratory mindset that permits to observe and evaluate interactions in place and time with coded objects.

2   Research Questions

Our main goal is to observe and evaluate the socio-technical assemblages on how interactions (in place and time) between people and coded urban objects affect citizens engagement with their surroundings. The term "engagement" comprises the interactions and understanding that happen between citizens and pervasive socio-technical systems in urban contexts. The main goal comprises two research questions:

1. How and to what extent do novel interactions with coded objects encourage empathic relations?
2. How and to what extent can these interactions raise awareness in citizens with their urban context?

To answer these research questions, our intention is to observe these socio-technical relations and provide evidence on how engagement, awareness and empathy may or may not be affected. To do so, we propose a novel Framework to serve us as a conceptual basis to scientifically design and develop the research activities and interventions, and to validate or refute our research questions.

3   The Framework

The term behaviour is commonly used in recent theories of design, society and technology [2], which takes their roots in cognitive and psychology theories to explain peoples decision based on systemic models. Systemic models alone, though, cannot fully account for the complexity of behaviour required to fully explain individual decisions, especially for non-expert people [3]. Among other factors, Yvonne Rogers argued that these behaviour-related theories cannot achieve the expected results in the practical field [4].

Connected to the Rogers statement, the Situational Awareness model described by Mica Endsley [5–7] determines that the context can influence people's actions and decisions. Despite Situational Awareness is often framed in safety-critical systems where failure may cause loss of life, closely related terms like location-awareness or context-awareness, which are about being aware of what is happening around, some authors found it helpful for collaboration processes and interactions at the scale of a city [8].

From another perspective, Zinnbauer [9] proposed the concept of Ambient Accountability as an explicit way to bring context awareness to citizens in the place and time of the interaction to deal with potential situations that could go right or wrong, and helps them to make decisions based on it. Ambient Accountability differs from Situational-Awareness in that the former accounts for the controversies in the public space and the actors involved in all the systems that the citizens struggle with.

By providing a conceptual framework to frame the concepts above for the purpose of the research, we should open the opportunity to designers and researchers to understand how they can design technologies in order to help citizens promoting awareness on what is coming next, and to establish specific interactions, based on truth and confidence. We next describe the Framework in two parts, the core and the observational methods, to introduce its novel elements, although the framework should be regarded as an interrelated whole.

3.1   From the Frameworks Core: Double-Fiction Devices [DFD]

By definition, a device is a thing designed and adapted for a purpose or function. As proposed in Law & Ruppert [10], social sciences methods can be considered devices. In the realm of this research, we understand devices as a method for analyse socio-technical assemblages where chaos and uncertainty are part of the system, much nearer to the messiness than to structured and organized relations, where side effects are both explicit and implicit. Our intention is to define this type of devices, as we call them Double-Fiction Devices [DFD], as conceptual constructions, that allow us to observe embedded context-aware coded systems as actants [11, 12].

On the contrary, the tangible entity - stabilized unit - can be defined as an object [OBJ], and is what creates the effect of affordance [13] and agency [14]. At the same time, using the categories adopted by Martin Dodge and Rob Kitchin [15], we can say that a blogject is our focus of research, in the form of coded objects, or software enabled, with the ability to transform physical objects into living objects. The concept of blogject constitutes a code/space [15], by which the traditional notion of static urban infrastructure augmented with code turns into a platform of infinite opportunities to transform and mold our relations with them. Furthermore, what defines the proposed Double-Fiction Devices [DFD] is not the system itself but the type of agency that coded objects exert over people and the environment: the Situational-Awareness (SA) and the Future-Awareness (FA).

Situational-Awareness, referred to the traditional concept in HCI, is the contextual feedback that is motivated by real-time information and accountability in time and place. In the case of Future-Awareness, fiction, expectation and uncertainty are its defining characteristics. Based on the Design Fiction concept postulated by Bleecker [16], devices [DFD] motivate the user to imagine and to create new futures, while interacting with coded objects, through two main drivers: aesthetics and narrative.

The recently development of conversational bots [14,17] and Internet of Things [18,19] brought to light several coded objects that could be analysed through the lens of DFD. Furthermore, devices [DFD] intend to comprise the two agencies even though the new opportunities that these devices [DFD] may bring to our world are yet largely unknown; what is clear is that they might improve our life in very different ways that traditional? technologies and interfaces have done until now.

3.2 The Framework as an Observational Method

Similar to the Ambient Accountability, Albretch Schmidt [20] introduced the concept of Implicit HCI for Interactive Context-Aware Systems, as a model for managing interactions with invisible? technology that benefits from contextual information and data. This model assumes that there are some implicit assumptions about the expected relation with the environment and with artefacts [20], that belong both to the user and to the designer of the system. Those assumptions are critical to accomplish a successfully interaction, while being aware of possible misunderstandings and communication errors between the user and the system, that otherwise are inevitable. The difference between the expected, the sensed and the desired reaction from a system, exemplified by the Schmidts implicit assumptions, was also schemed by Benford et al. [21] in an early stage of the HCI field. But these frictions between the context and the user-interface do not have to be necessarily a negative experience as argued by Cox and Gould [22]. Conversely, it could unfold and raise awareness between present and future situations.

We consider the notion of Aristotles tragedy as a metaphor [23,24], where the drama and storytelling help to build the relation between the character and the public. This analogy allow us to build a narrative that helps to understand how people get engaged which often provokes the rise of empathy with physical, coded objects. The three stages of the tragedy are also represented in our Framework time-flow (Fig. 1). The proposed time-flow illustrates a performance over time during the human-object interaction. Performance is a sequence of observable and accountable actions in a specific period, and it is differentiated from behaviour that corresponds to a pattern of regular movements that responds to a set of cultural, social and cognitive understandings.

By this model, we understand a relation is built upon the habit of interaction and is perceived by different insights. For that reason, we decided to understand it, from a socio-technical perspective, as empathic relations?. That is why only direct observation can bring some insights of what happens during the construction of meaning.

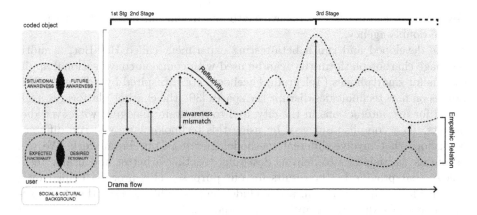

Fig. 1. The Framework

4   Work Plan

4.1   Methodology

As Kientz & Wobbrock [25] pointed out, contributions in HCI can be quite
diverse, ranging from empirical research, to artefact design, to methodological and theoretical frameworks. The use of mixed methodologies to bring new
insights to research is not new. Semi-Structured Qualitative Studies [26] and
design-as-research [27] have been tested in HCI [28, 29] and other fields.

To demonstrate the feasibility and validity of the proposed Framework, we
take methodologies from diverse fields that, altogether, provide us with the right
tools to accomplish the required multi-scale approach through the experiments
(see next section). For example, for understanding the construction of meaning
we will use Ethnomethodology and Deep Cover HCI as a direct observation
approach. Semi-structured surveys and ethnography process will help us to build
the conceptual construction under the lens of an Anthropological understanding.
Quantitative methods, like data analysis will be useful for uncovering hidden
patterns during people and coded objects interactions.

4.2   Designed Experiments

For our purpose of promoting care to the urban heritage, we will use the term
urban infrastructure not as simple as it is commonly viewed - roads and sewage
systems for example. We formalize it as all what is around us in an urban
context - objects, services, systems, etc. - which become actants between code
and space. In this respect, conversational agents or *chatbots* are particularly
interesting because they are gaining great attention nowadays on the public
spheres due to Google and Facebook recently released its own platforms for
assistive conversational agents, accompanied by recent developments in NLP and
ML, which have reached a mature stage to bring chatbots into the mainstream.

Given their social nature, we believe chatbots can suit our needs for experiments on the double-agency.

We developed and run a beta-testing experiment called HolaBot, a multi-language chatbot platform that can be used with common conversational applications for smartphones (Telegram, Facebook, etc.). Inspired by different possibilities on how technologies disrupt the spaces [30], the chatbot platform is itself a tool for live interactions in the city, and to maintain dialogues with everyday objects. To accomplish our goal by using this technology, we will run different workshops that involve different methodologies from our Framework. We will encourage participants to help us designing together a better and usable technology that provide better results for our purpose. This process, helped by a Design Fiction approach, will also include the possibility to use other technologies, like public displays, maps, websites and others.

5   Conclusions

The construction of new concepts during the course of this research will be an important contribution for the Social Studies of Technology and Human-Computer Interaction fields, based on a social sciences background and empirical results. In particular, we will conceive and provide a conceptual framework (Sect. 3) with an comprehensive guide and to articulate experiments with coded objects (Sect. 4). Based on it, the interpretation of the observed patterns of use could lead to novel insights to propose new socio-technical artefacts, technologies and design patterns for future objects.

As Dodge and Kitchin did once [15], we also are intrigued by the question of how code/software reshapes the city? We are willing to provide some insights to the evolution of this idea and the creation of new conscious objects for promoting awareness in the citizenship. Meanwhile, as preliminary results, we found that the unexpected, and the creation of opportunistic interactions in the space, should not be considered a problem but an opportunity to engage in different scales. Moreover, the effects and consequences of including new coded objects in the public space, could lead not only to new opportunities but also to new behaviours that are far from being clear.

Acknowledgements. The authors gratefully acknowledge funding from the European Union through the GEO-C project (H2020-MSCA-ITN-2014, Grant Agreement Number 642332, http://www.geo-c.eu/). Carlos Granell has been partly funded by the Ramón y Cajal Programme (grant number RYC-2014-16913).

References

1. Venturini, T., Latour, B.: The social fabric: digital traces and quali-quantitative methods. Proc. Future En Seine **2009**, 87–101 (2010)
2. Lockton, D.: Design with Intent: A design pattern toolkit for environmental & social behaviour change. No. May 2013

3. Rogers, Y.: Interaction design gone wild: striving for wild theory. Interactions **18**(4), 58–62 (2011)
4. Rogers, Y.: Moving on from weiser's vision of calm computing: engaging ubicomp experiences. In: Dourish, P., Friday, A. (eds.) UbiComp 2006. LNCS, vol. 4206, pp. 404–421. Springer, Heidelberg (2006)
5. Endsley, M.R.: Toward a theory of situation awareness in Dinamic Systems. Hum. Factors J. Hum. Factors Ergon. Soci. **37**(1), 32–64 (1995)
6. Endsley, M.R., Bolté, B., Jones, D.G.: Designing for Situation Awareness (2003)
7. Endsley, M.R.: Designing for Situation Awareness: An Approach to User-Centered Design, 2nd edn. CRC Press (2011)
8. Nova, N., Girardin, F., Dillenbourg, P.: The effects of mutual location-awareness on group coordination. Int. J. Hum. Comput. Stud. **68**(7), 451–467 (2010)
9. Zinnbauer, D.: Ambient Accountability - Fighting Corruption When and Where it Happens. Technical Report, October 2012
10. Law, J., Ruppert, E.: The social life of methods: devices. J. Cult. Econ. **6**(3), 229–240 (2013)
11. Latour, B.: On actor-network theory. A few clarificaitons plus more than a few complications. Soziale Welt **25**(3), 1–16 (1996)
12. Latour, B.: Reassembling the Social: An introduction to Actor-Network Theory. Oxford University Press, Oxford (2006)
13. Gibson, J.J.: The Theory of Affordances (1977)
14. Latour, B.: Networks, societies, spheres: Reflections of an actor-network theorist. Int. J. Commun. **5**(1), 796–810 (2011)
15. Kitchin, R., Dodge, M.: Code, Space: Software and Everyday Life. MIT Press, Cambridge (2011)
16. Bleecker, J.: Design Fiction: A Short Essay on Design, Science, Fact and Fiction. Near Future Laboratory, no. March, p. 49 (2009)
17. Goth, G.: Deep or shallow, NLP is breaking out. Commun. ACM **59**(3), 13–16 (2016)
18. Balestrini, M., Diez, T., Marshall, P., Gluhak, A., Rogers, Y.: IoT community technologies: leaving users to their own devices or orchestration of engagement? EAI Endorsed Trans. Int. Things **1**, 150601 (2015). 10
19. Brambilla, G., Picone, M., Cirani, S., Amoretti, M., Zanichelli, F.: A simulation platform for large-scale internet of things scenarios in urban environments. In: Proceedings of the The First International Conference on IoT in Urban Space, pp. 50–55 (2014)
20. Schmidt, A.: Interactive context-aware systems interacting with ambient intelligence. In: Riva, G., Vatalaro, F., Davide, F., Alcañiz, M. (eds.) Ambient Intelligence, pp 159–178. IOS Press (2005)
21. Benford, S., Schnadelbach, H., Koleva, B., Anastasi, R., Greenhalgh, C., Rodden, T., Green, J., Ghali, A., Pridmore, T., Gaver, B., Boucher, A., Walker, B., Pennington, S., Schmidt, A., Gellersen, H., Steed, A.: Expected, sensed, and desired: A framework for designing sensing-based interaction. ACM Trans. Comput. Hum. Interact. (TOCHI)D **12**(1), 3–30 (2005)
22. Cox, A.L., Gould, S.J., Cecchinato, M.E., Lacovides, I., Renfree, I.: Design frictions for mindful interactions. In: Proceedings of the CHI Conference Extended Abstracts on Human Factors in Computing Systems - CHI EA 2016, pp. 1389–1397. ACM Press, New York (2016)
23. Boal, A.: Theater of the Oppressed. Pluto Classics, Pluto (2000)
24. Laurel, B.: Computers as Theatre. Addison Wesley Longman (1993). ISBN: 0201550601

25. Kientz, J.A., Wobbrock, J.: Research contributions in human-computer interaction. Interactions **25**, 38–44 (2016)
26. Blandford, A.: Semi-Structured Qualitative Studies. The Encyclopedia of Human-Computer Intreraction (2013)
27. Fallman, D.: The interaction design research triangle of design practice, design studies, and design exploration. Des. Issues **24**(3), 4–18 (2008)
28. Crabtree, A., Chamberlain, A.: Introduction to the special issue of the turn tothe wild. ACM Trans. **20**(3), 3 (2013)
29. Girardin, F.: Aspects of implicit and explicit human interactions with ubiquitous geographic information. Contract **9**, 1–171 (2009)
30. Crang, M., Graham, S.: Sentient cities: Ambient intelligence and the politics of urban space. J. Bus. Ethics **44**, 103 (2004)

Easing Students' Participation in Class with Hand Gesture Interfaces

Orlando Erazo[1,2(✉)], Nelson Baloian[1], José A. Pino[1], and Gustavo Zurita[3]

[1] Department of Computer Science, Universidad de Chile, Santiago, Chile
{oerazo,nbaloian,jpino}@dcc.uchile.cl
[2] Escuela de Informática, Universidad Técnica Estatal de Quevedo, Quevedo, Ecuador
[3] Department of Management Control and Information Systems,
Universidad de Chile, Santiago, Chile
gzurita@fen.uchile.cl

Abstract. Students' participation in traditional classroom settings may be hindered due to various reasons, which interrupt the class flow or cause distraction among the rest of the class members. To tackle that problem, we propose using applications based on touchless hand gestures (THG) that would allow students to interact from their own places. The feasibility of this proposal is analyzed in this work. To do it, we requested students to use two applications from their physical locations. Obtained qualitative results suggest the proposal may be used in an acceptable way as the use of applications based on THG becomes widespread. Actually, students who participated recommend the use of this proposal, since they may be more motivated to participate actively in the development of classes, which would result in better teaching-learning processes.

Keywords: Classroom teaching · Touchless hand gestures · Natural user interface

1 Introduction

Encouraging students' participation in traditional classroom lectures frequently makes teachers ask questions, require students to solve a problem on the blackboard or suggest them to ask questions about the lecture [1]. However, some students may be reluctant to participate in class because they may be shy or nervous, or simply they may be afraid of making mistakes or seem unintelligent. Actually, teachers may experience a drop in participation when these practices are not properly applied [2]. These problems can appear when the teacher asks a student to perform a task on the board in front of the class. This may also interrupt the normal flow of the lecture and cause distraction. One way to tackle the problem is to equip the classroom with enough computers so that each student may use one of them [3]. Alternatively, each student may use her own laptop (e.g., [1]). Given the accessible costs of mobile devices, the teacher could permit the use of students' personal devices, tablets or smartphones instead of laptops to participate in class [2]. Unfortunately, these settings also let students perform activities different than those required for the class [4].

© Springer International Publishing AG 2016
C.R. García et al. (Eds.): UCAmI 2016, Part I, LNCS 10069, pp. 393–399, 2016.
DOI: 10.1007/978-3-319-48746-5_40

The interaction using touchless hand gestures (THG) for educational purposes is another option that has been studied especially in recent years. Works reporting about user interfaces (UIs) based on THG are described in [5]. They can be applied with the aim of enhancing classrooms and immersing students in their learning [6–9]. However, most of them require students stand in front of a screen at a certain distance to interact with the applications. This approach has the same problems than the classical one in which a student works in front of the class. The fact that the student has to go to the right place may interrupt the class flow, and cause disorders and students' distraction.

Alternatively, the interaction using THG from students' location may help to promote participation in class, but this approach has yet to be explored. Therefore, and as a first step, the goal of this paper is to analyze the feasibility of using UIs based on THG in classrooms from students' own physical location. We report on initial qualitative results that support this proposal and provide the basis to further investigate it.

2   Touchless Hand Gestures in the Classroom

The development of devices like Kinect and Leap Motion (LM) has induced the emergence of applications allowing users to interact without using intermediate input devices such as mice and keyboards [10]. Applications of this type use as input the information conveyed by gestures performed in the air, and hence, physical contact is not required to manipulate content. Though gestures can be executed with various body parts, we focus only on THG. This interaction style can be "natural" to users [10], and it can be used in scenarios where other interaction styles are inadequate.

Education is an application field where the use of THG can be advantageous. UIs of this type can ease and improve teaching and learning by fabricating meaningful classroom interactions [5]. They may contribute to increase participation, provide a better way to present and manipulate teacher's material, create opportunities for discussion, and overall create enjoyable classes [5]. Several works have been proposed to support/complement/improve the learning of different subjects and languages at the various educational levels [6, 7], to control presentations [8], etc.

Although THG can be employed in several scenarios, we focus just on classrooms. The most frequent use is the learning of specific topics. In this case, a student is required to stand on a specific place in the classroom (e.g., between the whiteboard and the other students) to interact with the application. For example, she can use the hands to manipulate 3D models of organs [9] in an anatomy class. An approach slightly different is the simulation of educational scenarios; e.g., a virtual laboratory [6]. Additionally, devices that enable the use of THG can also ease the development of interactive whiteboards. Works of this type demonstrate that THG can be used to increase the participation and/or motivation of students in classrooms. However, their main disadvantage is that they require a physical space reserved specifically to allow students to use the applications. Alternatively, we propose the use of THG to allow students to interact with applications from their own physical locations.

Our interaction model consists of three phases (Fig. 1): *transferring control* (TC), *participation* (P) and *finishing* (F). A teacher controls the application, and hence, she must transfer control to a student who will perform the required task. Therefore, *transfer control* means the teacher stops being the user who controls the application and the student is able to use it from that moment onwards. Next, the student starts the interaction to carry out the task. Several aspects should be considered for this goal: interaction style (i.e., type of gestures to use), gesture space (i.e., the space to input gestures), gesture set (e.g., see [10]), and student representation (i.e., how a user recognizes her actions). Finally, the student concludes the interaction and control returns to the teacher, who continues with the class or transfers control to another student.

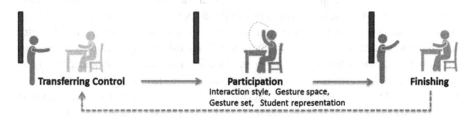

Fig. 1. Proposed concepts for designing hand gesture interfaces for classrooms

A couple of hypothetical examples can further explain our proposal. A teacher is showing slides projected on a screen. A student has a question which refers to the content presented some slides back, but the student does not remember exactly which one. Instead of having the teacher going slides back one by one, the student could take control (TC) of the presentation from his/her spot, and browse through the slides quickly with hand gestures until finding the right one (P). Also, the student can move a cursor over the slide and make marks to highlight the part the question refers to. After this, another student or the teacher can take control (F) and perform other tasks. Another scenario is a Grammar class in primary school. The teacher shows a sentence and asks about mistakes it contains. The teacher selects a student (TC) who starts interacting with the application to answer the question. The student can use various options (P), such as selecting one from several answers via a push gesture, encircling the answer, highlighting it with a marker, etc. Another student or the teacher can then correct a wrong answer, or the application itself can automatically give feedback (F).

3   Initial Evaluation

Taking into account that we were interested in learning about the students' feelings, beliefs, etc. regarding the proposal, we decided to carry out a focus group to collect qualitative data about student perceptions as a starting point. The major goal was to get students' opinions about the proposal by using the developed prototypes.

3.1   Design

The hardware setup consisted of a notebook, a projected display, and two gesture input devices, mounted in a classroom in our university campus. Taking into account there are several devices that can be used to track users' hand positions and recognize gestures, we decided to use and test two of them: Kinect and LM. Both devices were connected to a notebook equipped with an Intel Core i7 processor, 8 GB of RAM. The Kinect was placed at a height of 1 m, and 2.5 m in front of participants, whereas the LM was placed on participant's desk. The wall-projected display, connected to the notebook, had a size of 2×2 m and a resolution of 1360×768 pixels.

Two prototypes were developed to verify our proposal. Both used a gesture space in front of the user, and students were represented with a hand cursor and a silhouette (at the bottom right). A first application (A1, Fig. 2a) allows users to control a program for presentations (specifically, we used MS Power Point) performing several THG. Students may also make some annotations like circling a word or answer, drawing a shape, etc. Thus, the application allows browsing between slides using swipe gestures; sketching on a slide by tapping a button to enter to and exit from the drawing mode, gripping to start drawing, and releasing for finishing; and erasing the sketch by a wave gesture, all when the Kinect is used. Tap gesture is exchanged for a *thumb gesture* (that is recognized when the user extends her thumb) when the LM is employed. The second application (A2, Fig. 2b) is more specific. It was developed thinking on students of a Data Structures course. A2 allows the building of binary trees based on tap, grip, and release gestures using Kinect, and thumb gestures using LM (the user opens the thumb for gripping and hides it for releasing). To do this, the teacher enters the value of a new node and the student has to insert it in the right place by gripping the node, moving it to the right place, and releasing it. The application lets students perform node rotations to balance the tree according to the AVL-tree rules, make tree traversals and show them, clean the working area, and undo actions.

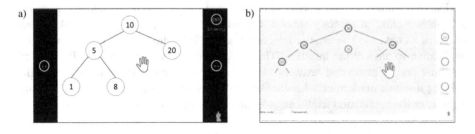

Fig. 2. The developed applications: (a) control a presentation program; (b) build binary trees.

Nine male computer science students (who were not UI designers) volunteered in the focus group. Seven undergraduate students were attending a course on Data Structures; two graduate students completed the group. All participants declared having a basic experience using Wii or Kinect for playing games.

The focus group started with the moderator's (a researcher) explanation about the goal and the use of THG. The moderator explained the idea of using applications based on THG from students' spot, and then he asked the participants to sit down only on the first row to start using the applications. First, the moderator explained the goal and use of A1, and the participants then tried it, first using Kinect, and secondly using LM.

Afterwards, A2 was introduced and used but interchanging the order of the devices. Finally, the moderator encouraged the participants to have a discussion on their preferences, beliefs, and general opinions about the possibility of using this interaction style according to our proposal, the elements included in the applications, the used devices, the perceived comfort, and the interaction (in general) by asking open-ended questions. The focus group lasted about 2 h.

Each participant had to perform several tasks when they were trying the applications. With three slides they had to advance forward and go backwards, and draw their initials (two letters) using A1. Concerning the other application (A2), each participant had to add a node and make a rotation (the options clear and undo were used occasionally when they were needed). Also, the participants took turns performing each task as they would do in a class; i.e., there was a moderator assuming the teacher's role who *transferred control* to each student to participate at the proper moment.

3.2 Results

The results described in this section were obtained from the discussion between the participants after performing the tasks. In general, they gave initial evidence of the feasibility of using THG to interact with applications from students' locations.

Concerning the main topic of interest, all participants agreed this style of interaction could help encourage students to participate in class, and they had no suggestions about the elements of the interfaces. A few comments in this sense were: "*classes will be more interesting if software of this type is used*", "*this proposal is ideal for students like us who love technology*", and "*this proposal could encourage students from secondary and maybe primary schools to participate in class*".

Concerning the used devices, it was not easy to get an agreement because the participants experienced greater precision using LM than using Kinect, but they said they preferred the Kinect interaction. At the end, they decided to choose Kinect as the input device suggesting that it was *fun, intuitive, involved more body parts*, and they expected an improvement in device precision in the near future.

Despite participants considered the applications as not difficult to learn and use, they mentioned the need to have a short learning curve for best results. They also provided further comments on the interfaces that led to the corresponding improvements. Some examples of this fact were: using both swipe gestures and buttons to navigate, moving the initial node to another place, and changing a couple of colors.

4 Discussion and Conclusion

With the aim of easing students participation during traditional classes and avoiding negative aspects (e.g., distraction and nervousness), we propose to use applications based on THG to allow students to interact from their physical locations. We have thus requested students to use two applications in the proposed manner, and the initial results demonstrate this type of applications could be used in an acceptable way. This proposal takes advantage of the benefits that THG can offer in the learning process. For instance, some activities/tasks could be done in a playful and interactive way contributing to enhance classroom interactions and to ignite student creativity [5].

This proposal may help manage some of the common problems experienced during the delivery of face-to-face classes, but today there are some practical limitations to implement it in real classrooms. They mainly refer to gesture acquisition devices. For example, LM offers acceptable precision to track hands and recognize gestures. However, its tracking space may be not large enough to allow recognizing some gestures. Moreover, student locations would have to be equipped with LMs, which could be comparable with having a mouse on each desktop. On the other hand, current versions of Kinect (and similar devices) can only track up to six people and the performance worsens with a distance over four meters. An alternative may be to use more than one Kinect to track more students and put the sensors at different places (e.g., on the ceiling). This configuration could be tried in the future, but we envision new and better gesture input devices that will track more people, at greater distances and fields of view, and with lower noise levels (e.g., Google's Project Soli).

This work has reported initial results, but it is necessary to perform further research. For example, we should analyze the degree at which this kind of applications would help encourage students to participate in class and avoid negative aspects. We also consider important to ask teachers their opinions about our proposal.

Acknowledgments. This work was partially supported by SENESCYT (Ecuador), NIC (DCC, Universidad de Chile), and Fondecyt 1161200 (Chile).

References

1. Anderson, R.J., Anderson, R., VanDeGrift, T., Wolfman, S., Yasuhara, K.: Promoting interaction in large classes with computer-mediated feedback. In: Wasson, B., et al. (eds.) Designing for Change, pp. 119–123. Kluwer Academic Publishers (2003)
2. Ratto, M., Shapiro, R.B., Truong, T.M., Griswold, W.G.: The activeclass project: experiments in encouraging classroom participation. In: Wasson, B., et al. (eds.) Designing for Change, pp. 477–486. Kluwer Academic Publishers (2003)
3. Baloian, N., Pino, J.A., Hardings, J., Hoppe, H.U.: Monitoring student activities with a querying system over electronic worksheets. In: Baloian, N., Burstein, F., Ogata, H., Santoro, F., Zurita, G. (eds.) CRIWG 2014. LNCS, vol. 8658, pp. 38–52. Springer, Heidelberg (2014). doi:10.1007/978-3-319-10166-8_4
4. Fried, C.B.: In-class laptop use and its effects on student learning. Comput. Educ. **50**(3), 906–914 (2008)
5. Hsu, H.J.: The Potential of Kinect in Education. Int. J. Inform. Educ. Technol. **1**(5), 365–370 (2011)
6. Jagodziński, P., Wolski, R.: Assessment of application technology of natural user interfaces in the creation of a virtual chemical laboratory. J. Sci. Educ. Technol. **24**(1), 16–28 (2015)
7. Lin, T.Y., Chen, C.F., Huang, D.Y., Huang, C.W., Chen, G.D.: Using resource of classroom and content of textbook to build immersive interactive learning playground. In: ICALT 2014, pp. 244–248. IEEE Press (2014)

8. Sommool, Worapot, Battulga, Batbaatar, Shih, Timothy K., Hwang, Wu-Yuin: Using kinect for holodeck classroom: a framework for presentation and assessment. In: Wang, Jhing-Fa, Lau, Rynson (eds.) ICWL 2013. LNCS, vol. 8167, pp. 40–49. Springer, Heidelberg (2013)
9. Blum, T., Kleeberger, V., Bichlmeier, C., Navab, N.: mirracle: an augmented reality magic mirror system for anatomy education. In: VRW 2012, pp. 115–116. IEEE Press (2012)
10. Erazo, O., Pino, J. A.: Predicting task execution time on natural user interfaces based on touchless hand gestures. In: IUI 2015, pp. 97–109. ACM Press (2015)

Sign Language Recognition Model Combining Non-manual Markers and Handshapes

Luis Quesada[1,2(✉)], Gabriela Marín[1,2], and Luis A. Guerrero[1,2]

[1] Escuela de Ciencias de la Computación e Informática, Universidad de Costa Rica,
San Pedro, Costa Rica
{luis.quesada,gabriela.marin,luis.guerreroblanco}@ucr.ac.cr
[2] Centro de Investigaciones en Tecnologías de La Información y Comunicación,
Universidad de Costa Rica, San Pedro, Costa Rica

Abstract. People with disabilities have fewer opportunities. Technological developments should be used to help these people to have more opportunities. In this paper we present partial results of a research project which aims to help people with disabilities, specifically deaf and hard of hearing. We present a sign language recognition model. The model takes advantage of the natural user interfaces (NUI) and a classification algorithm (support vector machines). Moreover, we combine handshapes (signs) and non-manual markers (associated to emotions and face gestures) in the recognition process to enhance the sign language expressivity recognition. Additionally, non-manual markers representation is proposed. A model evaluation is also reported.

Keywords: Sign language recognition · Handshapes recognition · Non-manual markers recognition · Intel RealSense

1 Introduction

In our human computer interaction (HCI) research group, we believe that technological advances should help diminishing the gap between people living with and without disabilities. To bridge that gap, it is essential to provide inexpensive tools.

Our work integrates natural user interfaces (NUI) and automatic sign language recognition (SLR) algorithms. There are more than 100 sign languages worldwide which are spoke mostly by deaf people [1]. Some researchers have achieved SLR using recent technological devices, i.e. Microsoft Kinect and Leap Motion. However, many of these works are still under development or their contributions were the evaluation of techniques and algorithms used in the context of some sign languages.

Sign language recognition is a complex task because includes several characteristics [2]. Within a dialogue, any of the characteristics can change the phrase's meaning. By example, the interlocutor's eyebrows position (a non-manual marker) makes the difference between an informative sentence and an interrogative sentence.

NUI use 3D cameras, which by infrared technology and depth sensors, recognize handshapes, face configuration and body position allowing recognition in a given moment of time. The device used for experimentation was the Intel RealSense.

© Springer International Publishing AG 2016
C.R. García et al. (Eds.): UCAmI 2016, Part I, LNCS 10069, pp. 400–405, 2016.
DOI: 10.1007/978-3-319-48746-5_41

The goal of this paper is to show a holistic model to achieve sign language recognition. This model recognizes sign language parameters: handshapes and non-manual markers using NUI and support vector machines (SVM). The main contribution of the paper is scalable SLR model using NUI (Intel RealSense). Also, this work aims to promote the development of tools to take advantage of new technologies for the benefit of the Deaf Community around the world.

In the next section we refer to sign language recognitions main components. In Sect. 3, the sign recognition model is proposed. In Sect. 4 the assessment system is presented. Finally, the discussion and the conclusions are presented in the final section.

2   Sign Language Recognition

This section describes sign languages main features: levels and parameters. Moreover, related work is described.

2.1   Sign Language Levels and Parameters

In Costa Rica, *Centro Nacional de Recursos para la Educación* (CENAREC) developed a project to describe the *Lengua de Señas Costarricense* (LESCO). LESCO description project 5 parameters: (1) handshape, (2) non-manual markers, (3) movement, (4) palm orientation and (5) location. These parameters described most of the sign languages [3].

This work considered only 2 parameters: handshapes and non-manual markers. The handshapes associate hand postures and concepts (words). Non-manual markers are changes in eyebrows position, facial expressions and head gestures uses to add grammatical information [4].

2.2   Related Work

Research related to sign language recognition include a variety of devices, i.e. 3D cameras, gloves and specialized hardware. This paper will focus its literature review only on the Microsoft Kinect and the Intel RealSense.

Microsoft Kinect has been tested recognizing small groups of signs, including ASL [5] and Japanese Sign Language (JSL) [6]. These works applied mixed recognition techniques with promising results. The techniques include Artificial Neural Networks (ANN), Hidden Markov Models (HMM) and SVM.

Intel RealSense has been involved in work in progress applications. Huang et al. [7] use this device to recognize fingerspelling alphabet. They predict the handshapes using SVM and Deep Neural Networks (DNN). Results are promising [7].

Moreover, automatic recognition systems for non-manual markers have been explored. Using multi-scale and spatial-temporal analysis, Liu et al. [8] proposed a system to recognize raised and lowered eyebrows, head nods, and head shakes [8].

There are few automatic SLR systems recognizing handshapes and non-manual markers at same time. These works are prior to the NUIs. Hence, they use conventional cameras [9]. NUI represents a new trend in the use of technologies to support HCI.

3   Sign Language Recognition Model

This section proposes a sign recognition model using the Intel RealSense and SVM. The device of Intel is a set of cameras and development libraries that allow users to use gestures to interact with computers. SVM predicts performed handshapes and non-manual markers. Figure 1 shows the proposed model. The combination handshape – non-manual markers enhance the SLR semantic.

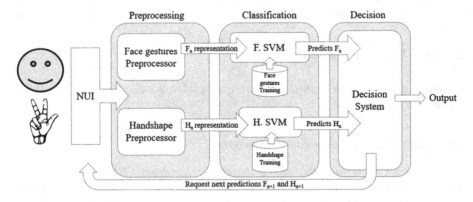

Fig. 1. SLR model.

Main components of the SLR model are 3D Camera (NUI), preprocessing module, classification module and decision module. This model assumes prior training of each SVM. Once the training is complete, the system is prepared to predict concepts performed by a signer using the trained sign language.

The NUI module includes hardware and software (libraries) provided by the device manufacturer. The hardware recognizes the position of each finger and the software provides the key points describing the performed sign. The hardware also recognizes the non-manual markers (eyebrows, eyes, etc.)

The preprocessing module transforms the raw data gathered from the device. The transformation allows the data be used by SVMs. The data correspond to non-manual markers and handshapes. Non-manual markers include key features: eyebrows config-uration (position), gaze and mouth configuration. Each feature was represented by an integer number between 0 and 100.

Therefore, F representation flowing between preprocessing module and classifica-tion module (see Fig. 1) is a list of 7 integer numbers. These numbers represent a face gesture associated to an emotion or a discursive modifier. Different non-manual markers configurations enhance the handshape significance [10].

Handshapes representation contains fingertips coordinates $<x, y, z>$ and direction vectors between phalanges. These data are gathered for each finger. This handshape representation allows the distinction between several [11]. Consequently, H represen-tation (see Fig. 1) is a list of real numbers corresponding to fingertips coordinates and vectors between phalanges.

Classification module receives preprocessed data from previous module. Two SVMs (previously trained) predict a face gesture and a handshape. SVMs are supervised learning models that use training observations to recognize patterns [12].

Based on information provided by the SVMs, the decision module chooses which sign is performing in the device vision range. Every 6 milliseconds the SVM predict two values: a face gesture prediction and a handshape prediction.

The answer of the SLR cannot be based on only one prediction. In an instant of time, the signer could be moving the hand to achieve the final position. The intermediate handshapes predictions could not be the final one.

Decision system main components are: a face gestures buffer (capacity: 5 predictions), a handshape buffer (capacity: 5 predictions), two buffer handlers (one handler per buffer) and a rules engine. Each prediction is evaluated by the respective buffer handler. Circular buffers are used. When new predictions F_n and H_n get in the decision system, the handler assigns them to a buffer space. Index n represents a frame of time. Therefore, each SVM prediction represents the sign performed in different frames of time. Each frame is separated by milliseconds between them.

As soon as the 5 buffer spaces are equal (5 equal consecutive predictions), a recognized face gesture (F_i) or handshape (H_j) is send it to the rules engine. If a rule applied to the recognized face gesture and handshape, then the system outputs a recognized sign S_r. This solution was explored in [11] recognizing handshapes only.

4   Evaluation

We selected a list of signs (handshapes) and a list of face gestures. Rules were created for the handshapes and face gestures selected. Each face gesture is defined by non-manual markers configuration. Afterwards, the SVMs were trained. Each SVM was trained separately by one person. The trainer is acquainted with ASL and LESCO. Only one person was considered because the nature of the test. Each person express emotions differently. Further, physical features of each person are different (i.e. eyebrows position or neutral gaze).

When the SVMs were ready, they were tested individually. Then, we attempted to recognize simple signs according to the implemented rules. The handshapes selected were: "today", "monday", "friday", and "now". Face gestures selected were: "interrogative", "informative", "anger", and "happy". Handshapes are LESCO signs. Each sign is performed using one hand. Face gestures were selected from LESCO description [2] and basic emotions expressed in sign languages [13].

Twenty rules were defined combining handshapes and face gestures. Four performances by rule were requested. Therefore, 80 sign performances were tested (5 face gestures, 4 handshapes, 4 attempts per combination). The requested performances were randomly ordered. One person performed all the tests. Figure 2.a shows the results considering the attempts (performances in front of the NUI) per face gesture.

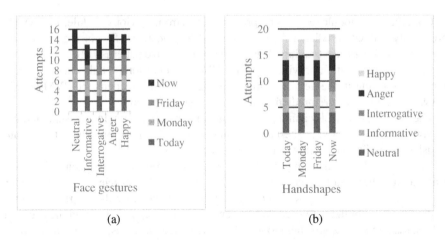

Fig. 2. (a) Accuracy results per face gesture, (b) Accuracy results per handshape.

Neutral face gesture achieved 100 % of gesture accuracy. Hence, all handshapes were recognized when the person expressed a neutral face. The worst recognition rate was 81.25 % (informative face gesture). While tests were performed, informative face gesture was misclassified as neutral face gesture; and anger gesture was misclassified as interrogative face.

No handshape was recognized with perfect accuracy. However, the signs were misclassified at most 2 times per handshape (total 20 attempts). Considering the 80 tests, 73 (91.25 %) were classified correctly. Only 3 of 7 misclassified signs do not match both features (face gesture and handshape). Remaining 4 misclassified signs do not match one of the features (see Fig. 2.b). Next section discusses the evaluation results.

5   Discussion and Conclusion

We presented a sign language recognition model. The model recognizes two important parameters of sign languages: handshape and non-manual markers. Although we choose a specific technology (Intel RealSense) and a specific classification algorithm (SVMs), these components could be substituted by different devices or algorithms. By example, an ANN can predict signs or a new NUI can gather data more efficiently.

Furthermore, additional parameters can improve the automatic sign language recognition model. Remaining parameters are: movement, palm orientation and location. Adding these parameters require: (1) to define a parameter representation, (2) to select and evaluate a classification algorithm and (3) to create rules including the new parameters.

Non-manual markers representation was tested. More face gestures must be defined to express more emotions associated to the sign languages specific grammar. Recognizing more face gestures require more non-manual markers recognition. Evaluation combining handshapes and face gestures recognition was executed. More than 90 % of the tests were classified correctly. As shown, selected parameters recognition adds semantic richness to signed dialogues.

We hope that this proposal will encourage research and development of new tools that help deaf people. People living with disabilities in developing countries need to take advantage of technological advances to achieve a better quality of life.

Acknowledgments. This work was partially supported by the Escuela de Ciencias de la Computación e Informática at Universidad de Costa Rica grant No. 320-B5-291, by Centro de Investigaciones en Tecnologías de la Información y Comunicación de la Universidad de Costa Rica, and Consejo Nacional para Investigaciones Científicas y Tecnológicas (CONICIT) of the Government of Costa Rica.

References

1. Lewis, P., Simons, G., Fennig, C.: Ethnologue: Languages of the World. SIL International (2009)
2. Oviedo, A.: Descripción General Básica de la LESCO (2012)
3. Woodward, J.: Sign language varieties in Costa Rica. Sign Lang. Stud. **73**(1), 329–345 (1991)
4. Caridakis, G., Asteriadis, S., Karpouzis, K.: Non-manual cues in automatic sign language recognition. Pers. Ubiquit. Comput. **18**(1), 37–46 (2014)
5. Zafrulla, Z., Brashear, H., Starner, T., Hamilton, H., Presti, P.: American sign language recognition with the kinect. In: Proceedings of the 13th International Conference Multimodal Interfaces, pp. 279–286 (2011)
6. Agarwal, A., Thakur, M.K.: Sign language recognition using Microsoft Kinect. In: Sixth International Conference on Contemporary Computing, pp. 181–185 (2013)
7. Huang, J., Zhou, W., Li, W., Li, H.: Sign language recognition using real-sense. In: EEE China Summit and International Conference on Signal and Information Processing (ChinaSIP), pp. 166–170 (2015)
8. Liu, J., Liu, B., Zhang, S., Yang, F., Yang, P., Metaxas, D.N., Neidle, C.: Non-manual grammatical marker recognition based on multi-scale, spatio-temporal analysis of head pose and facial expressions. Image Vis. Comput. **32**(10), 671–681 (2014)
9. Yang, H.D., Lee, S.W.: Robust sign language recognition by combining manual and non-manual features based on conditional random field and support vector machine. Pattern Recognit. Lett. **34**(16), 2051–2056 (2013)
10. Nguyen, T.D., Ranganath, S.: Facial expressions in American sign language: tracking and recognition. Pattern Recognit. **45**(5), 1877–1891 (2012)
11. Quesada, L., López, G., Guerrero, L.A.: Sign language recognition using leap motion. In: García-Chamizo, J.M., et al. (eds.) UCAmI 2015. LNCS, vol. 9454, pp. 277–288. Springer, Heidelberg (2015)
12. Cortes, C., Vapnik, V.: Support-vector networks. Mach. Learn. **20**, 273–297 (1995)
13. Antonakos, E., Roussos, A., Zafeiriou, S.: A survey on mouth modeling and analysis for Sign Language recognition. In: International Conference on Automatic Face and Gesture Recognition, pp. 1–7 (2015)

Automatic Generation
of User Interaction Models

Cristina Tîrnăucă$^{(\boxtimes)}$, Rafael Duque, and José Luis Montaña

Departamento de Matemáticas, Estadística y Computación,
Universidad de Cantabria, Santander, Spain
{cristina.tirnauca,rafael.duque,joseluis.montana}@unican.es

Abstract. A prominent requirement in the field of human-computer interaction is to make mobile applications more usable and better adjusted to their users' needs. In particular, designers of groupware applications face the task of developing software for many users while making it work as if it was designed for each single individual. User modeling research has attempted to address these issues. A precondition for achieving this task is to find predictive and generative models of the user interactions. In this paper we develop a methodology for modeling the user behavior when interacting with a computer system. The byproduct of this methodology is a low level representation of the user interactions in the form of weighted automata, which can be easily transformed into user profiles in text form. Profiles can then be used by the designer to configure and verify the task model of the system.

Keywords: Human computer-interaction · User modeling · Mobile interfaces · Weighted automaton · Clustering

1 Introduction

Nowadays, we can observe a proliferation of groupware applications (social networks, shared editors, messaging services, etc.) that enable the collaboration between users. The Computer-Supported Collaborative Work (CSCW) research field [6] has focused on studying how technology can effectively support these collective processes. One of the main purposes of the CSCW has been the identification of methodologies that provide a systematic approach to discovering the users' requirements and to evaluating the degree to which these systems allow users to be aware off, to modify or to interact with the work of other users.

One of the most frequent characterizations of the groupware systems is based on the following two dimensions of their contexts of use [3]: (i) *time*, whether users collaborate synchronously (they collaborate at the same time) or asynchronously (they collaborate at different moments) and (ii) *space*, whether users are co-located or geographically distributed. Currently, most users of smart-phones use groupware applications that allow them to collaborate synchronously and/or asynchronously while being geographically distributed. Therefore, the evaluation

© Springer International Publishing AG 2016
C.R. García et al. (Eds.): UCAmI 2016, Part I, LNCS 10069, pp. 406–418, 2016.
DOI: 10.1007/978-3-319-48746-5_42

of these groupware applications should assess the versatility of the systems to support synchronous and asynchronous interactions and whether the system is adapted to the users' mental model so they do not have to make any effort to use the system's features.

In order to carry out these evaluations, this article describes a methodological approach that identifies the context of use in which the users perform the interactions (synchronous or asynchronous) and generates descriptive models of how these users orchestrate the interactions with the system. Finally, these models are processed to create descriptive text in natural language of the main characteristics of the users' interaction with the system. Thus, the designer can verify whether the system offers a natural interaction experience to its users in each context of use and whether users deviate substantially from the task model used to design the system. The task models are specifications widely used in the Human-Computer Interaction field to describe the logical activities that have to be performed in order to reach the users' goals. Therefore, the evaluation of the system should analyze the users behaviors to verify that it is not hard for them to follow the sequence of actions specified by the task model. Moreover, the users of the system can have different behaviors so the task model must also be flexible enough to enable the users to reach their goals in different ways. With this aim, we propose a methodology that processes log repositories with information of the user interactions and also models the behavior of the users. Then, the users with similar behavior are grouped together and for each set of similar users, a profile (in the form of a weighted automaton) is generated. Finally, these weighted automata are transformed into descriptive text that capture the

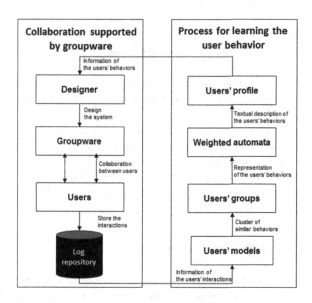

Fig. 1. Main steps of the methodology

characteristics of those different users profiles, which is a valuable information that allows to design a task model according to the users' natural behavior (Fig. 1).

2   Related Work

Suarez et al. [10] establish a classification of interactive systems and point out that specific evaluation criteria should be applied to each one, according to their features and complexity. This classification includes the groupware as a specific type of application. Among the specific features of the groupware applications, it is noteworthy that they enable not only the communication between users but also the collaboratively building of artifacts in shared workspaces. The groupware applications support user interactions whose effects can be perceived by at least another member of the group or another community. Therefore, the evaluation should consider specific criteria such as the effectivity of the awareness and social support of the application. Molina et al. [7] propose a combination of techniques (questionnaires, empirical testing, heuristic evaluation, eye tracking) to analyze the awareness support of groupware applications. Neale et al. [8] propose some specific measurements to evaluate the degree to which an application intuitively enables social interactions.

These evaluations have been automated using tools such as Tatiana, which is independent of any groupware system and allows us to configure and to automate the analysis of interactions recorded in log files by means of several socio-cognitive methodologies. Moreover, Tatiana provides support to perform non-automated analysis, where collaborative activity is reproduced by video and the users introduce annotations or categorizations about the users' interactions. ProM [1] is another tool that facilitates this kind of analysis: it allows users to select different data mining algorithms in order to analyze the work-flows recorded in log files.

Thaler [11] uses the term *usability mining* for the evaluation process of information systems based on analyzing log traces. In this case, the goal is to derive a model of usage of the system that includes information about the users behavior (irrelevant actions, undo actions, using help function, etc.). The users' actions can be analyzed using statistical techniques that generate quantitative information. These measures are known as low-level indicators [2], as they usually do not provide an interpretation of the user's activity. The indicators whose values provide an interpretation (cognitive, technological, etc.) of the user's activity are known as high-level indicators.

3   Data Flow Representation

The data flow generated by the interactions of users with a computerized system can be seen as a stream of tuples $\mathcal{D}$ of the form (id, t, a), where id is the user's identifier in the system and t represents the instant of time when the action a took place.

More precisely, $\mathcal{D}$ is a sequence of the form $\mathcal{D} := [\mathcal{D}[i]]_{1 \leq i \leq N}$, where $\mathcal{D}[i] := (id_i, t_i, a_i) \in \mathcal{U} \times \mathcal{T} \times \mathcal{A}$; $\mathcal{U}$ is a finite set of user identifiers, $\mathcal{T}$ is a finite set of instants in which the process is observed and $\mathcal{A}$ is a finite set of actions. For convenience, we denote by $\mathcal{D}[i].id = id_i$, that is, the id-component of tuple $\mathcal{D}[i]$. Analogously $\mathcal{D}[i].t$ and $\mathcal{D}[i].a$ represent (respectively) the t-component and the a-component of tuple $\mathcal{D}[i]$. We assume that $\mathcal{D}[i].t \leq \mathcal{D}[i+1].t$, for $1 \leq i < N-1$. The information contained in $\mathcal{D}$ can be segmented according to different criteria. If we are interested in the case in which $\mathcal{D}$ is partitioned according to the user identifiers, $\mathcal{U} := \{u_1, ..., u_l\}$, each segment of information is of the form:

$$\mathcal{D}(k) := [(a_i, t_i) : \mathcal{D}[i].id = u_k] = [(a_{i_1}, t_{i_1}), (a_{i_2}, t_{i_2}), \ldots, (a_{i_n}, t_{i_n})]$$

That is, segment $\mathcal{D}(k)$ is the subsequence of $\mathcal{D}$ formed by those tuples (a_i, t_i) in which action a_i is performed by the user whose identifier is u_k (the user's id information is the same for all tuples in $\mathcal{D}(k)$ and thus it is omitted). We call segment $\mathcal{D}(k)$ a trace (also *path* or *trajectory*) of user u_k in the system.

For data analysis and user profiling, one might be interested in the duration of transitions between actions and not in the exact instance of time in which actions take place. In such cases, we can rewrite the trace $\mathcal{D}(k)$ as a new path of the form:

$$\pi(k) : [(a_{i_1}, d_{i_1}), \ldots, (a_{i_{n-1}}, d_{i_{n-1}}), a_{i_n}] \tag{1}$$

where $d_{i_j} := t_{i_{j+1}} - t_{i_j}$ is the time elapsed between action a_{i_j} and action $a_{i_{j+1}}$, for $1 \leq j < n$, and thus, a continuous attribute. We can discretize these durations into a fixed number of categories, say $\mathcal{C} := \{c_1, \ldots, c_L\}$, where each value c_i represents a time interval chosen *ad hoc* for the system under study.

4   User Interaction Models and Group Profiles

The problem of *modeling the user interactions* can be stated as follows: given a path π of a certain user, find a generative model that behaves in the same way as the user does in the interactive system. *A priori* there is no restriction on the nature of the generative model, which could be a Markov model, an automaton, a Bayesian network, etc. We explore here a Markov-like structure called *weighted automaton*.

Definition 1 *(Weighted automaton, see [4]). Let Σ be a finite alphabet of symbols and n a positive natural number. A weighted automaton over Σ with n states is a tuple $\mathcal{M} := (in, out, \{W_\sigma\}_{\sigma \in \Sigma})$, where in and out are vectors in $\mathbb{R}^n$ representing features of the empty prefix and of the empty suffix, respectively, and W_σ is an $n \times n$-matrix with real entries representing transition weights. In some situations we can omit in and out if they are not relevant for the problem.*

Let $\mathcal{A} = \{a_1, a_2, ..., a_m\}$ be the set of actions that can be performed by a user in a given interactive system. For each user u_k, we build the path $\pi(k)$ as in (1). In this path, actions a_{i_j} are in $\mathcal{A}$ and durations d_{i_j} belong to some interval c in $\mathcal{C}$, where $\mathcal{C} = \{c_1, \ldots, c_L\}$ is a finite set of time intervals as explained in Sect. 3. We define the *user interaction model* as the weighted automaton $\mathcal{M}_{u_k} := (\{W_c^k\}_{c \in \mathcal{C}})$ over the alphabet $\mathcal{C}$ with states $\{a_1, a_2, ..., a_m\}$, in which the matrices of weights are defined as follows:

$$W_c^k(a, a') := count_c(a, a'), \text{ for all } c \in \mathcal{C} \text{ and } a, a' \in \mathcal{A}$$

where $count_c(a, a') := |\{j \in \{1, \ldots, n-1\} \mid a = a_{i_j}, a' = a_{i_{j+1}}, d_{i_j} \in c\}|$, that is, the number of times action a precedes action a' in the trajectory $\pi(k)$ of the respective user and the time elapsed between the two actions is in the time category c.

Sometimes we identify the weighted automaton $\mathcal{M}_{u_k}$ with a point of the affine space $\mathbb{R}^{Lm^2}$. This point is defined by

$$P_{u_k} := (W_c^k(a, a'))_{(c,a,a') \in \mathcal{C} \times \mathcal{A} \times \mathcal{A}} \in \mathbb{R}^{Lm^2}$$

Determining whether two users have a similar behavior can then be done via distance measures or similarity measures. Given two vectors $x = (x_1, \ldots, x_p)$ and $y = (y_1, \ldots, y_p)$, the distance between them can be calculated using the *Minkowski metric*:

$$d_g(x, y) = (|x_1 - y_1|^g + |x_2 - y_2|^g + \ldots + |x_p - y_p|^g)^{1/g} \tag{2}$$

The commonly used *Euclidean distance* is obtained for $g = 2$, the *Manhattan distance* (also called *city block*) for $g = 1$ and the *Chebychev distance* for $g = \infty$.

An alternative concept to that of the distance is the similarity function. When the angle between the two vectors is a meaningful measure, one may consider the *cosine measure*

$$cos(x, y) := \frac{\langle x, y \rangle}{\|x\| \cdot \|y\|}, \tag{3}$$

where $\langle \cdot, \cdot \rangle$ is the Euclidean inner product in $\mathbb{R}^N$, and $\|\cdot\|$ is the norm induced by the inner product, or the *normalized Pearson correlation*:

$$cor(x, y) := \frac{\langle x - \bar{x}, y - \bar{y} \rangle}{\|x - \bar{x}\| \cdot \|y - \bar{y}\|}, \tag{4}$$

where $\bar{x}$ denotes the average feature value of x over all dimensions.

In practice, we use $d_{cos}(x, y) := 1 - cos(x, y)$ and $d_{cor}(x, y) := 1 - cor(x, y)$ in order to have $d_{cos}(x, x) = d_{cor}(x, x) = 0$ as in the case of the above mentioned distances.

Next, we are interested in clustering the users into a certain non specified quantity of *representative user profiles* such that users in the same group (cluster) behave more similarly to each other than to users in other clusters. To this end, we use agglomerative hierarchical clustering with three linkage criteria: single, complete and average (see [9] for more details). Given a set of l users to be clustered and a fixed number $k \leq l$ of desired clusters, the basic process of our hierarchical clustering is as follows.

- Step 1. Start by assigning each user to its own cluster, so that if we have l users, in this initial stage we have l clusters, each containing just one user.
- Step 2. Set the distances between the clusters equal the distances between the users they contain.
- Step 3. Find the closest (most similar) pair of clusters and merge them into a single cluster, so that now we have one less cluster.
- Step 4. Compute distances between the new cluster and each of the old clusters.
- Step 5. Repeat steps third and fourth until users are clustered into k clusters.

Depending on the type of linkage chosen, the distance between two clusters is computed with one of the three formulas:

- single linkage: $d(C, C') = \min\limits_{x \in C, x' \in C'} d(x, x')$
- complete linkage: $d(C, C') = \max\limits_{x \in C, x' \in C'} d(x, x')$
- average linkage: $d(C, C') = (\sum\limits_{x \in C, x' \in C'} d(x, x'))/(|C| \cdot |C'|)$

where $d(x, y)$ can be any of the distances previously defined.

We denote by k the number of representative user profiles in an interactive system. The correct choice of k depends most of the times on the application. The optimal k will strike a balance between maximum compression of user profiles using a single cluster, and maximum accuracy by assigning each profile to its own cluster (having one cluster per user). If an appropriate value of k is not apparent from prior knowledge on the properties of the profile set, it must be somehow determined. In the literature, there are several proposals for making this decision effective (see [9] for a survey). Since in this particular application we are interesting in outlining and analyzing a smallish number of profiles, the k will be chosen *ad hoc* (more details are given in Sect. 5).

Once k is chosen and the groups of similar users are identified, next step is to find a model that describes the profile of each group of users. Note that groups of users that contain less than 10 % of the population are discarded as *outliers* (the threshold can be modified depending on the application). We propose to train a weighted automaton for each group of users (representing a cluster). We define the *group profile* of cluster C as the weighted automaton $\mathcal{M}_C := \{W_c^C\}_{c \in \mathcal{C}}$ over alphabet $\mathcal{C}$ with states $\{a_1, \ldots, a_m\}$, in which the weights matrices are defined as follows.

$$W_c^C(a, a') = \frac{\sum\limits_{u_k \in C} W_c^k(a, a')}{\sum\limits_{c \in \mathcal{C}} \sum\limits_{a \in \mathcal{A}} \sum\limits_{u_k \in C} W_c^k(a, a')}, \text{ for all } c \in \mathcal{C} \text{ and } a, a' \in \mathcal{A} \tag{5}$$

Initial and final probabilities can be similarly defined, but they are not relevant in this case so we omit giving explicit formulas. According to [5], the previous automaton maximizes the likelihood of the observations.

5   Case Study: Collaborative Sports Betting

Our proposal was applied to a case study in which thirty users interacted with a mobile groupware application that supports sports betting. These thirty users were randomly grouped in ten groups of three members. They were requested to collaboratively make five bets. The interactions of the users with the application were stored in a log repository. Finally, our proposal was used to extract a description of the users profiles.

The process of creating a bet is made up of three main steps. First, a user proposes a bet to the other members of the group. This proposal includes a result of a sport event and an amount of money. Second, the members of the group use a chat tool (see Fig. 2-right) to analyze the result and the stake of the bet. Third, the members of the group use a voting panel (see Fig. 2-center) to accept or reject the bet that has been proposed. Figure 2-left shows the main user interface of this application, that allows the user to: propose a new bet to the other members of the group, see the state of the bets or proposals made previously, use a chat to discuss about a proposal, create a new group of users or see a tutorial that explains how to use the application. The appendix of this paper includes a specification of the actions supported by the application.

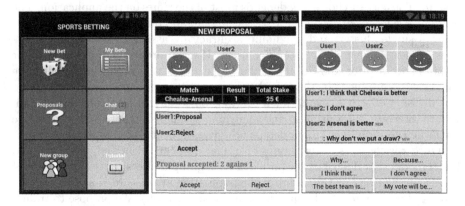

Fig. 2. User interface of the groupware system

Each user is represented by a vector of Lm^2 components with $m = 12$ (only twelve actions were used by users) and $L = 4$ (we discretized the set of all time intervals into four intervals). The precise four intervals are (time is expressed in seconds): $c_1 = [0, 46], c_2 = [47, 104], c_3 = [107, 295], c_4 = [297, 5251]$, that is, c_1 corresponds to actions that take less than three quarters of a minute, c_2 corresponds to longer actions that take less than one minute and three quarters, c_3 corresponds to actions that take less than 5 min, and c_4 corresponds to actions that are longer than 5 min.

After performing agglomerative hierarchical clustering with the three linkage criteria and the five distinct metrics described in Sect. 4, we reached the following conclusions:

- the single-link or average-link clustering methods detect many outliers before starting to output reasonable sized groups: a second group of at least three users is identified, on average, with $k = 9$ for single linkage, $k = 5.2$ for complete linkage and $k = 7.8$ for average linkage; moreover, in the case of single linkage, none of the three Minkowski-type distances produces a second group of at least three users,
- the complete-link clustering methods usually produce more compact clusters and more useful hierarchies than the other two clustering methods.

Once chosen the type of linkage, we had to determine which of the five distances should be used. First, we discarded from our analysis the Chebychev distance because of the many outliers detected before starting to identify reasonable-sized groups (7 in this case, compared to 2, 0, 3 and 4 for the other metrics used). Then, for each k, we plotted the distance between the last two clusters merged in order to obtain k clusters from the previous $k + 1$ clusters.

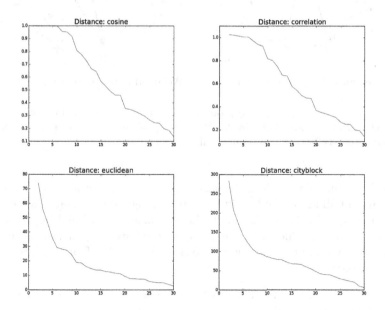

Fig. 3. Distance against number of clusters

We observe that for the similarity-type of metrics, choosing a k that justifies increasing the number of partitions from k to $k + 1$ (see Fig. 3) is much more difficult than for the Euclidean distance (where the obvious k is 6) or the Manhattan distance (where the best k seems to be 8). Therefore, the metric chosen in the end was the Euclidean one, with $k = 6$.

The weighted finite automaton generated for each of the two bigger groups identified with this metric are presented in Fig. 4 (the other 4 groups contained only one user, and their characteristics are described in Table 1). A description for each action is provided in the Appendix. A transition from a state a_p to a state a_r labeled i/x has to be interpreted as $W^C_{c_i}(a_p, a_r) = x$. Note that for a better readability, transitions with weights less than 0.1 are omitted.

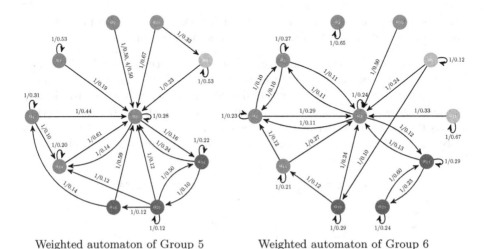

Weighted automaton of Group 5   Weighted automaton of Group 6

Fig. 4. Weighted automata for two profiles; colors indicate the panel to which a given action belongs: orange for Chat, blue for New Bet, green for Proposals, pink for Tutorial and salmon for My bets. (Color figure online)

These automata provide information used to generate a set of rules that enables us to build a description in natural language of the main characteristics of each user profile. Thus, this methodology allows us to build expert system that take as input log files with the users' interactions and generate as output a textual description of the main user profiles. The following four rules are applied for this purpose:

- Rule 1: If $|C| < 10\% * l$ for a cluster $C \rightarrow$ *The members of C can be considered as outliers.*
- Rule 2: If $\exists a, a'$ such that $W^C_{c_4}(a, a')! = 0 \rightarrow$ *The members of C have used the system in an asynchronous context.*
- Rule 3: If $\exists a, a'$ such that $W^C_{c_1}(a, a')! = 0 \rightarrow$ *The members of C have used the system in a synchronous context.*

Table 1. Description of the profiles

Group number/number of users	Description of profiles and rules that are activated
1/1	The members of this group can be considered as outliers (Rule 1). The members of this group have used the system in a synchronous context (Rule 3)
2/1	The members of this group can be considered as outliers (Rule 1). The members of this group have used the system in a synchronous context (Rule 3). During the interaction process the members of this group never used the following tools: voting panel, tutorial, my bets, new bet (Rule 4)
3/1	The members of this group can be considered as outliers (Rule 1). The members of this group have used the system in a synchronous context (Rule 3). During the interaction process the members of this group never used the following tools: tutorial (Rule 4)
4/1	The members of this group can be considered as outliers (Rule 1). The members of this group have used the system in a synchronous context (Rule 3). During the interaction process the members of this group never used the following tools: voting panel (Rule 4)
5/4	The members of this group have used the system in a synchronous context (Rule 3). The members of this group have used the system in an asynchronous context (Rule 2). During the interaction process the members of this group never used some of the actions supported by the following tools: voting panel (Rule 4)
6/22	The members of this group have used the system in a synchronous context (Rule 3). During the interaction process the members of this group never used some of the actions supported by the following tools: voting panel (Rule 4)

- Rule 4: If $\exists a$ such that $W_{c_i}^C(a, a') = W_{c_i}^C(a', a) = 0, \forall i \in \{1, \ldots, 4\}, \forall a' \in \mathcal{A}$ $\rightarrow$ *During the interaction process, the members of C never used some of the actions supported by the tools: (list of tools that support action a).*

Table 1 includes the textual description of the profiles generated in this case study by means of these four rules. We can observe that the system was often used in a synchronous way. Only the members of the fifth profile carried out often asynchronous interactions. Moreover, we can observe that most users never perform some of the actions supported by the voting panel. If the evaluators or designers focus the attention on the states of the automaton that models these actions, they can discover that the actions of accept and reject are very seldom used. Most users use the chat to answer the proposal of bets that other users made. Therefore, the automaton and the textual information of these profiles can be used by the designers to adapt the system to this natural user behavior and to design new evaluations in which the interactions can be carried out in an asynchronous context.

6   Conclusions

We have proposed a methodology for the automatic generation of user interaction models in interactive systems that combines unsupervised and supervised learning. We record the logs of the users in the system in form of traces and, after a preprocess consisting in describing actions and durations, we compress these traces into feature vectors. Feature vectors are then clustered using agglomerative hierarchical clustering techniques (unsupervised phase) into groups of users by similarity of the empirical distributions of actions, durations and transitions. Once this process is completed, we model each group of users by means of a weighted automaton (supervised phase). This finite state machine is what we call an user profile. User profiles, as intended in this paper, constitute a low level representation of user patterns in interactive systems. From the low level representation we derive a profile in text form using rules that automatically generate a text identifying some features being representative of the group of users under consideration. As future work we plan to apply our technique to inverse software engineering, using the weighted automaton to infer a task model of the interactive system under study that may help the software engineer to improve the system's design.

Acknowledgments. This work was partially supported by project PAC::LFO (MTM2014-55262-P) of Ministerio de Ciencia e Innovación (MICINN), Spain.

A   Appendix

The following Table 2 describes the semantics of the actions of the interactive groupware system used for the experimentation. The actions supported by the tool to generate groups of users are omitted because they were managed by the evaluators and the users of the system never performed these actions.

Table 2. Actions of the groupware system

Identifier	Panel	Description of the action
a_1	Chat	Access to this space
a_2	Chat	Send a "free" message
a_3	Chat	Send a "Why..." message
a_4	Chat	Send a "Because" message
a_5	Chat	Send a "I think that" message
a_6	Chat	Send a "I don't agree" message
a_7	Chat	Send a "The beast team is" message
a_8	Chat	Send a "My vote will be" message
a_9	Proposals	Access to this space
a_{10}	Proposals	Reject a proposal
a_{11}	Proposals	Accept a proposal
a_{12}	Proposals	A proposal was accepted by the group
a_{13}	Proposals	A proposal was rejected by the group
a_{14}	My Bets	Access to this space
a_{15}	Tutorial	Access to this space
a_{16}	New Bet	See sport events
a_{24}	New Bet	Access to this space
a_{25}	New Bet	Send a proposal

References

1. van der Aalst, W.M.P.: Exploring the CSCW spectrum using process mining. Adv. Eng. Inform. **21**(2), 191–199 (2007)
2. Bravo, C., Redondo, M.A., Verdejo, M.F., Ortega, M.: A framework for process-solution analysis in collaborative learning environments. Int. J. Hum. Comput. Stud. **66**(11), 812–832 (2008)
3. Cruz, A., Correia, A., Paredes, H., Fonseca, B., Morgado, L., Martins, P.: Towards an overarching classification model of CSCW and groupware: a socio-technical perspective. In: Herskovic, V., Hoppe, H.U., Jansen, M., Ziegler, J. (eds.) CRIWG 2012. LNCS, vol. 7493, pp. 41–56. Springer, Heidelberg (2012)
4. Culik, K., Karhumaki, U.: Finite automata computing real functions. SIAM J. Comput. **23**(4), 789–814 (1994)
5. Dupont, P., Denis, F., Esposito, Y.: Links between probabilistic automata and hidden markov models: probability distributions, learning models and induction algorithms. Pattern Recognit. **38**(9), 1349–1371 (2005)
6. Grudin, J.: Computer-supported cooperative work: history and focus. Computer **27**(5), 19–26 (1994)
7. Molina, A.I., Gallardo, J., Redondo, M.A., Bravo, C.: Evaluating the awareness support of collece, a collaborative programming tool. In: Proceedings of the XV International Conference on Human Computer Interaction (Interacción 2014), pp. 11:1–11:2. ACM, New York (2014)

8. Neale, D.C., Carroll, J.M., Rosson, M.B.: Evaluating computer-supported cooperative work: models and frameworks. In: Proceedings of the 2004 ACM Conference on Computer Supported Cooperative Work (CSCW 2004), pp. 112–121. ACM, New York (2004)
9. Rokach, L.: A survey of clustering algorithms. In: Maimon, O., Rokach, L., et al. (eds.) Data Mining and Knowledge Discovery Handbook, pp. 269–298. Springer, Heidelberg (2010)
10. Torrente, M.C.S., Prieto, A.B.M., Gutiérrez, D.A., de Sagastegui, M.E.A.: Sirius: a heuristic-based framework for measuring web usability adapted to the type of website. J. Syst. Softw. **86**(3), 649–663 (2013)
11. Thaler, T.: Towards usability mining. In: Plödereder, E., Grunske, L., Schneider, E., Ull, D. (eds.) 44. Jahrestagung der Gesellschaft für Informatik, Informatik 2014, Big Data - Komplexität meistern, 22-26 Stuttgart, Deutschland, LNI, vol. 232, GI (2014)

Examining the Usability of Touch Screen Gestures for Elderly People

Doris Cáliz[1]([⊠]), Xavier Alamán[2], Loic Martínez[1], Richart Cáliz[3],
Carlos Terán[3], and Verónica Peñafiel[4]

[1] CETTICO Research Group, ETSIINF, Polytechnic University of Madrid,
Campus de Montegancedo, 28660 Boadilla del Monte, Madrid, Spain
doriscalizramos@outlook.com, loic@fi.upm.es
[2] Department of Computer Science, Autonomous University of Madrid,
C/Francisco Tomás y Valiente, 11, 28049 Madrid, Spain
Xavier.Alaman@uam.es
[3] FIS Group, Departamento de Informática y Ciencias de la
Computación (DICC). EPN, Escuela Politécnica Nacional,
Ladrón de Guevara E11-25 y, Andalucía, Quito, Ecuador
richartharold@hotmail.com, carlos.teran@cobiscorp.com
[4] Datos Análisis Estadístico. Análisis de datos,
Allcuquiro 2-75 y, Paseo de los Cañaris, Cuenca, Ecuador
veropenafielm@gmail.com

Abstract. This paper presents an experimental study to assess the capabilities of older adults to interact with multi-touch surfaces. The study involved 100 elderly people between 61–92 years old. We selected two different elderly centres in Madrid, with different characteristics in terms of income level. The "Gesture Games" tool was used because it allows experimenting with the seven more used multi-touch gestures: Tap, Double tap, Long press, Drag, Scale up, Scale down and One-finger rotation. The analysis of the data showed that older adults have total capacity to execute these seven tasks. Some of the tasks, such as "scale down" and "scale up" were found easier for them, while other tasks, such as "double tap" were more difficult.

Keywords: Multi-touch · Human computer interaction (HCI) · Usability evaluation · Multi-touch in elderly

1 Introduction and Previous Work

As people age, their cognitive and/or physical abilities start to degrade and could prevent them from properly using a tablet. For this reason is important to study what kind of skills have the elderly people when they use multi-touch superficies such as smartphones, tablets and netbooks [1]. According to Abascal, what older users expect from mobile communications is not very different from what the generic user expects from these services: mostly, fully reliable personal communications and services to improve, as much as possible, safety and quality of life [2].

There are already several works studying these problems. For example, "Anshin", is a software application for mobile devices to prevent solitary death and to provide a

© Springer International Publishing AG 2016
C.R. García et al. (Eds.): UCAmI 2016, Part I, LNCS 10069, pp. 419–429, 2016.
DOI: 10.1007/978-3-319-48746-5_43

social network. The tool use touch gestures (select and drag) to change the configuration [3]. "Dance! Don't Fall" is an application for elderly people that teach them to dance, in which drag gestures are intensively used. The project senSAVEr is a system that provides a continuous mobile health monitoring service for people with hypertension. The interface was characterized by displays of graphical symbols and animations which contain the possibility to check parameter values [4] using touch gestures. Moderne Kijkbuis' is an entertainment application for elderly with physical and/or cognitive impairments in which the elderly had major difficulties pressing two dimensional buttons with basic touch gestures [5].

This paper presents an experimental study to assess the capabilities of older adults to interact with multi-touch surfaces.

2 Experimental Study

The overall objective of this experimental study was to identify the skills of elderly adults to handle tablets with suitable gestures, taking into account their limitations, in order to determine the best suited to applications for this population segment [6]. Using the Metric Question (GQM) Meta-template, our goal can be defined in the following way: to analyse a set of multi-touch gestures for the purpose of assessing their suitability from the point of view of the usability of multi-touch technologies in the context of the elderly people (Fig. 1).

Fig. 1. Elderly people during the workshop.

Gender and the group age were the two main variables considered independent. Execution time and success rate were the two dependent variables for each task (Tap, Double tap, Long press, Drag, Scale up, Scale down, One-finger rotation). Consequently, the hypotheses to be tested statistically, as defined for each task performed (type of gesture), were formulated as follows: H1, completion time of task k is not affected by gender; H2, completion time of task k is not affected by age group; H3, the degree of success for task k is independent of gender; H4, the degree of success for task k is independent of age group; H5, the degree of success is independent of the task.

In order to test these hypotheses, we measured the manipulation time of each gesture as well as it success, with the ultimate goal of obtaining a set of guidelines specifically focused on designing touch-enabled applications for elderly people.

2.1 Participants

The evaluation was performed with a total of 100 seniors in two different centres of the Community of Madrid, Spain. The Sagasta Centre is located in an area with a high purchasing power while the San Blas Centre is located in a low-income area. In each centre 50 seniors participated, 25 women and 25 men, making a total of 100 participants. The age varied between 61 and 92 years.

2.2 Equipment

The interaction framework for the experiment was implemented in Java using JMonkeyEngine SDK v.3.0beta. The application name is Gestures Games [7]. The device used for the experiment was a Szenio 10.1, 1 GB RAM, 32 GB tablet with Android 4.2.2 with capacitive multi-touch screens.

2.3 Procedure

For each task, the elderly were given a 5-minute learning phase with an instructor. The task were performed in a sequential order by each participant. All the participants hold the tablet in the same way. The same instructor carried out all the experiments. The experimental platform then asked them to perform the task without any assistance. They had to perform three repetitions of each gesture under specific conditions. When the gesture was completed successfully, the platform gave a positive audio-visual feedback. If the instructor saw that the participant did not carry out the task in a given time, it was marked as undone and the elderly went on to the next one. For each interaction, the system recorded the start time (seconds needed to go into action after the visual stimulus was shown), completion time, success (performed correctly or incorrectly), and the number of contacts with the surface (in order to detect unsuccessful actions or whether the user had made any attempt to interact). A qualitative analysis was also carried out from the notes taken by an external observer during the experimental sessions.

2.4 Tasks

There were 7 tasks that the elderly had to perform:

Task 1: Tap. A static image of an animal appears in a random position on the screen (see Fig. 2). Participants are requested to tap on the target image in order to pass the test.

Fig. 2. Example of a simple tap, double tap or long pressed test

Task 2: Double Tap. A static image of an animal appears in a random position on the screen (see Fig. 2). Participants are requested to double tap on the target image with one finger.

Task 3: Long Press. A static image of an animal appears in a random position on the screen (see Fig. 2). Participants are requested to carry out a long press gesture on the target image until the target disappears.

Task 4: Drag. A static image of an animal appears in a random position on the screen and the same (reference) image appears in a white profile in another random position, always at the same distance (Fig. 3). Participants are requested to drag the target to the reference image with one finger.

Fig. 3. Example of a drag test.

Task 5: Scale up. A static image of an animal appears in the centre of the screen within a similar but 1.5 times larger reference shape. Participants are requested to scale up the target image to the size of the reference shape.

Task 6: Scale down. A static image of an animal appears in the centre of the screen superimposed on a similar reference shape half its size (see Fig. 4-b). Participants are requested to scale down the target image.

(b)　　　　　　　　　　　　　　(a)

Fig. 4. Example of a scale test: (a) scale up and (b) scale down.

Task 7: One-finger rotation. A static image of an animal appears in the centre of the screen in front of a blank profile of the same image in a different orientation. Participants are requested to rotate the target image to the position of the reference image.

3   Results

We have selected the following aspects to analyse: number of tasks completed, rate of task compliance (All, Sex, Age, Centre, Experience), ratio of task compliance, task completing time (All, Sex, age, Centre, Experience), and ratio of task completing times. Each participant has tried at least two of the gestures proposed in the application: 48.51 % of participants have achieved successful completion of at least two repetitions of the same task.

- **Task success**

The incidence of success in fulfilling tasks using different gestures according to sex and age showed no statistically significant associations. However, the gesture "one-finger rotation", in the case of analysis by centres, presented an association, as exposed by Chi-square variable test ($p < 0.05$). Previous experience in the use of smartphones marked differences in the incidence of performance in the tasks "tap", "double tap", "long press" and "drag" ($p < 0.05$). (See Table 1).

- **Inter-gesture correlations in task success**

They were found moderate-low correlations between the success in the "tap" task and success in the "double tap" and "one-finger rotation".

The correct accomplishment of the "double tap" has a strong correlation with the "long press" task. Furthermore, the "long press" task has a moderate-low correlation with "drag" and with "scale-up" tasks. Success in the "Drag" task is positively correlated with "scale-up", "scale-down" and "one-finger rotation". In addition, "scale-up" and "scale-down" tasks are correlated with each other.

Table 1. Test x2, incidence of success with gesture VS Gender, Centre, Age, Previous Experience

Gesture	Gender		Centre		Age		Experience	
	x2	p	x2	p	x2	p	x2	p
Tap	0,000	0,992	1,282	0,257	2,248	0,134	8,189*	0,004
Double tap	0,209	0,648	0,246	0,620	3,749	0,053	6,831*	0,009
Long press	0,323	0,570	0,469	0,494	0,009	0,926	5,755*	0,016
Drag	0,027	0,869	0,190	0,663	0,153	0,696	6,815*	0,009
Scale-Up	1,575	0,209	2,000	0,157	2,165	0,141	2,643	0,104
Scale-Down	0,034	0,853	0,000	0,989	0,002	0,966	0,034	0,853
One-finger rot.	0,008	0,927	5,983	0,036*	0,050	0,823	0,001	0,978

*Note: * significative correlation (p < 0.05)*

Finally, "scale-up" and "scale-down" are strongly correlated with the success in the "one-finger rotation" task (see Table 2).

Table 2. Inter-gesture correlations

		Double-tap	Long press	Drag	Scale up	Scale down	One-finger rotation
Tap	v	0,391	0,187	0,043	0,092	0,077	0,243
	p	0,00**	0,060	0,203	0,354	0,438	0,015*
Double tap	v		0,333	0,018	0,097	0,097	0,084
	p		0,010*	0,237	0,331	0,331	0,401
Long press	v			0,333	0,277	0,102	0,076
	p			0,001**	0,050*	0,304	0,445
Drag	v				0,295	0,49	0,249
	p				0,003*	0,000**	0,013*
Scale-up	v					0,295	0,653
	p					0,003*	0,045*
Scale-down	v						0,653
	p						0,045*

Note: * p < 0.05 (moderate corr.) **p < 0.001 (strong corr.)

- **Task completing time**

The tasks with a longer average completion time corresponds to the gesture of "one-finger rotation" with a value of 5.42 s (SD = 4.16 s), followed by the activity of "drag" with an average value of 4, 96 s (SD = 2.88). The activity with a shorter completion time was the activity of "two taps", although this action had also the lower incidence of success.

The activities that showed highest variances were "tap" and "scale-down" (see Table 3).

Table 3. Completing time of tasks

Gesture	Min.	Max.	Average	Standard deviation	Variance
Tap	0,72	78,54	4,56	9,19	84,40
Double tap	0,72	6,83	2,14	1,22	1,49
Long press	1,35	9,71	3,23	1,78	3,17
Drag	1,54	16,54	4,96	2,88	8,30
Scale up	0,68	22,43	2,71	2,72	7,37
Scale down	0,92	50,87	4,05	5,47	29,91
One-finger rotation	1,32	29,83	5,42	4,16	17,34

- **Task completing time correlations with Gender, Age Centre and previous touch screen experience.**

The time of completion of the tasks showed significant differences between men and women in the gestures "tap", "long press" and "drag" ($p < 0.05$). In terms of age, significant differences were found between the group of people over 71 years and the group of people under 71 years of age in the gesture "tap". The previous experience with the use of smartphones showed a significant difference in the gesture of "scale down" (see Table 4).

Table 4. Mann-Whitney U test on task completing time

Gesture	Gender	Age	Centre	Experience
	P	p	p	P
Tap	0,039*	0,050*	0,932	0,333
Double tap	0,274	0,405	0,674	0,378
Long press	0,004*	0,456	0,992	0,493
Drag	0,022*	0,218	0,660	0,483
Scale up	0,924	0,249	0,585	0,399
Scale down	0,338	0,059	0,263	0,042*
One-finger rotation	0,307	0,136	0,422	0,383

*Note: * significative correlation, $p < 0.05$*

The women showed an average completion time greater than that of men in the gestures related to "long press" and "drag", with averages of 3894.5 ms (SD = 2224.2 ms), and 5299.9 ms (DE = 2589.9 ms) respectively, compared to 2694.5 ms (DE = 1067.7 ms) showed by men for the "long press" and 4688.0 (SD = 3084,5 ms) for "drag". On the other hand the time required to complete the activity "tap" was greater for men with an average of 5221.7 ms (SD = 12174.4 ms) (See Fig. 5).

The group of people under 71 years showed smaller completion times with an average difference of 3426,23 ms. The behaviour for each task is shown in Fig. 6.

The behaviour of the time taken for the completion of tasks, depending on the centre or depending on the previous experience of the elderly, are shown in Figs. 7 and 8.

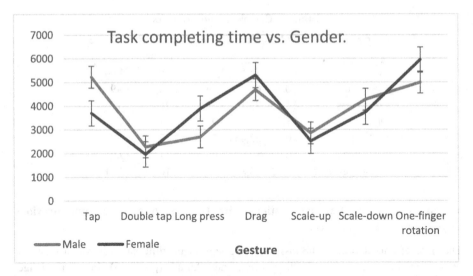

Fig. 5. Task completing time vs. gender.

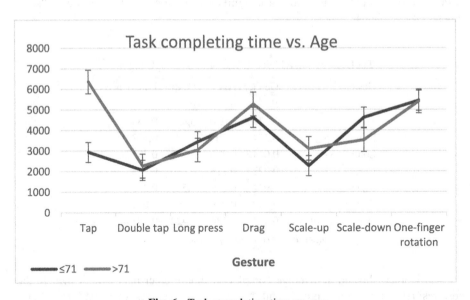

Fig. 6. Task completing time vs. age

The action "scale down" correlated with the previous experience of the elderly: people with previous experience in management smartphones used an average of 4760.2 ms (DE = 6940,2 s) compared to 3140.1 ms (DE = 2427,9 s) for the inexperienced people.

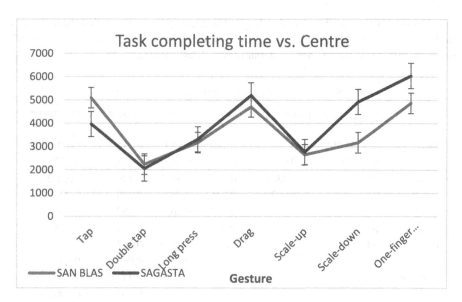

Fig. 7. Task completing time vs. centre

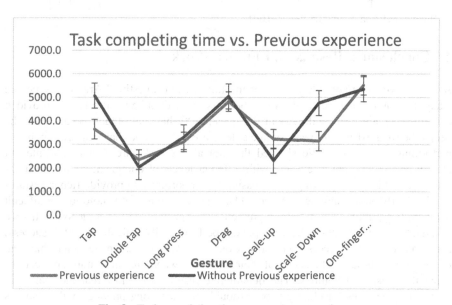

Fig. 8. Task completing time vs. previous experience

- **Inter-gesture correlation in task completing times**

The time taken to complete the task "tap" is slightly correlated with the time spent performing "double tap" and "drag". The time taken to complete the task "double tap" has a moderate-low correlation with the "long press" and "scale up". In addition "Long press" is positively correlated with "drag". The time spent in the action "drag" has a moderate-low correlation with "scale up", "scale down" and "one-finger rotation". Scale up and "scale down" are moderately correlated (see Table 5).

Table 5. Inter-gesture correlation in task completing times

		Double-tap	Long press	Drag	Scale up	Scale down	One-finger rotation
Tap	Rh	0,270*	0,208	0,246*	0,159	0,131	−0,057
	p	0,032	0,094	0,031	0,165	0,255	0,632
Double tap	Rh		0,335**	0,208	0,339**	0,189	−0,012
	p		0,007	0,085	0,004	0,120	0,927
Long press	Rh			0,333**	0,165	0,157	−0,004
	p			0,003	0,143	0,168	0,976
Drag	Rh				0,424**	0,254*	0,349**
	p				0,000	0,013	0,001
Scale-up	Rh					0,342**	0,176
	p					0,001	0,100
Scale-down	Rh						0,072
	p						0,500

Note: correlation *$p < 0,05$ **$p < 0,001$

4   Conclusions, Results and Future Work

After this work we are able to answer the fundamental question "Are elderly people ready for multi-touch technology?" The answer is definitely affirmative, provided certain issues are dealt with. About the question "What multi-touch gestures are the people between 61 and 92 years of age able to use?" we found that they are capable of performing all gestures. We showed that not all the tasks are equally feasible but elderly people are able to execute with different levels of complexity. Current applications for elderly people might be missing the opportunity to provide richer gestures within elderly people abilities, and could be using a gesture that is notoriously difficult for them (e.g., double tap, tap, long pressed). The special elderly people skills that we found in this test, was that elderly people can perform easily scale down (99 % success) and scale up (98 % success) gestures. Consequently, interaction designers have an opportunity to broaden the scope of their interfaces when creating future applications using these especial abilities. The quantitative results also show that there are still challenging gestures for elderly people (double tap, tap, long pressed) with relative's low success rates ranging. These gestures have to be discussed in the context of the interaction aids or design guidelines that application designers should take into account if these touch interactions are included in future applications. Designers would be improve the way to execute these gestures in to do easily to use or execute these tasks for this special segment of population. For example, increasing the time between the first tap and the second (for the double tap gesture), so that they have time to react and this fit their actual motor abilities.

In addition to the automatic data logging that was performed to measure completion times and degree of success, an external observer gathered valuable information regarding the behaviour of elderly people during the experiments. These observations revealed different problems that will now be described.

The task was more difficult for them was the double tap, as it is well known that motor skills at their age can be somewhat severed, and possibly are not flexible enough to perform two taps in a short time interval. The task they preferred, according to the data collected and the final questionnaire, was to scale up and scale down, possibly because in this task they can use both hands on the tablet and this gives them security and firmness.

Based on this research, future work have be done in the following areas:

- Incorporating smart elements on mobile applications what can react with tutorials or modify the appearance of the application. This would allow the application to be used by different types of users, including the elderly.
- Expanding the scope of the study to other domains or types of applications and for other types of devices.
- Applying artificial intelligence elements where the tool is able to understand and learn the user behaviour in order to formulate the criteria for improvement.
- Incorporation of audio-visual tools into the assessment tool to better enable user interaction.

References

1. Cáliz, D., Alamán, X.: Usability evaluation method for mobile applications for the elderly: a methodological proposal. In: Pecchia, L., Chen, L.L., Nugent, C., Bravo, J. (eds.) IWAAL 2014. LNCS, vol. 8868, pp. 252–260. Springer, Heidelberg (2014)
2. Díaz-Bossini, J., Moreno, L.: Accessibility to mobile interfaces for older people. Procedia Comput. Sci. **27**, 57–66 (2013)
3. Takami, S., Torii, I., Ishii, N.: Development of system for prevention of solitary death with mobile devices. Procedia Comput. Sci. **35**, 1193–1201 (2014)
4. Lorenz, A., Oppermann, R.: Mobile health monitoring for the elderly: Designing for diversity. Pervasive Mob. Comput. **5**(5), 478–495 (2009)
5. Muskens, L., van Lent, R., Vijfvinkel, A., van Cann, P., Shahid, S.: Never too old to use a tablet: designing tablet applications for the cognitively and physically impaired elderly. In: Miesenberger, K., Fels, D., Archambault, D., Peňáz, P., Zagler, W. (eds.) ICCHP 2014, Part I. LNCS, vol. 8547, pp. 391–398. Springer, Heidelberg (2014)
6. Nacher, V., Jaen, J., Navarro, E., Catala, A., González, P.: Multi-touch gestures for pre-kindergarten children. J. Hum. Comput. Stud. **73**, 37–51 (2015)
7. Guía, E.D., Lozano, M.D., Penichet, V.M.R.: Co-StiCap: Sistema Basado en Interfaces de Usuario Distribuidas y Tangibles Para Mejorar las Capacidades Cognitivas en Niños con TDAH. Interacción, enseñanza y Aprendiz, 61–68 (2014)

A Proposal for Using Virtual Worlds for the Integration

María J. Lasala[1], Xavier Alamán[2(✉)], and Miguel Gea[3]

[1] IES Narcis Oller, Valls, Spain
mlasala3@xtec.cat
[2] Universidad Autónoma de Madrid, Madrid, Spain
xavier.alaman@uam.es
[3] Universidad de Granada, Granada, Spain
mgea@ugr.es

Abstract. This paper presents a proposal for integrating people in risk of exclusion by means of Virtual Worlds. Different studies show the benefits of using virtual worlds for educational purposes, where you can develop a wide variety of innovative teaching and learning activities. In particular we are working with immigrants; with high school students with learning disabilities; and with people with cognitive disabilities (autism, Asperger, Down syndrome). In this paper we present three experiences in this area, one of them already finished and the other two being currently implemented.

Keywords: Virtual worlds · e-Learning · Educational systems for the integration

1 Introduction and Previous Work

Different studies show the benefits of using virtual worlds for educational purposes, where you can develop a wide variety of innovative teaching and learning activities. A review of such systems can be found in [1, 2]. The nature of virtual worlds allows the application of innovative learning methodologies, such as the constructivist approach [3]. In a virtual world the students may explore; interact with the environment; interact with other students and with the teacher; and build their own constructions. These are all elements that make up the idea of constructivist learning [4].

One area that may be specially benefited by such educational systems is the collective of people in risk of discrimination. In particular we are working with immigrants; with high school students with learning disabilities; and with people with cognitive disabilities (autism, Asperger, Down syndrome). Virtual worlds can provide the opportunity to try out alternative social interactions reflecting upon feelings and thoughts [5]. Therefore, virtual worlds can be used for inclusive education for these collectives.

On example of this kind of work is Brigadoon [6]. Brigadoon is a private island in Second Life aimed to Autism or Asperger Syndrome people, where students can improve their social skills without face to face interactions. Students can build objects in a virtual world, sitting and chatting with other people in a virtual garden, sailing boats, and in general performing activities that provide them new experiences.

C.R. García et al. (Eds.): UCAmI 2016, Part I, LNCS 10069, pp. 430–436, 2016.
DOI: 10.1007/978-3-319-48746-5_44

There is work also in other areas of integration. For example, "Accessibility in Virtual Worlds" is an example of a virtual world project aimed to blind students. The position is communicated by sound, allowing blind students to navigate the virtual world and to interact with other students [7].

The experiences described in this paper are taking place in the virtual world based on the Open Simulator platform that has been created within the eIntegra project (Spanish Research Plan, project TIN2013-44586-R), which is researching on educational technologies for the social integration of groups at risk of discrimination.

2   Integrating Immigrant Students Using Virtual Worlds

This educational application took place at the IES Ernest Lluch, a high school in Tarragona, Spain. In this school the rate of immigrant students is high and they have a problem with the newcomers, which need to learn the Catalan language in order to be incorporated into regular classrooms. To this end, a number of courses are offered by the Catalan educational system, which are called "Welcome Courses". These courses allow immigrant students (between 12 and 15 years old) to receive specific training in Catalan language and culture, as well as other transversal skills.

Different types of activities for practicing creating sentences or identifying the main elements of a sentence were developed in a virtual world. Figure 1 shows an example in which the student had to guess what kind of word was missing in the blank space (a noun, a verb or an adjective). The student manipulated a tangible element corresponding to the type of the missing word.

Fig. 1. Language exercises in the Virtual World

Another type of activity was to identify the subject and predicate of a sentence. To do this, the sentences were divided into two parts, and the student placed the part he believed was the subject is in its place, followed by the part he identified as the predicate. All the activities in the virtual world produced feedback after completion, indicating whether the activity was completed successfully or not.

The system was used in four sessions in 2 days, involving students from several regions of Spain and from several other countries: China, Ukraine, England, Colombia, Cuba, and Morocco. The students came from various course levels and had various levels of background knowledge of Catalan language and culture. The activities were performed by the students, and the teacher assessed the grade of success of their performance. According to these assessments (obtained from semi structured interviews with the teacher after each experiment), the students found the system easy to interact, helping them to understand the different parts of speech, especially in cases of students whose language is quite different from Catalan.

The use of virtual worlds encouraged the students to learn concepts that normally are quite abstract and boring to them, achieving a strong motivation through the "gamification" of their learning activities.

3   Integrating Students with Learning Difficulties Using Virtual Worlds

The Institut Narcís Oller in Valls (Tarragona, Spain) is a public high school that is experimenting with a collaborative model in which the students themselves develop the educational contents that other students would use. There is an additional interesting feature in this experiment: the students that are creating the educational contents are students in the "reinforcing group", a special group for students with learning disabilities such as Attention Deficit Disorder (ADD), hyperactivity, etc., in the 3rd year of Secondary Education (ESO). The materials are used afterwards by students that are also in the 3rd year of ESO, but in the ordinary group.

Students in the reinforcement course, under the supervision of their teacher, create within the virtual world landscapes and situations that exemplify the 3D concepts they are studying in the subject of human geography. Examples of such concepts, related to the primary economic sector, are: factors affecting the agricultural area, farming systems, market agriculture, forestry and deforestation, intensive and extensive farms, fisheries resources and typology, aquaculture, etc. (see Figs. 2 and 3).

These students often have problems of attention deficit and/or hyperactivity and/or understanding (some of them already diagnosed). Building three-dimensional structures to exemplify the abstract concepts being studied greatly improves their motivation and understanding. The rest of the students of the course that are not in the reinforcement group visit this virtual world and have to give an account of what they see in it, in the form a travel book, practicing the concepts they were taught at the classroom. These students also receive the benefit of studying a topic which can be arid and abstract in a practical and motivating way.

Fig. 2. A virtual world for human geography (2)

Fig. 3. A virtual world for human geography (1)

The idea is that this virtual world will grow over several years, accumulating landscapes, forests and farms, so that more and richer materials will be available for the study of this subject.

4   Integrating Students with Cognitive Disabilities

This experience focuses on and specific target group (people with cognitive disabilities) and how this new technologies may be potentially suitable to help them in their social and labour integration. This experience involves building a transmedia experience of a virtual immersive museum in a school of special education (Fig. 4).

Fig. 4. Outdoors exposition of the works of the children

The aim is to develop a collaborative and immersive museum using a virtual reality environment (Open Simulator). The users can build their rooms for exhibit their art crafts, put their content materials and include comments and personal comments. Further goals are to promote collaborative activities (guided tours) and exporting to other media (cardboard, and mobile devices using alternative technologies).

Our focus group is composed of 6 children with different ages (ranging from 8 to 20 year old) with different levels of cognitive disabilities, including autism disorders. The students have various possible objectives with different levels of difficulty:

- Walk through and discover the 3D immersive world, acquiring skills for 3D movement, orientation and object localization.
- Character building: identify their avatar, and personalize according to their preferences,
- Building activities: create walls, upload media content and putting on the 3D environment.
- Communication activities. Manipulating chat and other interactive elements where they can interact with the 3D world.
- Collaborative activities, such as follow a group, meet someone, etc.

Once we have achieved their attention in this 3D world, the next step is to promote creativity on this scenario, encouraging the opportunity of creating contents and stories within this world. For example, storytelling is a good technique to promote their abilities, both as a therapeutic activity, as well as an opportunity for creating contents (interactive

3D world, objects, etc.) that may be collected and viewed by others as a public or private spaces. A potential use of this tool may be a collaborative activity to create contents and incomes (using virtual stores, ticket visit or any other kind of business models) (Fig. 5).

Fig. 5. 3D Virtual Museum

This work shows the advances and outcomes of this activity, which is part of a more general project: the e-Integra project in the context of Information Society, particularly in the area of attention to diversity, and focusing on the development of technology to

Finally, we want to thank the IES Ernest Lluch at Cunit (Tarragona), the Intitut Narcis Oller at Valls (Tarragona), and the ASPROGRADES non-profit association at Granada for all their support during the experiment. The work reported in this paper was partially funded by the Spanish Research Plan (project TIN2013-44586-R) and by the Madrid Research Plan (project S2013/ICE-2715).

References

1. Hew, K.F., Cheung, W.S.: Use of three-dimensional (3-D) immersive virtual worlds in K-12 and higher education settings: a review of the research. Br. J. Educ. Technol. **41**, 33–65 (2010)
2. Mateu, J., Lasala, M.J., Alaman, X.: Developing mixed reality educational applications: the virtual touch toolkit. Sensors **15**(9), 21760–21784 (2015)
3. Vygotsky, L.S.: Mind in society: the development of higher psychological processes. In: Cole, M., John-Steiner, V., Scribner, S., Souberman, E. (eds.) (Luria, A.R., Lopez-Morillas, M., Cole, M. [with Wertsch, J.V.], Trans.) Harvard University Press, Cambridge (Original manuscripts [ca. 1930–1934])
4. Jonassen, D.H.: Designing constructivist learning environments. In: Reigeluth, C.M. (ed.) Instructional-Design Theories and Models: A New Paradigm of Instructional Theory, pp. 215–239. Lawrence Erlbaum Associate, Mahwah (1999)
5. Sheehy, K., Ferguson, R.: Educational inclusion, new technologies. In: Scott, T.B., Livingston, J.L. (eds.) Leading Edge Educational Technology. Nova Science, NY (2008)

6. Lester, J.: About brigadoon. brigadoon: an innivative online community for people dealing with Asperger's syndrome and autism. http://braintalk.blogs.com/brigadoon/2005/01/about_brigadoon.html. Accessed 14 June 2016
7. Sheehy, K.: Virtual environments: issues and opportunities for researching inclusive educational practices. In: Peachey, A., Gillen, J., Livingstone, D., Smith-Robbins, S. (eds.) Researching Learning in Virtual Worlds. Human Computer Interaction Series (2010)

Designing the Human in the Loop
of Self-Adaptive Systems

Miriam Gil[✉], Vicente Pelechano, Joan Fons, and Manoli Albert

Centro de Investigación en Métodos de Producción de Software,
Universitat Politècnica de València, Camí de Vera s/n, 46022 Valencia, Spain
{mgil,pele,jjfons,malbert}@pros.upv.es

Abstract. Self-adaptation is a key requirement in emerging software
systems that must become capable of continuously adapting its behavior at run-time to their context (new environmental conditions, resource
variability, unpredictable situations, changing user needs, etc.) without
human intervention. However, experience in autonomous systems shows
that people cannot be excluded entirely of the adaptation loop. For example, in the case of autonomous cars, they still need humans to drive in
certain situations (e.g., complex driving situations, emergencies, etc.).
This work defines the key factors to design the human participation in
the control loops by introducing a framework to design human participations. Our framework considers human attention as a critical factor
for user participation. Also, it pays attention to the dynamism between
different types of human participation depending on the different system
limitations (e.g., uncertainties in sensing, conflicts in goals, etc.) and
the current user situation (e.g., user attention, environmental situation,
etc.). We illustrate our approach by applying it to manage some actual
autonomous cars situations that require human intervention.

Keywords: Human in the loop · Self-adaptation · Human-computer
interaction · User attention

1 Introduction

In an increasingly dynamic, intelligent and decentralized open world, the technology and types of computing systems evolves towards an ecosystem made of
a wide variety of devices and distributed services of clear mobile and ubiquitous
nature, and in a continuous technological evolution. Facing this situation it is
needed to develop systems that are capable of continuously adapting its behavior
at run-time to new environmental conditions, unpredictable situations, changing user needs, new types of devices, new technologies to interact with or new
services to consume. Self-adaptive systems (SAS) have emerged as a solution
to manage this situation [2] and facilitate the development and management of
services in the domain of Smart Cities and Buildings, Autonomous Cars, etc.

Adaptations in this context play a key role since its goal is not only to offer
more specialized and appropriate services for each situation, but also to manage

© Springer International Publishing AG 2016
C.R. García et al. (Eds.): UCAmI 2016, Part I, LNCS 10069, pp. 437–449, 2016.
DOI: 10.1007/978-3-319-48746-5_45

and resolve conflicts and emergent situations that allow more resilient systems. Even though these adaptations have to be managed autonomously, the capability of these systems to provide reliable services in presence of (internal and external) changes is affected for its growing complexity and the unpredictable nature of the environments in which they typically operate. For this reason, in many situations is interesting to involve humans in the adaptation process to help the system facing conflicts difficult to solve autonomously and to improve the adaptation strategy with their feedback ("human in the loop") [3,4]. For example, today humans tend to be better than computers at recognizing faces in crowds or drive in complex situations or emergencies.

Typically, self-adaptive systems based their behavior in a closed-loop mechanism (e.g. implementing the MAPE-K loop [2]) that comprises four key activities: *monitor, analyze, plan* and *execute.* A challenge to involve the humans in self-adaptation is how to expose and involve the user in the control loop so that users can participate in the adaptation process (e.g., providing input, changing the decision-making process or executing adaptations). This involvement of the user has to be made in a robust manner even in situations where users have limited attentional, cognitive, or physical bandwidth for interaction. Although systems do not require human intervention, it is important that they show their state and behavior to users in order to provide transparency, understandability, controllability and trust to users and avoid the appearance of a "magic back box" [21]. Moreover, for such involvement to be successful the human must be aware of the autonomy and react to it appropriately.

However, existing SAS have been developed with the primary goal of achieve a full autonomy without considering the human participation or the interaction of these systems with the humans. This situation has caused the appearance of certain problems. For example, the implementation of semi-autonomous vehicles have exhibit several problems such as the inadequate feedback from the vehicle to the driver or the handoff problem when the system cannot longer handle by itself and requires that the driver takes the control of the car, among others [19].

The goal of this work is to explore the range of ways to involve humans within the control loop of SAS so they can participate in adaptation decisions, but always maximizing the system autonomy and avoiding intrusive and annoying systems. To accomplish this task, we present a framework for designing user-empowered control loops of self-adaptive systems. This framework pays attention to the dynamism between types of user participation depending on different circumstances (e.g., changing goals, uncertainty, ambiguity, unpredictability, etc.) and the current user situation. An important element of our framework is the consideration of the human attention as a critical factor for user participation in order to avoid overwhelming users and allow a "natural" involvement.

The rest of the paper is structured as follows. Section 2 presents where humans can participate in the control loop. In Sect. 3, we discuss the importance of the human involvement in SAS and sets the requirements for human participation. Section 4 presents the proposed framework to design the human in the loop. Section 5 discusses some related work, and Sect. 6 concludes the paper.

2   Humans in Self-adaptive Loops

Typically, autonomous systems embody an adaptation loop that consists of several processes (*collect, analyze, decide, act*), as well as sensors and effectors, as depicted in Fig. 1 [2]. This loop is composed by an autonomic manager software element and a (hardware or software) managed element. The autonomic manager continually executes a collect-analyze-decide-act loop in which it observes sensor readings, analyzes and plans an appropriate management decision, and then executes that decision via effectors. A central knowledge base contains knowledge pertaining to the likely effectiveness of various possible management decisions in achieving the managers overall policy objectives. Typically, such knowledge takes the form of an explicit system model.

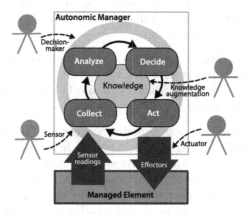

Fig. 1. Control loop for autonomic computing with human roles.

One of the problems that arise in these systems is the interaction with humans. Usually, the user has no option at runtime to intervene in the adaptive behavior in case that an anomalous situation or malfunction appears, and consequently understand and control the system. What happens when behavior varies from the expected, when the user wants to do something different, when errors arise, or when complex behavior emerges? Model-based evaluation methods have been proposed as a viable solution to build software that executes with the appropriate quality and behavior [5]. However, they only guarantee quality execution at design time and cannot always provide accurate results at runtime because the environment where systems operate may not be completely known when applications are designed. For this reason, adaptation in some classes of systems (especially safety-critical systems) can benefit from human involvement.

2.1   Where Can Humans Participate in the Control Loop?

The tasks of the control loop that can be potential for human participation are:

- **At sensor level:** System decisions are based on sensed information that can be imprecise [8]. Sensors can deliver uncertain data or they can fail, and consequently the control loop may have problems with this anomalous input calculating wrong values that do not represent the context reality correctly.
- **At decision-making level:** When the system is deciding about how to adapt to reach a final state, it may have to deal with a conflict in satisfying system goals due to multiple goals conflicting with one another, or a high degree of uncertainty due to automatic learning or evolution of systems [15].
- **At effector level:** Once an adaptation is decided, to implement a decision the system must act via available actuators and effectors. However, during the execution stage of adaptation may arise problems for example when adaptations involve physical changes to the system that cannot be automated or a fallback mechanism is required [3].

Besides the above intrinsic problems due to the inherent variability of the systems, and the environment in which they operate with the associated randomness of events, human participation can also be seen from the viewpoint of humans who are interacting with the systems.

- At **knowledge level**: Users can have different concerns or preferences depending on the situation, and consequently they might not always prefer the same behavior for a particular situation. As system decisions are based on a variability model with associated behavioral information (e.g. adaptation rules, utility function, etc.) that cannot be changed by the user at run-time, this can lead to a lack of control from users and a bad user experience.

Considering the participation of the users in these levels of the control loop of SAS, the various roles that humans can take are the following (see Fig. 1):

- *Sensor*: humans can act as sophisticated sensors by incorporating information difficult to monitor or correcting the sensed anomalous value.
- *Actuator*: humans can act as system-level effectors to execute adaptations.
- *Decision-maker*: humans can incorporate input into the decision-making process to provide better insight about the best way of adapting the system.
- *Knowledge augmentation*: users may provide personal input to personalize the systems and better fit their preferences by providing new knowledge.

Thus, these roles should be supported when considering the user involvement.

3   Human-Computer Interaction Challenges

A potential problem to involve the humans in self-adaptation is that usually systems are designed to achieve the maximum possible autonomy without considering the interaction with the user. Although having a high degree of autonomy is probably a necessary precondition for the future growth of SAS, humans will always be part of computational processes. Bad designs can lead users to mistrust autonomous systems, misuse it, or abandon it altogether [13]. But yet, interacting with well-designed systems is limited and ofter uninformative for the user because their inherent complexity. Some of the threats that affect the quality of interaction with SAS are [10]:

1. *Diminished predictability and transparency:* Predictability refers to the extent to which a user can predict the effects of his/her actions and transparency the extent to which a user can understand system actions or know how the system works. A measure to deal with this threat is providing explanations of actions to users.
2. *Diminished controllability:* Controllability refers to the extent to which the user can shape a system's decisions or personalization. Measures to increase controllability are (1) letting the system has to submit actions to users for approval (finding ways of making this unobtrusive) and allowing users to set parameters that controls systems behavior.
3. *Obtrusiveness:* Obtrusiveness refers to the extent to which the system makes demands on the user's attention. This threat can be minimized by adapting the timing and interaction style of messages to users' activity and context.

Barkhuss and Dey [1] examined the degree of autonomy that self-adaptive applications should have from users' view. They defined three levels of inter-activity: personalization (applications let the user specify application behavior in a given situation), passive context-awareness (applications present updated context to the user and lets him decide how to change its behavior), and active context-awareness (the system autonomously changes the application behavior based on sensed context information). They observed that users preferred self-adaptive features over personalization, but at the same time they experience a lack of control. Thus, they pointed out the **need to manage a suitable balance between user control and system autonomy at run-time.**

In order to increase the user experience of autonomous systems, Russell et al. [16] proposed a shift in the way of thinking about the interaction between humans and autonomous systems and stated that human-computer interaction aspects must be present in autonomic computing design from its beginnings to support: (a) **behavior-reporting mechanisms** that will allow users to understand what the system is doing with a measure of trust and confidence, (b) **system inspectability and control** for post-failure analysis, understanding, and recovery, and (c) **user attention management** models to avoid overwhelming users. These requirements are clearly mapped to the threats listed above.

3.1 What Should SAS Support to Involve the Human?

Taking the identified limitations and threats as the basis, we can list a set of requirements that a solution to introduce the user in the loop should support:

R1. Supporting transparency. Systems cannot be seen like magic, humans need to understand what is going on in the system to be effective participants in the joint activity of changing or adjusting the behavior [16]. Providing the user with feedback and explanations about the system state is crucial to establish and keep users' trust [4]. To that effect, a self-adaptive system needs to expose aspects of its control loop to the user.

R2. Managing controllability. People cannot be removed from interacting with systems because either there could be critical tasks that need to be manually resolved or users may prefer more control. To mitigate this, it is important to give users control, but always managing a balance between systems autonomy and user control [9]. Thus, systems should provide mechanisms to adjust dynamically the degree of user control (e.g., user participation) depending on different circumstances (e.g., changing goals, emergent behaviors, uncertainties, or simply that users prefer more control).

R3. Managing user attention. A way of managing user attention and making systems unobtrusive is by means of implicit interactions, those that occur without the explicit behest or consciousness of the user [18]. Implicit interactions occur in the attentional periphery and are non-exclusive. Users should be able to interact with a SAS in a robust manner even in situations where they have limited attentional, cognitive, or physical bandwidth for interaction [16].

Besides these requirements, it is important to provide support for the different human roles since they will determine the concrete interaction with the user. In the following section, we present a framework to design the human participation in the control loop of SAS and support the presented requirements.

4   A Framework to Describe the Human in the Loop

With the goal to support the identified requirements to integrate the human in the control loop, we propose a conceptual framework to design human participations and capture the participation requirements at design time. Specifically, we based our framework on the implicit interaction framework presented in [11] to design implicit interactions. The basic idea of using implicit interactions to integrate the human in the control loop is that the system can perceive the users interaction with the SAS and adjust its behavior without overwhelming users.

The proposed framework defines the degree of human participation taking into account which agent (the human or the system) *initiates interactions* with the system/human (related to the degree of autonomy and user control specified in R2) and to which degree the *user attention, concentration or user consciousness* is required to interact with the system (related with R3 to manage user attention). Also, by means of changing the degree of attention required, we manage the transparency of the system giving more or less feedback and explanations to users (related with R1). However, it is worth noticing that more attention may have a negative impact on obtrusiveness if this information is not provided in the right way and timing.

This framework is intended to model human participations as the exchange of information between a human and a SAS and provide the basis for designing

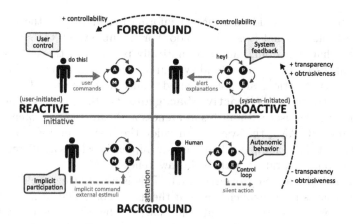

Fig. 2. Conceptual framework used for the definition of user participation.

the human in the loop. In particular, it divides the participation space along two axes (see Fig. 2): the initiative and the attention. Specifically, the **initiative** dimension indicates which agent (and to what degree) initiates an interaction participation, the human or the system. According to this factor, the participation can be *reactive* (the user initiates the interaction, and consequently takes control) or *proactive* (the system takes the initiative). Usually, in self-adaptive applications the initiative always comes from the system proactively without engaging the user's explicit attention. However, with this framework we show how this initiative can be shifted to the user's side in order to enable his/her reactive participation. Regarding the **attention** dimension, it corresponds to the degree of cognitive and perceptual load imposed on user by the SAS (related with the obtrusiveness). With regard to this factor, the participation can take place at the *foreground* of human consciousness (the user is fully conscious of the interaction) or at the *background* (have less demand and may elude notice). The attentional demand can be manipulated using the different human perceptual channels for interaction (e.g., visual, auditory, etc.) to achieve participations more natural such as using speech, hand gestures, etc. In the next subsection we give more detail of each quadrant.

4.1 Semantics of Basic Human Participation Types

The following cases are descriptions of human participation types based on the framework and illustrating examples for each quadrant (see Fig. 2):

Autonomous Behavior (Proactive/background). This case is the representative example of a fully autonomous system where human intervention is not necessary and feedback is hidden from the user. The system carries out all actions autonomously with low supervision or input.

System Feedback (Proactive/foreground). This participation takes place in the attentional foreground of the human but is initiated by the system.

The system may provide unsolicited information or inform the user about their decisions or what it is going to do. For example when the system shows the user what it is doing, and automatically performs actions. This participation allows users to understand system decisions and actions. Note that it is possible that actions are not executed immediately afterwards.

Implicit Participation (Reactive/background). In this case, the system takes input from user without his awareness and can change system's behavior based on it. Also, the system can guide the user to perform a task with low oversight. For example, when the user implicitly selects a different variant and carry out adaptation without his awareness.

User Control (Reactive/foreground). This is a classic example where participation takes place explicitly and at the user's command in which the user takes a conscious decision about some part of the adaptation. Users select decisions, stop the system from engaging in an undesired adaptation or take actions manually. Users are given explicit and detailed oversight over adaptations and feedback on results. For example when the user manually modify the system's adaptation behavior or confirms an action.

Designers may divide the participation space into many disjoint fragments as they need depending on the system to provide more degrees of user participation types. For example, we can define a medium level of attention (e.g., *slightly-noticeable*) to denote subtle participations in which the user has to make some effort to perceive the interaction. The only rule that must be followed when dividing an axis is that the ordering must be preserved in each axis for the defined values ($Background < Slightly - Noticeable < Foreground$ to indicate that *Foreground* human participations require more attention than *Slightly-Noticeable* participations that require more attention than *Background* participations).

In our approach, we use these divisions to drive the selection of the interaction mechanisms that are better suited for each particular system domain. For example, in the case of the autonomous car a high degree of attention can be mapped into speech interaction and a medium degree of attention by using the screen board. However, this selection falls out of the scope of the present work.

4.2 Model of Human Participation Loop

Although we have characterized basic human participations, in order to achieve an effective human participation when it was required, this human intervention has to follow a feedback loop in which canonical models of computer-human interactions are based [7]. In these models, information flows from a system (e.g. a computer, a car, etc.) through a human and back through the system again. According to Norman [14] (see the left side of Fig. 3), the physical system presents signals (e.g., feedback in a display), which the human interprets, evaluates, and acts via an input device connected to the physical system (e.g., a wheel).

Thus, we follow the feedback loop to design the complete cycle of human participation (see right side of Fig. 3). As an ideal SAS just takes care of itself, we can consider that the system generally is in the autonomous behavior quadrant

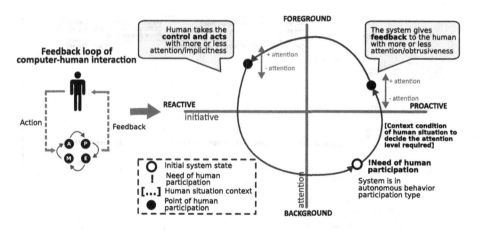

Fig. 3. HCI feedback loop in the human participation framework

(marked as initial system state in the figure; however it could start from another quadrant). The cycle is triggered by the need of human intervention at some part of the control loop (e.g., uncertainty in sensing, conflict in goals, etc.) that will determine the human role, as explained in Sect. 2. Note that this need of human participation has to be detected by the autonomic manager. In this way, when the human participation is required, the system first may give feedback to the user (proactive quadrants) requiring a specific level of attention depending on the human situation (e.g., context, capabilities, etc.). Then the system should pass the control to the user (reactive quadrants) to gather his/her input with more or less implicitness. Once the input from the human is gathered, the system should come back to the initial state quadrant, unless another participation is required. Throughout the cycle, designers should specify the points of human participation to define the way in which the interaction with the human is provided (feedback and action points). Note that the degree of attention demanded for the points of human participation will depend on the context conditions (current human situation) associated to each particular domain.

For example, consider an autonomous car, such as the Google car [12], a project by Google that involves developing technology for autonomous cars by means of a robot chauffeur. The system works with video cameras, radar sensors and a laser range finder to "see" other traffic, as well as detailed maps to navigate the road ahead. Although the car is designed to have a fully autonomous driving for most cases, it has still some limitations that require human supervision and control to achieve a fully functionality, especially when it encounter complex driving situations or emergencies. In order to integrate the human in the autonomous car, we use our framework to design the human participation as illustrated in Fig. 4.

In particular, for this example we have divided the participation space into six quadrants (left side of Fig. 4). We also show an example of the interaction mechanisms selected for each each quadrant. In the right side of Fig. 4, we illustrate the

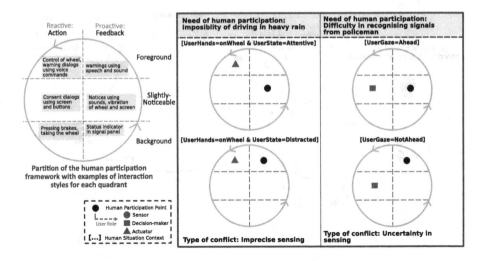

Fig. 4. Designing the user participation of the autonomous car

design of the human participation based on the human situation context (context conditions between brackets as introduced in Fig. 3). In both cases, we identify the need of human participation and the type of conflict (e.g., imprecise sensing) and analyze the human situation to select the adequate level of attention. Based on this human situation (e.g., user attentive or distracted) we represent the attention level required throughout the cycle as human participation points of feedback and action. In the case of the action, we also represent the role that play the human (different shapes in the figure) because this information will be important to select the interaction mechanisms to use in each case. For example, in the case of the impossibility of the system to drive autonomously in a heavy rain, the system first has to give feedback to the user to alert him/her. In this particular case, if the user is attentive to the situation the feedback may demand less attention. However if the user is distracted, the system will demand more attention to alert the user. Once the user is alerted and the system checks that s/he has the hands on the wheel, the human can take the control of the car with the role of actuator (because the human is driving the car). In the case of the uncertainty in recognizing the signals from policeman, the feedback is provided more notorious or less depending on the user gaze (user looking at the policeman or not) and then the user acts as a decision-maker by selecting between different options (e.g., stop, continue, etc.).

The framework facilitates the analysis of a wide range of human participations and the variability in terms of the attention level required. It provides a conceptual framework that can be used by designers to systematically analyze the human participation requirements and set up the mechanisms to be used at the operating phase to involve the user.

5 Related Work

Some works have considered the importance of the user involvement in SAS [4,17] and stated the importance of distinguishing the different roles between user and system. Shin et al. [20] presented a mixed-initiative conflict resolution approach that combines automatic resolution with user-driven resolution according to user's preferences. However this solution only considers two kind of participation: automatic or manually by asking the user. Hardian et al. [9] presented a design space to provide user control by means of revealing to users system state and they highlighted the need to manage a suitable balance of user control and system autonomy at run-time.

Recently, Dorn and Taylor [6] introduced a framework to reason about the effect of software-level changes on human interactions and vice versa. This approach offers a collaboration-aware system adaptation process for enable more sophisticated system adaptation, however, it does either not provide support to the explicit involvement of users in the adaptation process nor the different user roles and uncertainty aspects. Evers et al. [8] provided interaction practices to influence the application's behavior according to the user's focus. Although the presented solution addresses some kind of user participation, the generic integration of the user in the control loop according to the different roles that the user can take is still missing. Cámara et al. [3] provided an extension to the Rainbow framework to reason about when involve humans in self-adaptation. However they focus on the role of human participants as actors (i.e., effectors) during the execution of adaptation. Although the approaches described above satisfy some of the requirements proposed in Sect. 3, none of them provide a complete solution to our current problem of introducing the user in the loop.

6 Conclusions

As we have discussed in this paper, SAS are powerful enough to take over control that used to be done by people, but not powerful enough to manage all misbehaviors that could negatively affect in meeting system requirements and user expectations. Our conceptual framework is an attempt to address this issue by exploring the range of ways in which the human can participate. This work provides a basis for introducing the user in the control loop of any SAS to mitigate, correct or adjust problems that could arise in the adaptation process. By framing user participation in terms of the dynamics of initiative and attention (key factors to any SAS, regardless the domain) the framework manages the trade-off between autonomy and human control from different roles (sensors, actuators, decision-makers) and with different attentional demands. We are currently applying the framework to several SAS to analyze its completeness. In parallel, we are working in evaluating the solution with users in real scenarios to validate their user experience when they can be involved in SAS. By means of this evaluation we also can check the improvements in system adaptations when involving the human. Future work is devoted to provide methodological guidance and tools to apply the framework in existing self-adaptive systems.

Acknowledgments. This work has been developed with the financial support of MINECO under the project SMART-ADAPT TIN2013-42981-P.

References

1. Barkhuus, L., Dey, A.K.: Is context-aware computing taking control away from the user? Three levels of interactivity examined. In: Dey, A.K., Schmidt, A., McCarthy, J.F. (eds.) UbiComp 2003. LNCS, vol. 2864, pp. 149–156. Springer, Heidelberg (2003)
2. Brun, Y., et al.: Engineering self-adaptive systems through feedback loops. In: Cheng, B.H.C., Lemos, R., Giese, H., Inverardi, P., Magee, J. (eds.) Software Engineering for Self-Adaptive Systems. LNCS, vol. 5525, pp. 48–70. Springer, Heidelberg (2009). doi:10.1007/978-3-642-02161-9_3
3. Cámara, J., Moreno, G., Garlan, D.: Reasoning about human participation in self-adaptive systems. In: SEAMS 2015, pp. 146–156 (2015)
4. Cheng, B.H.C., de Lemos, R., Inverardi, P., Magee, J.: Software Engineering for Self-Adaptive Systems. Programming and Software Engineering, vol. 5525, p. 261. Springer, Heidelberg (2009)
5. Cortellessa, V., Di Marco, A., Inverardi, P.: Model-Based Software Performance Analysis. Springer, Heidelberg (2011)
6. Dorn, C., Taylor, R.N.: Coupling software architecture and human architecture for collaboration-aware system adaptation. In: ICSE, pp. 53–62 (2013)
7. Dubberly, H., Pangaro, P., Haque, U.: On modeling: what is interaction?: are there different types? Interactions 16(1), 69–75 (2009)
8. Evers, C., Kniewel, R., Geihs, K., Schmidt, L.: The user in the loop: enabling user participation for self-adaptive applications. FGCS J. 34, 110–123 (2014)
9. Hardian, B., Indulska, J., Henricksen, K.: Balancing autonomy and user control in context-aware systems - a survey. In: Fourth IEEE International Conference on Pervasive Computing and Communications Workshops, pp. 6–56 (2006)
10. Jameson, A., Gajos, K.Z.: Systems that adapt to their users. In: Jacko, J.A. (ed.) The Human Computer Interaction Handbook, pp. 431–456 (2012)
11. Ju, W., Leifer, L.: The design of implicit interactions: making interactive systems less obnoxious. Des. Issues 24(3), 72–84 (2008)
12. Litman, T.: Autonomous vehicle implementation predictions: implications for transport planning. In: Transportation Research Board 94th Annual Meeting (No. 15-3326) (2013)
13. Muir, B.M.: Trust in automation: Part I. Theoretical issues in the study of trust and human intervention in automated systems. Ergonomics 37(11), 1905–1922 (1994)
14. Norman, D.A.: The Design of Everyday Things. Basic Books, Inc., New York (2002)
15. Perez-Palacin, D., Mirandola, R.: Uncertainties in the modeling of self-adaptive systems: a taxonomy and an example of availability evaluation. In: 5th ACM/SPEC International Conference on Performance Engineering, pp. 3–14 (2014)
16. Russell, D.M., Maglio, P.P., Dordick, R., Neti, C.: Dealing with ghosts: managing the user experience of autonomic computing. IBM Syst. J. 42(1), 177–188 (2003)
17. Salehie, M., Tahvildari, L.: Self-adaptive software: landscape and research challenges. Trans. Auton. Adaptive Syst. 4(2), 1–42 (2009)
18. Schmidt, A.: Context-aware computing: context-awareness, context-aware user interfaces, and implicit interaction. In: The Encyclopedia of HCI, 2nd edn. (2013)

19. Shaikh, S.A., Krishnan, P.: A framework for analysing driver interactions with semi-autonomous vehicles. In: Proceedings First International Workshop on Formal Techniques for Safety-Critical Systems (FTSCS), pp. 85–99 (2012)
20. Shin, C., Dey, A.K., Woo, W.: Mixed-initiative conflict resolution for context-aware applications. In: UbiComp 2008, pp. 262–271 (2008)
21. Stumpf, S., Burnett, M., Pipek, V., Wong, W.K.: End-user interactions with intelligent and autonomous systems. In: CHI 2012 Extended Abstracts on Human Factors in Computing Systems, pp. 2755–2758 (2012)

Exploring the Benefits of Immersive End User Development for Virtual Reality

Telmo Zarraonandia[✉], Paloma Díaz, Alvaro Montero, and Ignacio Aedo

Computer Science Department, Universidad Carlos III de Madrid, Leganés, Madrid, Spain
{tzarraon,pdp,ammontes}@inf.uc3m.es, aedo@ia.uc3m.es

Abstract. We present an immersive virtual reality tool, called VR GREP, to empower end users with the capacity to design and develop virtual reality environments by themselves. To investigate the potential benefits that this technology might provide to support the end user development of virtual environments we conducted a study in which 23 participants collaborated. The participants designed and implemented two virtual environments using their favourite interaction style. They reported that the immersive environment contributed to making them feel more creative and engaged in the process. They also agreed that the perspective provided by the tool was more adequate for the process, as it is closer to the one perceived by the final user. In general, the results suggest that the technology could have a great potential for supporting the authoring tasks, although to make it a viable alternative to desktop based solutions the precision and accuracy when interacting with the virtual environment will need to be improved.

Keywords: Virtual reality · End user development · Natural interaction · Authoring tool

1 Introduction

Thanks to the commercialization of a new generation of affordable Virtual Reality (VR) devices, such as Oculus Rift or HTC Valve, it is expected that the immersive VR technology will experience a rapid expansion in the next few years. However, the full potential of this technology might not be realised unless the authoring process evolve in an usable way [1]. VR applications already need to be flexible enough to allow non-specialized users, such as educators or trainers, to adapt and modify the content of the virtual environment to their current needs [2]. But as more people get used to and appropriate VR devices, more applications will be required. It would be necessary to provide tools to personalize or adapt the VR applications to new requirements that emerge from new uses devised by end users. In order to enable an user driven innovation process [3], end user development tools are required. End User Development (EUD) is defined as *"a set of methods, techniques and tools that allow users of software systems, who are acting as non-professional software developers, at some point to create, modify, or extend a software artefact"* [4].

© Springer International Publishing AG 2016
C.R. García et al. (Eds.): UCAmI 2016, Part I, LNCS 10069, pp. 450–462, 2016.
DOI: 10.1007/978-3-319-48746-5_46

In this paper we advocate for the use of EUD tools to be able to author and modify VR environments without having technical knowledge. Since one of the most distinctive features of VR is immersion, that is, the capacity to give the user the sensation of being "present" in a virtual environment [5], we consider that EUD tools should also be immersive and let users modify the VR environment in the virtual space, not in a desktop representation of it. This will support carrying out a design process following the principles of situated design. At the same time the benefits derived from the feeling of presence might also be enjoyed during the creation process. Furthermore, non-experienced users could find easier to carry out the authoring process interacting naturally in an immersive VR environment than using the current metaphors provided for the task by the desktop based solutions.

To investigate these issues we developed VR GREP (Game Rules scEnarios Platform), an immersive EUD tool for authoring and modifying general purpose immersive VR environments that allows to choose and personalize the interaction style for each edition tasks. The VR GREP platform provided us with the basis to carry out an exploratory study in which 23 participants designed and developed a VR virtual environment while fully immersed in the VR space. The participants acknowledged the potentiality of the approach, and they appreciated its capacity to provide a closer perspective to the final user's view, and to enhance the engagement in the process. It was also interesting to note that, despite the limited accuracy currently provided by the hardware used, most of them preferred to perform the edition tasks using a direct interaction style based on hands movements.

In the remaining of the paper we will first review VR uses and applications and EUD environments to provide the context of this research. Then we introduce the VR GREP platform, and summarize its main features and architecture. Next the study and the results obtained are detailed. The paper ends with some conclusions and future lines of work.

2   VR Uses and Applications

Although VR has been traditionally associated with the area of games and sophisticated flight simulators, there are many other fields in which the possibilities offered by this technology have already been exploited. For example, in the medical area VR applications have been developed for treatment of acrophobia [6], fear of flying [7], brain injury rehabilitation [8] or post-stroke rehabilitation [9]. Education and learning is another field for which immersive VR is specially appealing. Although so far most of the educational VR applications are desktop-based [10–12], it is possible to find some examples of fully immersive HDMs-based VR environments for teaching modelling virtual words [13, 14] or to help to understand scientific concepts [15], and CAVE (CAVE Automatic Virtual Environment) systems that implement virtual laboratories for students [16] or help them to learn chemistry [12, 17]. In the area of digital arts, VR applications have been used to support immersive installations [18], and Goggle has just recently announced the upcoming release of Tilt Brush [19], an application for the HTC Vive device that allows artist to paint in a 3D space. Museums and cultural heritage institutions are also starting to adopt this technology, either to enrich the visit to art exhibitions [20], or to virtually reproduce the original appearance of archaeological and historical sites [21, 22].

3   EUD in Immersive VR Environments

As described in the previous section, the affordances provided by VR can be useful in many different interaction scenarios. If this technology is put into the hands of those that experience problems that could be improved with it, that is, the end users, we will witness an explosion of innovative applications coming form the imagination of non professional developers as it has happened with other technologies [3]. But for that to be possible we need to have adequate EUD tools. However, EUD solutions for VR environments are still scarce. Most applications are created ad-hoc and there is no chance to reuse and adapt them without having a specialised technical background. There are some desktop-based VR versions [10, 11], but in this work we posit the need to explore the contribution of immersive environments to support situated end-user design of VR environments.

According to the principles of situated design, the solutions conceived during design practice are influenced by the situation and position from which the design activity is carried out [23–25]. If the design of VR spaces could take place in the same immersive space users will experience, designers will be able to act upon the real user experience and not over 2D representations where relevant affordances are lost, including the sense of presence, the immersion, and the physical navigation and interaction with the space. An immersive EUD tool will put designers into the end users shoes; they will work on a WYSIWYG (What You See Is What You Get) approach, and will be able to test the user's view even from an early stage of the process [1]. Furthermore, an immersive environment could also report benefits in terms of engagement [26] or increasing spatial understanding [27]. Another key aspect to facilitate the adoption of a EUD tool is to provide an interface that is easy to learn and to operate by non-technical users. However, how these potential benefits can be translated into useful and usable EUD tools is still an open issue. In this paper we describe a first step in this direction, an EUD tool that explores some interaction capabilities in an immersive environment as described in the next section.

4   The VR GREP Tool

VR GREP (Virtual Reality Game Rules scEnario Platform) is an immersive EUD platform designed to allow non-expert users to create general purpose immersive VR environments, without requiring technical assistance. Using the tool an author equipped with a VR Head Mounted Display, as the Oculus Rift, can carry out the creation process within the virtual environment itself. VR GREP tool has been implemented using the Unity game engine, and it is built on top of GREP (Game Rules scEnario Platform) [28], an EUD platform for supporting the design and implementation of digital games, with an special focus on educational ones.

The VR GREP Tool supports two modes of use: edition and exploration (Fig. 1). In the edition mode the user designs a virtual "scene" with the "VR Scenes Editor". Before starting the edition process, the author needs to upload to the platform two XML files, the *entities file* and the *controls file*, and to select a background for the scene. The *entities file* contains the list of elements that the author can use to define his or her scenes. Each of the entities in the list is linked to one asset of the platform repository that will be used to represent it. For example, a specific *entities file* might define a correspondence between the entity "house" and an asset in the platform that depicts a cartoonish house, whereas another *entities file* might link the entity "house" with a more realistic representation of a building. On the other hand, the *controls file* specifies the commands and interactions preferred by the author to perform each edition task, as described in the next section. Finally, the background provides an initial setting for the scene. Most backgrounds consist of just an empty terrain or a floor with a texture of concrete or grass, for example. However, and to speed up the design, it is also possible to select backgrounds that provide a more elaborate pre-defined representation of an environment, as a room or a forest, and which already include trees, bushes, etc.

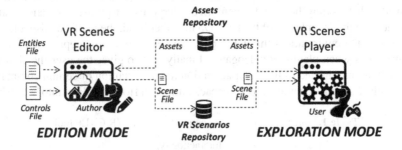

Fig. 1. Edition and exploration modes of the VR GREP Tool

Once the background of the scene has been selected, the author can start exploring and transforming the virtual scene, walking around it, placing entities, and adjusting its size and orientation. It is also possible to add entry points to other scenes so that more complex VR scenarios can be created. The final design can be exported as an XML file containing the description of all the elements in the scene. These scenes files can be stored in the *scenarios repository* of the platform, making them available to other users, who can retrieve them and reproduce them using the platform in exploration mode with the VR Scenes Player.

4.1   Personalizing the Interaction Style

The way the user interacts with the VR environment has a direct effect in the level of immersion and presence he or she will experience [29]. For this reason, it is often assumed that natural interaction techniques are the most adequate solution for immersive VEs, as they allow to mimic more closely the way the user would perform the task in the real world. However, some tasks require a level of precision that the input device that support the gestures or movement detection, for example, might not be able to deliver. At the same time there might be other less natural techniques that the user could find easier to remember and to use. In general, it is difficult to think of a single interaction technique that could result adequate to support the wide range of tasks the user might require during the authoring of a VR environment. In fact, the interaction design needs to be informed by the user's characteristics and the specific requirements of the task [30]. In our case, the system is intended to be used by designers who might not have a high level of technological expertise. Therefore, it is paramount to minimize the cognitive effort required to learn to use the system, and to provide alternative options to perform each task so that different users' preferences and backgrounds can be accommodated.

Following these ideas, the VR GREP edition tool implements a flexible interaction model that allows the designer to chose and configure the way he or she wants to carry out each of the edition tasks. Table 1 summarizes the different interaction styles VR GREP currently supports. On the one hand, the system allows the user to directly interact with the environment via hand gestures, voice commands and her own gaze. This type of interaction is frequently used is immersive VR environments as the user does not need to manipulate a physical artefact to execute the command [31]. However, it is necessary to consider that asking the user to memorize a large list of phrases or hand gestures might increase the complexity of the task. On the other hand, the platform also allows to interact with the environment through a physical device like a gamepad, using it in a similar way as when playing a videogame. Finally, it also gives the user the choice to define virtual buttons and to link their activation to the execution of certain commands. It is possible to specify icons and labels for each button, and to group them into button bars.

Table 1. Interaction modalities supported by the VR GREP tool.

Style	Interaction type
Direct interaction	Hands gestures, voice, gaze
Physical interaction	Joystick, gamepad
Virtual input	Virtual button

Before starting the edition process the user specifies the interaction technique he or she prefers to use for performing each of the tasks, and uploads the selection as an XML file, the controls file. Table 2 summarizes the tasks the author might perform while editing a virtual environment in the VR GREP tool. Following the VE interactions classification proposed in [32] the tasks can be organized in three major categories or universal tasks: navigation or viewpoint manipulation, selection and manipulation, and system control. Navigation refers to the process of moving around the environment and changing the user's point-of-view. The most common navigation technique in VR systems is the First Person Perspective, which means that the virtual world is rendered from the perspective of the user. The VR GREP tool also implements this approach, adopting a walking metaphor to maintain the user immersion in the VR world. Selection has been implemented using another common interaction solution in VR environments: raycasting the user's gaze. A crosshair marks the centre of the user's vision, and to select an object or position he or she only needs to look and place the crosshair on top of it. Once selected the user can manipulate the object's position, orientation and size. To modify the first one the users needs to first grab the object, and then release it at a new location. On the contrary, the orientation and size of an object can be directly modified just by selecting the object and triggering the appropriate command depicted in the table. Finally, the application control is relatively simple as it only includes commands for saving the design, exiting the platform, confirming or discarding an action, display or hide the buttonbars, and navigate and activate the buttons.

Table 2. Summary of tasks the author can perform and personalize.

Category	Task
Navigation	Move forward/backward/left/right, walk/run
Selection and manipulation	Select entity, select position, add entity, remove entity, add entrance, remove entrance grab entity, release entity, increase scale, reduce scale, rotate left, rotate right.
Application control	Save, exit, confirm/discard, Click button, previous/next button, display/hide buttonbar

5   Exploratory Study

In this section we present an exploratory case study conducted to gain insights on the potential benefits that immersive VR might report for supporting end users in the process of designing and developing VR environments. Exploratory case studies are frequently used in the HCI area for the initial investigation of a new problem, so that it can be better understood [33]. More specifically the objectives of the study were to investigate:

– the potential benefits than immersive authoring environments could report in terms of creativity enhancement.
– the benefits non-experts users might perceive of using an immersive environments over desktop based authoring solutions.
– users' interaction preferences for carrying out the edition task.

5.1   Participants

The study was organized in the context of a technology fair that took place in the University Carlos III of Madrid. In total 23 volunteer participants (4 female) collaborate in the study. Participants ranged from 20 to 46 years, and they had a wide range of different backgrounds. 19 participants reported to have some previous experience on designing virtual scenarios using sandboxes and platforms such as Minecraft or Garry's Mod. 10 participants never used immersive VR before and the rest of them had tried some kind of VR device. None of them was an experienced VR user.

5.2   Apparatus

The hardware consisted of an Oculus Rift and a Leap Motion device connected to an Apple Mac computer (Apple Mac Pro or Apple iMac), and an Android mobile phone that capture the voice commands and send them wirelessly to the computer. The software used was an installation of the GREP VR platform described in the previous section.

5.3 Procedure

The experiment was organized in the following way. Firstly, participants were asked to fill in a pre-test questionnaire to gather demographic data and information about their background and previous experience. Next, they carried out two activities. In the first one they were asked to design a VR environment depicting a medieval village. They started with a semi-completed scenario to which they added different types of animals and vegetation. This activity was guided by one of the workshops organizers, who explained the participant how to navigate the scene, add elements to it and modify them using each of the different interaction techniques available. The organizer made sure that the participant performed each of the tasks using each type of interaction styles at least once. Once the design was completed the participant could test it by playing a pre-defined game in which she had to search and capture all the animals in the village previously designed.

In the second activity the participant was asked to design a western village. In this case the design was carried out almost from scratch, starting with an empty terrain that the participant populated with different buildings, trees, and structures. The guidance provided during this second activity was kept to a minimum, and the participant freely chose the way he or she wanted to interact with the system for carrying each design task.

The total time for completing the two designs was about 20 min. After that time the participants filled in a second questionnaire and were briefly interview to gather their opinions and reactions to the experience. Figure 2 depicts some pictures taken during the activities and some screenshots of the virtual environments produced.

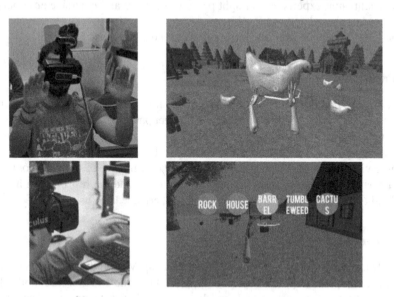

Fig. 2. Participant of the study editing virtual environments with the VR GREP tool

5.4 Data Collection

The primary data source were questionnaires that include both close and open questions. The questionnaires were divided in three sections. The first one (Table 3) aimed to provide insights into the potentiality of immersive environments as a mean to enhance creativity during the authoring process. The questions in this section were adapted from the Creativity Support Index (CSI) survey presented in [34], a validated instrument to measure the creativity support provided by a system or interface. This survey considers six orthogonal factors related to creativity support: results worth the effort, expressiveness, exploration, enjoyment, immersion and collaboration. In our study only the first five were taken into account (Q1–Q5), as collaboration is not currently supported in the platform used in the study. To obtain a measure of the users' general satisfaction we also asked them if they would like to repeat the activity again (Q6).

Table 3. Responses to the 1st section of the questionnaire: creativity support

Questions			M	SD
Results worth	Q1	What I was able to produce was worth the effort I had to exert to produce it	4,30	0,55
Expressiveness	Q2	I was able to be expressive and to include the things I wanted	3,70	0,91
Immersion	Q3	My attention was fully tuned to the activity, and I forgot about the system/tool that I was using	3,61	1,10
Exploration	Q4	It was easy for me to explore different options and design choices	3,43	1,06
Enjoyment	Q5	I feel engaged in the tasks and I really enjoyed it	4,22	0,51
Satisfaction	Q6	I would repeat the activity again	4,30	0,81

In the second section, the participants who had some previous experience with desktop based authoring tools were asked to compare it with the one provided by the immersive EUD tool. More specifically, they were asked if they felt more creative (Q7), if they perceive better the way the final user would experience the environment (Q8), if they were more motivated (Q9), and if they think it was superior in general terms (Q10).

Finally, the third section of the questionnaire included some open questions that participants could use to explain their ratings, to describe which were their interaction preferences, the major benefits and shortcomings of the environment, and any possible suggestion to improve the system.

The information gathered from the questionnaires was completed with the direct observation of the activities, and with the responses of the participants to brief semi-structured interviews conducted at the end of the experiment.

5.5 Results

With regards to the questions about the creativity factors, the participants' responses (Table 3) suggest that there was a general agreement on the fact that using an immersive tool to carry out the authoring task was really worth the effort ($M = 4,30$ SD $= 0,55$). They also considered the experience very enjoyable ($M = 4,22$ SD $= 0,51$), and they would repeat it again ($M = 4,30$ SD $= 0,81$). The score obtained for the other three creativity aspects, although positive, did not score so high. Among the three of them, expressiveness was the most valued aspect of the experience ($M = 3,70$ SD $= 0,91$), followed by immersion ($M = 3,61$ SD $= 1,10$), and the possibility to explore different options ($M = 3,43$ SD $= 1,06$).

When asked to compare the design activity with the ones performed in a desktop platform (Table 4), participants considered the VR system as clearly more motivating ($M = 4,30$ SD $= 0,87$), helpful for understanding the experience of the final user ($M = 4,13$ SD $= 0,92$), and useful for enhancing creativity ($M = 4,00$ SD $= 0,93$). However, when asked directly if they consider that VR is better for this task the responses, although positives, were less enthusiastic ($M = 3,52$ SD $= 1,18$).

Table 4. Responses to the 2nd section of the questionnaire: comparison with desktop

Questions			M	SD
More creative	Q7	Being immersed in the scenario made me feel more creative	4,05	0,89
Better perception	Q8	Creating the scenario in the VR environment allowed me to perceive better the way the player will experience it	4,15	0,93
More engagement	Q9	The VR environment made me feel more engaged in the task than the desktop version	4,36	0,87
Better in general	Q10	It is better to carry out the design task in the VR environment rather in the desktop version	3,52	1,19

The participants' answers to the open questions of the questionnaire and to the interview can help to understand better these results. For example, the advantages more often reported about an VR environment over a desktop one were immersion (5 participants) and closeness to the final experience of the user (5 participants). With regards to the drawbacks, 2 participants reported that desktop solutions are easier to use and another one explained that they are more precise. In addition, although most reactions to the system were very positive, 2 participants reported feeling a bit dizzy after the experience.

Finally, and as expected, the participants did not agree about the best way to interact in the VR during the design process (Table 5). As shown in the table, 8 participants reported to prefer using the hands, 4 the gamepad, 5 the hands combined with voice commands, 3 the hands combined with buttonbars, and the last 3 the gamepad in combination with voice commands. It is interesting to note that when asked to explain the reason behind their choice most participants reported that "it was the way it felt more natural", regardless the interaction style they preferred. The interviews revealed that, not surprisingly, the gamepad was the favourite option for those participants who played

Table 5. Summary of responses regarding interaction preferences

Preferred interaction	Total participants
Hands	11
Gamepad	5
Hands + voice	4
Gamepad + voice	3

videogames regularly. On the contrary, the use of hands was preferred by those participants who do not play videogames or that were less technologically skilled.

5.6 Discussion

The participants' responses suggest that most of them were satisfied with the experience. The potentiality of the technology for supporting the task was widely acknowledged. This point is greatly significant, specially considering that none of the participants had designed a virtual environment using an immersive platform previously, and many not even had any prior experience with VR technology. The benefits in terms of engagement of the user normally reported when analysing experiences with VR environments were also present in this case, when the system was used as a support for the design task. Most importantly, the study indicates that the participants felt natural and appropriate to create the virtual world using the same tool and same perspective as the users who will explore it latter on. Also, and with regards to the interaction styles, the experience confirmed the necessity of providing alternatives so that the user can choose the modality he or she feels more natural for the task.

The results regarding the utility of the approach for enhancing user's creativity were less clear. On the one hand the answers to the question Q5 suggests that the participants felt more creative than when using a desktop platform. However, the questions about the ability to express oneself and to explore design alternatives did not obtain very positive responses. A possible explanation to this might lie in the limited number of graphical resources available in the platform at the moment of carrying out the experience. This clearly imposed a restriction in the range of designs that the participants could envision during the activity. Also, the limitations of the interaction devices used might also help to explain the low score for the level of immersion, and why, despite the good ratings obtained in the other factors, the VR platform was not more clearly preferred over the desktop ones. This way, during the experience we observed how sometimes participants experienced difficulties when carrying out the tasks. For example, sometimes the voice commands were not recognized or the system failed to identify the gesture the user performed. Although these problems not impeded most participants to appreciate the potential of the platform, they could have suggested that the technology was not ready to allow to carry out designs with the level of precision provided by desktop platforms. As one of the participant stated "I would use a desktop platform to carry out the initial design work, and then I would test it and finish it in the VR platform".

Finally, it is also necessary to consider some limitations of the study. Firstly, the novelty of the experience could have clearly influenced the level of satisfaction of the participants. Also, precision and accuracy were not crucial requirements for the designs produced. In general, it is possible that if the users were asked to produce a specific design that require working with an authoring tool during a continued period, they might prefer to do it using a traditional desktop based platform. Further studies would be required to clarify this point.

6   Conclusions and Future Work Lines

We presented a study that aim to provide some insights into the benefits that VR technology might report for supporting EUD tasks of VR environments. The results of the experience suggest that the use of immersive EUD platforms could report benefits at several levels. The participants reported to appreciate its advantages to foster creativity, engagement and provide a more appropriate perspective of the design. However, metaphors and solutions appropriate for VR environments that exploit the benefits that natural interaction styles provide while maintaining the accuracy of desktop solutions are needed. Our current work goes in that direction. We aim to investigate different ways in which techniques currently used in videogames and sandboxes for designing virtual environments can be translated into a totally immersive platform. In addition, work is being carried out to expand the VR GREP Editor functionalities so that the designer could also specify rules to govern the interaction between he virtual entities. This would allow them to design and implement VR interactive experiences that could be used not only for entertainment but also to support educational activities, for example.

References

1. Dörner, R., Kallmann, M., Huang, Y.: Content creation and authoring challenges for virtual environments: from user interfaces to autonomous virtual characters. In: Brunnett, G., Coquillart, S., van Liere, R., Welch, G., Vasa, L. (eds.) Virtual Realities. LNCS, vol. 8844, pp. 187–212. Springer, Heidelberg (2015)
2. Dörner, R., Grimm, P.: Etoile - an environment for team, organizational and individual learning in emergencies. In: Proceedings of the 9th IEEE International Workshops on Enabling Technologies: Infrastructure for Collaborative Enterprises (WETICE 2000), pp. 27–34. IEEE Computer Society (2000)
3. Von Hippel, E.: Democratizing Innovation. MIT Press, Cambridge (2005)
4. Lieberman, H., Paterno, F., Klann, M., Wulf, V.: End-user development: an emerging paradigm. In: Lieberman, H., Paterno, F., Wulf, V. (eds.) End User Development. Human-Computer Interaction Series, vol. 9, pp. 1–8. Springer, Heidelberg (2006)
5. Slater, M.: Measuring presence: a response to the witmer and singer questionnaire. Presence 8(5), 560–566 (1999)
6. Krijn, M., Emmelkamp, P.M.G., Biemond, R., de Ligny, C.D., de Ligny, M.J., van der Mast, C.A.: Treatment of acrophobia in virtual reality: the role of immersion and presence. Behav. Res. Ther. 42(2), 229–239 (2004)
7. Mühlberger, A., Herrmann, M.J., Wiedemann, G., Ellgring, H., Pauli, P.: Repeated exposure of flight phobics to flights in virtual reality. Behav. Res. Ther. 39(9), 1033–1050 (2001)
8. Rose, F.D., Brooks, B.M., Rizzo, A.A.: Virtual reality in brain damage rehabilitation: review. CyberPsychol. Behav. 8(3), 241–262 (2005)

9. Deutsch, J.E., Latonio, J., Burdea, G.C., Boian, R.: Post-stroke rehabilitation with the Rutgers Ankle system: a case study. Presence: Teleoperators Virtual Environ. **10**(4), 416–430 (2001)

10. Shih, Y.C., Yang, M.T.: A collaborative virtual environment for situated language learning using VEC3D. J. Educ. Technol. Soc. **11**(1), 56–68 (2008)

11. Virvou, M., Katsionis, G.: On the usability and likeability of virtual reality games for education: the case of VR-ENGAGE. Comput. Educ. **50**(1), 154–178 (2008)

12. Huang, H.M., Rauch, U., Liaw, S.S.: Investigating learners' attitudes toward virtual reality learning environments: based on a constructivist approach. Comput. Educ. **55**(3), 1171–1182 (2010)

13. Bricken, M., Byrne, C.M.: Summer students in virtual reality. In: Virtual reality: Applications and exploration, pp. 199–218 (1993)

14. Hay, K.E., Crozier, J., Barnett, M., Allison, D., Bashaw, M., Hoos, B., Perkins, L.: Virtual gorilla modeling project: middle school students constructing virtual models for learning. In: International Conference of the Learning Sciences: Facing the Challenges of Complex Real-World Settings. Psychology Press (2013)

15. Dede, C., Salzman, M.C., Loftin, R.B.: ScienceSpace: virtual realities for learning complex and abstract scientific concepts. In: Proceedings of the IEEE Virtual Reality Annual International Symposium (1996)

16. Ren, S., McKenzie, F.D., Chaturvedi, S.K., Prabhakaran, R., Yoon, J., Katsioloudis, P.J., Garcia, H.: Design and comparison of immersive interactive learning and instructional techniques for 3D virtual laboratories. Presence **24**(2), 93–112 (2015)

17. Limniou, M., Roberts, D., Papadopoulos, N.: Full immersive virtual environment CAVETM in chemistry education. Comput. Educ. **51**, 584–593 (2008)

18. Cavazza, M., Lugrin, J.L., Hartley, S., Libardi, P., Barnes, M.J., Le Bras, M., Le Renard, M., Bec, L., Nandi, A.: New ways of worldmaking: the Alterne platform for VR art. In: Proceedings of the 12th Annual ACM International Conference on Multimedia, pp. 80–87 (2004)

19. Google. Tilt Brush. http://www.tiltbrush.com/. Accessed 10 Jan 2016

20. Bergamasco, M.: Le musee del formes pures. In: 8th IEEE International Workshop on Robot and Human Interaction (RO-MAN 1999) (1999)

21. Bruno, F., Bruno, S., De Sensi, G., Luchi, M.L., Mancuso, S., Muzzupappa, M.: From 3D reconstruction to virtual reality: a complete methodology for digital archaeological exhibition. J. Cult. Herit. **11**(1), 42–49 (2010)

22. Carrozzino, M., Bergamasco, M.: Beyond virtual museums: Experiencing immersive virtual reality in real museums. J. Cult. Herit. **11**(4), 452–458 (2010)

23. Haraway, D.: Situated knowledges: the science question in feminism and the privilege of partial perspective. Feminist Stud. **14**(3), 575–599 (1988)

24. Suchman, L.A.: Plans and situated actions: the problem of human-machine communication. Cambridge University Press, Cambridge (1987)

25. Suchman, L.A.: Human-Machine Reconfigurations: Plans and Situated Actions. Cambridge University Press, Cambridge (2007)

26. Dalgarno, B., Lee, M.J.: What are the learning affordances of 3-D virtual environments. Br. J. Educ. Technol. **41**(1), 10–32 (2010)

27. Bowman, D., McMahan, R.P.: Virtual reality: how much immersion is enough? Computer **40**(7), 36–43 (2007)

28. Zarraonandia, T., Diaz, P., Aedo, I.: Using combinatorial creativity to support end-user design of digital games. Multimed. Tools Appl. 1–26 (2016). doi:10.1007/s11042-016-3457-4

29. Jennett, C., Cox, A.L., Cairns, P., Dhoparee, S., Epps, A., Tijs, T., Walton, A.: Measuring and defining the experience of immersion in games. Int. J. Hum Comput Stud. **66**(9), 641–661 (2008)
30. Foley, J.D., Wallace, V.L., Chan, P.: The human factors of computer graphics interaction techniques. IEEE Comput. Graph. Appl. **4**(11), 13–48 (1984)
31. Bowman, D.A., Kruijff, E., LaViola Jr., J.J., Poupyrev, I.: An introduction to 3-D user interface design. Presence Teleoperators Virtual Environ. **10**(1), 96–108 (2001)
32. Hand, C.: A survey of 3D interaction techniques. Comput. Graph. Forum **16**(5), 269–281 (1997). Blackwell Publishers
33. Lazer, J., Fenq, J.H., Hochheiser, H.: Research Methods in Human-Computer Interaction. Wiley, New York (2010)
34. Carroll, E.A., Latulipe, C., Fung, R., Terry, M.L.: Creativity factor evaluation: towards a standardized survey metric for creativity support. In: Proceedings of the Seventh ACM Conference on Creativity and Cognition, pp. 127–136. ACM (2009)

An Assisted Navigation Method for Telepresence Robots

Francisco Melendez-Fernandez[✉], Cipriano Galindo,
and Javier Gonzalez-Jimenez

Departamento de Ingeniería de Sistemas y Automática,
Universidad de Málaga, Málaga, Spain
fco.melendez@uma.es

Abstract. Telepresence robots have emerged as a new means of interaction in remote environments. However, the use of such robots is still
limited due to safety and usability issues when operating in human-like
environments. This work addresses these issues by enhancing the robot
navigation through a *collaborative control* method that assists the user
to negotiate obstacles. The method has been implemented in a commercial telepresence robot and a user study has been conducted in order to
test the suitability of our approach.

Keywords: AAL · Telepresence robotics · Assisted driving · Collaborative control

1 Introduction

Telepresence robotics integrates solutions from Mobile Robotics (MR) and Information and Communication Technologies (ICTs) to provide a fruitful interaction
between two distant locations: (i) the *robot environment*, where a mobile robot
performs, and (ii) the *visitor environment*, where an user teleoperates the robot
and actively interplays with the surroundings through its sensory system.

This form of communication is increasingly gaining attention in Ambient
Assisted Living (AAL) contexts, particularly in applications aimed at supporting services for ageing-well at home. In such applications, the final goal is to
support the remote social interaction between caregivers and elderly people in
a more natural fashion than traditional methods do (e.g., phone calls or video-
conference). To this goal, robotic telepresence envisages the robot's mobility as
an added-value to enable the visitor to freely move within the remote environment. In this way, the assisted person is relieved from being at a specific location,
i.e. in front of a computer, and/or holding a device while the interaction occurs.

Achieving the required levels of safety in the robot motion when guided by the
user is the first, unavoidable requisite for a teleprecesence robot. Usability, also,

Authors are with the Mapir Group. This work is supported by the research
project DPI2014-55826-R, funded by the Spanish Government, financed by European
Regional Development's funds (FEDER).

C.R. García et al. (Eds.): UCAmI 2016, Part I, LNCS 10069, pp. 463–468, 2016.
DOI: 10.1007/978-3-319-48746-5_47

is highly necessary since the robot, as a mobile multimedia platform, must permit a visitor to put the focus on the main purpose of the visit, the social interaction, instead of on negotiating obstacles along the commanded path. Meaningful use cases of robotic telepresence affected by this issue are presented by Tsui et al. in [7,8]. The first study discusses the limitations of a telepresence robot to operate in scenarios involving movement while simultaneously having a conversation, while the second one points the difficulties of visitors to explore an art gallery because of the presence of people near the robot, long hallways, and network latency.

Enhancing the robot mobility with obstacle avoidance and assisted driving features (i.e., *collaborative control*) has been proved to be a suitable approach to deal with such problems [1,5,6].

For example, in [6] a method based on the readings of a 2D laser range finder is proposed, reporting increased levels of safety in assisted driving at the cost of longer times required to complete the same task.

Macharet and Florencio propose in [5] a system with increased perception capabilities based on the 3D range information of a RGBD camera. They report benefits provided by the collaborative method in both terms, safety and task time performance, but they also point out a negative effect of the assistance on the level of usability perceived by the users. In particular, users found assisted driving less intuitive than manual, and most of the participants demanded some feedback about the autonomous behavior during the task.

Other approaches, like the system presented in [1], address the problem of designing collaborative control methods using low-cost sensory systems, e.g. an array of ultrasonic sensors. However, low cost sensory systems are, in general, insufficient to deal with typical problems of mobile robotics like, for example, self-localization, and, thus, most of the robotic telepresence platforms targeting autonomous behaviors rely on laser scanner and RGBD approaches.

In this work, we describe our collaborative control method for telepresence robots that integrates off-the-shelf robotic algorithms relying on the scans of a laser rangefinder and a RGBD camera to provide assisted driving. The method provides a natural and transparent way to assist the user in typical maneuvers like door-crossing, narrow passages, and cluttered spaces. The collaborative control has been integrated into a commercial telepresence robot (see Fig. 1) equipped with the required sensors and a control architecture based on the MOOS robotic framework [3]. In addition, a convenient web-based visitor interface has been implemented to solve usability and accessibility issues of other existing approaches and, finally, a user study ($N = 24$, 12 visitors performed manual driving and the other 12 used the collaborative control) has been conducted to experimentally assess the suitability of the assisted guiding method.

2   A Collaborative Control Method for Telepresence Robots

The main features that characterize a collaborative control method for telepresence robots are (i) *collision avoidance*, to ensure the security of the robot

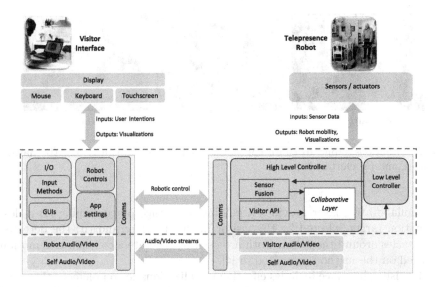

Fig. 1. Overall architecture of the considered robotic telepresence application. The collaborative control combines information from the user intentions and sensory data to guide the robot to the destination marked by the user, while automatically negotiate obstacles.

workspace, and (ii) *obstacle negotiation*, to relieve visitors from complex maneuvers, helping them to concentrate in the social interaction instead of on the robot teleoperation.

Relying on the abilities of the visitor guiding the robot, the collaborative control overcomes current limitations of mobile robotics to handle with the intricacies and complexities of human-like environments. Thus, the challenge is to coherently merge user intentions with autonomous behaviors in order to provide an intuitive assisted driving. Figure 2 illustrates some common situations from our experiments in which navigation assistance is typically required, namely, crossing doors (Fig. 2(a)), going through narrow passages and/or hallways (Fig. 2(b)), and negotiating obstacles in cluttered/dynamic environments (Fig. 2(c)).

Our approach provides a suitable solution to these cases through a collaborative control with the following features:

1. The sensory system provides 3D range data of the proximity of the robot exploited to detect obstacles. To that aim, the 3D sensed data is projected into a 2D occupancy grid by selecting the minimum measured distance from each column of the range image and fused with the scan of the 2D laser rangefinder. If the closest obstacle point is under a specified threshold, the collision avoidance mechanism is activated, stopping the robot to prevent any crash.

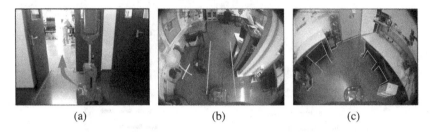

(a)   (b)   (c)

Fig. 2. Situations prone to cause collisions. (a) passing through doors, (b) narrow passages, and (c) cluttered spaces.

2. A collaborative layer provides a guiding assistance by combining (i) a destination target selected by the visitor in the interface and (ii) the detected obstacles around the robot. Both are used to generate a collision-free motion based on the method presented in [4].
3. The visitor interface includes effective visualizations to complement the video received from the telepresence robot (see Fig. 3(b)). More specifically, a set of graphical user interfaces (GUIs) have been integrated in order to (i) provide the visitor with feedback on the obstacles in the robot surroundings and (ii) inform about the operations being conducted autonomously in the collaborative layer, which helps in keeping teleoperation intuitive. Furthermore, the interface allows the user to easily enable/disable the guiding assistance of the robot motion at any time, and considers controllers for multiple input devices (i.e., keyboard, mouse, and touchscreens), which is a key aspect in terms of user accessibility.

3   Experiments

In order to test the collaborative control, it has been implemented as part of the MOOS-based robotic control architecture deployed in one of our commercial Giraff robots [2]. The set of trials involved $N = 24$ participants (12 of them performed fully manual driving and the other 12 used collaborative control) that were requested to steer the robot through a specific path (see Fig. 3(a)). Two metrics are taken into account to evaluate the execution of the task: *time spent* and *number of collisions made*.

Conducted tests included a training period of 45 s. in which the participants familiarized with the controls. A task is given to the visitor at locations 1, 2, and 3 to simulate the social interaction of the visitor in a real situation. Tasks consisted on searching and identifying an specific item printed in an A5 paper size. Note that in intermediate paths 0–1 and 2–3 the participant must deal with additional obstacles included in the setup to clutter the workspace (the additional obstacles are depicted in Fig. 3(a) as starred objects).

Table 1 presents the test results. The results point out that the collaborative control fulfills its purpose of enabling safer and faster robot operations: it

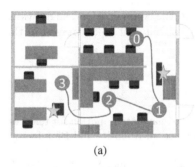 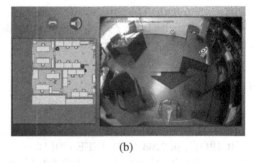

(a)   (b)

Fig. 3. (a) Floorplan of the robot workspace considered in the experiments. Locations identified by users as problematic for teleoperation are mark with stars. (b) User interface showing one of such locations.

improves the performance of manual driving in both metrics *number of collisions* and *task completion time*. Based on the ANOVA test of the data collected, we can report strong evidence on the *collisions* and safety indicators ($p < 0.05$), while the results obtained for the rest of indicators point out soft tendencies of the difference between control modes ($p \approx 0.1$). The tests also revealed a weak point of the system in terms of usability reported by users as sporadic incoherent behavior in the assistance provided. This effect is mainly due to the limited perception capabilities of the telepresence robot, which leads to a misinterpretation of the free-space and, therefore, to a robot motion incoherent with the visitor intentions. Dealing with this issue requires a more systematic study of the autonomous behavior integrated in the collaborative layer and a deeper understanding of the user expectations in the problematic maneuvers, problems that will be addressed in future work.

Table 1. Test Results

Driving mode	Collisions *(mean, sd)*	Seconds on task *(mean, sd)*	Perceived safety 0–7 scale *(mean, sd)*	Perceived usability 0–7 scale *(mean,sd)*
Manual	1.2, 0.75	114, 7.4	3.33, 2.06	**5.66, 1.55**
Collaborative	**0, -**	**93.5, 9.28**	**5.83, 0.75**	5.33, 1.86
ANOVA results	*F = 7.35, p = 0.022*	-	*F = 7.75, p = 0.019*	-

4   Conclusion

In this paper we have described a collaborative control for telepresence robots and a first working prototype which has been tested with 24 users in a controlled environment. The study has pointed out that visitors performed safer and more efficient when using the collaborative control, and the comments and suggestions of the participants have revealed particular issues that will be addressed in the extension of the presented work.

References

1. Chung, W.K., Lam, T.L., Xu, Y.: A natural assisted navigation motion for telepresence robots. In: 2014 IEEE International Conference on Robotics and Biomimetics (ROBIO), pp. 2268–2273. IEEE (2014)
2. Coradeschi, S., Cesta, A., Cortellessa, G., Coraci, L., Galindo, C., Gonzalez, J., Karlsson, L., Forsberg, A., Frennert, S., Furfari, F., et al.: GiraffPlus: a system for monitoring activities and physiological parameters and promoting social interaction for elderly. In: Hippe, Z.S., Kulikowski, J.L., Mroczek, T., Wtorek, J. (eds.) Human-Computer Systems Interaction: Backgrounds and Applications 3. AISC, vol. 300, pp. 261–271. Springer, Heidelberg (2014)
3. Gonzalez, J., Galindo, C., Blanco, J., Fernandez-Madrigal, J., Arevalo, V., Moreno, F.: Sancho, a fair host robot. a description. In: IEEE International Conference on Mechatronics, ICM 2009, pp. 1–6. IEEE (2009)
4. Jaimez, M., Blanco, J.L., González-Jiménez, J.: Efficient reactive navigation with exact collision determination for 3D robot shapes. Int. J. Adv. Robot. Syst. 12(63) (2015)
5. Macharet, D.G., Florencio, D.A.: A collaborative control system for telepresence robots. In: 2012 IEEE/RSJ International Conference on Intelligent Robots and Systems (IROS), pp. 5105–5111. IEEE (2012)
6. Takayama, L., Marder-Eppstein, E., Harris, H., Beer, J.M.: Assisted driving of a mobile remote presence system: system design and controlled user evaluation. In: 2011 IEEE International Conference on Robotics and Automation (ICRA), pp. 1883–1889. IEEE (2011)
7. Tsui, K., Norton, A., Brooks, D., Yanco, H., Kontak, D.: Designing telepresence robot systems for use by people with special needs. In: Proceedings of International Symposium on Quality of Life Technologies, vol. 2 (2011)
8. Tsui, K.M., Desai, M., Yanco, H.A., Uhlik, C.: Exploring use cases for telepresence robots. In: 2011 6th ACM/IEEE International Conference on Human-Robot Interaction (HRI), pp. 11–18. IEEE (2011)

A Sensor-Driven Framework for Rapid Prototyping of Mobile Applications Using a Context-Aware Approach

Borja Gamecho[1,2(✉)], Luis Gardeazabal[1,2], and Julio Abascal[1]

[1] Egokituz Laboratory, University of the Basque Country (UPV/EHU), Donostia, Spain
{luis.gardeazabal,julio.abascal}@ehu.eus
[2] Wimbi Technologies S.L. (WimbiTek), Donostia, Spain
borja.gamecho@wimbitek.com

Abstract. The development of mobile context-aware applications using sensors require the developers to understand several diverse issues: signal acquisition, network protocols, embedded systems, data filtering, etc. We designed and implemented a software framework in order to assist developers in prototyping. Our framework facilitates the use of sensors from wearable devices and supports the reusability of components following a modular approach. This paper describes the design of our approach and highlights the benefits of the framework for the development of mobile applications. To evaluate the framework, representative context-aware applications are described as a case study. The usability of the applications were tested with 26 participants and good results were obtained.

Keywords: Context-aware computing · Mobile and wearable computing · Rapid prototyping framework

1 Introduction

Mobile context-aware applications take into account what is happening in the real world to provide a better adaptation than those offered by regular mobile applications. Usually these applications are deployed in smartphones or tablets and react to changes in the environment or in the user activity, in order to adapt the device's behavior to be more effective in its interaction with the user. A drawback is that developers of mobile applications (commonly called apps) have to deal with several challenges, especially those related to the use of sensors.

The development of a mobile context-aware application requires studying which sources of contextual information would be available when the application is used. Among others, physical sensors stand out for this purpose. Conventional smartphones incorporate a number of embedded sensors which are used to obtain context information. For instance, the work of Hervas et al. [1] combine the use of the GPS with other smartphone features to provide suitable context information for people with mild cognitive impairments. Other works, such as that proposed by Fontecha et al. [2], use smartphone accelerometer signals combined with clinical information records to obtain assessment for elderly frailty detection. Both works provide context-aware services based on a single smartphone sensor.

C.R. García et al. (Eds.): UCAmI 2016, Part I, LNCS 10069, pp. 469–480, 2016.
DOI: 10.1007/978-3-319-48746-5_48

When data from different sensors are combined, hidden context information, such as user activity, emotional state or phone location, can be revealed (see Table 1). For example, in the work by Wiese et al. [3], four different sensors installed in the smartphone are used in order to know if the smartphone is located in a pocket, on a table, or inside a bag. Moreover it detects whether or not the owner is manipulating the smartphone. This information can be used by the applications to adapt their behavior more suitably.

Table 1. Examples of combinations of physical sensors.

Author(s)	Physical sensors	Context information
Schmidt et al. [8]	Temperature, Pressure, CO Gas Meter, Photodiode, ACC, PIR, Microphone	User activity. Mobile phone placement and usage
Wiese et al. [3]	ACC, Light/Proximity, Capacitive, Multispectral	Smartphone placement
Jang et al. [9]	ST, ECG, EDA, PPG	User emotional state
Haag et al. [10]	EMG, EDA, ST, BVP, ECG, Respiration	User emotional state
Chon & Cha [11]	GPS, ACC, Compass, Bluetooth, WiFi and GSM	User Activity
Parkka et al. [12]	Air Pressure, Microphone, ACC, Humidity … (25 sensors)	User Activity

ACC: Accelerometer, ECG: Electrocardiography, EDA: Electro Dermal Activity, PPG: Photoplethysmography (also known as BVP, Blood Volume Pulse), PIR: Passive InfraRed, ST: Skin Temperature.

Usually smartphone sensors obtain contextual information about the device itself or the activity being performed by its owner. Therefore the number of contexts that can be recognized using only a smartphone are limited. However the proliferation of wearable devices has extended the sensing capabilities of smartphones. Nowadays it is possible to have access to a variety of sensors to get more contextual information from the user (including physiological signals).

Wireless sensor devices, such as BITalino [4] or SHIMMER [5], enable the acquisition of physiological signals such as electrocardiography (ECG) or electromyography (EMG) among others. By combining data from wearable sensors, useful background information about the user can be obtained [6]. For instance, Banos et al. 2014 [7] use a SHIMMER device to get information about the physical activities being performed by the users. However, the addition of wearable devices to the set of devices available in the smartphone also makes the programming task more difficult for developers. In order to deal with this ecosystem of devices, sensors and algorithms, a number of context-aware frameworks have been proposed in the research community.

2   Related Work in Context-Aware Frameworks

Several frameworks contributing to deal with these issues have been proposed in the past. For instance Dey's Context Toolkit [13] was a very influential framework for building Context-Aware applications. Dey's work identified and established the features necessary for architectural support to Context-Aware applications. It also contributes with a reusable set of components to define context aware applications. Meanwhile Schmidt's Computing in Context [14] is also a reference in the field and proposed a three level architecture to support context-aware systems. Both, Dey's and Schmidt's works were proposed before the emergence of the smartphone, nevertheless they laid the groundwork for context-aware rapid prototyping frameworks.

First generation smartphones, such as the Nokia S60, also received attention from the researchers to develop their frameworks. For instance, the work of BeTelGeuse [15] focuses on designing a multiplatform and extensible context-aware system. Among other contributions the use of Context Parsers is outlined, these are abstractions of sensors that read and parse data and share they information using a blackboard model proposed by Winograad [16]. Korpipää's work [17] proposes the use of an ontology for managing context information in mobile phones. This system, like BeTelGeuse also uses a central node to store context information following the blackboard model.

Nowadays, with the ubiquitous presence of modern smartphones and wearable devices, mobile context-aware frameworks are a valuable tool not only for researchers but also for application developers. For instance, the AWARE framework [18] proposes a mobile instrumentation toolkit using the smartphone in order to study human behavior, routines and concepts, focusing on four activities: sensing context, storing context, sharing context and using context. Paspallis et al. [19] presents a pluggable and modular middleware architecture for developing context-aware mobile applications. A very interesting property of the system is that the middleware is able to activate or deactivate plug-ins as needed.

Several related works have been enumerated in this Section, covering the main aspects of context-aware applications prototyping. We contribute to this area with a framework for describing mobile context-aware applications and to facilitate sensor management for inexperienced developers. Our software framework allows rapid prototyping and testing at different stages of the development.

3   Programming Mobile Context-Aware Applications from the Developers' Perspective

In order to design a context-aware application four sequential steps are usually followed. The developers need to decide (1) which context information is suitable for the application; (2) which sensors are able to provide such context information; (3) how the data coming from the sensors can be transformed into suitable context-information; and, (4) how the context information can be used to extend the functionalities of the proposed mobile application.

The purpose of our framework is to assist the developers in the third step. In addition, it facilitates the use of context information in mobile applications by means of the use of a context delivery interface in order to separate the rest of the application from the context acquisition.

3.1   Delivery of Context, Characterizing Entities in Mobile Environments

We adopted the Deys definition [20] to define "context": "Context is any information that can be used to characterize the situation of an entity. An entity is a person, place or object that is considered relevant to the interaction between a user and an application, including the user and the application themselves". For this reason we focus on characterizing the situation of entities. These entities can be a person, such as the user, an object, such as the smartphone or a place, such as the bus stop. All the entities involved in the interaction of the application must be identified by the developer. The context information is represented in our approach as messages that contain the following information:

- Entity: Who is affected.
- Context: What is affected.
- Value: What is the actual value of the context or how has it changed.
- Timestamp: When has it happened.

In our framework, context information is delivered in messages to the application using a dedicated channel that communicates the context acquisition with the applications main area. For instance, the following JSON [21] message indicates that the user of the smartphone is performing the running activity, with a probability of 95 %:

```
{
"Context-Information":
    {
       "Entity":"User",
       "Context":"Activity",
       "Values":[{"Running":0.95},{"Walking":0.05}],
       "Timestamp":"13:30:21"
    }
}
```

The context information must be modeled by the developers of the application and varies significantly from one application to another. That is why the mechanism to define the context information should be flexible and the reason to choose JSON specification. Once the information is delivered from the context acquisition module, the developer only needs to take into account the context updates to make their application context-aware.

3.2   Technical Challenges of Context Acquisition

Developers have to face many challenging tasks when programming the acquisition of context. Among these, they have to deal with:

- *Seamless integration of the different devices.* The system should work as a whole. The main obstacle to achieving this goal is the heterogeneity of sensors, devices, network or platforms that require the use of different APIs and libraries.

- *Context recognition processing techniques and algorithms complexity.* Developers dedicate considerable time to recognizing context information and improving models to match the adequate context values.
- *Performance of the application.* Continuous sensor readings and heavy processing of the context aware applications critically affect the performance of the mobile device battery.

If these technical challenges are not properly addressed the resulting application will have poor usability, only serving to frustrate the users. In our framework we want to achieve a layered vision to deal with these challenges and alleviate the programming tasks.

3.3 Virtualization and Abstraction of Sensors

Regarding the context aware applications described in Table 1, two interesting issues can be underlined. On the one hand, the combination of data from different sensors produces context information. This abstraction can be considered as a new virtual sensor that provides higher level information. On the other hand, equivalent context information is obtained from different combinations of sensors as instances of an abstract sensor. We consider that a framework capable of representing both virtual and abstract sensors facilitates context acquisition management in mobile applications.

For instance (see Fig. 1), from a set of four different physical sensors (ACC, ECG, BVP and GPS), an activity monitor (AM1) can be obtained combining data from two of them (ECG and the ACC). This activity monitor, acting as a virtual sensor, contains all the processing to obtain the information of the activities carried out by a person. In addition to AM1, the other two sensors (GPS, BVP) can be combined to obtain an alternative activity monitor (AM2). Both AM1 and AM2 are instances of the same abstract sensor, which provides context information to the mobile application. This way some independence of sensors can be achieved.

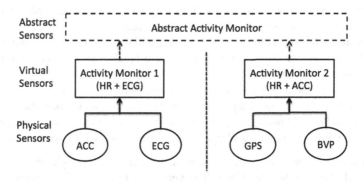

Fig. 1. Example of abstracts and virtual sensors.

Developers can use the abstraction of virtual sensors and abstract sensors to design the context acquisition of their applications and separate concerns. All the features described in Sect. 3 are implemented in the framework described in Sect. 4.

4   Software Framework for Context-Awareness

In order to instantiate our proposal, we adopted and extended an existing software framework proposed in Canovas et al. [21] known as MobileBIT. This was conceived to develop sensor driven mobile applications for telemedicine and mobile health domains to deal with the following tasks: real-time data acquisition, data processing, data storing and data visualization. The architecture of MobileBIT is divided into four elements (see Fig. 2):

- **Functional blocks**: These are the basic components of MobileBIT, each block encapsulates a task and they are communicated with each other via "channels".
- **Data Processing Language (DPL)**: This is the configuration language to set up the applications in MobileBIT. It is based in JSON language and defines how the functional blocks are connected through channels.
- **Workflow Manager (WFM)**: This is the core engine of the framework, when the application is in runtime WFM instantiates the functional blocks and ensures that all the modules are working properly.
- **Hybrid application approach**: MobileBIT uses two different layers, for the above-mentioned features, the framework uses a native application layer. Conversely for the applications user interface a web layer is used in order to visualize and manage the interaction with the user.

We have developed a prototype of this framework in Android and extended it to deal with context information. In our approach there are three types of Functional Blocks:

- **Physical device block**: This represents the mobile device with all the embedded sensors. It can be a wireless wearable device or a smartphone. Inside this block networking issues are addressed and raw data is acquired.
- **Processing block**: This contains data filtering and algorithms to transform raw data into higher level embedded information. These blocks can be chained in order to obtain context information.
- **Context blackboard block**: When a processing block obtains the context values for the characterization of an entity, the context blackboard block writes the message as described in Sect. 3.1 and delivers it to the web application layer. This block has only one generic implementation and must be configured in the DPL to work properly.

The main advantage of using functional blocks is their high reusability once programmed. Another benefit is that it is very easy to change the configurations of functional blocks using the DPL configuration file, allowing fast prototyping and comfortable testing of the applications.

Our MobileBIT extension implements all the mechanisms described in the previous Section. The hybrid approach separates the context acquisition part of the application

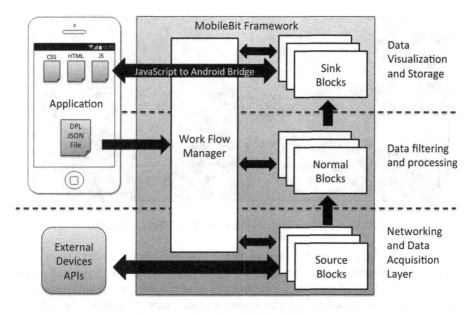

Fig. 2. Architecture of MobileBIT system.

from the rest of functionalities as required in Sect. 3.1. Thus context information updates are delivered using JavaScript to the web application.

Regarding the abstraction layers, virtual sensors can be implemented using processing blocks and DPL. On the other hand, abstract sensors are not explicitly represented but they can be defined as DPL files with a different block configuration.

As a result, developers have different resources to deal with the developing of mobile context-aware applications while using our framework.

5   Case Study with a Representative Applications

Representative Context-Aware applications were developed in order to test whether the proposed framework fits our requirements. The evaluation had the following goals:

- Create virtual and abstract sensors and test them.
- Test the generation of context information and delivery mechanisms.
- Evaluate the usability in order to check the applications' functionality and identify problems in applications.

Two applications were developed: the ToBITas Case Study [22] and the Rehabilitation Exercise System (RESapp) [23]. The former is a smartphone application designed to control a mobile robot in real time with movements of the right arm. The latter was designed to exercise the right arm in rehabilitation therapy tested in two scenarios: under laboratory conditions and in a retirement day center. For this last application, there are two different possibilities, with and without the help of the robot. Figure 3 shows the different experiments performed with the applications.

Fig. 3. Images of the experimentation with ToBITas and RESapp.

The applications focus on the "user" as the main entity to obtain context information. The context available for the developers is the movement of the user's arm and user's hand and the position of the user's arms. In order to obtain the context information we use a BITalino sensor platform [4]. The following blocks were developed in the software framework to obtain the delivery of the context information:

- **BITalino Device Block**: In order to use all the sensors available in the BITalino board, a Device Block was developed to obtain information from the accelerometer (ACC) and two electromyogram (EMG) sensors.
- **Muscle Processing Block**: Using an EMG signal as an input, it is attached to one muscle and it returns if the muscle is contracted. A threshold must be configured to tune this block depending on the person and the muscle.
- **Tilt Movement Processing Block**: Using an ACC signal as an input it is attached to one body joint and it returns if a joint a position from a range of possible values is reached. A list of thresholds must be configured in order to obtain the desired behavior.
- **Context Blackboard Block:** This block is a resource that is only programmed once but can be used many times. Using the DPL we configured the following Context Blackboards:
  - **Arm action:** Require an EMG sensor attached to the *biceps* which is connected to a Muscle Processing Block, it returns when the user arm is folded. The context values generated for the "arm action" are "folded" or "released".
  - **Hand action:** Require an EMG sensor attached to the *thenar eminence* and works in the same way as the Arm action. In this case, the context values generated for the "hand action" are "closed" or "open".
  - **Arm position**: Require an ACC sensor attached in the wrist and the use of a Tilt Movement processing block to get the joint to form positions from a predefined list. The context values generated for the "arm position" are "Wrist up", "Wrist down" and "Wrist side".

Figure 4 depicts all the abstractions required to obtain the context information for the demonstrative applications. Once the context acquisition module is configured the context is delivered to the application side where it can be handled to create the ToBITas and RESapp applications.

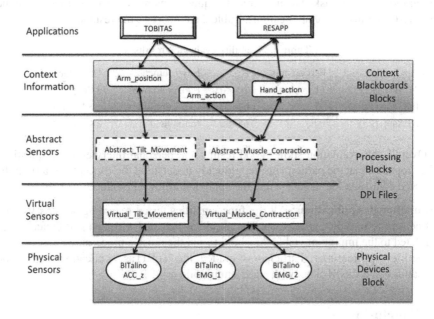

Fig. 4. Developed modules for the software.

The software framework allowed us to develop the application in progressive steps from the bottom side of the BITalino to the top side of the context applications. Programming this prototype we have reused modules and saved development time in different ways:

- It was required to develop the muscle processing block once only for it to be used for both muscles: biceps and thenar eminence. This processing block is general purpose and can be used to extend the application to other muscles of the human body.
- Context Blackboards enabled us to label the output of the Processing Blocks and to create suitable context information for the application side by means of a DPL JSON file.
- Due to the modularity of the blocks and taking advantage of MobileBIT's existing blocks to visualize and store sensor data, we were able to easily test the functionality of the Physical Device and the Processing blocks during the development process.
- ToBITas and RESapp applications use the same context information but they address different functionalities. Once the acquisition module was ready, we only focused on the final functionality coded in the web layer of the hybrid application.

Both applications were tested with 27 volunteers. Two participants reported problems to run the application with regard to the EMG sensor signal acquisition, one of those participants was able to finish the tasks and the other was discarded during the configuration of the thresholds for the processing blocks. The participants who finished the routines (26) were asked to answer a SUS questionnaire [24] in order to measure the perceived usability of the applications. Table 2 summarizes the results.

Table 2. Usability evaluation results.

Application	Participants	Age	Environment	SUS value
ToBITas [22]	11	20–40	Lab. conditions	73.86 ± 12.58
RESapp (Pilot)	5	64–80	Lab. conditions	84 ± 4.64
RESapp [23]	10	64–80	In the field	88.5 ± 7.2

Overall, the evaluation shows good results and personal interviews and questionnaires reported that the participants very quickly understood the concepts regarding the proposed control mode. It seems that the approach followed produces:

- **Functional Applications**: All the functionalities tested regarding sensors worked fine for 93 % of the participants. The problems detected with two participants were related to the minimum viable threshold to run the muscle processing.
- **Usable Applications**: Participants graded the ToBITas application with good usability and the RESapp with excellent usability.

6 Conclusion

This work presents a rapid prototyping framework for the rapid development of mobile context-aware applications. The framework is based in two main concepts, the abstraction and virtualization of sensors in order to obtain context information, and the context delivery mechanism to separate the rest of the application from the context acquisition. In this way, the prototyping of context-aware applications is simplified.

We conducted an evaluation based on the development of a representative application that uses the framework. It was tested in three iterations with a total of 26 users focusing on usability. From the positive results we conclude that the software framework is adequate to produce usable Context-Aware applications. Nevertheless, the abstract sensor mechanism has not been fully tested as two equivalent virtual sensors were required. For future work, we want to modify the application in order to use different sensor platforms to BITalino to validate the abstraction mechanism.

The main benefits of our approach are the reusability of the programmed modules, and the configuration options which allows the creation of virtual and abstract sensors. However, developers must still be aware of other concerns such as discovery and pairing of sensor devices before initializing the framework components. In order to improve our software framework we are working on complementary tools to assist developers in such tasks.

Acknowledgements. This work has been supported by the Ministry of Economy and Competitiveness of the Spanish Government and by the European Regional Development Fund (projects TIN2013-41123-P and TIN2014-52665-C2-1-R), and by the Department of Education, Universities and Research of the Basque Government under grant IT980-16. The last two authors belong to the Basque Advanced Informatics Laboratory (BAILab), grant UFI11/45, supported by the University of the Basque Country (UPV/EHU). B. Gamecho is backed by the "Convocatoria de contratación de doctores recientes hasta su integración en programas de formación postdoctoral en la UPV/EHU 2015".

References

1. Hervás, R., Bravo, J., Fontecha, J.: An assistive navigation system based on augmented reality and context awareness for people with mild cognitive impairments. IEEE J. Biomed. Health Inform. **18**(1), 368–374 (2014)
2. Fontecha, J., Navarro, F.J., Hervás, R., Bravo, J.: Elderly frailty detection by using accelerometer-enabled smartphones and clinical information records. Pers. Ubiquit. Comput. **17**(6), 1073–1083 (2013)
3. Wiese, J., Saponas, T.S., Brush, A.B.: Phoneprioception: enabling mobile phones to infer where they are kept. In: Proceedings of the SIGCHI Conference on Human Factors in Computing Systems, CHI 2013, pp. 2157–2166. ACM, New York (2013)
4. Silva, H., Fred, A., Martins, R.P.: Biosignals for everyone. IEEE Pervasive Comput. **13**(4), 64–71 (2014)
5. Burns, A., Greene, B.R., McGrath, M.J., O'Shea, T.J., Kuris, B., Ayer, S.M., Stroiescu, F., Cionca, V.: Shimmer a wireless sensor platform for noninvasive biomedical research. IEEE Sens. J. **10**(9), 1527–1534 (2010)
6. Morris, D., Scott, T., Tan, D.S.: Emerging input technologies for always-available mobile interaction. Found. Trends HCI **4**(4), 245–316 (2011)
7. Banos, O., Garcia, R., Holgado-Terriza, J.A., Damas, M., Pomares, H., Rojas, I., Saez, A., Villalonga, C.: mHealthDroid: a novel framework for agile development of mobile health applications. In: Pecchia, L., Chen, L.L., Nugent, C., Bravo, J. (eds.) IWAAL 2014. LNCS, vol. 8868, pp. 91–98. Springer, Heidelberg (2014)
8. Schmidt, A., Aidoo, K.A., Takaluoma, A., Tuomela, U., Laerhoven, K., Velde, W.: Advanced interaction in context. In: Gellersen, H.-W. (ed.) HUC 1999. LNCS, vol. 1707, pp. 89–101. Springer, Heidelberg (1999). doi:10.1007/3-540-48157-5_10
9. Jang, E.H., Park, B.J., Kim, S.H., Chung, M., Park, M.S., Sohn, J.H.: Classification of three negative emotions based on physiological signals. In: Proceedings of Intelli 2013, pp. 75–78 (2013)
10. Haag, A., Goronzy, S., Schaich, P., Williams, J.: Emotion recognition using biosensors: first steps towards an automatic system. In: Proceedings of ADS, pp. 36–48. Springer (2004)
11. Chon, J., Cha, H.: Lifemap: a smartphone-based context provider for location-based services. IEEE Pervasive Comput. **10**(2), 58–67 (2011)
12. Parkka, J., Ermes, M., Korpipaa, P., Mantyjarvi, J., Peltola, J., Korhonen, I.: Activity classification using realistic data from wearable sensors. IEEE Trans. Inf. Technol. Biomed. **10**(1), 119–128 (2006)
13. Dey, A.K.: Providing architectural support for building context-aware applications. Ph.D. thesis, Georgia Institute of Technology (2000)
14. Schmidt, A.: Ubiquitous computing-computing in context. Ph.D. thesis, Lancaster University (2003)

15. Kukkonen, J., Lagerspetz, E., Nurmi, P., Andersson, M.: Betelgeuse: a platform for gathering and processing situational data. IEEE Pervasive Comput. **8**(2), 49–56 (2009)
16. Winograd, T.: Architectures for context. Hum. Comput. Interact. **16**(2), 401–419 (2001)
17. Korpipa, P.: Blackboard-based software framework and tool for mobile device context awareness. Ph.D. dissertation, University of Oulu, Faculty of Technology (2005)
18. Ferreira, D.: Aware: a mobile context instrumentation middleware to collaboratively understand human behavior. Ph.D. dissertation, University of Oulu, Faculty of Technology (2013)
19. Paspallis, N., Papadopoulos, G.A.: A pluggable middleware architecture for developing context-aware mobile applications. Pers. Ubiquit. Comput. **18**(5), 1099–1116 (2014)
20. Crockford, D.: The application/json media type for javascript object notation (json) (2006)
21. Cânovas, M., Silva, H., Lourenço, A., Canento, F., Fred, A.: MobileBIT: a framework for mobile interaction recording and display. In: Proceedings of the 6th Conference on Health Informatics (HEALTHINF), pp. 366–369 (2013)
22. Gamecho, B., Guerreiro, J., Alves, A.P., Lourenço, A., Silva, H.P., Gardeazabal, L., Abascal, J., Fred, A.: Evaluation of a context-aware application for mobile robot control mediated by physiological data: the tobitas case study. In: Hervás, R., Lee, S., Nugent, C., Bravo, J. (eds.) UCAmI 2014. LNCS, vol. 8867, pp. 147–154. Springer, Heidelberg (2014). doi: 10.1007/978-3-319-13102-3_26
23. Gamecho, B., Silva, H., Guerreiro, J., Gardeazabal, L., Abascal, J.: A context-aware application to increase elderly users compliance of physical rehabilitation exercises at home via animatronic biofeedback. J. Med. Syst. **39**, 135 (2015)
24. Brooke, J.: SUS: a retrospective. J. Usability Stud. **8**(2), 29–40 (2013)

Risk Elicitation for User-Generated Content in Situated Interaction

Pedro Coutinho[1(✉)] and Rui José[2(✉)]

[1] School of Technology and Management, Polytechnic Institute of Viana do Castelo,
Viana do Castelo, Portugal
p.coutinho@estg.ipvc.pt
[2] Centro Algoritmi, University of Minho, Guimarães, Portugal
rui@dsi.uminho.pt

Abstract. Digital public displays have a unique capability to enable situated shared experiences, especially when open to user-generated content from people in their vicinity. The challenge, however, is how to open public displays to user-generated content, while being able to efficiently support conformity with place and display owner expectations. Sharing the display with users potentiates many risks, which go far beyond the feared appropriation of the display for presenting offensive content. In this study, we conducted a systematic elicitation of the risks involved. Based on a qualitative analysis of moderation situations referred in the literature, we identify and describe 7 specific risks that display owners should manage to be able to support user-generated content.

1 Introduction

Ubiquitous and mobile technologies are creating many new opportunities for situated interaction, in which digital services deliver a shared experience to nearby people. Digital public displays are a representative example of this type of situated experiences. They are becoming increasingly ubiquitous in smart cities and they have a unique capability to expose their message in a contextually relevant way to all those people nearby, breaking personal filter bubbles and enabling situated shared experiences. However, before they can evolve to become an effective communication medium for everyone, public displays need to move away from a world of closed display networks and allow users to contribute with their own content [1]. This would be a key enabler to transform those displays into truly situated devices that reflect the contexts in which they are inscribed and the social practices around them.

The major challenge faced by the idea of user-generated content is how to share control with users while being able to guarantee that published content matches the wider social expectations and practices. Despite its obvious potential, there are also multiple risks associated with user-generated content. In the absence of appropriate moderation, the potential value generated from user-generated content would be overshadowed by the negative impact of inappropriate content.

Objectives and methodology. Our research is concerned with the issue of how can we open public displays to user-generated content while mitigating the risks associated with

© Springer International Publishing AG 2016
C.R. García et al. (Eds.): UCAmI 2016, Part I, LNCS 10069, pp. 481–486, 2016.
DOI: 10.1007/978-3-319-48746-5_49

inappropriate content. We consider that a risk event is when something harmful or undesirable happens, causing a certain negative impact. A risk is the probability that a risk event may occur. In this study, we conducted a systematic elicitation of the risks associated with user-generated content in situated interaction scenarios. While previous work has studied specific moderation techniques for particular risks, we aim to provide a systematic identification of those risks. This should enable moderation to be approached from a broader risk management perspective, allowing display owners to identify the minimal set of techniques that mitigates their risk to an acceptable level, while still being able to attract publishers and minimise the moderation effort.

The methodology was based on a qualitative analysis of moderation situations referred in the literature. We selected 26 scientific publications addressing different facets of this topic, 10 of which correspond to the papers included in the related work section of this paper and which were the ones generating more references. The 26 papers were coded using a process based on a Grounded Theory approach and a coding tool. We coded any elements that were somehow related with user-generated content and moderation processes, including the different techniques, concerns, motivations and results. The result was a collection of 100 coded segments corresponding to 23 unique codes. We then conducted a consolidation process of the codes in 5 top-level concepts, corresponding to the various perspectives of moderation that arise from the selected literature, more specifically: heuristics (experiences on moderation usage); inappropriate content (issues of inappropriate content presentation in the display); moderation approaches (references to moderation approaches and techniques); moderation evaluation (evaluation of the impact and consequences of moderation in publications' quantity and quality); and motivations (examples of motivations for moderation processes). The codes referring to different views of what was regarded as inappropriate content were used to consolidate the key risks outlined in this paper.

2   Related Work

The need for moderation and other control mechanisms has already been widely acknowledged in previous research. Examples of possible conflicts on content being published were reported by Hosio et al. [2], in the context of a motivating session for taking pictures to be published on public displays. The wide range of public display systems and their particular publication requirements lead to the emergence of many different approaches on moderations. Greis et al. [3] present a broad study of pre-moderation techniques. Elhart et al. [4] describe a distributed post-moderation process involving the collaboration of University staff. Taylor et al. [5] study how moderation could be delegated to users that act as trusted curators for a specific content category. Alt et al. [6] study a report abuse functionality included in the Digifieds system. Social accountability is referred as the key driver for moderation in the Plasma Network [7]. Storz et al. [8] suggest the use of social media on public displays, not simply for creation of content, but also for moderation in a long-term basis.

Publication practices around traditional public notice areas have been studied by Alt et al. as a design inspiration for the emergence of new practices around digital displays [5].

They address the issue of the motivations that venue owner can have to share their public boards and also their practices for controlling that content. The Instant Places framework [9] enabled people to influence display content through the selection of thematic pins that are recognised when the user checks-in to a display.

Despite these contributions, the current state of the art has not yet provided a systematic framework for approaching the issue of moderation from its many perspectives and help to define the control sharing strategy for a concrete scenario. This work is novel in how it takes this broader perspective on the risks associated with user-generated content.

3 The Risks of Control Sharing

In this section, we summarise the key findings of our study, which essentially correspond to the identification of 7 key risk categories that need to be addressed to support user-generated content on public displays.

Offensive content. The possibility to see offensive content posted on the public display is the most obvious fear associated with user-generated content. Without proper control it is very likely that someone will end up posting explicit material. This may include adult content, horrible injury or ostensively aggressive messages, although in many contexts even swear words or rude language may also be interpreted as offensive. Regardless of its specific nature, this is content that most people will find disturbing. Even if they see it as being the result of an obviously malicious and intentional act by a third-party, they will still interpret it as a gross failure of the duties of the display owner. This impact on the image of the place can be so negative that avoiding offensive content will normally be seen by display owners as their key concern in regard to user-generated content.

Spam. Another common fear, and indeed one of the most recurring problems in social platforms, is spam. This may include more or less obvious forms of advertising, but also posts that are presented as normal content but are only aimed at promoting people, businesses or content sources, often including branded images with URLs or other contact information. In most cases, spam content will not be perceived as offensive and occasional spam content can even go unnoticed. Still, a system that is not able to handle spam properly can easily see the value of user-generated content being undermined by the noise produced by widespread spam.

A key challenge with spam is that it can be very subjective. A previous study on the distribution of paper leaflets in cafés has shown the diffuse nature of what is acceptable [9]. Café owners were very sensitive to content from possible competitors, but they often accepted it as long as it was part of a reciprocal relationship. These tacit connections show how this assessment can be strongly embedded with implicit local knowledge.

Soft Hacking. In this study, we are not considering the risk associated with security breaches, but there are many forms of hacking that simply try to explore the borderlines of normal system usage to accomplish what may be described as a slightly marginal behaviour. This tends not to be offensive, because the key motivation is the reward for being able to beat the system. It will, however, be something that is provocative enough to show that the frontier is being crossed. This risk is particularly relevant when there are automated moderation procedures involved. For example, in Instant Places [10], users could post words on their Bluetooth names that were then used for selecting images from Flickr. Even though it was difficult to get the system to fetch an image that could be provocative, some users applied considerable time and creativity to the challenge. While this is not necessarily armful, it still needs to be considered to avoid opening the door to more serious and ill-intentioned efforts.

Etiquette breach. Etiquette rules can help to define what are the acceptable posting behaviours. These etiquette rules, whether they are written or not, need to be shared by the community. Common examples of etiquette breach include posting off-topic posts or trolling. A troll is a person who publishes deliberately provocative messages to cause trouble, start a contentious topic, derail a discussion or incite an emotional response from others. This is not necessarily offensive, it is just inappropriate and regarded as undesirable behaviour by the community. For example, many on-line forums ban topics such as religion or politics because of the strong emotional and heated discussions that these topics often generate.

Editorial conflict. An editorial conflict happens when a user posts something that is perfectly acceptable, certainly not abusive, perhaps even appreciated by the audience, but which somehow fails to meet what the display owner had envisioned as appropriate. This is the hardest form of moderation because it is based on implicit rules that even the display owner may have difficulty in stating explicitly. Previous research on non-digital community boards has shown that their creators did not have a pre-defined profile for those boards. The actual content that composed the boards had emerged from a continuously evolving social negotiation and the interplay of the interests of the board owners and users [6]. To attract user-generated content, a display owner may have to accept some flexibility in regard to topics that may be of the interest to the display audience, even when they do not correspond to what the display owner had initially envisioned for the public display.

Copyrighted material. Even if unintentionally, people are likely to post images, branded logos, text, videos, music or other materials that are protected by copyrights laws. This can be hard to track, but at least some mechanism is needed to deal with reports of copyright infringement. In this case, the problematic cases can be analysed and potentially removed. Also, the specific liabilities associated with potential law infringement need to be considered.

Personal exposure. Content involving individuals can be regarded as inappropriate whenever it exposes those individuals without their consent. Even public data from social networks, such as name and photo, may be perceived as excessive exposure when shown on public displays. Previous research by Hosio et al. [2] has shown that many people see a possible conflict when posting to a public display photos with friends in them, even if these photos are already publicly available online.

In the moment machine [2], people were in general excited about the idea of taking a photo to be presented at the public display, but the authors also report cases where privacy concerns were raised in regard to where and when were those photos being shown. Also, some people were simply not happy about their photos and wanted to have them removed. The authors report on a particular case where a women contacted the researchers to remove her photo. She did not want to have photos where she was not looking good, especially not in a place where she passed-by on a regular basis.

4 Discussion and Conclusions

Enabling users to contribute with their own content is a defining feature for most situated interaction scenarios, and for open public displays in particular. However, this control sharing needs to be bounded to avoid abusive appropriation by users. This study has taken a comprehensive approach to this issue and focused on uncovering the broad range of risks involved in user-generated content. This elicitation of the diverse risks involved constitutes the first step in analysing a specific scenario for user-generated content.

As future work, we expect to conduct interviews with display owners to get their perception about the probability and potential impact of the risks identified in this study. With such data, we expect to generate and calibrate a risk matrix that can help display owners to get a global view of priorities and define the appropriate control strategies. This should make the assessment process even easier and provide a path towards generalised approaches for managing the risk of user-generated content in situated interaction.

Acknowledgments. This research is partially funded by FCT – Fundação para a Ciência e Tecnologia within Project UID/CEC/00319/2013 and by project 11304 (16/SI/2015), supported by Norte Portugal Regional Operational Programme (NORTE 2020), under the PORTUGAL 2020 Partnership Agreement, through the European Regional Development Fund (ERDF).

References

1. Davies, N., Langheinrich, M., José, R., Schmidt, A.: Open display networks: a communications medium for the 21st century. Computer **45**, 58–64 (2012). (Long. Beach. Calif.)
2. Hosio, S., Kukka, H., Riekki, J.: Social surroundings: bridging the virtual and physical divide. IEEE Multimed. **17**, 26–33 (2010)
3. Greis, M., Alt, F., Henze, N., Memarovic, N.: I can wait a minute: uncovering the optimal delay time for pre-moderated user-generated content on public displays. In: Proceedings of the Conference on Human Factors in Computing Systems (CHI 2014), pp. 1435–1438 (2014)
4. Elhart, I., Memarovic, N., Langheinrich, M., Rubegni, E.: Control and scheduling interface for public displays. In: Adjunct Proceedings of the International Conference on Pervasive and Ubiquitous Computing (UbiComp 2013), pp. 51–54 (2013)
5. Taylor, N., Cheverst, K., Fitton, D., Race, N.J.P., Rouncefield, M., Graham, C.: Probing communities: study of a village photo display. In: Proceedings of the 19th Australasian conference on Computer-Human Interaction: Entertaining User Interfaces (OzCHI 2007), pp. 17–24 (2007)

6. Alt, F., Kubitza, T., Bial, D., Zaidan, F., Ortel, M., Zurmaar, B., Lewen, T., Shirazi, A.S., Schmidt, A.: Digifieds - insights into deploying digital public notice areas in the wild. In: Proceedings of the 10th International Conference on Mobile Ubiquitous Multimedia, pp. 165–174 (2011)

7. Churchill, E.F., Nelson, L., Denoue, L., Murphy, P., Helfman, J.I., Helfma, J.: The plasma poster network: social hypermedia on public display. In: O'Hara, K. (ed.) Public and Situated Displays. Social and Interactional Aspects of Shared Display Technologies, pp. 233–260. Kluwer Academic Publishers, London (2003)

8. Storz, O., Friday, A., Davies, N., Finney, J., Sas, C., Sheridan, J.: Public ubiquitous computing systems: lessons from the e-campus display deployments. IEEE Pervasive Comput. 5, 40–47 (2006)

9. José, R., Pinto, H., Silva, B., Melro, A.: Pins and posters: paradigms for content publication on situated displays. IEEE Comput. Graph. Appl. 33, 64–72 (2013)

10. José, R., Otero, N., Izadi, S., Harper, R.: Instant places: using bluetooth for situated interaction in public displays. IEEE Pervasive Comput. 7, 52–57 (2008)

GoodVybesConnect: A Real-Time Haptic Enhanced Tele-Rehabilitation System for Massage Therapy

Cristina Ramírez-Fernández[1,2(✉)], Eloísa García-Canseco[1],
Alberto L. Morán[1], Oliver Pabloff[1], David Bonilla[1],
Nirvana Green[1], and Victoria Meza-Kubo[1]

[1] Facultad de Ciencias, UABC, Universidad Autónoma de Baja California,
Ensenada, Mexico
{cristina_ramirez, eloisa.garcia,
alberto.moran, opabloff, david.bonilla,
nirvana.green, mmeza}@uabc.edu.mx
[2] Instituto Tecnológico de Ensenada, Ensenada, Mexico

Abstract. We present the design, development and evaluation of a haptic enhanced tele-rehabilitation system for massage therapy of the back using the Vybe haptic gaming pad. The proposed haptic system includes features that allow (i) administering online therapy programs, (ii) self-adjustable and safety treatment of back massages using a virtual environment, the gesture sensor LEAP Motion controller and the Vybe haptic device, and (iii) save and replay messages according to the therapy program. A usability evaluation with 25 elders suggests that the haptic tele-rehabilitation system is perceived as relaxing, useful and usable, while providing a supervised, real-time and secure way to treat the patient and adjusting the therapy haptic feedback intensity.

Keywords: Hapto-virtual environment · Tele-rehabilitation · Back therapies

1 Introduction

Nowadays, mainly due to a combination of demographic changes, a lack of resources in the field of Public Health and technology improvements, the development of new rehabilitative practices seems mandatory in order to build sustainable models for rehabilitation from the clinical, organizational and economic perspectives [1]. In recent years, haptic feedback has shown promise to enhance user experience in tele-rehabilitation [2]. However, current tele-rehabilitation systems have yet to use the richness of haptic modality within its content. The lack of haptic methods to provide real-time back rehabilitation in a supervised and remote way inhibits the attention of patients that require massage therapy. Massage has become one of the most popular complementary and alternative medical (CAM) therapies for back pain, the condition for which CAM therapies are most commonly used [3]. Massage is defined as "a mechanical manipulation of body tissues with rhythmical pressure and stroking for the purpose of promoting health and wellbeing" [4]. However, although some mechanical

© Springer International Publishing AG 2016
C.R. García et al. (Eds.): UCAmI 2016, Part I, LNCS 10069, pp. 487–496, 2016.
DOI: 10.1007/978-3-319-48746-5_50

support tools for back massage intervention have been created e.g. [5–7], massage therapy is still provided mainly in a traditional way, where both patient and therapist need to be in the same place [8].

In this paper we propose, implement and evaluate a real-time haptic enhanced tele-rehabilitation system for massage therapy. We introduce GoodVybesConnect, a real-time haptic enhanced tele-rehabilitation system for massage therapy that contains a combination of a WEB system, virtual environment (VE), the Vybe haptic gaming device [9] and the Leap Motion Controller (LMC) gesture sensor [10]. Firstly, the input parameters of the therapy are individualized and calibrated according to the patient characteristics. Secondly, the execution of the therapy depends on the therapist's hands movements in the VE, which generate multimodal feedback to patients (i.e. visual, audible and vibrotactile feedback). Finally, therapy results are automatically updated in the patient clinical record.

The main contribution of this research is a method that allows physical therapists to provide back massage therapy to their remote patients. Massage therapy with visual, auditory and haptic feedback can be run in real-time depending on the availability of the therapist. In addition, the client may share a session previously stored by the therapist to be played at home according to a scheduled therapy program.

Our pilot evaluation results suggest that the haptic telerehabilitation system is perceived as a relaxing, useful and usable tool, while providing effective and safety remote massages with mechanisms to monitor and support the patient, and to recon-figure the therapy programs.

2   Related Work

According to the literature, there are various forms of intervention for back treatment, including physical therapy, acupuncture, chiropractic treatment and massage therapy [11]. However, these procedures require the patient to be in the same place as the therapist, and they are mainly carried out in the traditional way using non-mechanical instruments [3, 11].

In recent years, the integration of mechanical instruments to support the imple-mentation of massage therapies such as massage chairs [5, 7] or automatic massage systems [6] has benefited therapists and their patients. These instruments allow serving more patients at a time. Nevertheless, the implementation of massage therapy with these mechanical instruments require "hard-wired" programmed routines, local supervision of the therapist and manual therapy management programs [12].

Our proposal is innovative in comparison to those found in related works due to several reasons, including, (i) a haptic method to provide real-time back rehabilitation in a supervised and remote way, (ii) a Web system to administer the therapy programs, (iii) the combination of emerging tools to perform therapies, i.e., a VE, the Vybe haptic gaming device [9] and the Leap Motion Controller (LMC) gesture sensor [10], and (iv) a secure way for patients to replay their massages according to the therapy program.

3   User-Centered Design

Qualitative study. In order to supplement our understanding of the therapists work during therapy sessions, we conducted a contextual study to explore the use of ambient intelligence technologies (e.g. haptic and gestural interfaces, and ICT's). We carried out two sessions of participatory design (6 h total) with two experienced physical therapists at Serena, a therapy center in Ensenada Baja California. After the study, therapists recommended: (a) to implement a therapy management web-based system in which they can keep track of their schedule as well as their patients clinical records and therapy sessions; (b) to implement a VE in which they can give a massage therapy of the back in a remote and safe way, and furthermore in real time. They also asked for configuration options (i.e., intensity of the haptic feedback, music, etc.) before and during executing therapy. In addition, therapists recommended that therapy should be recorded and shared with patients for later playback according to their therapy program. Finally, therapists indicated that such a tool will allow them to treat patients who change residence or those who can not leave home.

4   Real-Time Haptic Enhanced Rehabilitation System: GoodVybesConnect

Description of the system. Figure 1 shows the architecture of proposed real-time haptic enhanced rehabilitation system. Following the therapists' recommendations, the web-based application (Fig. 2) is a therapy administration system in which therapists can manage their schedule of therapy sessions, their patients and their corresponding clinical records. Besides, therapists can configure the therapy by adjusting the visual feedback, intensity, and kind of music, among others. The web application also shows

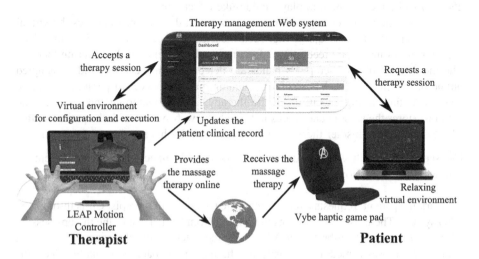

Fig. 1. The GoodVybesConnect architecture.

Fig. 2. Therapy management web system. The therapist can accept, communicate and update the patient therapy record. In addition, the patient can request a therapy session, communicate and obtain his/hers therapy files.

the results of patients' past therapy sessions through tables and graphs (Fig. 2). Moreover, patients can schedule a therapy session, view their therapy record, access past therapy sessions, and communicate via chat with their therapist.

The VE is a haptic enhanced tele-rehabilitation system that was developed using Unity 5.3.4, the Vybe haptic game pad [9] and the Orion library for the Leap Motion controller (LMC) [10]. The main objective of the VE is to provide a real-time and remote back massage therapy to patients. We used the LMC gesture sensor as input device and the Vybe haptic gaming pad as the output device to execute therapy (Fig. 1). Used as a massage bed, the Vybe haptic gaming pad is a vibro-tactile grid display that has six voice-coil actuators located on the upper back and six DC-motors located on the seat and lower back. The voice-coils play smooth vibrations (150–250 Hz) while the DC-motors play rumble-like effects [9].

Figure 3 shows the configuration screen in which the therapist chooses the virtual back that s/he wants to visualize (i.e. back muscles, surface or intermediate muscles), the intensity of the haptic feedback and the music the patient will hear during therapy. The movements of the therapist's hands are detected with the LMC and transmitted online in real time to the VE and Vybe gaming haptic device. All parameters can be changed online during execution of the therapy. After concluding the massage, the therapist stores the session and shares it through the web system with the patient so that s/he can reproduce his/her therapy again if indicated by his/her therapy program.

Use scenario: To illustrate the use of the GoodVybesConnect platform we present the following use scenario:

Carl, the patient, requests a remote massage session with therapist Chris through the Web system. Therapist Chris accepts the request from Carl. To start the therapy session Chris configures and calibrates the VE setting the external muscles view of the virtual back. She chooses a medium intensity for the haptic feedback and finally selects the

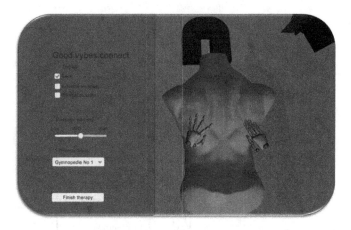

Fig. 3. VE for the configuration and execution of back massage therapy.

relaxing music Carl will hear. Then Carl starts the VE and turns on the Vybe haptic gaming pad. Chris starts moving her hands to conduct the massage therapy. The movements of Chris' hands are recognized by the gesture LMC sensor and sent through the Internet to the remote site. At the same time, Carl, lying on the Vybes haptic game pad on the remote site safely receives his back massage.

During the remote therapy, Chris, the therapist, can update the therapy parameters (i.e. type of music, intensity of haptic feedback). When Chris decides to end the therapy, she saves the session and shares it with Carl by means of the Web server. Thus Carl can see the patients' results and even replay his therapy whenever he needs it. This scenario is shown through a sequence diagram in Fig. 4.

5   Pilot Evaluation and Results

Study description. The study was conducted with older adults that participated in a usability test to evaluate the application. In the usability study, participants were adults aged 55 or older, with gender and social status indistinct. Participants signed a consent form and agreed to be video-recorded during the execution of the back massage (see Fig. 5(1)). The evaluation was carried out in the research laboratory of a local public university, equipped with two computers. The GoodVybesConnect VE was installed on one, and the Emotiv brain-computer interface was set up and calibrated on the other [13] (see Figs. 5(2) and (3). In addition, the Vybe haptic device was used as a massage bed, while the Emotiv was used to get the emotional responses of the participants during the massage execution (see Figs. 5(4) and (5)). Our predictions were that: (1) participants will respond that they feel calm after receiving the massage, (2) the usability perception of the massage system is high, and (3) the perception of the massage haptic feedback is good.

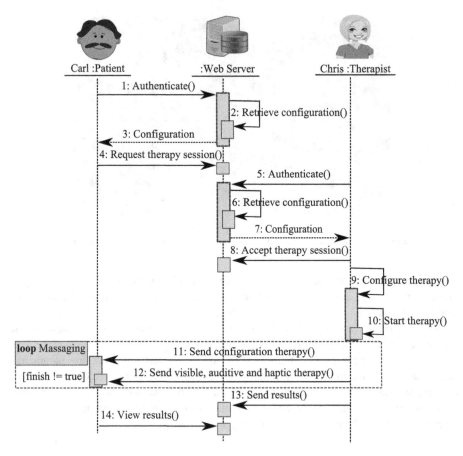

Fig. 4. Sequence diagram of the main use scenario. The patient requests a therapy session and the therapist accepts it and configures it. The therapist configures the therapy for the patient. The VE and Vybe haptic device receive the configuration. The therapist provides the massage with visible, auditive and haptic feedback. Finally, the therapist finishes the massage, saves the therapy, and the patient receives the therapy results.

The evaluation procedure consisted of a welcome message, initial explanation, and a questionnaire about demographic data. Then, the Emotiv device was calibrated for each participant with the help of an expert, and the GoodVybesConnect application was used for 5 min to provide the back massage to each participant. Each participant received a massage previously recorded by a physical therapist. The intensity of the haptic feedback of the provided massage was set randomly (i.e., ¼, ½, ¾ and 1). All participants experienced the same auditive feedback during the massage.

System Usability Scale (SUS) [14] and Technology Acceptance Model (TAM) [15] questionnaires (5-point Likert scale) were applied at the end of the study. During both the on-entry demographic questionnaire and the on-exit questionnaire participants were asked about their emotional state at that moment, e.g., if they were stressed, nervous,

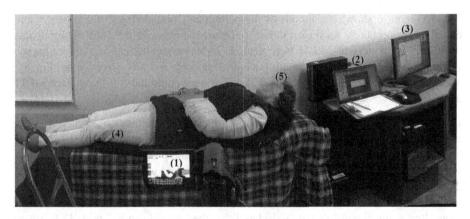

Fig. 5. Participant during back massage therapy. Materials: (1) video camera, (2) computer running the VE for back massage therapy, (3) computer used to calibrate the Emotiv device, (4) haptic Vybe gaming pad used as massage bed and (5) Emotiv device used to obtain brain signals.

relaxed, happy or neutral. Also, while answering the on-exit questionnaire participants were asked for which of the aforementioned moods prevailed during the massage and their perception of the haptic feedback received through the Vybe gaming device.

Study Results. Participants were 25 older adults (age mean ± std: 63.68 ± 7.98 years, 11 males, 14 females), 32 % of the participants have received physical therapy due to various reasons (e.g. neck or spine problems, parkinson disease or depression), 60 % were under a medical treatment and 72 % use the computer on a regular basis.

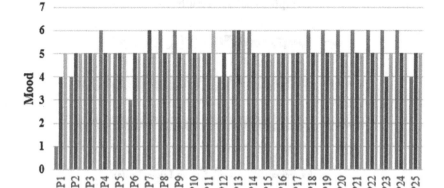

Fig. 6. Mood results as reported by participants (i.e., 1 = stressed, 2 = scared, 3 = nervous, 4 = neutral, 5 = calm, 6 = happy).

Mood. Figure 6 shows the moods of the participants obtained with the on-entry and on-exit questionnaires. As shown in Fig. 6, before the massage 8 % of the participants were stressed or nervous, 12 % were neutral, 28 % were calm and 52 % were happy. During the massage 8 % were neutral, 84 % were calm and 8 % were happy. Finally, after the massage 4 % were neutral (P12), 88 % were calm and 8 % were happy (P11 and P13).

Usability. 72 % of participants declared to have contact with the computer. Regarding usefulness, the massage was perceived as useful for back therapy (median 4.73/5), and with high intention to use (median 4.72/5). 28 % of the participants stated that if they would have the system available at their home they would use it once or twice a week, 28 % stated that they would use it three or four times a week, 12 % stated that they would use it 5 times a week, and 32 % stated that they would use it 6 times a week or more. Regarding time of use, 4 % declared that they would use it 5 min, 32 % stated that they would use it 10 min, 32 % stated that they would use it 15 min, and 32 % stated that they would use it 20 min or more.

In addition, several participants indicated that this type of system would be very good for them being elderlies, and they asked when it would be available for commercial use. Finally, participants mentioned that it is very important to have this kind of systems at home (median 4.84/5).

Perception of haptic feedback. Figure 7 shows the perception of safety, pleasure and comfort of the haptic feedback received through the massage. Participants said that they could not even imagine receiving a back massage from the physical therapist by means of the computer. They said that this (the system) is something very new that it should be used as a support tool in hospitals, waiting rooms and in their own homes. Finally, they highlighted the importance of the feature of generating a massage online and receiving it in a safely manner, under the supervision of the physical therapist.

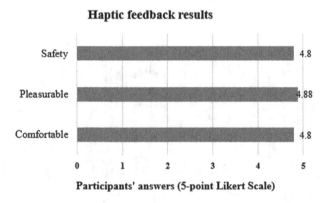

Fig. 7. Haptic feedback results on safety, pleasurable and comfortable features.

6 Conclusions and Future Work

Regarding this work in progress report, our main findings are that (i) the proposed haptic enhanced tele-rehabilitation system was well received by the elderly - after the massage most of them (96 %) were calm (88 %) or happy (8 %); (ii) elderly subjects found the application as being highly useful (4.73/5) and 100 % reported having a high intention of use if they had it available at home; (iii) elderly subjects became relaxed after receiving the back massage, and (iv) the therapists that contributed in the participatory design sessions suggested that this way of conducting on-line remote massages benefited them as they will be able to treat patients that moved away or that cannot leave their home. In particular, the therapists highlighted the feature that allows them to configure, adapt and perform their therapy massage in real time and remotely as the most useful and secure feature, along with the feature of storing the therapy session to share it with clients according to their therapy program.

These results provide promising evidence towards the feasibility of developing a haptic enhanced tele-rehabilitation system that would extend the possibility for a remote and supervised massage therapy for the elderly. However, it is necessary to further evaluate the proposed tool with therapists, the management features with a higher number of participants of both kinds, for a longer time, so as to actually confirm the observed trends, and better establish the scope and impact of these results. Also, as a future work, we will analyze the EEG brain signals and the videos of the participants during their using the system to compare them with the self-report results obtained in this research work.

References

1. McCaskey, M.A., Schuster-Amft, C., Wirth, B., Suica, Z., de Bruin, E.D.: Effects of proprioceptive exercises on pain and function in chronic neck- and low back pain rehabilitation: a systematic literature review. BMC Musculoskelet Disord. **15**, 382 (2014)
2. Rogante, M., Grigioni, M., Cordella, D., Giacomozzi, C.: Ten years of telerehabilitation: a literature overview of technologies and clinical applications. NeuroRehabilitation **27**, 287–304 (2010)
3. Cherkin, D.C., Sherman, K.J., Kahn, J., Erro, J.H., Deyo, R.A., Haneuse, S.J., et al.: Effectiveness of focused structural massage and relaxation massage for chronic low back pain: protocol for a randomized controlled trial. Trials **10**, 96 (2009)
4. Romanowski, M., Romanowska, J., Grześkowiak, M.: A comparison of the effects of deep tissue massage and therapeutic massage on chronic low back pain. Stud. Health Technol. Inf. **176**, 411–414 (2012)
5. Zullino, D.F., Krenz, S., Frésard, E., Cancela, E., Khazaal, Y.: Local back massage with an automated massage chair: general muscle and psychophysiologic relaxing properties. J. Altern. Complement. Med. **11**, 1103–1106 (2005)

6. Buselli, P., Bosoni, R., Buse, G., Fasoli, P., La Scala, E., Mazzolari, R., et al.: Effectiveness evaluation of an integrated automatic thermomechanic massage system (SMATH(R) system) in non-specific sub-acute and chronic low back pain - a randomized double-blinded controlled trial, comparing SMATH therapy versus sham therapy: study prot. Trials **12**, 216 (2011)

7. Engen, D.J., Wahner-Roedler, D.L., Nadolny, A.M., Persinger, C.M., Oh, J.K., Spittell, P.C., et al.: The effect of chair massage on muscular discomfort in cardiac sonographers: a pilot study. BMC Complement. Altern. Med. **10**, 50 (2010)

8. McEwen, S.: Social work in health care when conventional meets complementary: nonspecific back pain and massage therapy. Health Soc. Work **40**, 19–25 (2015)

9. Disney: Disney Research (2015). https://www.disneyresearch.com/

10. Smeragliuolo, A.H., Hill, N.J., Disla, L., Putrino, D.: Validation of the Leap Motion Controller using markered motion capture technology. J. Biomech. **49**(9), 1742–1750 (2016). Elsevier

11. Chen, W.L., Liu, G.J., Yeh, S.H., Chiang, M.C., Fu, M.Y., Hsieh, Y.K.: Effect of back massage intervention on anxiety, comfort, and physiologic responses in patients with congestive heart failure. J. Altern. Complement. Med. **19**, 464–470 (2013)

12. Clar, C., Tsertsvadze, A., Court, R., Hundt, G.L., Clarke, A., Sutcliffe, P.: Clinical effectiveness of manual therapy for the management of musculoskeletal and non-musculoskeletal conditions: systematic review and update of UK evidence report. Chiropr Man Therap. **22**, 12 (2014)

13. Cernea, D., Olech, P.-S., Ebert, A., Kerren, A.: Measuring subjectivity. KI - Künstliche Intelligenz. **26**, 177–182 (2012)

14. Brooke, J.: SUS - a quick and dirty usability scale. In: Usability Evaluation in Industry, pp. 189–194 (1996)

15. Davis, F.: Perceived usefulness, perceived ease of use, and user acceptance of information technology. MIS Q. **13**, 319–340 (1989)

Evaluation of a Usability Testing Guide for Mobile Applications Focused on People with Down Syndrome (USATESTDOWN)

Doris Cáliz[1(✉)], Javier Gomez[2], Xavier Alamán[2], Loïc Martínez[1],
Richart Cáliz[3], and Carlos Terán[3]

[1] CETTICO Research Group, ETSIINF, Technical University of Madrid,
Campus de Montgancedo, 28660 Boadilla del Monte, Madrid, Spain
doriscalizramos@outlook.com, loic@fi.upm.es
[2] Department of Computer Engineering, Autonomous University of Madrid,
C/Francisco Tomás y Valiente, 11, 28049 Madrid, Spain
{jg.escribano,xavier.alaman}@uam.es
[3] FIS Group, Departamento de Informática y Ciencias de la Computación (DICC), EPN,
Escuela Politécnica Nacional, Ladrón de Guevara E11-25 y Andalucía, Quito, Ecuador
richartharold@hotmail.com, carlos.teran@cobiscorp.com

Abstract. Usability testing of mobile applications involving people with Down syndrome is an issue that has not been comprehensively investigated. There is no single proposal that takes on board all the issues that could potentially be taken into account to deal with the specific needs of people with Down syndrome. We propose a guide for a usability testing process involving participants with Down syndrome. This guide is called USATESTDOWN. It is based on a literature review and experience gained at a number of workshops where people with Down syndrome used mobile devices. This paper briefly describes USATESTDOWN and its application at a special employment centre called PRODIS with 10 participants.

Keywords: Usability testing · Mobile applications · Cognitive disability · Down syndrome · Human computer interaction (HCI) · Mobile devices

1 Introduction

An essential property of mobile devices and applications is usability. Usability is defined by three main attributes: effectiveness, efficiency and satisfaction [1]. Usable systems are easy to learn, efficient, not prone to errors and generate user satisfaction [2].

This paper is part of a research focused on usability for people with Down syndrome (DS). DS is a cognitive disability with specific characteristics. People with DS have impaired cognitive processing, language learning and physical abilities, as well as different personal and social characteristics [3]. Children with DS differ from neurotypical children or children with other types of developmental disabilities in that all three major types of abilities (cognitive, motor, and perceptual) are affected but the disability

© Springer International Publishing AG 2016
C.R. García et al. (Eds.): UCAmI 2016, Part I, LNCS 10069, pp. 497–502, 2016.
DOI: 10.1007/978-3-319-48746-5_51

often is slight [4]. The functional abilities of individuals with DS, related to the extent of the impairment in the sensory and motor channels [4], memory, cognition and communication skills, vary hugely [5]. Both the research and clinical literature report difficulties in the auditory [6], visual [2] and tactile [7] sensory areas. With regard to motor skills, low muscle tone and weak muscles are often a problem [8]. Researchers aiming to evaluate a mobile application in individuals with DS should take into consideration these sensory and motor issues.

On the grounds of the particular characteristics of people with DS, the products that they use need to be highly usable. Usable design calls for a user-centred approach, where users are involved in several steps of the process, including usability testing. In this context, the process of usability testing should fit the needs of people with DS. We have developed a guide to improve this process [9]. This paper explains how the guide was applied to one particular usability testing process.

The paper is structured as follows. Section 2 describes related work on usability evaluation involving people with DS. Section 3 provides a brief overview of the USATESTDOWN guide. Section 4 describes the evaluation of USATESTDOWN. Finally, Sect. 5 reports the findings and outlines future work.

2   Related Work

2.1   Usability Evaluation Methods

There are three types of evaluation methods: observational, analytical and inquiry evaluation methods [10]. Observational methods (such as usability testing and user performance testing) collect data by observing user experiences with a product [2]. Analytical methods (such as heuristic evaluation and cognitive walkthrough) rely on the opinion of experts rather than collecting data from user experiences [11]. Inquiry methods (such as user satisfaction questionnaires or focus groups) take a user-oriented view and identify broad usability problems or opinions on a product as a whole.

Given the specific characteristics of people with DS, inquiry methods are not adequate as they require communication skills and abstract logical thinking [12]. Likewise, analytical methods are unsuitable because people with DS have a wide range of different abilities. This means that observational and, in particular, usability testing methods are preferred. This is the focus of the research presented in this paper.

2.2   Usability Testing of Mobile Applications Involving People with DS

We have not found much research on the usability evaluation of ICT involving users with DS. Devan is a tool for detailed video analysis of user test data. It makes use of a table format for representing an interaction at multiple levels of abstraction. Devan has been successfully applied among children with DS [13]. Kumin and Lazar evaluated the usability of multi-touch tablet devices by adults with DS for workplace-related tasks. They concluded that people with DS can use a multi-touch-screen device to complete office-related tasks [14]. AR BACA SindD is a usability evaluation framework for an augmented reality framework for learners with DS. The framework has been applied to the usability evaluation of learning courseware based on augmented reality [15].

2.3 Analysis of Related Work

While there is some related research, it is incomplete. Additionally, we failed to find a single proposal that took on board all the issues that might be taken into account. The paper on Devan does not consider mobile or touchscreen devices and does not describe a complete usability testing guide [13]. The usability evaluation by Kumin and Lazar set out to understand potential interface improvements and gave several tips on usability evaluation. However, they failed to define a usability test guide [14]. Although AR BACA SindD is a usability evaluation framework for an augmented reality framework for learners with DS, it focused specifically on AR systems. This evaluation cannot be generalized to other systems [15]. In short, there is no guide for evaluating usability in mobile applications focused on people with DS.

3   Overview of USATESTDOWN

USATESTDOWN [9] is a guide to support usability testing of mobile applications when the participants are people with DS. It has been developed by combining information collected from a literature review [16] and experience acquired during four workshops with approximately 100 children with DS [17, 18].

Table 1. Summary of recommendations provided by USATESTDOWN

Step	Recommendations
1. Recruit participants	• Recruit a minimum of 10–15 participants • Take into account the mental age (rather than their chronological age) of people with DS • Involve usability experts, DS experts and DS tutors
2. Establish tasks	• Define tasks with increasing levels of difficulty • Tasks should be simple and short (plan for 10 min. sessions) • Cooperate with experts in DS to define tasks • Do not limit time to finish a task
3. Write instructions	• Prepare an oral presentation of the test for participants • Use simple language to communicate with participants • Speak slowly when explaining the test
4. Define test plan	• Simplify evaluation scales down to 3 values (agree, neutral, disagree) and use faces (happy, neutral, sad) when possible • Minimize the amount of text presented to participants • Use short interview questions
5. Run pilot tests	• Have a meeting with the participant before the test • Make sure that parent, tutors or teachers are present during the test
6. Refine test plan	• Update the plan quickly if participants are found to have trouble during the pilot test
7. Run the test session	• Record videos of the session taking care not to film the participants' faces • Pay special attention to the reactions of the participants, as they may have trouble explaining their feelings during the test
8. Analyse data	• It is essential to combine quantitative and qualitative results • Carefully compare quantitative data with qualitative results, as they might be different
9. Report results	• Report the results to all stakeholders, including family or teachers of the participants

The guide reproduces the usual usability testing steps. The usability process is divided into the following steps: (1) recruit participants, (2) establish tasks, (3) write instructions, (4) define the test plan, (5) run the pilot test, (6) refine the test plan, (7) run the test session, (8) analyse the collected data, and (9) report results.

The guide provides recommendations taking into account the needs of people with DS in the usability testing process. Table 1 summarises some of the recommendations provided in the guide.

4   Evaluation of USATESTDOWN at PRODIS

This paper describes the application of USATESTDOWN in a real case at the PRODIS Centre in Madrid, Spain [19]. The goal was to evaluate the usability of the AssisT-Task tool [20], a mobile technology system that was especially designed to assist people with cognitive disabilities in their workplace. AssisT-Task is based on assistive technologies using QR codes and mobile devices. It is meant to help these people perform their daily life activities and gradually gain autonomy through its use. This application generates step-by-step manuals that can be adapted to the circumstances and needs of the user such as support for a wider set of tasks, enabling user interaction during application use.

USATESTDOWN was applied to the AssisT-Task tool, as described below:

1. **Recruit participants.** Participants were selected by the experts in the PRODIS Centre. The workshop was attended by seven women and four men aged from 21 to 28. The participants had no prior experience handling the insurance policy selection process.
2. **Establish tasks.** The tasks were defined by a team composed of two specialized tutors working on a daily basis with people who have DS, a usability evaluation expert and an expert in the AssisT-Task application. The test was held in the employment centre to assure that participants were in a familiar and normal environment. The tasks defined for the test where based on the common use of AssisT-Task.
3. **Write instructions.** Short documents were prepared to help participants understand what they were supposed to do.
4. **Define the test plan.** The defined test plan included a specific section on the training of the participants before performing the test. In addition, the test plan included an easy-to-read version of the System Usability Scale (SUS) questionnaire, which was put together with the support of experts in DS.
5. **Run the pilot test.** The pilot test showed that the cameras were not in the best position. In addition, the user seemed a little confused with the short explanation of the application.
6. **Refine the test plan.** It was decided that the tutors should be involved in task execution. The camera positions were modified, and more time was set aside for explanations.
7. **Run the test session.** The modified test plan was applied for all the participants.
8. **Analyse the results.** We viewed the videos and annotations and created a document with the collected data. The results for success (task completion), satisfaction and frustration were then analysed. Most participants were able to complete their tasks

and were satisfied with the tasks that they had completed. However, levels of frustration were higher, indicating that they had some trouble with each of the tasks. In addition, we analysed timing as recorded by the application, as well as the responses to the SUS questionnaire. In both cases, the results were positive.

9. **Report the results.** The results were reported to the development team and to the managers. These results will be taken into account to improve the AssisT-Task system.

5 Conclusions and Future Work

First, it was necessary to adapt the SUS questionnaire for people with DS because the language in which it is written is complex. The test results were overwhelmingly positive, and participants commented that they had enjoyed both the application and the process, which is also confirmed by the recorded videos.

Generally, the USATESTDOWN guide proved to be viable and can be successfully used and modified to meet the needs of specific projects. Expert tutors rated the guide positively.

The participation of these expert tutors was very important for the implementation of the test according to the guide. Additionally, it is critically important for the expert tutors to be in attendance during the participants' interactions with the application in order to create a relaxed and familiar environment.

A negative factor of this evaluation was the time limits placed during the application of the pilot test on participants. Participants found it stressful being subjected to the times taken by the first participant.

Note also that the participants quickly forgot the process. We suggest that an evaluation stage be added where devices are given back to participants in order to determine how long it takes for them to work independently and be able to do the activity unaided by a tutor or the application.

References

1. International Standards Organization. ISO 9241–11. Ergonomic requirements for office work with visual display terminals (VDTs) – Part 11: Guidance on usability (1998)
2. Nielsen, J.: Usability Engineering. Morgan Kaufmann, San Francisco (1993)
3. Yussof, Rahmah Lob, Badioze Zaman, Halimah: Usability evaluation of multimedia courseware (MEL-SindD). In: Badioze Zaman, Halimah, Robinson, Peter, Petrou, Maria, Olivier, Patrick, Schröder, Heiko, Shih, Timothy K. (eds.) IVIC 2009. LNCS, vol. 5857, pp. 337–343. Springer, Heidelberg (2009)
4. Feng, J., Lazar, J., Kumin, L., Ozok, A.: Computer usage by children with down syndrome: challenges and future research. ACM Trans. Accessible Comput. (TACCESS) 2(3). Article no. 13 (2010)
5. Haro, B.P.M., Santana, P.C., Magaña, M.A.: Developing reading skills in children with Down syndrome through tangible interfaces. In: Proceedings of the 4th Mexican Conference on Human-Computer Interaction - MexIHC 2012, p. 28 (2012)

6. Kirijian, A., Myers, M.: Web fun central: online learning tools for individuals with Down syndrome. In: Lazar, J. (ed.) Universal Usability: Designing Computer Interfaces for Diverse Users, pp. 195–230. Wiley, Chichester (2007)
7. Schulze, E., Zirk, A.: Personalized Smart Environments to Increase Inclusion of People with Down's syndrome. Results of the Requirement Analysis State of the Art, p. 144 (2014)
8. Brandão, A., Trevisan, D.G., Brandão, L., Moreira, B., Nascimento, G., Vasconcelos, C.N., Clua, E., Mourão, P.T.: Semiotic inspection of a game for children with Down syndrome. In: Proceedings - 2010 Brazilian Symposium Games Digital Entertainment, pp. 199–210 (2011)
9. Cáliz, D., Martínez, L., Alamán, X., Terán, C., Cáliz, R.: 'USATESTDOWN' a proposal of a Usability testing guide for mobile applications focused on persons with Down syndrome. Ar-chivo Digital UPM, vol. 1, pp. 1–17 (2016)
10. Lepistö, A.: Usability evaluation involving participants with cognitive disabilities. In: Proceedings of the Third, pp. 305–308 (2004)
11. Nielsen, J.: Heuristic Evaluation. Usability Insp. Methods, pp. 25–62 (1994)
12. Zaman, B., Vanden Abeele, V., De Grooff, D.: Measuring product liking in preschool children: an evaluation of the Smileyometer and This or That methods. Int. J. Child-Comput. Interact. 1(2), 61–70 (2013)
13. Macedo, I., Trevisan, D.G.: A Method to Evaluate Disabled User Interaction: A Case Study with Down Syndrome Children. Univers. Access Human-Computer Interact. Des. Methods, Tools, Interact. Tech. eInclusion, pp. 50–58 (2013)
14. Kumin, L., Lazar, J.: A usability evaluation of workplace-related tasks on a multi-touch tablet computer by adults with down syndrome. J. Usability Stud. 7(4), 118–142 (2012)
15. Ramli, R., Zaman, H.B.: Designing usability evaluation methodology framework of Augmented Reality basic reading courseware (AR BACA SindD) for Down Syndrome learner. In: Proceedings of the 2011 International Conference on Electrical, Engineers Informatics, ICEEI 2011 (2011)
16. Cáliz, D., Martínez, L., Alamán, X., Terán, C., Cáliz, R.: Usability testing in mobile applications involving people with down syndrome: a literature review. In: ICAIT 2016 Conference (2016)
17. Cáliz, D., Alamán, X.: Usability Evaluation Method for Mobile Applications for the Elderly: A Methodological Proposal, pp. 252–260 (2014)
18. Jadán-Guerrero, J., Guerrero, L., López, G., Cáliz, D., Bravo, J.: Creating TUIs using RFID sensors—a case study based on the literacy process of children with down syndrome. Sensors 15(7), 14845–14863 (2015)
19. Fundación PRODIS (2016). http://www.fundacionprodis.org/
20. Gómez, J., Alamán, X., Montoro, G., Juan, C., Plaza, A.: Am ICog – Mobile technologies to assist people with cognitive disabilities in the work place. Adv. Distrib. Comput. Artif. Intell. Jornual 2(1), 9–17 (2011)

Objective Learnability Estimation
of Software Systems

Alexey Chistyakov[1]([⊠]), María T. Soto-Sanfiel[2], Enric Martí[1], Takeo Igarashi[3],
and Jordi Carrabina[4]

[1] Computer Science Department, Universitat Autónoma de Barcelona (UAB),
Bellaterra, Spain
alexey.chistyakov@e-campus.uab.cat, enric.marti@uab.cat
[2] Audiovisual Communication and Advertising Department, UAB, Bellaterra, Spain
mariateresa.soto@uab.es
[3] Department of Computer Science, The University of Tokyo, Bunkyō, Japan
takeo@acm.org
[4] UAB, CEPHIS, Escola d'Enginyeria, Bellaterra, Spain
jordi.carrabina@uab.cat

Abstract. Learnability is a fundamental usability factor. It is included
in several well known and widely used software usability evaluation
models such as: IBM's Computer Usability Satisfaction Questionnaire
(CUSQ), System Usability Measurement Inventory (SUMI), System
Usability Scale (SUS), and others. However, all of them assess learnability only subjectively. Taking into account the fact of presence of differences in perceived duration in interaction between human and computer,
development of a new approach targeting usability, as well as learnability,
in objective measures could be of great interest. This paper describes our
endeavour in pursuing this task. We present our approach to the problem, introduce an instrument for calculating objective learnability out
of times of completion, and reveal results of a user study among 101
participants conducted to test adequacy of the method.

Keywords: Human-Computer Interaction · Learnability · Usability ·
Usability Measurement · Usability Engineering

1 Introduction

Usability is one of the core terms in human-computer interaction studies. It is
described by International Standards Organisation (ISO) [15] as "the effectiveness, efficiency, and satisfaction with which specified users can achieve goals in
particular environments". Following this definition, better usability of an application brings more efficient human-computer interaction (HCI), which is the
main objective of this branch of the computer science. Thus, measuring, testing
and correct understanding of the problems impacting the usability is seen by the
researchers and practitioners as of extreme importance.

© Springer International Publishing AG 2016
C.R. García et al. (Eds.): UCAmI 2016, Part I, LNCS 10069, pp. 503–513, 2016.
DOI: 10.1007/978-3-319-48746-5_52

There are many recognised approaches, guidelines and methods to predict [13], test [19] and measure [3,14] usability. Most of them try to manage the term by clustering it into components. The number and the definition of those components varies from one measurement model to the other. Moreover, there is no consistent characterisation of them among software developers and researchers. Nevertheless, some of these usability factors can be distinguished.

Learnability is one of those factors. It is included in a considerably large number of the measurement models. As of today, learnability is recognised as an important part of the usability and, consequently, the software quality. It characterises an effort needed to be proficient with a system: less effort required to learn a way to operate the system efficiently, defines its higher learnability. It is closely related to usability even without necessarily implying high performance. Nowadays, "easy to learn" is one of the key positive characteristics of a well designed user interface, moreover the task of getting as efficient as possible with a system at as few time as possible could be vital for some applications.

Proper evaluation of the learnability of a system is an important and, apparently, underestimated part of the usability research. The comprehensive review [6] of user studies involving usability measurements reveals that the majority of studies make no attempt to assess learnability. The currently existing tools assessing the ability to learn a system are great in number, though strictly limited to subjective evaluation and strongly rely on user's subjective perception. Taking into account the proven fact of presence of a difference between subjectively experienced duration and objective time [18], we find existing measurement tools insufficient. We consider advancing in the definition of objective learnability measurement important for related industries and researchers. New approach could help to (i) more clearly understand a system's ability to get familiar with, (ii) localise existing learnability problems more efficiently, (iii) design better usability and, consequently, better user interfaces.

With hereby paper we offer a method for calculation of learnability from times of completion. Further we analyse current practices in measuring the learnability, describe the method, and reveal results of a user study conducted to test the proposed approach.

2   State of the Art

Learnability is mentioned as one of the forming factors of the usability in number of standards and evaluation models. Ease of learning and comprehensibility indicated as factors directly impacting the usability in IEEE Std. 1061 [9]. At the same time ISO [15] defines usability as combination of understandability, learnability, operability, attractiveness and compliance. Back in 1984, Shackel [17] proposed a new usability definition, which became one of the most useful operational statements of usability at the time. According to his model a system should have to pass the usability criteria, one of which is learnability. Nielsen [14] introduced user acceptance framework which defines learnability as the most fundamental usability attribute. According to Nielsen, highly learnable systems have a steep incline for the first part of the learning curve shown in Fig. 1, thus allow users to reach a reasonable level of usage proficiency in a shorter time. Dix et al. [2] specifies learnability as one of the three factors defining the overall usability. Löwgren [12] introduced REAL a software evaluation method. REAL splits the usability into (R)elevance, (E)fficiency, (A)ttitude and (L)earnability. Kirakowski et al. [7] designed Software Usability Measurement Inventory (SUMI), which clusters usability into efficiency, effectiveness, helpfulness, control and learnability.

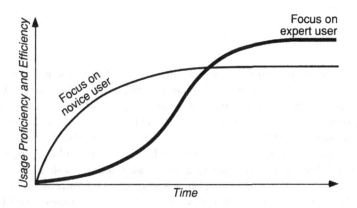

Fig. 1. Learning curves for a hypothetical system that focuses on the novice user, being easy to learn but less efficient to use, as well as one that is hard to learn but highly efficient for expert users. As seen in Nielsen's Usability Engineering

Despite the importance of learnability for a system quality evaluation, there are surprisingly few known approaches focused solely on learnability. Hoffman [5] proposed a method in which learnability is interpreted as:

$$\bar{i} = 2/\left(B + W\right) \tag{1}$$

where (B) stands for trials-to-criterion (predefined user's efficiency threshold) for the best performing participant and (W) the same for the least performing participant. This way closer i to 1.00, higher the learnability of a system under test, and the otherwise, closer i gets to zero, more difficult the cognitive work, thus learnability is lower. Rafique et al. performed [16] a thorough analysis of the past learnability studies and proposed an evaluation model aimed specifically at learnability. The measurement is performed by using four-item questionnaire, divided into two parts responsible for (i) interface understandability and (ii) task match. The questions, except one formulated by Rafique et al., were derived from SUMI [7] and IUI [4] questionnaires.

A number of methods designed to measure usability have learnability as a sub construct. SUMI, for instance, represents a questionnaire consisted of 50 questions and includes subscale of control and learnability. IBM's Computer Usability Satisfaction Questionnaire (CUSQ) [10] is a set of 19 questions with a part

Table 1. Reliability of the currently existing learnability measurement tools compared

Method	Reliability	Learnability construct reliability	Author
CUSQ	.95	.91	Lewis [10]
SUMI	.92	.82	Kirakowski [7]
WAMMI	.90	.74	Kirakowski [8]
SUS	.92	.71	Brooke [1]
Rafique	.70	-	Lewis [16]
Hoffman	-	-	Hoffman [5]

- Not applicable or not tested

dedicated to information quality, which could be used to assess a system's learnability. Perhaps, the most popular among practitioners is the System Usability Scale (SUS) - a 10-item questionnaire developed by Brooks to measure usability, which is proven [11] to have a cluster of 2 items intended to measure learnability of a given system. All of the aforementioned tools recommended themselves as reliable instruments for user studies. For further comparison of existing tools and methods involving learnability assessment please refer to Table 1. Nevertheless, all of them reflect only perceived usability and provide measurements of software quality only from end user's point of view, which in some cases could be insufficient. In his review [6] of usability studies Hornbæk justifies the importance of pursuing the subjective/objective distinction usability measurement, for they could improve objective performance and user experience.

3   Objective Learnability Estimation Model

Learnability is a complex underestimated concept directly influencing system's usability and software quality. The overwhelming majority of currently used methods are questionnaire based subjective estimations of perceived learnability. However, almost none of them try to approach the problem objectively. Therefore, we designed a method (Method) intended to alleviate this problem. The Method represents a statistical approach, based on a definition of the term given by Jakob Nielsen [14] as *"the effort for the user to reach a reasonable level of proficiency or a steeper incline for the first part of the learning curve"* (as shown on Fig. 1).

We assumed the learnability curve as a logarithmic approximation trendline built over a graphical representation of a System's efficiency progression over time. A logarithmic trendline is defined by the equation:

$$y = c \cdot \ln(x) + b \tag{2}$$

where (x) and (y) - coordinates, (b) - a constant defining the displacement of a curve, and (c) is a sought-for parameter defining the inclination of the curve: higher (c) produces steeper incline of the trendline. This parameter of the equation (2) can be calculated using the least squares fitting:

$$c = \frac{n \sum_{i=1}^{n} y_i \ln(x_i) - \sum_{i=1}^{n} y_i \sum_{i=1}^{n} \ln(x_i)}{n \sum_{i=1}^{n} \ln(x_i)^2 - (\sum_{i=1}^{n} \ln(x_i))^2} \qquad (3)$$

In our interpretation (x) and (y) are the time (or trials) and the corresponding system's efficiency respectively. (c) in this case, following the Nielsen's assumption, characterises learnability of a system. By applying (3) on the problem in hand it is possible to calculate a comparable objective measure of the learnability. Thus (c) of a single session would be:

$$c = \frac{n \sum_{i=1}^{n} e_i \ln(t_i) - \sum_{i=1}^{n} e_i \sum_{i=1}^{n} \ln(t_i)}{n \sum_{i=1}^{n} ln(t_i)^2 - (\sum_{i=1}^{n} \ln(t_i))^2} \qquad (4)$$

where (n) - total number of tests within a session, (e_i) - calculated efficiency for a task (i), and (t_i) - time of completion of the task (i) or a number of the tasks completed, depending on chosen definition of a system's efficiency.

Efficiency (e_i) could be calculated in different ways. For instance, in case of identical tasks, it could be a relation of time of completion to the number of tasks performed, or, in case of a sequence of tasks of different complexity, a number of basic interactions (e.g. clicks, key presses, etc.) per second or anything that could characterise user's confidence in interacting with a system.

Further on, we defined overall system's learnability (c) as a mean of all the sessions:

$$\bar{c} = \frac{1}{N} \sum_{j=1}^{N} c_j \qquad (5)$$

where (N) - number of sessions, (c_j) - calculated learnability for a session (j).

Therefore, higher (c) indicates higher learnability, close to zero or negative values in this case would mean that the initial efficiency, recorded when participant completed the first task, was the same or lower than efficiency obtained at the end of an experiment. Negative value could be an indicator of fundamental flaws either in a system or experimental design.

It is necessary to emphasise, that this approach is only true for systems having the standard learnability curve (Fig. 1). In other cases the learnability curve will be distorted and the described approach would not produce any sensible result.

4   Method

To validate the Method for the objective measuring of learnability, we designed and conducted an experimental study with human subjects that is described next.

4.1   Participants

A total of 101 participants including 65 males and 36 females ($M = 32.41$, $SD = 9.32$, $Rg = 20 - 60$ years old) took part in the study. Later, on the data analysis phase, subjects were divided into 4 age groups (20–29, 30–39, 40–49, and 50–60 years old). All responded to an online call for participation sent through social networks in two languages (English and Russian). Two versions of the stimulus were created, one for each of those languages. The final sample consisted of 70 individuals exposed to the English version and 31 individuals exposed to the Russian version. The participant's contribution was anonymous and voluntary, no economical compensation was offered. As the call for participation was distributed via online, the choice of the browser and operating system was left for the user's discretion. In the majority of cases (87.6 %) the stimulus was reproduced on desktop PCs, while 12.4 % used handheld devices to complete the tasks. Mainly the stimulus was viewed under different versions of Windows operating system (58.1 %), while the rest used: OSX (25.7 %), Android (9.5 %), Linux (4.8 %), and iOS (1.9 %). The list of browsers used to perform the tasks included Google Chrome (64.8 %), Mozilla Firefox (20 %), Apple Safari (12.4 %), and different versions of the Internet Explorer (2.8 %). None of the participants had previous experience using the Tomtom Multisport watch user interface, which interpretation was used as a test system.

4.2   Materials

To test the Method we used an imitation of the Tomtom Multisport's (TTMS) wrist watch user interface. This device represents a wrist watch with a sophisticated system of sensors, allowing users to track their sport activities. The device is consisted of an e-Ink display and a four-way controller serving as the only user input device. We considered this limitation of the system a good subject for learnability study.

For the sake of the experiment it was decided to recreate the TTMS UI using HTML (see Fig. 2) and distribute the stimulus through social networks. Functionality of the implementation was limited to the very basics: function to setup clock, date, alarm, and 24/12h format toggle switch. The UI included the device's display on the top, the four-way UID on the bottom, and the "I give up" button below the UI. When pressed, a current task is indicated as failed and the next task in the sequence is displayed.

4.3   Procedure

To test the learnability of the stimulus we defined a particular sequence of 10 consequent tasks (see Table 2). The order of the tasks in the sequence and the tasks themselves remained the same across all the sessions. The call for participation contained brief explanation of the experimental setup and the goals of the study. Participants who answered the call received the link to the stimulus. When opened, the demographic information form was displayed along with an explanation of the course of the experiment and a "Start" button triggering the test and the session timer. The list of tasks was always visible during the test. Every time a task was completed a corresponding notification was displayed. In case participant can not finish a task she was advised to click the "I give up"

Fig. 2. Graphical representation of the stimulus, imitating the user interface of the Tomtom Multisport watch. The Standby mode to the left and the Main Menu to the right. The "I give up" button below the UI finishes a current task and switches to next one in the sequence. When pressed, the current task is considered failed.

Table 2. Sequence of tasks in the experimental sequence and number of clicks necessary to complete a corresponding task.

Task	c_n
1. Set the alarm to 05:15 PM	25
2. Go back to the initial screen	2
3. Set the time to 10:10 PM	26
4. Go back to the initial screen	2
5. Set the date to April 12th 2016	26
6. Go back to the initial screen	2
7. Set the watch to 24-h format and set the time to 12:05	28
8. Go back to the initial screen	2
9. Set the watch to 12-h format and set the alarm to 09:00 AM	32
10. Go back to the initial screen	2

c_n - *minimum number of clicks needed to complete the task*

button to switch to the next task in the sequence (the current task is indicated as failed). Time to complete the task was not limited, the session timer went on until the sequence was finished. Results from the users who left the session without completing it were discarded.

4.4 Results

A significance level of $\alpha = 0.05$ was chosen for the study.

During the test, times of completion and number of clicks made on the stimulus were recorded using a respective javascript function. The mean time spent to complete a session was equal to ($N = 101$, $M = 237.07sec.$, $SD = 91.51sec.$),

the mean amount of clicks made at the end of the session was $(N = 101,$
$M = 203.356, SD = 38.845)$.

In the described experimental setup session's efficiency (e) of a participant
(p) was defined as:

$$e = \sum_{i=1}^{N} \frac{E_i n_i}{t_i} \qquad (6)$$

where (E_i) - the participant's effectiveness performing a task (i), a binary value
which takes 1 when the task is completed successfully and 0 otherwise, (n_i) -
number of clicks allowed by a participant prior finishing the task, (N) - a total
number of tasks within a session, (t_i) - time of completion of the task. In this
particular case the efficiency is seen as a number of clicks over the stimulus per
second.

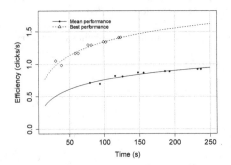 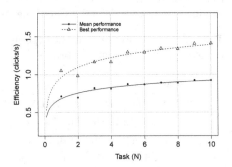

Fig. 3. Observed efficiency regression. Time based to the left and task based to the
right

We applied the described approach on the obtained dataset, the graphical
representation of the result of this computation is shown on Fig. 3. The results
are similar to those predicted by Nielsen (see Fig. 1). The overall observed mean
efficiency of the stimulus at the end of the experiment was equal to $(N = 101,$
$M = 0.92, SD = 0.24)$.

Further, to calculate learnability of the stimulus we applied the Method (4)
on the obtained mean efficiency progression values. The overall observed mean
learnability of the stimulus was calculated as $(N = 101, M = 0.21, SD = 0.17)$
and displayed normal distribution (Fig. 4). The highest detected learnability
value was $(c_{max} = 0.8875)$, 7 users displayed negative learnability, with the
lowest detected $(c_{min} = -0.1825)$.

T-Test and ANOVA methods were used to analyse the obtained dataset.
The analysis revealed significant differences between desktop and mobile users
$(t = 1.983, p \geq 0.001)$. The learnability in the desktop group was higher $(N = 90,$
$M = 0.217, SD = 0.176)$ than in the mobile group $(N = 11, M = 0.119,$
$SD = 0.054)$, and similar difference in the observed efficiency in the desktop

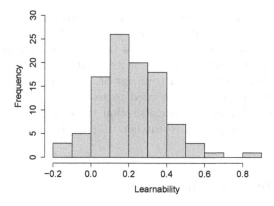

Fig. 4. Calculated learnability distribution

$(N = 90, M = 0.963, SD = 0.212)$ and the mobile $(N = 11, M = 0.581, SD = 0.136)$ groups (Fig. 5). This could be explained by the fact that the layout of the implemented UI was not properly adapted for use on mobile devices, thus the efficiency of interactions and, consequently, the learnability was lower. At the same time the analysis shown no influence of age, gender, operating system or browser of choice on the ability to learn the user interface.

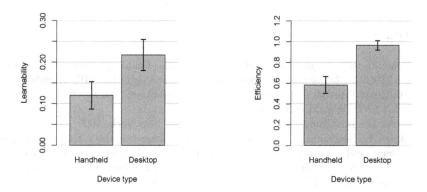

Fig. 5. Observed differences in calculated learnability (to the left) and efficiency (to the right)

5   Conclusion

Learnability measurements is an important part of usability assessment. This work introduced the statistical model capable of generating a comparable objective measure based solely on recorded times of completion. It is intended to be used during the data analysis phase, when the experiment is over, which could save a considerable amount of data collection time for both researchers and participants. In perspective it could bring less time-consuming and more efficient tests, more participants, larger datasets, more reliable data. It could be used as a supplement to already existing instruments or, in some cases, as a standalone tool. With the conducted study, we tried to test and justify adequacy of the approach and revealed results for consideration of the scientific community and practitioners. We encourage HCI researchers to consider our approach for their tests.

6   Future Work and Discussion

Despite the potential benefits, the proposal is rather bold. Therefore, there is work to be done to shape the approach and improve its reliability. Studies containing (i) larger samples, (ii) split tests between two or more stimuli, (iii) tasks different in nature and complexity could help to test reliability of the presented Method. A comparison of objective learnability calculated with the Method and perceived learnability measured with the usability questionnaires could prove really useful for evaluation of the method's performance. It is also of great interest for us to test the approach over prolonged periods of time. Researchers interested in tackling the specified problems are invited to discussion and potential collaboration.

References

1. Brooke, J.: SUS-A quick and dirty usability scale. Usability evaluation in industry (1996). https://books.google.es/books?hl=en&lr=&id=IfUsRmzAqvEC& oi=fnd&pg=PA189&dq=system+usability+scale&ots=G9nzEaok2k& sig=loVNNDnWmvkLWHmkrfrdgCy8HZY
2. Dix, A.: Human-Computer Interaction. Springer, New York (2009)
3. Frøkjær, E., Hertzum, M., Hornbæk, K.: Measuring usability: are effectiveness, efficiency, and satisfaction really correlated? In: CHI 2000 Proceedings of the SIGCHI conference on Human, vol. 2, pp. 345–352 (2000) http://doi.acm.org/ 10.1145/332040.332455
4. Gediga, G., Hamborg, K.C., Düntsch, I.: The isometrics usability inventory: an operationalization of ISO 9241–10 supporting summative and formative evaluation of software systems. Behav. Inf. Technol. **18**(3), 151–164 (1999)
5. Hoffman, R., Marx, M.: Measurement for evaluating the learnability and resilience of methods of cognitive work. Theor. Issues Ergon. Sci. **11**, 561–575 (2010). http://www.tandfonline.com/doi/abs/10.1080/14639220903386757
6. Hornbæk, K.: Current practice in measuring usability: challenges to usability studies and research. Int. J. Hum Comput. Stud. **64**(2), 79–102 (2006). http://linkinghub.elsevier.com/retrieve/pii/S1071581905001138
7. Kirakowski, J., Corbett, M.: SUMI: the software usability measurement inventory. Br. J. Educ. Technol. **24**, 210–212 (1993). http://onlinelibrary.wiley.com/doi/ 10.1111/j.1467-8535.1993.tb00076.x/abstract

8. Kirakowski, J., Cierlik, B.: Measuring the usability of web sites. In: Proceedings of the Human Factors and Ergonomics Society Annual Meeting, vol. 42, pp. 424–428. SAGE Publications (1998)

9. Kitchenham, B.A., Hughes, R.T., Linkman, S.G.: Modeling software measurement data. IEEE Trans. Softw. Eng. **27**(9), 788–804 (2001)

10. Lewis, J.R.: IBM computer usability satisfaction questionnaires: psychometric evaluation and instructions for use. Int. J. Hum. Comput. Interact. **7**(1), 57–78 (1995)

11. Lewis, J.R., Sauro, J.: The factor structure of the system usability scale. In: Kurosu, M. (ed.) HCD 2009. LNCS, vol. 5619, pp. 94–103. Springer, Heidelberg (2009). doi:10.1007/978-3-642-02806-9_12. http://link.springer.com/chapter/10.1007/978-3-642-02806-9_12

12. Löwgren, J.: Human-Computer Interaction: What Every System Developer Should Know. Studentlitteratur, Lund (1993)

13. Molich, R., Nielsen, J.: Improving a human-computer dialogue. Commun. ACM **33**(3), 338–348 (1990)

14. Nielsen, J.: Usability Engineering, vol. 11. Elsevier Science (1994). https://books.google.com/books?hl=en&lr=&id=DBOowF7LqIQC&pgis=1

15. Padayachee, I., Kotze, P., van Der Merwe, A.: ISO 9126 external systems quality characteristics, sub-characteristics and domain specific criteria for evaluating e-learning systems. In: The Southern African Computer Lecturers' Association, University of Pretoria, South Africa (2010)

16. Rafique, I., Weng, J., Wang, Y., Abbasi, M.Q., Lew, P., Wang, X.: Evaluating software learnability: a learnability attributes model. In: 2012 International Conference on Systems and Informatics (ICSAI2012), pp. 2443–2447. IEEE, May 2012. http://ieeexplore.ieee.org/articleDetails.jsp?arnumber=6223548

17. Shackel, B.: Usability-context, framework, definition, design and evaluation. In: Shackel, B., Richardson, S. (eds.) Human Factors for Informatics Usability, pp. 21–37. Cambridge University Press, Cambridge (1991)

18. Tractinsky, N., Meyer, J.: Task structure and the apparent duration of hierarchical search. Int. J. Hum. Comput. Stud. **55**(5), 845–860 (2001)

19. Wharton, C., Rieman, J., Lewis, C., Polson, P.: The cognitive walkthrough method: a practitioner's guide. In: Nielsen, J., Mack, R.L. (eds.) Usability Inspection Methods, pp. 105–140. John Wiley & Sons, Inc., New York (1994)

Using Smart TV Applications for Providing Interactive Ambient Assisted Living Services to Older Adults

José M. Tapia, Francisco J. Gutierrez(✉), and Sergio F. Ochoa

Department of Computer Science, University of Chile, Beauchef 851, 3rd Floor, Santiago, Chile
{jtapia,frgutier,sochoa}@dcc.uchile.cl

Abstract. The irruption of computer-based technology in social interaction has negatively affected the way in which elderly people interact with their family members, because they are, in some cases, reluctant to adopt new digital media. Given that literature suggests that seniors spend a significant part of their day watching television, we argue that Smart TV applications can be an effective way to provide them access to ambient assisted living services. This paper reports the design and use of a Smart TV-based application that promotes social interaction between older adults and their family members through social media. The system runs on a LED screen, extended with smart functionalities provided by Google Chromecast. The social interaction features provided by the system include exchanging email messages and sharing photos that are automatically retrieved from the accounts of family members in social media feeds. The system was evaluated with a group of expert users as well as with a sample of end-users. Older adults participating in the study praised the new possibilities offered by the proto-type application as a way to better engage with family-generated content, thus facilitating their social integration.

Keywords: Older adults · Interactive AAL services · Technology appropriation · Social isolation · Design challenges · Chromecast

1 Introduction

The use of social media applications and services has inadvertently increased the risk of social isolation among older adults, given that family members tend to overlook the traditional interaction spaces that the elderly traditionally used for socializing [7, 18, 24]. A recent survey conducted in Chile [6] shows that almost 25 % of older adults consider themselves excluded or socially isolated, while 40 % declare to miss the company of people around them. Similarly, a study conducted with a random sample of 3,858 older adults in Finland shows that 77 % of them suffered from social isolation or continuously feel lonely [26]. Although the proportion of socially isolated people varies across different cultures and societies, it is clear that this is currently a global issue [4].

Broadly speaking, the notion of wellbeing in older adults is not restricted to main-taining a good physical health state –such as being autonomous with sustainable levels of mobility and functionality–, but it also considers maintaining a good social health – such as keeping active within close social networks– [25]. Previous research in

© Springer International Publishing AG 2016
C.R. García et al. (Eds.): UCAmI 2016, Part I, LNCS 10069, pp. 514–524, 2016.
DOI: 10.1007/978-3-319-48746-5_53

gerontology and social psychology has also shown that the quantity and quality of social relationships impacts the overall mental and physical health of older adults, their behavior, and their mortality rate [10, 11, 27].

The social isolation suffered by older adults during the last two decades seems to be rooted in several causes. One of them is the increasing use of computer-mediated technology for communicating in informal settings, given because that these tools offer provide more flexibility and reduce help optimize the invested time in the interaction [22]. However, a large number of older adults are still reluctant to use technology for communicating with their families and friends, so this reduces their available interaction space [9]. Another cause that explains an increasing social isolation in elderly people is the underlying time and media preference asymmetries among older adults and the other members within their social networks, which are documented in several studies (e.g., [9, 14–16]).

Unfortunately, the challenge of socially integrating older adults to their families is not easy to address, as the elderly usually suffer from cognitive and motor impairments that limit their technology adoption [13]. In that respect, it is desirable to consider a smooth technology appropriation approach when designing systems for older adults, thus respecting the people preferences, practices, and routines [12]. Following such an approach, and trying to find a sound way to introduce ambient assisted living (AAL) services that help the elderly reduce their social isolation, we developed a Smart TV-based system with that purpose.

In a previous work, we discussed how to design tablet-based applications and services to increase family connection with older adults through the system prototype SocialConnector [17]. This paper builds on such work to explore the effectiveness of using Smart TV applications to reach the same goal. In fact, older people tend to spend more time watching television than younger people, although they enjoy this experience less [5].

Next section discusses related work regarding the usage and design challenges of TV-based services targeted to older adults. Section 3 presents the software architecture of the proposed system and explains its main components. Section 4 is devoted to describe the evaluation process and present the preliminary results of the system in terms of usability and perceived usefulness. Based on this, we discuss design alternatives and open challenges for providing AAL services for elderly people through Smart TVs. Finally, we conclude and provide perspectives on further work.

2 Related Work

Prior literature suggests several principles aimed to guide the design of TV-based applications for older adults (e.g., [3, 8, 19, 21, 28]). Recognizing the heterogeneous set of digital skills among older adults, Rice and Alm [23] designed a set of prototypes and interaction metaphors aimed to ease the appropriation of TV-based applications by this population. According to the authors, there are two main challenges to address: (1) provide an appropriate input control and (2) actively take into consideration on-screen interaction. Therefore, the main concepts that need to be considered in design and prototyping are: *providing clear and concise navigation*, as well as *satisfying the achievement of goals in an easy way*. Moreover, the design of simplified remote controls allows a more successful navigation over the screen, whereas navigational techniques miming aspects of real-world artifacts provide concrete affordances to older adults [23].

Designing engaging experiences using TVs as the main interaction device is not restricted to just providing clean and accessible interfaces. An important extension of the involvement with the visual content is provided by the remote control, which is largely the key input device for interacting with TV-based services. In that respect, Bobeth et al. [2] studied the overall performance and older adults' preference on using three different input devices for controlling interactive TV-based applications: tablets, freehand gestures, and a physical remote control. The results show that a mirrored TV screen on a tablet outperforms the other two options to control linear TV applications according to the opinion of older adults. In addition, according to the authors, it is also wise to avoid unnecessary display switches.

TV-based applications are also useful as a way to mitigate the negative effects of social isolation, by providing interactive means to engage with the content and surrounding elements and actors in the physical world. For instance, Orso et al. [20] conceived SeniorChannel, a TV application that allows users to access and interact with TV content through a simple interface. According to the authors, interactive multimedia has the potential not only to turn TV watching to an active experience, but also as a way to improve social inclusion. Similarly, Alaoui and Lewkowicz [1] designed Smart TV applications aimed to support social activities for elderly people.

In this paper, we extend the design of the latest version of SocialConnector [17], with the goal of observing the possible effects of changing the interaction device as a way to facilitate social interaction and to enhance the overall perception of social integration. The new system, named SocialConnectorTV, is a lite version of the original system, which runs in a smartphone and displays in the Smart TV the visual information delivered by the social interaction services. Next we present the system architecture and its main components.

3 System Architecture

Different Smart TV manufacturers have mounted their displays upon several middleware and operating systems (e.g., Android, LG WebOS, and Samsung Tizen). This diversity led us to make decisions about the hardware to test for deployment.

Given that our initial system prototype runs over a native Android tablet-based platform [17], we opted to maintain this line of development and stick to a Smart TV device capable of running the same operating system. The rationale behind this decision is to reduce development effort, mitigate software compatibility issues during migration, and the possibility to comparatively study the performance and overall user experience between the deployed system running on a Smart TV and on a state-of-the art tablet PC. Therefore, we initially opted to deploy our system on a standard LED TV equipped with a Google Chromecast device[1], which is a digital media player that streams multimedia content and runs software applications casted from a third-party device. In this case, we used a smartphone running SocialConnector TV to cast the software to the TV display. This workaround is not noticed by end-users and older adults therefore assume that the developed application is running in the Smart TV.

In order to interact with the application, older adults use an ad-hoc remote control. Such a device is implemented as a software application that runs in a smartphone, acting as the "controller" of the system and embedding most of the social interaction services considered in the original SocialConnector system. This application uses Chromecast as a mediator to display visual content on the TV screen (Fig. 1).

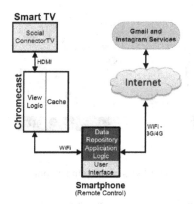

Fig. 1. Operational environment of the solution

Fig. 2. Software architecture of SocialConnector TV

The communication between the smartphone and the Internet can be performed using WiFi or a regular mobile phone network (3G or 4G). The communication between the

---

[1] https://www.google.com/chromecast/tv/ .

smartphone and the Chromecast uses WiFi, and that between the Chromecast and the Smart TV is done through an HDMI cable. Next we briefly explain these components (Fig. 2).

3.1 Remote Control Application

At launch time, the remote control application senses the environment and identifies all devices (typically TVs) that are equipped with a Chromecast device and are up to one hop of distance from the smartphone acting as remote control. The list of devices is displayed to the user through the GUI of the application. Using such a list, the user can choose a target device (i.e., a particular Smart TV display) and then the application creates a work session that includes such a smartphone and the selected Smart TV. After this synchronization stage is concluded, the application is in control of the content to be displayed in the Smart TV, wirelessly casting the content through Chromecast.

The remote control application has a layered architecture that considers a user interface, the application logic, and a data repository. The user interface allows older adults to access and use the provided social interaction services. Figure 3.a shows the main user interface through which the elderly can send/respond messages (emails), view the incoming messages, view new photos of their family members (automatically retrieved from Instagram), or browse the photo album.

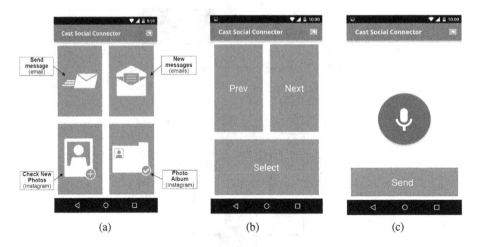

Fig. 3. User interfaces of the remote control application

When the user chooses the option to send a message or view the photo album, the list of contacts is shown in the TV displaying a photo of the available family members to be contacted; i.e., the contact list is a carrousel of pictures of people that the user can navigate by using the interface presented in Fig. 3.b. This interface also allows the elderly to select the contact that is expected to receive a message, or the contact whose pictures will be fetched from his/her Instagram account. If the older adult wants to send or respond to an incoming message, a microphone will be activated for dictating the message (Fig. 3.c). Then, a speech-to-text service transforms the voice message into text and shows the content for approval. If the content of the message is approved, then it is transferred to the intended receiver as a regular email; otherwise, it is discarded.

The application logic of the remote control implements the services that allow the exchange of messages between the older adult and his/her contacts, automatically retrieving photos using the Instagram API and processing any attached comments within the original source. This layer is also in charge of packaging this information and sending it to the Chromecast for its rendering and display in the Smart TV screen.

The application also has a data repository that manages a local record of the information that is required for the normal operation of SocialConnector TV; for instance, the list of contacts, the most recent photos and messages for each one of them, the list of messages and photos already seen by the user, and the information for automatically logging in to the local user email and Instagram accounts.

3.2   SocialConnector TV

The commands prompted by the user on the remote control application trigger a response in both the smartphone and the Smart TV screen. For instance, when the user chooses the option "*photo album*" (Fig. 3.a), the system displays the contact list in the smart TV (Fig. 4.a), and simultaneously, the interface to control the interactive system navigation in the smartphone (Fig. 3.b). If the user selects a contact (e.g., "Natalia"), then he/she can view Natalia's photos and navigate through them.

(a)   (b)

Fig. 4. User interface of the SocialConnector TV: (a) list of contacts, (b) picture of the selected contact

3.3   Chromecast

Finally, the Chromecast component comprises two services: the view logic and the cache (temporal data repository). The first one is a gateway that encapsulates the logic required to interact with the Smart TV and the remote control application running on the smartphone. The second service records the information that is required to maintain the coordination between these two devices (e.g., work session information and communication status) and the information to be displayed on the Smart TV screen.

Typically, the view logic of the Chromecast receives two kinds of inputs from the remote control application: HTML files and commands. On the one hand, the HTML files have the content and graphical elements to be rendered in the Smart TV screen (e.g., the information shown in Fig. 4). On the other hand, the commands are used to control such an interface; for instance, for making focus on a certain option, changing the information that is displayed, or navigating through the information architecture (e.g., advance to the next photo or message). More complex interactions can also be implemented using the Chromecast as intermediary, since this device is able to process HMTL, CSS, Javascript, and several formats of digital information.

4   Usability Evaluation

We evaluated the system usability and perceived usefulness in two stages. First, we conducted a laboratory-based inspection with the aim to identify major usability concerns. Once these identified issues were corrected in the system prototype, we conducted a study with a sample of end-users in a simulated setting.

4.1   Heuristic Inspection with Expert Users

We conducted a first usability inspection aiming to identify major issues in the design of the Smart TV application before evaluating the system with end-users. This inspection was conducted in two stages: (1) a cognitive walkthrough session performed by the authors, and (2) a heuristic evaluation by expert users in user interface design for mobile devices.

Regarding the cognitive walkthrough study session, we defined a set of tasks that covered the different functionalities offered by the system. These tasks were: (1) composing and sending a message to a given contact, and (2) browsing through the photos of a given family members. While fulfilling these tasks, each author assumed different roles aiming to navigate through the different interaction paths provided by the system, as a way to understand how easy it would be for inexperienced end-users to engage with the application. Once completed the evaluation session, we identified a set of key usability concerns that needed to be fixed in order to improve the user experience of the system.

Subsequently, a panel of three expert users in mobile user interfaces performed a heuristic evaluation following Nielsen's usability guidelines, and lifted a second set of potential usability and user experience concerns. Initially, the identified usability concerns were related to the complexity of the navigation schema, a lack of feedback on the system status, as well as few meaningful affordances and fit to the mental model of older adults. All of these concerns were redesigned and corrected for evaluating the system with older adults.

4.2 Usability Study with End-Users

Through snowball and convenience sampling, we recruited eight participants acting as end-users, aged 60 and over (4 women, 4 men), with a low-level of technology appropriation. None of the recruited participants has used nor heard about Chromecast before, and they rarely used computers and smartphones before. We simulated a home setting as a living room in our lab, and we asked participants to interact with the system using as remote control a smartphone provided by us.

Users were individually and independently asked to complete a set of tasks following the thinking aloud protocol, where they were prompted to express their thoughts as they were performing the evaluation. As with the first usability inspection, the required activities to be performed by end-users were: (1) compose and send a message to a family member, and (2) browse the photos of a given family member.

The first author introduced the system to participants and moderated the session, the second author observed how the participants interacted with the system and kept hand-written notes throughout the process, and the third author kept track of the number of errors and spent time in completing the proposed tasks. By error we note any action that does not fit within the expected interaction flow, such as misunderstanding the elements displayed in the user interface. Table 1 summarizes the tasks performed by the participants and the obtained results.

Table 1. Summary statistics of the evaluation results.

Assigned task	Mean time spent (minutes)	Std. Dev.	Mean number of errors	Std. Dev.
1. Compose and send a message to a family member	1.4	0.5	1.9	0.9
2. Browse through the photos of a given family member	1.1	0.2	1.3	0.5

The first result that we can highlight is that all participants were able to complete the assigned tasks, although most of them never interacted with a Smart TV before. The time spent for completing the tasks was in the same range as that observed in our previous experience evaluating the system running in Tablet PCs [17]. Therefore, if we consider that the participants were interacting with Smart TVs for the very first time, the observed values become highly promising due to a possible continuous learning effect over time during actual use.

In addition, we observed that some participants asked many questions to the assistant, showing that they were afraid to making mistakes. Therefore, self-confidence in the use of the application will also contribute to further reduce times and quantity of errors when using the application. This consideration should be noted when improving the design of our system and further developments aiming for providing AAL services to older adults. An alternative to deal with this issue is proposing meaningful and contextualized tutorials, which would contribute to helping older adults smooth their learning curve, consequently improving their confidence on interacting with the system.

Once all users individually and independently completed their tasks, they were invited to discuss altogether with the authors in a focus group session aiming to assess the perceived usefulness of the evaluated application. Most participants were highly enthusiastic of using the system. Overall, they perceived the application as quite useful and praised the new possibilities offered by SocialConnector TV as a way to better engage with family-generated content, thus facilitating their social interaction within their social networks. Although participants appreciated the design and aesthetics of the main user interface displayed on the TV screen, as well as the remote control application embedded in the smartphone, most of them stated they were not confident enough on using the system without external assistance.

> P4: *"I liked the application and it seems to be quite useful for me. However, I am not sure if I will be able to browse its different features when alone at home".*

Following on the number of errors made while fulfilling the proposed tasks, one of the most significant sources of trouble for participants is concerned with understanding the semiotics of the proposed service icons (Fig. 3.a). Given that expert users also raised a concern related to the design and meaning of the proposed icons, we conclude that more attention should be devoted to improving the design and understanding of the service icons in further developments. Following the comments suggested by some users, short labels could be added to the redesigned icons as a way to enhance the meaning of such actions. All in all, the metaphors used to represent the list of contacts and messages were not clear for end-users and will be improved in a next iteration of the evaluated system.

> P7: *"I think I got lost somewhere, because I did not understand quite well what those buttons did on the TV. Perhaps it would be useful if they had some short text or labels to enhance what they try to mean".*

In summary, although the evaluation results show the application still has space for improvement, the most important aspect to highlight is the fact that the participants were able to accomplish the assigned tasks and were engaged during the activity. This leads us to expect more interesting results for the next iteration of this system.

5   Conclusions and Future Work

In this paper we present a prototype application running on Smart TVs for facilitating the social integration of older adults within their family networks. The system was developed using Google Chromecast, a promising technology for allowing interactive applications to be deployed in home TV settings.

The development of our system raised two main challenges: (1) conceive a usable remote control application, and (2) providing a useful layout in the TV screen. Although the preliminary evaluation of the system shows that older adults participating in the study consider it to be useful, there is still some space for improvement, particularly in terms on the design of user feedback, the proposed affordances, and providing meaningful metaphors to assist the end-users in learning how to interact with the application.

We argue that by addressing these concerns, older adults would improve their engagement with the system.

As future work, we aim to deploy a second prototype running on AndroidTV devices. This would allow us to conduct a 3-factor in-the-wild study, aiming to compare in the usage and appropriation of our technology to mediate family interaction between: (1) state-of-the-art tablets, (2) TVs equipped with Chromecast, and (3) Smart TVs running dedicated software.

Acknowledgments. This work has been partially supported by the Fondecyt Project (Chile), grant: 1150252. The work of Francisco J. Gutierrez has been supported by the Ph.D. Scholarship Program of Conicyt Chile (CONICYT-PCHA/Doctorado Nacional/2013-21130075).

References

1. Alaoui, M., Lewkowicz, M.: Struggling against social isolation of the elderly – the design of SmartTV applications. In: Dugdale, J., Masclet, C., Grasso, M.A., Boujut, J.-F., Hassanaly, P. (eds.) From Research to Practice in the Design of Cooperative Systems: Results and Open Challenges, pp. 261–275. Springer, London (2012)
2. Bobeth, J., Schrammel, J., Deutsch, S., Klein, M., Drobics, M., Hochleitner, C., Tscheligi, M.: Tablet, gestures, remote control? influence of age on performance and user experience with iTV applications. In: Proceedings of the ACM International Conference on Interactive Experiences for TV and Online Video (TVX 2014), pp. 139–146 (2014)
3. Carmichael, A.: Style Guide for the Design of Interactive Television Services for Elderly Viewers. Independent Television Commission, Winchester (1999)
4. Cloutier-Fisher, D., Kobayashi, K., Smith, A.: The subjective dimension of social isolation: a qualitative investigation of older adults' experiences in small social support networks. J. Aging Stud. **25**(4), 407–414 (2011)
5. Depp, C.A., Schkade, D.A., Thompson, W.K., Jeste, D.V.: Age, Affective Experience, and Television Use. Am. J. Prev. Med. **39**(2), 173–178 (2010)
6. Fernández, B., Herrera, M.S., Valenzuela, E.: Chile and their elderly people – third national survey on quality of life in elderly people. Ministry of Social Development, Chile (2014)
7. Giddens, A.: Conversations with Anthony Giddens: Making Sense of Modernity. Stanford University Press, Stanford (1998)
8. GIll, J., Perera, S.: Accessible universal design of interactive digital television. In: Proceedings of the European Conference on Interactive Television (EuroITV 2003), pp. 83–89 (2003)
9. Gutierrez, F.J., Ochoa S.F.: Mom, i do have a family!: attitudes, agreements, and expectations on the interaction with chilean older adults. In: Proceedings of the ACM Conference on Computer-Supported Cooperative Work and Social Computing (CSCW 2016), pp. 1400–1409 (2016)
10. House, J.S., Landis, K.R., Umberson, D.: Social relationships and health. Science **241**, 540–545 (1988)
11. House, J.S.: Social isolation kills, but how and why? Psychosom. Med. **63**(2), 273–274 (2001)
12. Janneck, M.: Recontextualizing technology in appropriation processes. In: Whitworth, B., de Moor, A. (eds.) Handbook of Research on Socio-Technical Design and Social Networking Systems, pp. 153–166. IGI Global, Hershey (2009)
13. Koltay, T.: The media and the literacies: media literacy, information literacy, digital literacy. Media Cult. Soc. **33**(2), 211–221 (2011)

14. Lindley, S.E., Harper, R., Sellen, A.: Designing for elders: exploring the complexity of relationships in later life. In: Proceedings of the British HCI Group Annual Conference on HCI (BCS-HCI 2008), pp. 77–86 (2008)
15. Lindley, S.E., Harper, R., Sellen, A.: Desiring to be in touch in a changing communications landscape: attitudes of older adults. In: Proceedings of the ACM SIGCHI Conference on Human Factors in Computing Systems (CHI 2009), pp. 1693–1702 (2009)
16. Muñoz, D., Cornejo, R., Gutierrez, F.J., Favela, J., Ochoa, S.F., Tentori, M.: A social cloud-based tool to deal with time and media mismatch of intergenerational family communication. Future Gener. Comput. Syst. 53, 140–151 (2015)
17. Muñoz, D., Gutierrez, F.J., Ochoa, S.F.: Introducing ambient assisted living technology at the home of the elderly: challenges and lessons learned. In: Cleland, I., Guerrero, L., Bravo, J. (eds.) IWAAL 2015. LNCS, vol. 9455, pp. 125–136. Springer, Heidelberg (2015). doi: 10.1007/978-3-319-26410-3_12
18. Neal, A.G., Collas, S.F.: Intimacy and Alienation: Forms of Estrangement in Female/Male Relationships. Garland Publishing, New York (2000)
19. Nunes, F., Kerwin, M., Silva, P.A.: Design recommendations for TV user interfaces for older adults: findings from the eCAALYX project. In: Proceedings of the ACM SIGACCESS Conference on Computers and Accessibility (ASSETS 2012), pp. 41–48 (2012)
20. Orso, V., Spagnolli, A., Gamberini, L., Ibañez, F., Fabregat, M.E.: Interactive Multimedia Content for Older Adults: The Case of SeniorChannel. Multimedia Tools and Applications (2016). http://dx.doi.org/10.1007/s11042-016-3553-5
21. Pak, R., McLaughlin, A.: Designing Displays for Older Adults. CRC Press, Boca Raton (2010)
22. Preece, J., Rogers, Y., Sharp, H.: Interaction Design: Beyond Human-Computer Interaction. John Wiley & Sons, Chichester (2015)
23. Rice, M., Alm, N.: Designing new interfaces for digital interactive television usable by older adults. Comput. Entertainment 6(1), 6:1–6:20 (2008)
24. Thomas, P.A.: Trajectories of social engagement and limitations in late life. J. Health Soc. Behav. 52(4), 430–443 (2011)
25. Thumala, D., Arnold, M., Massad, C., Herrera, F.: Social Inclusion and Exclusion of Elderly People in Chile – Fourth National Survey on Social Inclusion and Exclusion. Ministry of Social Development, Chile (2015)
26. Tilvis, R.S., Routasalo, P., Karppinen, H., Strandberg, T.E., Kautiainen, H., Pitkala, K.H.: Social isolation, social activity and loneliness as survival indicators in old age: a nationwide survey with a 7-year follow-up. Eur. Geriatr. Med. 3(1), 18–22 (2012)
27. Umberson, D., Montez, J.K.: Social relationships and health: a flashpoint for health policy. J. Health Soc. Behav. 51, 54–66 (2010)
28. Zaphiris, P., Ghiawadwala, M., Mughal, S.: Age-centered research-based web design guidelines. Extended Abstracts of the ACM SIGCHI Conference on Human Factors in Computing Systems (CHI-EA 2005), pp. 1897–1900 (2005)

Analyzing Human-Avatar Interaction with Neurotypical and not Neurotypical Users

Esperanza Johnson[1(✉)], Carlos Gutiérrez López de la Franca[1],
Ramón Hervás[1], Tania Mondéjar[1,2], and José Bravo[1]

[1] University of Castilla-la Mancha (MAmI Research Lab),
Paseo de la Universidad 4, Ciudad Real, Spain
{MEsperanza.Johnson, Carlos.Gutierrez5}@alu.uclm.es,
{ramon.hlucas, jose.bravo}@uclm.es,
Tania.mondejar@esmile.es
[2] eSmile, Psychology for Children and Adolescents,
Calle Toledo 79 1ºE, Ciudad Real, Spain
http://mami.uclm.es

Abstract. Assistive technologies have been used to improve the quality of life of people who have been diagnosed with health issues. In this case, we aim to use an assistive technology in the shape of an affective avatar to help people who have been diagnosed with different forms of Social Communications Disorders (SCD). The designed avatar presents a humanoid face that displays emotions with a subtlety akin to that of real life human emotions, with those emotions changing according to the interactions that the user chooses to perform on the avatar. We have used Blender for the design of the emotions, which are happiness, sadness, surprise, fear and anger, plus a neutral emotion, while Unity was used to dictate the behavior of the avatar when the interactions were performed, which could be positive (caress), negative (poke) or neutral (wait). The avatar has been evaluated by 48 people from different backgrounds and the results show the overall positive reception by the users, as well as the difference between neurotypical and non-neurotypical users in terms of emotion recognition and chosen interactions. A ground truth has been established in terms of prototypic empathic interactions by the users.

Keywords: Affective computing · Affective avatar · Human-avatar interaction · Social communication disorder · Cognitive disabilities · Empathy

1 Introduction

Some kinds of disabilities entail Social Communication Disorders (SCD) that usually carry problems related with social interaction and social understanding [1]. Assistive technologies can help people who suffer from these conditions have a better quality of live by improving on certain aspects of their day-to-day life [2]. The approach explored in this work is an affective avatar to engage the users in interactions with it, while the avatar reacts to those interactions by displaying certain emotions. The long term goal of this is to improve the social skills, emotional management and empathy of the users,

© Springer International Publishing AG 2016
C.R. García et al. (Eds.): UCAmI 2016, Part I, LNCS 10069, pp. 525–536, 2016.
DOI: 10.1007/978-3-319-48746-5_54

while the short term goal for an experiment conducted for this work was the validation of the model.

The users that took part in the experiment were both of neurotypical as well as non neurotypical backgrounds (with neurotypical being an umbrella term for people without any neurological pathology or disorder), while the experiment consisted on those users interacting with the avatar, identifying the emotions displayed by the avatar, and establishing both their own emotional response to the emotion shown by the avatar and the logic of the avatar's reaction.

Apart from this development, there was a previous paper [13] that explored a taxomy for the different kinds of human-avatar interactions that support certain cognitive processes, instantiating this prototype by adapting it to support a particular cognitive process related to communication, which for this case would be emotional states and empathic behavior.

Given this, the order of the paper will be as follows: In Sect. 2 we will explore related work that has been studied in order to obtain knowledge applicable to our own work; Sect. 3 will deal with the interactions the affective avatar is capable of, as well as the process towards configuring the interactions themselves, Sect. 4 is a more in depth talk of the basis of the affective avatar and its design. Sections 5 and 6 explore the experiment performed and its results, respectively; Sect. 7 speaks of the future work that we intend to do, finalizing with Sect. 8 with the conclusions to this paper.

2   Related Work

We have explored a variety of works, in different areas. Firstly, we explored any possible works regarding affective avatars, which yielded results when it came to the design of avatars, or the design of affective systems to detect emotions in the user. After these findings, we focused on exploring works related to avatars for disability.

Concerning the topic of avatars to help people with disabilities, we have found a wide arrange of works in that area, such as a proposal that uses serious games and avatar to aid people with intellectual disabilities in several daily tasks [7]; a collaborative virtual environment for people with autism and avatars that represent emotions [3]; an eye tracker system for people with severe motor disability to interact with an avatar [6]; and training systems that assist older people with mental and physical damages through the use of an avatar in their televisions [4]. This process allowed us to observe previously explored proposals and extract knowledge in terms of what had already been done in this area and propose a novel idea. In this case, we saw that the avatars that were used were not affective, nor did they focus on emotional health or empathy, which is the focus of this proposal.

In the area of avatar design, we have found another battery of interesting proposals, of which we have looked into a small collection which range from a work on human-avatar interaction in a simulation game that helps teenagers deal with peer pressure [8], user interfaces based on 3D avatars for interactive television, and how the user interacts and reacts to it [9], an AI Framework for the supporting behavioral animation of avatars, to make them behave more realistically [10], as well as research works that discuss children's avatar preferences [11] and the interaction of children with Autism with an interactive avatar in which they could modify its facial characteristics [12]. These proposals have been key in giving us a better understanding on the impact of the avatar's design in users, which has helped the creation of the avatar proposed in this paper.

Finally in the area of computer-human interaction, we have found works that deal with the design of an affective system, specifically, a work that presents a novel architecture for the development of intelligent multimodal affective interfaces, based on the integration of Sentic Computing [14], where Sentic Computing is an area that exploits computer and human sciences to better interpret and process social information. This will help us gain more knowledge in the area of interactions with an avatar.

3   Interactions of the Affective Avatar

The interactions were decided by looking at the basic types of interactions among humans, which can be positive, negative or neutral, looking also at the arousal of the emotions that were chosen [15]. After that, we decided on a way to reflect this in the simplest terms for interactions with a tablet. For this, we have decided that there would be three types of interactions with the avatar. A good type of interaction (caress), a bad type (poke) and a neutral interaction (wait), and according to which interaction the user has engaged in, it will affect the avatar in a different way. The neutral interaction has the distinction of having the wait time be different according to the start and end emotions, and the difference in arousal between those emotions [15].

After establishing the kinds of interactions we would use, we had to decide on how those interactions would affect the avatar. For that, we had to settle on a variety of emotions, which are the named universal emotion categories proposed by Paul Ekman in 1972, from which we removed disgust due to it not being relevant to the conducted work. This left us with the emotions of happiness, sadness, anger, surprise and fear, plus an idle state that has a neutral expression. These emotions can be seen in Fig. 1. All of the details of the design will be discussed in the next section.

Following the decision of the emotions that the avatar would show and the interactions that could be done to affect it, we tied both concepts into a model that would show how those interactions affect the emotions. This model corresponds to a state machine where each emotion is a state, and each interaction is a transition between two states. The state machine shown in Fig. 2 works in a way in which the user will first see an Idle state in the avatar (with a Neutral expression), and from there depending on each action of the user, the avatar's emotion will change according to the input. The emotions, as well as the transitions between emotions, have been validated in a previous work [16].

4   Basis of the Affective Avatar

In this point we will discuss the design of the affective avatar and the reason for some of the choices made in terms of design. The affective avatar was designed with a focus on a cognitive process mentioned in the previous point, which is Emotional State (E),

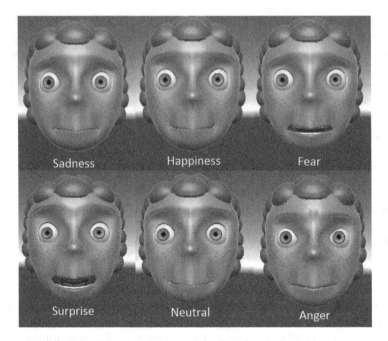

Fig. 1. Emotions shown by the avatar

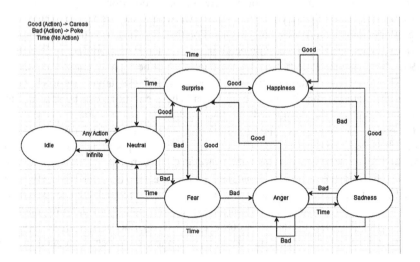

Fig. 2. The state machine that controls the transition between emotions.

with the intention of being of assistance in the management of the user's emotions. The reasoning for this is the support of cognitive function and the theory of the mind that are important research lines in SCD [1].

Before we started the 3D design of the avatar using the software Blender[1] we had to decide how the avatar would look like. For this, we gathered knowledge from previous works dealing in the area of avatar design. This involved making the avatar have a humanoid aspect over others and a friendly disposition [5], as well as attempting to make the avatar seem as gender neutral as possible, as in seems that children design avatars showcasing their own gender [11].

After establishing these points, we proceeded to the design with Blender, of which one of the key elements was the creation of shape keys, which represents the deformation of the object's vertices from the basis, enabling us to design the different expressions that we wish for the avatar to have. To these we later add bones that will act as drivers for those deformations. The bones that we have added are for the head, brows, eyelids, lower jaw and three for the mouth (upper lip and the corners of the lips), as well as eye control and a bone master. The hierarchy of these bones is a tree, in which the BoneMaster is the root, and the EyeCtrl and Head bones hang from it, and finally all the other facial bones are children of the Head bone. The bones have been changed to the black lines that can be seen in Fig. 3, where the circular base is the BoneMaster, and the circle surrounding the head vertically is the Head bone.

Fig. 3. Bones that control the facial expressions of the avatar.

After this, the model was implemented into Unity[2] and the behavior was implemented using Mecanim, a tool that allows the programming of the behavior of animations by means of a state machine and a script (in this case in C#), for which the states represent animations and the transitions are conditions that must be true in order

[1] https://www.blender.org/.

[2] https://www.unity3d.com.

for them to occur, which are specified in the script. In this case, the animations and the transitions implemented in Mecanim correspond with the state machine in Fig. 2.

5 Experiment

We used an empirical approach, as the purpose of this experiment is to establish patterns of interaction in neurotypical and non-neurotypical users, and to observe if there is any discernible difference in how they interact. The reason for this experiment was mainly to validate the 3D model of the avatar, as well as to determine if the users showed empathy towards it. From the gathered data, we have also been able to see if there is a pattern in terms of repetitive actions in some groups of users (Fig. 4).

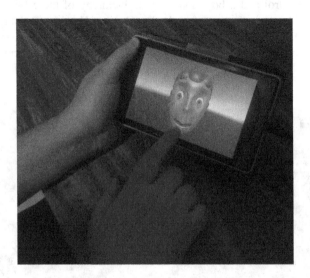

Fig. 4. User interacts with the avatar.

There were 48 participants in the study, which can be subdivided into two groups: neurotypical and not neurotypical, where not neurotypical is an umbrella term for anyone with any kind of neurological disorder. The group of neurotypicals was made up by 30 people divided by age into three cohorts, C1 (< 12), C2 (12–21) and C3 (22–30), whereas the not neurotypical group was made up by 18 people, 10 with an intellectual deficiency (Cn1) and 8 with Down syndrome (Cn2). The protocol was as follows: (1) participants were informed about the purpose of the experiment and the information to be collected; (2) the avatar, in its neutral emotional state, was shown to participants and the different possible interactions were explained; (3) participants performed 20 interactions with the avatar (at a total of 960 interactions during the experiment) and were asked to identify the emotions shown by the avatar. The following data was collected: initial emotion of the avatar, final emotion after interaction (as identified by the user), interaction the user chose, reflected emotion in the user (if any), and the opinion of the user about the logical (or not logical) emotion of the avatar.

From these collections of data we were able to obtain results concerning accuracy when identifying the emotions of the avatar, recall, precision, f-score, confusion matrix, number of continuous interactions, etc. All of these were done globally as well as by groups and cohorts, whereas some of the data (confusion matrix) we also distinguished between the total amount of interactions (20) and the last 10 interactions as we considered the first 10 interactions a learning period for the user to become used to the facial expressions of the avatar.

Further details of the experiment, as well as the analyzed data and our findings, can be seen in previous work [16], which mainly dealt with the validation of the facial expressions of the avatar.

6   Results of the Experiment

In terms of mean accuracy in the correct identification of the emotions by the users during the whole test, neurotypical users performed better at a **73.69 %**, whereas not neurotypical users performed worse at a **53.61 %**. This number increased when only taking into account the last 10 interactions, though the increase for the non-neurotypicals was smaller (~3 %) than the increase for the neurotypicals (~6 %). This vast difference can be seen in its most extreme example when analyzing the recognition of each particular emotion, where Neutral was the emotion with the worst recognition accuracy when identifying it. In the case of neurotypicals, the results were **59.88 %** and **65.15 %**, whereas the not neurotypicals had results that were much worse at an accuracy of identification of **12.77 %** total, with the result improving (but still quite low) after 10 interactions to a mean accuracy of **21.43 %**, result that obviously affects the global results for overall mean recognition accuracy. In general, the rest of emotions had better recognition percentages, and they improved after the first 10 interactions. Tables 1 and 2 show the exact data for the accuracy in recognizing each emotion by both groups.

Table 1. Accuracy in the recognition of the avatar emotions by neurotypical users.

	Neutral	Fear	Anger	Happy	Surprise	Sadness
Accuracy	59.88	65.26	61.90	94.16	82.05	73.68
Accuracy-10	65.15	75.56	64.10	94.27	92.00	79.31

Table 2. Accuracy in the recognition of the avatar emotions by non-neurotypical users.

	Neutral	Fear	Anger	Happy	Surprise	Sadness
Accuracy	12.77	25.58	72.92	69.70	47.69	72.00
Accuracy-10	21.43	17.65	76.00	69.86	60.87	64.29

In terms of cohorts within these groups, the highest accuracy was for Surprise for C3 and C2, whereas Happiness was the emotion with the highest recognition percentage in C1. For non-neurotypicals, the emotion with the highest percentage of recognition was Anger for both groups.

Most of the issues with low accuracy were due to the confusion of the emotion with a different one, which can be seen in the confusion matrix for both groups. In the case of the neurotypical group of users, Neutral was confused with a variety of emotions, though after a learning process and taking into account the last 10 interactions, it can be seen that it is mostly confused with Happiness, though the opposite does not happen nearly as frequently. Other notable confusions are Anger and Fear with Sadness.

For the non-neurotypical users, Neutral is also the most confused emotion, as it is confused with all the other emotions, mostly with Sadness, which is also the case for Fear. Happiness also is confused with other emotions, like Neutral, but the amount of times it was identified correctly make up for the overall number of incorrect identifications. All of this information can be seen in Table 3, which shows the confusion matrix for both groups for the last ten interactions.

Table 3. Confusion matrix for neurotypical users (Top) and non-neurotypical users (Bottom) for the last 10 interactions.

Actual/Predicted - 10	N	Fe	An	Ha	Su	Sa
Neutral	43	0	0	15	3	5
Fear	0	34	1	0	1	9
Anger	4	1	25	0	0	11
Happiness	4	0	0	67	0	0
Surprise	0	1	1	0	46	0
Sadness	0	1	4	0	1	23
Actual/Predicted - 10	N	Fe	An	Ha	Su	Sa
Neutral	6	2	4	2	1	13
Fear	0	3	1	0	0	13
Anger	0	2	19	0	0	2
Happiness	9	5	2	51	7	0
Surprise	0	5	0	4	14	0
Sadness	0	0	4	0	0	9

In terms of interactions, all users showed a preference for caressing the avatar, though some difference can be seen. The most notable is that cohorts C2 and C3 from the neurotypical users have a more even distribution between the three types of interactions that can be chosen, whilst cohort C1 from the neurotypical users and both cohorts of the non-neurotypical users show a preference for interactions with the avatar instead of waiting, though caressing was still the most chosen option, which was particularly true from Cn1 of non-neurotypicals. All of this can be seen in Table 4.

While this gives us an overall idea of the kinds of interactions that users chose, it does not show how those interactions were carried out. With the collected data and careful observation of it, we have determined that neurotypical users tend to not repeat the same action more than 3 consecutive times, choosing a different action afterwards. With this, we wanted to draw conclusions of possible differences in interactions between groups as well as cohorts. Thus, we observed the cases in which users chose to perform the same interaction on the avatar 4 consecutive times, considering such

Table 4. Total actions done by neurotypical users (Above) and non-neurotypical users (Below), as well as by cohort (Poke (unpleasant), Caress (pleasant) and Wait (no action)) Between parenthesis is the percentage for how often each interaction was chosen (Number_Interactions_Cohort/Total_Interactions_Cohort).

	Poke	Caress	Wait
C3	64 (32 %)	70 (35 %)	66 (33 %)
C2	72 (36 %)	70 (35 %)	58 (29 %)
C1	69 (34.5 %)	113 (56.5 %)	18 (9 %)
Total	205 (34.2 %)	253 (42.2 %)	142 (23.6 %)
	Poke	Caress	Wait
Cn2	71 (35.5 %)	97 (48.5 %)	32 (16 %)
Cn1	42 (26.3 %)	93 (58.1 %)	25 (15.6 %)
Total	113 (31.4 %)	190 (52.8 %)	57 (15.8 %)

actions as repetitive. We would consider 4 consecutive interactions as one repetitive action, and add a unit for every time it was repeated after this (for example, if the user repeats the same action 8 consecutive times, we would have 5 repetitive actions).

As it can be seen in Table 5, for the neurotypical users most of the repetitive actions come from the cohort C1 (ages < 12), and those repetitive actions tend to be caressing the avatar. Observationally speaking, most of these actions were done by children who were on the younger end of the spectrum (ages 4–6).

Table 5. Repetitive actions made by the users divided by groups (NT – Neurotypical, NNT – Non-Neurotypical) and cohorts, per interaction, as well as the percentages of those repetitive interactions over the total interactions.

	Poke	Caress	Wait
NT-C3	2 (1 %)	2 (1 %)	5 (2.5 %)
NT-C2	1 (0.5 %)	0 (0 %)	0 (0 %)
NT-C1	1 (0.5 %)	24 (12 %)	0 (0 %)
NT-Total	**4 (0.6 %)**	**26 (4.3 %)**	**5 (0.8 %)**
NNT-Cn2	13 (8.1 %)	20 (12.5 %)	0 (0 %)
NNT-Cn1	9 (4.5 %)	15 (7.5 %)	2 (1 %)
NNT-Total	22 (6.1 %)	35 (9.7 %)	2 (0.5 %)
Total	**52 (5.4 %)**	**122 (12.7 %)**	**14 (1.5 %)**

On the other hand, for the non-neurotypical users we can observe that the amount of repetitive actions increases considerably, and not just in caressing, but also in poking the avatar. This shows us the difference in the ways neurotypical and non-neurotypical users interact, in that non-neurotypical users tend to be more repetitive in their actions. We also observed that many times there were 6–8 consecutive interactions of the same kind in several of the cases, as well as the fact that most repetitive interactions were of a positive nature.

7 Future Work

Part of the future work that has already been developed, is a machine learning algorithm to support the diagnosis of SCD by training that algorithm with the results of the conducted experiments to be able to predict empathic behavior of the users. With this, we can classify the users according to the observed empathic behavior, which could point us towards a possible SCD.

We would also like to develop an avatar-based game, which would be of a role playing type for which the user will be put in a real-life situation so that they will become more emotionally comfortable in those situations, as well as acquiring skills to navigate them, both by gaining a level of comfort and by being able to identify the emotions of the people surrounding them. With this in mind, we would also like to observe any possible correlation between the game mechanics and the improvement in executive function [17], as well as use some other devices to further engage the user and also gather more data [18].

Finally we would like to include a wider array of participants in future tests with the avatar to give us a better understanding of possible differences among different types of non-neurotypical users and a better way to address and improve the avatar with the gained knowledge.

8 Conclusions

This work contributes to the field of affective systems, particularly to help understand how users react before an affective avatar, and how the interact with it.

With the results of the experiment we performed with 48 participants, we have been able to learn the following lessons:

- Subtle redesign of the avatar is needed for the most conflicting emotion, though the intention of the design is to reflect the subtlety of the spectrum of human emotions.
- An improvement after the first 10 interactions was observed, meaning that it is important to let the user become familiar with the avatar and how to interact with it.
- We found evidence that the state machine that represents the changes between emotions was a logical behavior for the avatar.
- Major differences between cohorts can be seen in the way they interact, particularly between neurotypical users of C1 and C2-C3.
- Younger neurotypical users and non-neurotypical users tend to be repetitive in their interactions with the avatar, which will have to be taken into account when designing an avatar aimed at these groups of people.
- Said repetitive actions tend to be caressing, though non-neurotypicals also engage in repetitively poking the avatar.

These findings can be useful to help the diagnosis of SCDs, though more tests should always be conducted, but it points to a tendency from people with SCD towards repetitive actions. Considering the nature of the affective avatar, this could also be useful to improve social abilities of people with SCD and to better understand how they interact with other people, leading to a possible adaptation of the avatar to these specific needs and understandings of interaction and empathy.

Acknowledgments. This work was conducted in the context of UBIHEALTH project under International Research Staff Exchange Schema (MC-IRSES 316337).

References

1. Gibson, J., Adams, C., Lockton, E., et al.: Social communication disorder outside autism? A diagnostic classification approach to delineating pragmatic language impairment, high functioning autism and specific language impairment. J. Child Psychol. Psychiatry Allied Disciplines **54**(11), 1186–1197 (2013)
2. LoPresti, E.F., Mihailidis, A., Kirsch, N.: Assistive technology for cognitive rehabilitation: state of the art. Neuropsychol. Rehabil. **14**(1–2), 5–39 (2004)
3. Cheng, Y., Moore, D., McGrath, P., Fan, Y.: Collaborative virtual environment technology for people with autism. In: Fifth IEEE International Conference on Advanced Learning Technologies (ICALT 2005), pp. 247–248. IEEE, July 2005
4. Cereghetti, D., Kleanthous, S., Christophorou, C., et al.: Virtual partners for seniors: analysis of the user's preferences and expectations on personality and appearance. In: AmI 2015, European Conference on Ambient Intelligence, Athens, Greece, 11–13 November 2015 (2015)
5. Hanke, S., Sandner, E., Stainer-Hochgatterer, A., et al.: The technical specification and architecture of a virtual support partner. In: AmI 2015, European Conference on Ambient Intelligence, Athens, Greece, 11–13 November 2015 (2015)
6. Adjouadi, M., Sesin, A., Ayala, M., Cabrerizo, M.: Remote eye gaze tracking system as a computer interface for persons with severe motor disability. In: Miesenberger, K., Klaus, J., Zagler, W.L., Burger, D. (eds.) ICCHP 2004. LNCS, vol. 3118, pp. 761–769. Springer, Heidelberg (2004)
7. Lanyi, C.S., Brown, D.J.: Design of serious games for students with intellectual disability. IHCI **10**, 44–54 (2010)
8. Norris, A.E., Weger, H., Bullinger, C., et al.: Quantifying engagement: measuring player involvement in human–avatar interactions. Comput. Hum. Behav. **34**, 1–11 (2014)
9. Ugarte, A., García, I., Ortiz, A., Oyarzun, D.: User interfaces based on 3D avatars for interactive television. In: Cesar, P., Chorianopoulos, K., Jensen, J.F. (eds.) EuroITV 2007. LNCS, vol. 4471, pp. 107–115. Springer, Heidelberg (2007)
10. Iglesias, A., Luengo, F.: AI framework for decision modeling in behavioral animation of virtual avatars. In: Shi, Y., van Albada, G.D., Dongarra, J., Sloot, P.M. (eds.) ICCS 2007, Part II. LNCS, vol. 4488, pp. 89–96. Springer, Heidelberg (2007)
11. Inal, Y., Sancar, H., Cagiltay, K.: Children's avatar preferences and their personalities. In: Society for Information Technology & Teacher Education International Conference, Florida, USA, 20–25 March 2006 (2006)
12. Carter, E.J., Hyde, J., Williams, D.L., Hodgins, J.K.: Investigating the influence of avatar facial characteristics on the social behaviors of children with autism. In: Proceedings of the 2016 CHI Conference on Human Factors in Computing Systems, pp. 140–151. ACM, May 2016

13. Johnson, E., Hervás, R., Mondéjar, T., et al.: Improving social communication disorders through human-avatar interaction. In: Ambient Intelligence for Health, Puerto Varas, Chile, 1–4 December 2015, pp. 237–243 (2015)

14. Cambria, E., Hupont, I., Hussain, A., Cerezo, E., Baldassarri, S.A.: Sentic avatar: multimodal affective conversational agent with common sense. In: Esposito, A., Esposito, A. M., Martone, R., Müller, V.C., Scarpetta, G.Y. (eds.) COST 2012. LNCS, vol. 6456, pp. 81–95. Springer, Heidelberg (2011)

15. Balconi, M., Pozzoli, U.: Face-selective processing and the effect of pleasant and unpleasant emotional expressions on ERP correlates. Int. J. Psychophysiol. **49**(1), 67–74 (2003)

16. Johnson, E., Hervás, H., Gutiérrez López de la Franca, C., Mondéjar, T., Ochoa, S.F., Favela, J.: Assessing empathy and managing emotions through interactions with an affective avatar. Health Inf. J., 1–12, September 2016

17. Mondéjar, T., Hervás, R., Johnson, E., Gutierrez, C., Latorre, J.M.: Correlation between videogame mechanics and executive functions through EEG analysis. J. Biomed. Inform. **63**, 131–140 (2016)

18. de la Franca, G.L., Hervás, R., Bravo, J.: Activity recognition in intelligent assistive environments through video analysis with body-angles algorithm. In: García-Chamizo, J.M., Fortino, G., Martone, R., Müller, V.C., Scarpetta, G.Y. (eds.) UCAmI 2015. LNCS, vol. 9454, pp. 162–173. Springer, Heidelberg (2015)

Findings About Selecting Body Parts to Analyze Human Activities Through Skeletal Tracking Joint Oriented Devices

Carlos Gutiérrez López de la Franca$^{(\boxtimes)}$, Ramón Hervás,
Esperanza Johnson, and José Bravo

Escuela Superior de Informática de Ciudad Real,
Laboratorio MamI, Universidad de Castilla-La Mancha,
Paseo de la Universidad 4, 13071 Ciudad Real, Spain
{Carlos.Gutierrez5,MEsperanza.Johnson}@alu.uclm.es,
{Ramon.Hlucas,Jose.Bravo}@uclm.es

Abstract. Analyzing activities (either static postures or movements) made by a user is a complex process that can be done through a wide range of approaches. One part of these existing approaches support doing the recognition focusing their analysis on specific body parts. In fact, in previous publications a method was introduced for activity recognition (**Body-Angles Algorithm**) capable of analysing only using a single sample of those activitites and allowing the selection for each activity which are the *relevant joints*. But being able to analyse the body of the user selecting only a subset of the same, has both advantages and disadvantages. Therefore throughout this article we will expose those disadvantages, the applied solution to mitigate them and the results of an evaluation destined to clear which body parts make it easier to obtain high accuracy rates in recognition. Through this work we aim to give the scientific community lessons learned about the usage of different body areas in the analysis of activity recognition.

Keywords: Activity recognition · Computer vision · Body-Angles Algorithm · Ubiquitous computing · Ambient intelligence · Kinect

1 Introduction

Regarding the research area of activity recognition, there are an innumerable amount of proposals with several types of focus and devices: machine learning methods, video analysis, mobile devices, wearable sensors and many more. Though some of the works focus their analysis on *specific body parts*, it is not common to evaluate the existing differences between using some parts or not. Given that these works demonstrate that it can be interesting to center the analysis *only on certain parts of the body*, throughout this text we will attempt to analyse the influence that this factor has on the results of the **Body-Angles Algorithm** [12] (as this allows to personalize each activity to the analysed body parts). This way we can improve the results and the usage of the *Body-Angles Algorithm* on top of obtaining a series of general conclusions applicable in any other work that uses skeletal tracking joint oriented devices.

© Springer International Publishing AG 2016
C.R. García et al. (Eds.): UCAmI 2016, Part I, LNCS 10069, pp. 537–548, 2016.
DOI: 10.1007/978-3-319-48746-5_55

In previous work the *Body-Angles Algorithm* and the *Extended Body-Angles Algorithm* were presented. The **Body-Angles Algorithm** (*BA-A*) [12] allows to compare the similarity between two *postures* shown by two human bodies without needing to use a dataset with multiple instances of each supported posture. It is capable of performing the analysis with a *single instance* thanks to the use of the *angles* that are formed by each pair of joints as a unit of information.

The **Extended Body-Angles Algorithm** (*E-BA-A*) [13] is an evolution and generalization of the *Body-Angles Algorithm*. It allows to compare the similarity between two *movements* performed by human bodies from a single instance of each considered movement. Its functionality is based on the *Body-Angles Algorithm* adding a layer of checks to take into account which one of the *frames* that compose the movement is being analysed.

These publications also include the results of the evaluations performed on each algorithm. Obtained results showed how both obtained high accuracy rates in the recognition and were no significant differences between each of the participants of the test. Specifically the *BA-A* obtained a global accuracy rate of **88.36 %** and *E-BA-A* obtained an accuracy rate of **93.01 %**. The implementation of both algorithms is independent of the sensor used, and to carry out the evaluations the chosen device was the first version of *Microsoft Kinect*.

For this the article will have the following points: Sect. 2 will explore in depth the contemplated state of the art; Sect. 3 will expose the goal of this work and will enumerate the possible improvements to apply to the *Body-Angles Algorithm* to solve the analysed problems; Sect. 4 will describe the tests that have been performed; Sect. 5 will introduce alternatives that have not been considered for this study, and finally Sect. 6 accumulates all the general conclusions extracted from the evaluation.

2   State of the Art

There are wide range of proposals centered on the area of *monitorization* or *activity recognition*, as it is a topic of study that generates a lot of interest. There are proposals to evaluate the performance of a dancer [1], to allow physical rehabilitation [19], activity recognition for the physical rehabilitation through mobile devices with accelerometer [23], detection of elderly frailty with accelerometry [9], detection of stereotypical behaviour in autistic children [11], a review of human activity recognition methods and different examples of each method [27], an analysis of the current outlook of research in the field of activity recognition [6] and a system that monitors the activities that occur in an isolation room of a psychiatric hospital [26].

There are also proposals that support themselves on *objects from the environment* (taking context into account) to do the activity analysis. Some of those examples are monitoring the activities and state of a dog through sensors embedded in their collar [18], a system of activity recognition of daily living that takes context into account (the objects the user interacts with) [10] and lastly the detection of activities done in a house with simple ubiquitous sensors [25].

Another kind of proposals centre around the use of *alternative recognition strategies*, like the recognition of activities in which the observer in 1st person takes part [24], a study of activity recognition when information from skeleton tracking is not available [28], or gesture recognition [4] and hand gesture [22].

Though some of the studied works analyse activites focusing only on *a specific body part* (like a system to guide people with dementia in the performance of activities of daily living [5], a system based on context centered around culinary activities and objects [3] and a method capable of recognize activities from a videocamera in an egocentrical point of view analizing the hands of the user and the objects [8]) those that approach the possible differences in recognition, fruit of this different analysis, are mostly related with *variations in the disposition of the accelerometers* on the human body.

Therefore there are studies that analyse the impact that these variations of the accelerometers from their initial position in which they were put have [2, 16], studies about the *optimal placement position of accelerometers* and how to improve recognition combining the data from several of them [7] and a method capable of *obtaining the position of the body* in which an accelerometer has been placed based only on the signal of the device [15] as knowing where the sensor is located is very important information about context.

Lastly, most similar related work to our proposal corresponds to two proposals opposite to each other. The first of them proposes to analyse human activities distinguishing among the different body parts of the person and applying a relational representation by means of graphs [17]. This way they attempt to try if this representation obtains better results than considering the whole body as a single object. The second proposal aims for the opposite [21] and maintains that it is possible to recognise repetitive activities without discerning between the different parts that compose the human bodies. For this they present a method capable of performing this analysis through sequences of images in greyscale.

Given that during the study of the state of the art we have not found any precedent whose focus is exactly the same as this proposal, a comparative analysis of the body parts that faciliate and improve the recognition can be beneficial for future works frame din this area.

3 Activity Analysis Based on Relevant Joints

3.1 Description of the Problem

In the evaluations done to validate the **E-BA-A** [13] we identified different types of activities that, due to their nature, have traits that make them more or less susceptible to error depending what kind of joint selection is made. From a general perspective we can identify two traits to classify activities:

- **Global/Limited Use of the Body:** The activity is characterized by using all or most of the monitored joints (*Global*) or by using a reduced subset of the same (*Limited*).
- **Symmetry:** There are activities that use both halves of the body, either symmetrically or with an inverted symmetry, while others are characterized by using only one half of the body.

According to the monitored activites and the results of the evaluation, the movements that use the joints in a global way (like *Walk* or *Forward Bend*) obtained very good accuracy percentages. But in the case of activities that only took into account one subset, like for example the joints of the right arm, the results were significantly worse. This is due to, when making these types of movements, the rest of the joints don't give any relevant information for its recognition, but its positions coincide with the ones they are at for other more general activities.

To illustrate this we can describe as an example the activity *Grab Object*, an activity that is limited with a high significancy to the joints of the right arm. If this activity is done standing up, it can be easily confused with the activity *Stand* as the position for the rest of the joints is very similar. These observations motivate the creation of this paper and guide the development of the evaluation described in Sect. 5.

3.2   Possible Solutions

As it can be seen in the previous point, allowing the selection of relevant joints for each activity is a possibility that should be used with precaution. The solution to the problem is to evaluate the elimination of irrelevant joints in the postures and movements. The problem is that having the possibility of selecting the relevant joints for each activity, gives the algorithm both positive and negative points in activity recognition.

As there are less *relevant bones*, each bone has a greater weight and if its result is good or bad it affects the result more in total. For the same reason any movement that has less relevant bones will be more exposed to possible precision errors that the sensor device can make. Also there are certain parts of the body (mainly the trunk), that due to its limited range of movement, give an extra of stability to the activities that consider it relevant.

For this reason, those activities that do not consider those body parts as relevant, can be at a certain disadvantage. Therefore it is convenient to study the possibility of not eliminating the irrelevant joints, meaning, studying if using this characteristic of the algorithm to maximize the efficacy of the analysis has more benefits or more problems.

The problem of this option is that we would *lose* some *flexibility* in terms of using the samples of the activities. As there are no differences between activities, and using in all of them the same subset of relevant joints (all the body except hands and feet, as it will be detailed later), those activities that could be done from different positions can no longer be monitored with a single sample.

If we have an activity whose relevant joints are only the arms, and we perform the analysis removing irrelevant joints, the algorithm can monitor the performance of that activity with the user either standing or sitting on a chair or the floor. But if we don't eliminate irrelevant joints and perform the analysis of all the activities with the same subset of joints, it is necessary to *record a sample* of the activity being done standing, another for sitting on a chair and another sitting on the floor (as the position of the legs in each case is different).

Within the exposed solution there is a particular case conditioned by technological limitations, and that is some of skeletal tracking joint oriented devices make a very basic analysis of the hand of the users. Specifically with the first version of Kinect it estimates its position as if it were another joint, so it reduces each hand to a single point. So even though Kinect gives the hands as joints, the union of these with its adyacent joint (wrist) cannot be considered a bone as such, and in consequence is not a *natural angle* that can be formed by the human body.

But the problem is not that it is not really a bone but that its tracking is less stable that the rest of the bones of the body. As the hand is the element of the body with the greatest mobility, its tracking and analysis is more complex. Therefore, even though the *"bone"* formed by the wrist and hand can be taken into account in the calculations of the algorithm, it is not advised as we have observed in an experimental manner that it tends to worsen results. Given this, when recording the sample for the activities in previous evaluations, the hand was marked as a relevant joint, favouring the activities that used a more reduced subset of joints that obtained lower similarities. In consequence, the evaluation done will check the behaviour of the system omitting hands and feet as relevant parts of the activities.

There is a second approximation, but as its application to the problem is not part of the work, we will speak of it in a future point titled *Discusion and Alternatives*.

4 Evaluation

4.1 Objetive of the Evaluation

Once the antecedents and the possible solutions to the described problem have been exposed let us see the evaluation made as part of this work. The evaluation consisted in applying the described solutions throughout the previous point and observe their effect on the results obtained by the **E-BA-A**. Thus the goal after this test is to find out if on the activity recognition systems oriented towards *monitorization of joints* it is more convenient to consider all or only those joints important for each activity.

4.2 Description of the Evaluation

To study if it is more beneficial to include or omit the irrelevant joints we will compare the recognition results obtained taking into account three different sets of joints.

The first set (**vB**) only considers the *joints of the extremities* used in the movement *without including the hands* (when the movement is done with the arm/s) *and the feet* (when the movement is done with the foot/feet). This way we want to check is just the elimination of these elements is enough to improve the recognition results of the movements whose relevant joints are a reduced subset. Or if otherwise, having less relevant joints and being more penalized in the case that the sensor device makes a precision mistake, eliminating the hands is insufficient to improve similarity percentages. The joints corresponding to the shoulders and hips are also part of the set **vB**, as the union points between the trunk and the extremities belong to both.

The second set (**vT**) considers the same joints as the set **vB** but adding those belonging to the *trunk*. With this we try to test if considering the trunk (as it is one the parts with a more stable tracking) it is viable to obtain high rates of accuracy without giving up the possibility of using samples of these movements from different positions.

It is a compromise engagement, an option that involves more joints but is not as radical as to stop omitting irrelevant joints (solution presented in point **4.2**).

The last set (**vC**) corresponds to *all the joints of the body* except hands, feet and head. With this set we pretend to test if accuracy rates in recognition improve notable in comparison with sets **vB** and **vT**. If so, it would be convenient to give up omitting all irrelevant joints to obtain better results, as using all the body theoretically eases the differentiation between activities. Therefore theoretically it would be easier to avoid confusions such as the ones that occured between *Drink* and *Grab Object* with *Stand* when the analysis of the former was done only with the joints of the right arm.

When using the three sets the four different selected activitites will have three versions: **vB**, **vT** and **vC**; corresponding to the joints used in the recording by the set of the same name. The four selected activitites are *Drink [D]* and *Grab Object [D]*[1], from the previous evaluation and done with the arms, and *Leg Flexion [I]* and *Leg Circular Swing [I]* as new additions that use the legs as the extremity. The reason to select these activities, and also their common denominator, is that the relevant joints in these activities correspond only to the extremities. So they prove ideal for the goals of this evaluation as they are compatible with the set **vB**.

Even though these will be the only four activites whose accuracy rates will be monitored during the experiment, this does not mean that they are the only activities that are considered by the **E-BA-A**. The goal is to test if the proposed solution allows to improve the recognition of activities with a more reduced subset of joints. Hence it is necessary that the algorithm also contemplates other activites to make the recognition of these four activitites more complicated. The total of activitites used in the evaluation of the **E-BA-A** can be seen in Table 1 (which contemplates the characteristics previously mentioned about *Symmetry* and *Global/Limited Use*).

Table 1. Taxonomy of the evaluation monitorized activities

	Symmetric	Asymmetric
Global	**Forward Bend**	**Walk**
	Sit Down	**Walk Backwards**
	Stand Up	
	Stand	
	Stay Seated	
Enclosed	**Squat**	**Drink**
		Grab Object
		Leg Flexion
		Leg Circular Swing

The evaluation has been done thanks to the participation of **5** volunteers of different ages, genders (**2** men and **3** women) and complexions. These last are detailed in

---

[1] The activities identified with **[D]** are done with the right side of the body. These are the **asymmetric activities**, those that can be performed with either the left **[I]** or right side of the body, and therefore two versions must be recorded in the system, one for each half of the body.

Table 2. Test subjects corporal information

Test Subject	Height (m)	Shoulder width (cm)	Hip width (cm)	Age
#1	1.60	39	45	25
#2	1.81	50	42	56
#3	1.56	44	38	55
#4	1.68	37	34	22
#5	1.84	45	44	25

Table 2. The participants have no disabilities nor specialized background in any athletic discipline, save for Subject #1, who has an intermediate level of Yoga.

4.3 Evaluation Results

The Fig. 1 shows the results obtained from each subject for each of the activities in addition to the totals by activity and totals per subject. Each unit of information (intersection between subject and activity) contains four data. **Suc** indicates the number of times that the algorithm which guessed correctly the movement performed by the voluntary. **Vic** indicates the number of times that the set of joints corresponding to the data has obtained a similarity with the activity greater than the rest of considered sets. Both fields are accompanied by his corresponding success rate (**Rate**) taking into account that the volunteers performed all activities a total of 50 times.

The only exception to the last data happens with the subject #2, who was not able to perform the *Leg Circular Swing [I]* movement due to the loss of balance during its performance. Therefore the results of this have been omitted from total calculations, and this fact does not affect neither the results nor the findings of this work.

4.4 Analysis of the Results

We will go over the obtained results for each one of the three subsets considered for evaluation. Regarding the set **vB**, is able to get high rates of success but only in the recognition of some of the activities (**96.4 %** for *Drink [D]* and **95.06 %** for *Grab Object [D]* but **0 %** and **9 %** respectively for *Leg Flexion [I]* and *Leg Circular Swing [I]*). Therefore, even with improved outcomes in some cases, omitting the hands and feet is not enough to ensure recognition of those activities with a smaller subset of relevant joints (the set **vB** has obtained an overall success rate of **52.42 %**). But in contrast, the improved results in the recognition of *Drink [D]* and *Grab Object [D]* indicates that omit these elements is beneficial for recognition. Consequently it is a measure that should be implemented in combination with others because it is positive, but is not a solution by itself.

On the other hand the use of the set **vC** is recommended as it has obtained an overall success rate of **92.42 %**. The drawback is that even though it is a very good rate, it is not the set that has achieved the best results of the evaluation. The best global success rate obtained during the evaluation has been **97.37 %**, corresponding to the set **vT**.

Extended Body-Angles Algorithm Test Results UCAmI 2016

vB

	Drink [D]				Grab Object [D]				Leg Flexion [l]				Leg Circular Swing [l]				Total			
	Suc	Rate	Vic	Rate	Suc	Rate	Vic	Rate	Suc	Rate	Vic	Rate	Suc	Rate	Vic	Rate	Suc	Rate	Vic	Rate
Subject #1	49	98 %	0	0 %	39	78 %	4	8 %	0	0 %	0	0 %	10	20 %	3	6 %	98	49 %	7	3.5 %
Subject #2	45	90 %	0	0 %	50	100 %	1	2 %	0	0 %	0	0 %	0	0 %	0	0 %	95	63.33 %	1	0.667 %
Subject #3	50	100 %	0	0 %	50	100 %	48	96 %	0	0 %	0	0 %	0	0 %	0	0 %	100	50 %	48	24 %
Subject #4	50	100 %	0	0 %	50	100 %	10	20 %	0	0 %	0	0 %	8	16 %	0	0 %	108	54 %	10	5 %
Subject #5	47	94 %	0	0 %	50	100 %	44	88 %	0	0 %	0	0 %	0	0 %	0	0 %	97	48.5 %	44	22 %
Total	241	96.4 %	0	0 %	239	95.6 %	107	42.8 %	0	0 %	0	0 %	18	9 %	3	1.5 %	498	52.42 %	110	11.58 %

vT

	Drink [D]				Grab Object [D]				Leg Flexion [l]				Leg Circular Swing [l]				Total			
	Suc	Rate	Vic	Rate	Suc	Rate	Vic	Rate	Suc	Rate	Vic	Rate	Suc	Rate	Vic	Rate	Suc	Rate	Vic	Rate
Subject #1	50	100 %	1	2 %	49	98 %	45	90 %	50	100 %	49	98 %	40	80 %	40	80 %	189	94.5 %	183	91.5 %
Subject #2	50	100 %	0	0 %	50	100 %	49	98 %	49	98 %	15	30 %					149	99.33 %	114	76 %
Subject #3	50	100 %	1	2 %	50	100 %	2	4 %	45	90 %	15	30 %	50	100 %	41	82 %	195	97.5 %	107	53.5 %
Subject #4	50	100 %	0	0 %	50	100 %	40	80 %	48	96 %	10	20 %	49	98 %	10	20 %	197	98.5 %	110	55 %
Subject #5	50	100 %	0	0 %	50	100 %	6	12 %	49	98 %	0	0 %	46	92 %	12	24 %	195	97.5 %	68	34 %
Total	250	100 %	2	0.8 %	249	99.6 %	142	56.8 %	241	96.4 %	89	35.6 %	185	92.5 %	103	51.5 %	925	97.37 %	582	61.26 %

vC

	Drink [D]				Grab Object [D]				Leg Flexion [l]				Leg Circular Swing [l]				Total			
	Suc	Rate	Vic	Rate	Suc	Rate	Vic	Rate	Suc	Rate	Vic	Rate	Suc	Rate	Vic	Rate	Suc	Rate	Vic	Rate
Subject #1	50	100 %	1	2 %	36	72 %	0	0 %	50	100 %	1	2 %	29	58 %	0	0 %	165	82.5 %	2	1 %
Subject #2	50	100 %	0	0 %	50	100 %	0	0 %	49	98 %	35	70 %					149	99.33 %	35	23.33 %
Subject #3	50	100 %	1	2 %	50	100 %	0	0 %	48	96 %	34	68 %	21	42 %	9	18 %	169	84.5 %	44	22 %
Subject #4	50	100 %	0	0 %	50	100 %	0	0 %	50	100 %	40	80 %	50	100 %	40	80 %	200	100 %	80	40 %
Subject #5	50	100 %	0	0 %	47	94 %	0	0 %	50	100 %	50	100 %	48	96 %	36	72 %	195	97.5 %	86	43 %
Total	250	100 %	2	0.8 %	233	93.2 %	0	0 %	247	98.8 %	160	64 %	148	74 %	85	42.5 %	878	92.42 %	247	26 %

Fig. 1. Evaluation results for the sets vB-vT-vC

5 Discussion and Alternatives

The fact that the algorithm fails for confusing the performed action with another very common [13] was already planned that may occur and is what we call *sink* postures or movements. The most basic and common activities, such as stand, will have many joints and bones in common with others. This means it could happen that, although we are doing a different posture or movement, get a fairly high percentage of similarity with any of the sink postures or movements, and then the response of the algorithm to that instant is any of the sink activities.

Hence, another possible solution to this problem is to introduce a stricter *minimum limit of prediction* for sink activities. The minimum limit of prediction represents the percentage of similarity that the activity with the greater similarity at that instant has to overcome to be considered the result or prediction of the algorithm. If the activity does not exceed the minimum limit is considered that what the user has done does not seem enough to any of the activities covered by the system. And if this happens, the result for that instant is *unknown activity*. Establishing a stricter limit for sink activities we difficult that these are chosen as prediction when they are not realized, because having a higher minimum limit of prediction, this generally only be overcome when the user is really doing that activity and no something similar.

Finally, a third way of solution would be to combine the two alternatives, with the aim of strengthening the recognition algorithm.

6 General Conclusions and Future Work

After analyzing the results obtained in the evaluation (Sect. 4.4), these indicates that the best option to analyze those activities whose relevant joints correspond only with extremities, is used with them also the trunk. The trunk provides stability to the results and reduces the factor that, to contemplate less *relevant bones*, they have more influence on the obtained similarities and at the same time they are more exposed to the sensor device possible failures. By including the trunk is achieved that the activity have an *intermediate amount of relevant joints* (and therefore *relevant bones*), which ensures a balanced weight distribution in the obtaining similarities process.

In addition, the set **vT** not only has obtained greater overall success rate but it has also obtained the *highest percentage of wins*. In a **61.26 %** of the times it has been the subset that has gained greater similarity to the activity performed by the test subjects. This means that it being able to get a greater similarity than the other sets with the performed activity, potentially also may obtain a greater difference between that similarity and the similarities obtained with the other considered activities. And if the difference with the rest of similarities is greater, the differentiation between some activities and others is simpler, which ease the work of the concrete activity recognition algorithm used.

Another finding was about how to use the joints in the analysis is that, whenever we are considering an *asymmetrical activity*, it is also necessary to consider as relevant the joints corresponding to the other half of the body. If this is not done, the differentiation between activities becomes difficult. If we consider an activity that can only be done with the right half of the body, it is not regarded as relevant the left half, and then a new activity that does the same but with the two halves at once is included as above, it will not be possible differentiate between them. What is done with the right side of the body is identical in both cases. Therefore, to avoid such situations, should always be included as relevant joints those homonyms corresponding to the other half of the body.

Finally, future work passes through evaluating the alternative solution presented in Sect. 6 and maximizing the use of the algorithms collaborating with other authors. Consequently it will be checked if the use of a different *minimum limit of prediction* for the sink activities is beneficial. For this, the first step will be continue to include more neutral movements in the system apart from *Stand* and *Stay Seated*. We identified as *neutral movements* those that serving for modeling situations where the user is doing nothing. That is, what happens between activities. Therefore the neutral movements are also potentially sink activities because they occur regularly.

In regards to the collaborations the idea is to add value to other works. On the one hand we will combine this system with an affective avatar [14] in order to give this last one information about the activities that the user is doing. On the other hand we will develop a videogame whose main mechanic will be the realization of physical activities. This will allow to analyse the relationship between the game mechanic and the executive function [20]. The activities performed during the game will be analysed through the *Extended Body-Angles Algorithm*.

Acknowledgments. This work was conducted in the context of UBIHEALTH project under International Research Staff Exchange Schema (MC-IRSES 316337) and the coordinated project grant TIN2013-47152-C3-1-R (FRASE), funded by the Spanish Ministerio de Ciencia e Innovación.

References

1. Alexiadis, D.S., Kelly, P., Daras, P., O'Connor, N.E., Boubekeur, T., Moussa, M.B.: Evaluating a dancer's performance using kinect-based skeleton tracking. In: Proceedings of the 19th ACM International Conference on Multimedia, Scottsdale, Arizona, USA, pp. 659–662. ACM (2011)
2. Banos, O., Toth, M.A., Damas, M., Pomares, H., Rojas, I.: Dealing with the effects of sensor displacement in wearable activity recognition. Sensors **14**(6), 9995–10023 (2014)
3. Bansal, S., Khandelwal, S., Gupta, S., Goyal, D.: Kitchen activity recognition based on scene context. In: International Conference on Image Processing (ICIP), Melbourne, Australia, pp. 3461–3465. IEEE (2013)
4. Biswas, K.K., Basu, S.K.: Gesture recognition using microsoft kinect®. In: Automation, Robotics and Applications (ICARA) 5th International Conference, Wellington, New Zealand, pp. 100–103. IEEE (2011)
5. Boger, J., Hoey, J., Poupart, P., Boutilier, C., Fernie, G., Mihailidis, A.: A planning system based on Markov decision processes to guide people with dementia through activities of daily living. IEEE Trans. Inf Technol. Biomed. **10**(2), 323–333 (2006)

6. Brush, A., Krumm, J., Scott, J.: Activity recognition research: the good, the bad, and the future. In: Pervasive Workshop How to do Good Research in Activity Recognition. Helsinki, Finland (2010)

7. Cleland, I., Kikhia, B., Nugent, C., Boytsov, A., Hallberg, J., Synnes, K., Finlay, D.: Optimal placement of accelerometers for the detection of everyday activities. Sensors **13**(7), 9183–9200 (2013)

8. Fathi, A., Farhadi, A., Rehg, J.M.: Understanding egocentric activities. In: International Conference on Computer Vision (ICCV), Barcelona, Spain, pp. 407–414. IEEE (2011)

9. Fontecha, J., Navarro, F.J., Hervás, R., Bravo, J.: Elderly frailty detection by using accelerometer-enabled smartphones and clinical information records. Pers. ubiquitous Comput. **17**(6), 1073–1083 (2013)

10. Fu, J., Liu, C., Hsu, Y.P., Fu, L.C.: Recognizing context-aware activities of daily living using RGBD sensor. In: IEEE/RSJ International Conference on Intelligent Robots and Systems (IROS), Tokyo, Japan, pp. 2222–2227. IEEE (2013)

11. Goncalves, N., Costa, S., Rodrigues, J., Soares, F.: Detection of stereotyped hand flapping movements in Autistic children using the Kinect sensor: A case study. In: Autonomous Robot Systems and Competitions (ICARSC), Espinho, Portugal, pp. 212–216. IEEE (2014)

12. Gutiérrez López de la Franca, C., Hervás, R., Bravo, J.: Activity recognition in intelligent assistive environments through video analysis with body-angles algorithm. In: García-Chamizo, J.M., et al. (eds.) UCAmI 2015. LNCS, vol. 9454, pp. 162–173. Springer, Heidelberg (2015). doi:10.1007/978-3-319-26401-1_16

13. Gutiérrez López de la Franca, C., Hervás, R.: Reconocimiento de Actividades de Propósito General mediante Kinect y el Algoritmo de Ángulos Corporales. Internal Report, University of Castilla-La Mancha (2016)

14. Johnson, E., Hervás, R., Gutiérrez López de la Franca, C., Mondéjar, T., Ochoa, S.F., Favela, J.: Assessing empathy and managing emotions through interactions with an affective avatar. Health Inf. J., 1–12 (2016). doi:10.1177/1460458216661864

15. Kunze, K., Lukowicz, P., Junker, H., Tröster, G.: Where am I: recognizing on-body positions of wearable sensors. In: Strang, T., Linnhoff-Popien, C. (eds.) LoCA 2005. LNCS, vol. 3479, pp. 264–275. Springer, Heidelberg (2005). doi:10.1007/11426646_25

16. Kunze, K., Lukowicz, P.: Sensor placement variations in wearable activity recognition. IEEE Pervasive Comput. **13**(4), 32–41 (2014)

17. Kusumam, K.: Relational learning using body parts for human activity recognition videos. Technical report, University of Lincoln (2012)

18. Ladha, C., Hammerla, N., Hughes, E., Olivier, P., Plötz, T.: Dog's life: wearable activity recognition for dogs. In: Proceedings of the ACM International Joint Conference on Pervasive and Ubiquitous Computing, Zurich, Switzerland, pp. 415–418. ACM (2013)

19. Leightley, D., Darby, J., Li, B., McPhee, J.S., Yap, M.H.: Human activity recognition for physical rehabilitation. In: IEEE International Conference on Systems, Man, and Cybernetics (SMC), Manchester, United Kingdom, pp. 261–266. IEEE (2013)

20. Mondéjar, T., Hervás, R., Johnson, E., Gutiérrez, C., Latorre, J.M.: Correlation between videogame mechanics and executive functions through EEG analysis. J. Biomed. Inform. **63**, 131–140 (2016)

21. Polana, R., Nelson, R.: Low level recognition of human motion (or how to get your man without finding his body parts). In: Proceedings of the 1994 IEEE Workshop on Motion of Non-Rigid and Articulated Objects, Austin, Texas, USA, pp. 77–82. IEEE (1994)

22. Ramirez-Giraldo, D., Molina-Giraldo, S., Alvarez-Meza, A.M., Daza-Santacoloma, G., Castellanos-Dominguez, G.: Kernel based hand gesture recognition using kinect sensor. In: XVII Symposium on Image, Signal Processing, and Artificial Vision (STSIVA), Antioquia, Turkey, pp. 158–161. IEEE (2012)

23. Raso, I., Hervás, R., Bravo, J.: m-Physio: personalized accelerometer-based physical rehabilitation platform. In: Proceedings of the Fourth International Conference on Mobile Ubiquitous Computing, Systems, Services and Technologies, Florence, Italy, pp. 416–421 (2010)

24. Ryoo, M.S., Matthies, L.: First-person activity recognition: what are they doing to me?. In: Computer Vision and Pattern Recognition (CVPR), Portland, USA, pp. 2730–2737. IEEE (2013)

25. Tapia, E.M., Intille, S.S., Larson, K.: Activity recognition in the home using simple and ubiquitous sensors. In: Ferscha, A., Mattern, F. (eds.) Pervasive 2004. LNCS, vol. 3001, pp. 158–175. Springer, Heidelberg (2004). doi:10.1007/978-3-540-24646-6_10

26. Veltmaat, M.J.T., van Otterlo, M., Vogt, J.: Recognizing activities with the Kinect. Technical report, Radboud University Nijmagen (2013)

27. Vrigkas, M., Nikou, C., Kakadiaris, I.A.: A review of human activity recognition methods. J. Frontiers Robot. AI **2**, 28 (2015)

28. Yang, Z., Zicheng, L., Hong, C.: RGB-Depth feature for 3D human activity recognition. Communications, China **10**(7), 93–103 (2013)

Author Index

Printed in the United States
By Bookmasters